Critical Theory and Early Christianity

Studies in Ancient Religion and Culture

Series Editors:

Philip L. Tite, University of Washington

Michael Ng, Seattle University

Studies in Ancient Religion and Culture (SARC) is concerned with religious and cultural aspects of the ancient world, with a special emphasis on studies that utilize social scientific methods of analysis. By "ancient world," the series is not limited to Greco-Roman and ancient Near Eastern cultures, though that is the primary regional focus. The underlying presupposition is that the study of religion in antiquity needs to be located within cultural and social analysis, situating religious traditions within the broader cultural and geopolitical dynamics within which those traditions are located.

This series also encourages cross-disciplinary research in the study of the ancient world. Due to the historical development of various academic disciplines, there has arisen a set of largely isolated and competing fields of study of the ancient world. Often this fragmentation in academia results in outdated or caricatured scholarly products when one discipline does use research from another discipline. A key goal of this series is to help facilitate greater cross- and inter-disciplinary work, bringing together those who study ancient history (especially social history), archaeology (of various methods and geographic focuses, as well as theorists in archaeology), ancient philosophy, biblical studies, early patristics/church history, Second Temple and formative Judaism, and Greek and Roman classics, as well as philologists.

Given the focus on the social and cultural context within which religion functions, the series also publishes studies which explore the various social locations in which real people in antiquity practiced or interacted with their religious traditions. Examples include the domestic cult, food production and consumption, temple worship, funerary practices/monuments, development of social networks, military cult, and ancient medicine.

Finally, the series encourages a broader application of theoretical and methodological tools to the study of the ancient world. While the main perspective is social-scientific (understood broadly), specific analyses from the reservoir of critical theory, narrative theories, economic theory, bio-archaeology, gender analysis, anthropology of religion, and cognitive theory are welcome.

Critical Theory and Early Christianity

Edited by
Matthew G. Whitlock

SHEFFIELD UK   BRISTOL CT

Published by Equinox Publishing Ltd.

UK: Office 415, The Workstation, 15 Paternoster Row, Sheffield, South Yorkshire S1 2BX

USA: ISD, 70 Enterprise Drive, Bristol, CT 06010

www.equinoxpub.com

First published 2022

© Matthew G. Whitlock and contributors 2022

All rights reserved. No part of this publication may be reproduced or transmitted in any form or by any means, electronic or mechanical, including photocopying, recording or any information storage or retrieval system, without prior permission in writing from the publishers.

British Library Cataloguing-in-Publication Data

A catalogue record for this book is available from the British Library.

ISBN-13   978 1 78179 412 8 (hardback)
          978 1 78179 413 5 (paperback)
          978 1 80050 129 4 (ePDF)
          978 1 80050 183 6 (ePub)

Library of Congress Cataloging-in-Publication Data

Names: Whitlock, Matthew G., editor.
Title: Critical theory and early Christianity / edited by Matthew G. Whitlock.
Description: Sheffield, South Yorkshire ; Bristol, CT : Equinox Publishing Ltd, 2022. | Series: Studies in ancient religion and culture | Includes bibliographical references and index. | Summary: "This volume aims to create-in Walter Benjamin's terms-dialectical images from early Christian texts and the twentieth and twenty-first centuries"-- Provided by publisher.
Identifiers: LCCN 2021050313 (print) | LCCN 2021050314 (ebook) | ISBN 9781781794128 (hardback) | ISBN 9781781794135 (paperback) | ISBN 9781800501294 (epdf) | ISBN 9781800501836 (epub)
Subjects: LCSH: Christian literature, Early--History and criticism. | Christianity and the social sciences. | Critical theory. | Religion and sociology.
Classification: LCC BR67 .C655 2022 (print) | LCC BR67 (ebook) | DDC 270.1--dc23/eng/20220126
LC record available at https://lccn.loc.gov/2021050313
LC ebook record available at https://lccn.loc.gov/2021050314

Typeset by ISB Typesetting, Sheffield, UK

Contents

Preface: Dialectical Images and Critical Theory   vii

1. Introduction: Making Early Christian Texts Strange (Again)   1
   Matthew G. Whitlock

PART I: WALTER BENJAMIN

2. Walter Benjamin and Early Christian Texts   35
   Matthew G. Whitlock

3. Reading, Libraries, and Urban Change in the Shadow of Capitalism and Apocalypse: Reading Walter Benjamin and John of Patmos   50
   Robert Paul Seesengood

4. "On the Concept of History": St. Augustine and Walter Benjamin   66
   Carl A. Levenson

PART II: GILLES DELEUZE

5. Gilles Deleuze and Early Christian Texts   99
   Matthew G. Whitlock

6. The Deleuzioguattarian Body of Christ without Organs   127
   Bradley H. McLean

7. The Many Acts of the Apostles: Simulacra and Simulation   147
   Matthew G. Whitlock and Philip L. Tite

8. Face-ing the Nations: Becoming a Majority Empire of God Reterritorialization, Language, and Imperial Racism in Revelation 7.9-17   184
   Sharon Jacob

PART III: ALAIN BADIOU

9. Alain Badiou and Early Christian Texts   213
   Matthew G. Whitlock

10. Christianity Appears First, as Itself   236
    Bruce Worthington

11. Towards a Vulgar Marxist Reading of Christian Origins Today   252
    James Crossley

12. Recapitulating the Event: Reading Irenaeus with Badiou   268
    Hollis Phelps

PART IV: JUDITH BUTLER

13. Judith Butler and Early Christian Texts   295
    Matthew G. Whitlock

14. Paul Exposed: Reading Galatians with Judith Butler   314
    Valérie Nicolet

15. Mattering Bodies:
    Animacy and Justice in Origen's *On First Principles*   350
    Peter Anthony Mena

    Index of Biblical References   367
    Index of Classical References and Authors   371
    Index of Early Christian Writings   372
    Index of Jewish Writings   374
    Index of Modern Authors   375
    Index of Subjects   380

Preface

Dialectical Images and Critical Theory

Matthew G. Whitlock

> It's not that what is past casts its light on what is present, or what is present its light on what is past; rather, image is that wherein what has been comes together in a flash with the now to form a constellation.[1]
> —Walter Benjamin, *The Arcades Project*

This volume aims to create—in Walter Benjamin's terms—dialectical images of early Christian texts and the twenty-first century. It blasts the past and the present into one another, creating new constellations of thought, ones connected with tensions and mediated by theory (mediation being what Theodor Adorno adds to Benjamin's concept of the dialectical image). The images derive from early Christian texts, while other thought images and theories derive from Walter Benjamin, Gilles Deleuze, Alain Badiou, and Judith Butler. The images and theories are not called upon because they connect directly between eras. We do not analyze, for instance, only those passages in the Deleuzian canon that discuss early Christianity, nor do we look only at those passages in Badiou's *Saint Paul: The Foundation of Universalism*. This volume is not about Butler's, Badiou's, Deleuze's, or Benjamin's writings on early Christianity. Rather, we invoke their theories and thought images because they offer new ways of conceptualizing early Christian texts and images *in our time*—whether or not they refer to these texts directly.

The chapters in the volume do not aim to resolve, through seamless syntheses, the tensions in dialectical images. That is not theory's chief purpose—at least in the minds of our four theorists. Theory here mediates between images, between the past and the present. What is more, the analyses in this volume are not organized under categories of biblical theology and synthesized by them. Rather, we try to discuss early Christian texts without recourse to biblical and traditional theological categories, even in their secular remains. We offer images from biblical texts: the New Jerusalem,

---

1. Walter Benjamin, *The Arcades Project* (trans. Howard Eiland and Kevin McLaughlin; Cambridge, MA: Belknap Press, 1999), 462. For more on Benjamin's dialectical image, see Chapter One.

the worshiping nations in Revelation, for example. We also offer thought images not typically associated with early Christian texts: malls, arcades, and libraries; automaton chess players, chess boards, and the Chinese game of Go; bodies without organs, machines, rhizomes, national anthems, and call centers; Lenin, Stalin, and mathematical sets; drag, and mattering bodies, both human and non-human, earthly and celestial. And we offer mediating theories, concepts, and categories not typically associated with interpreting early Christian texts: gentrification; body-of-Christ-without-organs, deterritorialization and reterritorialization, simulacra and simulation, facialization; evental sites, mathematics, set theory, and queer theory. These images and theories challenge unspoken premises of our scholarship, and they produce new constellations of thought.

This volume does not aim to uncover the true, hidden elements of the past through present theory, that is, to uncover "the true origins" or "the true intentions" of early Christian texts. Instead, to borrow the terms of science fiction theorist Darko Suvin, this volume aims to create "cognitive estrangement" and "novum." That is, by creating new constellations between the past and present, mediated by theories, this volume hopes to make early Christian literature strange (again), to make the present strange (again), and by doing so renew our understanding of both. Perhaps Alain Badiou sets the ideal when he discusses the role of philosophy: to find "the means of saying 'Yes!' to the previously unknown thoughts that hesitate to become the truths that they are."[2]

This volume is organized as follows. First, the introductory chapter, "Making Early Christian Texts Strange (Again)," expands on the ideas summarized in this preface, connecting the work of our four theorists with the essays in this volume, especially in light of critical theorists associated with the Institute for Social Research (ISR; also known as the Frankfurt School). Second, the introduction is followed by four parts, each part devoted to one of our four theorists. Each part contains an introduction to the theorist and two to three essays applying their theories to early Christian texts. More specifically, each introduction provides concrete context of the theorist's life and work, a brief overview of her or his concepts, and a summary of the essays in this volume that apply these concepts. The introductions do not give comprehensive biographical or philosophical overviews of each theorist. Rather, the introductions aim to provide enough context of each theorist's thoughts so as to collide them with early Christian texts—both in how

---

2. Alain Badiou, *Logics of Worlds: Being and Event II* (trans. Alberto Toscano; London: Bloomsbury, 2009 [2006]), 3.

they have been received and how they have proliferated. Then, the essays that follow the introductions embark on this task.

While there are certainly philosophical categories by which to compare our four theorists (e.g., new materialism, multiplicity, Marxism, capitalism, the subject, etc.), as well as common philosophical influences (e.g., Nietzsche for all four; Sartre for Badiou, Deleuze, and Butler; Althusser for Badiou and Butler), this is not the focus of the volume. This volume is not a philosophical text comparing the ideas of the four theorists. This comparative task is best done by scholars of Benjamin, Deleuze, Badiou, and Butler. Rather, the task here is to collide contexts, ideas, and images of early Christian literature with the twenty-first century using these theorists. And by such collisions, discussions of materialism, the subject, Marxism, and so on, do come to the fore. But when similar categories are discussed, by no means do we assert that the theorists agree on their meanings. These categories are simply called upon as *entry points* into the contexts of each theorist and how their theories can be uniquely applied to early Christian texts.

Lastly, each of the four theorists has personal connections to the horrors of the twentieth century: Benjamin took his own life when fleeing from the approaching Nazi presence in France; Deleuze's brother was killed in the resistance; Badiou's father was a leader in the resistance; and Butler lost family members to the Holocaust. There is no doubt that these horrific events of the twentieth century had a lasting impact on these theorists and their theories. May their theories guide us as we encounter the twenty-first century.

Matthew G. Whitlock, Seattle University.

Bibliography

Badiou, Alain. *Logics of Worlds: Being and Event II*. Translated by Alberto Toscano. London: Bloomsbury, 2009 [2006].

Benjamin, Walter. *The Arcades Project*. Translated by Howard Eiland and Kevin McLaughlin. Cambridge, MA: Belknap Press, 1999.

Chapter One

Introduction:
Making Early Christian Texts Strange (Again)

Matthew G. Whitlock

> Anyone who resists can survive only by being incorporated. Once registered as diverging from the culture industry, they belong to it as the land reformer does to capitalism. Realistic indignation is the trademark of those with a new idea to sell.[1]
>
> — Max Horkheimer and Theodor Adorno, "The Culture Industry"

> They packaged our fight into product, turned our dissent into intellectual property, televising our revolution with commercial breaks. They backdoored into our minds, refurbished the facts, and then marked up the price.[2]
>
> — *Mr. Robot*

Early Christian Texts and the Culture Industry

Season Three of the television series *Mr. Robot* begins with the commodification of an idea, of a revolution. After F**k Society successfully hacks ECorp and erases all its financial records, including records of debt, the show's protagonist, Elliot Alderson, walks through the streets of a collapsed society. Thanks to his hack, Elliot bemoans how "they"—the one percent who are benefiting from the revolution that meant them harm—have hijacked his revolution, packaging "fight into product," turning "dissent into intellectual property," and televising "revolution with commercial breaks." His movement is no longer strange. It is no longer unpopular. He walks by a souvenir stand of masks (similar to the Guy Fawkes masks of *V for Vendetta* and the Anonymous movement), of F**k Society T-shirts, and of posters for a new television series based on the radical movement he started. So the viewer is presented with a television series about a revolution that has become a television series. This scene captures what critical theory reveals about the culture industry: it co-opts a revolution in order to

---

1. Max Horkheimer and Theodor Adorno, "The Culture Industry: Enlightenment as Mass Deception," in *Dialectic of Enlightenment: Philosophical Fragments* (ed. Gunzelin Schmid Noerr; trans. Edmund Jephcott; Stanford, CA: Stanford University Press, 2002), 94–136, here 104.
2. Mr. Robot. "eps3.0_power-saver-mode-h," *USA*, 53:22, 11 October 2017.

appease the revolutionary desires of its consumers, thereby both protecting the status quo and using revolutionary art and literature as objects for its own gain, including early Christian literature.[3]

This co-opting of art and literature with the culture industry is a refrain of the writers associated with the Institute for Social Research (ISR; the so-called Frankfurt School), a key node out of which critical theory expanded.[4] In their essay "The Culture Industry: Enlightenment as Mass Deception," Max Horkheimer and Theodor Adorno observe how resistance and divergence inevitably are enlisted by the culture industry, being "incorporated" into it and ultimately belonging to it. In doing so, it makes indignation "realistic" and harmless, and then it trademarks it.[5] This is especially true with a revolutionary work of literature. Its popularity marks the downfall of its resistance. Stephen Eric Bronner sums up how this downfall is expressed in Horkheimer and Adorno's thought: "…the extent to which a work becomes popular—regardless of its political message—is the extent to which its radical impulse will be integrated into the system."[6] So while the popularity of a work may mark its influence, a surface treatment of its

---

3. Recent, less subtle examples include the Kendall Jenner Pepsi ad (2017), using the Black Lives Matter movement, and the Dodge Ram Super Bowl ad (2018), using MLK's "Drum Major Instinct" sermon. Judith Butler points to the movies *Victor, Victoria* and *Tootsie,* which domesticate and normalize the radical impulse of the drag movement, only reinforcing the gender norms drag itself challenges. According to Sara Salih, these two movies are examples of hijacked subversions, ones that "merely [consolidate] existing power structures." See Sara Salih, *Judith Butler* (Routledge Critical Thinkers; New York: Routledge, 2002), 96–8; Judith Butler, *Bodies That Matter: On the Discursive Limits of "Sex"* (New York: Routledge, 1993), 126.

4. The following theorists are most commonly associated with the Institute for Social Research (ISR): Walter Benjamin (1892–1940), Max Horkheimer (1895–1973), Herbert Marcuse (1898–1979), Erich Fromm (1900–1980), Theodor Adorno (1903–1969), Jürgen Habermas (1929–present). Discussions of critical theory often begin with ISR. This is an important node within a vast network of critical theorists and philosophers. It is important to note here ISR's intersection with Western Marxism and the early writings of Marx, who called for a "ruthless critique of everything existing" and a "criticism [that] must not be afraid of its own conclusions, nor of conflict with the powers that be" (Karl Marx and Friedrich Engels, *The Marx-Engels Reader* [ed. Robert C. Tucker; 2nd edn; New York: W. W. Norton, 1978], 13). The ideas of ISR also intersect later with the three other theorists and philosophers in this volume: Gilles Deleuze, Alain Badiou, and Judith Butler, whose ideas will also be noted throughout this introduction.

5. Horkheimer and Adorno, "The Culture Industry," 104.

6. See Stephen Eric Bronner, *Critical Theory: A Very Short Introduction* (Oxford: Oxford University Press, 2001), 6. Bronner's statement here underscores what he says earlier in his book about the ISR: they were not as focused on Marx's economic determinism as they were about his thoughts on the influence of "the political and cultural 'superstructure' of society" (p. 2).

influence misses a subtle move: how its "radical impulse" becomes integrated into the system, into the status quo, supporting what it protests.[7] The radical impulse, in short, becomes a realistic, yet undetectable impulse in support of the status quo, largely because it becomes so common. Gilles Deleuze and Félix Guattari note a similar pattern in literature, when a work moves from a being "minor literature" to "major literature," losing the radical impulse as it is assimilated into the majority voice.[8] Commenting on Deleuze's and Guattari's concept of minor/major literature in light of Shakespeare, Claire Colebrook writes:

> Shakespeare can be considered a "minor" author precisely because his works do not offer a unified image of man, or even unified image of Shakespeare. His texts are more like question marks with each production or reading raising new questions. Of course, when Shakespeare becomes an industry (of tourism, culture and academia) he becomes a major author: we seek to find the real Shakespeare, the origin of his ideas and the true sense of his works. He becomes minor, again, only if we recognize the potential of his work to be read as if we did not know who Shakespeare was.[9]

In the twenty-first century, the popularity of the early Christian literature in the western world is undeniable.[10] So is its integration into the culture industry. To borrow Colebrook's terms about Shakespeare, early Christian literature has become *an industry of tourism, culture and academia*. A unity is sought in this diverse literature, a unity on which to locate and justify our culture and its industry. Again, borrowing Colebrook's terms, *we seek to find the real* Christianity, *the origin* of its ideas, and *the true sense* of what it means—all of which provides a foundation for the predominant system,

---

7. Note that the radical impulse of a text is not the same as its historical origin, essence, or intent. More will be said on this below.

8. See Gilles Deleuze and Félix Guattari, *Kafka: Toward a Minor Literature* (trans. Dana Polan; Minneapolis, MN: University of Minnesota Press, 1986).

9. Claire Colebrook, *Gilles Deleuze* (New York: Routledge, 2002), 105. One can argue how Deleuze's body of work has become major literature. See, for example, Andrew Culp, *Dark Deleuze* (Minneapolis, MN: University of Minnesota Press, 2016), 3, where Culp finds irony in Michel Foucault's famous statement about Deleuze: "Perhaps one day, this century will be known as Deleuzian." Culp reads Foucault's statement as Deleuze being "all too timely," all too integrated into this age. Deleuze's work on connectivity—read by Google execs and venture capitalists alike—has become major in the estimation of Culp.

10. Here I do not draw a clear-cut demarcation between sacred and secular literature. While there are certainly differences along a spectrum between so-called "sacred" and "secular" texts, especially in function, this binary is quite modern and arbitrary. What's more, secular possesses structures and functions of the sacred—and these differences are matters of degree not kind. Note that Benjamin did not make this distinction as well (see Chapter Two).

and even a ground from which critiques of that system often begin. Hence, critiques of the system are framed with the same methodological assumptions of the system itself. And if not careful, critiques themselves can potentially center on the *essence* of Christianity—its *true* origins and *true* roots.[11] Critiques can potentially place New Testament origins at the center of the debate and plant themselves at the root of a tree-like structure, often with the assumption that the branches (i.e., what is being critiqued) have veered from the assumed, true origin.[12]

The rhetoric of the Museum of the Bible, which opened in Washington DC in 2017, serves as an example of how literature has been incorporated into the system. Steve Green, the president of Hobby Lobby and the chairman of the board of the Museum of the Bible, claims on the museum's website: "The Bible is the best-selling, most translated book of all time and is arguably history's most significant piece of literature … It has had an unquestionable influence on science, education, democracy, arts and society. This book has also profoundly impacted lives across the ages, including my own."[13] Indeed, the Bible is popular. It is "best-selling"; it is the

---

11. See the sections on Gilles Deleuze below (Chapters Five and Seven), where we challenge the assumptions behind this tree-like, "arborescent" approach, offering instead a rhizomatic approach to early Christian "origins," one that recognizes the complexity of the early Christian era and our own. For an alternative approach to origins, see the sections on Alain Badiou below, particularly where Bruce Worthington derives truth from the Christ event using Badiou's theory of the event (Chapter Eleven), without recourse to traditional, theological approaches.

12. Besides Deleuze's critique of origins (n. 7 above), see Judith Butler, "What is Critique? An Essay on Foucault's Virtue," in *The Political Readings in Continental Philosphy* (ed. David Ingram; London: Basil Blackwell, 2001), 212–26, here 223. Butler refers to both Foucault and Nietzsche to question the authority of "origins," especially in relation to values. Nietzsche, for example, critiques and counters "fictive origins" not by grounding his thought on the true historical origin, but by referring to his own "fictive origins" about origins. For a history-of-scholarship on the quest for "the purest expression of biblical truth," see Philip R. Davies, "Biblical Studies: Fifty Years of a Multi-Discipline," *CBR* 13.1 (2014): 34–66, here 43–4.

13. "Steve Green, Chairman of the Board," https://www.museumofthebible.org/leadership. Note how this website points to Green's success—at least as defined by the culture industry—as a qualification for the chairman of the board of the bible museum: "Steve Green is also president of Hobby Lobby, the world's largest privately owned arts and crafts retailer. Founded in 1972 by his father, David, in 300 square feet of retail space, the chain has grown to more than 600 stores. Along with its affiliated companies, Hobby Lobby employs some 30,000 people companywide. Today, Hobby Lobby and its affiliates (including Hemispheres and Mardel Stores, a Christian bookstore and educational supply chain) have combined sales of more than $3.3 billion." For a critical analysis of Steve Green and the Museum of the Bible, see Candida R. Moss and Joel S. Baden, *Bible Nation: United States of Hobby Lobby* (Princeton, NJ: Princeton University Press, 2017).

"most translated book." And with this popularity comes "unquestionable influence," but Green fails to acknowledge the nuances of this "unquestionable influence." First, the popularity of a "best-selling" and a "most significant piece of literature" does not generate only positive influence. Popularity brings significant influence and impact, but this impact moves across the spectrum of positive and negative effects. One can point to the numerous ways the Bible and early Christian texts have been integrated into the status quo and undergirded it, sometimes subtly and sometimes not so subtly.[14] In cases where the motives of "sharing" these texts may *appear* harmless (e.g., "spreading the good news"), the outcome can be quite the opposite, as James Baldwin observed: "The spreading of the Gospel, regardless of the motives or the integrity or the heroism of some of the missionaries, was an absolutely indispensable justification for the planting of the flag."[15] Early Christian texts have undergirded nationalism, capitalism, neoconservatism, and neoliberalism; they have set foundations for slavery, anti-Semitism, colonialism, racism, white supremacy, xenophobia, and gentrification; they have supported sexism, sexual abuse, domestic violence, heterosexism, homophobia, and transphobia; they have justified state-sponsored violence, terrorism, torture, and family separations.[16]

Second, while Green clearly qualifies "influence" with "unquestionable" in order to argue for the Bible's impact, there is irony here: *unquestionable influence* implies that something becomes so popular that its influence, and

---

14. The degree of subtlety, of course, is relative to the location of the reader (i.e., social location, time period, etc.): "A literary work is not an object which stands by itself and which offers the same face to each reader in each period," Hans Robert Jauss, "Literary History as a Challenge to Literary Theory," *New Literary History* 2.1 (1970): 7–37, here 10.

15. James Baldwin, *The Fire Next Time* (New York: The Dial Press, 1963), 46.

16. A few critiques are noteworthy for the purposes of this chapter. On white supremacy, see Angela N. Parker, *If God Still Breathes, Why Can't I? Black Lives Matter and Biblical Authority* (Grand Rapids, MI: Eerdmans, 2021). On neoliberalism, see James Crossley, *Jesus in an Age of Neoliberalism: Quests, Scholarship and Ideology* (Sheffield: Equinox, 2012). On state-sponsored violence and "the war on terror," see James Crossley, *Jesus in an Age of Terror: Scholarly Projects for a New American Century* (New York: Routledge, 2014; London: Equinox, 2008). On domestic violence and the New Testament, see Barbara E. Reid, OP, *Taking Up the Cross: New Testament Interpretation through Latina and Feminist Eyes* (Minneapolis, MN: Fortress, 2007). On heterosexism and homophobia, see Dale B. Martin, *Sex and the Single Savior: Gender and Sexuality in Biblical Interpretation* (Louisville, KY: Westminster John Knox, 2006). Most recently, former United States Attorney General Jeff Sessions used Romans 13 to justify separating immigrant families at the southern border. See Julia Jacobs, "Sessions's Use of Bible Passage to Defend Immigration Policy Draws Fire," *New York Times,* 15 June 2018, https://www.nytimes.com/2018/06/15/us/sessions-bible-verse-romans.html.

in some cases unjust influence, is not questioned by the population. As a result, it not only becomes undebatable, but undetectable; it becomes too familiar; it becomes the status quo; it becomes "common sense," a phrase Deleuze often critiques in *Difference and Repetition*.[17] In sum, the influence of early Christian texts becomes so thorough, so universal, and so common, and so self-evident that it becomes latent, undetectable, unquestionable. It becomes the proverbial "blue pill," contributing to a Matrix-like sleep of twenty-first century capitalism.[18] Its "function is to tame"—to apply the words of Deleuze and Guattari to uncritical readings of early Christian literature—"and the result is the fabrication of docile and obedient subjects."[19]

The ISR was quite aware of this slumber. Benjamin's philosophy, in Adorno's words, describes a slumber of the modern world, depicting bourgeois society as "the trance-like captivity of the bourgeois immanence."[20] Or, when speaking about popular literature and art—more specifically, the effect of Frank Capra's Oscar winning movie *You Can't Take It With You*—Benjamin describes "a certain kind of harmlessness—a narcotic in which the 'education of the heart' and 'tomfoolery' are the most important

---

17. See Gilles Deleuze, *Difference and Repetition* (trans. Paul Patton; New York: Columbia University Press, 1994), 129–68. For a summation of Deleuze's philosophy against common sense, and a critique of common-sense approaches in academia, see Itay Sneer, "Making Sense in Education: Deleuze on Thinking Against Common Sense," *Educational Philosophy and Theory* 50.3 (2018): 299–311. Judith Butler also critiques common sense and "self-evident" truths, especially in how they are, according to Sara Salih, "often vehicles for ideological assumptions that oppress certain groups in society, especially those in the minority or on the margins." See Salih, *Judith Butler*, 4. Indeed, in response to a *New York Times* review and critique of her writing style, Butler asserts: "… scholars are obliged to question common sense, interrogate its tacit presumptions and provoke new ways of looking at a familiar world." Judith Butler, "A 'Bad Writer' Bites Back," *New York Times,* 20 March 1999, https://archive.nytimes.com/query.nytimes.com/gst/fullpage-950CE5D61531F933A15750C0A96F958260.html

18. See Chapter Five below for how "the blue pill" in *The Matrix* expresses the lure of twentieth-century capitalism, which keeps humanity in an unquestionable slumber. In Chapter Five, the machinery of the Matrix is paralleled with Deleuze and Guattari's concept of machines.

19. Gilles Deleuze and Felix Guattari, *Anti-Oedipus: Capitalism and Schizophrenia* (trans. Robert Hurley, Mark Seem, and Helen R. Lane; Minneapolis, MN: University of Minnesota Press, 1983), xxii. In this context, Deleuze and Guattari are discussing the effect of Christian figures, icons, and signs.

20. Theodor Adorno, "A Portrait of Walter Benjamin," in *Prisms* (trans. Samuel and Shierry Weber; Cambridge, MA: MIT Press, 1967), 227–42, here 236. Badiou, similarly, calls out the "structural passivity" and "routine" of the world. See Alain Badiou, "Philosophy as Biography," *The Symptom* 9 (2007), http://www.lacan.com/symptom9_articles/badiou19.html.

ingredients."[21] In short, in borrowing the words of ISR—it is this *trance like captivity*, this *certain kind of harmlessness* that an "unquestionable" approach to early Christian literature can nurture, similar to Capra's *You Can't Take It With You*. The literature becomes an instrument of the dominant culture and discourse, and so does scholarship about it, even scholarship underscoring the radical impulses of early Christianity.

Scholarship, too, can become, in the words of Horkheimer and Adorno, a place of "realistic indignation." Robert Myles critiques scholarly brands of "realistic indignation" in his essay "The Fetish for a Subversive Jesus," particularly those of John Dominic Crossan and N. T. Wright.[22] Here Myles uses phrases similar to Horkheimer's and Adorno's "realistic indignation": the "cultural mainstreaming of subversion," "containable subversion," and "gestural subversion."[23] The sum game of this brand of subversion, according to Myles, is "economic and ideological compliance" and a distancing from "militant revolutionary action."[24] So in the end "wider social formations like capitalism or neoliberalism" are not undermined, and "the rhetoric of subversion ultimately just reinforces them."[25] Myles cites Crossan's *The Historical Jesus: The Life of a Mediterranean Jewish Peasant*, for example, to show how Jesus' homelessness is viewed as an individual lifestyle choice as opposed to the result of the systemic injustices of the economic system.[26] Jesus is portrayed one "who co-opts aspects of poverty culture to progress an

---

21. Walter Benjamin, *Gesammelte Briefe* (ed. Christoph Gödde and Henri Lonitz; 6 vols.; Frankfurt: Suhrkamp Verlag, 1995–2000), 6:304–5. Quoted and translated in Howard Eiland and Michael W. Jennings, *Walter Benjamin: A Critical Life* (Cambridge, MA: Belknap Press, 2014), 640. Benjamin, according to Eiland and Jennings, saw the film as "meretricious" and "reactionary" and "as evidence of the film industry's complicity with fascism."

22. Robert Myles, "The Fetish for a Subversive Jesus," *Journal for the Study of the Historical Jesus* 14.1 (2016): 1–14. Crossan and Wright are examples of broader patterns in Anglo-American New Testament scholarship, ones in which I certainly implicate myself first.

23. Myles, "Fetish for a Subversive Jesus," 1–4.

24. Myles, "Fetish for a Subversive Jesus," 1.

25. Myles, "Fetish for a Subversive Jesus," 4.

26. See John Dominic Crossan, *The Historical Jesus: The Life of a Mediterranean Jewish Peasant* (San Francisco, CA: Harper, 1991), xi–xxi. Myles astutely links this portrayal to the genre of Crossan's own work: "Part of this is simply a consequence of writing in the genre of historical biography which almost inevitably heightens the role of individual agency in generating cultural, political, and religious change" ("Fetish for a Subversive Jesus," 7). This assertion connects well with Benjamin's suspicions about historical narratives, a suspicion discussed later in this chapter.

ethical programme undergirded by liberal values."[27] On N. T. Wright's *Jesus and the Victory of God*, Myles demonstrates how Wright internalizes Jesus' subversion for his readers: "What primarily matters for Wright's Jesus, it would seem, is the symbolic and internal revolution of the individual believer."[28] To borrow Benjamin's terms on the Capra movie, this internalization of subversion can serve as a narcotic, moving people away from broader, structural issues in society. In short, Myles argues how these examples from Wright and Crossan show how "academic discourse is itself implicated in a form of containment."[29]

This sort of containment not only involves academic discourse, but also the discourse *in* early Christian texts themselves. Though not *yet* integrated into the modern culture industry in their original contexts, these texts were certainly prone to integration into the Roman Empire and its structures. Three chapters in this volume illustrate this point, one by Bradley McLean, one by Sharon Jacob, and another by James Crossley. In Chapter Six, "The Deleuzoguattarian Body without Organs," McLean looks through the lens of Deleuze and Guattari to analyze early Christian communities in Corinth, showing how first-century Christ groups "were coopted by the state apparatus for the purposes of its own social production." In Chapter Eight, "Faceing the Nations, Becoming a Majority Empire of God," Sharon Jacob uses Deleuze and Guattari (i.e., their ideas on deterritorialization and reterritorialization) in order to show how Revelation shares a vision countering the one of the Roman Empire; however, in depicting this new vision, which includes all the nations worshiping before the throne of God, it employs the imagery of the Empire itself. Diverse nations sing in *one language* before God, much like a modern anthem. Revelation's radical vision of countering the Empire, in other words, ultimately becomes a vision of another empire, the empire of God. And in Chapter Eleven, "Towards a Vulgar Marxist Reading of Christian Origins Today," James Crossley examines how the revolutionary impulse of the Jesus movement is appropriated by Paul and becomes "hardened ideology" in the Johannine literature.

Even more, aside from early Christians texts and scholarship about them, critique itself is quite vulnerable to being integrated or integrating itself

---

27. Myles, "Fetish for a Subversive Jesus," 8. See, for example, N.T. Wright, *Jesus and the Victory of God* (Minneapolis, MN: Fortress, 1996), 594.

28. Myles, "Fetish for a Subversive Jesus," 10. Gilles Deleuze also critiqued this internalization in "Du Christ à la bourgeoisie," *Espace* 1 (1946): 93–106. English translation: "From Christ to Bourgeoisie," trans. Raymond van de Wiel, http://documents.raymondvandewiel.org/from_christ_to_the_bourgeoisie_translation.pdf. This essay is discussed in Chapter Five below.

29. Myles, "Fetish for a Subversive Jesus," 10.

into the system, as this introduction itself does not rise above its own condition. Critique, too, must be aware of its own vulnerability and be open to critique. Steven Helmling, commenting on Adorno's own awareness, notes: "Critique must refuse the hubris of supposing it can escape, or has escaped, has risen above, its ideological condition."[30] Integration, in the end, is inevitable and inescapable in critique, especially popular critique. Helmling continues:

> Adorno's immanent critique is not to exempt his own critical practice from the liabilities of the dominant ideology, but precisely to attest ideology's ubiquity and power by enacting in the writing itself (his own) critique's implication— even (his own) critique's implication—in the very predicaments (his own) critique aims to address, protest, elucidate, redeem.[31]

Thus, we see the inevitability of being integrated in an ideological system, and even more of being popularly read within that system. Again, in applying the words of Eric Bronner to our subject matter, we see that the *extent to which* an early Christian text (or scholarship about it, or critique of it and its scholarship) *becomes popular—regardless of its political message—is the extent to which its radical impulse will be integrated into the system*. In the next section and in this volume, we examine creative ways theorists—while being self-aware of their own vulnerabilities—have tried to blast through the inevitable.

Early Christian Texts and Congealed Ideologies

All four theorists in this volume discuss, in their own ways and contexts, the inescapabilty of the status quo, the inevitability of being integrated into the system, a system that constructs, reiterates, and congeals everything into itself, everything from texts to subjects to genders.[32] Each theorist's unique approach will be discussed in the chapters that follow. But here I

---

30. Steven Helmling, "Constellation and Critique: Adorno's Constellation, Benjamin's Dialectical Image," *Postmodern Culture* 14.1 (2003).

31. Helmling, "Constellation and Critique." Here Helmling also notes how Adorno directs his critique of critique to fellow critics. On Lukács, Adorno states: "Under the guise of an ostensibly radical critique of society he smuggled back the most pitiful clichés of conformism to which that critique had once been directed." See Theodor Adorno, *Notes on Literature* (trans. Shierry Weber Nicholson; 2 vols.; New York: Columbia, 1992), 1:217.

32. Judith Butler, for example, uses the imagery of congealment to discuss socially constructed gender norms/frames. See *Gender Trouble: Feminism and the Subversion of Identity* (New York: Routledge, 1999 [1990]), 33. On the image of congealment in Butler's work, see Salih, *Judith Butler*, 62–3, 82.

focus chiefly on the ISR (particularly Adorno and Benjamin), who offer the thought image of congealment, a starting point to help us move beyond literature's inevitable integration into the system.[33] For Adorno, critique begins with a recognition of congealed ideologies. Congealment involves the solidifying of substances by cooling or freezing. Adorno describes immanent critique as the reverse process of congealment, reliquifying what has been solidified, that is, reliquifying ideologies that have been hardened: "The thought movement that congealed in [concepts] must be reliquified, its validity traced, so to speak, in repetition."[34] In further explaining Adorno's idea of *immanent critique*, Steven Helmling couples Adorno's above assertion with another assertion, one from Adorno's "A Portrait of Walter Benjamin," where he describes Benjamin as one who "awaken[s] congealed life in petrified objects."[35] Helmling then summarizes Adorno's thought image as follows: "Adorno likewise figures 'reification' as a process of freezing, hardening, or congealing, and the critical process, by contrast, as one of softening, loosening, reliquifying (as in … Benjamin's attempt to 'awaken congealed life in petrified objects')."[36]

Four observations about Adorno's thought image are noteworthy in relation to early Christian texts. First, and as argued in the first section above, popular texts are massified, calcified, reified, and congealed within the contexts of their receptions. As a result, they simply cannot be read at self-evident or common-sense levels. Read this way, they replicate, reinforce, and justify the structures and categories into which they have already been congealed.[37] What is more, rational, objective inquiry does not escape this congealment,

---

33. In the next two sections, I follow Helmling's discussion of Adorno's and Benjamin's ideas of critique: immanent critique and the dialectical image. See Steven Helmling, *Adorno's Poetics of Critique* (Continuum Studies in Continental Philosophy; New York: Continuum, 2009), 100–37, and "Constellation and Critique."

34. Theodor Adorno, *Negative Dialectics* (trans. E. B. Ashton; New York: Seabury, 1973), 97. Here Adorno is discussing the ideological congealment of Heidegger's ontology.

35. Adorno, *Prisms*, 233. Regarding the past, Benjamin "was drawn to the petrified, frozen or obsolete elements of civilization." See Helmling, *Adorno's Poetics of Critique*, 113.

36. Helmling, *Adorno's Poetics of Critique*, 105.

37. Badiou refers to this type of thinking as "ethical ideology," as opposed to "the ethics of truth." The former is expressed in the phrase "love only that which you have always believed"; the latter is expressed in the phrase "love what you will never believe twice." Ethical ideology, according to Badiou, "tells [individuals] to stick with what they know and have always believed." See *Ethics: An Essay on the Understanding of Evil* (trans. Peter Hallward; London: Verso: 2001 [1993]), 52–6. For an analysis of ethical ideology and the ethics of truth in Badiou's philosophy, see Ed Pluth, *Badiou: A Philosphy of the New* (Cambridge: Polity, 2010), 137–8.

including scientific and historical analyses.[38] These analyses include the historical analysis of early Christian texts (for example, see Myles on Wright and Crossan above). In this volume, we aim to expose congealed ideologies in our own time, ones that affect the way we read early Christian texts, for example, exposing congealed assumptions about city planning and gentrification and how they affect reading of the New Jerusalem in book of Revelation (Seesengood, Chapter Three); or exposing our congealed assumptions about gender and sexuality and how they affect our reading of the Pauline corpus (Nicolet, Chapter Fourteen).

Second, in order to move beyond a type of reading that reinforces present ideologies, some sort of method needs to expose and break this congealment, much like a flame reliquifies the congealed in chemistry.[39] We will return to this point in the next section below.

Third, what has been congealed must be traced—a tracing that includes the contexts from and into which the texts have been congealed. On Adorno's immanent critique above ("... its validity traced ... in repetition"), Helmling notes that critique must be immanent, starting from inside "the ruse" of the ideological system it is critiquing: "critique must suffer the ruse of ideology, and even in a sense reproduce it from within, the very course of the attempt to unmask it and undo its power."[40] Herein lies the value of the historical-critical method. Whereas it certainly can serve as an escape route from conducting critical analyses—both of the present and past, as Lewis Gordon points out—or serve as a reinforcement of present ideologies, it ought not be abandoned in immanent critique.[41] The historical-critical

---

38. For a critique of rationality (instrumental rationality), see Horkheimer and Adorno, *Dialectic of Enlightenment: Philosophical Fragments*; Bronner, *Critical Theory*, 51–62. See also Butler, "What is Critique?" 221, who discusses positivism and rationalization in light of the Frankfurt School and Foucault.

39. Note Badiou's comment on truth: "It depends on an irruption, not on a structure." See Alain Badiou, "Philosophy as Biography," *The Symptom* 9 (2007).

40. Helmling, "Constellation and Critique," section 3.

41. For a critique on how historicism and textualism serve as retreats, see Lewis R. Gordon, *Disciplinary Decadence: Living Thought in Trying Times* (New York: Routledge, 2016), 2, 42. Gordon critiques religious studies for its overreliance on cataloguing historical "facts" while failing to articulate an overall understanding that integrates pressing, present questions. He argues that religious studies retreats into historicism and textualism, a retreat that is "a kind of unreasoned rationality." It is rational because "it has a logical order or method or process." It is unreasonable because "genuine thinking," which Gordon defines as bringing unsettled questions to the fore, is taken out of the process. The result of this unreasoned rationality is valuing disciplinary method over the pursuit of understanding. Disciplines themselves, therefore, become isolated and fetishized and reified and congealed. This isolation reduces disciplines and their sub-disciplines into "a stalemate of subjectivities." On fetishizing disciplinary methods, see

method can reveal how congealed ideologies have concealed themselves today, a concealment that Judith Butler discusses in her own work.[42] Sara Salih, commenting on Butler, notes how discourses and ideologies often hide their genealogies, their own histories, and by doing so, they appear as timeless.[43] In light of what Butler and Salih are claiming, the historical-critical method helps us trace the genealogies of congealed, "timeless," and "unquestionable" readings of early Christian texts. The danger, however, is when the historical-critical method is fetishized as an end in itself—outside of the context of critical theory, outside of tracing the genealogies of ideologies. When fetishized as ends, historical analyses halt at repeating and tracing texts and their ideologies, *supposedly* leaving texts in their own eras without conscious interaction with the present.[44] Hence, the results of historical analyses are relativized, placed into, in the words of Lewis Gordon, a "stalemate of subjectivities."[45] Philip Davies notes the resulting stalemate in biblical and early Christian studies: "historical-critical exegesis had managed to avoid addressing the question of contemporary meaning and thus avoided a great deal of conflict with religious interpretations, enabling many scholars to keep the classroom and chapel apart."[46] As a result, present ideologies remain congealed and timeless, unquestionable and unchallenged—and so do ancient texts—when historical methods are used as ends. But this is not the case when historical-critical methods are co-opted with immanent critique, supposedly. Benjamin does not place confidence in solely tracing movements and sequences. In "On the Concept of History," Benjamin argues against a historicism that "culminates in universal history," preferring "arrest" over "movement of thoughts," preferring spatial (dialectical images) to sequential

---

also Lewis R. Gordon, "Disciplinary Decadence and the Decolonisation of Knowledge," *African Development* 39.1 (2014): 81–92.

42. See Butler, *Bodies That Matter*, 12: "Performativity is thus not a singular 'act,' for it is always a reiteration of a norm or set of norms, and to the extent that it acquires an act-like status in the present, *it conceals or dissimulates* the conventions of which it is a repetition" (italics are my own).

43. Salih, *Judith Butler*, 95.

44. I say *supposedly* here with New Historicism in mind, which challenges the idea that ancient texts can be purely repeated and traced, as if historical methods really can recapture texts in their own eras apart from the influence of our own.

45. Gordon, *Disciplinary Decadence*, 42.

46. Davies, "Biblical Studies: Fifty Years of a Multi-Discipline," 50. For a similar critique of the historical-critical method in light of reception history, see William John Lyons, "Hope for a Troubled Discipline? Contributions to New Testament from Reception History," *JSNT* 33.2 (2010): 208–20, here 215 and 217.

tracing. Benjamin aims for "thinking [that] suddenly comes to a stop in a constellation saturated with tensions."[47]

Fourth, immanent critique breaks apart and recombines; however, in doing so, it neither destroys nor synthesizes. Or to put it another way: this thought image involves recovery, not destruction; juxtaposition, not synthesis.[48] Helmling accordingly states: "Immanent critique seeks as much to recover what is valid in ideological congealments as to undo what is false."[49] This recovery, however, does not result in a synthesis into a seamless system, nor a narrative without gaps or tensions, nor a new congealment.[50] Nor does it result in a correction or refinement of a present congealment. Rather, recovery involves parataxis. It involves montage: new juxtapositions, new tensions, new and strange relationships, or in Adorno's own terms, constellations—a term he derives from Benjamin's *The Origin of German Tragic Drama*.[51] These constellations can include pieces from the present and the past—montages across history. With constellations in mind, this volume intentionally creates constellations. For example, though appearing on the surface as an "anachronistic thought-experiment," James Crossley (Chapter Eleven) creates a constellation of Marx, Lenin, Stalin, and early Christianity in light of modern English and American liberalism. Constellations such as these strike at the strongholds of congealed ideologies. In Benjamin's terms, the relationships create dialectical images and blast through eras and their congealments. In the next section, I connect this fourth point with Benjamin's concept of the dialectical image and show

---

47. Benjamin, *Selected Writings*, 4:396.

48. In applying Deleuze's ideas about "the unfinished whole," Kristien Justaert, derives a "non-reductive theology" from Deleuze, one I contend is similar to Adorno's ideas about the (non-reductive) constellation. See Kristien Justaert, "Gilles Deleuze (1925–1995)," 370–82 in *Religion and European Philosophy: Key Thinkers from Kant to Žižek* (ed. Philip Goodchild and Hollis Phelps; New York: Routledge, 2017), 370–82, here 377.

49. Helmling, "Constellation and Critique," section 8.

50. Helmling, "Constellation and Critique," section 8. Adorno prefers the language of parataxis here. Perhaps a reference to Adorno's aesthetics, where he compares impressionism to montage, best illustrates this distinction: "Impressionism dissolved objects ... into their smallest elements in order to synthesize them gaplessly into the dynamic continuum. It wanted aesthetically to redeem the alienated and heterogenous in the replica ... It was against this that montage protested, which developed out of the pasted-in newspaper clippings and the like during the heroic years of cubism." Theodor Adorno, *Aesthetic Theory* (ed. Gretel Adorno and Rolf Tiedemann; trans. Robert Hullot-Kentor; Theory and History of Literature, 88; Minneapolis, MN: University of Minnesota Press, 1997), 154–5.

51. Helmling, *Adorno's Poetics of Critique*, 101. For "constellation," see Adorno, *Negative Dialectics*, 162–6.

how it informs the reading of early Christian texts, and most importantly, how it can blast through the inevitable and unquestionable lure of the culture industry, of its status quo, of its common sense.

Early Christian Texts and the Dialectical Image

Just as all four theorists in this volume, in their own ways, discuss the inevitability of "congealed" ideologies, they also propose their own ways of breaking through them, or subverting them. For Butler, this involves drag, subversion of norms, and resignification. For Badiou, this involves "the event," intervention, resurrecting truths, and forcing (a mathematical concept depicting the naming of a new, radical event). For Deleuze, this involves becoming animal, becoming woman, or playing the game of Go instead of being confined to the boundaries and borders of a chess board. All of these ways are discussed in more detail in the chapters that follow. But here I focus on Benjamin's dialectical image and Adorno's immanent critique and the constellation.

Adorno's ideas of immanent critique and the constellation connect with Benjamin's methodology of "reading" history, which in Adorno's words, is "… to awaken congealed life in petrified objects … but also to scrutinize living things so that they present themselves as being ancient …"[52] Benjamin, like Adorno, awakens congealed life.[53] But he also presents living things as ancient: "to scrutinize living things so that they present themselves as being ancient …" This unique combination of the past and the present, of the old and the new, is best expressed in Benjamin's *Arcades Project*, where he forms and explains the "dialectical image":

> It's not that what is past casts its light on what is present, or what is present its light on what is past; rather, image is that wherein what has been comes together in a flash with the now to form a constellation. In other words, image is dialectics at a standstill. For while the relation of the present to the past is a purely temporal, continuous one, the relation of what-has-been to the now is dialectical: is not progression but image, suddenly emergent. —Only dialectical images are genuine images (that is, not archaic); and the place where one encounters them is language.[54]

---

52. Adorno, *Prisms*, 233. See Helmling, "Constellation and Critique," section 2.

53. See Agata Bielik-Robson, "Walter Benjamin" in *Religion and European Philosophy*, 115–26. Here Bielik-Robson describes Benjamin's method in relation to theology: "the liquidation of theology"; "making the theological message fluid again, before it has congealed into religious dogma"; "theology turned into liquid ink … used once again to compose a new scripture."

54. Walter Benjamin, *The Arcades Project* (trans. Howard Eiland and Kevin McLaughlin; Cambridge, MA: Belknap Press, 1999), 462.

The dialectical image is a constellation. It views the past and the present together not as a seamless progression, but as an image at a standstill, as a dialectics at a standstill.⁵⁵ The place of encounter, according to Benjamin, is language. This encounter, therefore, is also one of "reading" history. Noting Benjamin's disenchantment with the German academy's models for reading historically, Gerhard Richter describes Benjamin's "model of reading historically that breaks with received academic wisdom and that is applicable not only to literary works but also to cultural objects and social texts in the widest sense."⁵⁶ Objects of the past have continual value when they are captured in dialectical images with the present. Colby Dickinson sums up well the value of these images for Benjamin: "In essence, history contains a limitless series of images, of those marginalized (or 'dangerous') memories which hold the power to overthrow our present perceptions of the past, that is, our traditions as we have constituted them."⁵⁷ Recovering these images counters the academy's way of reading history, which, according to Richter, involves confirmation of what is already assumed to be true, that is, "arranging works in their own chronological configuration and locating in them, in a mimetic arrest, the material content necessary for the confirmation of what one already assumes to be true of a particular historical moment."⁵⁸

Here I delineate four key points for reading historically through Benjamin's dialectical image, in particular for reading early Christian texts in the twenty-first century. First, while awakening congealed life is an important piece of Benjamin's approach to ancient texts, so is stillness, that is, "dialectics at a standstill," a phrase Benjamin uses in contrast to viewing a narrative progression in history.⁵⁹ Benjamin embraces "image" and the "suddenly emergent" instead of narrative. So Helmling sums up Benjamin's approach: "history as *image* rather than *story*."⁶⁰ In this way, Adorno describes Benjamin's methodology with another thought image: "the glance of his phi-

---

55. Note that "standstill" is in tension with liquefying the congealed. This tension is discussed below.

56. Gerhard Richter, *Thought-Images: Frankfurt School Writers' Reflections from Damaged Life* (Stanford, CA: Stanford University Press, 2007), 63. Here I follow Richter's chapter on Walter Benjamin (pp. 43–71).

57. Colby Dickinson, "The Relationship of Canon and Messiah: The Convergence of Jan Assmann and Walter Benjamin on a Theory of Monotheistic Canon," *The Bible and Critical Theory* 7.1 (2011): 1–15, here 6–7.

58. Richter, *Thought-Images*, 64.

59. In this volume, both Seesengood (Chapter Three) and Levenson (Chapter Four) underscore Benjamin's antipathy for viewing history as a progression.

60. Helmling, *Adorno's Poetics of Critique,* 137. For the contrast between image an narrative, see Helmling, "Constellation and Critique," section 6.

losophy is Medusan."[61] While the Medusan glance is perhaps problematic in coupling it with the thought image of the reliquified past, the Medusan glance sheds more light on Benjamin's approach to the present than the past, or more specifically, in Helmling's words, to "nascent ideology."[62] For Adorno uses the Medusan image in the context of Benjamin's discussion of his contemporaries.[63] Helmling notes that Benjamin himself uses similar Medusan imagery to discuss the present and future market economy of the bourgeoisie, speaking of "the monument of the bourgeoisie as ruins."[64] All this to say: while early Christian scholarship has set its sights on the past, it is vital to have a Medusan gaze upon the present, exposing its ideology, its assumptions about the progression of history, and its relationship with the culture industry. Moreover, without this Medusan gaze at the present, dialectical images are incomplete (and not dialectic), thereby returning to and repeating the predicaments outlined in the first section above.

Another image Adorno uses here to depict Benjamin's "stillness" methodology—one perhaps highlighting what Benjamin does with layered images from different time periods—is the palimpsest, an image quite familiar to early Christian scholarship: "All creation becomes for [Walter Benjamin] script that must be deciphered though the code is unknown. He immersed himself in reality as in a palimpsest. Interpretation, translation, critique are the schemes of his thought."[65] Benjamin saw in his study scripts of "complex layers that compose the world."[66] These are buried layers of script that may be recovered in a palimpsest. However, older layers are not hidden origins superior to what is written over them. Adorno was not the first to use the palimpsest in this manner. The image has its own layers. Perhaps Benjamin himself thought about the palimpsest's relation to reality while reading one of his favorite thinkers, the nineteenth-century French poet and essayist Charles Baudelaire, who in *Artificial Paradises* quotes another writer one

---

61. Adorno, *Prisms*, 233. Quoted in Helmling, "Constellation and Critique," section 2. Note the implications here as pointed out by Helmling. If Benjamin is Perseus, he freezes and kills Medusa with a mirror, beheads her, and uses her image to freeze and kill adversaries. Perhaps this image informs the scholar of early Christians texts: holding a mirror to the past from the present, while freezing the present with the past.

62. Helmling, "Constellation and Critique," section 13.

63. Helmling, "Constellation and Critique," section 13.

64. Helmling, "Constellation and Critique," section 13.

65. Theodor Adorno, "Introduction to Benjamin's *Schriften*," in *On Walter Benjamin: Critical Essays and Recollections* (ed. Gary Smith; Cambridge, MA: MIT Press, 1988), 8–9.

66. Benjamin, *Selected Writings*, 1:284. See also Howard Eiland, "Reality as Palimpsest: On Benjamin's Arcades Project" (The Program in Critical Theory lecture, UC Berkeley, Berkeley, CA, 15 April 2010).

generation before him, the English essayist Thomas De Quincy.⁶⁷ Both connect memory to the palimpsest.⁶⁸ To De Quincy, the brain has "everlasting layers of ideas, images and feelings," where "each succession has seemed to bury all that went before," but "in reality, not one has perished." Baudelaire takes this thought one step further, focusing on the difference between the palimpsest and memory. The former, from a "Greek tragedy" to a "knightly romance," amasses "a collision between heterogeneous elements," while the latter "imposes a harmony among the most disparate elements." Richard Terdiman sums up Baudelaire's point well: "[the texts of memory] were always already overwritten by the process of writing itself."⁶⁹ Each new layer *seemingly* overwrites the older ones. They are connected, but not synthesized. Benjamin concretizes this thinking in his *Arcades Project*, where he captures the nineteenth-century Paris arcades in the images of his own twentieth-century Paris, palimpsesting the present with the past, and the past with the present. So, like Adorno, Eiland and Jennings appropriately summarize Benjamin's writing—and view of history—as "a kind of vertical montage."⁷⁰ And vertical montage is a thought image useful for the study of early Christian origins. But to study early Christian origins by scraping off what is written over them is a betrayal-in-reverse of the palimpsester: erasing the present with the hope of uncovering a "purer," more authoritative past.

Second, given the image of a vertical montage, to what extent should scholarship mediate between the layers, between the dialectical images? It is montage after all, or in Baudelaire's terms, a "collision between heterogeneous elements." In connecting the past and the present, to what extent should scholars of early Christian texts mediate between the two? A famous exchange between Adorno and Benjamin addresses similar questions, with Benjamin arguing for montage with very little mediation (if at all), and with Adorno arguing for mediation through theory. Benjamin submitted a piece to ISR's *Journal for Social Research*, a piece on Baudelaire that was part of his larger *Arcades Project*.⁷¹ Adorno criticized Benjamin's piece because it brought together materials from Baudelaire and social history without

---

67. Eiland and Jennings make this suggestion in *A Critical Life*, 708.

68. Charles Baudelaire, *Artificial Paradises* (ed. and trans. Stacy Diamond; New York: Citadel, 1996), 147–9.

69. Richard Terdiman, *Present Past: Modernity and the Memory Crisis* (Ithaca, NY: Cornell University Press, 1993), 109.

70. Eiland and Jennings, *A Critical Life*, 383.

71. See Helmling, *Adorno's Poetics of Critique*, 112. For Adorno's response to Benjamin's piece, see Theodor Adorno and Walter Benjamin, *The Complete Correspondence, 1928–1940* (ed. Henri Lonitz; trans. Nicholas Walker; Cambridge, MA: Harvard University Press, 1999), 281–3. For a rendering of this exchange more sympathetic to Benjamin's point of view, see Eiland and Jennings, *A Critical Life*, 622–9, who describe

mediation. Adorno states: "Motifs are assembled but they are not elaborated."[72] He again states: "Unless I am very much mistaken, your dialectic is lacking in one thing: mediation. You show a prevailing tendency to relate the pragmatic contents of Baudelaire's work directly and immediately to adjacent features in social history, and whenever possible, economic features, of the time."[73] And again, Adorno states: "The 'mediation' which I miss and find obscured by materialistic-historiographic evocation, is simply the theory which your study has omitted."[74]

Though ultimately agreeing to revise the work for the journal, Benjamin did counter Adorno, appealing to the constellation. Eiland and Jennings note: "Benjamin was intent on working out a method of historical encapsulation through typifying images in shifting constellations, and he was convinced that the knowledge to which this motivic method gave access, knowledge of present and past in light of each other, could not be recuperated through any amount of abstract theorizing."[75] In the context of his larger *Arcades Project,* Benjamin originally crafted this Baudelaire piece to be this type of constellation. Sections coming before and after this piece in the *Arcades Project* then would include theory. But in the end, Benjamin revised the center section, entitled "On Some Motifs in Baudelaire."

The importance of this Benjamin-Adorno conversation is twofold: first, in light of Benjamin's claims, it expresses due caution about providing too much mediation and synthesis between the past and the present, a synthesis leading to the inevitable integration of the past into present norms, as articulated the first section above;[76] second, in light of Adorno's claims, it expresses the need to provide at least some theoretical mediation between the present and the past. Without theoretical mediation, the same danger is also present as with too much mediation: integrating an unquestioned past into unquestioned norms of the present, that is, integrating present norms which the traditions of the past themselves have established (e.g., gender norms). Theory ought not unify constellations into an already existing common sense or status quo, but highlight discontinuities in and between

---

the exchange as "the most crushing rejection of [Benjamin's] career" and Adorno's letter as plunging Benjamin "into a deep, immobilizing depression."
72. Adorno and Benjamin, *The Complete Correspondence*, 282.
73. Adorno and Benjamin, *The Complete Correspondence*, 282.
74. Adorno and Benjamin, *The Complete Correspondence*, 283.
75. Eiland and Jennings, *A Critical Life*, 625.
76. Perhaps this is best illustrated by a potential "Walter Benjamin Bible Commentary" series. Each biblical book would only include quotes about it (often obscure and juxtaposed) from over two millennia, without mediation from its author/scholar/compiler, the result being a vertical montage.

and within the past and the present.[77] Judith Butler accordingly states: "not only is it necessary to isolate and identify the peculiar nexus of power and knowledge that gives rise to the field of intelligible things, but also to track the way in which the field meets its breaking point, the moments of its discontinuities, the sites where it fails to constitute the intelligibility for which it stands."[78] In this volume, we aim to read the past and present together, but not in the service of a unified field of knowledge or faith. Rather, our aim is to identify cracks and fissures in dialectical images of the past and present. In Chapters Fourteen and Fifteen, for example, Valérie Nicolet and Peter Anthony Mena read the theories of Judith Butler alongside Paul and Origen, bringing together contemporary and ancient ideas of gender, the body, and bodies. Without theoretical mediation, analyses of gender and the body in these ancient texts would be too prone to projections from "common sense" approaches derived from present structures of power and knowledge, including assumptions within theories themselves. With theoretical mediation and dialectical images, deeper, more nuanced questions are asked. Nicolet exposes Paul as both "disciplinary" and "liberating," showing how "any liberating discourse is also always at the same time a disciplining discourse." Mena expands Butler's theories of the body to both human and non-human bodies, creating a dialectical image that exposes cracks and fissures in hierarchical assumptions (both past and present) about bodies. In doing so, Mena orients us "toward justice for all matter ... a justice that extends beyond care for only matter viewed as animate."

Third, the dialectical image blasts out pieces from the past, past objects petrified in the present, caught in present ideological congealments, often unquestionable ones. These are, again in Dickinson's words, "marginalized memories" holding "the power to overthrow our present perceptions." And I also suggest here that, in referencing the first part of this chapter, "marginalized memories" hold "radical impulses." To stay true to Benjamin's concepts, these impulses are found in dialectical images, not apart from them—for we cannot capture historical moments apart from the present. They are recovered only in the present. In Benjamin's words, it is a "consciousness of the present which explodes the continuum of history."[79] Shock

---

77. See Helmling, "Constellation and Critique," section 21: "For Adorno, the point of mediation would be to render, even 'exaggerate,' the disjunctions, the contradictions that, for Lukács, they should unify."
78. Butler, "What is Critique?" 222.
79. Walter Benjamin, "Eduard Fuchs, Collector and Historian," in *Selected Writings* (ed. Michael W. Jennings; trans. Rodney Livingstone, et al.; 4 vols.; Cambridge, MA: Belknap Press, 1991–1999), 3:262. We turn to this piece on Fuchs in Chapter Two below.

and explosion both occur in the present, in the dialectical image. In shock, which is Adorno's motif, we see the ability to "awaken numbed perception" and "subvert received habits of synthesizing" (Helmling's words).[80] And in explosion, which is Benjamin's motif, we see how these "obscure constellations" disrupt history: "both the past and present are torn from their immediate contexts … 'exploded' out their putative teleology," (Richter's words).[81]

In the study of early Christian texts, these disrupting pieces and constellations are often found and formed by writings marginalized by the status quo: for instance, Howard Thurman's *Jesus and the Disinherited*.[82] More recently, Mitzi Smith and Yung Suk Kim challenge the congealed centering of white male scholarship in New Testament Introductions. In *Toward Decentering the New Testament: A Reintroduction*, Smith and Kim assert "agency and creativity and resistance to a status quo that systematically or routinely silences the concerns of nonwhite communities and the scholarship they produce."[83] And lest the work challenging the center remain on the margins, Smith and Kim assert: "This text attempts to honor and give space to minoritized scholars; as an aggregate, we *majoritize* our work and perspectives as authoritative voices and resources for understanding the New Testament for further study."[84] Sharon Jacob, furthermore, calls out what she terms "White Incredulity" and "White Amnesia": "scholars and particularity white scholars in academia collectively experience *White Amnesia* when it comes to engaging with the work of scholars of color. Sometimes our work might be relegated to footnotes or works cited sections, thus illustrating the marginal ways in which our scholarship is engaged and interacted with in the mainstream."[85] The present, ideological congealments of scholarship must continually be blasted through. Below Sharon Jacob critiques assumptions

---

80. See Helmling, "Constellation and Critique," section 18.

81. Richter, *Thought-Images*, 64.

82. Howard Thurman, *Jesus and the Disinherited* (Nashville, TN: Abingdon Press, 1949). The formation of constellations, especially ones challenging present norms, is not new to the reception of early Christian texts, especially in writings marginalized by the norms. Referring to Hegel, Bronner points out that "progress is ultimately furthered by the person who is out of step with the majority" (*Critical Theory*, 77).

83. Mitzi J. Smith and Yung Suk Kim, *Toward Decentering the New Testament* (Eugene, OR: Cascade Books, 2018), 4.

84. Smith and Kim, *Toward Decentering the New Testament*, 3.

85. Sharon Jacob, "White Incredulity and Why It Matters? Distrust, Disbelief, and the Immigrant Experience." 2 August 2020. Cited 25 November 2020, https://medium.com/@sharonjacobpts/the-term-white-fragility-coined-by-robin-dangelo-refers-to-the-defensiveness-or-disbelief-that-4a80bf0095b8.

scholarship makes about majority language and the "one voice" of worshiping nations in Revelation 7 (see Chapter Eight).

Obscure constellations are also formed when marginalized biblical texts (i.e., non-canonical texts) are read alongside majority texts (i.e., canonical texts). Or they are formed when the sacred is found "in the advertising kiosk," as Benjamin himself points out in "The Religious Position of the New Youth."[86] Or they are formed when modern and obscure ideas (at least ones obscure to the first few centuries) are connected with early Christian texts. We aim to do in this volume: for example, when Walter Benjmamin dialogues about progress with Augustine over a game of chess (Levenson, Chapter Four), or when modern national anthems are connected with the worship language in Revelation (Jacob, Chapter Eight), or when modern mathematics (set theory) comes into contact with allegory, Adam, Jesus, Paul, and Irenaeus (Phelps, Chapter Twelve).

Fourth, dialectical images bring strangeness to both the past and the present. On Adorno (in light of Benjamin's dialectical image), Helming observes: "he may present an unfamiliar or even shocking juxtaposition, whose *estrangement* is to provoke a new and heightened consciousness of the ideological condition in which we are entrapped."[87] (I add here: a new and heightened consciousness of the ideological conditions in which early Christian texts are entrapped.) Richter draws similar conclusions about the strangeness effect of the dialectical image—making both the past and present strange. Richter references Benjamin's essay "Literary History and Literary Scholarship" in order to articulate this point. Benjamin asserts: "What is at stake is not to portray literary works in the context of their age, but to represent the age that perceives them—our age—in the age during which they arose. It is this that makes literature into the organon of history; and to achieve this, and not to reduce literature to the material of history, is the task of the literary historian."[88] On this passage, Richter makes two important points. First, by "organon," Benjamin does not mean that reading historically involves "arranging works in their own chronological configuration" and confirming "what one already assumes to be true of a particular historical moment."[89] Second, Benjamin does not mean "retroactively imposing

---

86. Walter Benjamin, "The Religious Position of the New Youth," in *Walter Benjamin: Early Writings, 1910–1917* (ed. Howard Eiland; trans. Howard Eiland, et al.; Cambridge, MA: Belknap Press, 2011), 168–70, here 169. See also the question and answer period in Howard Eiland, "Reality as Palimpsest," where this Benjamin piece is referenced in relation to early Christianity.
87. Helmling, "Constellation and Critique," section 17.
88. Benjamin, *Selected Writings*, 2:464.
89. Richter, *Thought-Images*, 64.

on texts of the past the concerns and issues of a later age in which they are read."[90] Rather, reading historically involves analyzing a text outside of the time in which it is embedded (e.g., "our time … comes to presentation only in what it is not").[91] In other words, "the historicity of a text may only become legible subsequent to its removal from its historical embeddedness," the embeddedness of our own texts in our own time and past texts in their time; hence, the value of a "double rupture" of both the past and present in a dialectical relationship.[92]

Below I conclude by working with this fourth point about Benjamin's dialectical image: strangeness, and in our case, making early Christian texts strange again. This motif also returns us to the beginning of this chapter, that is, Claire Colebrook's discussion of Deleuze and how minor (and strange) literature becomes major (and common), and how—in borrowing from the ISR to explain Deleuze and Colebrook—minor literature becomes part of the culture industry. Below I discuss the reverse process: how—through immanent critique and reading history as a dialectical image—major (and common) literature becomes strange again, how constellations of the past and present, mediated by theory, bring a newness and strangeness to the present and its reading of the past. Recall Colebrook's words on Shakespeare: "He becomes minor, again, only if we recognize the potential of his work to be read as if we did not know who Shakespeare was."[93] An early reception theorist, Hans Robert Jauss, similarly argues: "Their [i.e., major literary works] *self-evident* beauty and their seemingly *unquestionable* 'eternal significance' bring them, from the point of view of the aesthetics of reception, into dangerous proximity with the irresistible and enjoyable 'culinary' art, and special effort is needed to read them 'against the grain' of accustomed experience so that their artistic nature becomes evident again."[94] I argue that early Christian texts become minor and strange again if we read them as if we did not know what they were. Critical theory, immanent critique, constellations, and dialectical images all help us to read them as if we did not know what they were.

90. Richter, *Thought-Images*, 64.
91. Richter, *Thought-Images*, 64.
92. Richter, *Thought-Images*, 64.
93. Claire Colebrook, *Gilles Deleuze*, 105
94. Jauss, "Literary History as a Challenge to Literary Theory," 15. While Jauss is talking about aesthetical reception here, later in the essay (Part VII), he discusses the social effects of "shattering" familiar expectations (pp. 31–7). I assert here that the Adorno-Benjamin approach offers more than the ironically popular phrase "reading against the grain."

Conclusion: Making Early Christian Texts Strange (Again)

Making early Christian texts strange again is further explained by turning to literary theory and one of its sub-disciplines, Science Fiction Theory, a sub-discipline that also involves across-time and time-out-of-joint images, ones that create a "double rupture," more often involving the present and the future than the present and the past, although its alternative histories do direct readers strangely back in time. Here I end with the work of Darko Suvin, who derives his theories about Science Fiction from Marx and circles associated with ISR, namely Berthold Brecht (estrangement) and Ernst Bloch (novum).[95] He also draws upon the work Walter Benjamin.[96] Suvin brings two terms into relations with the study of Science Fiction, which I propose are also helpful to bring to the study of early Christianity and help illuminate the effects of Benjamin's dialectical image in the future: *cognitive estrangement* and *novum*. Gerry Canavan, commenting on Suvin's first term, notes: "Cognitive estrangement constitutes precisely this twofold move: we transport to the other world (estrangement) so that we can better think about this one (cognition)."[97] Early Christian texts, when accompanied by historical-critical tools and critical theory, transport readers into other worlds, creating estrangement; however, for Benjamin the estrangement happens in two worlds (the past and present); hence, Benjamin's double rupture. The transport is not a reactionary move, as if it opens a purer, utopian, early Christian world of true origins and morals, a world critiquing eras that follow it, including this one. (Note that in Science Fiction the transport is not only to utopias, but to dystopias or alternative histories.)

---

95. For Suvin's influences, see *Metamorphoses of Science Fiction*, xxxix and 18–9. On pp. 18–9, Suvin first points to Russian Formalist Viktor Shklovsky for the idea of estrangement (*ostranenie*), from whom I also have derived the title of this introduction: "making strange." See Viktor Shklovsky, *Theory of Prose* (trans. Benjamin Sher; Normal, IL: Dalkey Archive Press, 1990 [1929]). Suvin then points to a term from Berthold Brecht, a close friend of Walter Benjamin: *Verfremdungseffekt*. Suvin quotes Brecht's *Short Organon for the Theater*: "A representation which estranges is one which allows us to recognize its subject, but at the same time makes it seem unfamiliar."

96. See Darko Suvin, *Metamorphoses of Science Fiction: On the Poetics and History of a Literary Genre* (ed. Gerry Canavan; Bern, Switzerland: Peter Lang, 2016), 1. Here Suvin begins his classic work on Science Fiction with a familiar Benjamin quote (quoted above, n. 82) about reading across time in "Literary History and Literary Scholarship." He also looks to Benjamin as a scholar who writes at a crisis point in history; Suvin asserts we are in one today, e.g., "there were over 30 wars in 1999 alone!" (pp. 392, 450).

97. Gerry Canavan, "The Suvin Event," in *Metamorphoses of Science Fiction*, xi–xxxvi. Canavan, whom I follow here, provides an excellent introduction to Suvin's work and its effect on literary and Science Fiction theory.

Rather, the transport creates estrangement throughout, a breakage of old and current worlds and norms, thereby opening up the future to *novum*, new worlds that bring further estrangement. *Novum* is the second term used by Suvin.[98] Suvin writes:

> The escape [into other worlds] is ... one to a better vantage point from which to comprehend the human relations around the author. It is an escape from constrictive old norms into a different and alternative timestream, a device for historical estrangement, and an at least initial readiness for new norms of reality, for the novum of dealienating human history.[99]

Here dialectical images and alternative timestreams provide a transport for *better vantage points* to *escape from constrictive old norms*—and in our case, from constrictive norms of both the past and present.[100] This transport is what delivers early Christian texts (or scholarship about them) from their integration into the system, from their integration into common norms and categories. At the same time, it brings readiness for *novum,* new ways of viewing reality and history. And this readiness, this *novum* is neither temporary nor the latest fashion.[101] It further breaks apart current categories and introduces the unfamiliar.

My assertion here is certainly not a call for early Christian scholarship to write Science Fiction, although such an effort may be quite estranging, like

---

98. I am intentionally combining (1) Benjamin's double rupture of the past and present with (2) Suvin's rupture of the present (estrangement) by a new reality (novum), which is usually a future world or sometimes an alternative history. For Suvin, *novum* is an alternative reality that can be rationally explained by science or a future science. It is a vehicle for cognitive estrangement.

99. Suvin, *Metamorphoses of Science Fiction*, 101.

100. Transport creates distance. Note Adorno's words on distance: "The value of thought is measured by its distance from the continuity of the familiar. It is objectively devalued as this distance is reduced; the more it approximates to the preexisting standard, the further its antithetical function is diminished." See Theodor Adorno, *Minima Moralia: Reflections on a Damaged Life* (trans. E. F. N. Jephcott; London: Verso, 2005 [1951]), 80.

101. Gerry Canavan ("The Suvin Event, xxiii), quoting Suvin (*Metamorphoses*, 87), states: "A novum which fails to produce such a politically charged vision of genuine historical difference will be 'of brief and narrow' relevance, precisely because 'they make for a superficial change rather than for a true novelty that deals with or makes for human relationships so qualitatively different from those dominant in the author's reality that they cannot be translated back to them merely by change in costume.'" Suvin's focus on a novum's qualitative difference offers an answer to Marcuse's critique of estrangement through art and literature, a critique which asserts that it, like mass culture, is fleeting and illusory. For a summation of Marcuse's critique of estrangement, see Galin Tihanov, "The Politics of Estrangement: The Case of the Early Shklovsky," *Poetics Today* 26.4 (2005): 665–96, here 689–91.

Philip K. Dick's unfulfilled wish to write an alternative "non-Christian" history, *The Acts of Paul*, where, according to his biographer Lawrence Sutin, "Manichaeism ... is the dominant world religion," and "by contrast, Christianity all but died out in the third century ..." Dick's "proposed narrator [is] a scholar out to locate 'secret Christians' who carry on the faith..."[102] Estranging scholarship need not be fictive, alternative histories. Scholarship about literature and art can aim to be just as estranging as Science Fiction, as exemplified by Adorno, Benjamin, and Suvin.[103] This estranging scholarship is best exemplified in our field by the journals *Bible and Critical Theory* and *Biblical Interpretation*, both mediating between the past and the present and the future with new transdisciplinary theories.

Estrangement can also be cultivated by the example Benjamin sets in *The Arcades Project*. While this volume focuses on early Christian texts and modern texts/theories in an Adorno-Benjamin sense, Benjamin's work alone calls for projects focusing on modern and early Christian artifacts. These projects include, for example, analyses of early Christian objects in light of modern Christian artifacts, such as those included in Colleen McDannell's book *Material Christianity: Religion and Popular Culture in America*.[104] Such analyses would place modern material objects in dialectic with artifacts and texts from early Christianity, much like Benjamin did with Paris in *The Arcades Project*, between the nineteenth and twentieth centuries. They would conjure an estranging effect. Like *The Arcades Project*, which Susan Buck-Morss describes as "a secular, sociopsychological theory of modernity as a dreamworld," such a project would look at modern Christian artifacts in popular culture.[105] However, as Buck-Morss points out, through dialectical images, today's dreamworld would not only

---

102. Lawrence Sutin, *Divine Invasions: A Life of Philip K. Dick* (New York: Carroll & Graff, 2005), 266. According to Sutin, Dick wrote a brief plot synopsis in January 1980. He died two years later without further work on the idea.

103. Mark Bould argues that Suvin's work itself is a work of estrangement. See "Introduction: Rough Guide to a Lonely Planet, from Nemo to Neo," in *Red Planets: Marxism and Science Fiction* (ed. Mark Bould and China Miéville; Middletown, CT: Wesleyan University Press, 2009), 1–26, here 18–9. Note also that Deleuze categorizes his prose philosophy as Science Fiction. See Deleuze, *Difference and Repetition*, xx–xi.

104. Colleen McDannell, *Material Christianity: Religion and Popular Culture in America* (New Haven, CT: Yale University Press, 1995).

105. Susan Buck-Morss, *The Dialectics of Seeing: Walter Benjamin and the Arcades Project* (Cambridge, MA: MIT Press, 1989), 253. Suvin, *Metamorphoses*, 432, asserts that Benjamin here counters Weber's critique of disenchantment: "the Weberian disenchantment of the world provokes a compensatory collective dream that Benjamin, like Marx, wanted to interrupt 'by dissolving mythology into the space of history.'" See Benjamin, *The Arcades Project*, 468.

be disclosed, but a "collective awakening from it" would also occur. Benjamin's theory "takes mass culture seriously not merely as the source of the phantasmagoria of false consciousness, but as the source of collective energy to overcome it."[106] Hence, such a project would find palimpsestic power in modern and early Christian artifacts together—connecting both, estranging both, apart from both eras.

Finally, it is by "making strange" that novum emerges in early Christian studies: that is, new norms, new texts, new categories, and new transdisciplinary contributions. But the two concepts are interrelated: it is also through novum that the process of "making strange" endures. First, this novum (at least in the Suvin/Benjamin sense) is not the recovery of a true past, nor new discoveries about the past, nor new interpretations about what the texts meant in the past; rather, novum is novum in the present and future—saying something about present reality by estranging the past and present together. Even as "non-canonical" texts are discovered, rediscovered, or newly translated, it is not so much what they reveal or confirm about "*the* past," that is, what their contrast reveals about "*the* roots" of accepted forms of Christianity; rather, their value is found in making early Christianity (in all its diversity) strange and unfamiliar again, opening up avenues for future ways of thinking about Christianity (novum). For Suvin points out, in reference to Benjamin, that "any healthy tradition is necessarily not ... only a canonic or 'high lit.' one."[107] And just as Benjamin allocated his resources not simply for high or canonical literature, early Christian studies ought to allocate more resources to what is strange, not common. William Lyons accordingly calls for a better allocation of resources in New Testament studies, away from texts that are most often studied.[108]

Second, making early Christianity strange again challenges the way people, artifacts, and texts are categorized, largely because novum does not yet have a category. Estrangement and novum fail to confirm what we already know and conform to how we know. Critique, according to Judith Butler, exposes the limits of current knowledge, showing that its categories are inadequate, that its discourse is inadequate.[109] The same can be said about estranging methodology, that is, the inadequacies it exposes and

---

106. Buck-Morss, *The Dialectics of Seeing*, 253.
107. Suvin, *Metamorphoses*, 8.
108. Lyons, "Hope for a Troubled Discipline?," 216.
109. Butler, "What is Critique?" 215–6. In the context of norms in relation to "I" and "other," see Judith Butler and Athena Athanasiou, *Dispossession: The Performative in the Political* (Cambridge: Polity, 2013), 67. Butler notes: "None of us know who precisely we will 'be' under regimes of ontology that we struggle against or seek to displace. It may be, for instance, that as we struggle against the categories of gender that

shows. Cracks and crevices have been exposed in different eras of reception, creating novum as new historical pieces are introduced or reintroduced, for example, the Jewishness of Jesus, Greco-Roman rhetoric, narrative criticism, and so on. Estrangement and novum also take place at an individual level, such as a student reading the New Testament in Greek for the first time, or no longer reading the New Testament at face value, but with historical context in mind. But "making strange" aims for something more radical here: blasting through familiar categories, queering familiar categories, or resurrecting truths anew, a concept from Badiou, which Hollis Phelps articulates in Chapter Twelve below.[110]

Finally, reading for estrangement and novum looks for a lens beyond a particular discipline. It looks for a transdisciplinary lens, the widened lens that Benjamin, Adorno, and the ISR were committed to examining the world through.[111] Widening the lens creates estrangement and novum, providing new perspectives, ones helping early Christian scholarship move beyond the norms of its own the discipline, as well as beyond supporting the norms of the culture industry.[112] A disciplinary lens hides and hardens these norms. Ward Blanton accordingly points out the cost of not engaging with "interdisciplinary traffic," and in particular not engaging with philosophy. To Blanton, it has "taken a heavy toll on our ability to produce creative

secure contemporary ideas of personhood, we no longer know exactly how we are to be named."

110. In this volume, Phelps expands on what he discusses earlier concerning Badiou's depiction of "the faithful subject" and Badiou's concept of "resurrecting truths": "This possibility corresponds with a faithful subject that does not so much produce a new truth as reactivate or resurrect an old truth for the production of something new in the present. To resurrect a truth, then, is to put that truth to a new use in the present, in an entirely different context." See Hollis Phelps, "Alain Badiou (1937–)," in *Religion and European Philosophy*, 438–51, here 445.

111. Tyrus Miller, "The Frankfurt School and Models of Interdisciplinarity," *Crosspollenblog*, 3 March 2014, http://crosspollen.files.wordpress.com. Miller identifies two types of interdisciplinary approaches in ISR. The first involves "problem based ventures into interdisciplinary criticism by individual scholars," exemplified in the work of Walter Benjamin and Theodor Adorno; the second involves the more radical approach of several scholars from several disciplines converging on the same problem or topic, an approach exemplified in the Institute's journal, *Zeitschrift für Sozialforschung*.

112. See Chapter Ten below, where Bruce Worthington applies the work of Badiou to discuss the events of early Christianity without recourse to traditional theology and its categories. For an argument on why biblical studies needs to move beyond simply serving theology, see James A. Kelhoffer, "New Testament Exegesis as an Academic Discipline," *CBR* 11.2 (2013): 218–33, here 222.

new historiographical modes of thinking about early Christian religion."[113] Indeed, "... with the sacrifice of breadth goes [a scholar's] ability to see the larger pictures, movements, or networks within which its methods and monuments have come to exist. The result can only be the repetition or naturalization of received modes of scholarship."[114] Bruce Worthington explores new modes below (Chapter 10) using Badiou's concept of the event. Trans- and interdisciplinary traffic potentially avoids repetitions, introducing strangeness, producing novum at the same time. What is more, widening the lens helps inform other disciplines, facilitating early Christian studies to contribute to dialogues outside its own boundaries, not simply taking methods from other disciplines in order to discover some supposed center of its own, but reaching outward and blasting through its norms and centers, ones which all disciplines, texts, and critiques are susceptible.[115]

Biographical Note

Matthew G. Whitlock (PhD, The Catholic University of America, 2008) is Associate Professor of New Testament at Seattle University. His research focuses on Acts of the Apostles, the Apostle Paul, New Testament Poetry, Critical Theory, and Science Fiction. His publications have focused on topics ranging from New Testament poetry in the *Catholic Biblical Quarterly* to the Body without Organs and Christianity in *Deleuze and Guattari Studies*. He is currently working on two books on dialectical images, one on images from the Science Fiction of Philip K. Dick and images from the letters of Paul, and the other on the theme of fame in images from the life of Kurt Cobain and early Christian writings about Jesus of Nazareth.

Bibliography

Adorno, Theodor. "A Portrait of Walter Benjamin," 227–42 in Adorno, *Prisms*. Translated by Samuel and Shierry Weber. Cambridge, MA: MIT Press, 1967.
—*Negative Dialectics* Translated by E. B. Ashton. New York: Seabury, 1973.
—"Introduction to Benjamin's *Schriften,"* 8–9 in *On Walter Benjamin: Critical Essays and Recollections*. Edited by Gary Smith. Cambridge, MA: MIT Press, 1988.

---

113. Ward Blanton, *Displacing Christian Origins: Philosophy, Secularity, and the New Testament* (Religion and Postmodernism; Chicago: University of Chicago Press, 2007).
114. Blanton, *Displacing Christian Origins*, 2.
115. Kelhoffer, "New Testament Exegesis as an Academic Discipline," 223. Kelhoffer urges New Testament Studies to consider what insights it can add to other disciplines, instead of simply being "beneficiaries" of their insights.

—*Notes on Literature*. Translated by Shierry Weber Nicholson. 2 volumes. New York: Columbia, 1992.
—*Aesthetic Theory*. Edited by Gretel Adorno and Rolf Tiedemann, translated by Robert Hullot-Kentor. Theory and History of Literature, 88; Minneapolis, MN: University of Minnesota Press, 1997.
—*Minima Moralia: Reflections on a Damaged Life*. Translated by E. F. N. Jephcott. London: Verso, 2005 [1951].
Adorno, Theodor, and Walter Benjamin. *The Complete Correspondence, 1928–1940*. Edited by Henri Lonitz and translated by Nicholas Walker. Cambridge, MA: Harvard University Press, 1999.
Badiou, Alain. *Ethics: An Essay on the Understanding of Evil.* Translated by Peter Hallward. London: Verso: 2001 [1993].
—"Philosophy as Biography," *The Symptom* 9 (2007): http://www.lacan.com/symptom9_articles/badiou19.html
Baldwin, James. *The Fire Next Time.* New York: The Dial Press, 1963.
Baudelaire, Charles. *Artificial Paradises.* Edited and translated by Stacy Diamond. New York: Citadel, 1996.
Benjamin, Walter. "Eduard Fuchs, Collector and Historian," in *Selected Writings*. Edited by Michael W. Jennings, translated by Rodney Livingstone, et al. 4 volumes. Cambridge, MA: Belknap Press, 1991–1999.
—*Gesammelte Briefe*. Edited by Christoph Gödde and Henri Lonitz. 6 volumes. Frankfurt: Suhrkamp Verlag, 1995–2000.
—*The Arcades Project*. Translated by Howard Eiland and Kevin McLaughlin. Cambridge, MA: Belknap Press, 1999.
—"The Religious Position of the New Youth," 168–70 in *Walter Benjamin: Early Writings, 1910–1917*. Edited by Howard Eiland, translated by Howard Eiland, et al. Cambridge, MA: Belknap Press, 2011.
Bielik-Robson, Agata. "Walter Benjamin," 115–26 in Goodchild and Phelps, eds., *Religion and European Philosophy*.
Blanton, Ward. *Displacing Christian Origins: Philosophy, Secularity, and the New Testament.* Religion and Postmodernism; Chicago, IL: University of Chicago Press, 2007. https://doi.org/10.7208/chicago/9780226056883.001.0001
Bould, Mark. "Introduction: Rough Guide to a Lonely Planet, from Nemo to Neo," 1–26 in *Red Planets: Marxism and Science Fiction*. Edited by Mark Bould and China Miéville. Middletown, CT: Wesleyan University Press, 2009.
Bronner, Stephen Eric. *Critical Theory: A Very Short Introduction.* Oxford: Oxford University Press, 2001.
Buck-Morss, Susan. *The Dialectics of Seeing: Walter Benjamin and the Arcades Project.* Cambridge, MA: MIT Press, 1989.
Butler, Judith. *Bodies That Matter: On the Discursive Limits of 'Sex'.* New York: Routledge, 1993.
—*Gender Trouble: Feminism and the Subversion of Identity.* New York: Routledge, 1999 [1990].
—"A 'Bad Writer' Bites Back." *New York Times,* 20 March 1999. https://archive.nytimes.com/query.nytimes.com/gst/fullpage-950CE5D61531F933A15750C0A96F958260.html (accessed 11/11/2021).
—"What is Critique? An Essay on Foucault's Virtue," 212–6 in *The Political Readings in Continental Philosophy.* Edited by David Ingram. London: Basil Blackwell, 2001.

Butler, Judith, and Athena Athanasiou, *Dispossession: The Performative in the Political.* Cambridge: Polity, 2013.
Colebrook, Claire. *Gilles Deleuze.* New York: Routledge, 2002. https://doi.org/10.4324/9780203241783
Crossan, John Dominic. *The Historical Jesus: The Life of a Mediterranean Jewish Peasant.* San Francisco, CA: Harper, 1991.
Crossley, James. *Jesus in an Age of Neoliberalism: Quests, Scholarship and Ideology.* Sheffield: Equinox, 2012.
—*Jesus in an Age of Terror: Scholarly Projects for a New American Century.* New York: Routledge, 2014; London: Equinox, 2008. https://doi.org/10.4324/9781315710914
Culp, Andrew. *Dark Deleuze.* Minneapolis, MN: University of Minnesota Press, 2016. https://doi.org/10.5749/9781452958392
Davies, Philip R. "Biblical Studies: Fifty Years of a Multi-Discipline," *Currents in Biblical Research* 13.1 (2014): 34–66. https://doi.org/10.1177/1476993X13508083
Deleuze, Gilles. "Du Christ à la bourgeoisie," *Espace* 1 (1946): 93–106. English translation: "From Christ to Bourgeoisie." Translated by Raymond van de Wiel, http://documents.raymondvandewiel.org/from_christ_to_the_bourgeoisie_translation.pdf
—*Difference and Repetition.* Translated by Paul Patton. New York: Columbia University Press, 1994.
Deleuze, Gilles, and Félix Guattari. *Anti-Oedipus: Capitalism and Schizophrenia.* Translated by Robert Hurley, Mark Seem, and Helen R. Lane. Minneapolis, MN: University of Minnesota Press, 1983.
—*Kafka: Toward a Minor Literature.* Translated by Dana Polan. Minneapolis, MN: University of Minnesota Press, 1986.
Dickinson, Colby. "The Relationship of Canon and Messiah: The Convergence of Jan Assmann and Walter Benjamin on a Theory of Monotheistic Canon," *The Bible and Critical Theory* 7.1 (2011): 1–15.
Eiland, Howard, and Michael W. Jennings. *Walter Benjamin: A Critical Life.* Cambridge, MA: Belknap Press, 2014.
Goodchild, Philip, and Hollis Phelps, eds. *Religion and European Philosophy: Key Thinkers from Kant to Žižek.* New York: Routledge, 2017. https://doi.org/10.4324/9781315642253
Gordon, Lewis R. "Disciplinary Decadence and the Decolonisation of Knowledge," *African Development* 39.1 (2014): 81–92. https://doi.org/10.4324/9781315635163
—*Disciplinary Decadence: Living Thought in Trying Times.* New York: Routledge, 2016.
Helmling, Steven. "Constellation and Critique: Adorno's Constellation, Benjamin's Dialectical Image," *Postmodern Culture* 14.1 (2003).
—*Adorno's Poetics of Critique.* Continuum Studies in Continental Philosophy; New York: Continuum, 2009. https://doi.org/10.1353/pmc.2003.0036
Horkheimer, Max, and Theodor Adorno. "The Culture Industry: Enlightenment as Mass Deception," 94–136 in *Dialectic of Enlightenment: Philosophical Fragments.* Edited by Gunzelin Schmid Noerr, translated by Edmund Jephcott. Stanford, CA: Stanford University Press, 2002.
Jacob, Sharon. "White Incredulity and Why It Matters? Distrust, Disbelief, and the Immigrant Experience." 2 August 2020. https://medium.com/@sharonjacobpts/the-term-white-fragility-coined-by-robin-dangelo-refers-to-the-defensiveness-or-disbelief-that-4a80bf0095b8 (accessed 12/11/2021).

Jacobs, Julia. "Sessions's Use of Bible Passage to Defend Immigration Policy Draws Fire." *New York Times,* 15 June 2018. https://www.nytimes.com/2018/06/15/us/sessions-bible-verse-romans.html (accessed 11/11/2021).

Jauss, Hans Robert. "Literary History as a Challenge to Literary Theory," *New Literary History* 2.1 (1970): 7–37. https://doi.org/10.2307/468585

Justaert, Kristien. "Gilles Deleuze (1925-1995)," 370–82 in Goodchild and Phelps, eds., *Religion and European Philosophy*, 2017. https://doi.org/10.4324/9781315642253-32

Kelhoffer, James A. "New Testament Exegesis as an Academic Discipline," *Currents in Biblical Research* 11.2 (2013): 218–33. https://doi.org/10.1177/1476993X12467129

Lyons, William John. "Hope for a Troubled Discipline? Contributions to New Testament Studies from Reception History," *Journal for the Study of the New Testament* 33.2 (2010): 207–20. https://doi.org/10.1177/0142064X10385518

Martin, Dale B. *Sex and the Single Savior: Gender and Sexuality in Biblical Interpretation.* Louisville, KY: Westminster John Knox, 2006.

Marx, Karl, and Friedrich Engels. *The Marx-Engels Reader*. Edited by Robert C. Tucker. 2nd edn. New York: W. W. Norton, 1978.

McDannell, Colleen. *Material Christianity: Religion and Popular Culture in America.* New Haven, CT: Yale University Press, 1995.

Miller, Tyrus. "The Frankfurt School and Models of Interdisciplinarity." *Crosspollenblog*, 3 March 2014. http://crosspollen.files.wordpress.com

Moss, Candida R., and Joel S. Baden. *Bible Nation: United States of Hobby Lobby.* Princeton, NJ: Princeton University Press, 2017. https://doi.org/10.2307/j.ctvc77jbk

Myles, Robert. "The Fetish for a Subversive Jesus," *Journal for the Study of the Historical Jesus* 14:1 (2016): 1–14. http://booksandjournals.brillonline.com/content/journals/10.1163/17455197-01401005

Parker, Angela N. *If God Still Breathes, Why Can't I? Black Lives Matter and Biblical Authority.* Grand Rapids, MI: Eerdmans, 2021.

Phelps, Hollis. "Alain Badiou (1937-)," 438–51 in Goodchild and Phelps, eds., *Religion and European Philosophy*, 2017. https://doi.org/10.4324/9781315642253-37

Pluth, Ed. *Badiou: A Philosophy of the New.* Cambridge: Polity, 2010.

Reid, Barbara E., OP. *Taking Up the Cross: New Testament Interpretation through Latina and Feminist Eyes.* Minneapolis, MN: Fortress, 2007.

Richter, Gerhard. *Thought-Images: Frankfurt School Writers' Reflections from Damaged Life.* Stanford, CA: Stanford University Press, 2007.

Salih, Sara. *Judith Butler.* Routledge Critical Thinkers. New York: Routledge, 2002. https://doi.org/10.4324/9780203118641

Shklovsky, Viktor. *Theory of Prose*. Translated by Benjamin Sher. Normal, IL: Dalkey Archive Press, 1990 [1929].

Smith, Mitzi J., and Yung Suk Kim. *Toward Decentering the New Testament.* Eugene, OR: Cascade Books, 2018.

Sneer, Itay. "Making Sense in Education: Deleuze on Thinking Against Common Sense," *Educational Philosophy and Theory* 50.3 (2018): 299–311. https://doi.org/10.1080/00131857.2017.1344537

Sutin, Lawrence. *Divine Invasions: A Life of Philip K. Dick.* New York: Carroll & Graff, 2005.

Suvin, Darko. *Metamorphoses of Science Fiction: On the Poetics and History of a Literary Genre.* Edited by Gerry Canavan. Bern: Peter Lang, 2016. https://doi.org/10.3726/978-3-0353-0735-1

Terdiman, Richard. *Present Past: Modernity and the Memory Crisis.* Ithaca, NY: Cornell University Press, 1993. https://doi.org/10.7591/9781501717604

Thurman, Howard. *Jesus and the Disinherited.* Nashville, TN: Abingdon Press, 1949.

Tihanov, Galin. "The Politics of Estrangement: The Case of the Early Shklovsky," *Poetics Today* 26.4 (2005): 665–96. https://doi.org/10.1215/03335372-26-4-665

Wright, N.T. *Jesus and the Victory of God.* Minneapolis, MN: Fortress, 1996.

PART I
Walter Benjamin

Chapter Two

Walter Benjamin and Early Christian Texts

Matthew G. Whitlock

Introduction

But whatever form [the present] takes, our task is to seize it by the horns so that we can interrogate the past. It is the bull whose blood must fill the grave if the spirits of the departed are to appear on its edge.[1]

— Walter Benjamin, "Against a Masterpiece"

And the man who merely makes an inventory of his findings [in an archeological dig], while failing to establish the exact location of where in today's ground the ancient treasures have been stored up, cheats himself of his richest prize.[2]

— Walter Benjamin, "Excavation and Memory"

Walter Benjamin (1892–1940) wrote about history in thought images, images of sacrifices and archaeological digs—all to illustrate his approach to interpreting the past around the present. I focus particularly on the present here because the study of early Christian texts by its very nature often moves into recapturing the past without full, intentional consideration of the past's relation with the present. For Benjamin, the present stands at the center of interpreting the past. In his review of Max Kommerell's *The Poet as Leader in German Classicism,* titled "Against a Masterpiece," Benjamin critiques Kommerell's interpretation of literary artists of the past (e.g., Goethe), arguing how Kommerell fails to seize the horns of the present to interpret the past. Kommerell fails to offer up "sacrifices to the present," avoiding the "deadly thrust of ideas," thereby not giving literature "the interpretation [he] owes it."[3] An interpretation of the past without consideration of the present falls short of a complete interpretation.

---

1. Walter Benjamin, "Against a Masterpiece," in *Selected Writings* (ed. Michael W. Jennings; trans. Rodney Livingstone, et al.; 4 vols.; Cambridge, MA: Belknap Press, 1991–1999), 2:383.
2. Benjamin, "Excavation and Memory," *Selected Writings*, 2:576.
3. Benjamin, "Excavation and Memory," *Selected Writings*, 2:576. See also Howard Eiland and Michael W. Jennings, *Walter Benjamin: A Critical Life* (Cambridge, MA: Belknap Press, 2014), 329, where this passage is cited to illustrate Benjamin's "key hermeneutic principle—namely, the operative power ('life-blood') of the present

In another image, Benjamin compares memory to an archeological dig, where "ancient cities lie buried."[4] There objects are uncovered that are "severed from all earlier associations," residing now "as treasures in the sober rooms of our later insights—like torsos in a collector's gallery." The past is stored in a gallery of later insights (i.e., the present) and cannot simply be catalogued apart from them.[5] Indeed, the person "who merely makes an inventory of his findings, while failing to establish the exact location of where in today's ground the ancient treasures have been stored up, cheats himself of its richest prize." The awareness of the exact present location even outweighs the exactitude of the memory: "It is far less important that the investigator report on [authentic memories] than that he mark, quite precisely, the site where he gained possession of them."

Benjamin himself marked the sites where he began his sacrifices and digs. In his *Arcades Project*, Benjamin dug into nineteenth-century Paris arcades not only to archive capitalism in the nineteenth century, but also to mark urban life in Paris under capitalism in his own twentieth century, interrogating the past with the present, conjuring spirits of the departed Paris arcades to encircle the Paris of his own time. Less famously, Benjamin explored and experimented with ancient texts of the Bible, most often Genesis 1–11, as Roland Boer points out.[6] In his studies of language and translation, Benjamin analyzes the two creation stories and the Tower of Babel narrative. On the one hand, Boer notes Benjamin's failure to archive important narrative details of these three stories: not interpreting the key roles Eve and the Serpent play in Genesis 3, and not interpreting the play and humor of the language in the second creation story and the Tower of Babel story.[7] On the

---

in all interpretation or interrogation of the past." This hermeneutic is articulated in Benjamin's final lines of "Literary History and the Study of Literature," which is also quoted in Chapter One above: "What is at stake is not to present literary works in the context of their age but to present of the age that perceives them—our age—in the age during which they arose. It is this that makes literature into an organon of history; and to achieve this, and not reduce literature to the materials of history, is the task of the literary historian" (*Selected Writings*, 2:464).

4. Benjamin, "Excavation and Memory," *Selected Writings*, 2:576.
5. For Benjamin's concept of history see Michael P. Steinberg, "The Collector as Allegorist: Goods, Gods, and the Objects of History," in *Walter Benjamin and the Demands of History* (ed. Michael P. Steinberg; Ithaca, NY: Cornell University Press, 1996), 89–118. Steinberg asserts: "History is not the history of thought but the history of experience (a material entity), and the experience of the present is directly implicated in the reconstruction of past experience (not the experience of *the* past, because there never can be *the* past)," 92–3.
6. Roland Boer, "From Plato to Adam: The Biblical Exegesis of Walter Benjamin," *The Bible and Critical Theory* 3.1 (2007): 6.1–6.13.
7. Boer discusses three texts from Benjamin. Each of these texts provides unique

other hand, Boer shows how Benjamin succeeds in bringing these ancient stories into conversation with his point of entry: his critique of the bourgeois linguistic theory of the twentieth century, which saw language as an instrument of communication. So Benjamin shows how humankind's pre-Fall state, exemplified in Adam's naming of creation, is an instance of truth found *in* language as opposed to *through* language.[8] What is important here for our purposes is not what Benjamin argues (which Boer does well in capturing), but how Benjamin makes his case: conjuring spirits of the past to encircle and encounter his era's engrained thoughts about language.[9]

In light of Benjamin's approach, our task here and in the next two chapters is twofold: first, to conjure up Walter Benjamin to encircle our present moment, that is, to bring new "Benjamin-like" approaches to the study of early Christianity and its texts; second, to conjure up early Christian authors and texts to stand along the periphery of Benjamin's ideas and our own present moment, ideas blasting into our eras from previous ones. This approach does not give us reason to be inaccurate or uniformed in archiving historical, rhetorical, and narratival details about early Christian texts—for in many ways this type of archiving is the strength of biblical and early Christian studies. But here we also refuse to retreat into merely archiving pieces from the past, pieces which, no matter how well we reconstruct them, will remain torsos in *our* galleries "severed from its prior associations." Thus what we strive to avoid, in Benjamin's words, is merely making an inventory of the collective memories of Benjamin's era and the first few centuries of early Christianity and failing to "establish the exact location of where in today's ground the ancient treasures have been stored up," which is the richest prize. To begin this pursuit, we bring our time together with Benjamin's, exploring his biography, his key concepts (especially those discussed in the

---

insights into language and translation, especially important for the interpretation of biblical and early Christian texts in the twenty-first century: Walter Benjamin, *The Origin of German Tragic Drama* (trans. George Steiner; New York: Verso, 1998), 27–56; "On Language as Such and the Language of Man," in *Selected Writings*, 1:62–74; "The Task of the Translator," in *Selected Writings*, 1:253–63.

8. Boer, "The Biblical Exegesis of Walter Benjamin," 5. See also Brian Britt, *Walter Benjamin and the Bible* (New York: Continuum, 1996), 35.

9. Benjamin is quite aware that he is valuing the starting point of his dig over archiving the details of what is found underneath, calling his investigation in the Bible "only initially indispensable" because he returns to his present argument about linguistic theory, returning to his starting point of the dig ("On Language as Such and the Language of Man," *Selected Writings*, 1:67). On Benjamin's own awareness of his method here, see Boer, "The Biblical Exegesis of Walter Benjamin," 8: "The Bible provides Benjamin with the linguistic—and ultimately the philosophical and literary—theory that he needs in order to develop a critique of contemporary schools of thought."

two chapters that follow), and his key works, along with important secondary works in biblical studies, early Christian studies, and theology, which are listed at the end of this chapter. Then in the two chapters that follow, we focus on libraries and gentrification, and time and history, conjuring early Christian texts from John of Patmos to Augustine to "the edge" of Benjamin and the twenty-first century.

The Aura and Context of Walter Benjamin's Work (1892–1940)

Benjamin's life is itself difficult to capture and archive, not because we lack details about it, but because in so many ways it is an expression of aura as defined in Benjamin's own terms. In his most famous work, "The Work of Art in the Age of Technological Reproducibility," Benjamin defines aura as "the unique apparition of a distance, however near it may be."[10] It is not the lack of available details that creates aura. Rather, it is distance, no matter how near or far (and thus not simply spatial distance). "To follow with the eye—while resting on a summer afternoon—a mountain range on the horizon or a branch that casts its shadow on the beholder is to breathe the aura of those mountains, of that branch," says Benjamin.[11] Indeed, an aura can be traced around Benjamin but, in his own words about art, his "unique existence in a particular place" cannot be reproduced or captured from a distance or even from up close in his own time.[12] Even his closest friends experienced this "distance."[13] He was elusive and, in his own words, a "contradictory and mobile whole."[14] What is more, his writings remain at a distance: many were left unfinished and unpublished, only be resurrected and translated after his death, and some were never recovered.[15] Here we provide a brief sketch of

---

10. Walter Benjamin, "The Work of Art in the Age of Technological Reproducibility" (Third Version), *Selected Writings,* 4:255. Quite fittingly, there is no definitive version of this essay; there are three different versions.

11. Benjamin, "The Work of Art in the Age of Technological Reproducibility" (Third Version), *Selected Writings,* 4:255.

12. Benjamin, "The Work of Art in the Age of Technological Reproducibility" (Third Version), *Selected Writings,* 4:253.

13. Eiland and Jennings, *A Critical Life*, 4–5. See also see Irving Wohlfarth, "Walter Benjamin and the 'German-Jewish Parnassus,'" *New German Critique* 70 (1997): 3–85. Linking Benjamin's friendships with aura, Wohlfarth states: "It is surely no accident that Benjamin's definition of aura should have captured with such uncanny precision the impression that he himself invariably left with his foreign friends" (p. 20).

14. *The Correspondence of Walter Benjamin and Gershom Scholem, 1932–1940* (trans. Gary Smith and Andre Lefevere; New York: Shocken Books, 1989), 108–9. See also Eiland and Jennings, *A Critical Life*, 4, 448.

15. On the way to the border and his eventual suicide, Benjamin carried an attaché

Benjamin's life, enough for building a context for understanding Benjamin's concepts, enough to form a dialectical image of today and early Christianity.

Benjamin was born into a wealthy and assimilated Jewish family in Berlin on 15 July, 1892. Berlin, a city of "modern urban commercialization," foreshadows the focus of his work: "the birth of Walter Benjamin and that of German urban modernity were more or less conterminous; it is in some ways not surprising that he produced the twentieth century's most influential theory of modernity."[16] Benjamin's family provided the means for a well-rounded and advanced education. Initially, Benjamin had a negative experience with schooling, largely based on his experience of an authoritarian and conventional approach to education. After this experience, Benjamin was sent to an expensive middle school, Haubinda, where his educational experience was transformed, setting the foundation for his transdisciplinary approach to learning and scholarship.[17] This foundation ultimately led Benjamin to earning a doctorate in 1919 from the University of Bern, Switzerland, where his dissertation focused on art criticism and German romanticism. Later, between 1924–1925 he wrote his *Habilitationsschrift*, *The Origin of the German Tragic Drama*, but it was not accepted by the University of Frankfurt. Because the *Habilitationsschrift* was the means of becoming a university lecturer, Benjamin's career as an academic was stifled. As a result, he never held a full-time academic appointment. He struggled to earn a reputation as an academic and scholar, and when he did earn the reputation as a scholar, it was through publishing without affiliation with a university. Eventually *The Origin of the German Tragic Drama* was published in 1928, and his career between 1925 and his death in 1940 was a constant struggle for financial support. Between the early 1930s and his death, Benjamin received stipends from the Institute of Social Research and published often with its journal *Zeitschrift für Sozialforschung,* where the French translation of "The Work of Art in the Age of Its Technological Reproducibility" was published in 1936. It is during this period that Benjamin also planned, collated, and composed pieces of the unfinished *Arcades Project.*

Benjamin's interlocutors reflected his eclecticism, including Karl Marx and Karl Korsch (on Marxism), the latter of whom Benjamin quotes in *The*

---

case with a manuscript in it. This manuscript was not saved and remains a mystery. See also Eiland and Jennings, *A Critical Life*, 673.

16. Eiland and Jennings, *A Critical Life*, 13.

17. Also Eiland and Jennings, *A Critical Life*, 21–5. At Haubinda Benjamin met teacher and educational reformer Gustav Wyneken, whose approach to education was unconventional. Eiland and Jennings note: "the Wynekenian educational program moves toward an integration of academic disciplines in a unified world view (*Weltbild*), both scientific and poetic," 25.

Arcades Project more than Marx himself;[18] the nineteenth-century French poet Charles Baudelaire, whose relationship to the city as a flâneur became the ideal model for Benjamin's relationship with Paris; Gershom Scholem, the most prominent scholar of Jewish mysticism in the twentieth century, and a lifelong friend of Benjamin, whose important correspondences with Benjamin through letters are well-preserved; Theodor Adorno, a friend and disciple of Benjamin, with whom Benjamin frequently corresponded; Berthold Brecht, the Marxist playwright and poet, a close friend of Benjamin, probably the friend whom Benjamin most admired. Aside from these interlocutors, Benjamin read Goethe, Kant, German theology, detective novels, and children's books, collecting all of these and much more in his library. He also collected visual art, including the now famous aquarelle by Paul Klee, *Angelus Novus*, which once hung above his library, and about which he was inspired to write "On the Concept of History." It is in all of these eclectic "texts" that Benjamin found inspiration.[19]

Tragically, on 27 September, 1940, Benjamin died at the age of 48 on the border of Spain while trying to escape France as the German army advanced, fearing internment and the concentration camps. Not having the proper papers, he attempted to cross the border illegally through the Pyrenees into Spain; however, by the time his party had arrived there, Spain had closed the border. That night Benjamin killed himself by taking a lethal dose of morphine. Spain reopened the border the next day.

Earlier that year, Benjamin wrote the following to his friend Gershom Scholem: "Every line we succeed in publishing today—no matter how uncertain the future to which we entrust it—is a victory wrested from the powers of darkness."[20] It is his surviving lines (and those published after his death) that are now collected and translated into English in the four volume *Walter Benjamin: Selected Writings* and in *The Arcades Project*. It is these lines and their unique concepts to which we now turn.

Key Concepts and Theories Covered in this Volume

Benjamin created concepts from his eclectic interlocutors and experiences. His approach to research was transdisciplinary. There is no discipline with

---

18. Eiland and Jennings, *A Critical Life*, 640.
19. See Britt, *Benjamin and the Bible*, 13: "Benjamin does not differentiate sacred and secular texts a priori. While the Bible constitutes the prototypical sacred text, Benjamin finds the same principle at work in baroque allegory, Baudelaire, surrealism, and many other intellectual currents of the nineteenth and twentieth century."
20. *The Correspondence of Benjamin and Scholem*, 262. Quoted in Eiland and Jennings, *A Critical Life*, 657.

which we can chiefly associate him: he's neither a philosopher, nor a theologian, nor a literary critic, nor a film critic, nor a political theorist. He operated beyond these labels. Roland Boer sums up Benjamin's eclecticism as paradoxical and tension-filled: "his great creative tension lies in the intersection between metaphysics and materialism, theology and Marxism."[21] Here Boer points primarily to Adorno and Scholem to underscore the tension between theology and dialectical materialism, a tension both interlocutors find problematic. What is more, there is a tension between the chief source of this "theology," whether it comes from German Christian theology or Jewish thought, especially in the form of Jewish mysticism.[22] One can also see this tension expressed in the polar opposite critiques of Benjamin's "Theses on the Philosophy of History" by Scholem (metaphysics and mysticism) and Brecht (Marxism and materialism).[23] But here it is not a matter of *the most influence* but of *the variety of influences*. These elements are part of Benjamin's creative tension, his montage. What is more, Benjamin being a collector and a flâneur allows for this tension and the development of his ideas. The images and concepts Benjamin was so adept at capturing were not simply derived from books, but from paintings, from cities, from arcades, from "petrified objects." Benjamin was a theologian of the profane, according to Scholem: "His insights are those of a theologian marooned in the realm of the profane."[24]

There is also a contextual element that cannot be forgotten here. Benjamin is developing concepts in the shadows of fascism, as the Nazi army is encroaching on his life. His ideas cannot be separated from this moment.

---

21. Roland Boer, *Criticism of Heaven: On Marxism and Theology* (Leiden: Brill, 2006), 58.

22. For a brief summary evaluating arguments about the competing influences of Christian theology and/or Jewish mysticism on Benjamin's thought, see Boer, "From Plato to Adam," 5. On the one hand, Scholem and Susan Buck-Morss make the case for Benjamin as a Jewish mystical thinker, an argument Boer finds anachronistic and unconvincing. See Gershom Scholem, *Walter Benjamin: The Story of Friendship* (trans. H. Zohn; Philadelphia, PA: Jewish Publication Society of America, 1981), 10–4, 28–30); Susan Buck-Morss, *The Dialectics of Seeing: Walter Benjamin and the Arcades Project* (Cambridge, MA: MIT Press, 1989), 229–40. On the other hand, note the influence of German Christian theology, see Wohlfarth, "Walter Benjamin and the 'German-Jewish Parnassus." Boer finds Wohlfarth's argument about Benjamin being an assimilated Jew familiar with Christian theology more convincing.

23. Boer, "From Plato to Adam," 14.

24. Gershom Scholem, "Walter Benjamin," in *On Jews and Judaism in Crisis: Selected Essays* (ed. Werner J. Dannhauser; Philadelphia, PA: Paul Dry Books, 2012), 187.

So in the confluence of his political moment, his conflicting ideologies, and his diverse images, we are invited into a conversation about concepts, concepts that can be placed side by side with events of today and those of the early Christian era, creating dialectical images. Below three central ideas in Benjamin's work are discussed, the first two setting up the two chapters that follow, and the third anticipating further connections made between Benjamin and early Christian studies: (1) urban change, libraries, and the messianic in Benjamin and Revelation; (2) the messianic, time, and history in Benjamin and Augustine; (3) aura, the work of art, and technology in Benjamin and early Christian manuscripts.

A. Robert Paul Seesengood: Urban Change, Libraries, and the Messianic

In his chapter on "Reading, Libraries, and Urban Change in the Shadow of Capitalism and Apocalypse," Robert Paul Seesengood brings Walter Benjamin's ideas into dialectic with John's Apocalypse. He focuses on urban growth—a prominent theme in Benjamin's work (Marseille in "'Chambermaids' Romances of the Past City" and Paris in *The Arcades Project*)—and gentrification, particularly "gentrification" in John's Apocalypse (i.e., from Rome to the New Jerusalem), a reading derived from Stephen Moore's work. Urban growth and gentrification stand at the center of our experience today, the location of most modern universities and scholarly conferences, which in Seesengood's case, include Albright College in Reading, Pennsylvania and the 2016 AAR/SBL in San Antonio, itself having an "arcade-like" river walk. While noting that urban change in Benjamin's writing can neither be limited to decline nor progress, Seesengood examines the veneer of progress. For Benjamin urban progress is illusory, says Seesengood, masking "the real life of the proletariat, replacing it with a gloss, a veneer." Seesengood contrasts the gritty life in the city of Marseille celebrated by Benjamin with the Paris Arcades, which involved a "planned program of reorganization," a reorganization that "alienates, dehumanizes, and transforms reality into fantasy," into phantasmagoria. The latter is reflected in Seesengood's experience of the river-walk in San Antonio and his reading of Revelation, where John replaces a human city with a divine city. In reading Revelation alongside Benjamin and Stephen Moore, Seesengood sees the New Jerusalem as the "ultimate urban renewal program" and "the ultimate consumer and master." There, "urban decay is replaced by divine arcade."

From urban renewal Seesengood turns to a connected theme in Benjamin: libraries. Here Seesengood contrasts two poles in his own experience: the proposed transformation of Albright College's library into an open space with glass and steel and the West Reading public library, "a dingy ruin," a pre-war building "lovingly maintained." It is in the latter where Benjamin would celebrate "the literacy of commoner." It is also here where the proletariat have free public access to books, building the hope of "less disparity of wealth." For Benjamin, a library also represents a montage of ideas, a desire to "preserve" and "(re)assemble." Seesengood shows how Revelation itself is a similar montage, drawing together "a host of scenes, characters, phrases, and texts" from second-temple Judaism. It is a collection of scrolls and codices, gathered from times past to create for John's unique messianic time, though Benjamin's idea of the messianic is quite different than John's. But how John infuses meaning in his time is a key move for Seesengood as he reads Revelation through the lens of Benjamin: John infuses meaning "in disparate acts and moments, creating a knot of messianic time."

Benjamin's idea of the messiah is materialist and not grounded in idealism. This conception of the messianic is clear, as Seesengood points out, in Benjamin's "Theses on the Philosophy of History." Here, as Benjamin's angel of history looks back upon humanity's bleak past, Benjamin rejects any conception of progress, idealism, or the hope of modernism. Gentrified, urban life does not bring about a messianic age through erasure. Instead, according to Benjamin, the messianic is the erasure of history at moments in time.

B. Carl Levenson:
History and Progress

In Benjamin-like fashion, Carl Levenson creates a montage of Augustine and Benjamin, bringing their thoughts into a dialectic based on images from Benjamin's "On the Concept of History," images from a chess-playing automaton to the angel of history blown facing backward into the future, what Benjamin calls "progress." What is gained from this dialogue is not a synthesis of Benjamin's thought into Augustine's, or Augustine's into Benjamin's. They are not objects of each other's thoughts; they serve as subjects playing off one another's imagery—with Levenson's mediation, of course. The end results are not synthesized answers, but three constellations centering on three questions: (1) Where do patterns in our lives and history come from? (2) May we hope to find redemption from them in the future? (3) May we hope to redeem them and the past?

Levenson's chapter is composed of three parts, answering the aforementioned questions, as well as imagining both Augustine and Benjamin in direct dialogue over each. In the first part, Levenson considers patterns in life in light of Augustine's and Benjamin's biographies. Both certainly have different biographies, different fates, and different interpretations, but here

Levenson recall's Benjamin's famous chess-playing-machine, where "you find your moves answered by patterns that come from outside you," hidden behind a facade. In the second part, in answering whether the future holds redemption for Augustine and Benjamin, Levenson points to the Empire's dissolution of the former and the fascist victories of the latter to contextualize what each faced. While Augustine looked to Christ's future victory, Benjamin looked to the Marxist hope, and doubted both. Benjamin looked to the past, where the angel of history is blown backward from paradise (i.e., "progress") looking upon the trash heap of history. So in the third part, Levenson considers this image alongside Benjamin, seeing the angel of history neither being able to reach the past nor see the future. But pulling common pieces on memory from both Augustine and Benjamin, Levenson explicates Benjamin's mysterious concept of a weak but real messianic power, where the present is momentarily interrupted by a time outside itself.

C. For Further Consideration: Technological Reproducibility of Early Christian Texts

Scholarly discussion about Benjamin's views on sacred texts is sparse.[25] But even more, one topic in Benjamin's writings especially sparse and ripe for development in early Christian studies is the relationship between technology and the reproduction of art, and in the case of textuality, the reproduction, translation, and interpretation of biblical and early Christian manuscripts.[26] Although "The Work of Art in the Age of Technological Reproducibility" focuses chiefly on art, photography, film, and new forms of art that do not require the authority of an original, its assertions can be applied to sacred texts and offer insight into Christian texts: their origins, their auras, their authority, and their reproduction, and more specifically, how their multiple reproductions in manuscripts and commentaries affect the way we perceive them. In other words, Benjamin's essay moves beyond considering how technology can be a means for improving the scholar's and the masses' comprehension of and access to art or sacred texts (i.e., the instrumentalist position of technology) and considers how technological

---

25. See Colby Dickinson, "The Relationship of Canon and Messiah: The Convergence of Jan Assmann and Walter Benjamin on a Theory of Monotheistic Canon," *The Bible and Critical Theory* 7.1 (2011): 6.
26. George Aichele is one of the few scholars who considers Benjamin in the context of "the virtual Bible" and the manuscript tradition, from hand-written copies without an original, to mass-printed copies, to digital copies—the Bible itself being a simulacrum. See George Aichele, *Simulating Jesus: Reality Effects in the Gospels* (Abingdon: Routledge, 2014), 14–6. In the first chapter, "The Virtuality of the Bible" (3–23). Aichele focuses on how print and digital technology affect the way the Bible is perceived.

development determines how and what we think and feel about art and sacred texts (i.e., the essentialist position).[27] It moves from technology as a means to technology determining affect.

For example, in the section of the "Work of Art" essay discussing how humanity's "mode of existence" changes over historical periods along with its "mode of perception," Benjamin points out the tension of reproducing singular works of art—or in our case, sacred texts.[28] The tension involves "the desire of the present-day masses to 'get closer' to things spatially and humanly, and their equally passionate concern for overcoming each thing's uniqueness by assimilating it as a reproduction."[29] The uniqueness, aura, and authority of an object all attract people to it; as a result, when it becomes examined and reproduced and examined again, or even more, mechanically produced without an original (e.g., art produced to be reproduced), it loses what may draw people to it: its singularity, aura, and authority. To paraphrase Benjamin: sameness is extracted from uniqueness.[30] By mass technological reproduction of sacred texts, not only in early manuscript traditions, but also in modern, online access for the masses, to what extent is sameness extracted from the uniqueness? What is more, to what extent do the overabundance of commentaries, repeating the similar insights, extract sameness from the uniqueness of a text?

The answers to these questions are complicated by our access to early Christian texts and artifacts. Unlike some forms of art, what makes early Christian tradition unique in light of Benjamin's ideas is that we do not have the original. The original always evades us, protecting the aura and the authority of the New Testament text, no matter how many times it is reproduced or interpreted. The ideal of the original remains. The same can be said about the quest for the "original" Jesus of history. His aura remains veiled because we cannot uncover "the original," though Jesus has arguably been the most mass-reproduced "object" in Western art and literature. The illusion and the mystery, the singularity and uniqueness, and the aura and authority remain because the original cannot be found, yet continues to be pursued. As early Christian texts are placed under the lenses

---

27. For the distinction between instrumental and essentialist theories, see Paul A. Taylor and Jan Ll. Harris, *Digital Matters: The Theory and Culture of the Matrix* (New York: Routledge, 2005), 11–2.
28. Benjamin, "The Work of Art in the Age of Technological Reproducibility," *Selected Writings*, 4:255–6.
29. Benjamin, "The Work of Art in the Age of Technological Reproducibility," *Selected Writings*, 4:255.
30. Benjamin, "The Work of Art in the Age of Technological Reproducibility," *Selected Writings*, 4:256.

of critique—and particularly their authority—it is important that these tensions and issues are brought to the fore. To what extent, in other words, does our inability to find original texts and artifacts of early Christianity protect them from the disintegration of their aura and authority? Aesthetically speaking, the auratic distance of a work of art or literature "aims at the beautiful" and provides "a gaze that will never get its fill."[31] However, politically and institutionally speaking, the preservation of aura upholds a system of power's seduction over its people. Benjamin makes this clear at the end of "The Work of Art Essay," derived from his firsthand observations of fascism.[32] Benjamin, therefore, does not lament the loss of aura. Eiland and Jennings sum up well the value that Benjamin—through Baudelaire's poetry—sees in shattering of the illusions of aura, a shattering just as relevant to the study of early Christian texts as tracing the aesthetical value of each text's aura:

> Baudelaire's poetry breaks through the brutal and seductive "magic of distance" with which it is nevertheless thoroughly conversant; it is like a viewer who "steps too close to the depicted scene" and thus shatters the illusions—not the least the illusions fostered by auratic phenomena and, through them, by traditional systems of power.[33]

Likewise, is it not the task of scholarship of early Christianity (at least one embracing critical theory) to break through the seductive "magic of distance" and step "close to the depicted scene"—not simply an intellectual task, but a just one, shattering "illusions fostered by traditional systems of power"?

Biographical Note

Matthew G. Whitlock (PhD, The Catholic University of America, 2008) is Associate Professor of New Testament at Seattle University. His research focuses on Acts of the Apostles, the Apostle Paul, New Testament Poetry, Critical Theory, and Science Fiction. His publications have focused on topics ranging from New Testament poetry in the *Catholic Biblical Quarterly* to the Body without Organs and Christianity in *Deleuze and Guattari Studies*. He is currently working on two books on dialectical images, one

---

31. Benjamin, "On Some Motifs in Baudelaire," *Selected Writings*, 4:338.
32. Benjamin, "The Work of Art in the Age of Technological Reproducibility," *Selected Writings*, 4:270.
33. Eiland and Jennings, *A Critical Life*, 645. Benjamin, "On Some Motifs in Baudelaire," 4:341.

on images from the Science Fiction of Philip K. Dick and images from the letters of Paul, and the other on the theme of fame in images from the life of Kurt Cobain and early Christian writings about Jesus of Nazareth.

Bibliography: Key Primary and Secondary Texts

A. Primary Literature

The Correspondence of Walter Benjamin and Gershom Scholem, 1932–1940. Translated by Gary Smith and Andre Lefevere. New York: Schocken Books, 1989.
The Arcades Project. Translated by Howard Eiland and Kevin McLaughlin. Cambridge, MA: Belknap Press, 1999.
Illuminations: Essays and Reflections. Edited by Hannah Arendt. Translated by Harry Zohn. New York: Schocken Books, 2007.
The Origin of German Tragic Drama. Translated by George Steiner. New York: Verso, 1998.
Selected Writings. Edited by Michael W. Jennings, et al. Translated by Rodney Livingstone, et al. 4 vols. Cambridge, MA: Belknap Press, 1991–1999.

B. Secondary Literature: Life and Context

Benjamin, Andrew, ed. *Adorno and Benjamin: Problems of Modernity*. New York: Routledge, 1989.
Eiland, Howard, and Michael W. Jennings. *Author as Producer: A Life of Walter Benjamin*. Cambridge, MA: Harvard University Press, 2007.
—*Walter Benjamin: A Critical Life.* Cambridge, MA: Belknap Press, 2014.
Ferris, David. *The Cambridge Introduction to Walter Benjamin*. Cambridge: Cambridge University Press, 2008. https://doi.org/10.1017/CBO9780511793257
Jay, Martin. *The Dialectical Imagination: A History of the Frankfurt School and the Institute for Social Research, 1923–1950.* Berkeley, CA: University of California Press, 1996.
Lane, Richard J. *Reading Walter Benjamin: Writing through the Catastrophe*. New York: Manchester University Press, 2005.
Leslie, Esther. *Walter Benjamin.* London: Reaktion Books, 2007.
Scholem, Gershom. *Walter Benjamin: The Story of Friendship.* Translated by H. Zohn. Philadelphia, PA: Jewish Publication Society of America, 1981.

C. Secondary Literature: Theology, Religious Studies, and Biblical Studies

Aichele, George. *Simulating Jesus: Reality Effects in the Gospels* (Abingdon: Routledge, 2014). https://doi.org/10.4324/9781315729237
Bielik-Robson, Agata. "Walter Benjamin (1892-1940)," 115–26 in *Religion and European Philosophy: Key Thinkers from Kant to Žižek*. Edited by Philip Goodchild and Hollis Phelps. New York: Routledge, 2017. https://doi.org/10.4324/9781315642253-11
Boer, Roland. "Walter Benjamin: The Impossible Apocalyptic of Daniel," 204–28 in *Marxist Criticism of the Bible*. New York: T&T Clark, 2003.

—"Benjamin's Perpetuation of Biblical Myth," 57–105 in *Criticism of Heaven: On Marxism and Theology*. Leiden: Brill, 2006. https://doi.org/10.1163/ej.9789004161115. i-472.14
—"From Plato to Adam: The Biblical Exegesis of Walter Benjamin," *The Bible and Critical Theory* 3.1 (2007): 6.1–6.13. https://doi.org/10.2104/bc070006
Britt, Brian. *Walter Benjamin and the Bible*. New York: Continuum, 1996.
Dickinson, Colby. "The Relationship of Canon and Messiah: The Convergence of Jan Assmann and Walter Benjamin on a Theory of Monotheistic Canon," *The Bible and Critical Theory* 7.1 (2011): 1–15.
Dickinson, Colby, and Stéphane Symons, eds. *Walter Benjamin and Theology*. New York: Fordham University Press, 2016. https://doi.org/10.5422/fordham/9780823270170.001.0001
Khatib, Sami. "Derrida & Sons: Marx, Benjamin and the Spector of the Messiah," *Anthropological Materialism*. February 2013. https://anthropologicalmaterialism.hypotheses.org
—"The Messianic without Messianism: Walter Benjamin's Materialist Anthropology," *Anthropology and Materialism* 1 (2013): 1–17. https://doi.org/10.4000/am.159
Pizer, John. "Reconstellating the Shards of the Text: On Walter Benjamin's German/Jewish Memory," *German Studies Review* 18.2 (1995): 275–90. https://doi.org/10.2307/1431833
Plate, Brent. *Walter Benjamin, Religion, and Aesthetics: Rethinking Religion through the Arts*. New York: Routledge, 2005. https://doi.org/10.4324/9780203997734
Rabinbach, Anson. "Between Enlightenment and Apocalypse: Benjamin, Bloch and Modern German Jewish Messianism," *New German Critique* 34 (1985): 78–124. https://doi.org/10.2307/488340
Scholem, Gershom. "Walter Benjamin," in *On Jews and Judaism in Crisis: Selected Essays*. Edited by Werner J. Dannhauser. Philadelphia, PA: Paul Dry Books, 2012.
Taubes, Jacob. *The Political Theology of Paul*. Translated by Dana Hollander. Stanford, CA: Stanford University Press, 2004.
Ullmann, Wolfgang. "Walter Benjamin und die jüdische Theologie," in *Aber ein Sturm weht vom Paradiese her: Texte zu Walter Benjamin*. Edited by M. Optitz and E. Wizisla. Leipzig: Reclam-Verlag, 1992.
Wohlfarth, Irving. "Walter Benjamin's Image of Interpretation," *New German Critique* 17 (1979): 70–98. https://doi.org/10.2307/488011
—"Walter Benjamin and the 'German-Jewish Parnassus,'" *New German Critique* 70 (1997): 3–86. https://doi.org/10.2307/488499

D. Other Secondary Literature

Buck-Morss, Susan. *The Dialectics of Seeing: Walter Benjamin and the Arcades Project*. Cambridge, MA: MIT Press, 1989.
Eagleton, Terry. *Walter Benjamin or Towards a Revolutionary Criticism*. London:New Left Books, 1981.
Gilloch, Graeme. *Myth and Metropolis: Walter Benjamin and the City*. Cambridge:Polity Press, 1996.
Hanssen, Beatrice, and Andrew Benjamin. *Walter Benjamin and the Arcades Project*. New York: Routledge, 2002.
Missac, Pierre. *Walter Benjamin's Passages*. Cambridge, MA: MIT Press, 1995.

Richter, Gerhard. *Walter Benjamin and the Corpus of Autobiography*. Detroit, MI: Wayne State University Press, 2000.
Smith, Gary, ed. *On Walter Benjamin: Critical Essays and Recollections.* Cambridge, MA: MIT Press, 1988.
Steinberg, Michael P. "The Collector as Allegorist: Goods, Gods, and the Objects of History," 89–118 in *Walter Benjamin and the Demands of History*. Edited by Michael P. Steinberg. Ithaca, NY: Cornell University Press, 1996.
Taylor, Paul A., and Jan Ll. Harris, *Digital Matters: The Theory and Culture of the Matrix.* New York: Routledge, 2005.

Chapter Three

Reading, Libraries, and Urban Change in the Shadow of Capitalism and Apocalypse: Reading Walter Benjamin and John of Patmos

Robert Paul Seesengood

Walter Benjamin's Marxist critique of the city, as exemplified in his description of the gritty French seaport Marseille, in his essay "Chambermaids' Romances of the Past City," and in other work, focused upon urban space transformed by the growth—or loss—of capital. What superficially appears to be either stark decline into slum or hopeful progress in gentrification is neither. In his essay "Unpacking My Library," Benjamin brings his attention to the dynamics of collection and ownership: How is this process a secret attempt to commodify and control ideas, a capitalistic urge that shapes the center of even philosophy and spiritual transformation. All these themes merge in Benjamin's last major work, *The Arcades Project*. *Arcades* takes as its subject the renovation and renewal of public commercial space within Paris using the format of an unfinished "book of books," of fragments and quotes from various books, inter-cut with Benjamin's own reflections. Benjamin's interests in renovation, renewal, and writing also merge in his complex category of the Messianic.

The canonical Apocalypse by John of Patmos also features urban transformations: the city of Rome (called "Babylon") and its commercial enterprises (Revelation 17–18) are replaced with New Jerusalem (Revelation 21). Revelation also has a library; its catalog includes a seven sealed scroll (Revelation 4 and 5) that initiates God's wrath and a Living Book (Rev. 20.12-15). It is also a collection of citations, allusions and authorial reflections all assembled, sometimes pastiche, into a new work. In this essay, I want to read John alongside Benjamin. Their readings of the city, the use of literacy, and the Messiah overlap in concern and, at times, vocabulary; but, in the end, their views of city and messiahship differ markedly, even if, read side by side, they enrich one another's discourse. Where John sees historical progress and longs for the replacement of human governments and cities with God's own, Benjamin sees less progress than change and cautions that apparent improvement is, often-as-not, illusory.

Cities

In his essay on Marseilles, France, and his extensive review of Parisian arcades, Benjamin muses on one of the central issues of urban growth: the decline and change of urban spaces.[1] Benjamin notes that changing cityscapes certainly do alter the circumstances in which a person of leisure, a wealthy man, can feel safe or protected.[2] But economic "progress" often masks the real life of the proletariat, replacing it with a gloss, a veneer.

Benjamin's description of Marseilles' grimy quarters certainly doesn't pull punches. He describes the view as one arrives in its ports from the sea as "the yellow-studded maw of a seal which has salt water running out between the teeth."[3] His descriptions grow in vividness, but also complexity. Describing the wharfs further:

> When this gullet opens to catch the black and brown proletarian bodies thrown to it by ship's companies according to their time tables, it exhales a stink of oil, urine, and printers ink. This comes from the tartar baking hard on the massive jaws: newspaper kiosks, lavatories, and oyster stalls.[4]

Benjamin celebrates Marseilles' proletarian appeal. The city's grit becomes the basis of its art. As he walks his reader further into the city, passing through its red light district, he points out the city's architectural bones, perhaps, better, its fossils, which preserve the record of its prosperous past, even if presently repurposed:

> On this bashful, dripping hand, however, shines a signet ring on a fishwife''s hard finger, the old Hotel de Ville. Here just two hundred years ago stood patricians' house, the high breasted nymphs, the snake-ringed Medusa heads over their weather-beaten doorframes have only now become unambiguously signs of a professional guild.[5]

---

1. On Benjamin's life and context see Esther Leslie, *Walter Benjamin* (London: Reaktion Books, 2007); Richard J. Lane, *Reading Walter Benjamin: Writing through the Catastrophe* (New York: Manchester University Press, 2005); Howard Eiland and Michael W. Jennings, *Author as Producer: A Life of Walter Benjamin* (Cambridge, MA: Harvard University Press, 2007); Martin Jay, *The Dialectical Imagination: A History of the Frankfurt School and the Institute for Social Research, 1923–1950* (Berkeley, CA: University of California Press, 1996).

2. On Benjamin and the city, generically, see Graeme Gilloch, *Myth and Metropolis: Walter Benjamin and the City* (Cambridge: Polity Press, 1996).

3. Walter Benjamin, "Marseilles," in *Selected Writings* (ed. Michael W. Jennings; trans. Rodney Livingstone, et al.; 4 vols.; Cambridge, MA: Belknap Press, 1991–1999), 2:233.

4. Benjamin, "Marseilles," in *Selected Writings*, 2:232.

5. Benjamin, "Marseilles," in *Selected Writings*, 2:233.

The vivid description of noises, smells, and scenes of poverty proceeds as if the essay were a travel catalog; the cathedral is described, as are markets and residential streets. Benjamin avoids lament. It is a city filled with decent, working-class, *literate* citizens.

Benjamin celebrates the (admittedly gritty) "realness" of Marseilles.

But what of Benjamin's Paris? Paris at the dawn of the twentieth century was a city of mixed spaces: the gentrified and desolate. Describing Paris a century before Benjamin, Honoré de Balzac offers a vivid description:

> If you wander along the streets of the Ile Saint-Louis, look for no other cause of the uneasy sadness that takes possession of you other than the solitariness, the dejected appearance of its houses and forsaken mansions. This island, the cemetery so to speak of the Old Regime tax-farming magnates, is as it were the Venice of Paris. Stock Exchange Square is all rattle, bustle and harlotry. It is beautiful only in the moonlight, at two in the morning; in the day-time an epitome of Paris, at night-time a dream-vision from Greece.[6]

Balzac's Paris is a mixed city with

> murderous streets; streets which are more aged than aged dowagers; respectable streets; streets which are always clean; streets which are always dirty; working-class, industrious, mercantile streets ... Some of them, like Rue Montmartre, are like mermaids—lovely heads, but fish tails at the other extremity.[7]

In his large, unfinished work on the Paris arcades, Benjamin examines the outcomes of urban transformation in Paris, from Balzac's to his own.[8] Beginning in the early-and-mid nineteenth century, the seamier "mercantile streets" of Paris became, by benefit of new construction technologies, transformed into commercial and "promenade" spaces, the arcades. The (planned) transformation of Parisian city blocks clearly fascinated Benjamin. His unfinished book about them consists of a series of (often incomplete) essays, brief notes on subjects inter-related (in Benjamin's mind) with Parisian culture and the arcades. These copious reading notes and quotations from other writers are inter-spliced with his own musings. The rest is a montage of various motifs—provocatively inter-laced and intertextually resonant, but with final connections left undrawn, inviting the reader to discover, or even to create, meaningful connections.

---

6. Honoré de Balzac, *History of the Thirteen* (trans. Herbert J. Hunt; New York: Penguin, 1974), 31.

7. de Balzac, *History of the Thirteen*, 31.

8. For general criticism of *Arcades*, see Beatrice Hanssen and Andrew Benjamin, *Walter Benjamin and the Arcades Project* (New York: Routledge, 2002); Susan Buck-Morss, *The Dialectics of Seeing: Walter Benjamin and the Arcades Project* (Cambridge, MA: MIT Press, 1989).

The Parisian arcades, winding streets of shops and markets, closed to non-pedestrian traffic and covered over with glass ceilings, Benjamin notes, were architectural marvels enabled by early nineteenth-century shifting prices in steel. As Ferris notes, the arcades are "the coming together of a capitalist economy with the dominant technological advance of the age."[9] Benjamin refers to the subsequent space as "phantasmagoria" that "allows the display of goods within 'fairyland' space."[10] Not only is the space protected from elements, an outdoors that is not outdoors, but it invites ever more dramatic presentation on the street below, wooing and seducing pedestrian promenade-goers, inviting them, seducing them, to leisure and consumption:

> The fairyland subsequently becomes a phantasmagoria, a dreamworld created by the arcades as a means of sustaining an economy based on the consumption of commodities. The arcades thus provide a concrete example of the moment in which the relation between capitalism and the work of dreams is revealed.[11]

Indeed, the system results in the commodification of dream, of desire for Modernity itself, for the new. The arcades foster a hunger for objects, objects which commodify and embody desires (particularly sexual desires); the possession of these objects, however, does not satiate. Instead, it dulls and awakens even more consumption. The repeated inflammation of (sexual) desire to possess or own becomes a perpetual, un-satiated, cycle of desire-without-release. Benjamin terms this "commodity fetish."

Urban change in arcades is a planned program of reorganization that, while lovely, results in alienation, dehumanization, and the transformation of reality into fantasy. It sublimates then dulls desire into commodity consumption.[12] It produces wonder, but results in alienation. It is clean, but sterile. It is marvelous, but its beauty is phantasmagoria. It is full of desire, but not satiation. It is timeless, changeless, but also purposeless joy. In contrast, the grit and grime of Marseilles is the patina of use, an honest proletarian space. Its streets smell of work-a-day reality, but also printers' ink. Benjamin's proletarian city is grimy, but its denizens are literate.

---

9. David Ferris, *The Cambridge Introduction to Walter Benjamin* (Cambridge: Cambridge University Press, 2008), 116.
10. Ferris, *Cambridge Introduction to Walter Benjamin*, 116.
11. Ferris, *Cambridge Introduction to Walter Benjamin*, 116.
12. See Terry Eagleton, *Walter Benjamin or Towards a Revolutionary Criticism* (London: New Left Books, 1981).

Books

A champion of authentic, hetero-economic city spaces, Benjamin was a staunch advocate for communal proletarian literacy. A friend and critic of such elevated literary voices as Proust, Benjamin, in his essay "Chambermaids' Romances of the Past Century" challenged the social stratification of literature and reading, the bifurcation between "high" and "serious" reading (done by the educated and the wealthy) and "common" or "escapist" reading done by the masses. The essay famously has scenes of proletarian urban life woven through it, yet its larger interest is in how books form the self and proletarian reading. "Since when are works of literature categorized according to the class that consumes them?" he asks, challenging assumptions of cultural bias in the recognition of "literacy."[13] Benjamin goes on to celebrate the literacy of the commoner, noting the long tradition of itinerant booksellers, the *colporteurs*, who took their books to the masses. Ordinary readers preserve literacy, and a literate proletariat is an empowered one.

Benjamin's idea of the connection between literacy and a strong proletariat would prove a lasting one in the twentieth century. Perhaps the most famous example is Richard Hoggart's seminal *The Uses of Literacy*.[14] Hoggart foresaw a moment, via literacy, of the "massification" of culture, a collapse into cultural homogeneity, effectively the "gentrification" of media. More reflective of Benjamin's day is the use of literacy among the pre-war proletariat as laid out in Jonathan Rose's magnificent *The Intellectual Life of the British Working Classes*.[15] In Benjamin's day, workers read. Openly and prolifically. And public spaces for reading prospered. Later economic review and analysis has borne out Benjamin's intuition: times of broad proletarian literacy have enjoyed narrower disparity of wealth.[16]

Benjamin's most familiar celebration of books, however, is his justly famous "On Unpacking My Library."[17] Benjamin uses the occasion of uncrating his books to reflect upon the process and dynamic of book ownership generally. (Benjamin frequently interwove autobiography and cultural

---

13. Walter Benjamin, "Chambermaids' Romances of the Past Century," *Selected Writings*, 2:225.
14. Richard Hoggart, *The Uses of Literacy: Aspects of Working-Class Life with Special Reference to Publications and Entertainments* (London: Penguin, 1969).
15. Jonathan Rose, *The Intellectual Life of the British Working Classes* (New Haven, CT: Yale University Press, 2001).
16. Thomas Piketty, *Capital in the Twenty-First Century* (Cambridge, MA: Harvard University Press, 2015).
17. Walter Benjamin, "Unpacking My Library: A Talk About Book Collecting," in *Illuminations: Essays and Reflections* (ed. Hannah Arendt; trans. Harry Zohn; New York: Schocken, 2007), 59–68.

context into his philosophical writing.)[18] The randomness of the packed library's disorder exposes, for Benjamin, the essence of the library itself. Authors write to assemble new books out of the old, creating the order of their insight, if not library sequence. For Benjamin, owning books and maintaining libraries is a very different urge than conventional reading; it arises from a desire to preserve, but also to own and serves as a seductive invitation to (re)assemble.

Again, these themes merge in the Arcade. For Benjamin, the reading and writing of books themselves is the bricolage aggregation of other books. Each book is, itself, a small library. Describing the *Arcades Project*, David Ferris writes:

> What remains of the project is an immense collection of notes divided and organized into different sections known as "convolutes." Each convolute corresponds to one of the principal subjects under which Benjamin organized his research, such as "Fashion," "Boredom," "Panorama," "Mirrors," "Flâneur," "Baudelaire," and so on. Each convolute is dominated by quotations removed from the contexts and placed in montage-like relation to each other. Interspersed among these are notes and observations by Benjamin.[19]

Arcades is an openly, unapologetically bookish work. It is by both its intention and its unfinished status a production that foregrounds books, reading, and the library.

The Messianic and the Apocalyptic

Among Benjamin's last works, perhaps his final, is the collected "Theses on the Philosophy of History." Composed at roughly the same time as *Arcades* (and saved for posterity by being hidden alongside that manuscript in a library until after the war) the theses articulate Benjamin's conviction that history, while possessing an "end" is not teleotic. There is no "goal" or progress of history, merely repeated making, unmaking and replacement until History's cessation. This end, as he describes it in his final thesis, is the Messianic.

For Benjamin, like many Jewish intellectuals of his epoch, the idea of the Messianic was only a partially hopeful idea, and always a materialistic one. The reality of the Messianic was, instead, an indictment of the present and any hope or expectation of "progress" or improvement. In a sense, the Messianic becomes the proto-postmodern in that it is a rejection of the

---

18. See Gerhard Richter, *Walter Benjamin and the Corpus of Autobiography* (Detroit, MI: Wayne State University Press, 2000); Pierre Missac, *Walter Benjamin's Passages* (Cambridge, MA: MIT Press, 1995).

19. Ferris, *Introduction to Walter Benjamin*, 115.

idealism and (arrogant?) hopefulness of Modernity. Messiahs arrive precisely because of the collapse of the present age.[20] Influenced by correspondence with the Kabbalist philosopher Gershom Scholem, Benjamin's understanding of the *tikkun olam* led him to fuse the political, communal and (for lack of a better word) the "theological" into a surreal Messianism infused with both commodification and political Zionism.[21] The Messianic was intrusive, erasing by demolition the present, recreating the Zionist "new City." Benjamin's messianism was, in other words, always a Zionistic apocalypse and fantastic. Imagining the progress of history as a graph, a chiasmus, Benjamin writes:

> If one arrow points to the goal toward which the secular dynamic acts, and another marks the direction of messianic intensity, then certainly the quest of free humanity for happiness runs counter to the messianic direction. But just as force, by virtue of the path it is moving along, can augment another force on the opposite path, so the secular order—because of its nature as secular—promotes the coming of the Messianic Kingdom."[22]

The erasure of Marseilles in some future hypothetical urban renewal, the transformation of Parisian streets in the arcades, is not "progress" but an erasure of the real (transformed) essence of the city itself. History, like the decline of Marseilles or the restoration of Paris, is not progress. The restoration of history can only be achieved by the erasure and rebuilding of history via the Messianic, and the Messianic is inherently Marxist. History is ideology and commodity combined—or, perhaps better, ideology expressed in commodity. The Messianic is history's end and always ethereal, yet any sense of the "realness" of history, like progress, is illusory, a dream.

John's Apocalypse: The City, the Book, and the Messianic Meet

The Apocalypse of John also merges themes of urban renewal, literature and writing, fantasy space and the Messianic/apocalyptic. In Revelation, earthly cities of Empire are replaced by the ultimate urban renewal program,

---

20. Lane, *Writing through the Catastrophe*, 15–6.
21. See Sami Khatib, "Derrida & Sons: Marx, Benjamin and the Spector of the Messiah," *Anthropological Materialism,* February 2013, https://anthropologicalmaterialism.hypotheses.org; Sami Khatib, "The Messianic without Messianism: Walter Benjamin's Materialist Anthropology," *Anthropology and Materialism* 1 (2013): 1–17; Lane, *Writing through the Catastrophe*, 15–6. Cf. Gershom Scholem, *Walter Benjamin: An Intellectual Biography* (Philadelphia, PA: Jewish Publication Society of America, 1981); Andrew Benjamin, ed., *Adorno and Benjamin: Problems of Modernity* (New York: Routledge, 1989).
22. Benjamin, "Theological-Political Fragment," *Selected Writings*, 3:305

a "new heaven and a new earth" whose capital is New Jerusalem.[23] Some critics of Revelation 20–22 remain ambivalent about the inherent politics of Revelation's transformation.[24] John's promised New Jerusalem is, indeed, wealthy, but its mass totally consumes New Earth, crowding out any non-urban space, nonhuman entity, and winnowing out undesirables, leaving all subject to the constant surveillance of the deity who now reigns alone and supreme, the ultimate consumer and master. John writes:

> Then I saw a new heaven and a new earth; for the first heaven and the first earth had passed away, and the sea was no more. And I saw the holy city, new Jerusalem, coming down out of heaven from God, prepared as a bride adorned for her husband … And the sprit carried me away to a great high mountain and showed me the holy city Jerusalem coming down out of Heaven from God having the glory of God, its radiance like a most rare jewel … It had a great, high wall, with twelve gates, and at the gates twelve angels, and on the gates the twelve tribes of the sons of Israel were inscribed … The city lies foursquare, its length the same as its breadth … twelve thousand stadia; its length and breadth and height are equal … And I saw no Temple in the city, for its Temple is the Lord God Almighty and the Lamb. (Rev. 21.1-22 RSV)

New Jerusalem's walls are a massive 144 cubits (21.17) and made of jewels (22.19-21). In its center is the throne of God (22.1) and "the river of the water of life, bright as crystal" that flows from it. The river descends through the city's central streets, a paradisiacal river-walk park with its central feature being the "Tree of Life" (22.3) transplanted from Genesis 2, with its twelve types of fruit aligning the river. The city is perpetually lit by God's presence (22.5).

The elegant city replaces other cities that also appear in Revelation. John condemns the Roman city and offers, in its place, a divine plan for urban renovation and renewal; these evil cities will be destroyed to make space for God's new construction. It is walled and gated; nothing "unclean" nor "those that practice abomination or falsehood" shall enter the city (21.27) even though the kings of the rest of the world will send it tribute (21.24). Within New Jerusalem are "those who wash their robes that they may have the right to the tree of life and they may enter the city by the gates" (22.14), but "outside" the city "are dogs and sorcerers and fornicators and murderers

---

23. See Craig R. Koester, *Revelation: A New Translation with Introduction and Commentary* (The Anchor Yale Bible, 38A; New Haven, CT: Yale University Press, 2014), 793–836; David E. Aune, *Revelation* (WBC, 52; 3 vols.; Nashville, TN: Thomas Nelson, 1998), 1133–94, note especially 1191–4.

24. Stephen D. Moore, *Empire and Apocalypse: Postcolonialism and the New Testament* (The Bible and the Modern World, 12; Sheffield: Sheffield Phoenix Press, 2006); Wes Howard Brook and Anthony Gwyther, *Unveiling Empire: Reading Revelation Then and Now* (New York: Orbis, 1999).

and idolaters, and everyone who loves and practices falsehood" (22.15). The Revelation to John is also a book of books, but these books don't contain narrative.[25] Instead, they appear more as registers, lists of names, punishments, and actions.

Describing New Jerusalem, Stephen Moore observes John's plan for urban renovation where the "blighted landscapes of this disaster-ridden book" are gentrified.[26] Rome's gutters, stained with the blood of the martyrs are washed clean with the blood of the lamb. Soiled and battered city walls are replaced with gates of pearl. Grimy streets are repaved with gold. One wonders fairly if the New Jerusalem has sewers, baths, parks, or gymnasia. It does, however, have first-rate health care, safe streets, and abundant public lighting. It needs no theater because of the constant spectacle (and musical extravaganza) provided by the Lamb and the One on the Throne. New Jerusalem is entirely arcade, a fantasy space with constant weather, lighting and safety, a permanent promenade with constant Muzak soundtrack of familiar and new songs celebrating the worthiness of the Lamb. The gritty, "real" of Rome is replaced with the ethereal space for idle consumption and pleasure. Urban decay is replaced by divine arcade.

Stephen Moore cannot resist a peep over the walls of Jerusalem to see what sort of world lies beyond it (or perhaps his view is from the permanent space outside its walls). What he sees is striking: there's nothing there. Heaven has no suburb. As if in a dystopian science fiction narrative, the city of heaven descends to land upon an earth utterly desolate outside its walls, the (windswept?) space beyond its gates devoid of order and patrolled by restless dead, beasts, and dogs. Perhaps a better image yet is that beyond the airy, camera-monitored phantasmagoria of the New Jerusalem Mall is the desolate parking lot, litter flitting here and there, the decay of the world paved over; perpetually policed it is now populated only by the occasional stray dog sniffing dumpsters for a meal. The massive city (Moore notes it is "Brobdingnagian in its dimensions") "replaces the natural world."[27] Dismayed at the emptiness beyond the gates, he returns his attention to the Panopticonic city itself, "the sheep in the shopping mall."[28] Moore notes the

---

25. See Aune, *Revelation*, 1133–94, note especially 1191–4; Charles H. Talbert, *The Apocalypse: A Reading of the Revelation of John* (Louisville, KY: Westminster John Knox, 1994).

26. Stephen D. Moore, "Ecotherology," in *Divinanimality: Animal Theory, Creaturely Theology* (ed. Stephen D. Moore; New York: Fordham, 2014), 196–209, here 203; see also *Untold Tales from the Book of Revelation: Sex and Gender, Empire and Ecology* (Atlanta, GA: SBL Press, 2014).

27. Moore, "Ecotherology," 204.

28. Moore, "Ecotherology," 204. On the centrality of the Lamb, see p. 205.

city's central River of Life flowing form the Lamb in the city center alongside the Tree(s) of Life, returned from Eden.

> The metaphors on which we have been musing (stream, tree, animal) are themselves situated within another metaphoric structure (city) so surreally outsized as to look unsettling like a cartoon rendition of what we are so busily turning our planet into anyway, as though too impatient to await the arrival of the heavenly megalopolis.[29]

Moore continues:

> How should we classify the New Jerusalem—as a "living city," a "utopia," or a "dead mall?" Or simply as a megamall, whether living or dead? Is Revelation's heavenly city not all too readily—all too eerily—evocative of this most iconic postmodern urban spaces, complete with its central fountain, single stream, and token tree?[30]

But what about the New Jerusalem's library? Despite its reputation for revealing the end of the world, Revelation is best read as a series of beginnings, each world replacing another, Kafka-like in eternal reproduction and renewal.[31] Revelation is apocalyptic, and, so, the mediated recreation of the cosmos, the display of the ultimate Phantasmagoric space represented as the "real" reality, the ultimately real.[32] Benjamin's Messiah challenges any pursuit for meaning in history and the quest for causation. The desire to link together so many moments of history is akin to the desire to find meaning in intertextual montage (the apparatus of all our reading). The scholar's location and (auto)biography infuse meaning in disparate acts and moments creating a knot of "messianic" time. In the reading of books, the apparatus is constructed with its potential lightning strike of insight, the messianic moment. In the renewal of the city we face two poles: the clinical, clean and gentrified fantasy space of commodification and consumption; and the stark, but real, proletarian space filled with work and with words. The word of life resides within the streets filled with smells of flesh and ink.

Revelation foregrounds written words in its own self-conscious presentation of itself as a book (a writing). It seems to bestride the worlds of the scroll (appearing in the more traditional divine throne room scene of 5.1) and the codex (or traditional book, appearing in the highly progressive final

---

29. Moore, "Ecotherology," 204.
30. Moore, "Ecotherology," 204.
31. See Tina Pippin, *Apocalyptic Bodies: The Biblical End of the World in Text and Image* (New York: Routledge, 1999), 1; Robert Paul Seesengood, *Competing Identities: The Athlete and the Gladiator in Early Christian Literature* (Library of New Testament Studies, 346; Playing the Texts, 11; New York: T&T Clark, 2006), 68–70.
32. See John J. Collins, *The Apocalyptic Imagination: An Introduction to Jewish Apocalyptic Literature* (2nd edn.; Grand Rapids, MI: Eerdmans, 1998), 1–42.

judgment in Revelation 21). The "Book of Life" (or "living book") has a long tradition in Jewish speculative literature, remaining integral to rabbinic Judaism that emerged post Mishnah.[33] In predominantly Jewish traditions, the Book of Life (or, alternately, the "Living Book") is a catalog of the redeemed, but also a ledger listing the ultimate fate of each living thing in creation. Non-apocalyptic ancient Christian writing uses the idea of a "living book" as a shorthand way of describing God's decrees (2 Timothy; Hebrews). God's (written) word is "quick," alive, and active. In a technique not unlike Benjamin's montage, Revelation draws together a host of scenes, characters, phrases, and texts from across the Hebrew scriptures and second-temple traditions. In many ways, the text of Revelation is a montage with commentary from these traditions. *Tikkun olam* seems effected, the divine spark sent back to G-d, not by acts of charity and compassion and commandment, but in the utterance of words, and words, and words.

Reading Benjamin

Moore's analysis of New Jerusalem is a critique of theological and economic systems that have diminished the Animal and environment. These are, of course, degradations and losses that are the result of capitalism and its unchecked, indeed, insatiable need for growth. Yet reading Moore alongside Benjamin we see that the phantasmagoria of John's new Jerusalem is also an inherently economic concern.

I read Benjamin in Reading, Pennsylvania where I live and teach. Reading was founded in 1748 by Thomas Penn along the Schuykill River, 45 miles from Philadelphia. The cramped twisting downtown testifies that it was once a walled city, rare for the US. My neighborhood and campus are in northern historic districts. A century ago they were the affluent suburbs; now they are surrounded by blocks of decayed, pre-war row houses carved-up into low-cost apartments. The city is, and has been, polyglot. Reading is the gateway to Pennsylvania Dutch territory; German is still spoken in the rural county outskirts. The city population is now overwhelmingly Latino and Caribbean; city signs and street conversation are in Spanish. Reading is a typical, eastern Pennsylvania post-industrial town; wealthy in the nineteenth century, as the coal, steel and railroads declined, the city has been left in poverty with decaying infrastructure. The city's historic districts for decades have been on the knife-edge of early (or surrendered) gentrification. Most of the professional classes live across the Schuykill River in West Reading or in the suburbs. In the twentieth century, the economy shifted from steel and coal and

---

33. Aune, *Revelation*, 223–7, 1102–4.

shipping to textiles and retail. Reading piloted the model of the manufacturer outlet mall. Three and four-story warehouses were covered with glass roofs and converted to magical, seemingly endless shopping space, restaurants, and hotels. Now, post-NAFTA, these are largely closed. The malls on the city edge are now largely empty, their vacant lots and buildings are refuges for gangs and drugs. Reading city streets teem with evangelists and missionaries preaching, passing out tracts, clutching Bibles tucked high up under their arms. When the Messiah comes, they ask, will I be ready? "Depends," I usually answer without commentary.

I read Benjamin in various libraries. One is Albright College's F. Wilber Gingrich Library. To enter the building, a 1960s era brutalist building of concrete and glass, I pass a display for a new library renovation plan. The proposal, a tens-of-millions of dollar project, will transform the current cold façade with glass and steel. The interior will be a broad, warm, open space in lovely color with meeting rooms, computer labs and a learning commons. There will be less space for books. My other library is the West Reading branch of the public library. Reading had a library system established early in the nineteenth century and modeled on Ben Franklin's grand Free Public Library of Philadelphia, proposed as the necessary engine, the crucible for our Republic. Reading's main branch, downtown, is a dingy ruin. The roof leaks. Condom wrappers and drug paraphernalia appear in stairwells. West Reading has a children's section that my son adores. The building is prewar, but lovingly maintained. It is full, but always neat-as-a-pin, and nearly always almost empty outside of the children's section. I am usually alone in the reading room.

As I read Benjamin, the advance, not progress, of history is starkly foregrounded in my daily newspaper and social media. The 2016 US presidential campaign and election confirm that unprecedented access to information does not lead to real knowledge or meaningful public debate. Information access certainly does not unify. Disinformation and conversational silos proliferate. "Apocalyptic" is thrown around freely by both pundits and comics. The word "fascism" is all too common in editorials. The public spaces of my city are subdued. More and more people feel we are in the last days with barbarian forces of one type or another ready to break in, to tear down. One hears much rhetoric about building walls, talk that sounds very different in gated neighborhoods, college campuses, and urban streets.

I read a version of this essay at the annual meeting of the Society of Biblical Literature (held in tandem with the American Academy of Religion). The AAR-SBL, an academic conference that averages 10,000 attendees and parallels other humanities conferences like the Modern Language Association. It moves annually from one city convention center to another; the main floor of the convention space is filled with exhibitors of all sorts, mostly publishers. Thousands of new books line displays of publisher after publisher. Editors meet with authors. Students attend receptions for graduate programs. Graduates are interviewed by prospective employers. It is a tense congregation of anticipation, recruitment, and "networking." Alongside this charged (and economic) exchange, there are also about 1000 presentations, arraigned by common theme or topic or methodology, in convention center and hotel meeting rooms; scholars read work in process and report new findings. Uniting the chaos is the writing and editing and reviewing and promoting and discovering and reading of books, of The Book.

In November 2016, the AAR-SBL met in San Antonio, and I read a version of this essay there. San Antonio, named for the patron saint of beasts and lost things, is infectiously charming. Founded in 1718 along the San Antonio River, it has a major conference center and hotels downtown, all intertwined with a developed river walk, elegant parks, and the Alamo. Stone walkways line the river, bordered in turn by lovely hanging gardens, niches with stone statues of saints or Texas heroes, and happy shops and restaurants. Mild weather brings everyone outside on balconies and porches. Boats of delighted tourists ply the river. Mariachi bands stroll the restaurant porches to accompany children, dinner conversation, clinked glasses, water birds. The air is scented with lemon trees. In the evening, decorative lights are spun among the trees, balconies, and porticos.

The response to my reading was productive, but I left the conference irresolute. Perhaps it is middle age, perhaps politics, but I am brooding and uncertain these days. Reading Benjamin these days—*these* days—thinking through his Messianic and its development during the rise of fascism and nationalism amid a pandemic, reading about transitions and transformations of urban space, reading about books all left me with an array of unfocused ideas, rattled and distorted. I walked, in the evenings, along the river, a space transformed and lovely, arcade-like, a meandering river of life bordered by fruit trees, stray bits of books in my mind, distorted and fragmentary. I met, on each walk, a colleague, a friend, an old school mate, or a teacher. All these experiences rattle intertextually through my reading, cohering into ... What? What will become of the books we are all so lovingly collecting, reading, unpacking, interpreting, and reading? Toward what phantasmagoria, what messiah, what New Jerusalem are we drifting?

Benjamin's ideal city is not the New Jerusalem. Benjamin's Messiah is not John of Patmos's (nor, really, Agamben's). What is Benjamin's ideal city or Messiah? As he completes his essay "Unpacking My Library," Benjamin writes, "Now I am on the last half-emptied case and it is way past midnight. Other thoughts fill me than the ones I am talking about—not thoughts but images, memories. Memories of the cities in which I found so many things."[34] He, as well, seems to be dissolving into an assemblage of ideas and memories—some real, some only borrowed but still feeling real and somehow unique—arising from-and-through his books. The author becomes a collage of ideas; ideas are built, bricolage, into buildings of a sort. Benjamin concludes the essay:

> O bliss of the collector, bliss of the man of leisure! ... For inside him there are spirits, or at least little genii, which have seen to it that for a collector—and I mean a real collector, a collector as he ought to be—ownership is the most intimate relationship that one can have to objects. Not that they come alive in him; it is he who lives in them. So I have erected one of his dwellings, with books as the building stones, before you, and now he is going to disappear inside, as is only fitting.[35]

John of Patmos, of course, concludes with a book promising a city and an absent (but, really, soon to be here, any time now) Messiah:

> I warn everyone who hears the words of the prophecy of this book: if any one adds to them, God will add to him the plagues described in this book, and if anyone takes away from the words of the book of this prophecy, God will take away his share in the tree of life and in the holy city, which are described in this book. He who testifies to these things says "Surely I am coming soon." Amen. (Rev. 21.18-20 RSV)

In Benjamin, the idea of the book becomes as compelling—perhaps more so— than the ideas within the book. At minimum, the subjective and objective sense of the genitive inherent in "the ideas of a Book" fuse and mitigate. The city is a metaphor of history's change and flux. Its "decline" is often the space of independence. Its "redemption" is often a mask, a fantasy. Benjamin assembles identity via the library. In an equal way, in *Arcades*, he assembles Meaning by the amalgamation and aggregation of discrete portions and fragments of books, woven together into a new "thing," a not-book-book, a book that is an open interval, a book that integrates reader and text while reducing all authorship to redaction, a Living Book that squirms away from the dissection blade.

Biographical Note

Robert Paul Seesengood is Associate Dean of First-Year and General Education and Professor of Religious Studies at Albright College in Reading, Pennsylvania. His research is focused upon the Bible in/and American

34. Benjamin, "Unpacking My Library," 67.
35. Benjamin, "Unpacking My Library," 67.

popular culture and critical theory. He is author of several articles and monographs, most recently *Philemon: Imagination, Labor and Love* (T&T Clark). He is book review editor for the journal *Bible & Critical Theory*.

Bibliography

Aune, David E. *Revelation*. 3 volumes. World Biblical Commentary, 52. Nashville, TN: Thomas Nelson, 1998.

de Balzac, Honoré. *History of the Thirteen.* Translated by Herbert J. Hunt. New York: Penguin, 1974.

Benjamin, Andrew, ed. *Adorno and Benjamin: Problems of Modernity*. New York: Routledge, 1989.

Benjamin, Walter. *Selected Writings.* Edited by Michael W. Jennings, et al. Translated by Rodney Livingstone, et al. 4 volumes. Cambridge, MA: Belknap Press, 1991–1999.

—*Illuminations: Essays and Reflections*. Edited by Hannah Arendt. Translated by Harry Zohn. New York: Schocken, 2007.

Brook, Wes Howard, and Anthony Gwyther. *Unveiling Empire: Reading Revelation Then and Now.* New York: Orbis, 1999.

Buck-Morss, Susan. *The Dialectics of Seeing: Walter Benjamin and the Arcades Project.* Cambridge, MA: MIT Press, 1989.

Eiland, Howard, and Michael W. Jennings. *Author as Producer: A Life of Walter Benjamin*. Cambridge, MA: Harvard University Press, 2007.

Eagleton, Terry. *Walter Benjamin or Towards a Revolutionary Criticism.* London: New Left Books, 1981.

Ferris, David. *The Cambridge Introduction to Walter Benjamin*. Cambridge: Cambridge University Press, 2008. https://doi.org/10.1017/CBO9780511793257

Gilloch, Graeme. *Myth and Metropolis: Walter Benjamin and the City*. Cambridge: Polity Press, 1996.

Hanssen, Beatrice, and Andrew Benjamin. *Walter Benjamin and the Arcades Project.* New York: Routledge, 2002.

Hoggart, Richard. *The Uses of Literacy: Aspects of Working-Class Life with Special Reference to Publications and Entertainments.* London: Penguin, 1969.

Jay, Martin. *The Dialectical Imagination: A History of the Frankfurt School and the Institute for Social Research, 1923–1950.* Berkeley, CA: University of California Press, 1996.

Khatib, Sami. "Derrida & Sons: Marx, Benjamin and the Spector of the Messiah," *Anthropological Materialism.* February 2013. https://anthropologicalmaterialism.hypotheses.org

—"The Messianic without Messianism: Walter Benjamin's Materialist Anthropology," *Anthropology and Materialism* 1 (2013): 1–17. https://doi.org/10.4000/am.159

Koester, Craig R. *Revelation: A New Translation with Introduction and Commentary.* The Anchor Yale Bible, 38A. New Haven, CT: Yale University Press, 2014. https://doi.org/10.5040/9780300262148

Lane, Richard J. *Reading Walter Benjamin: Writing through the Catastrophe*. New York: Manchester University Press, 2005.

Leslie, Esther. *Walter Benjamin.* London: Reaktion Books, 2007.

Missac, Pierre. *Walter Benjamin's Passages*. Cambridge, MA: MIT Press, 1995.

Moore, Stephen D. *Empire and Apocalypse: Postcolonialism and the New Testament.* The Bible and the Modern World, 12. Sheffield: Sheffield Phoenix Press, 2006.

—"Ecotherology," 196–209 in *Divinanimality: Animal Theory, Creaturely Theology.* Edited by Stephen D. Moore. New York: Fordham, 2014. https://doi.org/10.5422/fordham/9780823263196.001.0001

—*Untold Tales from the Book of Revelation: Sex and Gender, Empire and Ecology.* Atlanta, GA: SBL Press, 2014. https://doi.org/10.2307/j.ctt9qh21k

Piketty, Thomas. *Capital in the Twenty-First Century.* Cambridge, MA: Harvard University Press, 2015.

Pippin, Tina. *Apocalyptic Bodies: The Biblical End of the World in Text and Image.* New York: Routledge, 1999.

Richter, Gerhard. *Walter Benjamin and the Corpus of Autobiography.* Detroit, MI: Wayne State University Press, 2000.

Rose, Jonathan. *The Intellectual Life of the British Working Classes.* New Haven, CT: Yale University Press, 2001.

Scholem, Gershom. *Walter Benjamin: An Intellectual Biography.* Philadelphia, PA: Jewish Publication Society of America, 1981.

Seesengood, Robert Paul. *Competing Identities: The Athlete and the Gladiator in Early Christian Literature.* Library of New Testament Studies, 346. Playing the Texts, 11. New York: T&T Clark, 2006.

Talbert, Charles H. *The Apocalypse: A Reading of the Revelation of John.* Louisville, KY: Westminster John Knox, 1994.

Chapter Four

"On the Concept of History": St. Augustine and Walter Benjamin[1]

Carl A. Levenson

My aim in this chapter is to imagine a conversation between Augustine, Bishop of Hippo, and Walter Benjamin, critical theorist. Fifteen centuries separate them, but strong voices span great distances.

Each thinker brings the context of his thinking. Augustine brings the Church, Platonic mysticism, the collapsing Greco-Roman order. Benjamin brings European culture, Jewish mysticism, the Fascist nightmare. Augustine died at 76, as his town fell to invaders. Benjamin died at 48, an apparent suicide, as the Holocaust threatened to claim him.

Both men were students of events. They looked for patterns, collective and personal. In their work, they speak of redemption but do so in different ways. Augustine looks to the future, to a *strong* Messianic figure who will redeem history in totality; Benjamin looks to the present, to each one of us, to our "*weak* messianic power" to redeem bits of the past we encounter as we wander.[2] Both men, indeed, speak of wandering. But Augustine was a Christian in a time of Christian ascendency; the empire was ending but as a Bishop he always had *authority*. Benjamin never had it. As an exile, he had friends but no position. When the Germans occupied France, he fled—and died in flight.

Certain pages in Augustine's writing echo the anti-Semitism found in earlier Church Fathers, the ancient Christian resentment that helped fuel Hitler's modern racism. But there was another side to Augustine. He loved Jewish texts, came to respect Jewish rites, and insisted that Jewish survival was ensured by prophetic tradition. "Slay them not ..." he writes, and his words—because of his fame—almost certainly saved Jewish lives. "*Slay them not ... but scatter them!*"[3] The Jewish exile, which began before Augustine's birth, was ending as Benjamin died.

---

   1.   I owe my interest in Augustine and Benjamin to David Tracy and Walter Odajnyk. I am grateful to Matt Whitlock for suggesting this essay and for insight and criticism.
   2.   *Walter Benjamin: Selected Writings* (ed. Howard Eiland and Michael W. Jennings; 4 vols.; Cambridge, MA: The Belknap Press of Harvard University Press, 1996–2003), 4:390.
   3.   See, for example, Augustine's exposition of Psalm 59, *Enarrat. Ps.* For

In spite of this tragic background, the encounter between Augustine and Benjamin, as I imagine it, has something festive about it. The past and present call to one another, as if the latter had always been expected and the former could still respond creatively. Such encounters, which Benjamin calls *dialectical*, point—beyond the tragic—to redemption; on the other hand, if we can't reach out to the past *in any way*, our tragic future may be preordained.

Any true dialogue takes on a life of its own; for both speakers say things that neither would have said singly. I lack the power to imitate their voices but, on three occasions, when the issues seemed most daunting, I found myself writing in dialogue form, as if to draw the speakers closer.

Our primary text will be Benjamin's last important work, "On the Concept of History" (*Uber den Begriffe der Geschichte*). Augustine sheds light on every part of it, but our focus will be on the three *implicit* questions that shape our grouping of the 18 sections of Benjamin's essay.

I. Where do event-patterns come from? (Section I of "On the Concept of History")
II. May we hope to find redemption in the future? (Sections II–IX)
III. May we hope to redeem the past? (Sections X–XVIII)

There is some awkwardness in discussing the first section because the exoticism in it troubles today's sensibilities. But Benjamin's goodwill is, I trust, unmistakable.

Section I: The Chess Master
Where Do Event-patterns Come From?

> There was once, we know, an automaton constructed in such a way that it could respond to every move by a chess player with a countermove that would ensure the winning of the game. A puppet wearing Turkish attire and with a hookah in its mouth sat before a chessboard placed on a large table. A system of mirrors created the illusion that this table was transparent on all sides. Actually, a hunchbacked dwarf—a master at chess—sat inside and guided the puppet's hand by means of strings. One can imagine a philosophic counterpart to this apparatus. The puppet, called "historical materialism," is to win all the time. It can easily be a match for anyone if it enlists the services of theology, which today, as we know, is small and ugly and has to keep out of sight.[4]

---

perspective, see Paula Fredriksen, *Augustine and the Jews: A Christian Defense of Jews and Judaism* (New Haven, CT: Yale University Press, 2010).

4. Benjamin, "On the Concept of History," *Selected Writings,* 4:444.

The chess-playing automaton, invented by Kempelen in Vienna in 1770, was exhibited in America by Maelzel. Its nickname was "The Turk." Poe, that master of mystery, described its exhibition. The Turk had a striking aura. It was tall, taller than a man, and its turban, hookah, and robe made it seem distant, exotic. In chess, the Turk was invincible. When it defeated you, you were almost willing to concede that your vanquisher, in this supremely mental game, really had been a machine. Its wheels and gears, housed in the cabinet beneath the table, had been displayed to you, section by section. Yet somehow this machine could *see*. It saw the moves you were making; and though, when you moved, you felt you were choosing freely between many possibilities, the machine stayed ahead of you, more than equal to any choice you made. So, it crushed you.[5]

Now, the opposite of déjà vu, Benjamin says, is an experience which, instead of striking us as strange because it feels like something that has "already" happened, strikes us because it foreshadows what *will* happen, as if "that invisible stranger the future" paid a visit, leaving tokens behind.[6] The charm of Maezel's "Turk" in its epoch was that it anticipated, almost mimicked, our current situation, where machines with their complex circuits surpass us in many ways (e.g., "Deep Blue's" victories in chess). On the other hand, the Turk pointed back to the past. That grandiose assemblage, inhuman, even inanimate, yet somehow conscious and purposeful, is like the god of an ancient visionary, a "god-image" of some kind (e.g., the wheels in Ezekiel's "chariot").[7] More than that: those who believe they have actually felt God approaching but, out of pride or terror, tried to run away, sometimes report having had the impression of being outplayed by their pursuer, defeated by a cosmic chess-master. Aryeh Kaplan, scientist and Kabbalist, writes as follows:

> How does God's providence interact with our free will? I often give the example of a chess game. Let us imagine that I would sit down with a grand master ... Could he maneuver some of my pieces over onto the side of the board, and then move them to the other side of the board? Could he get my king in the middle, then in one corner, and then in another corner ... He could obviously get me to do it. Yet I have free will in every move I make ...[8]

---

5. Edgar Allen Poe, "Maelzel's Chess Player," 1846, https://www.eapoe.org/works/essays/maelzel.htm.
6. Benjamin, "A Berlin Chronicle," *Selected Writings,* 2:634.
7. See Ezek. 1.1-27.
8. Aryeh Kaplan, *Innerspace* (New York: Moznaim Publishing Corporation, 1990), 72.

Using this analogy, we can say God is the ultimate Master and his game involves all mankind. The stakes are the ultimate triumph of good itself.[9]

Augustine could not have played chess, but when in the *Confessions* he looks back upon his life, he certainly finds that God— in order to reach him— had outplayed him exquisitely. The story is complex. Augustine tells it in his *Confessions*, which is a masterpiece of self-analysis. His mother Monica had pushed Catholicism too hard. It was for him too much like "mother's milk." Of course, he wished to outgrow it, wished to strike out on his own—wished to escape the maternal presence that might still, if he relaxed his guard, reclaim him. But a beneficent providence arranged that the Manichean Bishop Faustus, whom Augustine consulted in defiance of Monica, impressed him as uninspired; while a job offer in Milan, which promised to lead him away from his mother's influence, led instead to the Catholic Bishop Ambrose who represented, apart from his celibacy, exactly the ideal figure Augustine wished to embody: erudite, powerful, widely admired. But Ambrose had hardly any time for Augustine—he was the opposite, in that sense, of Monica the too attentive mother. And this very contrast allows the completion of the providential stratagem. The remote and powerful Ambrose in the end becomes Monica's ally, sensing in her authenticity a greatness her son hadn't noticed. A balance emerges—and a path to Catholicism opens.[10] And years later, remembering how he had been "played," Augustine concludes that God, being omniscient, could play anyone in the same way, playing on hopes and fears, however base, to draw us toward redemption. If many are lost, all the same, God intends that too.[11]

What, then, shall we say? What would Benjamin say? He could hardly have contested the first step in the argument, that there are patterns, collective and personal, shaping our life: he himself had observed such patterns.[12]

---

9. Kaplan, *Innerspace*, 34.

10. Augustine, *Confessions*, 5.6, 13. For a partial "diagram" of Augustine's life, see Carl Levenson, "Distance and Presence in Augustine's *Confessions*," *Journal of Religion* 65 (October 1985): 500–12.

11. Augustine writes: "Of the [elect], not one of them perishes, because God is not mistaken ... God is overcome by nothing." God chose us, indeed, "before the foundation of the world, not because we were going to be ourselves holy and immaculate, but ... that we might be so ..." *On Rebuke and Grace*, ch. 14; *On the Predestination of the Saints*, ch. 37; translated by Peter Holmes and Robert Ernest Wallis, and revised by Benjamin B. Warfield. From *Nicene and Post-Nicene Fathers, First Series* (Ed. Philip Schaff; Buffalo, NY: Christian Literature Publishing, 1887). Revised and edited for New Advent by Kevin Knight, http://www.newadvent.org/fathers/1512.htm.

12. Benjamin's insight into his own life-patterns came to him, he says, at the Café des Deux Magots in Paris. The insight faded like a dream, but Benjamin emphasizes that *it could only have come to him in Paris;* for the walls, quays, kiosks, etc. had thrown him

But he would certainly have warned us that if, in recollecting our life, we are looking for patterns whose function is promoting our "progress," we may be tempted to jump to conclusions from which later grief will dislodge us. And if we ask where event-patterns come from and form a picture—however subliminal—of some "Other" who is imposing them, the risk of idolatry is great.

The numinous Turk—God as intelligent machine—was, after all, a cheat. That grandiose figure, Poe theorized, was controlled by a *Buchlicht Mannlein*—a "little hunchback"—who managed to conceal himself in the machinery in the cabinet. Poe shows how, when the doors of the cabinet were opened one by one for inspection, the *Mannlein* would squeeze forward and backward through the wheels, so as never to be seen in the place where the audience was looking. In brief, the *Mannlein* had to merge with the machinery—somewhat like Chaplin in *Modern Times*—and then, when the game began and a secret signal disclosed the moves to be countered, he prevailed, as players then had to do, through sheer mental power.

The *Mannlein*, the Turk, and the one who is "played" form an allegorical triad. By stipulation, the Turk who is always to win stands for the Marxist Dialectic; and Benjamin's favorite chess-opponent—who indeed usually won—was Berthold Brecht, the Marxist poet. The Turk is beautiful and numinous, and like the Marxist Dialectic is a smooth-running machine, defeating, in the end, the capitalists who oppose it (Benjamin's father was a capitalist); but the *Mannlein*, who is hidden in the gears or behind mirrors, is the game's true master. If the game is redemptive, the *Mannlein* is the redeemer. If the *Mannlein* suffers (and how could he not?) his redemptive work gives him pain.

Augustine might have smiled when Benjamin told him that the Turk with his dreamy hookah was a false image of dominance, and that the true master, who "had no beauty … that we should desire him,"[13] was, after all—theology. We might imagine the following exchange.

> AUGUSTINE: *God the father can't be pictured—the "Turk" is an idol, a phantasm. The Father, however, manifests through the Son, the Son who is confined to the cross as the* Mannlein *to the machine. The Son is not a theologian but theology is ABOUT him.*
>
> BENJAMIN: *Or else the* Mannlein *could stand for the workers as Marx describes them. Confined, tormented, forced to conform to inhuman rhythms, they are cheated of their victories—"the fruits of their labor stolen from*

into a dream-state where meanings intertwined and thickened. A synchronicity: the Café des Deux Magots was a favorite haunt of Sartre, who would publish "On the Concept of History" in *les temps modernes*. See *Selected Writings*, 2:614.

13. See Is. 53.2.

them"—*but injustice might provoke rebellion. Only (and this is decisive) they aren't machines; they're free. We don't know what they'll do or when they'll do it.*[14] *As for the grandiose Turk—that is, the Marxist professor who believes in "iron laws" of history—won't he/she be astonished if the* Mannlein, *smashing the cabinet, rises up in full armor ... only to disclose theory's impotence?*

AUGUSTINE: *Hebrew scripture provides the link between Church teaching and Marxist dialectic. Marx came from a line of rabbis. Just as, for Marx, the growing wealth-gap brings justice through rebellion; so, in Christian doctrine, the "loosening of Satan" brings Satan's subduer: our redeemer.*[15]

BENJAMIN: *Sabbatai Sevi, the Jewish pseudo-Messiah—born in Turkey in 1626—believed he could descend into evil and by DOING evil overcome it. My Kabbalist friend Scholem made a study of him.*[16] *His followers did influence Marx. But a philosophy of history secretly driven by myth will depend, for better or worse, on "small, ugly" theology. That's what I intended in my allegory.*

AUGUSTINE: *In my time, at least, theology was not small and ugly*[17] *... But let me complete my interpretation. I believe that you yourself are a figure in your presentation. You are the player who is skeptical of the Turk, but equally, perhaps, of the* Mannlein. *You are the mediating "third" whose DOUBT unites the "first" and "second."*[18]

BENJAMIN: *Mediation, however, was not my particular strength, as my friend Adorno once contended.*[19]

And so—to sum up—where do event-patterns come from?
The chess-machine allegory addresses itself to this question. The Player, the Turk, and the *Mannlein* may be interpreted in many ways; but it will always

---

14. Sartre's point in "*Materialism et Revolution,*" *les temps modernes* (1946); repr., *Situations, III* (Paris: Gallimard, 1949), 135–229. His criticism is directed more toward Marx's expositors than Marx himself.

15. Augustine, *Civ.* 20.23. Citations from *City of God* (trans. Henry Bettenson; intro. G. R. Evans; London: Penguin Books, 1972).

16. Gershom Scholem, *Sabbatai Sevi: The Mystical Messiah* (Princeton, NJ: Princeton University Press, 1973).

17. Nor in Benjamin's time: Buber, Rosenzweig, Barth, Bultmann, Tillich, Rahner, Maritain, Marcel, Gilson, Weil, C. S. Lewis, etc.

18. The turning point of the narrative in Augustine's *Confessions*—the heart of the fifth of nine books—is an interval of radical doubt. "No part of the truth," he concludes during this period, "can be grasped by the human mind" (*Conf.* 5.19). It seems to me that this "core of doubt" not only divides, but also unites, the two halves of Augustine's story, with each half "echoing" the other. See Levenson, "Distance and Presence in Augustine's *Confessions,*" 500–12.

19. Benjamin and Adorno, "Exchange with Theodor W. Adorno on 'The Paris of the Second Empire in Baudelaire,'" *Selected Writings*, 4:99–105.

be the case that, if you are the Player, you find your moves answered by patterns that come from outside you, and while the divinely mechanical Turk seems to devise these patterns, they actually come from the *Mannlein* who is hidden but guaranteed to win. The question remains: What is the point of the exhibition? Will there be progress? Liberation? Or will the result be nothing more than amazement and confinement in the gears?

Sections II–VIII: "Infinite hope ... but not for us" May We Hope to Find Redemption in the Future?

> The tradition of the oppressed teach us that the "state of emergency" in which we live is not the exception but the rule. We must attain to a conception of history that is in keeping with this insight. Then we will clearly see that it is our task to bring about a real state of emergency and this will improve our position in the struggle against Fascism. One reason why Fascism has a chance is that, in the name of progress, its opponents treat it as a historical norm ... The current amazement that the things we are experiencing are "still" possible in the twentieth century is *not* philosophical.[20]

History is not about progress, according to Benjamin. The debris piles up too high, to use a famous image of Benjamin. What prevents us from noticing, Benjamin says, is that history is written by the victors who see progress in their successes; they do not name their victims whom they trample underfoot in their advance. Every triumph of culture is stained by the conditions of its origin. There is always the blood-bath of conquest. And we gladly confuse technical progress, which has been rapid since the enlightenment, with moral progress, which has not.[21]

The amazement felt across the Roman Empire that Rome, after centuries, was falling, not progressing, struck Augustine as untheological. *The City of God*, his longest book, conveys this lesson effectively. In the same way, the amazement felt by progressives in the twentieth century that the horrors of Fascism were "still" possible is not, Benjamin comments, the Socratic type of amazement[22] that opens the mind to reality; it is the amazement of the obtuse when reality intrudes on their dreams. Fascism has a chance, says Benjamin, because it presents itself as the new norm. That makes it harder to combat. The communists, whom Benjamin believed in, signed a pact with Hitler in 1939, explaining that their decision would facilitate future progress. "On the Concept of History" is his desperate response to their betrayal.

---

20. Benjamin, "On the Concept of History," *Selected Writings*, 4:392.
21. Benjamin, "On the Concept of History," *Selected Writings*, 4:391–2.
22. Plato, *Theaet.* 155c-d.

"Is there any hope?" Kafka was asked. "An infinite amount," he replied, "only not for us." Kafka's sisters later died in the Holocaust. Benjamin cites his words about hope[23]—and they are daunting words, because we do want hope *for ourselves*. We want to believe that, if we make things today a little better, we will have accomplished something for tomorrow—for ourselves or perhaps for our children. To renounce this kind of hope would mean breaking the spell of the future; in other words, getting a glimpse of Eternity. Augustine managed to do it.[24] And Eternity, we may suppose, would foreshadow the redemption toward which history, of itself, is unfortunately not progressing.

In fact, good and evil alternate in history. God the artist plays with lights and shadows, according to Augustine.[25] And even if there is not progress, there is the City of God. The honorable Abel, slain by his wicked brother Cain, was its first citizen and martyr. That *already* celestial city persists inside the earthly one.[26] Its members will not be strong enough to prevent the "loosening of Satan" because evil, still repressed to some extent in our time, must eventually be unshackled, as if to fulfill history's logic. Its unshackling, however, will bring about its defeat when the Messiah appears on the scene.[27]

Now, in one way, surely, Benjamin is close to Augustine. With his enemies, the Fascists, flourishing, and his friends, the Marxists, capitulating, Benjamin says that what matters is not victory in the struggle but "what is

---

23. Benjamin, "Franz Kafka," *Selected Writings*, 2:798. Max Brod had asked if there was any hope "outside this manifestation of the world that we know." Kafka replied, "Plenty of hope —for God—an infinite amount—only not for us." The deficits of the world, in other words, testify to divine lapses—"a bad mood for God, a bad day of his"—but not in the least to God's hopelessness. Only ours.

24. *Conf.* 7.10: "I entered under your guidance the innermost places of my being, but only because you had become my helper ... With the vision of my spirit, such as it was, I saw the Unchangeable Light far above my spiritual ken, transcending my mind ... All who know the truth know that light, and all who know it know eternity ..."

25. *Civ.* 1.18.

26. The two cities, Augustine says, were not created in two different spaces, but made out of "two kinds of love: the earthly city was created by self-love reaching the point of contempt for God, the heavenly city by the love of God carried as far as contempt for self," *Civ.* 14.8.

27. "The binding of the devil means that he is unable to exert his whole power of temptation either by force or by guile ... But 'the devil must be unloosed for a short time' ... for we are told he is going to rage with all his strength and the strength of his supporters ..." Fortunately, his rage will soon be spent. And just as capitalism fuels technology—which, Marx hopes, will one day serve the cause of Justice—so, Augustine says, "if [the Devil] had never been unloosed ... it would not have been manifest what good use the Omnipotent would make of his great wickedness ..." *Civ.* 20.23.

manifest in the struggle as courage, humor, cunning, and fortitude";[28] which is to say, *God's own city*—the elements in and among us that are better, therefore holier, than the adversarial forces whose "loosening" we cannot prevent. In a Gnostic mood, Benjamin contends that evil, by its nature, gets results ("bearing fruit," he says, "is the mark of evil acts ..."); "acts of good have no 'consequence.'" Indeed, expecting results from good is "the imperative of progress in its most dubious form."[29] Even so, Benjamin can't really object when the communists politicize redemption; thus, he praises "communist action." But he believes that communist "goals" are "non-sensical and non-existent," as he assures the non-Marxist Scholem.[30]

Our attitude toward such things may depend upon personal experience. Augustine strayed in his youth ("I wandered ... I strayed ... yet you did not restrain me"[31]); but, finally, at the age of 32, he found his voice and vocation. What is more, the encompassing structure of the narrative in the *Confessions* is like a progressive ("dialectical") triad: there is his rebellious early period (Books I–II) where he becomes his own person (so to say, a moment of "matter"); there is a period of spiritual striving (Books III–VII) where, rising from Manicheanism dualism, to Pantheism, to Platonism, he obtains, finally, a glimpse of transcendent reality, all the while declining morally; and there is finally a moment of conversion (Books VIII–IX) when, in the name of Christ (to which mysterious children direct him), he aligns his vision and life—and changes the world.[32] Now, the *young* Augustine whom we meet in the *Confessions* may not strike us today as quite unworthy of the older Bishop; indeed, the Bishop has a rigidity to which the youth would have been immune; and the youth has a questioning spirit we sometimes miss in the Bishop. Thus, the best in Augustine shines, early as well as late, sometimes brightening, sometimes dimming. Not even for saints is progress linear.

For Benjamin, there is no progress. For him, things always go wrong, as if some adverse presence were always there to undermine him. Hannah Arendt, another friend, speaks of this in her memorial essay.[33] Benjamin was haunted by the *buchlicht Mannlein* presented in a children's poem, a

---

28. Benjamin, "On the Concept of History," *Selected Writings*, 4:390.
29. Benjamin, "Try to Ensure that Everything in Life Has a Consequence," *Selected Writings*, 2:686.
30. *The Correspondence of Walter Benjamin and Gershom Scholem: 1932–1940* (trans. Gary Smith and Andre Lefevre; intro. Anson Rabinbach; Cambridge, MA: Harvard University Press, 1992), xix.
31. *Conf.* 2.1.
32. See Carl A. Levenson, "The Cycle of Triads and the Pattern of Distance and Flesh: A Study of the Plot of Augustine's Confessions" (PhD dissertation; Chicago: University of Chicago, 1980).
33. Hannah Arendt, "Introduction," in *Walter Benjamin, Illuminations*: *Essays and*

hidden figure who outplays us, defeats us repeatedly. Benjamin remembers that when, as a child, he spilt the milk, or broke the jar, or tracked dirt on the carpet, his mother would say, "*Mr. Bungle sends his regards*"; and he knew that "Mr. Bungle" was in reality the *Mannlein*, who lived in the realm of the invisible.

> When I go down to the cellar
> There to grab some wine
> A little hunchback in there
> Grabs that jug of mine.

It's not that the child intrudes on the *Mannlein* and gains a fatal glimpse of him, as sometimes happens with the Greek *daimones*. "Anyone whom the little man looks at pays no attention, not to himself and not to the little man." But the milk spills, the jug breaks. The child, outplayed, stands "in consternation … before a pile of debris."[34]

Now, it really does seem, says Arendt, that some hidden power was always outplaying Benjamin; for otherwise how was it possible that he, whose family had been rich, whose genius had been recognized, who was diligent in writing, cherished by friends—how was it possible that he was usually broke, without a job, without students, and unable to publish writings that now, after 70 years, are regarded as cultural treasures? Benjamin had been shrewd enough to flee Germany for France, and then, as the Nazis advanced, to arrange to leave France for America … but he had tried to pass through Spain on the one day the border was closed, and on that day—with the Holocaust threatening to claim him—he took his own life. As with Romeo in Juliet's tomb, he only needed a little patience. The border would soon have re-opened, just as Juliet soon revives. One cannot bear to think what Augustine would say about the suicide. Yet had Benjamin been persuaded, if only in his last terrible hours, of Augustine's too rigid view, he would have survived.

The *Mannlein* in the children's poem is surely the same as the *Mannlein* in the chess-machine: stunted, secretive, powerful; unfortunately, a bit like the "Jew" in Fascist caricatures. For Hannah Arendt, on the other hand, the *Mannlein* is Benjamin's genius. For Benjamin, she writes, lived "in the place at which weakness and genius coincide"; and the words of Riviere about Proust apply, Arendt contends, to Benjamin too:

> He "died of the same inexperience that permitted him to write his work. He died of ignorance … because he did not know how to make a fire or open

Reflections (ed. Hannah Arendt; trans. Harry Zohn; New York: Schocken Books, 2007), 1–55.
   34. Benjamin, "Berlin Childhood around 1900," *Selected Writings,* 3:385.

a window." But like Proust, he had every reason to bless the curse and to repeat the strange prayer at the end of the folk poem with which he closes his childhood memoir.

> O dear child, I beg of you
> Pray for the *buchlicht Mannlein* too![35]

Those who feel exiled in the world, who cannot learn to open windows or light fires, those who feel that the links between their aims and the implements that serve them have been *bent* somehow, as if a receding, shrinking world-space had acquired a "hump," as Benjamin says—or as if time had slipped "out of joint," as Hamlet says—all of us in that situation will understand Benjamin's suspicion that the *Mannlein*, and he alone, is shaped to fit worldly life.[36] When Benjamin's Messiah comes, the *Mannlein* will disappear. Perhaps the Messiah will slay him … or perhaps (as we gladly think) he will merge with the process of redemption, with which he has secretly conspired.[37] Redemption, in any case, says Benjamin (citing a "great rabbi" who turns out to be friend Scholem), may actually be quite *subtle*.[38] No clash of armies, no dying, no bleeding. Just a barely perceptible shift. Only in retrospect, perhaps, would we even notice we had been redeemed.

> *AUGUSTINE: When I wrote my* Confessions, *I was seeking my life in totality. I spoke the words in time, but I was focused on what held them together. So many patterns emerged that my mind could not comprehend them. But God's hand was there.*
>
> *BENJAMIN. If you see your life in totality, you are standing outside your life. Which means: in the place of death. When we are about to die, a sequence of images may be set in motion; then we see our life before us. Turning that around, if we see our life before us—even with death years away—death has started to do its work.*[39]

---

35. Arendt, "Introduction," 7.
36. Benjamin, "Berlin Childhood," *Selected Writings,* 3:385.
37. The "messianic arrow" writes Benjamins, flies against the "secular dynamic" that aims at human happiness; in that way, it enhances happiness, which means facing "downfall" authentically. Benjamin, "Theological Political Fragment," *Selected Writings*, 3:305.
38. Benjamin, "Franz Kafka," *Selected Writings*, 2:811. "The *Mannlein* is at home in distorted life; he will disappear with the coming of the Messiah, who (a great Rabbi once said) will not wish to change the world by force but will merely make a slight adjustment in it."
39. Benjamin writes: "Just as a sequence of images is set in motion inside a man as his life comes to an end—unfolding the views of himself in which he has encountered himself without being aware of it—suddenly in his expressions and looks the unforgettable emerges, and imparts to everything that concerns him that authority that even the poorest wretch in the act of dying possesses for the living around him." Benjamin, "The

AUGUSTINE. Death haunted my Confessions. My mother's death, my friend's death, my own death. Each moment flowed away as I evoked it; its disappearance made death manifest. But each moment of my life was like a word. I wanted the moments to pass by so I could grasp the meaning of the whole; or better, grasp what God was saying, since our moments are words in God's speech. God's intention began to emerge—like the pattern in a well-composed novel. I felt that everything would then be bound around me, in a manner certain to stand fast.[40]

BENJAMIN: There was no "standing fast" for me. The eternal feature of my life was simply—transience itself. As Germans, we lost much; as Jews, we lost nearly all. It occurred to me in youth, however, that an eternity of downfall would still be—eternity. As best I could, I welcomed rhythms of transience and in detachment tried to be happy.[41]

Storyteller," *Selected Writings*, 3:150–1. Socrates—who calls philosophy a "practice of death" because it "separates soul from body"— was perhaps the first to notice the epistemological value of mortality. In his last hour, he sees his life as a whole—at a distance, in perspective, with its twists and turns fully manifest—as if death, and death alone, could make this possible. "When I was young," he says, "I had a passion for natural science ..." With these apparently casual words, his magnificent life-review begins (*Phaed.* 64a; 96–107).

40. *Conf.* 4.4-12. A friend dies and, "Black grief closed over my heart ... Wherever I looked I saw death ... Everything I had shared with [him] turned into hideous anguish without him. My eyes sought him everywhere, but he was missing. I hated all things because they held him not, and could no more say to me, 'Look, here he comes!' as they had been wont to do in his lifetime when he had been away." And this tangible heart-breaking absence—non-being as the "reference" of beings—soon provides a hint about matter, *materia prima*; for God, in a sense, makes the world "out of" transience (12.6). "In rising, things begin to exist and grow toward their perfection but ... the more quickly they grow and strive to be, the more swiftly they hasten not to be ... Such is their law." On the other hand, to the degree that we grasp our life-story and its meaning (as we grasp any discourse in its meaning), we actively consent that our times (like words) "should fly on their way" so the meaning can be fully incarnate; we "are not glued fast by sensuous love" to any passing moment. Put differently: We apprehend in things the "Word through whom they are created" and we discern in that very Word the power to limit any condition's duration—which the telling of stories requires. "'*From here begin*,' says the Word; '*thus far you shall go* ...' 'But I,' says the Word of God, 'shall I depart to any place?'" "Entrust to Truth whatever truth is in you," and everything that passes will then "be restored and bound fast to you..." *Conf.* 4.4-12.

41. In the "Theological Political Fragment" of 1920, if we trust Scholem's dating—or 1936, if we trust Adorno's—Benjamin writes: "The spiritual *restitutio in integrum*, which introduces immortality, corresponds to a worldly restitution that leads to an eternity of downfall; and the rhythm of this eternally transient worldly existence, transient in its totality, in its spatial but also its temporal totality, the rhythm of messianic nature, is happiness," *Selected Writings*, 3:305. Judith Butler explores these lines. "Downfall," she says, frees us from self-attachment as we attend to these "rhythms of transience" which are more like music—the sound of swaying trees—than like ideas (in the usual

AUGUSTINE: Eternity as downfall? Yes, I see the mysticism in it. Things fade away; they grow silent; then God's Word becomes audible. So the passing of things can enlighten us—I noticed this more than once.[42] *But what IS the past? I asked myself. The distance of present memories. And what IS the future? The distance of present expectations.*[43] *Outside our minds, time is nothing: the ABSENCE of the past and future, emptily open to Eternity. No hope, no remorse to clutter it. Yet Eternity contains time's patterns.*

BENJAMIN: I see patterns in my life, too. The same kinds of people, the same adventures, the same disasters.[44] *What I don't see is progress and purpose. You led a different kind of life. You MADE your life cosmogonic. It mirrored the world's creation. There was matter—your early wandering. There was form—your glimpse of the highest. There was formative-conversion—your vision giving your life form. But for me, it was all wandering—all exile, straying, erring. At its best, it was a kind of strolling. Flanerie, I sometimes think, was paradoxically the aim of my life.*

AUGUSTINE: It was not, as you say, the aim of mine. But in my youth, as I let the world know, I did wander too much—around cities like Carthage and Thagaste. I stole forbidden fruit, literally as well as figuratively ... as if, "sinning in Adam," I had to enact Adam's sin. When I later looked back on those days, it seemed to me that God's silence had something inexplicable about it. God let me go, let me stray.[45]

sense). In this way, the rhythm of transience disrupts "progressive" time; just as, in "On the Concept of History" remembrance "flashes up" disrupting time's forward movement. See Judith Butler, "One Time Traverses Another: Benjamin's Theologico-Political Fragment," European Graduate School, 2013, https://www.youtube.com/watch?v=LA8hiT2nIAk.

42. *Conf.* 9.10. As death is about to separate them, Augustine and Monica share a moment of illumination. The world slips away; its meaning—the Word of God—emerges from it. "And so we said: If the tumult of the flesh fell silent ... and silent too were the phantasms of earth, sea and air ... silent the heavens, and the very soul silent to itself ... for if anyone listens, all these things will tell him, 'We did not make ourselves but he made us who abides forever' ... if, having said this they held their peace ... and God alone were to speak ... would not this, and this alone, be *Enter into the joy of your Lord*." Already in *Conf.* 7.10-11, the revelation of sheer transience accompanies the inner light.

43. "... Neither things past nor things future have any existence ... and it is inaccurate to say: 'There are three tenses or times: past, present and future,' though it might properly be said, 'There are three tenses or times: the present of past things, the present of present things, and the present of future things.' These are three realities in the mind, but nowhere else as far as I can see, for the present of past things is memory, the present of present things is attention, and the present of future things is expectation," *Conf.* 11.20. And, "In you, my mind, I measure my time. Do not interrupt me by clamoring that time has objective existence," *Conf.* 11.27.

44. Benjamin, "A Berlin Chronicle," *Selected Writings*, 2:614.

45. *Conf.* 2.1: "I was wandering away from you, yet you let me go my way. I was flung hither and thither, I poured myself out, frothed and floundered in the tumultuous

BENJAMIN: Do you regret it? Your wandering freed you. And consider this: Sometimes when you wander through a city, you encounter something that reminds you of something else, something that surfaced before. As the past opens up, you find treasures not revealed before. You are amazed, struck dumb—and you blast that moment out of history. You blast a life out of its epoch, a work out of its canon; you let it link with, form a passageway to, a moment that passed before. If there's redemption, it's probably like that: billions of minds redeeming—by re-entering—trillions of vanished moments. What is not "cited" that way is lost. The past, then, turns toward us ... and how could it not, if time's BEING, as you say, is just our own mental stretching? But I think we are endowed with a trace of messianic power—very weak, to be sure, but real[46]—a power to which the past lays claim.

AUGUSTINE: Such a claim would not be settled lightly. However, another thought comes to me. At the time of my conversion, Paul's much earlier writing spoke to me. My life changed greatly; did Paul's life change at all?[47]

BENJAMIN: His conversion drew strength from yours. You both draw strength from those who follow. A breath of air that pervaded earlier times caresses us as well. As flowers turn toward the sun, the past strives to turn— by dint of a secret heliotrope—toward the sun that, even now, is rising in the sky of history.[48]

AUGUSTINE: Sunlight and flowers? Quite a change from the Turk and Mannlein.

And so—to sum up—we've been asking in this section about hope. Augustine believes in the future. In spite of the Empire's dissolution and his own years of wandering, Augustine feels involved in a sacred drama,

---

sea of my fornications, and you were silent. O my joy, how long I took to find you! At that time you kept silent as I continued to wander far from you ... and sowed more seeds of grief."

46. Benjamin, "On the Concept of History," *Selected Writings*, 4:390. In the idea of "*weak* messianic power," Agamben sees the influence of Paul. "When I am weak," says Paul, "I am strong"—as if weakness belonged of necessity to the messianic force in each of us. Giorgio Agamben, *The Time That Remains* (trans. Patricia Dailey; Stanford, CA: Stanford University Press, 2005), 140–3.

47. *Conf.* 8.12.

48. Benjamin's exact words: "The past carries with it a secret index by which it is referred to redemption. Doesn't a breath of the air that pervaded earlier days caress us as well? In the voices we hear, isn't there an echo of now silent ones? Don't the women we court have sisters they no longer recognize? If so, then there is a secret agreement between past generations and the present one. Then our coming was expected on earth. Then, like every generation that preceded us, we have been endowed with a *weak* messianic power, a power on which the past has a claim. Such a claim cannot be settled cheaply ... As flowers turn toward the sun, what has been strives to turn—by dint of a secret heliotropism—toward that sun which is rising in the sky of history." Benjamin, "On the Concept of History," *Selected Writings,* 4:390.

at once personal and cosmic, in which evil rises to entangle us, only to be overcome by Christ. Marxists speak of a parallel drama in which the unleashing of "wicked" capitalism justly evokes revolution—and therefore the future saves us—but the sense that this happens necessarily, through mechanisms studied by "science," is nourished, Benjamin warns, by veiled and wizened theology; it is not as "scientific" as it seems. The Turk, then, is gone—dialectic is not a machine. And though the *Mannlein*, defeating all comers, might, suggests Arendt, in the end bestow a blessing, his intentions can hardly be relied on; and regarding history's happy ending, many doubts remain (in view of fascist victories, etc.). What, then? Uncertain about the future, Benjamin looks to the past. If the wind that drives us forward does not seem to favor us, we must learn to fly against the wind.

Sections IX–XVIII: Angels of Redemption May We Hope to Redeem the Past?

> There is a picture by Klee called *Angelus Novus*. It shows an angel who seems about to move away from something he stares at. His eyes are wide, his mouth is open, his wings are spread. This is how the angel of history must look. His face is turned toward the past. Where a chain of events appears before us, *he* sees one single catastrophe, which keeps piling wreckage upon wreckage and hurls it at his feet. The angel would like to stay, awaken the dead, and make whole what has been smashed. But a storm is blowing from Paradise and has got caught his wings; it is so strong that the angel can no longer close them. This storm drives him irresistibly into the future, to which his back is turned, while the pile of debris before him grows toward the sky. What we call progress is *this* storm.[49]

An angel, says Scholem (discussing the matter with Benjamin), has his entire reality in the mission assigned him. His *essence* is what the mission calls for. Born to it, confined to it, he'll vanish if ever he completes it … even if his mission is of the shortest possible duration, for example, to sing a note in God's praise.[50] And here is the angel of history, a perennial angel, surely; yet Benjamin first beheld him in Klee's painting of an angel who is *new*, a painting Benjamin had purchased and in the end bequeathed to Scholem. The history angel's mission consists entirely in remembrance. Therefore, he must always face the past. A storm is blowing in Paradise and its winds, which catch the angel's wings, hurl him backward toward the

---

49. Benjamin, "On the Concept of History," *Selected Writings*, 4:392.
50. Gershom Scholem, *On Jews and Judaism in Crisis: Selected Essays* (ed. Werner J. Dannhauser; Philadelphia, PA: Schocken Books, 1987), 210–3.

future which, since he lacks eyes behind his head, he can see only after it has "passed."

He does, however, grasp the past *as a whole*—from Eden to "a moment ago." Where we perceive a sequence of events, his more perfect (angelic) vision detects a single catastrophe. Wreckage keeps piling up. "The angel would like to stay, awaken the dead, make whole what has been smashed." But the Edenic storm drives him ceaselessly backward toward the future, away from those in need of rescue. We call the storm progress, says Benjamin. Or the fall, Augustine suggests.

Both names serve well. Plotinus' *teaching about time* provides a bridge between them. In the beginning, Plotinus says, the soul gazes into Eternity. Past and future are present as one. But in this situation, the soul feels inquietude. Possessing the prize, it has never played the game. Blessed with time-transcending plenitude, it grieves for, hopes for *nothing*—wants *nothing*. Yet it *wants to want*—wants to win for itself, not passively receive, fulfillment of desire. What to do? Trapped in the ever-abiding, it finds a way to expel past and future, thereby creating absence everywhere. Time emerges.[51]

Now, when Augustine reads Plotinus, he discovers the key to his youth. "I wanted to want; I despised myself having little want." In his hunt for satisfaction, he outruns the too nurturing Monica. "I hated security, and a path free from snares."[52] What he wants, however, is not some particular thing in the future, but futurity as such, the "openness" that beckons; or as Benjamin might have put it in his days as an advocate for youth, what young Augustine wants is something "inexperiencable"—for experience corrodes the still indeterminate hopes that drive the young into experience itself.[53] Which takes us straight to Edenic Eve. "You shall be as gods," the serpent tells her. Which means she is not yet one. But she hungers for this "not-yet," for an unimaginable height to be attained through her actions and decisions. The storm called progress now begins: begetting, herding, farming, murder (i.e., tales of Cain and Abel); then cities, the bronze age, the art of war, the flood. Thus, the debris is accumulating. God, the heavenly court, the human couple all know it. "The humans are now like us knowing good and evil." Eyes once closed have opened wide.[54]

Let us look again at Klee's painting. The angelic visage registers shock. His eyes are staring; his teeth are flashing. He'll never get used to this

---

51. Plotinus, *Enn.* 9.7.
52. *Conf.* 3.1.
53. Benjamin, "Experience," *Selected Writings*, 1:3–5.
54. Gen. 2.4–11.8.

nightmare. He seems more like a beast than a human (especially around the mouth and claws); and, with his huge angular head and shrunken angular body, he reminds us as well of a robot of some kind, a mechanical-spiritual entity (not unlike Ezekiel's angels). He would like, Benjamin says, to help, to make things whole. But he would have to enter the past, away from which the storm bears him. Can anyone fly against the wind?

Let us see. The angel's essence is remembrance; and "the faculty of memory," says Augustine, "is great—a vast, an infinite recess."

> People go to admire lofty mountains, and huge breakers of the sea, and crashing waterfalls, and vast stretches of ocean, and the dance of the stars, but they leave themselves behind out of sight. It does not strike them as wonderful that I could enumerate those things without seeing them with my eyes, and that I could not even have spoken of them unless I could ... contemplate them in mind, where they are as vast as they would be outside.[55]

The history angel *remembers*; can't he enter the past through memory? Everything is there: mountains, flowing water, the stars, crowded cities. Where, then, is the difficulty? Let the angel enter; let him fly where he wishes, healing, soothing, repairing. Yes, but what will be gained? Once we have lost Eternity, the past, growing distant, gets reduced to mere traces of itself. Its vastness remains, but its substance seems to be gone. "What we bring forth from memory," says Augustine, "is not the events themselves ... but words formed from [their] images ... which have left some kind of traces in the mind."[56] How repair, why repair, mere traces, emptied of the substance they had formerly?

A Jew with a weak heart watching Fascism triumph around him, a haunted man who does not bemoan his danger but denounces oppression across history, Benjamin's thought becomes fantastic, at once archaic and surreal. The Edenic storm is time's progression. Can we not, then, murder time? In 1830, insurrectionists in Paris shot at all public clocks. Benjamin cites their accounts.[57] Did time, then, die? Or (to change the metaphor) can we not find the brakes of time? Revolution, contends Marx, is history's locomotive, but Benjamin thinks just the opposite. Revolution, he declares in a note to "On the Concept of History," is "the grasping of the emergency brake" by those who discover—to their horror—where the train will bear them.[58]

And then Benjamin invites us to explore the festival calendar, which does not so much measure as *overcome* time. Every Christmas, he explains,

---

55. *Conf.* 10.8
56. *Conf.* 10.8.
57. Benjamin, "On the Concept of History," *Selected Writings*, 4:395.
58. Benjamin, "*Parolipomena* to 'On the Concept of History,'" *Selected Writings*, 4:402.

converges with every other; the "now" of Christmas keeps coming back. All festivals have this power.[59] And Benjamin speaks of Nietzsche, for whom cosmic history recurs like a festival. What the cosmos generates once, it generates repeatedly, eternally—"down to the last detail," "in the same succession and sequence."[60] This doctrine of eternal return, moreover, is itself a "return." In the distant Roman empire, Augustine, too, had examined it, having drawn it from a still more distant past.

> [It's as if the philosopher Plato,] in the same town, in the same school, with the same disciples [had already] appeared many times, will appear many times in the future. For the things which have been and those which are to be are always coinciding.[61]

Does memory consist of traces only? If Nietzsche is right, the traces will finally take on flesh again. Plato, whom we remember, will resurrect from a trace of himself, and his school and pupils, too, and his work with Socrates too. All will be bodied forth—"down to the last detail"—in full glory.

Does that help the angel help us? No, because the point of Nietzsche's doctrine is that everything will come back just as it was before. Memory-traces take on flesh but their repair and enhancement are forbidden. Athens is sure to fall to Sparta, Socrates will perish as before. *Act in such a way that you would will to live your life again*—and this applies to us collectively as well as individually. To will anything other than exactly *this present life* is to negate being itself, preferring nothingness and death. To worship God on the cross, Nietzsche contends, is especially to divinize death.[62]

From the past, Augustine answers: "Far be it from me to believe these things. Christ died only once for our sins!"[63] Those terrible hours bought redemption in a single iteration. Thus for Augustine, the cross, whose intersecting lines support and torment the human body, shatters the ancient cycles that make history repeat itself like nature. Indeed, every historical event now acquires an aura of uniqueness, for each is uniquely distanced from the event whose uniqueness is acknowledged. No doubt, we can now dream of progress—of a blither, freer, more equitable future. But Christianity, as the historian of religion Mircea Eliade comments, will remain the

---

59. Benjamin, "On the Concept of History," *Selected Writings*, 4:395.
60. Friedrich Nietzsche, *The Gay Sciences,* https://philoslugs.files.wordpress.com/2016/12/the-gay-science-friedrich-nietzsche.pdf *4:341.*
61. *Civ.* 4.14.
62. Friedrich Nietzsche, *The Antichrist,* section XVIII in *The Portable Nietzsche* (trans. and intro. Walter Kaufmann; London: Penguin, 1954).
63. *Civ.* 12.14.

religion of the fallen, for it bars us from Paradise which is the site of "eternal return" and delivers us to history's terrors.[64]

How, then, oppose time's wind? Consider Benjamin's *flanerie*. He was born, he says, under Saturn, planet of delays and detours. He would stroll through the streets of Paris, as if, when moving forward, an opposing force held him back, causing him to tarry and veer.[65] Meandering, he *sees*: a shop, a crowd, a beggar, a beckoning woman. Something in the scene might awaken a bit of the past—not in the normal sense of memory but as an echo awakened by a call vibrates across great distance. Baudelaire, famous for *flanerie*—whom Benjamin translates and explicates—evokes these echoing-places that hashish helps him discover.

> Nature is a temple whose living pillars
> Sometimes speak confused words ...
> Prolonged echoes ... mingle in the distance,
> A dark vast unity ...
> Expanding infinitely ...[66]

If we can't glimpse Eternity as Augustine says he managed to do, we might at least, following Baudelaire, seek these special places which, like "living pillars," support the edifice, the "temple," of nature. These are *confusing* places because sensations, along with epochs, flow together in them; but they are like shadowy fragments of Augustine's Unchangeable Light: tiny shards that suggest "dark, vast unity." And the *flaneur* Benjamin came to resemble the *flaneur* Baudelaire. He shared the poet's taste for hashish, for "diabolical" smiles and deep "Luciferian beauty";[67] and especially for the echoing places or, if you prefer, the *auras* around certain objects, auras that hint at the object's distant origin, that are the "distance" of the origin itself.[68] Now, these auratic (echoing) places have their opposite, Benjamin says, in the experience Baudelaire calls spleen: the moment reduced to mere transition. "*The void is always thirsty, the water-clock drips out*": here we encounter, says Benjamin, "the passing moment in all its nakedness."[69] In the same way, Augustine describes his encounters with cosmic formless

---

64. Mircea Eliade, *Cosmos and History: The Myth of Eternal Return* (trans. Willard Trask; New York: Harper Torchbooks, 1954).
65. Arendt, "Introduction," in *Illuminations*, 12.
66. Baudelaire, "Correspondences," *Fleurs du Mal*, https://fleursdumal.org/
67. Benjamin, "Main Features of My Second Impression of Hashish," *Selected Writings*, 2:85.
68. Benjamin, "The Work of Art in the Age of its Reproducability," *Selected Writings*, 3:103–6.
69. Baudelaire, "L'Horloge," *Fleurs du Mal*.

matter—a "something-nothing," an "is-is not"[70]—which grief, in particular, precipitates. "*My eyes sought for him everywhere... He was missing ... I saw only death.*" The "something-nothing" of matter is *death* which has swallowed one's friend.[71] It is therefore an emphatically "Augustinian" Baudelaire with whom Benjamin so readily identifies when he writes that, "to his horror, the [splenetic or] melancholy man [jostled by the crowd, by "modernity"] sees the earth revert to a mere state of nature [not nature the "living temple," but nature as "unformed matter"]; no breath of pre-history surrounds it—no aura."[72]

There is, of course, a purely mental wandering. Rhetoricians call it digression. Augustine's work seems at times almost composed of digression, as if indeed an opposing force prevented him from coming to the point, as if there were something else, more important than the point—as if in delay there was redemption. Benjamin, too, does not let his broader purpose tyrannize over his sentences. "On the Concept of History," for example—with its prologue about history's game ("The Chess Master") and its shift at the center (Section IX) from the future that will not save us (II–VIII) to the past that can still be redeemed (X–XVIII)—has a very simple structure which is not, however, overt because its themes keep comingling and scattering, as if the opposing force did not let the structure take hold. And suppose the opposing force grows stronger. Suppose it stops us, not merely from coming to the point, but—for a numinous moment—from saying anything at all, even inwardly. Then the mind, as Augustine puts it, "grows silent to itself ... and not thinking of itself, gets beyond itself ... Will that not be, 'Enter into the joy of your Lord'?" Silence thereby rises to rapture.[73]

Benjamin too believes in silences. In his youth, (in "The Metaphysics of Youth"), he writes that "all conversation strives for silence";[74] and at the end of his life, in the essay under discussion, he urges his readers to master the art of growing silent; for "thinking involves, not only the flow of thoughts, but their arrest as well."[75] One might wish that fascistic thinking had found a way to "arrest" itself as it hurled itself toward monstrous conclusions, but Benjamin has something else in mind. Thoughts are successive, time carries them; and thinking must therefore stop where time does—in the echoing places where past and present come together ... and especially in situations pregnant with political tension. The work of Luther, for example,

---

70. *Conf.* 12.6.
71. *Conf.* 4.4.
72. Benjamin, "On Some Motifs in Baudelaire," *Selected Writings*, 4:336.
73. *Conf.* 9.10.
74. Benjamin, The Metaphysics of Youth, *Selected Writings,* 1:7–8. *Writings*
75. Benjamin, "On the Concept of History," *Selected Writings*, 4:396.

echoes the work of Paul; the French revolution echoes events in ancient Rome. Marx notices this and finds it farcical,[76] but Benjamin sees opportunity. Just as, for Freud, repetition in the context of analysis permits, *if one stays lucid*, the lifting of repression,[77] so, too, here: these historical repetitions provide, Benjamin says, "a revolutionary chance in the fight for the oppressed past"—that is to say, a chance to redeem.[78]

To return to the angel of history: let us suppose that his strength is *exactly* equal to time's wind. What will happen? The wind blows from Eden; the angel flies against it. Motion stops in the midair. Is that messianic cessation? And suppose that the angel mounts higher, to find a wind more to his purpose. What sort of wind? Presumably a wind that blows from our apocalyptic future, a wind blowing back to Paradise where it meets the wind that blows forward.

Plato, the inventor of science fiction, imagines things like this. One day, time will screech to a halt as if (to use Benjamin's image) God had grasped the emergency brake. With cessation comes tribulation. Everything is shaken, uprooted. But just as a train, having screeched to a halt, proceeds to move backward on its tracks; so, time, having stopped, reverses its previous direction. The dead rise from their graves. Dry bones take on flesh. Disappointing outcomes give way to superb aspirations. What is scattered is gathered once more. God himself must preserve with his hands this backward-flowing time (since nature wants to move forward); and the closeness of the divine lends everything the aura of Paradise (i.e., the "golden age" of Saturn, for whom Benjamin's planet is named). Indeed, the backward flowing time must eventually lead back to Paradise, lost through Promethean defiance.[79]

Did Augustine ever study Plato's Apocalypse? Probably not; but Plato certainly influenced, directly or indirectly, conceptualizations of the biblical apocalyptic writing; and "backward-flowing time" would account for much apocalyptic imagery: death working in reverse, the reaper overtaking the sower, the scattered gathered, and so on. Did Benjamin dream of such things? We know quite well that he did. He was fascinated by regression—by Kafka's primal (hetaeric) world, with its talking beasts and docile,

---

76. Karl Marx, *The 18th Brumaire of Louis Napolean*, https://www.marxists.org/archive/marx/works/download/pdf/18th-Brumaire.pdf, 5

77. Sigmund Freud, "The Dynamics of Transference" and "Remembering, Repeating, and Working Through," in *Complete Psychological Works* (vols. I–XXIV; London: The Hogarth Press, 1958), 12:97–109;12:145–72. The classic study of "regression" in contrast to progressive dialectic is Paul Ricoeur's *Freud and Philosophy* (New Haven, CT: Yale University Press, 1965).

78. Benjamin, "On the Concept of History," *Selected Writings*, 4:396.

79. Plato, *Pol.* 269c–273e; Hesiod, *Theog.* 507.

sensuous humans—creatures he describes as "unfinished," "half-created," for they have not yet encountered the Law which for Augustine and Paul is undoable, unachievable and is by now, say Benjamin and Scholem, "indecipherable" in any case.[80] The longing for regression is acute in Benjamin; but beginnings are elusive and regression takes many paths. All mystery rites, for example—and here Benjamin cites hierophant Plutarch—involve "two opposing forces," a right-leaning one that drives forward and a left-leaning one that drives back; the retrograde force, says Benjamin, unseats the "onrushing conqueror" within us—or, rather, on top of us, "riding" us— and, retrospectively, "turns existence into script."[81] If we trust Plutarch, the retrograde force was strongly felt in ancient rites; and the aura of such solemnities still lingers among us … but "technical reproducibility," contends Benjamin, makes aura decline and decay. Why is that? Because technically replicated forms, which assuage the craving of the masses to "overcome uniqueness" and "get closer," have no direct physical connection with the past conditions that produced them (e.g., the painter's own hand); thus, they lack the backward-stretching aura.[82]

Regarding regression, we can go further. Seven years before writing "On the Concept of History," while contentedly staying in Ibiza, Benjamin thought about his Klee; and at that stage it didn't strike him that the angel was propelled from past to the future; it seemed, on the contrary, that the angel moved from future to past; and if we dragged the celestial visitant backward to the future where he came from, he would not, in order to grasp it, need to turn his eyes toward it: he'd *remember the future* perfectly.[83] In a statement salvaged by Scholem, Benjamin also speculates that his own ever-changing "secret name" belongs as well to the angel: *Agesilaus Santander*, an anagram for "the angel Satan."[84] The angel, however, may have failed in his only mission (to sing a note in God's praise) because of something Benjamin has done; and the angel is therefore sending Benjamin his feminine other half, a sacred gift and a torment (like Pandora or possibly Eve). A marvelous woman walks into the room. She is unique, different from others; she offers an entirely new experience; but she also points back to the past; for there is nothing "new to hope for," Benjamin maintains, except "on the road that leads home"; and the angel from the future

---

80. Benjamin, "Franz Kafka," *Selected Writings*, 2:798.
81. Benjamin, "Franz Kafka," *Selected Writings*, 2:815.
82. Benjamin, "The Work of Art in the Age of its Reproducibility," *Selected Writings*, 3:104–6.
83. Benjamin, "Agesilaus Santander (Second Version)," *Selected Writings*, 2:715.
84. Benjamin, "Agesilaus Santander," *Selected Writings*, 2:714.

must therefore resemble—"everything from which I've had to part."[85] Benjamin thinks to win the woman with an almost godlike patience; for no man, he claims, is more patient. "*O Lord, give me chastity,*" cries Augustine, "*but not yet.*"[86] Less patient than Benjamin, he sits in a garden wringing his hands and tearing his hair because, as he knows very well, he *can be* chaste if he wants to, but he cannot *make* himself want to: his "will cannot will itself wholly ... cannot will itself to be a will."[87] The name of Christ helps him. Words of Paul instruct him in its use. Chanting children direct him to the words. For Augustine, then, a backward flowing time-stream would mean regression to a life he despises, allegorically embodied by Unchastity who "tugs at [his] garments of flesh"; whereas redemption means a leap ahead, with Lady Continence calling him forward. And though he has wandered and strayed for many years, a Prince of Delay like Hamlet, the future does finally reach him[88]—though he still "burns for truth" too impatiently.[89]

Augustine's *Confessions* is one of the world's most significant texts, a turning point in the history of grace and self-analysis. Its modern analogue—which, like the *Confessions*, is steeped in Platonism—is Proust's *Remembrance of Things Past*, where distant spiritual laws are made visible as if through a telescope. Benjamin greatly admired Proust. He made translations, wrote commentaries. Like Baudelaire, Proust provides a bridge between Augustine and Benjamin; and my own recollections of Proust have certainly colored this dialogue. Proust's daunting novel—3,000 pages, each requiring patience—concerns love degraded into jealousy and transcendence reduced to social climbing. The Edenic storm blows relentlessly, propelling the narrator through betrayals and disappointments to a monstrous climax, the gratuitous death of Albertine, and then to a weird denouement where everyone grows grotesquely old. The story is redeemed, however, by the

---

85. Benjamin, "Agesilaus Santander," *Selected Writings*, 2:715. "Beauty, so ancient and so new!" cries Augustine (*Conf.* 10.27).

86. *Conf.* 8.17.

87. *Conf.* 8.9.

88. *Conf.* 8.9-12. Augustine on his conversion: "I was saying to myself, 'Now is the moment, let it be now ...' but I shrank from dying to death and living to live." "The frivolity of frivolous aims ... still held me back, plucking softly at my garment of flesh and murmuring in my ear, 'Do you mean to get rid of us?'" He wants to leap into the future, but when "I strove to tear myself free, [the past] held me completely." No doubt, his ambition is too entwined with fallenness. He can't make the leap, any more than Eve could leap into divinity. But then: "I heard a voice from a house nearby—perhaps a voice of some boy or girl—singing over and over again, 'Pick it up and read, pick it up and read ...'" He reads a text of Paul and channels back to his illustrious predecessor the future that, through the child, had reached him.

89. *Conf.* 3.4.

higher memory that generates it. What sort of memory? It sometimes happens that, as we meander through life without "progressing," we encounter an object that resembles something in the past—a taste, perhaps, or a scent, a sound, a color. Thanks to such "correspondences," the gates of the past open. Memory traces become real: *"real without being actual, ideal without being abstract."*[90] Thus, they hover between essence and instance, and they form their own kind of world, on which guests from the future may call.

> *BENJAMIN: Proust cites Celtic mythology to the effect that all the people we've lost, all those we've loved and grieved for, actually still exist but are confined within certain objects: trees, stones, bits of food, etc. If we stumble upon them—if we hear them cry out—we can liberate them. They are waiting for us, but all too often we never find them. Proust's narrator, a gentleman named "Marcel," eats a certain pastry (a madeleine, with its* plis religieuse*) and sips some herb tea. He dips the pastry into the tea. And suddenly the past calls out to him. It shines through the room—and will later shine through carefully written prose—like sunlight streaming through curtain lace.*[91] *For Marcel is reminded of that other tea and pastry served to him in his childhood when he spent summers in Combray with his parents. The rediscovered taste is like a call that awakens an echo—Baudelaire, too, speaks of "echoes" in such situations. And the people of Combray, the paths and shops, the church on the hill—all their memory-traces take on flesh again (a spiritual flesh, to be sure) as they stream toward the future's gifted emissary.*[92]

> *AUGUSTINE: Can the past receive visits from the future? When I wrote my* Confessions, *I felt the distance of all those happenings. Not that I minded: distance protected me.*

> *BENJAMIN: The same with Proust. He suffered badly from asthma. The closeness of the present could be crushing, suffocating. Also, he found it tempting. The intimacy of things drew him in, then cast him off. He wasted time in heartbreak and obsession. But in the madeleine-experience, presence is made out of distance. You learn to adore distance as the substance of that which you love.*

> *AUGUSTINE: As for me, I'm reminded of church doctrine. Forbidden fruit undid us—wine and bread lifts us up again.*[93] *Why, then, should not tea and pastry help us along the path? So: I sip the tea, I taste the pastry. The door of the past opens. What then?*

---

90. Marcel Proust, *Remembrance of Things Past* (trans. Scott Moncrieff; 7 vols.; New York: Henry Holt, 1922), 1:67; 6:264.
91. Benjamin, "On the Image of Proust," *Selected Writings*, 2:240.
92. Benjamin, "A Berlin Chronicle," *Selected Writings*, 2:634; "On the Concept of History," *Selected Writings*, 4:332–6.
93. Regarding the Eucharist—bread and wine—Jesus says: "Do this in memory of me" (Luke 22.19). But he adds that the bread and wine *are* him (Matt. 26.28): those who remember in the future will be in some sense present with him *now*.

BENJAMIN: *Sometimes when you dream you preserve a bit of waking consciousness, so you know that the dream is a dream. Then you empower yourself in the dream: you fly, lift heavy weight, read other people's thoughts, and so on. In the same way, when you enter the past while retaining a link to the present, you transcend your habitual condition. This is what happens to Marcel.*

> The vicissitudes of life had become indifferent to me, its disasters innocuous, its brevity illusory—this new sensation having had on me the effect which love has of filling me with a precious essence ... I had ceased now to feel mediocre, accidental, mortal ...[94]

You see: a new kind of being. And he will accomplish a new kind of deed ...

AUGUSTINE: *Ah, but he speaks of romance! I know all about that. You love a mortal as God should be loved; your love is returned, your ego inflates; you touch, you possess the god of your idolatry ... whom, however, you're terrified of losing.*[95] *Or perhaps it's wealth that you love, or power, or status, or a drug. That kind of love I call CUPIDITY. It rules the human city, in contrast to the City of God ...*[96]

BENJAMIN: *Patience, Augustine! Regarding romance, the law that was so clear to you became, for better or worse, indecipherable to me. In the women who might have favored me, I discerned, to the end of my days, an image of redemption.*[97] *Be that as it may, I would very much like to persuade you—and here I'll use your own vocabulary—that Proust's higher memory turns cupidity into charity, that is, into non-possessive love. Cupidity wants to cancel distance; the higher memory "embraces" it. And holiness, too, I feel to be a kind of distance: the aura of distance that encompasses rituals and prayer,*[98] *reminiscent of the distance of God. One thing I know. Proust tells a story redeemed through the manner of telling. And you, too, must have felt, when you were writing your* Confessions, *that you were THERE with your younger self, redeeming errors ....*

AUGUSTINE: *I felt closer to the God who redeemed them.*

BENJAMIN: *Eternity redeems all. But if you depart from Eternity a little, everything starts to breaks up. The shattered light of the future must, in the present, be channeled into the past.*[99]

AUGUSTINE: *I detect another Trinity: the three dimensions of time. They rest on a timeless archetype. God creates through his Word, which is also*

---

94. Proust, *Remembrance of Things Past*, 1:34.
95. *Conf.* 4.6.
96. *Civ.* 14.28.
97. Benjamin, "On the Concept of History, *Selected Writings*, 4:389.
98. Benjamin, "The Work of Art in the Age of its Reproducibility," *Selected Writings*, 3:104–7.
99. Benjamin, "On the Concept of History," *Selected Writings*, 4:389–91.

called—"Beginning."[100]

BENJAMIN. *Kabbalists say that too.*[101]

AUGUSTINE. *Then it's my turn to tell a story. It concerns your namesake, the biblical Benjamin. The Viceroy of Egypt had falsely accused him of theft and was about to put him in prison. His brother Judah offered to go in his place, explaining that Benjamin was his venerable father's favorite and that his father would die of grief without him. Judah did not say, but with anguish he remembered, that he had long ago helped destroy his father's earlier favorite: Joseph, the most gifted of the brothers. Judah had been jealous of the earlier favorite Joseph but is now willing to die for the current favorite Benjamin. I know: a father should love his children equally. But that's beside the point. Judah's crime was insuperable. Do you understand, then, what is happening? Judah is rising to a deed that will rectify his earlier wrong. The room grows porous; the past receives the present. And Judah is cleansed, not by mere echoes, but by deeds.*

BENJAMIN: *Thomas Mann wrote a novel about Joseph which—incredibly—is even longer than Proust's tremendous novel. Scholem seemed impatient with it;*[102] *but Mann intended it in part as a Kabbalistic exploration, emphasizing "temporal echoing" and "correspondence" and (if I may so put it) "messianic cessation of happening." Mann's earlier work,* Magic Mountain, *which I read aloud with my family, approaches the same basic themes and entirely won me over.*[103] *So ... let's consider Joseph; let's look at the great climactic moment. Judah lays down his life for Benjamin, and suddenly—right at the moment of danger—a memory flashes up*[104] *and the world changes like a dream. The Viceroy of Egypt is revealed as Joseph himself. Thrown into the pit, he had risen after three days. He organizes Judah's redemption—by letting Judah redeem Benjamin. God is hardly mentioned in the story (as if he had vanished into the sky, like the Kabbalistic* Ein Sof*) but Joseph's*

---

100. *Conf.* 12.5: "In symbolic form, a Trinity now dawns clear for me ... You, Father, made heaven and earth in that "Beginning" who originates our wisdom ..."

101. The Zohar renders Genesis 1: "With Beginning, [the Unnamable] created *Elohim.*" Usually taken as the subject of the sentence, "God" is here taken as its object; and "Beginning" (= "Wisdom") precedes God in that sense (Zohar, *Bereshit*, 1.15a). Regarding time and Divine Life, Kaplan, citing Kabbalistic authorities, explicates: "... Wisdom represents the undifferentiated potential of existence that God wishes to give ... Understanding is the 'Hand' that defines existence or, in this case, the future that holds what the past gives to it." Both flow from the Crown—"the infinite time that the human mind cannot penetrate or fathom." Aryeh Kaplan, *Innerspace* (New York: Moznaim Publishing, 1990), 47.

102. *The Correspondence of Benjamin and Scholem*, 143, 145.

103. Howard Eiland and Michael W. Jennings, *Walter Benjamin: A Critical Life* (Cambridge, MA: Belknap Press of Harvard University Press, 2014), 239.

104. "Articulating the past historically does not mean recognizing it 'the way it was.' It means appropriating a memory as it flashes up in a moment of danger." Benjamin, "On the Concept of History," *Selected Writings*, 4:391.

messianic power can't be described as weak, since he is, after all, *"Joseph the Provider,"* who fights hunger in the universe. Kabbalists call him *"the Righteous One."* They say he channels great erotic energy.[105]

AUGUSTINE: *To my mind, he foreshadows Christ. He, too, was sold for silver and having been cast down he rose again. Therefore future time is contained in the seeds of the past, and time is not empty or homogenous, for prophets read the future EXACTLY as the past.*[106] *But perhaps we Christians, letting "the dead bury the dead," emphasize too much a redemption yet to come. In so doing, we neglect our ancestors, as if resigned to their being lost.*

BENJAMIN. *The image of ancestors in chains rouses me more than any other. And our ancestors won't be safe—no more than our children—if the enemy isn't defeated.*

AUGUSTINE. *The enemy has not ceased to triumph. The iniquities invented in your time long ago damaged ours. But your last words—whose meaning, perhaps, we touched on—strengthens our heart:*[107]

> The soothsayers who queried time and learned what it had in store certainly did not experience time as either homogenous or empty. Whoever keeps this in mind will perhaps get an idea of how past times were experienced in remembrance, namely, in just this way. We know that the Jews were prohibited from inquiring into the future. The Torah and the prayers instruct them in remembrance, however. This stripped the future of its magic, which holds sway over all those who turn to soothsayers for

---

105. Gershom Scholem, *On the Mystical Shape of the Godhead* (trans. Joachim Neugroschel; ed. Jonathan Chipman; New York: Schocken books, 1991). See especially Chapter Three: "Tsaddik: The Righteous One."

106. According to Benjamin, an author's "lifework is preserved and sublated in the [particular] work, the era *in* the lifework, the entire course of history *in* the era. The nourishing fruit of what is historically understood contains time in its *interior* as a precious but tasteless seed." To see this, however, we must encounter a distant event as it corresponds (in the sense of Baudelaire) to the "now," thus de-emphasizing "causal significance." History, Benjamin says, should not be told "like beads on a rosary ("Concepts of History," *Selected Writings*, 4:396–7.)" As Freud says of interpreting dreams, the *sequence* of images matters less than the associations evoked in the dreamer by *each image taken separately*, associations from the day before as well as from the very distant past. Freud, *The Interpretation of Dreams*, in *The Complete Psychological Works*, 4:96–121.

107. Benjamin writes: "The Social Democrats preferred to cast the working class in the role of a redeemer of *future* generations, in this way cutting the sinews of its greatest strength. This indoctrination made the working class forget both its hatred and its spirit of sacrifice, for both are nourished by the image of enslaved ancestors rather than by the ideal of liberated grandchildren ("On the Concept of History," *Selected Writings*, 4:394). Also: "The only historian capable of fanning the spark of hope is the one who is firmly convinced that *even the dead* will not be safe from the enemy if he is victorious. And the enemy has not ceased to triumph," 4:391.

> enlightenment. This does not imply, however, that for the Jews the future became empty homogenous time. For every second was the small gateway in time through which the Messiah might enter.[108]

So—to sum up—the history angel is helpless.
The future is concealed from him and the past, which he sees, is out of reach. Our own case turns out to be different. We don't merely see the past "in" memory, we *enter* the past *through* memory. Recollection leads to resurrection. And we enter the past, says Proust, as beings of a higher order: we are, to be sure, very weak messiahs but we bear all the same "precious essence." Sometimes, as the biblical Joseph-story shows, we find bits of the distant past so near that they actually merge with the "now"; then the sun of our current adventure alters the sense of "long ago," just as some future sun shapes us through the future's current emissary. Nor will this surprise us if we believe—with Augustine—that *eternity comes before time*. Originally nestled in the One, moments scattered in time echo and alter one another, just as points scattered in space coalesce in a landscape or cityscape. This "correspondence," says Benjamin, citing Baudelaire's poem, contrasts with "the moment in all its nakedness"—that is, with Augustinian matter. Time's magic spell persuades us that the future, if we demand it, will justify our history and prove that we were never really wanderers. But this craving for a future, Scripture hints and Platonism echoes, caused our fall from eternity to time.

Biographical Note

Carl Levenson is Professor Emeritus of Philosophy at Idaho State University. He is the author of *Socrates among the Corybantes* (Spring Publications, 1999; reissued 2022), a study of Plato's *Euthydemus* in which Socrates tangles with sophists and mystical dancers, and he is currently writing a book on the prosecution and trial of Socrates in its prophetic, historical, and literary setting. Levenson has long been drawn to the writings of St. Augustine, especially the *Confessions*, and to comparative religion

---

108. Benjamin, "On the Concept of History," *Selected Writings*, 4:397. To correct our point of departure, namely, the chess-master allegory, let us now imagine the Turk as the *true* historical materialist who eschews divine mechanism (for God is not a machine) and through authentic dialectical practice reaches bits of the past concretely. Benjamin says of such historians that they won't spend themselves anymore "in historicism's bordello," focused on history's laws and sequences. They "remain in control of their powers"—"man enough [so runs the metaphor] to blast open the continuum of history (4:396)." And if, at first, only fragments can be retrieved, "a redeemed mankind … would be granted the fullness of its past," a past "citable in all of its moments" (4:390).

and European philosophy and literature. He has an evolving interest in Kabbalah and in the problem of time in physics.

Bibliography

Agamben, Giorgio. *The Time That Remains*. Translated by Patricia Dailey. Stanford, CA: Stanford University Press, 2005.

Arendt, Hannah. "Introduction," in *Illuminations: Essays and Reflections*. Edited by Hannah Arendt. Translated by Harry Zohn. New York: Schocken Books, 2007.

Augustine. *On the Predestination of the Saints*. See Schaff, ed., *Nicene and Post-Nicene Fathers, First Series*, 1887.

—*On Rebuke and Grace*. See Schaff, ed., *Nicene and Post-Nicene Fathers, First Series*, 1887. Revised and edited for New Advent by Kevin Knight. http://www.newadvent.org/fathers/1512.htm

—*City of God*. Translated by Henry Bettenson. Introduction by G. R. Evans. London: Penguin Books, 1972.

Baudelaire, Charles. "Correspondences," in Fleurs du Mal. https://fleursdumal.org/

Benjamin, Walter. *The Correspondence of Walter Benjamin and Gershom Scholem: 1932–1940*. Translated by Gary Smith and Andre Lefevre. Introduction by Anson Rabinbach. Cambridge, MA: Harvard University Press, 1992.

—*Selected Writings*. Edited by Howard Eiland and Michael W. Jennings. 4 vols. Cambridge, MA: The Belknap Press of Harvard University Press, 1996–2003.

Butler, Judith. "One Time Traverses Another: Benjamin's Theologico-Political Fragment." European Graduate School, 2013. https://www.youtube.com/watch?v=LA-8hiT2nIAk

Eiland, Howard, and Michael W. Jennings. *Walter Benjamin: A Critical Life*. Cambridge, MA: Belknap Press of Harvard University Press, 2014.

Eliade, Mircea. *Cosmos and History: The Myth of Eternal Return*. Translated by Willard Trask. New York: Harper Torchbooks, 1954.

Fredriksen, Paula. *Augustine and the Jews: A Christian Defense of Jews and Judaism*. New Haven, CT: Yale University Press, 2010.

Freud, Sigmund. *Complete Psychological Works*. Volumes I–XXIV. London: The Hogarth Press, 1958.

Kaplan, Aryeh. *Innerspace*. New York: Moznaim Publishing, 1990.

Levenson, Carl A. "The Cycle of Triads and the Pattern of Distance and Flesh: A Study of the Plot of Augustine's Confessions." (PhD dissertation: University of Chicago, 1980).

—"Distance and Presence in Augustine's Confessions," *Journal of Religion* 65 (October 1985): 500–12. https://doi.org/10.1086/487308

Marx, Karl. *The 18th Brumaire of Louis Napolean*. https://www.marxists.org/archive/marx/works/download/pdf/18th-Brumaire.pdf

Nietzsche, Friedrich. "The Antichrist," section XVIII in *The Portable Nietzsche*. Selected and translated with an Introduction and Notes by Walter Kaufmann. London: Penguin, 1954.

—"The Gay Sciences." https://krishnamurti.abundanthope.org/index_htm_files/The-Gay-Science-by-Friedrich-Nietzsche.pdf

Poe, Edgar Allen. "Maelzel's Chess Player." 1846. https://www.eapoe.org/works/essays/maelzel.htm

Proust, Marcel. *Remembrance of Things Past*. Translated by Scott Moncrieff. 7 volumes. New York: Henry Holt, 1922. https://doi.org/10.15697/10.5072/FK2ZP4489N

Ricoeur, Paul. *Freud and Philosophy*. New Haven, CT: Yale University Press, 1965.

Sartre, Jean Paul. "Materialism et Revolution." 1946. Reprinted *Situations, III.* Paris: Gallimard, 1949.

Schaff, Philip, ed. *Nicene and Post-Nicene Fathers, First Series.* Translated by Peter Holmes and Robert Ernest Wallis. Revised by Benjamin B. Warfield. Buffalo, NY: Christian Literature Publishing, 1887. Revised and edited for New Advent by Kevin Knight. http://www.newadvent.org/fathers/1512.htm

Scholem, Gershom. *Sabbetai Sevi: The Mystical Messiah*. Princeton, NJ: Princeton University Press, 1973.

—*On Jews and Judaism in Crisis: Selected Essays*. Edited by Werner J. Dannhauser. Philadelphia, PA: Schocken Books, 1987.

—*On the Mystical Shape of the Godhead*. Translated by Joachim Neugroschel. Edited by Jonathan Chipman. New York: Schocken Books, 1991.

PART II
Gilles Deleuze

Chapter Five

Gilles Deleuze and Early Christian Texts

Matthew G. Whitlock

Introduction

A rhizome has no beginning or end; it is always in the middle, between things, interbeing, *intermezzo.* The tree is filiation, but the rhizome is alliance, uniquely alliance. The tree imposes the verb "to be," but the fabric of the rhizome is the conjunction, "and ... and ... and ..." This conjunction carries enough force to shake and uproot the verb "to be." Where are you going? Where are you coming from? Where are you heading for? These are totally useless questions. Making a clean slate, starting or beginning again from ground zero, seeking a beginning or foundation—all imply a false conception of voyage and movement ...[1]

—Deleuze and Guattari, *A Thousand Plateaus*

It is at work everywhere, functioning smoothly at times, at other times in fits and starts. It breathes, it heats, it eats. It shits and fucks. What a mistake to have ever said the id. Everywhere *it* is machines—real ones, not figurative ones: machines driving other machines, machines being driven by other machines, with all the necessary couplings and connections.[2]

—Deleuze and Guattari, *Anti-Oedipus*

If Gilles Deleuze (1925–1995) and his frequent writing partner, Félix Guattari (1930–1992) were questing or voyaging after Christian origins, they would begin with a middle, a moving node (among many nodes) in a network.[3] They

---

1. Gilles Deleuze and Félix Guattari, *A Thousand Plateaus: Capitalism and Schizophrenia* (trans. Brian Massumi; Minneapolis, MN: University of Minnesota Press, 1987), 25; translation of *Capitalisme et schizophrenie tome 2: Mille plateaux* (Paris: Éditions de Minuit, 1980).
2. Gilles Deleuze and Félix Guattari, *Anti-Oedipus: Capitalism and Schizophrenia* (trans. Robert Hurley, Mark Seem, and Helen R. Lane; Minneapolis, MN: University of Minnesota Press, 1983), 1; translation of *Capitalisme et schizophrénie tome 1: l'Anti-Oedipe* (Paris: Éditions de Minuit, 1972).
3. What is the middle? "The middle is by no means an average; on the contrary, it is where things pick up speed. *Between* things does not designate a localizable relation going from one thing to the other and back again, but a perpendicular direction, a transversal movement that sweeps one *and* the other way, a stream without beginning or end that undermines it banks and picks up speed in the middle," Deleuze and Guattari, *Anti-Oedipus*, 1.

would "do away with foundations, nullify endings and beginnings."[4] Their model would not be a tree, but a rhizome, not envisioning early Christianity vertically and hierarchically—as if its past's supposedly untainted roots offered the foundation and truest form. They would envision it horizontally, examining and mapping all its lines and lines of flight. They would describe early Christianity without "any structural or generative model."[5] They would not trace but map its thought movements, like "a stream without beginning or end that undermines its banks and picks up speed in the middle," the middle where new concepts proliferate.[6] Like Adorno's and Benjamin's constellation, Deleuze and Guattari embrace conjunction and parataxis: "the fabric of the rhizome is the conjunction, 'and ... and ... and ...'"[7] Like Adorno and Benjamin, they would neither narrativize it nor hierarchize it, nor impose a logic of cause and effect. A rhizome, like early Christianity, has no one beginning, no foundation, and no definitive end. Early Christianity is many things and between many things. It is a rhizome, not a tree; it "assumes very diverse forms, from ramified surface extension in all directions to concretion into bulbs and tubers."[8] Deleuze and Guattari would talk not of early Christianity's filiations nor of its roots, but of its connections and its alliances. Early Christianity would not be one, but many; not isolated, but connected.

When it comes to texts, Deleuze and Guattari see rhizomes. In *A Thousand Plateaus*—a sequel published eight years after their first book together, *Anti-Oedipus*—they recognize their own multiplicity and connectivity:

> The two of us wrote *Anti-Oedipus* together. Since each of us was several, there was already quite a crowd. Here we have made use of everything that came within range, what was closest as well as farthest away.[9]

---

4. Deleuze and Guattari, *Anti-Oedipus*, 1.
5. Deleuze and Guattari, *Anti-Oedipus*, 12. This is not saying they would fail to see any hierarchical, tree-like structures in early Christianity (see, for example, McLean's analysis of Christ groups in Chapter Six below). However, what they would not do is impose a tree-like model (now) as a lens for seeing how "Christianity" evolved.
6. Deleuze and Guattari, *Anti-Oedipus*, 25. On mapping versus tracing: "Writing has nothing to do with signifying. It has to do with surveying, mapping, even realms that are yet to come" (5–6); "The rhizome is altogether different, *a map and not a tracing*. Make a map, not a tracing" (12); "All of tree logic is a logic of tracing and reproduction" (12).
7. On Adorno and Benjamin on parataxis and constellations, see Steven Helmling, *Adorno's Poetics of Critique* (New York: Continuum, 2009), 113–5. According to Helmling, "In Adorno's modernist account, 'parataxis' does with narratemes something like what 'constellation' is meant to do with the diverse fragments it constellates: presents them in an ensemble undomesticated by the familiar thought syntax, the habituated grammars, and thus the ideological presuppositions that familiarize the new ..." (113).
8. Deleuze and Guattari, *Anti-Oedipus*, 7.
9. Deleuze and Guattari, *A Thousand Plateaus*, 3.

In collaboration, Deleuze and Guattari did not pretend to close off their work, isolate their work, but they recognized themselves as open, layered, and moving bodies, and so also their books: "A book has neither object nor subject: it is made of variously formed matters, and very different dates and speeds."[10] A book (and an early Christian text), too, is a rhizome, and part of a larger rhizome. A reader (and a reader of an early Christian text), too, is a rhizome and part of a larger rhizome. There is no isolation. Indeed, a crowd of voices composes our texts today—our texts about ancient texts and all the texts in between—despite being the age of individual authors, copyrights, commodification of ideas, disciplines, and specializations. "Each of us is several"; a scholar's work is "made of variously formed matters, and very different dates and speeds."

While Walter Benjamin's palimpsestic thinking—as Adorno depicts it—reveals layers in thought and interpretation, layers often captured in the dialectical images, Deleuze and Guattari's thinking reveals immanent planes and lines of flight, planes and lines in motion.[11] The rhizome reaches in all directions at all times. Deleuze and Guattari reveal moving and fluid connections, not just in static layers.[12] Discourse is always in motion, always reaching, always connecting, always changing. To take Adorno's depiction of Benjamin's palimpsestic thinking one step further: textuality is a 4D palimpsest, neither static nor frozen, always in motion, always emerging, always being written over and reappearing anew, always differing while repeating. And for Deleuze and Guattari these moving parts are not only expressed in rhizomes, but in lines of flight, plateaus, and machines.

Like the thought image of a rhizome at the start of *A Thousand Plateaus*, eight years earlier the image of a machine stands on the first page of *Anti-Oedipus*, Richard Lindner's painting *Boy with Machine*.[13] Susan Ballard aptly describes it:

> A black-and-white full-page illustration of Richard Lindner's *Boy with Machine* (1954) shows a young boy about to set a sequence of machines in motion. The child smiles out at his audience, his chubby pleasure hard

---

10. Deleuze and Guattari, *A Thousand Plateaus*, 3.

11. See Theodor Adorno, "Introduction to Benjamin's *Schriften*," in *On Walter Benjamin: Critical Essays and Recollections* (ed. Gary Smith; Cambridge, MA: MIT Press, 1988), 8–9: "All creation becomes for [Walter Benjamin] script that must be deciphered though the code is unknown. He immersed himself in reality as in a palimpsest. Interpretation, translation, critique are the schemes of his thought."

12. Note that for Deleuze and Guattari intertextuality involves more than simply tracing connections between scriptures in a tree-like, chronological, and hierarchical (Old Testament in New Testament) fashion.

13. Deleuze and Guattari, *Anti-Oedipus*, i.

to avoid. He seems to be listening, waiting. His hands are tangled, knotted within the levers that will set one machine against the other. One foot is caught inside the lower bucket of a large machine while the other hovers, floating within a dark mass, not fully machine and not completely organic either. *Boy with Machine* is an artwork that welcomes us into a text that will result in the proliferation of machines both organic and technical.[14]

Deleuze and Guattari express reality here through machines and the connections between them—truly and not metaphorically: "Everywhere *it* is machines—real ones, not figurative ones: machines driving other machines, machines being driven by other machines, with all the necessary couplings and connections."[15] Later in the first chapter of *Anti-Oedipus,* Deleuze and Guattari interpret Lindner's painting: it "shows a huge, pudgy, bloated boy working one of his little desiring machines, after having hooked it up to a vast technical social machine—which, as we shall see, is what even the very young child does."[16] In distinguishing their work from Freudian psychotherapy (e.g., "playing mommy and daddy"), they offer a schizoanalysis based on multiplicity: multiple connections between multiple machines.[17] For it is "a mistake to have ever said *the* id. Everywhere *it* is machines."[18] Deleuze and Guattari's theories are not founded on familial relations, but on our desiring machines being hooked up to social machines, to vast technical machines, "machines driving other machines, machines being driven by other machines, with all the necessary couplings and connections."[19] Like the boy in Lindner's painting, we (as machines in motion) are all a part of and connected to other machines in motion. There is no reality or textuality apart from this motion, these connections, these machines.

What is more, just as Adorno and Benjamin were critiquing congealed ideologies through thought images, Deleuze and Guattari were, in the

---

14. Susan Ballard, "The Audience and the Art Machine: Janet Cardiff and George Bures Miller's *Opera for a Small Room*," in *Deleuze and the Schizoanalysis of Visual Art* (ed. Ian Buchanan and Lorna Collins; London: Bloomsbury, 2014), 125.

15. Deleuze and Guattari, *Anti-Oedipus*, 1.

16. Deleuze and Guattari, *Anti-Oedipus*, 7. See also p. 358, where they use Lindner's painting to show how a child plugs "a desiring-machine into a social machine, short circuiting the parents."

17. Deleuze and Guattari, *Anti-Oedipus*, 47. "The small child lives with his family around the clock; but within the bosom of this family, and from the very first days of his life, he immediately begins having an amazing nonfamilial experience that psychoanalysis has completely failed to take into account. Lindner's painting attracts our attention once again." Here they point to a child playing in a nursery, "a place where desiring-production and group fantasy occur, as a place where the only connection is that between partial objects and agents."

18. Deleuze and Guattari, *Anti-Oedipus*, 1.

19. Deleuze and Guattari, *Anti-Oedipus*, 1.

words of Claire Colebrook, putting "forward provocative claims that shattered the usual standards for theory and rational argument."[20] Deleuze and Guattari expose ideologies that falsely attempt to close off this machine-like motion, this rhizomatic and machinic connectivity, ideologies forcing truths, texts, and histories into a tree-like structures. Deleuze and Guattari's *Anti-Oedipus*, according to Colebrook, "worked by questions and interrogation: why *should* we accept conventions, norms and values? What stops us from creating new values, new desires, or new images of what is to be and think?"[21] For life itself is "an open and creative whole of proliferating connections."[22] So similar to *immanent critique*, Deleuze and Guattari sought new constellations of thought, new combinations, new connections. They valued "machinic experimentation," in the words of Susan Ballard, "new flows, new assemblages, new breakages, new experiments."[23] In Deleuze and Guattari's world, philosophy itself is creative. It involves creating concepts. Mediation between the past and the present is one of creativity, one of creating concepts and theories, one of experimentation, not simply interpretation.

Given the thought images of the rhizome and the machine, as well as the experimental and creative nature of Deleuze and Guattari's approach, how then do their approaches effect the way one reads early Christian texts? In his work on Deleuze and Guattari and hermeneutics, Bradley McLean argues that their approach moves scholarship beyond "the governing paradigm of historical positivism," avoiding "the nihilism inherent within its world-view."[24] Historical positivism relegates early Christian texts into closed systems, locking them into historical epochs, attempting to avoid the natural and inevitable interactions and connections between the present and the past. McLean refers to Nietzsche to illustrate the resultant nihilism of this approach: "Thus, just as Friedrich Nietzsche had previously prophesied, when early Christianity is analyzed into 'completely historical' knowledge, and is 'resolved … into pure knowledge,' it 'ceases to live' and is thereby 'annihilated' by the historicizing process itself."[25]

---

20. Claire Colebrook, *Gilles Deleuze* (Routledge Critical Thinkers; Abingdon: Routledge, 2002), 5.
21. Colebrook, *Gilles Deleuze*, 5.
22. Colebrook, *Gilles Deleuze*, 5. The appeal to "life" here is a transdisciplinary appeal; that is, Deleuze and Guattari based their theories and concepts on what research in multiple disciplines is revealing, from neuro-science to mathematics to biology.
23. Ballard, "The Audience and the Art Machine," 126.
24. Bradley H. McLean, "Re-imagining New Testament Interpretation in Terms of Deleuzian Geophilosophy," *Neotestamentica* 42.1 (2008): 51–72, here 52.
25. Bradley H. McLean, *Biblical Interpretation and Philosophical Hermeneutics* (Cambridge: Cambridge University Press, 2012), 3; Friedrich Nietzsche, *On the*

What is more, the study of early Christianity has functioned primarily in the arborescent, tree-like paradigm, resulting in hierarchical treatment of the textual tradition, searching for roots and origins, prioritizing texts that are not far removed from its "base" over fringe texts—those branching away from its roots. McLean points out that this "unified," tree-like paradigm is one that is imposed on early Christianity; it is a "pre-established pattern of development."[26] Along with imposing pre-conceived hierarchies, this arborescent paradigm "totalizes" and also creates binaries in its structure, including author/text, interpreter/text, original/copy, and so on.[27]

In contradistinction to historical positivism and the arborescent approach, McLean proposes a "rhizomatic hermeneutics," composed of three tenets. First, early Christian texts have no one center, foundation, or essence, but are themselves moving multiplicities connected to other moving multiplicities. "Rhizomatic hermeneutics," asserts McLean, "begins with the recognition that, not only the New Testament, but also the historical 'author' and 'context,' are dynamic 'multiplicities' that have been *aided, encoded,* and *multiplied* by other multiplicities."[28] Second, interpreters of early Christian texts are also moving multiplicities connected to other moving multiplicities. "Like the biblical text itself," McLean argues, "each interpreter is a tangled network, constituted by countless forces interacting with other multiplicities."[29] The modern interpreter is not isolated, nor can her work be isolated and relegated solely to capturing past historical epochs. Third, the interpreter and the text are not isolated from each other. They, too, are in a rhizomatic relationship. Thus, "in contrast to the contemporary practice of historical positivism," argues McLean, "rhizomatic interpretation … recognizes that the text and interpreter are not two independent entities— an object of interpretation and an inquiring subject."[30] Indeed, the text is not an object to be reified. Both the text and interpreter interact with one

---

Advantage and Disadvantage of History for Life (trans. Peter Preuss; Indianapolis, IN: Hackett, 1980), 39–40.

26. McLean, "Re-imagining New Testament Interpretation," 53–4.

27. McLean, "Re-imagining New Testament Interpretation," 54.

28. McLean, "Re-imagining New Testament Interpretation," 70. For an argument and demonstration of how Deleuze and Guattari's rhizomatic paradigm can help us "rethink 'reception history' as a dynamic and open-ended process, with multiple entries and exits, rather than linear trajectories," see Caroline Vander Stichele, "The Head of John and its Reception or How to Conceptualize 'Reception History,'" in *Scriptural Traces: Critical Perspectives on the Reception and Influence of the Bible* (ed. Claudia V. Camp, W. J. Lyons, and Andrew Mein; Library of Hebrew Bible/Old Testament Studies, 615; London: Bloomsbury, T&T Clark, 2015), 79–93, here 84–6.

29. McLean, "Re-imagining New Testament Interpretation," 70.

30. McLean, "Re-imagining New Testament Interpretation," 70.

another within a rhizomatic network, within many moving and changing and expanding rhizomatic networks.

Using the rhizome as a starting point, the first section below places Gilles Deleuze and his writing partner, Félix Guattari, within their own "tangled networks" of the mid to late twentieth century. Then, in the second section, the key concepts and theories of Deleuze and Guattari are delineated. Here particular attention is paid to the concepts and theories that mediate between early Christian texts and the twenty-first century in the following three chapters: machines and bodies without organs, simulacra and simulation, and language, deterritorialization, and reterritorialization. Here a brief overview of each chapter is given, as well suggestions for future connections. This chapter ends with a bibliography of primary and secondary sources.

Intersections: Contextualizing Deleuze's Work

Given Deleuze's rhizomatic approach and his and Guattari's insistence for their readers to start *A Thousand Plateaus* in any section, at any plateau, and not simply from the beginning, this section aims to contextualize the multiple points and connections of his work without conforming it to a tree-like structure.[31] Anne Sauvagnargues, speaking about contextualizing Deleuze and Guattari's work, accordingly notes: "… there is no key moment in a thinker's biography."[32] Here I focus on moments in Deleuze's life, moments pertinent to the concepts and theories discussed in the essays below.

Gilles Deleuze was born into a wealthy, bourgeoisie family on 18 January, 1925, in Paris, France. Deleuze, according to François Dosse, resented his family and "the stultifying world of the bourgeoisie."[33] But this was not his view of his brother. Deleuze's older brother, Georges, died as part of the Nazi resistance. He was captured and died on the way to a concentration camp. Deleuze stood in the shadow of his brother; hence, Dosse titles his chapter on Deleuze's childhood "A Hero's Brother."[34] Similar to Benjamin and Adorno, the events of World War II had a deep, personal impact on

---

31. Deleuze and Guattari, *A Thousand Plateaus*, 22. "For example, a book composes of chapters has culmination and termination points. That takes place in a book composed instead of plateaus that communicate with one another across microfissures, as in a brain? … Each plateau can be read starting anywhere and be related to any other plateau."

32. Quoted in François Dosse, *Gilles Deleuze & Félix Guattari: Intersecting Lives* (trans. Deborah Glassman; New York: Columbia University Press, 2010), 506. In this section, I primarily follow Dosse's biography of Deleuze and Guattari.

33. Dosse, *Intersecting Lives*, 89.

34. Dosse, *Intersecting Lives*, 88–107.

Deleuze's thinking. The impact was not only felt by the tragic death of his older brother, but also in his looking back on the horrors of Nazism, which demanded a new philosophy, new concepts—a demand Deleuze and Guattari articulate in *What Is Philosophy?*[35] Whereas the older Georges battled Nazism in his present, the younger Gilles Deleuze battled its hardened ideology in retrospect, by creating new, fluid concepts. "It was imperative," states Dosse, "to create new concepts: the trauma of Nazi barbarity made it necessary to carry out the tasks of thinking."[36]

Another event that impacted Deleuze's thinking was the student riots in May 1968, cultivating a radical ground for experimentation. This radicalness was not only nurtured by the events of 1968, but even more so by a person, Félix Guattari, who was much more involved in the revolutionary movement than Deleuze.[37] Félix Guattari was born on 30 March, 1930, the youngest of three brothers in a traditional and conservative family.[38] At the age of 15, it was clear, according to Dosse, that Guattari was "precociously politically aware," attending Communist Party meetings.[39] Guattari was a radical egalitarian who thought and acted outside the lines. A student of Lacan, Guattari's education was in psychoanalysis. Lacan's ideas would have a significant impact on Guattari's conception of the machine, a Deleuze and Guattari concept discussed at length in this chapter and Bradley McLean's that follows.[40] Yet Guattari's application of his intellectual training radicalized psychoanalysis, challenging both his teacher, Lacan, and the application of his psychoanalytical approach (hence, *Anti-Oedipus*). At La Borde, Guattari formed an egalitarian community for patients, focusing on group therapy, bridging the gap between doctor and patient. Nicole Guillet, Guattari's colleague at La Borde, for example, noted: "Félix really liked declassifying people, like having a doctor come work in the office. He had the psychologists doing the dishes."[41] Besides Lacan, Guattari was also influenced by the writings of Sartre, whose ideas on annihilation sparked Guattari's ideas on deterritorialization, a key Deleuze and Guattari concept discussed in this chapter and Sharon Jacob's chapter that follows.[42] It is this Guattarian love of experimentation—taking concepts beyond the thoughts of his teachers—that met

35. Gilles Deleuze and Félix Guattari, *What Is Philosophy?* (trans. Hugh Tomlinson and Graham Burchill; London: Verso, 1994), 106–8.
36. Dosse, *Intersecting Lives*, 520.
37. Dosse, *Intersecting Lives*, 177.
38. Dosse, *Intersecting Lives*, 21.
39. Dosse, *Intersecting Lives*, 26.
40. Dosse, *Intersecting Lives*, 39.
41. Dosse, *Intersecting Lives*, 57.
42. Dosse, *Intersecting Lives*, 29.

with Deleuze's ideas in 1969. Though meeting for the first time, they were not strangers. According to Deleuze they were "friends" before encountering one another, and their collaboration joined their streams of thought together. "We didn't collaborate like two different people," claimed Deleuze. "We were more like two streams coming together to make a third stream, which I suppose was us."[43] The result of May 1968 and their meeting in 1969 was their first book, *Anti-Oedipus*, which according to Guattari was a direct effect of the student riots.[44]

Prior to his intersection with Guattari, Deleuze experienced his educational awakening in high school, which was triggered by a teacher (similar to Benjamin's initial encounter with Gustav Wyneken), literature professor Pierre Halbwachs, who introduced the teenage Deleuze to French literature, in particular Baudelaire (also akin to Benjamin's early formation), saving Deleuze from the boredom and malaise of schooling.[45] Then, at the age of 18, Deleuze had another key encounter, this time with a spiritualist, Marie-Madeleine Davy, whom Dosse calls Deleuze's "high priestess."[46] Davy was a Catholic leftist with a doctorate in theology from the Paris Catholic Institute. Deleuze was a frequent visitor to Davy's estate, which, according to Dosse, was "a sanctuary for Jews, Resistance fighters, those who had refused to go on the forced labor convoys, and British and American pilots."[47] What is remarkable about this encounter is its effect on the young Deleuze's interpretation of modern Christianity, capitalism, and the dichotomy between the human interior and exterior—all expressed in his early essay "From Christ to Bourgeoisies," which was dedicated to Mary Davy.[48] Deleuze critiques modern Christianity's move to interiority and away from exteriority, that is, away from connecting to the world materially, historically, socially, and

---

43. Gilles Deleuze, *Negotiations: 1972–1990* (trans. Martin Joughin; New York: Columbia University Press, 1995), 136. When asked about his own background preceding his collaboration with Deleuze, Guattari said: "I had too many 'backgrounds,' four at least." These four were (1) his involvement with the Communist Path and the Left Opposition, (2) the La Borde clinic, (3) Lacan's seminars, and (4) his experience working with schizophrenics (14).

44. Deleuze, *Negotiations*, 15.

45. Dosse, *Intersecting Lives*, 90. Here Dosse notes that prior to this point Deleuze was bored by school and a mediocre student.

46. Dosse, *Intersecting Lives*, 93.

47. Dosse, *Intersecting Lives*, 91.

48. Gilles Deleuze, "Du Christ à la bourgeoisie," *Espace* 1 (1946): 93–106. For an English translation, see Gilles Deleuze, "From Christ to Bourgeoisie," trans. Raymond van de Wiel, http://documents.raymondvandewiel.org/from_christ_to_the_bourgeoisie_translation.pdf.

politically.⁴⁹ And when this form of Christianity does take into account exteriority, it is not primarily focused on nature, but human nature as distinct from broader social concerns and other animate and inanimate forms in the world. It is an internalized exteriority.⁵⁰ So too the "good news" of salvation is narrowly focused, according to Deleuze:

> ... but the good news that it brings us is not about the world, it concerns about that part of the world called human nature. The Gospel does not deal with politics and the social ... it brings everything back to the possibility of sin, and the possibility of saving man from sin.⁵¹

As a result of this narrow focus on human nature (as opposed to the broader, external focus on nature and society), this form of Christianity undergirds the ideology of the bourgeoisie and capitalism while contradicting the message of Christ: "Insofar as the bourgeoisie internalizes interior life and Christ alike, they do it in the form of property, of money, of having; all of which Christ hated, and that he had come to fight, to substitute it for being."⁵²

In contrast to this bourgeoisie Christianity, Deleuze offered a "new notion," one found in certain forms of Christian mysticism (e.g., William of St. Thierry, whom Mary Davy was translating), forms introduced to him through Davy, ones focusing on connectivity to the world. Indeed, Deleuze (along with his friends) created the journal in which "From Christ to the Bourgeoisie" was published, in which according to Raymond van de Wiel, they wanted "to establish a new *fraternité* between man and the world, an immediate contact between the interior and the exterior."⁵³ This connectivity,

---

49. See Raymond van de Wiel, "From Christ to the Bourgeoisie: Deleuze, Spiritualism, Sartre and the World" (paper presented at the Third International Deleuze Studies Conference, Amsterdam, The Netherlands, 13 July 2010), 1–8, http://raymondvandewiel.org/post/127463632357/from-christ-to-the-bourgeoisie-deleuze. Van de Wiel contextualizes this early essay and points out where Deleuze's critique of Christianity is directed: the Neo-Thomism of Jacques Maritain. Although Maritain argues for human rights at a key point in the twentieth century—offering the distinction between the individual and the person—he is chiefly concerned about human nature and the human person, according to van de Wiel, which for Maritain "is radically distinct from other beings" and the world (p. 3). This concern, therefore, internalizes (human) nature.

50. Van de Wiel, "Deleuze, Spiritualism, Sartre and the World."

51. Deleuze, "From Christ to the Bourgeoisie," 104. On this internalization of Jesus in modern scholarship, recall Robert Myles' critique of N. T. Wright, referenced in Chapter One above: "What primarily matters for Wright's Jesus, it would seem, is the symbolic and internal revolution of the individual being." See Robert Myles, "The Fetish for a Subversive Jesus," *Journal for the Study of the Historical Jesus* 14.1 (2016): 1–14, here 10.

52. Deleuze, "From Christ to the Bourgeoisie," 102. On Davy, see Van de Wiel, "Deleuze, Spiritualism, Sartre and the World," 5.

53. Van de Wiel, "Deleuze, Spiritualism, Sartre and the World," 2.

this *fraternité*—one without an internal/external dichotomy, one without a transcendent sky God-to-human relation—is explored by Bradley McLean's chapter below on Deleuze and Paul's "body of Christ without organs."

Aside from these intersections, at the university level as both a student and professor (from the Sorbonne to University of Paris VIII in Vincennes), Deleuze creatively conversed with the works of diverse philosophers, writers, and artists, producing works on Hume, Nietzsche, Kant, Proust, Bergson, Sacher-Macoch, Spinoza, Bacon, Leibniz, and Foucault, and another work with Guattari on Kafka.[54] In the words of Claire Colebrook, Deleuze's "career began with a re-reading of the philosophical tradition. He took quite traditional figures and argued that their works harbored a far more radical potential."[55] These writings were not strictly "history-of" texts; they were, in Deleuze's own problematic words, "monstrous offspring," the result of him fathering texts with other writers.[56] These texts disrupted the philosophical

---

54. Gilles Deleuze, *Empiricism and Subjectivity: An Essay on Hume's Theory of Human Nature* (trans. Constantin V. Boundas; New York: Columbia University Press, 1991); translation of *Empirisme et subjectivité: Essai sur la Nature humaine selon Hume* (Paris: Presses Universitaires de France, 1953); *Nietzsche and Philosophy* (trans. Hugh Tomlinson; London: Athlone, 1983); translation of *Nietzsche et la philosophie* (Paris: Presses Universitaires de France, 1962); *Kant's Critical Philosophy: The Doctrine of the Faculties* (trans. Hugh Tomlinson and Barbara Habberjam; London: Athlone, 1984); translation of *La Philosophie critique de Kant: Doctrine des facultés* (Paris: Presses Universitaires de France, 1963); *Proust and Signs: The Complete Text* (trans. Richard Howard; Minneapolis, MN: University of Minnesota, 2003); translation of *Proust et les signes* (Paris: Presses Universitaires de France, 1964); *Bergonsim* (trans. Hugh Tomlinson and Barbara Habberjam; New York: Zone, 1990); translation of *Le Bergsonisme* (Paris: Presses Universitaires de France, 1966); *Masochism: An Interpretation of Coldness and Cruelty* (trans. Jean McNeil; New York: G. Braziller, 1971); translation of *Présentation de Sacher-Masoch* (Paris: Éditions de Minuit, 1967); *Expressionism in Philosophy: Spinoza* (trans. Martin Joughin; New York: Zone Books, 1990); translation of *Spinoza et le problème de l'expression* (Paris: Éditions de Minuit, 1968); *Spinoza: Practical Philosophy* (trans. Robert Hurley; San Francisco, CA: City Lights Books, 1988); translation of *Spinoza: Philosophie pratique* (Paris: Presses Universitaires de France, 1981 [1970]); *Francis Bacon: Logic of Sensation* (trans. Daniel W. Smith; Minneapolis, MN: University of Minnesota Press, 1986); translation of *Francis Bacon: Logique de la sensation* (Paris: Editions de la différence, 1981); *Foucault* (trans. Sean Hand; Minneapolis, MN: University of Minnesota Press, 1988); translation of *Foucault* (Paris: Éditions de Minuit, 1986); *The Fold: Leibniz and the Baroque* (trans. Tom Conley; Minneapolis, MN: University of Minnesota Press, 1993); translation of *Le Pli: Leibniz et le Baroque* (Paris: Éditions de Minuit, 1988); Deleuze and Guattari, *Kafka: For a Minor Literature* (trans. Dana Polan; Minneapolis, MN: University of Minnesota Press, 1986); translation of *Kafka: pour une littérature mineure* (Paris: Éditions de Minuit, 1975).

55. Colebrook, *Gilles Deleuze*, 3.

56. Dosse, *Intersecting Lives*, 109. See Gilles Deleuze, *Negotiations: 1972–1990*, 6; translation of *Pourparlers 1972–1990* (Paris: Éditions de Minuit, 1990): "I saw myself

norms and assumptions of Deleuze's time, creating new concepts. Ultimately what Deleuze derived from this study of the history of philosophy was his own unique contribution to philosophy. Similar to Benjamin, the present is made strange again by interacting with the past, and the past becomes strange again by interacting with the present. By doing so, new constellations are formed. In Claire Colebrook's words: "If we were to *repeat* Shakespeare today then we would not don Elizabethan costumes, rebuild the Globe and take ourselves back in time—whatever that means—to a past that remains unchanged. Repeating the past always transforms the past, for the past is as much in production as the present."[57] Colebrook continues: "we should look to the past, not to find out what it was, but to allow the force of past problems, questions or direction to transform the present into the future."[58] While Deleuze's approach does not exclude the study of the past through historical-critical methods, it also does not exclude the present by trying to escape into the illusion of a historical-critical vacuum. Nor does it escape the present by exalting the "purity" and "authenticity" of past origins (i.e., "authentic" Shakespeare revivals or recovering the "authentic" early Christian experience). It forces the disruption of the present and the past, challenging scholarship to create new concepts, new monstrous offspring.

Deleuze creates new concepts by disrupting the present and the past in his "solo" efforts (as if there is such a concept of "solo" in a Deleuzian world): *Difference and Repetition, The Logic of Sense,* and his two works on cinema—*Cinema I: The Movement Image* and *Cinema II: The Time-Image*.[59] *Difference and Repetition,* sometimes referred to as Deleuze's magnum opus, bridges Deleuze's work on the history of philosophy with

---

as taking an author from behind and giving him a child that would be his own offspring, but monstrous." Kenneth Novis rightly interrupts Deleuzian scholarship, warning about repeating this metaphor without calling out its problems. See Kenneth Novis, "Deleuze and MeToo," *KennethNovis* (blog), *Wordpress,* 13 April 2020, https://kennethnovis.wordpress.com/2020/04/13/deleuze-and-metoo.

57. Colebrook, *Gilles Deleuze,* 84.
58. Colebrook, *Gilles Deleuze,* 84.
59. Gilles Deleuze, *Difference and Repetition* (trans. Paul Patton; New York: Columbia University Press, 1994); translation of *Différence et répétition* (Paris: Presses Universitaires de France, 1968); *The Logic of Sense* (trans. Mark Lester and Charles Stivale; New York: Columbia University Press, 1990); translation of *Logique du sens* (Paris: Éditions de Minuit, 1969); *Cinema I: The Movement-Image* (trans. Hugh Tomlinson and Barbara Habberjam; Minneapolis, MN: University of Minnesota Press, 1986); translation of *Cinéma I: l'Image-Mouvement* (Paris: Éditions de Minuit, 1983); *Cinema II: The Time-Image* (trans. Hugh Tomlinson and Barbara Habberjam; Minneapolis, MN: University of Minnesota Press, 1989); translation of *Cinéma II: l'Image-temps* (Paris: Éditions de Minuit, 1986).

"his own" philosophy. James Williams describes this work as "at the center of his philosophical works, not only chronologically but also methodologically and in terms of interpretation."[60] Its middle chapter attacks assumptions about common sense, as noted above (see Chapter One); its later chapters argue against "essences," asserting that reality itself is simulacra, that is, repetitions with differences. The latter argument is applied to the Acts tradition by Whitlock and Tite in Chapter Seven below, challenging assumptions scholarship makes about finding essences, foundations, and origins in early Christian text. Here we assert that Acts of the Apostles itself is a simulacrum, not the origin or essence of the tradition. At the same time, later Acts texts do not veer from "the origin," but rather do what Acts of the Apostles itself does: repeat with difference. Finally, *Logic and Sense* continues along the same trajectory of *Difference and Repetition,* while using a less traditional form of philosophical argument (e.g., employing paradoxes and referencing Lewis Carroll) to argue against common sense and Platonism. And Deleuze's two works on cinema, *The Movement Image* and *The Time-Image*, show what new forms of art can do: create new ways of seeing and perceiving, through which new concepts are created.

While Deleuze's ideas about the creative force of life persist, another force persists in his philosophy and life: his own suffering and death. Due to his health and his own preference to stay at home, Deleuze did not travel to conferences as one would expect a well-published scholar and philosopher to do. He suffered from respiratory problems throughout his life, the severity of which increased toward his death, including painful spells of suffocation. On 4 November, 1995, Deleuze killed himself, jumping from the window of his apartment. On Deleuze's suffering and death, his friend Yves Mabin commented: "He was absolutely suffocating; that he could stand it for so long is proof of his exceptional courage. He was unusually brave in hanging on to that point."[61] Roger Pol-Droit noted how Deleuze's life and death embodied his philosophy of becoming, countering philosophical assumptions about permanence: "Putting things into motion everywhere. The becomings, the emergences, whereas the history of philosophy more often thought about stable things, permanence."[62] Others question his

---

60. James Williams, *"Difference and Repetition as Transcendental Empiricism,"* in *The Cambridge Companion to Deleuze* (ed. Daniel W. Smith and Henry Somers-Hall; Cambridge: Cambridge University Press, 2012), 33–54, here 33.

61. Dosse, *Intersecting Lives*, 498.

62. Roger-Pol Droit, on "Le cercle de Minuit" (6 November 1995), INA Archives; quoted in Dosse, *Intersecting Lives*, 499–500.

suicide because it is in tension with his philosophy, contradicting his affirmation of life.[63]

On the subject of Deleuze's "affirmation of life," it is important to end here with Andrew Culp's recent book *Dark Deleuze*, perhaps providing balance and tension with how this introduction began, namely with ideas of connections, machines, and rhizomes.[64] Culp's work offers a portrait of Deleuze's philosophy that serves as a warning against surface readings of Deleuze's rhizome and machine, a warning appropriate to scholars using his concepts in the age of connectivity. Andrew Culp points out the dangers of being too affirmative about Deleuze's affirmation of life. In *Dark Deleuze*, Culp claims his own creation of "monstrous offspring," the product of Culp's interactions with the gaps in Deleuze's philosophy, especially the darker ones, ones more in line with the Christian crypt than Christ's ascension.[65] Indeed, in light of Deleuze's own classification of *Difference and Repetition*, Culp names his own work as "apocalyptic science fiction."[66] Culp questions surface readings of Deleuze's conception of connectivity (i.e., the rhizome) making it "*Dark Deleuze's* immediate target."[67] The ideology of connectivity, according to Culp, plays into the goal of a twenty-first century global-capitalism: world-building, namely, "to make everyone and everything part of a single world."[68]

---

63. See Andrew Culp, *Dark Deleuze* (Forerunners: Ideas First; Minneapolis, MN: University of Minnesota Press, 2016), 11: "Michel Serres ... remains steadfast that Deleuze's death must have been an accident because he felt that suicide was not in Deleuze's character or philosophy."

64. Culp, *Dark Deleuze*.

65. Culp, *Dark Deleuze*, 16–7. Here Culp is referencing Deleuze's *The Fold: Leibniz and the Baroque*. Culp writes: "Greco's great baroque mannerist painting *The Burial of Count Orgaz*, we are given a choice. Above the great horizontal line, a gathering of saints ascends to the height of Jesus, whose own ascension grants the heavens eternal lightness. Below, a communion of cloaked, pale men crowd together to lay the count to rest under a dark background illuminated by a torchlight" (17).

66. Culp, *Dark Deleuze*, 2. Deleuze, *Difference and Repetition*, xx–xi.

67. Culp, *Dark Deleuze*, 5.

68. Culp, *Dark Deleuze*, 6. Culp counters the typical science fiction trope: humanity losing control of its knowledge and technology; he asserts: "The problem is, *they know perfectly well what they are doing, but they continue doing it anyway.*" He points to Google ideas director Jared Cohen, who once held a position in the State Department during the Bush administration. Culp writes: "In a geopolitical manifesto co-written with then Google CEO Eric Schmidt, *The New Digital Age*, Cohen reveals Google's deep aspiration to extend US government interests home and abroad. Their central tool? Connectivity." See Jared Cohen and Eric Schmidt, *The New Digital Age: Reshaping the Future of People, Nations, and Business* (New York: Doubleday, 2013).

Since both Deleuze and Culp classify their work as apocalyptic science fiction, perhaps an apoc-sci-fi thought-image best illustrates Culp's critique of connectivity and its relation to twenty-first century global capitalism and its technology: "The Power Plant" from the movie *The Matrix*. Before becoming a set piece for the film, "The Power Plant" was drawn by comic book artist Geof Darrow. The Wachowski siblings—creators, writers, and directors of *The Matrix* trilogy—hired Darrow to storyboard their original script in images (like Deleuze and Benjamin, the Wachowskis thought and wrote in images). The Wachowskis were familiar with Darrow's work in the comic series *Hard Boiled*, where Darrow created complex and intricate images for writer Frank Miller, images expressing the gluttony and misogyny of the antagonist of the story, Mr. Willeford, the owner of Willeford Home Appliances, an archetype of the military-industrial capitalist, himself dependent on an intricate web of mechanical arms and pipes and robotic women washing, sustaining, and feeding him with Coke and Pepsi cans.[69] So it was Darrow who then drew "The Power Plant" for *The Matrix*, a vast network of pipes and wires connected to an infinite number of individual pods, where the majority of human beings lie asleep and complacent, dreaming about a virtual reality—not a utopian world without suffering, which humanity rejected as "a dream that [their] primitive cerebrum kept trying to wake up from"—but the "peak of [human] civilization," late twentieth-century urban capitalism.[70] While asleep in this twentieth century "dream world," fields of human beings are grown and harvested for energy by and to sustain AI machines in a post-apocalyptic world, while "the liquefied [human] dead are fed to the living."[71] And liberation, though quite rare, consists of taking a red pill, which locates the liberated in Darrow's Power Plant, where they wake up to view fields of human beings connected to countless numbers of chords and pipes and machines—human enslaved, objectified, and used as instruments by and for machines.[72]

---

69. Frank Miller and Geof Darrow, *Hard Boiled* (Milwaukie, OR: Dark Horse Books, 1993). The protagonist of *Hard Boiled*, a cyborg named Carl, lives a staged life, thinking he is a human being living a benevolent life in the suburbs as an insurance investigator. He wakes up from this false life. Destined to become a revolutionary upon his awakening, he revolts. Yet he ultimately succumbs to Mr. Willeford's power. Carl chooses to forget his revolutionary calling and reunite with his staged life, without any memory of his awakening to the truth. So Carl is rebuilt and returns to a "normal" suburban life with a wife, kids, a dog, and a new car. He does what Cypher wished for in *The Matrix*: to be re-inserted into the dream world without any memories of an awakening.

70. See Spencer Lamm, ed., *The Art of the Matrix* (New York: Newmarket Press, 2000), 262. Lana Wachowski and Lilly Wachowski, *The Matrix* (Warner Brothers, 1999).

71. Wachowski and Wachowski, *The Matrix*.

72. The phrase "red-pilled" is used by Alt-Right bloggers to represent someone waking up to conspiracies unveiled by the movement. See Andrew Marantz, "Trolls for Trump:

This imagery points back to how we started this chapter: Lindner's *Boy and the Machine*, where "hands are tangled, knotted within the levers that will set one machine against the other."[73] And in Deleuze and Guattari's machinic world, there is no release from connections: "Everywhere *it* is machines—real ones, not figurative ones: machines driving other machines, machines being driven by other machines, with all the necessary couplings and connections."[74] And by no means are all machines exploitive and villainous (see "war machines" below). Whereas in Freud we are bound and always connected to internal drives, in Deleuze we are always connected externally to machines: desiring machines to social machines.[75] It is not a matter of being released from machines, but a matter of which machine one is connected to.[76] There is no machine-neutrality; claims of neutrality are merely feigned detachment. We are born as machines into machines. In the university, we are machines born into scholarly machines, and sometimes administrative ones.[77]

Meet Michael Cernovich, the Meme Mastermind of the Alt-Right," *The New Yorker* (31 October 2016). The irony, however, is that both worlds in *The Matrix* (the dream world and real world) are quite similar to the world the Alt-Right supports. In the dream world, represented by the blue pill, not the red, humanity lives in late twentieth-century capitalism, satisfying the brain's primal drives for competition; in the real world, humans are enslaved and exploited while consuming one another for survival. So to be "red-pilled" in *The Matrix* is to wake up from the twentieth-century dream of urban capitalism and to see the reality hidden underneath: the commodification and exploitation of human beings. What's more, appropriate to Deleuze's thinking, taking the red pill involves new connections, not simply being released from corrupt ones. This is illustrated in recent interpretations of *The Matrix* as a trans allegory. The red pill transitions one from old connections to new, both in *The Matrix* and for trans patients. See Laura Dale, "With *The Matrix 4* Coming, Let's Talk About How the First Movie Is a Trans Allegory," *SYFY Wire*, 2020, https://www.syfy.com/syfywire/with-the-matrix-4-coming-lets-talk-about-how-the-first-movie-is-a-trans-allegory.

73. Ballard, "The Audience and the Art Machine," 125.
74. Deleuze and Guattari, *Anti-Oedipus*, 1.
75. See McClean, Chapter Six of this volume.
76. Perhaps our era's increasing knowledge about connectivity sheds new light on Paul's ideas (or vice versa). In his historical analysis of Pauline psychology, Klaus Berger shows how we project our enlightenment ideas of freedom and autonomy onto Paul's writing about freedom, whereas Paul's concept of freedom is about to whom/what one is connected (Rom. 6.15-23): a "freedom from" a power (e.g., death or Sin) to an "attaching oneself to a liberator" (the body of Christ). See Klaus Berger, *Identity and Experience in the New Testament* (trans. Charles Muenchow; Minneapolis, MN: Fortress Press, 2003), 35–7.
77. Recall Darko Suvin's point from Chapter One above: "Those who do not put an explicitly defensible civic cognition at the heart of their professional cognition at best adopt the dominant epistemology of the time when they were students, and at worst adapt their cognition to the new epistemology of the Powers-That-Be." Darko Suvin, "Circumstances and Stances: A Retrospect," in *Metamorphoses of Science Fiction: On*

We are born into state machines and have war machines (metaphoric) as alternatives. War machines are exterior to the state: "of another species, another nature, another origin than the State apparatus."[78] War machines function as "the agents of social and political transformation."[79] According to Culp, war machines are the heroes of *A Thousand Plateaus,* but also the potential villains. On the one hand, there are guerrilla war machines, revolutionary war machines, queer war machines, and thought war machines.[80] Thought war machines, for example, seek to "dethrone" structuralism.[81] On the other hand, there are war machines that are inevitably hijacked by the state: the commercial war machine, the fascist war machine, and the capitalist (military-industrial) war machine—the latter being "the worst of them all."[82]

Recognizing and having some agency within these machinic connections are important steps to a Deleuzian approach to early Christian texts. Recognizing the inevitable capture of war machines by the State is also an important step in a Deleuzian approach. However, as Clayton Crockett argues, the Deleuzian story does not end with the capturing of war machines.[83] While the State appropriates knowledge (for its own ends), it cannot create new concepts, new combinations, new ways of thinking. Hence, using Deleuzian concepts for viewing early Christian texts is one way of awakening us from "common sense" categories that inevitably tie us to normative machines, and enabling us to create new connections and combinations and categories.

Key Concepts and Theories in this Volume and Beyond

Because Deleuze's concepts are fluidic, rhizomatic, and nomadic, it is difficult to define them universally. Theory is the active and fluid creation

---

the Poetics and History of a Literary Genre (ed. Gerry Canavan; Ralahine Utopian Studies, 18; Bern: Peter Lang, 2016), 448.

78. On "war machines," see Deleuze and Guattari's chapter "1227: Treatise on Nomadology—The War Machine" in *A Thousand Plateaus*, 351–423, here 352.

79. Paul Patton, "Deleuze's Political Philosophy," in Smith and Somers-Hall, eds., *The Cambridge Companion to Deleuze*, 198–219, here 207.

80. Culp, *Dark Deleuze*, 22–3.

81. François Dosse, "Deleuze and Structuralism," in Smith and Somers-Hall, eds., *The Cambridge Companion to Deleuze*, 126–50, here 135.

82. Culp, *Dark Deleuze*, 22–3

83. Clayton Crockett, *Deleuze beyond Badiou: Ontology, Multiplicity, and the Event* (New York: Columbia University Press, 2013), 9–10. Here Crockett discusses the concept of the time-image, "a brain for the people who do not yet exist but can be brought into existence. The state cannot think, which is why the state cannot create a time-image, only appropriate it."

of concepts, according to Deleuze and Guattari in *What Is Philosophy?* Andrew Robinson sums their approach well:

> In *What Is Philosophy?* [Deleuze and Guattari] define the function of theory in terms of proliferating concepts—inventing new conceptual categories which construct new ways of seeing. In common with many constructivists, they take the view that our relationship with the world is filtered through conceptual categories. Distinctively, they also view agency in terms of differentiation—each person or group creates itself, not by selecting among available alternatives, but by splitting existing totalities through the creation of new differences. This approach leads to a proliferation of different concepts which, across [Deleuze and Guattari's] collaborative and individual works, total in the hundreds.[84]

Therefore, in secondary literature on Deleuze and Guattari, the lists vary and are by no means—in rightful tribute to their thought—systematic. What is more, with the exception of "rhizome," "affect," and "actual/virtual," the vast majority of these concepts have not yet been used in analyses of early Christian texts, especially New Testament Studies: assemblage, becoming woman, body without organs, deterritorialization and reterritorialization, event, expression (versus representation), fabulation, fold, immanence, intensity, lines of flight, minor and major literature, materialism, molar, multiplicity, noology, plateau, schizoanalysis, simulacrum, smooth space, stratification, time-image, transcendental empiricism, and transversality.[85] These concepts offer "new ways of seeing" early Christian literature. For a helpful guide to his concepts, see *The Deleuze Dictionary*.[86] In this volume, besides the concepts discussed above (i.e., rhizome, machines), we focus on four others: body without organs (McLean), deterritorialization and reterritorialization (Jacob), simulacra/difference and repetition (Whitlock and Tite), and stuttering and minor literature (summarized below).

A. Bradley H. McLean:
The Body of Christ as the Body without Organs

In his chapter "The Deleuzioguattarian Body of Christ without Organs," Bradley McLean moves beyond the common categories "Jesus of history"

---

84. Andrew Robinson, "In Theory—Why Deleuze Still Matters: States, War Machines and Radical Transformation," *Ceasefire Magazine*, 10 September 2010, https://ceasefiremagazine.co.uk/in-theory-deleuze-war-machine.

85. On the rhizome, see McLean, "Re-imagining New Testament Interpretation"; *Biblical Interpretation and Philosophical Hermeneutics*; Vander Stichele "How to Conceptualize 'Reception History.'" On actual/virtual, see George Aichele, *Simulating Jesus: Reality Effects in the Gospels* (Abingdon: Routledge, 2014).

86. Adrian Parr, ed., *The Deleuze Dictionary* (rev. edn.; Edinburgh: Edinburgh University Press, 2010).

and "Christ of faith" to offer a new, materialist conception of Christ's followers, based on Paul's Christ groups (ἐκκλησίαι), or in Pauline terms, "the body of Christ." While much has been said about the "Jesus of history" (in historical terms) and "the Christ of faith" (in transcendent terms), the dynamics of "the body of Christ" have yet to be articulated in Deleuzoguattarian-materialist terms. So, based on the Deleuze and Guattari's concept "the body without organs," McLean helps us conceive of the material dimensions of early Christian origins: "the body of Christ without organs." In McLean's words, "Pauline Christ groups were *materially* formed, *in a most literal sense, as a 'body of Christ* without organs,' which is to say, as a self-organizing system, without reference to a transcendental plane." McLean clarifies that the "body without organs actually *does* possess organs: the modifier 'without organs' merely implies that the connections between its organs and the organs of *other* bodies are just as significant as the connections between the organs of its own body."

After setting the stage, Mclean identifies and delineates "the body of Christ without organs" in two communities: Corinth and Philippi. Next, he delves deeper by defining these "bodies without organs" as desiring-machines connected with other desiring-machines. And within and between these machines are "flows" (e.g., sights, sounds, smells, sensations, foods, flows of production, etc.). Hence, "the bodies of Jesus, Paul, and indeed all first-century Christ followers were *porously* connected to the material, libidinal, and semiotic flows" of the Roman world. As a result, McLean asserts: "the scholar of Christian origins should ask, what desiring-machines were Jesus and the first Christ groups plugged into, and what symptoms were produced in them by being plugged into other desiring-machines?"

McLean then takes on this task, analyzing how the "body of Christ without organs" functioned as a desiring machine (composed of desiring machines) and plugged into other desiring machines in the Roman world. In doing so—and in staying faithful to a Deleuzoguattarian approach—McLean asserts "the body of Christ without organs emerged through "self-organization" like "an egg or embryo" and "without external agency, intentionality or goal." He then delineates three passive syntheses that took place in its emergence: (1) connective synthesis, (2) disjunctive synthesis, and (3) conjunctive synthesis. First, in the connective synthesis, desiring machines connect with other desiring machines, but without boundaries. It is purely parataxis: "and" plus "and" plus "and." Thus, in McClean's words, "Christ followers, as the organs of this body, simply connected to other organs, without being restricted (repressed) by pre-established social structures, hierarchies, laws, and doctrines, allowing the formation of extended chains of desiring-machines, *with no beginning, end or center*." Hence, these are "undifferenciated bodies of Christ without organs." Second, in the disjunctive synthesis, organized networks are formed through the connections of the first synthesis. "Good" and "bad" flows of production are named. Hence, flows begin to be regulated. Boundaries are drawn. Desiring machines are repressed. In the end, either "the desiring-production of the organs of the body of Christ is either overcoded by the social production of the state apparatus" or "repressed altogether." Third, in the conjunctive synthesis, external events interrupt the prior synthesis of "body of Christ without organs," disrupting it, creating new flows and mutations. Hence, a "resuscitation of desiring-production" occurs. Here "the system spontaneously self-organizes and achieves a new phase space." McLean names this phase as "the *full* body of Christ without organs." By applying these three syntheses to Paul's Christ groups, McLean provides a new, materialist lens for viewing the patterns and cycles of early Christ followers.

B. Whitlock and Tite: The Many Acts of the Apostles: Simulacra and Simulation

In their chapter "The Many Acts of the Apostles: Simulacra and Simulation," Whitlock and Tite explore Deleuze's theories about simulacra, contrasting them to those of Jean Baudrillard, and then applying them to the Acts tradition. On the one hand, Baudrillard views simulacra negatively, claiming that we have been so overcome by copies of copies that we have lost sight of the real. His theories affirm the dichotomy between the real and the virtual, and the original and the copy. In applying Baudrillard's theories to the quest for Christian origins, Whitlock and Tite conclude that we are left only with copies of copies of early Christian "origins." And if we seek the "authentic" or "authoritative" essence of Christianity behind these copies, we find, in Baudrillard's terms, "the desert of the real."

On the other hand, Deleuze views simulacra positively, claiming that life is a simulacrum of becoming, an infinite and evolving series of real images and real differences. Whitlock and Tite show how Deleuze's theories challenge the dichotomies between the real and the virtual, authentic and inauthentic, authoritative and apocryphal—dichotomies too often undergirding modern quests for Christian origins. Using Deleuzian theories, Whitlock and Tite examine early Christian texts not as authentic and authoritative representations of an original source or essence, but as a continuous and evolving series of real images and real differences, a simulacrum of becoming. Applying these theories to the Acts tradition, they examine how the story of Cornelius repeats and differs from Luke to Acts, and from Acts to the so-called apocryphal Acts, and how this series of forms, in Deleuze's words, leads to "the abandonment of representation."

C. Sharon Jacob: Face-ing the Nations: Becoming a Majority Empire of God

In her chapter, "Face-ing the Nations and Becoming a Majority Empire of God: Reterritorialization, Language, and Imperial Racism in Revelation 7.9-17," Sharon Jacob focuses on how the unanimity of language in Revelation helps create a new empire of God, one unintentionally mirroring the Roman Empire, the very empire it aims to dismantle in its visions. Jacob uses Deleuze and Guattari's theories on deterritorialization, reterritorialization, facialization, and language to highlight how the nations in Revelation 7.9-17 become "recognizable, controllable, and comprehensible entities as they are inserted into the nationalistic vision of the divine empire of God."

In the first part of her chapter, Jacob examines the historical and literary contexts of Revelation 7.9-17. Concerning the historical context, Jacob argues how the text of Revelation expresses both derision and desire for the culture of the Roman Empire. For "the performance of mimicking the colonizer's culture exposes both the desire and derision of the oppressed for the dominant and their culture." Jacob accordingly argues: "in the process of outwardly resisting the Roman Empire, John of Patmos internalizes the imperial values and reinscribes them in his vision." Concerning the literary context of 7.9-17, Jacob examines how biblical scholarship analyzes Revelation's (7.5-8) divergence from the way the tribes are traditionally listed. Biblical scholarship suggests that this divergence "gestures to a new divine order." However, Jacob argues that these interpretations are "limited to a Christian vision" and "fail to take into account the traces of imperialism that appear as the undercurrent in this vision." These traces are then explicated by Jacob in the second part of her chapter.

In the second part of her chapter, Jacob examines Revelation 7.9-17 through the lens of Deleuze and Guattari's theories, specifically calling attention to language, deterritorialization, reterritorialization, and facialization. First, referencing the work of Partha Chatterjee,[87] Jacob notes how "official languages become the common thread that stitch together nations, binding the tongues of its citizens, weaving them into a unique tapestry that displays nationalism on the world stage." By envisioning the nations worshiping the lamb in *a loud voice*, in Koine Greek, John of Patmos threads together a world stage of one voice and language, argues Jacob. To use Deleuze and Guattari's terms, "*minor languages* spoken by the multitude in Revelation 7.9-17 are replaced by the *major language* of the Empire." As

---

87. Partha Chatterjee, "Nationalism as a Problem," 126–8 in *The Post-Colonial Studies Reader 2nd Edition* (ed. Bill Ashcroft, Gareth Griffiths, and Helen Tiffin; New York: Routledge, 1995).

a result, "imperial visions and language mimicked in the text of Revelation facialize the empire of God by constructing a unified vision of the nations under one God." The new divine order "is a multinational, multicultural, multilinguistic multitude, *but speaking in the language of the empire*." It is the language, according to Jacob, that deterritorializes the nations, who in verse 9 are of many languages. And they are reterritorialized into *a loud voice*. In short, "the facialization of these nations, illustrated through an overt and deliberate reterritorialization of their language and dress, racialized in order to familiarize, constructs a nationalized vision where only one nation, speaking one language, wearing one dress, gathers to worship only the one and true God."

D. For Further Consideration: Early Christian Literature as Minor Literature

Sharon Jacob outlines the effects a major language has had upon those who oppose and mimic empire, highlighting the facialization that occurs in the process. The consequence is reterritorialization. And because deterritorialization/reterritorialization is an ongoing cycle in Deleuze and Guattari's theory, we expect that deterritorialization also occurs while subversive literature speaks a major language of empire. Hence, Deleuze and Guattari also highlight how writing in the major language of empire creates a "minor literature," one nuanced with both facialization and subversion, and reterritorialization and deterritorialization. So minor literature deterritorializes the major language of empire.

Minor literature is a modern literary category coined by Deleuze and Guattari, describing literature written by a marginalized group in the "major" language of its culture.[88] Minor literature does not emphasize the voice of the author, but the voice of a community. The author does not possess an "elite" style, but collects multiple styles, styles which together "stutter." Thus, writers of "minor literature," according to Deleuze, make their language "scream, stutter, stammer, or murmur," pushing it to its limits.[89] For Deleuze and Guattari, language falls short of expressing what is other than common sense.[90] Minor literature, however, takes language beyond

---

88. See G. Deleuze and F. Guattari, *Kafka: Toward a Minor Literature* (trans. D. Polan; Minneapolis, MN: University of Minnesota Press, 1986). For examples of how this category is applied in literary and cultural studies, see R. Pérez, "What Is 'Minor' in Latino Literature," *MELUS* 30 (2005): 89–108 (102).

89. G. Deleuze, "He Stuttered," in *Essays: Critical and Clinical* (trans. D. W. Smith and M. A. Greco; Minneapolis, MN: University of Minnesota Press, 1997), 107–14, here 110.

90. Note the similarity here with Badiou's claims about language's inability to fully

common sense and commonly held norms. Authors of minor literature do not write in their native language, but in the majority language of their time, such as Kafka writing in German, not his native Czech, or the New Testament authors writing in Koine Greek, not the Aramaic or Hebrew native to Jesus and his first followers. They are "foreigners in their own [major] language." They invent "a *minor use* of the major language within which they express themselves entirely."[91] They carve "out a nonpreexistent foreign language *within* [their] own language."[92] By doing so, they deterritorialize language and challenge the social boundaries of the major culture. There is, in other words, political immediacy to their work.

Jacob's work on Deleuze and Guattari, Revelation, and language sets the state not only for more nuanced work on Revelation, but also on other early Christian texts, which can fall victim to interpretations that either view these texts as entirely subversive or conforming. Jacob and Deleuze and Guattari, on the other hand, see these texts as containing both reterritorialization and deterritorialization, both having negative and positive effects.

Biographical Note

Matthew G. Whitlock (PhD, The Catholic University of America, 2008) is Associate Professor of New Testament at Seattle University. His research focuses on Acts of the Apostles, the Apostle Paul, New Testament Poetry, Critical Theory, and Science Fiction. His publications have focused on topics ranging from New Testament poetry in the *Catholic Biblical Quarterly* to the Body without Organs and Christianity in *Deleuze and Guattari Studies*. He is currently working on two books on dialectical images, one on images from the Science Fiction of Philip K. Dick and images from the letters of Paul, and the other on the theme of fame in images from the life of Kurt Cobain and early Christian writings about Jesus of Nazareth.

Bibliography: Primary and Key Secondary Texts

A. Primary Literature

The original French publications are listed for the sake of presenting a chronology of Deleuze and Guattari's work.

---

capture "the event." See John Mullarkey, "Deleuze," in *Alain Badiou: Key Concepts* (ed. A. J. Bartlett and Justin Clemens; Durham: Acumen, 2010), 168–75, here 169–70.
91. Deleuze, "He Stuttered," 109.
92. Deleuze, "He Stuttered," 109.

Deleuze and Guattari

Anti-Oedipus: Capitalism and Schizophrenia. Translated by Robert Hurley, Mark Seem, and Helen R. Lane. Minneapolis, MN: University of Minnesota Press, 1983. Translation of *Capitalisme et schizophrénie tome 1: l'Anti-Oedipe.* Paris: Éditions de Minuit, 1972.

Kafka: Towards a Minor Literature. Translated by Dana Polan. Minneapolis, MN: University of Minnesota Press, 1986. Translation of *Kafka: Pour une litterature mineure.* Paris: Éditions de Minuit, 1975.

A Thousand Plateaus: Capitalism and Schizophrenia. Translated by Brian Massumi. Minneapolis, MN: University of Minnesota Press, 1987. Translation of *Capitalisme et schizophrenie tome 2: Mille plateaux.* Paris: Éditions de Minuit, 1980.

What Is Philosophy? Translated by Hugh Tomlinson and Graham Burchill. London: Verso, 1994. Translation of *Qu'est-ce que la philosophie?* Paris: Éditions de Minuit, 1991.

Gilles Deleuze: Major Works

"Du Christ à la bourgeoisie," *Espace* 1 (1946): 93–106. For an English translation, see Gilles Deleuze, "From Christ to Bourgeoisie." Translated by Raymond van de Wiel. http://documents.raymondvandewiel.org/from_christ_to_the_bourgeoisie_translation.pdf

Empiricism and Subjectivity: An Essay on Hume's Theory of Human Nature. Translated by Constantin V. Boundas. New York: Columbia University Press, 1991. Translation of *Empirisme et subjectivité: Essai sur la Nature humaine selon Hume.* Paris: Presses Universitaires de France, 1953.

Nietzsche and Philosophy. Translated by Hugh Tomlinson; London: Athlone, 1983. Translation of *Nietzsche et la philosophie.* Paris: Presses Universitaires de France, 1962.

Kant's Critical Philosophy: The Doctrine of the Faculties. Translated by Hugh Tomlinson and Barbara Habberjam. London: Athlone, 1984. Translation of *La Philosophie critique de Kant: Doctrine des facultés.* Paris: Presses Universitaires de France, 1963.

Proust and Signs: The Complete Text. Translated by Richard Howard. Minneapolis: University of Minnesota, 2003. Translation of *Proust et les signes.* Paris: Presses Universitaires de France, 1964, 1970, 1976.

Bergsonim. Translated by Hugh Tomlinson and Barbara Habberjam. New York: Zone, 1990. Translation of *Le Bergsonisme.* Paris: Presses Universitaires de France, 1966.

Masochism: An Interpretation of Coldness and Cruelty. Translated by Jean McNeil. New York: G. Braziller, 1971. Translation of *Présentation de Sacher-Masoch.* Paris: Minuit, 1967.

Expressionism in Philosophy. Translate by Martin Joughin. New York: Zone, 1992. Translation of *Spinoza et le problème de l'expression.* Paris: Éditions de Minuit, 1968.

Difference and Repetition. Translated by Paul Patton. New York: Columbia University Press, 1994. Translation of *Différence et répétition.* Paris: Presses Universitaires de France, 1968.

The Logic of Sense. Translated by Mark Lester and Charles Stivale. New York: Columbia University Press, 1990. Translation of *Logique du sens.* Paris: Éditions de Minuit, 1969.

Spinoza: Practical Philosophy. Translated by Robert Hurley. San Francisco, CA: City Lights Books, 1988. Translation of *Spinoza: Philosophie pratique.* Paris: Presses Universitaires de France, 1981.
Francis Bacon: Logic of Sensation. Translated by Daniel W. Smith. Minneapolis, MN: University of Minnesota Press, 1986. Translation of *Francis Bacon: Logique de la sensation.* Paris: Editions de la difference, 1981.
Cinema I: The Movement-Image. Translation by Hugh Tomlinson and Barbara Habberjam. Minneapolis, MN: University of Minnesota Press, 1986. Translation of *Cinéma I: l'Image-Mouvement.* Paris: Éditions de Minuit, 1983.
Cinema II: The Time-Image. Translated by Hugh Tomlinson and Barbara Habberjam. Minneapolis, MN: University of Minnesota Press, 1989. Translation of *Cinéma II: l'Image-temps.* Paris: Éditions de Minuit, 1986.
Foucault. Translated by Sean Hand. Minneapolis, MN: University of Minnesota Press, 1988. Translation of *Foucault.* Paris: Éditions de Minuit, 1986.
The Fold: Leibniz and the Baroque. Translated by Tom Conley. Minneapolis, MN: University of Minnesota Press, 1993. Translation of *Le Pli: Leibniz et le Baroque.* Paris: Minuit, 1988.
Negotiations: 1972–1990. Translated by Martin Joughin. New York: Columbia University Press, 1995. Translation of *Pourparlers 1972–1990.* Paris: Éditions de Minuit, 1990.
"He Stuttered," 107–14 in *Essays: Critical and Clinical.* Translated by D. W. Smith and M. A. Greco; Minneapolis, MN: University of Minnesota Press, 1997.
Gilles Deleuze and Claire Parnet, *Dialogues.* Revised edition. Translated by Barbara Habberjam, et al. New York: Columbia University Press, 2002.

Félix Guattari: Selected Works

Psychoanalysis and Transversality: Texts and Interviews 1955–1971. Translated by Ames Hodges. South Pasadena, CA: Semiotext(e), 2015 [1972].
Schizoanalytic Cartographies. Translated by Andrew Goffey. New York: Continuum, 2012 [1989].
The Three Ecologies. Translated by Ian Pindar and Paul Sutton. London: Continuum, 2008 [1989].
Chaosmosis: An Ethico-Aesthetic Paradigm. Translated by Julian Pefanis. Bloomington, IN: Indiana University Press, 1995 [1992].
"Modèles de contraine et modélisation créative" (April 1991), in *Chimères* 28 (1996).
The Guattari Reader. Edited by Gary Genosko. Translated by Sophie Thomas. Oxford: Blackwell, 1996.

B. Secondary Literature: Life, Context, Work, and Concepts

Colebrook, Claire. *Gilles Deleuze.* Routledge Critical Thinkers; Abingdon: Routledge, 2002.
Crockett, Clayton. *Deleuze beyond Badiou: Ontology, Multiplicity, and the Event.* New York: Columbia University Press, 2013.
Culp, Andrew. *Dark Deleuze.* Forerunners: Ideas First. Minneapolis, MN: University of Minnesota Press, 2016.
Dosse, François. *Gilles Deleuze & Félix Guattari: Intersecting Lives.* Translated by Deborah Glassman. New York: Columbia University Press, 2010.

—"Deleuze and Structuralism," 126–50 in Smith and Somers-Hall, eds., *The Cambridge Companion to Deleuze*.
Flaxman, Gregory. *Gilles Deleuze and the Fabulation of Philosphy*. Minneapolis, MN: University of Minnesota Press, 2012.
Mullarkey, John. "Deleuze," 168–75 in *Alain Badiou: Key Concepts*. Edited by A. J. Bartlett and Justin Clemens. Durham: Acumen, 2010.
Parr, Adrian, ed. *The Deleuze Dictionary*. Revised edition. Edinburgh: Edinburgh University Press, 2010.
Patton, Paul. "Deleuze's Political Philosophy," 198–219 in Smith and Somers-Hall, eds., *The Cambridge Companion to Deleuze*. .
Smith, Daniel W., and Henry Somers-Hall, eds. *The Cambridge Companion to Deleuze*. Cambridge: Cambridge University Press, 2012.
Williams, James. "*Difference and Repetition* as Transcendental Empiricism," 33–54 in Smith and Somers-Hall, eds., *The Cambridge Companion to Deleuze*.

C. Secondary Literature: Theology, Religious Studies, and Biblical Studies

Aichele, George. *Simulating Jesus: Reality Effects in the Gospels*. Abingdon: Routledge, 2014. https://doi.org/10.4324/9781315729237
—"Deleuze on Film, and the Bible," 238–47 in *T&T Clark Companion to the Bible and Film*. Edited by Richard Walsh. London: T&T Clark, 2018. https://doi.org/10.5040/9780567666239.0026
Berger, Klaus. *Identity and Experience in the New Testament*. Translated by Charles Muenchow. Minneapolis, MN: Fortress Press, 2003.
Justaert, Kristien. "'*Ereignis*' (Heidegger) or 'La Clameur de l'etre' (Deleuze): Topologies for a Theology beyond Representation," *Philosophy and Theology* 19.1–2 (2007): 241–56. https://doi.org/10.5840/philtheol2007191/213
—*Theology after Deleuze*. Deleuze Encounters. New York: Continuum, 2012. https://doi.org/10.5040/9781350251908
—"Gilles Deleuze (1925–1995)," 37–82 in *Religion and European Philosophy: Key Thinkers from Kant to Žižek*. Edited by Philip Goodchild and Hollis Phelps. New York: Routledge, 2017. https://doi.org/10.4324/9781315642253-32
McLean, Bradley H. "Re-imagining New Testament Interpretation in Terms of Deleuzian Geophilosophy," *Neotestamentica* 42.1 (2008): 51–72.
—"The Embodied Interpreter: Deleuze and Guattari," 268–301 in *Biblical Interpretation and Philosophical Hermeneutics*. Cambridge: Cambridge University Press, 2012.
—"What Does *A Thousand Plateaus* Contribute to the Study of Early Christianity?" *Deleuze and Guattari Studies* 14.3 (2020): 533–53. https://doi.org/10.3366/dlgs.2020.0415
Myles, Robert. "The Fetish for a Subversive Jesus," *Journal for the Study of the Historical Jesus* 14:1 (2016): 1–14. http://booksandjournals.brillonline.com/content/journals/10.1163/17455197-01401005
Niemoczynsk, Leon. "Nature's Transcendental Creativity: Deleuze, Corrington, and an Aesthetic Phenomenology," *American Journal of Theology & Philosophy* 34.1 (2013): 17–34. https://doi.org/10.5406/amerjtheophil.34.1.0017
Sherman, Jacob Holsinger. "No Werewolves in Theology? Transcendence, Immanence, and Becoming-Divine in Gilles Deleuze," *Modern Theology* 25.1 (2009): 1–20. https://doi.org/10.1111/j.1468-0025.2008.01501.x

Van de Wiel, Raymond. "From Christ to the Bourgeoisie: Deleuze, Spiritualism, Sartre and the World." Paper presented at the Third Interanational Deleuze Studies Conference, Amsterdam, The Netherlands, 13 July 2010. http://raymondvandewiel.org/post/127463632357/from-christ-to-the-bourgeoisie-deleuze

Vander Stichele, Caroline. "The Head of John and its Reception or How to Conceptualize 'Reception History,'" 79–93 in *Scriptural Traces: Critical Perspectives on the Reception and Influence of the Bible*. Edited by Claudia V. Camp, W. J. Lyons, and Andrew Mein. Library of Hebrew Bible/Old Testament Studies, 615. London: Bloomsbury, T&T Clark, 2015.

Whitlock, Matthew G. "The Wrong Side Out With(out) God: An Autopsy of the Body Without Organs," *Deleuze and Guattari Studies* 14.3 (2020): 507–32. https://doi.org/10.3366/dlgs.2020.0414

D. Other Secondary Literature

Adorno, Theodor. "Introduction to Benjamin's *Schriften*," 8–9 in *On Walter Benjamin: Critical Essays and Recollections*. Edited by Gary Smith. Cambridge, MA: MIT Press, 1988.

Ballard, Susan. "The Audience and the Art Machine: Janet Cardiff and George Bures Miller's *Opera for a Small Room*," 125–48 in *Deleuze and the Schizoanalysis of Visual Art*. Edited by Ian Buchanan and Lorna Collins. London: Bloomsbury, 2014. https://doi.org/10.5040/9781472594303.ch-006

Chatterjee, Partha. "Nationalism as a Problem," 126–8 in *The Post-Colonial Studies Reader 2nd Edition*. Edited by Bill Ashcroft, Gareth Griffiths, and Helen Tiffin. New York: Routledge, 1995.

Cohen, Jared, and Eric Schmidt. *The New Digital Age: Reshaping the Future of People, Nations, and Business*. New York: Doubleday, 2013.

Dale, Laura. "With *The Matrix 4* Coming, Let's Talk About How the First Movie Is a Trans Allegory." *SYFY Wire*, 2020. https://www.syfy.com/syfywire/with-the-matrix-4-coming-lets-talk-about-how-the-first-movie-is-a-trans-allegory

De Landa, Manuel. *A Thousand Years of Nonlinear History*. Edited by Jonathan Crary, et al. New York: Swerve, 2000.

Elkaïm, Mony. *If You Love Me, Don't Love Me: Constructions of Reality and Change in Family Therapy*. New York: Basic Books, 1990.

Helmling, Steven. *Adorno's Poetics of Critique*. New York: Continuum, 2009.

Lamm, Spencer, ed. *The Art of the Matrix*. New York: Newmarket Press, 2000.

Marantz, Andrew. "Trolls for Trump: Meet Michael Cernovich, the Meme Mastermind of the Alt-Right." *The New Yorker*, 31 October 2016.

Massumi, Brian. *Parables for the Virtual*. Durham, NC: Duke University Press, 2002. https://doi.org/10.1215/9780822383574

Miller, Frank, and Geof Darrow. *Hard Boiled*. Milwaukie, OR: Dark Horse Books, 1993.

Nietzsche, Friedrich. *On the Advantage and Disadvantage of History for Life*. Translated by Peter Preuss. Indianapolis, IN: Hackett, 1980.

Nigianni, Chrysanthi. *Deleuze and Queer Theory*. Edinburgh: University of Edinburgh Press, 2009.

Novis, Kenneth. "Deleuze and MeToo." *KennethNovis* (blog). *Wordpress*, 13 April 2020. https://kennethnovis.wordpress.com/2020/04/13/deleuze-and-metoo

Penny, Laura. "Parables and Politics: How Benjamin and Deleuze & Guattari Read Kafka," *Theory & Event* 12.3 (2009). https://doi.org/10.1353/tae.0.0083

Pérez, R. "What is 'Minor' in Latino Literature," *Multi-Ethnic Literature of the United States* 30 (2005): 89–108. https://doi.org/10.1093/melus/30.4.89

Robinson, Andrew. "In Theory—Why Deleuze Still Matters: States, War Machines and Radical Transformation." *Ceasefire Magazine,* 10 September 2010. https://ceasefiremagazine.co.uk/in-theory-deleuze-war-machine

Suvin, Darko. "Circumstances and Stances: A Retrospect," 445–52 in *Metamorphoses of Science Fiction: On the Poetics and History of a Literary Genre.* Edited by Gerry Canavan. Ralahine Utopian Studies, 18. Bern: Peter Lang, 2016.

Wachowski, Lana, and Lilly Wachowski. *The Matrix.* Warner Brothers, 1999.

Chapter Six

The Deleuzioguattarian Body of Christ without Organs

Bradley H. McLean

The traditional distinction between the "Jesus of history" and the "Christ of faith" is as relevant to Pauline theology as it is anywhere in the New Testament.[1] But even Paul's Christ of faith had material dimensions in the form of the "Christ groups" (ἐκκλησίαι), each of which materially embodied the "body of Christ":[2] "Now you are the body of Christ (σῶμα Χριστοῦ) and individually parts of it" (1 Cor. 12.27, cf. Rom. 12.4-5). In this chapter I will argue that the Pauline "body of Christ" possessed material coordinates by virtue of being a Deleuzian "body without organs" (*corps sans organes*), abbreviated as "BwO" (CsO).[3] In making this point, I am not arguing that Paul conceptualized Christ groups in language that can be assimilated to Deleuze's "body without organs."[4] On the contrary, I will argue that each Pauline Christ group was formed, *in a most literal sense,* as a "body o*f Christ* without organs," which is to say, as a self-organizing system, without reference to a transcendental plane.

---

1. Gotthold Lessing (1729–1781) was the first to distinguish between the "Jesus of history" and the "Christ of faith," a distinction which was later expanded upon by Martin Kähler in his book, *The So-Called Historical Jesus and the Historic Biblical Christ* (trans. C. E. Braaten; Philadelphia, PA: Fortress Press, 1964 [1896]).

2. In place of the term "church," I employ the term "Christ group" or "Christ association" on the grounds that no recognizably "church," with a closed canon of scripture, bishops, doctrines, and creeds existed prior to the fourth century CE; cf. John S. Kloppenborg, *Christ's Associations: Connecting and Belonging in the Ancient City* (New Haven, CT: Yale University Press, 2019).

3. Deleuze was not a materialist. He understood the actual (material) plane and virtual plane as asymmetrical aspects of a single, univocal plane of becoming. He argued that the virtual is real, and immanent to the actual; cf. Gilles Deleuze, *Difference and Repetition* (trans. Paul Patton; New York: Columbia University Press, 1994), 208. However, this article will focus on the dynamics of the actual, material plane of existence.

4. Deleuze's creation of new terms goes hand in hand with his effort to transform thinking-as-representation (arguing that 'this is that') into thinking-as-experimentation. He demonstrates how the four elements of representational thinking subordinate difference to conceptual categories of identity, opposition, analogy, and resemblance; cf. Bradley H. McLean, "Deleuze's Interpretation of Job as a Heroic Figure in the History of Rationality," *Religions* 10.141 (Feb. 2019): 1–8.

In more general terms, the two primary aims of this chapter are, first, to introduce the Deleuzian concept of a "body without organs" to biblical scholars and, second, to apply this concept to the study of Christian origins. Since no significant encounter between Deleuze and Guattari and biblical studies has yet been established, this chapter constitutes a kind of conversation starter.[5] But since it is not possible to address the Pandora's box of related philosophical and theological issues, this chapter constitutes little more than a gesture towards future engagements with Deleuzian philosophy in the field of Christian origins. This chapter will argue that the concept of a "body *of Christ* without organs" opens up insights that are beyond the reach of standard historiographical methodologies.

Deleuze's distinctive term for a "body" formed through autoproduction is "body without organs" (*corps sans organes*). As I shall explain below, a "body without organs" actually *does* possess organs, but its organs have been disorganized (de-organ-ized). This is a body that has not (yet) been organized, or overcoded, by the State apparatus. This chapter will analyze the Pauline "body of Christ" in terms of a Deleuzian "body (of Christ) without organs."[6]

This application of Deleuzian terminology to Pauline theology is also defensible on Deleuzian grounds: In their book, *Anti-Oedipus*, Deleuze and Guattari explicitly state that "Christ's body is engineered on all sides and in all fashions, pulled in all directions, playing the role of a full body without organs."[7] The Deleuzian "body without organs" is ideally suited to elucidate Paul's "body of Christ" because the concept of a Deleuzian "body without organs" is not limited to individuals, but is equally applicable to supra-individual bodies such as religious voluntary associations, and even the entire Roman Empire. For Deleuzian philosophy there is no substantive difference between the "body without organs" of an individual, group, or the State.[8]

In what follows, I will describe how a "body *of Christ* without organs" could have formed in the Greco-Roman world through a series of three

---

5. For an overview of the potential contributions of Deleuzian philosophy to the study of Christian origins, see Bradley H. McLean, "What Does *A Thousand Plateaus* Contribute to the Study of Early Christianity?" *Deleuze and Guattari Studies* 14.3 (2020): 533–53.

6. "Overcoding is the operation that constitutes the essence of the State ... the dread of flows of desire that would resist coding, but also the establishment of a new inscription that overcodes, and that makes desire into the property of the sovereign"; see Félix Guattari, *Psychoanalysis and Transversality: Texts and Interviews 1955–1971* (trans. Ames Hodges; South Pasadena, CA: Semiotext(e), 2015 [1972]), 162.

7. Gilles Deleuze and Félix Guattari, *Anti-Oedipus: Capitalism and Schizophrenia* (trans. Robert Hurley; Minneapolis, MN: University of Minnesota Press, 1983), 369.

8. Guattari, *Psychoanalysis and Transversality,* 209–10.

passive syntheses, without reference to a transcendental plane. These three passive syntheses occur at a pre-individual level, lacking self-comprehension, intentionality, purpose, or goal. In the first passive synthesis, termed a *connective* synthesis, a proto "body of Christ without organs" was formed, outside of a determined state. In the second passive synthesis, termed a *disjunctive* synthesis, this BwO developed boundaries when a surplus value (Christ) formed from the accumulation of the recordings (memories) of good and bad flows over the course of time. This newly bounded "body of Christ without organs" fluctuated between two different behaviors: Alternating between a "paranoid" BwO and a "schizoid" BwO, its surplus value would first repel its organs (members), and then attract them. In the third passive synthesis, termed a *conjunctive* synthesis, the first and second passive syntheses conflated, whereby the "body of Christ without organs" became capable of distributing its flows and intensities in ways that did not conform to either the proto BwO, or the organizing principles of the paranoiac/schizoid BwO. At this point, either a "full" or "empty" "body of Christ without organs" was formed.

What Can a Body Do?

In 1 Corinthians 12.27, Paul declares to the Corinthian Christ followers, "you are the body of Christ (σῶμα Χριστοῦ) and individually organs (μέλη) of it." Similarly, in Romans 12.4-5 he declares "we, who are many, are one body (ἓν σῶμα) in Christ, and individually organs (μέλη) of it." The Greek term *melos* (μέλος, pl. μέλη) in 1 Corinthians 12.27 and Romans 12.5 designates an "organ" or "part" of a human body.[9] Paul employs this term repeatedly in 1 Corinthians 12.12-27 in his list of the organs (eyes and ears) and parts (hands and feet) that belong to the "body of Christ" (see my discussion below). At the outset, let us consider a simple example, found in 1 Corinthians 6.15, where Paul employs the same term in his rhetorical question, "Do you not know that your bodies are organs/parts (μέλη) of Christ?" One might suppose that Paul's language is metaphorical, but in 1 Corinthians 6.15-16 he makes no distinction between the "organs of Christ" (μέλη Χριστοῦ) and the very real, sexual "organs of a prostitute" (πόρνης μέλη). On this basis it can be argued that when Paul states that the Corinthians are "individually" (ἐκ μέρους) the organs and parts of Christ's body (σῶμα), his language is not figurative, but literal.

---

9. F. Danker, *A Greek-English Lexicon of the New Testament and other Early Christian Literature* (3rd edn.; Chicago, IL: University of Chicago Press, 2000), 628.

What can a body do by virtue of possessing organs? Spinoza defined a "body" dynamically in terms of its capacity for motion: "Bodies are distinguished from one another by reason of motion and rest, speed and slowness, and not by reason of substance."[10] According to Spinoza, the capacity of a body to affect, and be affected, is not a constant property, but rather is an attribute that changes according to "the nature of the body affected and at the same time from the nature of the affecting body, so that one and the same body may be moved differently according to the differences in the nature of the body moving it."[11] In taking up Spinoza's famous question, "What can a body do?" Deleuze defines a body *kinetically* in terms of the flows, and the ruptures of flows, between itself and other bodies. Following Spinoza, Deleuze defines bodies *dynamically* in terms of a body's overall capacity "for affecting and being affected" by these other bodies.[12] On the plane of consistency—our lifeworld—all bodies are perpetually in flux, affecting and being affected by other bodies, adjusting themselves to each other's shifting presences. It was this changing *capacity* of the "body of Christ" in Corinth, Philippi, and elsewhere to affect and be affected differently by other bodies at different times that defined their identity as groups.

Christ Followers and Christ Groups as Machines

A bounded set of machines, or organs, constitutes a body without organs.[13] For machines and a body without organs are two forms of one and the *same* body: Machines "are the direct powers of the body without organs, and the body without organs, the raw material" of machines.[14] Deleuze also

---

10. Baruch Spinoza, "Ethics," in *The Collected Works of Spinoza,* vol. 1 (ed. and trans. Edwin Curley; Princeton, NJ: Princeton University Press, 1985), 1:401–617, esp. 458.
11. Spinoza, "Ethics," 460.
12. Gilles Deleuze, *Spinoza: Practical Philosophy* (trans. Robert Hurley; San Francisco, CA: City Lights Books, 1988), 18, 123–4.
13. The term "body without organs" was first coined by the avant-garde poet and playwright, Antonin Artaud. The sixth chapter of *A Thousand Plateaus,* entitled "November 28, 1947: How Do You Make Yourself a Body without Organs?" is an oblique reference to Artaud's radio play entitled "To Have Done with the Judgment of God" ("*Pour en finir avec le jugement de dieu*"), which he recorded between 22–29 November 1947, just shortly before his death. Antonin Artaud, who suffered from schizophrenia, referred to his body as "this ill-assembled heap of organs"; cf. Susan Sontag (ed.), *Antonin Artaud: Selected Writings* (trans. Helen Weaver; New York: Farrar, Straus & Giroux, 1976), 571.
14. Félix Guattari, *The Guattari Reader* (ed. Gary Genosko; trans. Sophie Thomas; Oxford: Blackwell, 1996), 81.

conceptualizes bodies as "machines—real ones, not figurative ones," whose organs and parts interact with other bodies.[15] "Machines" and "machinic processes" entail the flow of non-exchangeable and non-substitutable a-signifying singularities that act on structures *from the outside*.[16] The concept of "machines" introduces uncertainty and indeterminacy into the fixity of bodily structures. Any bodily part or organ that connects to the part or organ of any other body *to produce a flow* between them is a "machine."[17] Hence, machines supply the "working parts" of a body, with the machines of one body connecting to, and disconnecting from, the machines of other bodies, allowing various kinds of flows—semiotic, material, and libidinal—to be conducted.[18]

Machines are always binary, with one machine coupled to another so as to produce, or draw in, a flow: one machine "produces a flow that the other (receives and) interrupts" it.[19] In the case of an infant, its mouth-machine temporarily connects to a breast-machine (of its mother) to draw in a flow of milk. In the case of a man and woman having sexual intercourse, a penis-machine is temporarily "joined" (κολληθήσεται) to a vagina-machine to transmit a flow of semen with the result that "the two bodies become *one flesh*" (Matt. 19.5 citing Gen. 2.24). Paul employs a similar example in the case of the coupling of the penis-machine of a Christ follower to the vagina-machine of a prostitute. Paul reasons that, since a Christ follower is also an organ or machine (μέλος) of the body of Christ, *Christ's* body actually becomes joined to the body of the prostitute through the act of sexual intercourse: a new "Christ-prostitute" body is thereby *formed* that is comprised of "one flesh" (σάρκα μία):

> Do you not know that your bodies are organs/machines (μέλη) of Christ? Should I then take the organs of Christ (μέλη Χριστοῦ) and make them organs of a prostitute (πόρνης μέλη)? ... Do you not know that he who is joined (κολλώμενος) to a prostitute becomes *one body* (with her)? (1 Cor. 6.15-16)

But prior to the flow of semen, these two bodies were in a *non-relation*: the networks of forces, which constituted each body were undifferenciated.[20]

---

15. Deleuze and Guattari, *Anti-Oedipus*, 1.
16. Despite my references to "Deleuzian" philosophy in this article, we should not forget that Félix Guattari contributed many of the primary concepts to their collaborative works including the concept of a "machine" and "machinic processes"; cf. Guattari, "Machine and Structure," in *Psychanalysis and Transversality*, 318–29.
17. Deleuze and Guattari, *Anti-Oedipus*, 36–9.
18. Deleuze and Guattari, *Anti-Oedipus*, 5.
19. Deleuze and Guattari, *Anti-Oedipus*, 1.
20. The behavior of a body is governed by its virtual "capacity" or "force" (*puissance*) and "power" (*pouvoir*). The term "force" refers the potential of a body to *affect* or

But, through the action of one of Christ's machines or organs (a Christ follower), Christ's own body was accorded the capacity "to penetrate sexually" the body of a prostitute, while the prostitute's body simultaneously possessed the corresponding capacity "to be sexually penetrated." In the moment of sexual penetration, these two bodily networks of forces interacted and were differentiated—actively and reactively—in terms of a relation of power. What is crucial for our own analysis of this differentiation is not the separate virtual networks of force of the body of Christ and the body of the prostitute respectively, but the result when these two networks of force become differentiated.[21] Through intra-action, a "Christ-prostitute" body formed, which did not conform to any pre-existing category of bodies.[22]

Desiring-production

The flows and rupture of flows between machines (organs) is termed "desiring-production." In its natural (unrepressed) state, the human body is comprised of a bounded group of machines—eyes, ears, nose, skin, stomach, mouth, and anus—which, by virtue of being porously connected to the lifeworld, are connected to other machines by various kinds of flows (sights, sounds, smells, sensations, and substances). A human mouth-machine wavers between functioning as an eating-machine, breathing-machine, speech-machine, and kissing-machine. When Paul visited the Corinthian church, his speech-machine was connected to the ear-machines of the Corinthians. But when he was absent, his speech-machine was connected to the eye-machines of the Corinthians by means of a writing-machine (amanuensis). At the outset of *Anti-Oedipus*, Deleuze describes the desiring-production that surrounds us in the most vivid language:

> [Desiring production] is at work everywhere, functioning smoothly at times, at other times in fits and starts. It breaths, it heats, it eats. It shits and fucks ... Everywhere *it* is machines—real ones, not figurative ones: machines driving other machines, machines being driven by other machines, with all necessary couplings and connections.[23]

---

be affected by another body. For example, a human body possesses the virtual capacity to be joyful, independently of any instance of actual rejoicing. The term "power" (*pouvoir*) entails the "differentiation" or resolution of networks of forces, by which affects are produced, which may be productive, destructive, aesthetic, informational, and so forth.

21. Brian Massumi, *Parables for the Virtual* (Durham, NC: Duke University Press, 2002), 15; Deleuze, *Spinoza: Practical Philosophy*, 125.

22. On "intra-action" see Karen Barad, *Meeting the Universe Halfway* (Durham, NC: Duke University Press, 2007), 56, 153.

23. Deleuze and Guattari, *Anti-Oedipus*, 1.

Similarly, the desiring-production of the body of Jesus was accomplished through his hand-machines, mouth-machine, and so forth, which conducted flows that healed, fed, and taught the bodies of the sick and disabled, of fishermen, tax collectors, the rich and poor alike. From this vantage point, understanding the life of Jesus does not entail an exegesis of his teachings, but grasping the desiring-production that was at work through his body.

Likewise, Christ groups can be theorized as little machines, connected to other machines of widely ranging types and magnitudes. From the perspective of these machinic processes, Christ groups were defined less by their beliefs, norms, and forms of organization, than they were by the countless machines that coupled with them. For example, Paul mentions flows of money (1 Cor. 16.1-4; 2 Cor. 8–9; Rom. 15.25-28), personal letters (1 Cor. 5.9; 7.1), and people between various types of machines.[24] In 1 Corinthians 11.23-24, he discusses how flows of Eucharistic bread and wine connected the machines (members) of the body of Christ, unifying it as a single body. As Deleuze observes, "Eating bread and drinking wine are interminglings of bodies; communing with Christ is also an intermingling of bodies, properly spiritual bodies that *are no less 'real'* for being spiritual."[25] Similarly, consider the flows of flows of people, information, and gifts between the Philippian Christ group, considered as such a "body," and the "body" of Paul during the period of his imprisonment in the governor's palace (Phil. 1.13).[26] Paul also illustrates this principle of co-functioning in 1 Corinthians 12.14-20, 27, in which the Greek term, μέλος (organ) can be glossed as "machine":

> ... the body is not made up of one machine (μέλος) but many. Now if the foot-machine should say, "Because I am not a hand-machine, I do not belong to the body," it would not for that reason stop belonging to the body. And if the ear-machine should say, "Because I am not an eye-machine, I do not

---

24. E.g., "Chloe's people" (1 Cor. 1.11), Stephanas, Fortunatus, and Achaïcus (1 Cor. 16.15-18), Apollo and Cephas (1 Cor. 1.11-12, 3.4, 3.22), and Timothy (1 Cor. 4.17. 16.10).

25. Gilles Deleuze and Félix Guattari, *A Thousand Plateaus: Capitalism and Schizophrenia* (trans. Brian Massumi; Minneapolis, MN: University of Minnesota Press, 1987), 81.

26. These flows can be mapped as follows: (1) news of Paul's imprisonment reached the Philippians (Phil. 4.18); (2) then Epaphroditus is dispatched to Paul with a gift of money (Phil. 4.18); (3) later, news of Epaphroditus' illness reaches Philippi (Phil. 2.26); and, (4) news reaches Epaphroditus about how the Philippians received this news (Phil. 2.26); (5) next, Epaphroditus returns to Philippi (and delivers Paul's letter to Philippians) (Phil. 2.28-29); lastly, (6) Timothy is then sent by Paul to Philippi (Phil. 2.19, 23); (7) he later returns to Paul with news (Phil. 2.19); (8) Paul himself later visits them (Phil. 2.24).

belong to the body," it would not for that reason stop belong of the body. If the whole body were an eye-machine, where would hearing happen? If the whole body were an ear-machine, where would smelling happen? But, in fact, God has placed the machines in the body, every one of them, just as God wanted them to be. If they were all the same machine, where would the body be? As it is, there are many machines, but one body ... Now you are the body of Christ and individually machines of it.

In the Greco-Roman world, machines functioned simultaneously at micro to macro scales of the desiring-production, from pre-individual and individual machines to progressively larger and more abstract machines, to the cosmos itself, the immense "body without organs," within which all machines had their place.[27] The Greco-Roman State apparatus was populated by countless machines of widely ranging kinds and magnitudes such as economic, judicial and military machines, not to mention kinship-machines, master-slave machines, honour-machines, benefaction-machines, funerary-machines, philosophical-school machines, synagogue-machines, Christ-machines, all of which overlapped, collided, and interpenetrated within differential networks. There is no privileged point of view from which to analyze the desiring-production that constituted the Greco-Roman world. Everywhere one looks, all one sees is the iterative process of machines connecting to machines, connected to yet more desiring-machines, *ad infinitum*.

The first Christ groups were porously connected by means of material, libidinal and semiotic flows to this vast world of machines. *Material* flows of wine, oil, grain, and slaves connected cities; there were flows of women between clans, flows of benefaction between patrons and clients, flows of soldiers between Roman provinces, flows of sacred texts between religious groups, flows of semen between men having sex with women and men having sex with men (1 Cor. 6.15-16; Rom. 1.26-27). There were flows of blood in battle fields and childbirth, during menstruation and animal sacrifice (1 Corinthians 8), flows of ships and money between ports. Of course, there were also *libidinal* flows of desire, disgust and hatred, trust and fear, joy and sadness, pride, shame, and passion between human bodies. What is more, *semiological* flows of discourse connected political assemblies and law courts; flows of hymns, prayers, and homilies connected the machines within Christ groups. In addition, we must not overlook the countless flows of a-signifying flows of particles-signs—percepts and affects—the "particles-waves" or "particles-signs" that animated all of life. In short, all that was observable and unobservable in the Greco-Roman world—the natural and

---

27. Guattari, *Psychoanalysis and Transversality,* 209–10; Gilles Deleuze and Félix Guattari, *Kafka: Toward a Minor Literature* (trans. Dana Polan; Minneapolis, MN: University of Minnesota Press, 1986), 64, 88.

cultural, the non-discursive and discursive—was interconnected by flows and the rupture of flows. The emergent Christ groups were situated at the intersection of many of these flows.

On this basis we can conclude that *the history of early Christianity was nothing more than a history of flows.* Consequently, any analysis of the historical emergence of early Christianity should include a study of the diverse flows that connected Christ groups to the Roman empire-machine, within which new bodies were continuously formed and unformed over the course of time. Scholars of Christian origins should ask, what machines were the first Christ groups plugged into, and what symptoms were produced in these groups through these couplings?

The Body of Christ without Organs

Each Christ group, being composed of machines, or organs (Christ followers), constituted a "body of Christ without organs": "Christ's body is engineered on all sides and in all fashions, pulled in all directions, playing the role of a full body without organs."[28] Comparable to the self-organization of an egg or embryo, the developmental process of becoming a "body of Christ without organs" occurred without external agency, intentionality or goal.[29] It was formed *immanently* through self-organization, without reference to an external transcendental plane.[30]

This is not to suggest that Deleuze rejects the concept of transcendence. He accords transcendence a derivative status by *defining it in terms of immanence,* arguing that transcendence is a secondary phenomenon that is produced within the plane of immanence. In Deleuzian philosophy, the term transcendence designates "that part within Being that keeps escaping our comprehension." Simply put, the transcendent is that which goes unthought: It is the "unthought … which cannot be thought and yet must be thought."[31] Deleuze's conceptualization of "immanent transcendence" opens up a way to understand an incarnational God of the cosmos, who is "non-hierarchical,

---

28. Deleuze and Guattari, *Anti-Oedipus*, 369.
29. Deleuze, *Difference and Repetition*, 97.
30. Leon Niemoczynsk, "Nature's Transcendental Creativity: Deleuze, Corrington, and an Aesthetic Phenomenology," *American Journal of Theology & Philosophy* 34.1 (2013): 17–34; Jacob Holsinger Sherman, "No Werewolves in Theology? Transcendence, Immanence, and Becoming-Divine in Gilles Deleuze," *Modern Theology* 25.1 (2009): 1–20.
31. Gilles Deleuze and Félix Guattari, *What Is Philosophy?* (trans. Janis Tomlinson and Graham Burchell III; New York: Columbia University Press, 1996), 59–60; Kristien Justaert, *Theology after Deleuze* (London: Continuum, 2012), 36.

non-representable ... and at the same time, as immanent."[32] From the perspective of immanent transcendence, "Christ was incarnated once, in order to show, that one time, the possibility of the impossible," that immanent transcendence is real.[33] Hence, we can still speak of the immanent transcendence of Christ within a Deleuzian framework.

A "body without organs" is formed immanently through three passive syntheses. Before explaining these syntheses in detail, I shall set out a brief overview of this process.

1. *Connective Synthesis:* In the first passive synthesis, an undifferenciated proto "body without organs," is formed, as a loosely bound group machines (organs).[34]
2. *Disjunctive Synthesis:* In the second passive synthesis, this proto "body without organs" forms a surplus value through internal self-repression, which gradually accrues the status of a quasi-cause, as a body "without (need of) organs," despite the fact that this surplus value is produced by, and is dependent on, the body's own organs. Over time, a relationship of repulsion and attraction develops between this surplus value (body without organs) and its organs.
3. *Conjunctive Synthesis:* In the third passive synthesis, the first and second passive syntheses become conflated, whereby the "body without organs" becomes capable of distributing its flows and intensities in ways that do not conform to either the BwO of the first or second passive syntheses. At this point a (productive) "full" or (self-destructive) "empty" body without organs, is formed.

---

32. Justaert, *Theology after Deleuze,* 36. We can catch a glimpse of an immanently transcendent Christ in Rom. 10.6-7, where Paul rewrites Deut. 30.12-14 to argue that the risen Christ did not "ascend into heaven" (i.e., to a transcendental plane above), nor "descend into the abyss" below, but rather now abides on earth, whereby Christ followers can attain righteousness before God (Rom. 10.9); cf. Francis Watson, *Paul and the Hermeneutics of Faith* (London: T&T Clark, 2004), 356–62.

33. Deleuze and Guattari, *What Is Philosophy?* 59.

34. For example, the Earth, before human habitation, was such a body without organs. Like a giant egg, it consisted of undifferenciated matter that developed through "involution"; cf. Deleuze and Guattari, *A Thousand Plateaus,* 40, 150–3. Deleuze and Guattari liken a "body without organs" to an egg, based on anthropological reports of Marcel Griaule on the creator goddess of the Dogon tribe of Mali. This goddess had the appearance of an egg. In the simplest version of the Dogon creation myth, the world originated from this egg; cf. Marcel Griaule and Germaine Dieterlen, "The Dogon," in Cyril Daryll Forde (ed.), *African Worlds; Studies in the Cosmological Ideas and Social Values of African Peoples* (London: Oxford University Press, 1954), 83–110, here 84.

A. The First Passive Synthesis: Connective Synthesis

In the first passive synthesis, machines (organs) connect to the other machines through intensive flows. This connective synthesis can be described as an "and then" iterative process, for it "ceaselessly establishes connections between semiotic chains, organizations of power ... and social struggles" through the exchange of material, libidinal and semiotic flows.[35] Through this "rhizomatic" process an undifferenciated proto "body without organs" is formed, which lacks determined boundaries. In point of fact, this undifferenciated "body without organs" actually *does* possess organs: The modifier "without organs" merely implies that the connections between its organs (machines) and the organs of other bodies are just as significant as the connections between the organs of its own body.

In the case of the Corinthian proto "body (of Christ) without organs," one would expect that during this connective synthesis no fixed boundaries would have existed between insiders (internal organs) and outsiders (organs of synagogues, pagan cults [1 Cor. 8.1–11.1], trade guilds [Acts 18.3], law courts [1 Cor. 6.1-11], prostitutes [1 Cor. 6.12-20], etc.). Indeed, this proto "body of Christ without organs" would have actually facilitated *ad hoc* connections to other organs. Christ followers, as the organs of this proto body, would have connected to other organs, without being restricted (repressed) by pre-established social structures, hierarchies, laws, or theological teachings, thereby facilitating the formation of extended intensive chains of machines, with no beginning, end, or center. Hence, this proto "body of Christ without organs" could be said to have the status of being "there" and not "there" at the same time.

B. The Second Passive Synthesis: Disjunctive Synthesis

In the disjunctive synthesis, the chains of organs, which were formed in the first passive synthesis, increasingly crisscross each other, forming interconnected networks that promote the transmission of flows between a select group of organs.[36] Productive and satisfying flows between organs are experienced as "good," while unproductive and unsatisfying flows are correspondingly experienced as "bad." For example, in the case of the body of an infant, its experience of the flow of breast milk into its mouth-machine, and the flow of feces out of its anus-machine, are both organized as "good" (satisfying, pleasurable) flows. The organs that produce and receive these flows

---

35. Deleuze and Guattari, *Anti-Oedipus*, 7, cf. 68–74.
36. Deleuze and Guattari, *Anti-Oedipus*, 75–83.

are termed "partial objects," a term borrowed from Melanie Klein.[37] Over time, the partial objects that produce and connect to good flows become more highly valued and accorded the status of "whole objects" (e.g., a mother's breast-machine), whereas partial objects that produce bad flows (such as pain) are repressed. Through the upgrading of some partial objects to the status of whole objects, and the downgrading and repression of other partial objects, a kind of virtual classificatory grid emerges.

All societies of the ancient world, each considered as a "body without organs," regarded unregulated flows of the human body as bad (dangerous), and therefore requiring repression, control, and prohibition. For example, in the case of Israelite society, the books of Leviticus and Deuteronomy are veritable handbooks on how to repress bodily flows of blood (Leviticus 12, 15), semen (Leviticus 15; Deut. 23.10), and feces (Deut. 23.12-14). Bad flows originating from women's reproductive organs, being inherently "leaky," posed a particular threat to the sanctity of the Temple.[38] Hence, parturition blood (Lev. 12.2-8), being impure (bad), is discussed in the same section as skin diseases, scabs, and weeping sores (Leviticus 13), and required control (Lev. 15.19-24). For this reason, when the twelve-year old Mary, the future mother of the Saviour of the world, approached the time of her menses, even *her* bodily flow of blood from her uterus-machine threatened to "defile the sanctuary" of the Lord (Prot. Jas. 8). The temple priests repressed her bad flows by expelling her from the Temple compound.

1. The Formation of a Surplus Value
Over the course of the disjunctive synthesis, what might be called "habitual" flows develop on the basis of the upgrading of good flows and repression of bad flows. These upgrading and downgrading processes are recorded in the raw substance of the body as a kind of memory. Even though this memory consists of nothing more than an accumulation of the recordings of past flows, it nonetheless gives rise to the illusion of a surplus value *that exists apart from, and in addition to,* the organs, that "remembers" them.[39]

Deleuze's theory of surplus value is rooted in Karl Marx's theorization of capital. In *Capital,* Marx explains how capitalism, through the expenditure

---

37. The term "partial objects" was first coined by Melanie Klein, who developed this term for body parts that take substances into their body and project substances outward because they are threatening; see Melanie Klein, *The Psychoanalysis of Children* (New York: Delacorte Press, 1975), 326–8.
38. Margrit Shildrick, *Leaky Bodies and Boundaries: Feminism, Postmodernism and (Bio)ethics* (New York: Routledge, 1997).
39. Deleuze and Guattari, *Anti-Oedipus,* 13, 326–7; Deleuze and Guattari, *A Thousand Plateaus,* 153.

of labor power, *adds value* to the commodity value of goods, resulting in a higher exchange value, the latter being linked to the cost of labor power.[40] Despite the fact that capital, as surplus value, depends on workers (the proletariat), it nonetheless gives rise to the illusion that that capital possesses an autonomous existence *apart from* the workers who create it.[41] Deleuze applies Marx's theory of surplus value to the development of the "body without organs."

In the case of the Corinthian "body *of Christ* without organs," the selection of good flows and repression of bad flows not only resulted in the formation of a body with distinct boundaries, it also simultaneously created a *surplus value*, a body of Christ without organs (members), which is to say, a body of Christ without the *need* of organs, having an autonomous existence apart from members, whose flows originally created it. Over time, this "body of Christ without organs," as a surplus value, accrued the status of a quasi-cause for the Christ group, its originating source, and regulator of all of its desiring-production, and residual memory of past flows.

2. The Paranoiac and Schizoid Body of Christ without Organs

The term "disjunctive synthesis" may seem contradictory: For the term "disjunction" implies a disorganization, whereas the term "synthesis" implies the opposite, a kind of organization into a larger whole. As I shall explain below, it is this very paradox that captures the essence of the body without organs. This body without organs actually alternates between disjunctive and synthesized forms, alternating between a paranoiac form, which *repels* its organs, and a schizoid ("miraculating") form, which attracts its organs:[42]

---

40. Commodity value is defined as the combined cost of raw materials and energy costs required for the production (constant capital) and the value of the labor power required to produce the product (variable capital). Surplus value *(Mehrwert)* is defined as the difference between the exchange value and commodity value. It is extracted from the working class as labor power, which accumulates in the form of capital. Marx makes a fundamental distinction between work *(Arbeit)* and labor power *(Arbeitskraft)*. He argues that while workers (the proletariat) may believe they sell their work to the ruling class (employers), what they actually sell is their labor power; cf. David Harvey, *The Enigma of Capital and the Crisis of Capitalism* (London: Profile Books, 2010), 11.

41. Karl Marx, *Capital: A Critique of Political Economy*, vol. 1 (1867), (trans. Ben Fowkes: Harmondsworth: Penguin, 1976), 169; cf. Mark Neocleous, "The Political Economy of the Dead: Marx's Vampires," *History of Political Thought* 24.4 (2003), 668–84, esp. 683.

42. The term to "miraculate" is derived from the memoire of Daniel Paul Schreber (1842–1911), who suffered from paranoiac schizophrenia. In his memoire entitled *Memoirs of My Nervous Illness*, Schreber chronicled the progress of his disease. One morning, he woke up with the thought that it would be pleasant to "succumb" to intercourse "as a woman" (i.e., a reference to anal intercourse). As his psychosis progressed,

> The paranoiac and the schizoid investments are like two opposite poles of unconscious libidinal investment, one of which subordinates desiring-production to the formation of sovereignty and to the gregarious aggregate that results from it, while the other brings about the inverse subordination, overthrows the established power, and subjects the gregarious aggregate to the molecular multiplicities of the productions of desire.[43]

In its paranoiac form, the BwO asserts its independence by repelling its organs as persecuting objects: For their very existence threatens to fragment the unity of the BwO. The result is a BwO that can be said to be "without organs" in the sense that it has repudiated its organs, which *do not belong* to it, but are only attached to it as *points of disjunction*.[44] In contrast, in its schizoid form, the same BwO attracts its organs by *repressing* their individual desiring-production, and organizing them as extensions of itself. Through attraction, these organs acquire the status of organs of the "body without organs." *This* body also can be said to be *without organs* in the sense that the individual organs have been repressed by combining them into a unified BwO. Over time, a rhythm is established in which the BwO oscillates between its paranoiac and the schizoid forms, as opposite poles ("attractors") of libidinal investment.

In the specific case of the paranoiac "body *of Christ* without organs," the organs (members) are sometimes characterized by disjunction: They are repelled by the "body of Christ"—a surplus value—as persecuting objects. For this "body of Christ" seemed to have an existence independently of them. Indeed, this "body of Christ" was *without* need of organs by virtue of having been *de-organ-ized*. This paranoiac body of Christ was organized *hierarchically*, with Christ situated at its apex (directly under God), to whose authority all members were subject. We find evidence of this paranoiac Christ in 1 Corinthians 11.3, where Paul states, "Christ is the head of every man, and the man is the head of a woman, and God is the head of Christ." Through Christ's authority, wives are subjected to the authority of their husbands, and husbands are subjected to the authority of a paranoiac Christ. Through the submission of women to men, and men to Christ, Christ (as surplus value) is accorded an autonomous existence and authority, which

---

he believed that God had *miraculously* turned his body into a woman's body by sending sunrays directly into his anus. Schreber's anus (organ) was miraculated by God so that his body seemed to emanate from God as a quasi-cause. Schreber figures prominently in the opening pages of *Anti-Oedipus*, as Deleuze and Guattari's primary example of an empty BwO (*Anti-Oedipus*, 2, 16, 18); cf. Chrysanthi Nigianni, *Deleuze and Queer Theory* (Edinburgh: University of Edinburgh Press, 2009), 157.

43. Deleuze and Guattari, *Anti-Oedipus*, 376.
44. Deleuze and Guattari, *Anti-Oedipus*, 18.

is independent of the desiring-production of the human bodies that created it.

The formation of this hierarchy through *internal* repression also rendered the Christ group suitable for additional *external* repression by the State apparatus. When the internal repression within the Christ group was reinforced by external the social repression of the State, all beliefs, behaviors, and meaning-effects that were not grounded in the social production of the State apparatus were prohibited. The Greco-Roman State apparatus overcoded the desiring-production of all its organs on the basis of illusory transcendentals. At this point, the desiring-production of Christ followers became little more than an *extension* of the social production of the State apparatus.[45] Thereafter, the individual bodies of male and female Christ followers were integrated into a set of normalizing, totalizing, and repressive social structures, such as we find in the household codes in Colossians 3.18–4.1, Ephesians 5.21–6.9 and 1 Peter 2.11–3.12. Thus, the paranoiac "body of Christ without organs" functioned as a societal system of judgment and social control.

But in its alternate, schizoid phase, the same "body of Christ without organs" was unified into a single "body of Christ," in which Christ followers functioned as living extensions of the body of Christ. This schizoid "body of Christ without organs" was organized as a circle, with Christ located at its center. The space between this center and the group's outer boundary was comprised of an amorphous continuum of organs (members) tasked with various ministries such as apostles, prophets, teachers, workers of miracles, healers, helpers, and so forth (1 Cor. 12.28-30). Paul argues that since these ministries are exercised in the *same* body of Christ, they are interdependent organs, and should therefore be valued equally.

C. The Third Passive Synthesis: Conjunctive Synthesis

Small groups such as Christ groups, which are characterized by the repressive determinism of the paranoiac and schizoid forms, nonetheless preserved the virtual capacity for limited degrees of freedom and creativity. For, in the course of a body without organ's oscillation between its paranoiac and schizoid forms, aleatory events sometimes occurred that produced function-based hybrids or mutations. Such mutations enable the BwO to distribute its flows and intensities in ways that do not conform to either the first or second passive synthesis.[46] By this means, a so-called "full" or "empty" "body without organs" can form. These are unpredictable

---

45. Deleuze and Guattari, *Anti-Oedipus*, 29.
46. Deleuze and Guattari, *A Thousand Plateaus*, 44.

hybrids in which the first and second passive syntheses become conjoined. A "full" BwO is a successful experiment: it is capable of resisting forms of both internal and external repression through deterritorialization in novel, productive ways. In contrast, an "empty" BwO is a failed experiment, one which has become self-destructive, through an excess of deterritorialization, such as the schizophrenic body of Daniel Schreber.[47] But in both cases, this body without organs has, to quote Antonin Artaud, managed to have done "with the judgment of God."[48]

The Contribution of Phase Space Theory

Deleuze and Guattari's theorization of the third passive synthesis received fresh stimulus when Ilya Prigogine and Isabelle Stengers published *Order Out of Chaos (1979)*. This book argued that the classical version of thermodynamics applied only to so-called "closed" systems, which is to say, to predictable, deterministic systems, whose range of behavior can be accurately predicted by standard methods of calculation. While complex or dynamical systems such as wind circuits, cyclones, tsunamis, and hurricanes, may behave like closed systems in the short-term, they are actually open systems that manifest long-term unpredictability and *display forms of self-organization*. When an intense flow of energy is injected into complex systems, such systems are pushed beyond their virtual attractors (thresholds) into a zone of sensitivity, in which minor increases in energy are amplified and force the system to change beyond its powers of recuperation.[49] When a bifurcation point or "schiz" is reached, such systems spontaneously self-organize and achieve a new phase space.[50] The term "phase space" refers to the multidimensional space where dynamic systems self-organize.

Deleuze and Guattari employed phase space theory to analyze how various types of complex bodies (systems) are capable of self-organization.[51] A case in point is the paranoiac/schizoid body without organs of the second

---

47. See note 42.
48. See note 13.
49. Manuel De Landa, *A Thousand Years of Nonlinear History* (ed. Jonathan Crary, et al.; New York: Swerve, 2000), 263.
50. Ilya Prigogine and Isabelle Stengers, *Order Out of Chaos* (London: Verso, 2017 [1984]), 177.
51. Guattari's first application of phase space theory was published in 1989 under the title *Schizoanalytic Cartographies* (trans. Andrew Goffey; New York: Continuum, 2012). Its translator, Andrew Goffey, describes this book as "one of the last big books of French 'theory'" (*Schizoanalytic Cartographies*, xv). Guattari developed his clinical schizoanalysis further in his next books, *The Three Ecologies (1989)*, and *Chaosmosis: An Ethico-aesthetic Paradigm* (1992).

passive synthesis, which behaves like a closed system, oscillating between its paranoiac to schizoid forms. In terms of phase space theory, one would say that its paranoiac and schizoid forms function as the attractors, and the fluctuation between these attractors represents "patterns of stability and becoming that are inherent in abstract dynamical systems."[52] The oscillation between the paranoiac and schizoid forms constitutes a BwO's "basin of attraction." However, when aleatory forces, so-called "rebel vibrations," flow into such a system, it is pushed beyond its attractors and sometimes propelled into a zone of sensitivity. When a bifurcation point or "schiz" is reached, a cybernetic feedback loop endogenously propels the BwO's phase state to transform on a molecular level.[53] "Schizoanalysis" is the Deleuzian term for the analysis of the effects of a schiz on different types of bodies.

In the case of a Christ group, considered as such a BwO, a schiz could function as the catalyst for dismantling a Christ group's structures of internal and external repression, and thereby give rise to a "full" BwO, and new forms of desiring-production beyond its former repertoires of behavior. As a starting point for the application of schizoanalysis to Christian origins, we must recognize that every "body of Christ without organs" was, to some extent, overcoded by the social production of the State apparatus, and hence was governed by a collective determinism. The net effect of such overcoding was to train Christ groups and Christ followers "to operate according to the norms of an established order."[54] Through overcoding, the State co-opted the desiring-production of Christ groups for the purposes of its own social production. A schizoanalysis of Christ groups would entail, first, identifying the organs of a particular Christ group, and understanding how these organs functioned in terms of the first and second passive syntheses. Next one would attempt to assess what surges of intensity could have induced, a schiz to precipitated the third passive synthesis. Alas, the question of whether or not Christ groups of the first three centuries did, in fact, experience such a schiz lies beyond the scope of this chapter. Suffice to say that Deleuze *does* maintain that forms of religion can be extricated from the social production of the State by entering "a more indistinct zone" in which there is a "possibility of undergoing a singular mutation or adaptation."[55] If Christ groups did undergo such a liberation of its desiring-production, the evidence of such a mutation would take the form of experimentation in ways of living together in relation to society at large.

---

52. De Landa, *Thousand Years of Nonlinear History,* 263.
53. Prigogine and Isabelle, *Order Out of Chaos,* 177.
54. Gilles Deleuze and Claire Parnet, *Dialogues II* (rev. edn.; trans. Barbara Habberjam; New York: Columbia University Press, 2002), 18.
55. Deleuze and Guattari, *A Thousand Plateaus,* 383.

Conclusion

What does the Deleuzian "body without organs" contribute to our understanding of first-century Christ groups? First, if we evacuate the transcendental plane from our analysis, then the formation of Christ groups can be theorized in terms of immanent processes, through which they emerged and developed through autoproduction. Like an egg or embryo, an emergent, undifferenciated "body of Christ" would have consisted of a loosely bound assemblage of organs, formed by means of a connective synthesis. In the second passive synthesis, a surplus-value-Christ emerged, when flows of intensities between machines were recorded in the raw matter of the group as a kind of residual memory. This self-organized "body of Christ without organs," would have oscillated between its paranoiac and schizoid forms, alternately repelling and the attracting its organs (members). Internal repression, augmented and complicated by the social repression, would have integrated the desiring production of this body of Christ into the social production of the State apparatus. But in the third passive synthesis, chance events in the daily life of this BwO would have introduced fresh intensities into this body, which, having reached sufficient intensity, would have induced schiz that functioned as a departure point for the re-organization of the body of Christ without organs. Through disruption of its structures of internal and external repression, its desiring-production could thereby be renewed, transforming it into a full body of Christ without organs.

Biographical Note

Bradley H. McLean is Professor of New Testament Language and Literature at the Toronto School of Theology and is cross-appointed to the University of Toronto's Department for the Study of Religion. He is the author of seven books, including *Biblical Interpretation and Philosophical Hermeneutics* (Cambridge University Press, 2012), as well as numerous articles on Deleuze and Guattari including 'What Does *A Thousand Plateaus* Contribute to the Study of Early Christianity? (*Deleuze and Guattari Studies,* 14.3, 2020) and 'Deleuze's Interpretation of Job as a Heroic Figure in the History of Rationality' (*Religions* 10.141, 2019). His latest volume is *Deleuze, Guattari and the Machine in Early Christianity: Schizoanalysis, Affect, and Multiplicity* (London: Bloomsbury Academic, 2022).

Bibliography

Barad, Karen. *Meeting the Universe Halfway.* Durham, NC: Duke University Press, 2007. https://doi.org/10.2307/j.ctv12101zq

Danker, F. *A Greek-English Lexicon of the New Testament and other Early Christian Literature*. 3rd edn. Chicago, IL: University of Chicago Press, 2000.
De Landa, Manuel. *A Thousand Years of Nonlinear History*. Edited by Jonathan Crary, et al. New York: Swerve, 2000.
Deleuze, Gilles. *Spinoza: Practical Philosophy*. Translated by Robert Hurley. San Francisco, CA: City Lights Books, 1988.
—*Difference and Repetition.* Translated by Paul Patton. New York: Columbia University Press, 1994.
Deleuze, Gilles, and Félix Guattari. *Anti-Oedipus: Capitalism and Schizophrenia*. Translated by Robert Hurley. Minneapolis, MN: University of Minnesota Press, 1983.
—*Kafka: Toward a Minor Literature*. Translated by Dana Polan. Minneapolis, MN: University of Minnesota Press, 1986.
—*A Thousand Plateaus: Capitalism and Schizophrenia*. Translated by Brian Massumi. Minneapolis, MN: University of Minnesota Press, 1987.
—*What Is Philosophy?* Translated by Janis Tomlinson and Graham Burchell III. New York: Columbia University Press, 1996.
Deleuze, Gilles, and Claire Parnet. *Dialogues II*. Revised edition. Translated by Barbara Habberjam. New York: Columbia University Press, 2002.
Griaule, Marcel, and Germaine Dieterlen. "The Dogon," 83–110 in *African Worlds; Studies in the Cosmological Ideas and Social Values of African Peoples*. Edited by Cyril Daryll Forde. London Oxford University Press, 1954.
Guattari, Félix. *The Guattari Reader.* Edited by Gary Genosko and translated by Sophie Thomas. Oxford: Blackwell, 1996.
—*Schizoanalytic Cartographies.* Translated by Andrew Goffey. New York: Continuum, 2012.
—*Psychoanalysis and Transversality: Texts and Interviews 1955–1971.* Translated by Ames Hodges. South Pasadena, CA: Semitist(e), 2015 [1972].
Harvey, David. *The Enigma of Capital and the Crisis of Capitalism*. London: Profile Books, 2010.
Justaert, Kristien. *Theology after Deleuze.* London: Continuum, 2012. https://doi.org/10.5040/9781350251908
Kähler, Martin. *The So-Called Historical Jesus and the Historic Biblical Christ*. Translated by C. E. Braaten. Philadelphia, PA: Fortress Press, 1964 [1896].
Klein, Melanie. *The Psychoanalysis of Children*. New York: Delacorte Press, 1975.
Kloppenborg, John S. *Christ's Associations: Connecting and Belonging in the Ancient City*. New Haven, CT: Yale University Press, 2019. https://doi.org/10.12987/9780300249309
Marx, Karl. *Capital: A Critique of Political Economy*. Volume 1 (1867). Translated by Ben Fowkes. Harmondsworth: Penguin, 1976.
Massumi, Brian. *Parables for the Virtual.* Durham, NC: Duke University Press, 2002. https://doi.org/10.1215/9780822383574
McLean, Bradley H. "Deleuze's Interpretation of Job as a Heroic Figure in the History of Rationality," *Religions* 10.141 (Feb. 2019): 1–8. https://doi.org/10.3390/rel10030141
—"What Does *A Thousand Plateaus* Contribute to the Study of Early Christianity?" *Deleuze and Guattari Studies* 14.3 (2020): 533–53. https://doi.org/10.3366/dlgs.2020.0415
Neocleous, Mark. "The Political Economy of the Dead: Marx's Vampires," *History of Political Thought* 24.4 (2003): 668–84.

Niemoczynsk, Leon. "Nature's Transcendental Creativity: Deleuze, Corrington, and an Aesthetic Phenomenology," *American Journal of Theology & Philosophy* 34.1 (2013): 17–34. https://doi.org/10.5406/amerjtheophil.34.1.0017

Nigianni, Chrysanthi. *Deleuze and Queer Theory*. Edinburgh: University of Edinburgh Press, 2009.

Prigogine, Ilya, and Isabelle Stengers. *Order Out of Chaos*. London: Verso, 2017 [1984].

Sherman, Jacob Holsinger. "No Werewolves in Theology? Transcendence, Immanence, and Becoming-Divine in Gilles Deleuze," *Modern Theology* 25.1 (2009): 1–20. https://doi.org/10.1111/j.1468-0025.2008.01501.x

Shildrick, Margrit. *Leaky Bodies and Boundaries: Feminism, Postmodernism and (Bio)ethics*. New York: Routledge, 1997. https://doi.org/10.1136/bmj.315.7117.1243a

Sontag, Susan, ed. *Antonin Artaud: Selected Writings*. Translated by Helen Weaver. New York: Farrar, Straus & Giroux, 1976.

Spinoza, Baruch. "Ethics," 401–617 in *The Collected Works of Spinoza*. Volume 1. Edited and translated by Edwin Curley. Princeton, NJ: Princeton University Press, 1985.

Watson, Francis. *Paul and the Hermeneutics of Faith*. London: T&T Clark, 2004.

Chapter Seven

The Many Acts of the Apostles: Simulacra and Simulation

Matthew G. Whitlock and Philip L. Tite

> Modern thought is born of the failure of representation, of the loss of identities, and the discovery of all the forces that act under the representation of the identical. The modern world is one of simulacra.[1]

In this modern world of simulacra, how—if at all—do we distinguish between the real and the simulated, the actual and the virtual, the model and the copy, and the original and the imitation? More specifically, in the study of early Christian origins in this modern world of simulacra, how—if at all— do we distinguish between the "authentic" acts and sayings of Jesus and his followers and those that are "inauthentic" or "imitations"? Can we uncover the "real" essence of early Christianity? An authentic Christianity? Our age of copies and simulacra is ripe with insight about the assumptions behind these questions, especially the insights of twentieth-century French philosophers Jean Baudrillard and Gilles Deleuze.[2] Here we argue that the concepts derived from their discussions about simulacra offer crucial insights about the quest for early Christian origins, especially when reading the canonical and non-canonical Acts together, the narratives of "the earliest" acts and sayings of Jesus' followers after his death. Jean Baudrillard's discussion of simulacra helps articulate the problem of this quest, namely the futility of finding "real" origins among the multiplicity of early Christian texts (simulacra),

---

1. Gilles Deleuze, *Difference and Repetition* (rev. edn.; trans. Paul Patton; New York: Columbia University Press, 1994), xix.
2. Plato described a simulacrum, which is the Latin term for Plato's use of the Greek φάντασμα, as a copy of a copy of a model. Because a simulacrum is a copy of a copy, it is seen as a corruption by Plato. For Plato's use of the term in contrast to Deleuze's, see Jonathan Roffe, "Simulacrum," in *The Deleuze Dictionary* (ed. Adrian Parr; rev. edn.; Edinburgh: Edinburgh University Press, 2010), 253. For the development of the term in Platonism and Deleuze's attempt to overturn its negative connotations, see Daniel W. Smith, "Platonism—The Concepts of the Simulacrum: Deleuze and the Overturning of Platonism" in *Essays on Deleuze* (Edinburgh: Edinburgh University Press, 2012), 3–26. Here Smith notes how the Church fathers used the term "against debauched representations of the gods on the Roman stage" (3).

texts simulating first-century acts and sayings. Gilles Deleuze's discussion further exposes the assumptions behind this quest (as well as assumptions behind Baudrillard's own quest for "the real") and how, from the start, the binary between the real and the simulacrum sets a course toward a dead-end. Deleuze's alternative—informed by philosophy, science, and art—sees the simulacrum as the vital force of life, of reality, a force repeating and differing, creating new forms and concepts for the present and future, a force co-opting the past for the present and the future. In short, *simulacrum for Deleuze is the real*. In applying Deleuze's insights to the Acts tradition, we argue that the tradition is not a simulacrum of corruption (i.e., a simulacrum of texts that moves further and further away from the canonical, "pure," and "real" acts of the apostles) but one that offers similarities and repetitions, and therefore differences, creating new concepts as Christian traditions move in their evolutionary drift—a drift that may not be limited by temporal constraints, but rather "drifts" both forward and backward in the infusion of difference and thus creative production of the "real" as the "simulacra" and the "simulacra" as the "real."

Articulating the Problem: Baudrillard on Simulacra and Simulation

Jean Baudrillard depicts the dilemma of simulation and the search for "the original" by turning to one of Jorge Luis Borges' fables, "On the Exactitude in Science"—and then turning it on its head.[3] In Borges' fable, cartographers in an unnamed empire strive to make a perfect map of their empire, so much so that a map of a province is the size of a city, and a map of the empire is the size of a province.[4] Unsatisfied with their work, the cartographers then create a map of the empire that is the same size as the empire, coinciding point by point. In later generations, the map becomes useless, not being able to serve the function of a map, becoming "tattered ruins" in the desert and "inhabited by animals and beggars."

Baudrillard's turn involves switching the map with the territory. In our age of simulation, it is not the map that is in ruins, but the territory itself, the real: "… it is the territory whose shreds slowly rot across the extent of the map. It is the real, and not the map, whose vestiges persist here and there in the deserts that are no longer those of the Empire, but ours. *The desert of the real itself.*"[5] In our age it is difficult to determine what is real—for what

---

3. Jean Baudrillard, *Simulacra and Simulation* (trans. Sheila Faria Glaser; Ann Arbor, MI: The University of Michigan Press, 1994), 1.
4. See Jorge Luis Borges, *Collected Fictions* (trans. Andrew Hurley; New York: Viking, 1998), 325.
5. Baudrillard, *Simulacra and Simulation,* 1 (italics are his own). In the film *The*

remains, according to Baudrillard, are maps, only the signs of the real.⁶ We are left with simulations (maps) among ruins, pieces here and there of reality.

While we certainly can apply Baudrillard's theory of simulacra to the quest for the "real" Jesus—his acts and sayings among the "simulated" maps found in the New Testament, in early Christian literature, or in the quests for the "historical Jesus"—here we focus on the early apostles and on the relationship between texts about them, between canonical and non-canonical texts, and more specifically between the canonical Acts of the Apostles and the many non-canonical Acts (e.g., *Acts of Andrew, Acts of John, Acts of Paul, Acts of Peter, Acts of Philip, Acts of Timothy, Acts of Thomas, Acts of Thomas and His Wonderworking Skin, Acts of Cornelius the Centurion,* and so many more ancient and medieval texts).⁷ So using Baudrillard's appropriation of Borges, we turn to the early Christian texts of the Acts tradition: they are maps of the territory, maps of the earliest, first-century acts and sayings of the apostles. When we extend our horizon beyond the canonical Acts,

---

Matrix, the Wachowski siblings use the phrase "the desert of the real" to depict the horrific reality that is concealed by "the Matrix," a simulated world hiding humanity's imprisonment. However, in the first film, they do not take Baudrillard's concept far enough—for they reveal "the real" to the audience, betraying Baudrillard's conception of the hyperreal, where the real is lost and irretrievable. On this criticism of *The Matrix*, see Seyda Öztürk, "Simulation Reloaded," *Cinetext*, August 2003, http://cinetext.philo.at/magazine/ozturk/seyda_ozturk-simulation_reloaded.pdf; William Merrin, "Did You Ever Eat Tasty Wheat: Baudrillard and the Matrix," May 2003, *Scope: An Online Journal of Film Studies,* https://www.nottingham.ac.uk/scope/documents/2003/may-2003/merrin.pdf.

6. In *Simulacra and Simulation,* Baudrillard describes simulation in four stages and three orders, the latter of which corresponds to historical eras. Our era is in the third order and in the fourth stage, where copies are far removed from originals, so much so that they cannot be distinguished from the real, so much so that they actually precede "the real." Brian Massumi succinctly defines Baudrillard's conception of simulation: "the substitution of signs of the real for the real." See Brian Massumi, "Realer than Real: The Simulacrum According to Deleuze and Guattari," *Copyright* 1 (1987), 90–7, here 90. He then states: "A common definition of the simulacrum is a copy of a copy whose relation to the model has become so attenuated that it can no longer properly be said to be a copy. It stands on its own as a copy without a model" (91).

7. For an analysis of the "virtual Jesus" in the canonical Gospels, see George Aichele, *Simulating Jesus: Reality Effects in the Gospels* (Abingdon: Routledge, 2014). For an application of Baudrillard's theory of simulacra to early Christian texts, see Willi Braun, "The Past as Simulacrum in the Canonical Narratives of Christian Origins," *R&T* 8 (2001), 213–28. Aichele uses both Baudrillard and Deleuze (primarily Deleuze) to discuss the virtual bible, the virtual Jesus, and the differences (in a Deleuzian sense) between the virtual Jesuses in the four Gospels. This chapter follows Aichele's use of Deleuze and simulacra for the study of the early Christian texts. It also follows Braun's use of Baudrillard and simulacra for understanding the "historical" production of the early Christian texts.

we witness a fascination with such mapping among early Christians over the centuries (the "map-makers"). What lies in ruins are not the maps; for we have plenty of them, and plenty of maps (secondary literature) about the maps. What lies in ruins is the territory. Living in an age far removed from the first century, we (as modern "map-makers" *qua* map-readers) simply cannot uncover the "real" acts and sayings of the first followers of Jesus; instead, we are left with maps, with simulations (the Acts simulacra) of "the earliest" followers, with the canonical Acts of the Apostles being perhaps the earliest one[8] and clearly the most authoritative for many modern Christians, albeit a map and simulation itself, a map and simulation without much corresponding territory that remains. In applying Baudrillard's metaphor to the Acts tradition and beginning with Acts of the Apostles, three questions come to the fore. First, how much territory is reflected in the canonical Acts of the Apostles? Second, how much territory can be recovered by scholarly study of Acts of the Apostles? Third, how much closer to the territory is the canonical Acts compared to the non-canonical Acts? Whereas all three of these questions have been dealt with at length in the study of the Acts tradition, they have yet to be framed with Baudrillard's lens, a lens which reveals underlying problems and assumptions, leading to another and, in our view, fuller lens on simulacrum, Deleuze's lens, one which also reveals problems and assumptions in Baudrillard's approach. So, the primary point in addressing these questions is not to review the plethora of secondary literature (e.g., on the historicity of Acts of the Apostles), but to address these questions with the concept of simulacrum, enabling us to rethink the Acts traditions as the Acts simulacra.

First, how much real territory is reflected in Acts of the Apostles? Willi Braun, applying the theory of Michel-Rolph Trouillot, argues that early Christian texts silence, suppress, and forget the "real" experiences from their inception, whether unintentionally or intentionally, and in the end create "the simulacrum of the canonical historical narrative in the present."[9] In Baudrillard's terms, through this process, the territory becomes minimized;

---

8. The canonical Acts is usually seen as the earliest text in the Acts tradition, with subsequent Acts being treated as derivate (simulacra) of the original (NT Acts). This traditional view needs clarification, however, given recent attempts to date the canonical Acts to the early second-century and, furthermore, the possible underlying written and oral sources incorporated into canonical Acts. Thus, canonical Acts needs to be treated as much originary and/or simulacrum as any other text in the Acts tradition. Consequently, a study of the Acts simulacra is enhanced though such a more dynamic intersection of the canonical and the non-canonical.

9. Braun, "The Past as Simulacrum," 223–4. See also Michel-Rolph Trouillot, *Silencing the Past: Power and the Production of History* (Boston, MA: Beacon, 1995).

the maps enlarged. According to Braun, this minimization of the territory involves a four-stage process: (1) making the facts ("the moment of doing, of lived history, in space and time"); (2) assembling the facts (an archive is created, a "retrospective selection that heralds some facts, side-lines others, and forgets some entirely"); (3) retrieving the facts (a narrative is constructed from the archive, involving filtering, connecting, valorizing, re-signifying, and fictioning); and (4) signifying the facts (archives and narratives canonized).[10] All four stages involve some element of filtering and silencing, leading to shifting moments of signification. In the first, for example, not all "acts" get recorded, especially those of the marginalized.[11] In the second, not all recorded acts are preserved or "archived." In the third, not all acts that are archived are highlighted in a narrative. In the fourth, not all acts become part of a canonized tradition. What remains are maps, simulations, or simulacra of early Christian experience; in Baudrillard's world, the territory is filtered out and lies in tattered ruins. However, with this minimization comes expansion, not only in the valorizing and fictioning stages of narrative creation, but also in the copying of the narratives themselves. As a result, we are left only with maps of a map, not an original map (which itself is simulation). Braun's four-stage process highlights increasing minimalization for the sake of expanded legitimation granted to some maps over other maps, all of which discursively point back to an imagined "territory" signified or embodied by the authorized map. Some narratives are marginalized and not copied frequently (e.g., the non-canonical Acts), while others are copied often (the canonical Acts of the Apostles). Thus, even the territory to which a map points is another map, another simulacrum albeit one imagined to be the real. Hence, we have numerous maps of the map of various Acts of the Apostles, but not the original. Rather, we have a desert of the real—and perhaps only a desert. The map of Acts of the Apostles was copied, forming textual traditions (and the field of textual criticism), some traditions expanding the map as much as ten percent (i.e., the Western tradition of Codex Bezae). So, from its outset, the (shifting) narrative of Acts of the Apostles is a map, a simulation, or more precisely a simulacrum of maps.

Second, how much real territory can be recovered by scholarly study of Acts of the Apostles? Given that the original copy has disappeared, scholars

---

10. Braun, "The Past as Simulacrum," 223.

11. Historiography, according to Deleuze, has been too anthrocentric, traditionally filtering out geo-history. So most historic events (i.e., non-human events) in space and time have been filtered and not recorded even at this first stage. For Deleuze's conviction that history encompass "the activities of non-human agents," see Hanjo Berressem, "Crystal History: 'You Pick Up the Pieces. You Connect the Dots,'" in *Time and History in Deleuze and Serres* (ed. Bernd Herzogenrath; London: Bloomsbury, 2012), 216–8.

are left with copies of copies and the task of discerning—through textual criticism—what the original may have been and how expansions such as Codex Bezae fit into the picture.[12] Once the "original" narrative is simulated by scholars (i.e., the NA[28]), scholars then theorize about sources of the narrative—but since there are no sources remaining, not even vestiges (unlike the Gospel tradition with at least Mark and a reconstructed Q), there is no agreement about sources.[13] The dating of the "original" narrative is also problematic.[14] But whether late first or early second century, the context of the composition of Acts and of its "original" territory are well-simulated by scholars.[15] Even more, working with and commenting on the narrative of Acts of the Apostles itself, Craig Keener most recently has provided us with four volumes, far outweighing the "original" text.[16] The maps extend far beyond the known territory of Acts of the Apostles, which itself is a map of a territory.[17] In this essay, we in no way intend to devalue the work of scholarship. Nor do we deny the reality of historical events, be that some events in the texts and the events of making the texts. However, we wish to frame it as it stands: maps far outweigh the territory of "the real" and these maps, more as many "map-readers," serve as more the "territory of the real" than

---

12. See, for example, the four-volume work comparing the Alexandrian textual tradition with Codex Bezae: Jenny Read-Heimerdinger and Josep Rius-Camps, *The Message of Acts in Codex Bezae: A Comparison with the Alexandrian Tradition* (4 vols.; London: T&T Clark, 2004–2009).

13. See Craig S. Keener, *Acts: An Exegetical Commentary* (4 vols.; Grand Rapids, MI: Baker, 2012–2015), 1:179. "Few source critical reconstructions agree ... Thus most scholars today are content to admit that Luke has sources in Acts but that we cannot reconstruct them."

14. The majority of scholars place the composition of Acts of the Apostles between 70–100. See, however, there are recent challenges to this position. See Joseph B. Tyson (*Marcion and Luke-Acts: A Defining Struggle* [Columbia, SC: University of South Carolina Press, 2006]), who places it in the second century. Keener (*Acts*, 401), whose own best guess is the early 70s, concludes: "All such dating, however, is at best educated guesswork, given the inadequacy of our data."

15. For example, two classic, multi-volume studies: Bruce W. Winter, ed., *The Book of Acts in First Century Setting* (5 vols.; Grand Rapids, MI: Eerdmans, 1993–1996); F. J. Foakes-Jackson and Kirsopp Lake, eds., *The Beginnings of Christianity. Part I: The Acts of the Apostles* (5 vols.; London: Macmillan, 1920–1933).

16. Keener's magnum opus, *Acts*, is over 4600 pages: vol. 1 is 1104 pages, vol. 2 1200, vol. 3 1200, and vol. 4 1152.

17. While secondary literature is not simulacrum in the strict sense of the term, secondary literature certainly provides "maps" for readings of ancient, primary texts. Hence, as an aid, secondary literature is part of the simulation, that is, a modern reading of an ancient text. See Aichele (*Simulating Jesus*) for a delineation of how reading an early Christian work today is an act simulation.

the territory upon which the maps reflect; these texts are simulations of a simulation, maps of a map.

What is more, the simulacrum precedes "the real." This insight is especially applicable to scholarly efforts to reach the territory through the maps. The acts and sayings of the apostles are researched only after their acts and sayings have been reproduced many times and studied with many maps. Indeed, they are researched because they have been reproduced many times. There is no way to experience the first-century acts and sayings without the influence of the maps of them, without the influence of the simulacra. The reality, essence, or primitiveness of the original acts and sayings of the earliest followers of Jesus, in other words, cannot be recovered. Even if we were able to place ourselves back in that place and time, we would still experience that place and time through the lens of the Acts simulacra.[18]

Third, how much closer to the territory is the canonical Acts compared to the non-canonical Acts? As we noted above, some maps were not copied as frequently and their contexts not as researched as frequently (e.g., the non-canonical Acts), but their copies remain. When we turn to these other Acts, they may not be as close in time to first-century territory as the canonical Acts of the Apostles; however, it does not follow that canonical Acts of the Apostles is "real" whereas the later Acts are "inauthentic," an assumption influenced by reading early Christian literature through a canonical lens; a lens that again is another map of a map. Baudrillard is aware of how overt simulations can cover up subtler, earlier ones, making the latter seem real: "Disneyland is presented as imaginary in order to make us believe that the rest is real."[19] In the same sense, it is the non-canonical Acts that are presented as inauthentic in order to make us believe that the canonical Acts of the Apostles is real, while *in reality*, all the Acts are simulacra. But where does this leave us? Are we left with the stark realization that nothing is real anymore? Or that everything is real in some sense? Baudrillard leaves us with problems, some of which are produced by his own assumptions, some of which Deleuze's theories on simulacra address.

---

18. Claire Colebrook (*Gilles Deleuze* [Routledge Critical Thinkers; Abingdon: Routledge, 2002], 97) uses Don Delillo's novel *White Noise* to illustrate Baudrillard's conception of simulacra preceding what is "real." In the novel, tourists come to see a famous barn, a barn made famous in photographs. Colebrook writes, "what the tourists are going to see is not what the barn *is* in concrete reality, but what the barn has become through repeated simulation."

19. Baudrillard, *Simulacra and Simulation,* 12.

Two Problems with Baudrillard's Conception of Simulacra in Light of Deleuze

There are two problems with Baudrillard's conception of simulacra, both pertinent to our study of the Acts tradition. First, given that we make a distinction between the real and the simulacra, and that the simulacra so outnumber the real that the real is irrecoverable, we are left with, in Brian Massumi's terms, nostalgia, lament, and hypercynicism—lament and hypercynicism because "the real" cannot be recovered; nostalgia because "the real" becomes idealized, a lost treasure, and in the case of Christian origins, the lost treasure of the past. Massumi accordingly states, "Baudrillard's framework can only be the result of a nostalgia for the old reality so intense that it has deformed his vision of everything outside it."[20] To Baudrillard, everything outside "the real" is deformed and distant. And Deleuze points to a source of this view: the Christian catechism, influenced by Platonism.[21] Here Deleuze offers his interpretation of the catechism:

> God made man in His own image and to resemble Him, but through sin, man lost the resemblance while retaining the image. Having lost a moral existence in order to enter into an aesthetic one, we have become simulacra ... The simulacrum is constructed around a disparity, a difference; it interiorizes a dissimilitude.

In applying a Platonic line of thought to the Acts tradition, we can see how the desire for early Christian origins falls into nostalgia. It is a pure, picturesque, and pastoral experience of the earliest followers of Jesus that has been lost. Because their acts and sayings have been copied and simulated multiple times, they become distant and deformed, that is, whether in the expanded Codex Bezae version of the canonical Acts of the Apostles or in the non-canonical Acts (in the light of the canonical Acts of the Apostles) or through human hermeneutical activation of the text (e.g., the Protestant criticism of Roman Catholicism resulting in a romanticized "New Testament Church" or original, unified community). Under this line of thought, a biblical scholar's task is to recover—or at least theorize an approximation of—this original essence or identity of early Christianity. And if we do not desire to reconstruct or theorize about essence or identity (for the sake of finding an original), then, following Baudrillard's framework, we are left with lament and cynicism: why should we even try to recover what cannot be recovered?[22]

---

20. Massumi, "Realer than Real," 96–7.
21. Gilles Deleuze, "Plato and the Simulacrum," trans. Rosalind Krauss, *October* 27 (Winter 1983): 45–66, here 48–9.
22. This question is a key starting point for the quest for Christian origins. Evoking an analogy from genetics, we ask: can a person recover the one original cell from her

Whereas Baudrillard's discussion of simulacra ends in lament, Deleuze's begins with possibility. The difference between these two outcomes is rooted in the second problem of Baudrillard's framework, a major problem that Deleuze exposes (without direct reference to Baudrillard), a point where our discussion of Baudrillard ends and our discussion of Deleuze begins.[23] In brief: Baudrillard bases his discussion of simulacra on *representation*, namely that a simulacrum represents an original model and fails in faithfully representing it. For Baudrillard, a "real origin" or "real model" exists, even though it is lost and unrecoverable. Simulacra, in this view, veer from original models (i.e., like the human image articulated in the catechism above); hence, simulacra no longer represent models; they pervert them. It is at this latter point where Deleuze exposes the fallacy in this conception:

> The simulacrum is constructed around a disparity, a difference; it interiorizes a dissimilitude. That is why we can no longer even define it with regard to the model at work in copies—the model of the Same from which resemblance of the copy derives. If the simulacrum still has a model, it is another one, a model of the Other from which follows an interiorized dissimilarity.[24]

Whereas Baudrillard wants to view simulacrum from a framework of *similarity*, Deleuze wants to view it from a framework of *difference*—for simulacra, by definition, are not faithful copies of a model, but rather repetitions

---

parents among the billions of cells, of copies? Is it still there? And even if so, why is this a worthwhile project? Why do we want to recover *one* "origin"? Is the motive simply curiosity? Scientific? Or is it ideological, grounding and supporting a particular notion about what comprises "true Christianity" in opposition to rival claims? Braun ("The Past as Simulacrum," 224) urges early Christian scholarship to be aware of the latter motive in the making of early Christian history. Smith ("Deleuze and the Overturning of Platonism," 4–10) suggests the quest for an original is rooted in Platonism: in trying to find the true claim among claims of rivals.

23. Roffe, "Simulacrum," 253. Roffe notes that Deleuze himself did not view simulacrum as a key part of his philosophy (see the Preface by Gilles Deleuze to Jean-Clet Martin, *Variations: The Philosophy of Gilles Deleuze* [trans. Constantin V. Boundas and Susan Drykton; Edinburgh: Edinburgh University Press, 2010], 8); however, Roffe rightly argues that Deleuze's discussion of simulacrum offers "one of the strongest forms of his critique of identity, and the affirmation of a world populated by differences-in-themselves which are not copies of any prior model." Smith ("Deleuze and the Overturning of Platonism," 26) traces Deleuze's abandonment of the term to publications after *Difference and Repetition* (1968), noting how simulacrum is replaced by the term "assemblage" in later works, surmising that in Deleuze's conception "things no longer 'simulate' anything, but rather 'actualize' immanent Ideas that are themselves real, though virtual." Smith, however, concludes that Deleuze's analysis of simulacrum "constitutes one of the fundamental problems of contemporary thought."

24. Deleuze, "Plato and the Simulacrum," 49.

with differences.²⁵ In Deleuze, simulacra are constructed around differences, not similarities. Simulacra do repeat with "an *effect* of resemblance; but that is a general effect, wholly external, and produced entirely different means from those that are at work in the model."²⁶ So on the surface there are semblances; however, these semblances bring about differences.²⁷ For Deleuze a real exists, but this real is the process of producing the Other, producing differences. Hence, it is not that the model is real or more real, and the simulacrum not. Rather, the "model" itself is simulacrum—a "model" that also differentiated itself from what it repeated or mimicked on the surface. It is the simulacrum, in other words, that is real.²⁸ In light of Deleuze's claims, Massumi sums up the problem with Baudrillard's conception of simulacrum: he "cannot clearly see that all things he says have crumbled [i.e., the real or model] were simulacra all along: simulacra produced by analyzable procedures that were as real as real, or actually realer than real, because they carried the real back to its principle production and in so doing prepared their own rebirth in the new regime of simulation."²⁹

Similarly, Claire Colebrook sums up both the reality of simulacra in Deleuze's conception and the problem of nostalgia in Baudrillard's:

> Jean Baudrillard argues that media culture has reduced everything to surface images with no reference to the real. Deleuze's notion of the simulacra both resists the nostalgia that would want to go back to a time when life was "more real" *and* rejects the idea that we now live in a postmodern world of mere images with no real causes. For Deleuze the simulacrum or image is real, and life is and always has been simulation—a power of production, creation, becoming and difference.³⁰

---

25. Massumi ("Realer than Real," 91) notes: "The simulacrum is less a copy twice removed than a phenomenon of a different nature altogether: it undermines the very distinction between copy and model."

26. Deleuze, "Plato and the Simulacrum," 49. Italics are Deleuze's.

27. See Massumi, "Realer than Real," 91. Here he refers to Lacan: "Mimicry … is camouflage" (Jacques Lacan, *The Four Fundamental Concepts of Psychoanalysis* [trans. Alan Sheridan; New York: Norton, 1981], 99). See also Gilles Deleuze and Félix Guattari, *Anti-Oedipus* (trans. Robert Hurley, Mark Seem, and Helen R. Lane; New York: Viking, 1977), 91.

28. See Colebrook, *Gilles Deleuze*, 98–9: "We tend to think that we have an actual world which precedes simulation, but for Deleuze there is an 'original' process of simulation. Beings or things emerge from processes of copying, doubling, imaging and simulation. Each unique work of art or each human individual is a simulation: genes copy and repeat, with deviation, while art works become singular not by *being* the world but by transforming it through images that are at once actual and virtual."

29. Massumi, "Realer than Real," 97.

30. Colebrook, *Gilles Deleuze*, 101.

In the study of the Acts tradition, it is this nostalgia for "the more real" that scholarship must avoid, as well as avoiding lament over a tradition of "mere images" with nothing real behind it. Instead, in the next section, we argue for the value of viewing the Acts tradition as real simulacra—simulacra composed from the power of repetition, newness, creativity, becoming, and difference.

Applying Deleuze's Conception of Simulacra to the Study of the Acts Tradition

> And the aim [of my empiricism] is not to rediscover the eternal or the universal, but to find the conditions under which something new is produced.[31]

In this section, we complete the move from Baudrillard to Deleuze, delineating concepts from Deleuze's discussion of simulacra and linking them to the study of the Acts tradition, especially in viewing the "canonical" Acts along with the "non-canonical." Then, in the next section, we apply these principles to trajectories in the tradition. This section begins with a panoramic view of how Deleuze approaches the past, largely based on how he conceives of simulacra in relation to history and literature.[32] Deleuze's quest is not about recovering a pure or pastoral past, the memory of which has been "corrupted" over time; rather, it involves finding "the conditions under which something new is produced."[33] This principle applies to the study of the Acts tradition, whether a given study grounds itself in historical

---

31. Gilles Deleuze, *Dialogues* (trans. H. Tomlinson and B. Habberjam; New York: Columbia University Press, 1987), vii.

32. Although Deleuze's conception of simulacrum often appears in discussions about art—both in his own and in discussions by others—his conception is helpful across disciplines and genres. In his article on Deleuze and aesthetics, James Williams argues: "In Deleuze's work, the definition of artwork as a simulacrum within a series of repetitions and variations has ramifications that extend beyond art into the epistemological and ethical" ("Deleuze," in *Encyclopedia of Aesthetics* [ed. Michael Kelly; 4 vols.; New York: Oxford University Press, 1998], 1:517).

33. For Deleuze's conception of history, see Jay Lampert, *Deleuze and Guattari's Philosophy of History* (London: Continuum, 2006); Eugene Holland, "Non-Linear Historical Materialism; Or, What is Revolutionary in Deleuze and Guattari's Philosophy of History?" in *Time and History in Deleuze and Serres* (ed. Bernd Herzogenrath; London: Bloomsbury, 2012), 17–30; Berressem, "Crystal History," 203–28. Berressem derives five implications from Deleuze's philosophy of history (along with the philosophies of Henry Adams and Michel Serres): historical studies should (1) look to chaos theory and physics to understand the movement and drift of history; (2) become "radically site specific" and "work from within the tangle of local spaces and times"; (3) take into account "the activities of non-human agents"; (4) work from a framework of contingency (as opposed to causality); (5) maintain that history emerges from an "'originary'

or literary studies. To make a quest for early Christian "origins" Deleuzian, one therefore must begin by asking not how early Christian texts (both canonical and non-canonical) veer from "origins," but *how they produce something new, and under what conditions this production happens.*[34] This would be the overarching principle of a Deleuzian study of Christian "origins." Such a Deleuzian study would shift our focus from territories, and even maps, to map-makers/map-readers. A Deleuzian study enables us to see maps as sites for creating or perceiving territories given the creativity erupting from dissimilitude. Below we outline four implications drawn from Deleuze's discussion of simulacra, all of which fall under the heading of this principle.

First, a Deleuzian study of Christian origins involves *not making a distinction between real and unreal, true original and false copy, and authentic and inauthentic.* By making such distinctions, we approach a given Acts text with preconceived notions of its value and how we are supposed to read/use such a text, as well as preconceived notions about what is "real" or "authentic" about the Christian tradition (resulting in a circular process of the assumed "real" affecting the reading of the "map" to reconstruct the "real"); by not making these distinctions, we approach a text as it is: a simulacrum with differences, creating something new under new conditions. What is more, we avoid making assumptions about the purity of the original, assumptions often formed for ideological reasons, just as they were formed in the Platonic tradition itself, a formation Deleuze himself brings to the fore.[35] As Daniel Smith points out, Deleuze takes aim at Platonism by examining the formation of the Platonic conception of the true Idea/Model

multiplicity." In other words, the historian him/herself is immersed in the constant movement and flow of his/her unstable and diverse milieu.

34. Note that "new" does not assume a teleological program. New neither assumes better nor worse, worse being too often assumed in quests for pure Christian origins, better too often assumed in studies informed by a realized eschatology. Indeed, like Nietzsche, Deleuze does not view history in a linear, teleological fashion. In his desire for newness, difference, and possibility, Deleuze—again like Nietzsche—wishes to invert Platonism. Perhaps Nietzsche's own words about "true being" help articulate the drive behind this desire for newness: "My philosophy is an *inverted* Platonism: the farther removed from true being, the purer, the finer, the better it is. Living is semblance as goal." Friedrich Nietzsche, *Grossoktavausgabe* (Leipzig, 1905 ff.), 9:190. Quoted in Smith, "Deleuze and the Overturning of Platonism," 4.

35. Note that what we are claiming here is not that later works in the Acts tradition are just as "original" or representative of the early followers of Jesus as Acts of the Apostles. We are claiming these works (including Acts of the Apostles) are not built on representation, but difference. Brian Massumi ("Realer than Real," 92), referencing Eric Alliez and Michel Feher, argues: "The best weapon against the simulacrum is not to unmask it as a false copy, but to force it to be a true copy, thereby resubmitting it to

(e.g., the "true" lover, the "true" philosopher), which was under the conditions of rivalry.[36] For Deleuze these claims of the "true" were formulated under conditions of rival claims within the democracy of the Greek *polis*. Who has the truer claim? The one who is closest to the true Idea. Who is the one farthest from the truth? The Sophist, who is farthest from the true Idea, the one embracing simulacra. Similarly, it is under the conditions of rivalries that claims to "real" Christianity, the "real" Jesus have historically surfaced in early Christian texts and in readings of them, even within the canon itself (e.g., Gal. 1.13-16). Hence, the scholarly study of early Christianity should take into account its own history of forming claims of authenticity under conditions of rivalries, whether theological or scholarly, and embrace new frameworks, ones not based on authenticity or faithfulness to an original, to a fixed Model; a Model that does not exist, but rather is the matrix serving as the subject of the next implication of "the authentic."

Second, asking under what conditions something new is produced involves recognizing that *there is no origin or original model*. Historically, there are certainly measurable events in the past, but these are events in a long series of events, neither original nor linear nor teleological, but points within a rhizome.[37] The past never was fixed; it was always in motion, always complex, always repeating, always repeating with differences. Aesthetically and literarily, works of art also neither represent nor copy an original model. James Williams sums up this Deleuzian principle well: "The artwork ... is neither an original nor a copy nor a representation. It is a simulacrum: a work that forms part of a series that cannot be referred to an original beginning or to a guiding ideal or model."[38] There is no original model or origin in the Acts tradition. Each piece, from Acts of the Apostles to the Acts of Cornelius, forms part of a series, a series with differences. And Acts of the Apostles does not stand at a fixed origin or even as a fixed origin—for it too is part of multiple series that precede it (e.g., events, sources, stories, scriptures—all of which too were preceded in complex simulacra) and follow it. In reading the Acts tradition, what we encounter is a kind of

---

representation and the mastery of the model." See Eric Alliez and Michel Feher, "Notes on the Sophisticated City," *Zone* 1.2 (1986): 40–55, here 55.

36. Smith, "Deleuze and the Overturning of Platonism," 4–5. See Deleuze, *Difference and Repetition,* 60.

37. For rhizome, see the introduction to the Deleuze section above. Note also that Deleuze is not arguing against historical-critical methods; he is, however, arguing against using these methods to establish a concrete and fixed origin that is then followed by a linear path of causality—whether that path be teleological or one of degradation, fading away from a "true" origin.

38. Williams, "Deleuze," 517.

"rhizomatic real"; that is, a series of erupting—and irrupting—moments of creativity relating various Acts traditions within contexts of creative difference, forming a dynamic constellation of multiplicity. The claim of an Ideal or Model, consequently, is another instance of the rhizomatic real.

Third, *there is no pure, essential, fixed moment of early Christianity. Everything is becoming.* Deleuzian thought, based largely upon twentieth-century science (here evolution and physics), sees everything in motion, everything in evolutionary drift.[39] In relation to science, art and literature express these moments of movement, becoming, and change—hence Deleuze's conviction of finding the conditions under which something new is produced.[40] Art, in Williams' words, "captures these movements and in so doing makes the perception permanent, in the sense that it can be reactivated in a spectator or audience."[41] The same applies to literature and the Acts tradition. Questions about Acts literature should involve how each text captures changes and movements—and how they are reactivated in their reception or map-reading. Such a focus on "becoming" need not follow modernity's fixation on social evolutionary theories, including most notably linear evolutionary theories of religious and cultural progression.[42] Again, the focus is on the rhizomatic and the interactive not the model-to-representation. Our approach to chronological influences needs to shift from a linear past-to-present paradigm to a more circular, interactive paradigm where the future shapes the past simultaneously while the past shapes the future.

Fourth, because there are no fixed states or identities or origins, and because everything is in motion and is becoming, *differences in a series are differences in intensity*. Here Deleuze grounds his thought on science and mathematics, on thermodynamics and differential calculus. Williams sums up Deleuze's thinking on how intensive differences relate to expression in aesthetics: "Expression captures changes in intensity, and, in effect, expression is to show the change [articulated in the third implication above]

---

39. Berressem, "Crystal History," 210–1.
40. In *What Is Philosophy?* Deleuze and Guattari summarize their philosophy and how science, art, and philosophy interact. See Gilles Deleuze and Félix Guattari, *What Is Philosophy?* (New York: Columbia University Press, 1996).
41. Williams, "Deleuze," 516. Williams continues (517): "Great art does not lie in the representation of an object, landscape, act, meaning, or, indeed, feeling. It lies in the capturing of the movements that bring about these things and that also lead to their destruction. The artwork reveals the falsity of representation and identity."
42. On social evolutionary models in the comparative study of religion, especially in the nineteenth century where Darwinian evolution served as the key scientific paradigm for not only the natural sciences but also the human sciences, see Eric J. Sharpe, *Comparative Religion: A History* (2nd edn.; London: Open Court, 1986), 47–71.

in terms of intensity, as opposed to a comparison of two fixed states."[43] In applying this implication to the Acts tradition, we can avoid common pitfalls of comparing two supposedly fixed states, for example, canonical versus non-canonical, proto-orthodox versus heretical, proto-orthodox versus "gnostic," high Christology versus low Christology, historiography versus novel, documentary versus literary, and so forth. Such fixed binaries result in a discourse of the authentic versus the inauthentic. In reality, as simulacra, Acts texts have intensive mixtures of various theologies, Christologies, genres, and so on. Neither the texts themselves nor their forms and contents can be compared as stable, fixed states, fitting neatly into one category or the other.

Fifth, *there is semblance in simulacra, but this semblance is a means to an end, the end being the production of something new*.[44] In the Acts tradition, we do not ask how one text veers from its source on which it is "dependent"; or how one text inauthentically portrays the acts or sayings of the apostles; rather, we ask how it uses surface semblances of acts or sayings of the apostles in order to become something new under new conditions.[45] What, in other words, is the text "evolving" or morphing into (through surface semblance of characters or motifs in other texts)? How does "the real" of the map lead to a new map of "the real"?

A Closer Look at the Acts Simulacrum: Acts of the Apostles and the Acts of Cornelius

In order to be concrete in our exploration of a Deleuzian approach to early Christian texts, we will refer to two texts in the Acts simulacrum: The

---

43. Williams, "Deleuze," 516.
44. For semblance as a means, see Deleuze and Guattari, *Anti-Oedipus*, 91. On the subject of means to an end, see also Massumi, "Realer than Real," 92: "The resemblance of the simulacrum is a means, not an end … Resemblance is a beginning masking the advent of whole new vital dimension." Perhaps a more precise Deleuzian terminology would call this external imitation "semblance" and not "resemblance." For, in Daniel Smith's analysis ("Deleuze and the Overturning of Platonism," 364, n. 33), the former denotes an internal likeness through and through, whereas the latter denotes only a surface likeness with differences.
45. For how "apocryphal" Acts use similar elements of the early Christian traditional differently, while not necessarily being literarily dependent, see Francois Bovon, "Canonical and Apocryphal Acts of the Apostles," *JSNT* 11 (2003): 165–94. Bovon's analysis, recognizing thematic similarities and differences within the Acts tradition, coincides well with a Deleuzian approach to simulacra, and is a good starting point for specific examples of the Acts tradition based on differences and repetitions, one example which we briefly take up in the next section.

canonical Acts of the Apostles and the Acts of Cornelius the Centurion. Space does not allow for a full analysis of these texts in light of Deleuze's theories on simulacra, but we suggest that the recent introduction and translation of the Acts of Cornelius the Centurion (Acts Corn.) by Tony Burke and Witold Witakowski offers us an in-depth analysis that is not built on canonical assumptions, but rather plays with and engages the canonical through processes of simulation.[46]

To begin, when identifying semblances between the Acts of the Apostles and the Acts of Cornelius, we cannot assume that the Acts of the Apostles is the original in a series of copies. Semblances are common points within a simulacrum, points from which *both* narratives create something new. Note that this insight does not reject that the Acts of the Apostles wrote a Cornelius story before the Acts of Cornelius, nor does it reject that the Acts of Cornelius is dependent on Acts of the Apostles.[47] At the same time, however, this textual relationship does not assume that Acts of the Apostles is the original point in the simulacrum nor that the Acts of the Apostles is untouched by processes of simulation. The Acts of the Apostles is a point in the Acts simulacrum that creates something new by repeating—and thus creating—the Cornelius story; so too the Acts of Cornelius is a point, possibly several points given the manuscript tradition (Greek and Ethiopic manuscripts with a now lost Arabic version), in the Acts simulacrum that creates something new by repeating the Cornelius story. The issue here, then, involves asking the same question about the Acts of the Apostles as one asks about the Acts of Cornelius, even if the former may involve speculation, largely because we do not have surviving copies of simulacra prior to the oldest manuscript of the Acts of the Apostles. Hence, we ask: *given the semblances in these two texts, what do these semblances reveal about the new elements that may have been produced in the Acts of the Apostles, as well as the ones that are produced in the Acts of Cornelius?* Asking this question about both texts not only protects against assumptions about the

---

46. Tony Burke and Witold Witakowski, "The Acts of Cornelius the Centurion," in *New Testament Apocrypha: More Noncanonical Scriptures* (ed. Tony Burke and Brent Landau; Grand Rapids, MI: Eerdmans, 2016), 337–61.

47. The Acts of Cornelius is extant in four Greek manuscripts dating from the eleventh to the fourteenth century, including an epitome or abbreviated excerpt. Paris, Bibliothéque nationale, gr. 1489 (fol. 95v-105v; = A), dated to the eleventh century, is a copy of the tenth-century collection by Symeon Magister the Logothete's collection of saints' lives. Thus, an earlier and longer version of the Acts of Cornelius may have been in circulation. There is also an Ethiopic version dated to the early fifteenth century (EMML 1824) that was transmitted via a no longer extant Arabic vorlage. For more on the manuscript tradition and translation history, see Burke and Witakowski, "Acts of Cornelius the Centurion," 338–40.

originality of the Acts of the Apostles, or the story of Cornelius, but also helps us identify points of creative production *in both or multiple texts*, focusing not only on *the what* (i.e., the semblances) within the simulacrum, but also *the how* (i.e., creative production) within the simulacrum.

The Acts of Cornelius is structured into four acts. There is also added material in the shorter form, where the hand of Cornelius, as a relic, is translated to Caesarea Palaestina.[48] The first act (1.1-9) is a close retelling of the New Testament account of Cornelius in three parts: gospel context for the story (1.1a); pre-conversion piety of Cornelius (1.1b); and the conversion of Cornelius (1.2-9). The second act (2.1–3.9) expands upon the Gentile mission motif found in the New Testament Acts account, with Cornelius serving a missionary function as a result of the dispersion of the Jerusalem church following a period of persecution. Cornelius comes to the city of Skepsis in Mysia (Asia Minor), where the ruler, Demetrius, attempts to force Cornelius to worship the gods Apollo and Zeus. When brought to the shrine of Zeus, Cornelius' prayers to God literally bring the house down, destroying the shrine, the idols, and trapping Demetrius' wife and son. The family is miraculously saved by God and Cornelius baptizes Demetrius and, through prayer, frees the family from the rubble. This second act ends with the conversion of the city. Act three (4.1–5.11) addresses the death and entombment of the holy Cornelius. Upon his death, he is buried where the shrine to Zeus had been. A great bush grows and hides the burial site, resulting in people forgetting where Cornelius had been laid to rest. The second part of this third act jumps forward in time, with dreams playing a central role in the emergence of the cult of this saint. Cornelius appears to the bishop of Troas, Silvanus, to reveal the burial site, while also appearing in another dream to Eugenius, a wealthy man (and thus a patron), to direct him to build a sanctuary for Cornelius' coffin. When the coffin is transferred to the sanctuary, where it will rest beside the altar, we have a further miracle in that the coffin moved on its own "as if alive" (5.9). This miracle is not dissimilar to the "walking and talking" Cross in the *Gospel of Peter* (39-42). The fourth and final act (6.1-5) jumps a bit further in time, after the death of Bishop Silvanus and Eugenius, when Encratius is ordered to paint the shrine and "carefully craft an image of Cornelius himself, as much as possible dressed accurately" (6.1). Encratius has no idea what Cornelius looked like and, in his frustration, says some offensive—perhaps we could say, blasphemous—words to the saint. The painter falls and dies, later to be raised by Cornelius

---

48. See Burke and Witakowski, "Acts of Cornelius the Centurion," 338, for a full description of this epilogue with translation on page 360–1.

and shown the image of the saint, thereby enabling him to finish the painting. The act ends with a worshipful affirmation of Trinitarian theology.

Each of these four acts, individually and in combination, are generative simulacra of the account of Acts 10, repeating and expanding the adventures of this character to advance a new, original—yet imitative—articulation of Cornelius. Rather than the despair of Baudrillard, these moments of dissimilitude, these narrative differences where the map veers into new terrain, is where a creative possibility arises. To walk with Deleuze, we see potential in differences for the generative creativity where maps create maps and then, in turn, the older maps are recreated through the newer maps. In a sense, all becomes original through the act of imitation. When we consider the manuscript variances, notably the Ethiopian translation, we have further moments of such rhizomatic creativity layered throughout the story. Although a detailed analysis of all such creative moments is beyond the scope of this essay, we will look at a few of these redactional moments through a Deleuzian lens.

The first act in the Acts of Cornelius parallels, or shares semblances with, Acts 10. The story begins with and clearly is drawing upon the vision of Cornelius, where an angel appears and declares, "Cornelius, your prayers and your alms have ascended as a memorial before God. Now, send men to Joppa and summon Simon, the one called Peter. When he comes he will tell you words of life" (Act. Corn. 1.2//Acts 10.3-6). The narrative framing is more instructive than the slight differences in the verbal exchange (e.g., Cornelius' question "What is it, Lord?" and the geographic details of where Peter is residing are eliminated). There is a direct intertextual reference to the Lukan account (1.2a "as the divine Luke most clearly reports"), a reference which could situate our apocryphal account within Baudrillard's distinction of "the real" and "the simulated" rather than a more Deleuzian understanding of both texts as mutual simulacra. However, the author(s) of Acts of Cornelius clearly anticipated the target audience evoking the biblical version of the story within the telling of this expanded narrative, thereby inviting the audience to reassess *both* accounts through the lens of the other. In other words, instead of an original and a copy, the narrator uses the intertextual link to adjust the interpretative engagement with the Lukan Acts account through the lens of the apocryphal Acts account, inviting the audience to re-read (or re-remember) Acts 10 through the prism of the Acts of Cornelius just as they are. Acts 10 is no longer just Acts 10, it is now Acts 10 + Acts of Cornelius. Something new emerges, and that is a new Acts of the Apostles—not by redactional adjustment of a text or manuscript variances, but by a new hermeneutical perspective brought to bear upon that earlier, now canonical version of the story of Cornelius the Centurion. The direct reference to the Lukan source, recognized as an authoritative source (i.e., scripture), is designed to evoke just such a perceptional adjustment by *pointing back* to the source material through a new narrative lens.

Other framing mechanisms play into this strategy. The Acts of Cornelius 1.1 serves as a preface, summarizing not only Cornelius' devout piety even prior to his conversion (1.1b), but also the sacral framework of the gospel within which that conversion occurs: "After the saving visitation of the Word upon the earth, and the voluntary cross and death for our sake, and the ascent into heaven, from where he came to build the fallen house of David, according to the prophets, there was the centurion Cornelius of the Italian Cohort …" (1.1a). This opening preface serves to summarize the Gospel of Luke and opening of Acts with a quick movement to Acts 10, bypassing most of Acts 1–9. This opening preface serves to establish two major points.

First, it establishes the devout piety of Cornelius even prior to his conversion. Cornelius is seen as worthy of inclusion into the Christian community because he has already demonstrated his godly character through acts of devotion: "abounding in good works—though not yet of his divine mercy … was devout, and both he and his entire family were fearing God and sharing from what he had with those in need. Furthermore, he prayed constantly to God." Cornelius embodies good works, devotion, fear of God, charitable giving, and prayerfulness.[49] All these virtues are then underscored by a possible Christ motif in verse 2, where the "angel came at about three o'clock" to give God's revelation to Cornelius. The time is highly symbolic and likely evokes the death of Christ when the darkness upon the earth was lifted (Matt. 27.45//Mark 15.33//Luke 23.44//Gos. Pet. 15-22). This temporal reference could evoke either (or both) an intertextual link between Cornelius and the centurion who witnessed Jesus' death (Matt. 27.54//Mark 15.39//Luke 23.47) or a typical martyrological motif where the saint/martyr is imbued with Christ-like motifs (perhaps the most notable example is

---

49. Cornelius embodies—both through actions and disposition—the virtues or "character" (*ēthos*) that are to be highly valued in Christians, notably in late antique and medieval literary contexts. On the significance of such characterization in ancient literary works, see Richard P. Thompson, "Reading Beyond the Text, Part I: Poetics, Rhetoric, and Religious Texts from the Greco-Roman World," *ARC: The Journal of the Faculty of Religious Studies, McGill University* 28 (2000): 115–42, and especially Thompson, "Reading Beyond the Text, Part II: Literary Creativity and Characterization in Narrative Religious Texts of the Greco-Roman World," *ARC: The Journal of the Faculty of Religious Studies, McGill University* 29 (2001): 81–122. Although Thompson focuses on historiography, his insights in the virtue-function of literary characters also applies to other narrative contexts such as hagiography, martyrdom accounts, and apocryphal acts.

Polycarp;[50] though note also, e.g., Potamiaena [Martyrdom of Potamiaena and Basilides 8-9], Fructuosus [Martyrdom of Fructuosus and Companions 3 and 4.3], Flavian [Martyrdom of Montanus and Lucius 17.4 and 22.3], and Pompeiana obtaining the body of Maximilian from the magistrate to bury it [Acts of Maximilian 3.4]).

Second, the narrator's use of the term "word" carries significance in the conversion account. Cornelius is informed that when Peter arrives, Peter will share "words of life" with him (1.2). The general proclamation of Peter is described as a universal missionary endeavor: "Thus, Peter going through *every land and sea* for proclamation, *everywhere* preached the truth ... for truly he was appointed for a light to the *gentiles and salvation for all*" (prior to settling in Joppa as a tanner; 1.3 emphasis added).[51] Rather than being the "apostle to the Jews" in contrast with the role of Paul as "apostle to the Gentiles" (cf. Gal. 2.7-8), the Peter of the Acts of Cornelius is an apostle to both Jews and Gentiles. Even more than the New Testament Acts, this apocryphal narrative establishes Peter as embracing the Gentile mission. This proclamation by Peter, especially his "words of life" to Cornelius, ties back to the gospel summary of Jesus' salvific accomplishment (as "the Word upon the earth") (1.1a). These two references to "word" nicely bracket the pious characterization of Cornelius, the Gentile centurion who will soon be converted and take on a significant missionary role in the church. Peter's dream of the descending unclean animals as food closely follows Acts 10.9-16 but infuses a few interpretative clues. The narrator adds an overt figurative reading of the dream, directly connecting the dream as symbols for Cornelius and those with him (1.7), whereas Acts 10.17 implies such a figurative reading. Both accounts repeat the virtues of Cornelius (Acts 10.22: "an upright and God-fearing man, who is well spoken of by the whole Jewish nation"// Acts Corn. 1.7b: "this symbolized his goodwill concerning his godliness

---

50. See the valuable discussion in L. Stephanie Cobb, "Polycarp's Cup: *Imitatio* in the *Martyrdom of Polycarp*," *Journal of Religious History* 38.2 (2014): 224–40. Perhaps the most significant exploration of the *imitatio Christi* motif in early Christian martyrdom remains Candida R. Moss, *The Other Christs: Imitating Jesus in Ancient Christian Ideologies of Martyrdom* (Oxford: Oxford University Press, 2010), especially the discussion of *alter Christus* in chapter 2 (on Polycarp, see pp. 57–9).

51. Note the difference between the Acts of Cornelius and the History of Simon Cephas, the Chief of the Apostles (ch. 7, the conversion of Cornelius) (dated roughly to the late fourth or fifth century), where in the latter the twelve apostles, including Peter, remain in Jerusalem in contrast to the wandering ministry of Philip of the seven (Hist. Sim. Ceph. 7.1-6). In this History of Simon Cephas, we only have a reworking of Acts 10 with no further legends of Cornelius. Cornelius' role seems to be to prompt the expansion of the ministry of the apostles beyond Jewish confines, partly building on deacon Philip's conversion of the traveling Ethiopian in ch. 6.

and zeal, and how he hungered for nothing so much ..."). After the baptism of Cornelius ("threefold immersion"), Peter "sowed the word of godliness in him and in the souls of those who had come with him" (1.8)—thus, fulfilling 1.7a's longing for "enlightenment" and the "bestow[ing] godliness." The baptism also has the Spirit "command Peter to go to them and [make] no discrimination" (1.7b).

The other interpretative redaction is set prior to the dream, where the narrator locates discrimination against Gentiles as belonging to "those who were not circumcised" (1.4). It is likely that this interpretation addition is an allusion to Galatians 2, where Paul, in conflict with Cephas (Peter), counters those of "the circumcision party" (Gal. 2.12). Unlike Galatians and perhaps Acts 10, the Acts of Cornelius does not present Peter as opposing the inclusion of Gentiles or as being dedicated to an exclusively Jewish demographic, but rather shifts the discrimination against Gentiles away from Peter. Thus, the Acts of Cornelius goes beyond Acts 10 (and even Galatians) by presenting Peter's reluctance to eat "anything profane or unclean" as mistaken interpretation by Peter not a rejection of the allegory. Peter takes the image as literal, whereas there is a deeper allegorical meaning to the image of unclean food. Peter stands completely in harmony with the Gentile mission.

The second act furthers the co-dependent simulacra of Acts and Acts of Cornelius by extending the narrative beyond Acts 10 rather than simply adjusting and reframing that narrative. The Acts of Cornelius again jumps forward from what is found in Acts, bringing us to the "dispersion of the apostles from Jerusalem after the grief over Stephen" with Cornelius "present also" (Acts. Corn. 2.1//Acts 11.19). A significant difference, however, is Acts 11.19-20: "and they spoke to no one except Jews" with "some among them ... spoke to the Hellenists also, proclaiming the Lord Jesus."[52] It is with this qualification that the two texts go their separate ways. Acts then follows the journey of Barnabas, whereas Acts of Cornelius follows Peter and Timothy (intriguing pairing, as one would have expected Timothy to be paired with Paul; again, aligning Peter to the Gentile mission as if the Petrine were the Pauline). The "spoke to no one except Jews" is completely

---

52. Significantly, the Greek *hellēnikos* is used differently in the two texts, likely reflecting historical and cultural differences. In Acts, the term refers to those Greek-speaking members of the community, whereas in the Acts of Cornelius the term follows the Byzantine usage meaning "heathen" (and is so translated by Burke and Witakowski on these grounds). For our purposes, this distinction nuances the respective characterization of the *hellēnikoi*: rather than an expanding ethnic identity from the inclusion of Jews to Gentiles (so Acts), we find a binary distinction of monotheistic Christians and polytheistic unbelievers (so Acts of Cornelius).

removed from the Acts of Cornelius. Rather, the narrative continues with Cornelius now participating in the missionary endeavors of Peter and Timothy to Ephesus, with him eventually chosen by lot (i.e., divination) to preach to the city of idols Skepsis.[53] The dispersion in the Acts of Cornelius is directly and affirmatively linked to a global missionary effort to Gentiles or, more specifically from this point on, polytheistic unbelievers. This "dispersion of the apostles" to various ends of the world is not uncommon in early Christian apocrypha. We find such allocation of the world to different apostles in, for example, the Acts of Thomas, the Acts of Thomas and His Wonderworking Skin, the Acts of Andrew and Matthias, the History of Philip, the History of Simon Cephas, the Chief of the Apostles (notably 6.1-7; cf. the acts of Philip at 6.8-11 preceding the conversion of Cornelius in chapter 7), and the Letter of Peter to Philip. Although the Synoptic gospel traditions may have been the basis for such narrative developments (Matt. 28.16-20 and Luke 24.44-49//Mark 16.14-16), it is with these apocryphal acts that we find the idea of universal mission with geographic allocations most fully developed. The Acts of Cornelius fits this development, though it does so by extending the geographic allocation beyond the eleven apostles to include—indeed, to focus upon—Cornelius. Cornelius ceases simply to be a link in an expanding chain of non-Jewish inclusion, as in Acts, to become an apostolic figure in his own right (even though never overtly declared "an apostle" in the Acts of Cornelius; his own self-presentation is as "the servant of the living God"; 2.3). Although not explicitly stated, Cornelius, if identified with the centurion at the Cross, may even fit the Lukan qualification for being an apostle, in that he was a "witness" to the death of Jesus (implied at Acts Corn. 1.2; cp. Matt. 27.54//Mark 15.39//Luke 23.47).

Beyond his participation in the apostolic division of the world, Cornelius, like many of the apostles in the apocryphal acts, further fits literary elements common for martyrological narratives. Thus, Cornelius is not only an apostle he is also a martyr. Although Cornelius does not die at the hands of Demetrius, he does serve as a witness ("martyr") before a heathen judge and faces imprisonment. There are several motifs present that are common in early Christian martyr acta. During the interrogation, Demetrius attempts to persuade Cornelius to offer sacrifice to the gods partly by an appeal to Cornelius' advanced age. Demetrius begins in confusion and frustration over Cornelius' self-description as "the servant of the living God" (2.3) and evokes the motif of age: "I will have no consideration for your old age, nor will I give concession to your years, nor respect your gray hair" (2.4). This

---

53. Burke and Witakowski, "Acts of Cornelius the Centurion," 347 n. d, observe that the Ethiopian text is corrupt, leaving Cornelius in Ephesus as the city of idols.

appeal is repeated, along with a command to offer sacrifice, after Cornelius identifies his military rank—and given the "old age" we can assume Cornelius is a veteran—and his evangelistic purpose: "At these (words) Demetrius saw now (his) old age. <He said>, 'I have pity on account of your years ... approach the gods and make sacrifice'" (2.6). This appeal to old age is not uncommon in the martyr acta. Age is a key aspect of the nobility of Polycarp and is the basis for the respect shown him by his persecutors (Mart. Polycarp 7, 9). Perpetua's father is also a tool for trying to persuade her to renounce her adherence to Christianity, that is, to pity his old age (Mart. Perp. 9). When Conon is called before the prefect, he is referred to as "grandfather" (Mart. Conon 2.5). Conon is an intriguing example of advanced age, as he is characterized as very simple, humble, and quiet—all virtues exemplifying his noble character. When we turn our attention to the military martyrs, Julius the Veteran stands out as an older person due his special pension as a veteran and possibly an *emeritus* soldier (Mart. Julius 2.3). Although his exact age is not noted, Julius served in the military for 27 years and Maximus tries to persuade him to take his bonus and enjoy the quiet retirement that he has earned.[54] Like Julius, Cornelius is likely a retired soldier of advanced years.

As with many martyr accounts, Cornelius is threatened with horrific torments if he does not offer sacrifice to the gods (Acts Corn. 2.6). It is from these threats that an antithesis between the gods and God arise: "There will be no god so powerful compared with these [torments] who will deliver you from my hands," Demetrius warns him. Cornelius replies, "My God is able to preserve me" to which he adds that God will destroy the gods or idols (2.6-7). Antithetical constructions are common literary techniques in martyr accounts to invert values and thereby undermine the persecutor's claims. What arises in the Acts of Cornelius is an antithesis of contraries (where one item is good, the other bad) rather than, as with Julius the Veteran, an antithesis of lesser-to-greater (cf. Aristotle, *Rhetorica* I.7.1-2). The antithesis between polytheistic idols and monotheism not only undercut Demetrius' threats by shifting the power dynamics from Demetrius to Cornelius (or, more correctly, to the Christian deity), it also foreshadows the destruction of the shrine of Zeus (which also leads to another antithesis in evaluating this destruction: Demetrius views it as an act of sorcery and experiences grief, whereas we are told that Cornelius enters the courtroom with joy due to the miracle). Again, an unexpected outcome from the Skepsaeans'

---

54. For a full rhetorical and social analysis of the Martyrdom of Julius the Veteran, see Philip L. Tite, "A Polite Conversation, an Edict, and a Sword: A Look at the *Martyrdom of Julius the Veteran*," Journal of Theological Studies NS 70.1 (2019): 184–238.

perspective—the gods' lack of power before a lone prisoner—that leads to the conversion of the city. The divine rescue of Evanthia and her son, which precedes the large-scale conversion including that of her husband Demetrius, is presented antithetically (they are in a "pit" or "abyss"—a place of darkness—yet "see here great miracles of God and angels crying out") (3.4). There may also be another antithesis between life and death motifs. When Cornelius goes to the fallen shrine to free the wife and son, his prayer is directed "toward the east into heaven" (3.7). Although this detail may simply evoke a directional focus to sacred geography (perhaps Jerusalem?), it could also evoke the idea of a rising sun and thus new life in a context of presumed death of the two trapped in the ruins.[55] The antitheses in this act are designed to undermine the legitimacy of the heathen worldview by contrasting it with the truth of the Christian reality that Cornelius proclaims.

All of these elements suggest that the Acts of Cornelius has extended the characterization of Acts 10 to infuse into the story of Cornelius a martyr motif to supplement the apostolic missionary motif. Through both of these character expansions, the "original" story of Cornelius in Acts 10 is reassessed or re-shaped into a fresh simulacrum, one generated from the rhizomatic matrix of the simulacrum-now-original. We find fresh layers of meaning laid over the potential interpretative outcomes of now reading the biblical account of this Christian centurion. Yet, the generative creativity does not end with the conversion of Demetrius, his family, and his city. Another layer is added in chapters 5 and 6. With the miraculous burial of Cornelius by the great bush, but also the later discovery of the coffin and its wonderous movement to a newly built shrine in honor of Cornelius, all done with visionary directions from Cornelius, we see this figure now belonging to the cult of the saints. As with most of the accounts in Gregory of Tours' *Glory of the Martyrs*, such hagiography—including visions, miracles, relics, and worship—places emphasis upon the postmortem wonders of the saint or martyr rather than the life of the martyr. Often such veneration is tied into holy relics and the power radiating from such items. This kind of hagiographic narrative is what we find in the closing chapters of the Acts of Cornelius. Thus, we have a richly layered presentation of Cornelius:

---

55. Raising up or ascending (especially when juxtaposed with death and disbelief as being brought down) seems to be a recurring motif in the Acts of Cornelius (e.g., 1.1-3; 2.3, 7; 3.4, 7; 4.1, 2; 5.4; and 6.3). This motif may be designed to link Cornelius back to "the voluntary cross and death for our sake, and the ascent into heaven" (1.1), thereby linking him to the centurion who witnessed Jesus' crucifixion in the Gospel of Luke. Furthermore, the goal "to build the fallen house of David" (1.1) may establish a parallel of the inversion of fallen and building for the destruction of the shrine of Zeus and the building of the shrine of the saint.

an apostle/missionary, martyr/witness, and venerated saint—all building on and thus creatively interpreting the Gentile mission motif found in Acts 10.

Perhaps the most unique version of the Acts of Cornelius is the Ethiopic translation (EMML 1824). Here we find several variants that serve to resituate the text to fit the political and theological context of the fourteenth and fifteenth centuries. Although many of the variants seemingly are minor translation choices, while others seem to reflect the intermediary Arabic vorlage, there are several redactional shifts that engage significant social, political, and theological controversies that defined the religious landscape of Ethiopia in the fifteenth century. This manuscript was likely commissioned by Yosef, the archimandrite after 1403 of the Dabrä Hayq 'Estifanos monastery north of Addis Ababa, and was the property of the monastery.[56]

The Ethiopian version of the Acts of Cornelius includes significant differences worth noting in order to better appreciate the rhizomes arising through and within this text. Many of these variances directly address concepts of God, especially in advancing Trinitarian theology (often while contrasting polytheism with monotheism):[57]

> 2.3—I am a servant of the living God, who can open the eyes of your heart that you may stop worshipping a worthless idol. Now, God has sent me to you that you may turn to the enlightenment and justice and venerate the Holy Trinity.

> 2.9—And you, O Prefect, why do you not turn away from the worship of gods that are worthless to you and turn to Christ, your God, to whom be glory? Now, you may save yourself and all who have the same faith as you. If you reject my words, show me those who say that there are gods, whereas I will show you the power of truth.

> 2.11—You are the God of truth and thus you will be worshipped and your holy name praised. Praise and glory are due to you—to the Father, the Son, and the Holy Spirit—forever and ever, Amen.

> 2.13—Bring that treacherous magician who by his sorcery destroyed the house of the gods.

> 3.7—I praise you, my God, who have created heaven, earth and sea and everything that is in them! You Lord, show your power and your miracles to those who believe in you, and to your servant Demetrius, and bring out his wife Atomia and his son Demetrius from imprisonment beneath, that your name be praised! Glorious is the Father, the Son, and the Holy Spirit, forever and ever! Amen.

---

56. See discussion in Burke and Witakowski, "Acts of Cornelius the Centurion," 339–40.

57. All translations are from Burke and Witakowski, "Acts of Cornelius the Centurion." The Ethiopic variants are translated by Witakowski in the notes.

172 *Critical Theory and Early Christianity*

> 3.8—Great is the God of the Christians, who revealed his power and glory by the hand of his servant Cornelius, and rescued us from the sin of the worship of idols!
>
> 3.9a— … and he would admonish and teach them the word of God. They received his admonitions and teachings and they praised and extolled our Lord Jesus Christ.
>
> 3.9b—Some of those who had remained pagans were drawn to the saint. He received them and made the sign of the cross of Christ over them, and baptized all of them in the name of the Father, the Son, and the Holy Spirit. He instructed them and commanded that they observe God's every commandment, and he prayed for them. When he finished his prayer all of them said "Amen."
>
> 4.2—O Lord, my God, you who have created the heaven, earth, sea and everything which is in them, you have created me. By your grace you helped me to complete my righteous struggle and to defeat Satan, the evil deceiver, who seduces your servants and maids! I give you thanks, good Lord, because you comforted my heart, woke up my troubled and tired soul, and enlightened my heart by (showing) the life of this transient world, so that I might turn to the enlightenment of truth. And you, O Lord, look from your heavens at your servants and maids and preserve their souls and bodies! Show to them favor out of the grace of your spiritual gifts and bequeath to them that they may not become old or decay, that they might praise your holy name. Praise is due to you—to the Father, the Son, and the Holy Spirit, forever, Amen.

There are two further and lengthy differences when Cornelius' coffin is transported to the shrine (5.8 and 5.9b). These two differences in chapter 5 both evoke "the Holy Trinity," "a Gospel book," and have a distinctly Ethiopian mention of "Saturday" as the day when "the bishop gathered the priests and all the faithful" as they engage liturgical activities (reciting prayers, burning incense, and "carrying a Gospel book") as they honor the placement of Cornelius' coffin. There are other differences, of course, such as the heightened hagiographic tone of the text in chapter 4, but these theological alterations are perhaps the most insightful ones for tracing the peculiar Ethiopian rhizomes at play in this version of the Acts of Cornelius.

The fifteenth and sixteenth centuries in Ethiopia were years of intense theological controversy.[58] Most of these debates occurred within the contexts

---

58. A very helpful and accessible overview of the history of Ethiopian Christianity in regard to these controversies is offered by Philip F. Esler, *Ethiopian Christianity: History, Theology, Practice* (Waco, TX: Baylor University Press, 2019), especially 43–73. More detailed discussions of these controversies are offered by Getatchew Haile, "Religious Controversies and the Growth of Ethiopic Literature in the Fourteenth and Fifteenth Centuries," *Oriens Christianus* 65 (1981): 102–36; Pierluigi Piovanelli, "Connaissance de dieu et sagesse humaine en Éthiopie: Le traité *Explication de la Divinité* attribué aux hérétiques 'mikaélites,'" *Muséon* 117.1–2 (2004): 193–227; and Aaron

of different monastic communities, yet also involved imperial authorities of the Solomonic dynasty. Most noteworthy is the role played by the emperor Zär'a Ya'əqob (b. 1399; r. 1434–1468), who took an adamant position on many of these theological disagreements and largely shaped the theological contours for the Ethiopian traditional church, such as with Ya'əqob's promotion of the veneration of the Virgin Mary.[59] These controversies predate Ya'əqob's reign, of course. Yet, it is on the concept of the Trinity and the sabbath controversy that the dissimilitude arising within the Acts of Cornelius can be explained. The controversy over the mystery of the unity of the Trinity centered on the image of God as either three different yet identical suns or one sun with three distinct properties. As Getatchew Haile nicely summarizes the conflict:

> The point of the controversy was whether the mystery of the unity and the trinity of God should be interpreted with three distinct suns, each representing one person of the Trinity, or with one sun, its disc representing the Father, its light the Son and its heat the Holy Spirit. According to Zär'a Ya'əqob the example of three suns would illustrate clearly the existence of three distinct persons in the Trinity. For the dissidents, however, this would be tantamount to saying three gods; they preferred, instead, the example of one sun. This was vehemently rejected by the Emperor, who saw Sabellianism in it, a limitation of the theology of the Trinity to *səm*, "name," only, and not extended to *mälkə'*, "appearance," "stature," "hypostasis," "figure," "form."[60]

Thus, the debate was over one object with three attributes (as advocated by the dissidents) and one attribute in three objects (as advocated by the emperor's party).[61] In addition, the conflation of God with the created order through his "likeness" was a point of contention, especially with the Zämika'elites and the emperor. The controversy revolved around claims that only God knows his likeness or form (*mälkə'*) or his self (*səm*) because God stands beyond the image of the creatures of the created order. When we turn our attention to the sabbath controversy, here we find a longstanding tension between Ethiopian Christianity and its Jewish heritage.[62] All accepted

---

Michael Butts, "Ethiopian Christianity," in *Eastern Christianity: A Reader* (ed. James E. Walters; Grand Rapids, MI: Eerdmans, 2021), 366–410. See also Getatchew Haile, "The Cause of the Ǝstifanosites: A Fundamentalist Sect in the Church of Ethiopia," *Paideuma* 29 (1983): 93–119. We also wish to express a word of appreciation to Sophia Dege-Müller for her helpful feedback while researching the theological context of fifteenth-century Ethiopian Christianity.

59. See also the discussion in Getatchew Haile, "A Hymn to the Blessed Virgin from Fifteenth-Century Ethiopia," *Worship* 65 (1991): 445–50.
60. Haile, "Religious Controversies," 108.
61. See Haile, "Religious Controversies," 109, 120–5.
62. See Esler, *Ethiopian Christianity*, 59–60.

that Sunday was to be kept as the sabbath, but what about Saturday? Should the church keep two weekly sabbaths or just the one? The argument against the two sabbaths was that the church would be reverting to its Jewish heritage rather than remaining Christian. This controversy revolved around the Ewosṭatewosites, who promoted the keeping of a Saturday sabbath. When Ya'əqob came to power, he sided with the Ewosṭatewosites' view that Saturday was to be kept as a Christian holy day. This debate was decided at the Council of Dābrā Matmaq in 1450, chaired by Ya'əqob.[63]

In turning to the Acts of Cornelius, this historical context of theological debate illuminates the differences in the Ethiopian translation of the text. During this energetic and tense period in Ethiopian theological formation, much of the debate occurred through the production of new texts, notably liturgical works, and the editing of older texts including translations of non-Ethiopian works.[64] The Acts of Cornelius fits the latter category. Although the Acts of Cornelius does not overtly declare a position on these debated points, it does seem to advance the "traditional" church position over against the so-called dissidents. Specifically, and most clearly, on Trinitarianism where the additions to the acts push against the dissident view of one sun with three attributes. It is noteworthy that these mentions of God as a triune being conflate the plural into the singular being, with all characteristics or functions either equally shared or not distinctly allocated. As in the traditional view, each person of the Trinity is interchangeable with regard to attributes but distinct entities ("three suns" though the image of "the sun" is not used in the Acts of Cornelius): The "living God" is equated with "the Holy Trinity" (2.3). At 3.7 the praise to God is due to his being the source of all creation, with power and miracles demonstrated through the rescuing of Atomia and the son Demetrius. The praise concludes on a high point of worship: "Glorious is the Father, the Son, and the Holy Spirit, forever and ever! Amen." This conclusion is preceded by a statement to "your name be praised!" The same kind of formula—"your holy name [be] praised" with the "God of truth" liturgically qualified as "the Father, the Son, and the Holy Spirit"—arises at 2.11 and similarly at 4.2. Often this Trinitarian formula is set in contrast with polytheism and idolatry (e.g., "the house of the gods" [2.13]; "a worthless idol" [2.3]; "the sin of the worship of idols" [3.8]), thereby using out-group conflict (in the narrative) to address in-group orthodoxy (pointing beyond the text). The Trinity is not presented

---

63. See Haile, "Religious Controversies," 131–3; Getatchew Haile, "The Letter of Archbishops Mika'el and Gäbrə'el Concerning the Observance of Saturday," *Journal of Semitic Studies* 26.1 (1981): 73–8.

64. Haile, "Religious Controversies," 102, 116.

as three gods, but is contrasted with polytheistic worship, thereby keeping the Trinity within a monotheistic system. Both the traditional church and the dissidents were concerned over polytheistic understandings of the Trinity, but it is with the presentation of the three persons as tied into the one without any distinction of attributes, that the Acts of Cornelius seems to articulate the position that a few decades later Zär'a Ya'əqob will support and enforce. In addition to the way the text presents the three persons of the Trinity, the continued mention of the *name* of God (2.11, 3.7, 3.9b, and 4.2) may evoke the controversy over the likeness or name of God. The Acts of Cornelius does not expound on this point of debate, however, and remains somewhat ambiguous. Rather, we find in the Acts of Cornelius that the "name" of God, which God has, properly belongs to the realm of worship. One does not know the name or likeness of God, one offers praise and worship to the name. It is also possible that the tale of the painter—specifically, the need to have the likeness of the saint revealed—may tie into this controversy while also reflecting the significant expansion of artistic religious expression during this period, if Cornelius' "unknown" image for his postmortem portrait serves as an analogy for the divine image.[65]

Finally, on the role of sabbath observance, the Ethiopic version distinguishes the day when Cornelius' coffin is miraculously moved to the new shrine as Saturday: "When the next day came, it was *Saturday*, the bishop gathered the priests and all the faithful. They went to the place where the casket (was), *reciting prayers, (burning) incense*, and *carrying a gospel book*. (The procession) moved *reciting praises* to the *Holy Trinity*" (5.9, emphasis added; cp. with parallels to "gospel book" "praising the Holy Trinity" and a procession filled with prayers at 5.8). Although there is no specific mention in the text of observing Saturday as a sabbath day, it is clear that the day is a holy day filled with both the worship of God and the veneration of the saint. That the text specifically adds "Saturday" is an important detail, given the sabbath debate dividing Ethiopian Christianity during this period. We can also see a hagiographic element here, as the text specifies that this is "the next day"—thus, it is possible that Cornelius is presented as a Christ figure, whose crucifixion on Friday may be alluded to here (though such an *imitatio Christi* motif is somewhat speculative). However, for a fifteenth-century reader in Ethiopia, the liturgical qualities in 5.9 would articulate a double sabbath position, an articulation that directly ties into Trinitarian debates. Thus, the differences found in the Ethiopic Acts

---

65. See the discussion in Butts, "Ethiopian Christianity," on the growth of artistic expression during this period. Cf. Piovanelli, "L'Explication de la divinité," 218–23 on conflicts over iconography.

of Cornelius situates this version within and arises from the historical and theological context of fifteenth-century Ethiopia.

The diverse simulacra of the story of Cornelius—from the possible sources underlying Acts 10, to canonical Acts 10, to the Greek differences and expansions on the canonical text in the apocryphal acts, and finally to the Ethiopic divergences—are all moments of repetitions with differences. All of these differences are based on an assumed *model*, yet it is the very model that is variable in each production of differences and thus the model is equally a simulacrum. The preface creates the (canonical) model to which it points the reader: editing, conflating, presenting, and obscuring the Lukan biblical account of Cornelius. It calls on the reader to identify the model as the original, while, simultaneously, framing the model in such a way that the original is only seen through the lens of the copy. Thus, as Deleuze notes, it is through such differentiation that the model itself is a simulacrum because, we could add, it functions as the model. The missional, martyrological, and hagiographic pieces extend the story so that even the simulacra are layers built upon other simulacra; each is a model that is transformed by new and different moments of creative play. Rather than linear historical distortions of the original, we have instead points along the rhizome where each moment of generative creativity is a moment of becoming.

Conclusion: Implications and Questions

By way of concluding, we want to propose a series of questions to ask when analyzing texts in the Acts trajectory (or more proper to Deleuze, texts within the Acts simulacrum). Here we simply want to highlight a process by which a Deleuzian hermeneutic can substantiate an approach to the Acts tradition that is not working from canonical assumptions. Hence, this conclusion will provide more questions than answers, but hopefully give concrete starting points for a Deleuzian approach to the Acts simulacrum. A key question to ask is: Why does it matter that we take a Deleuzian approach to the Acts simulacrum rather than using standard redactional and source analysis (vis-à-vis Baudrillard's original and copy model)? What do we gain that may not arise from more traditional exegetical and historical approaches such as source criticism, redaction criticism, and tradition criticism? To begin, we want to stress that these well-established exegetical approaches are not to be discarded, but rather subsumed under or utilized within a critical theory that may better elucidate the interpretative processes by which social actors creatively engage, transform, and activate unique works by using semblances to bring about differences. The simulation that arises is not merely something new or derivative, as if there is merely an original and a series of (distorted) copies, but rather the simulation is transformative of the world (or work) from which is arose. We move both forward and backward in time, or, more accurately, each point on the rhizome is continually in a state of becoming as they are interdependently being transformed by the other points on the rhizome.

First, we need to ask: under what conditions this production happens? Nothing happens in a vacuum. Transformations are contextual just as they are interdependent. To draw upon the metaphor of the strawberry plant, or the rhizome, we could ask ourselves what kind of soil is the plant growing in? How do the shoots adapt to the confines of space, weather, type of soil, access to light, and so on? Just as our berry bushes will reflect their context, so also with literature and art and thought. In our above example of the Acts simulacrum, we dedicated extra space to the historical, political, and theological "soil" where the Ethiopic simulacrum took root and grew. Yet, each point along the rhizome of the Acts tradition is nurtured by and thereby reflects the distinct soil (or conditions) where the semblances are produced through differences. Thus, to study points along the Acts tradition is to contextualize the process of producing the Other, the production of differences.

Second, what are the sources of Acts of Cornelius? It is not using modern critical editions, such as NA[28]! It is not repeating and differing from the Acts of Apostles that we see in our Bibles in 2022. Rather, it is repeating and differing from the Acts simulacrum, including the diverse layers of previous points along the rhizome. Our own simulation process should not be discounted. Each of us is a subject, contextualized within our own interpretative communities (to evoke Stanley Fish) and through which our sources are read and interpreted as authoritative. Beyond our own self-reflexivity, we also need to recognize the creative use of sources engaged in by both the Acts of Cornelius and the Acts of the Apostles. Perhaps instead of seeing "sources" as copies that fade (the analogy of the photocopy of the photocopy of the photocopy of the original), or objects that are building blocks for larger textual productions, we could instead see sources as "layers" of interpretative moments. Each moment is as "authentic," as "real," as "valid" as any other moment—even when those moments conflict. Indeed, we learn from Deleuze that when a simulation veers in different directions that this is when an original arises: the simulacrum is *an* original yet not *the* original.

Third, how does a given moment in the Acts tradition capture changes and movements—and how are they reactivated in their reception? In many ways, a Deleuzian approach to texts is an ongoing activity rather than an end product or object. We are dealing with *verbal* moments not delimiting *nouns* (to evoke a common metaphor in theory circles). To do Deleuzian exegesis is to look at similarities and differences that are processes of creativity. Our goal as scholars is to watch those processes, to analyze the activation and transformation of traditions. Source criticism is a contributing step in that kind of analysis. Thus, we are not identifying underlying texts or using texts to reconstruct some *Ur*-text that is "original" (such an effort would merely be our own process of creativity as we create a further simulacrum within the Acts tradition), but rather doing a non-linear exploration of the diverse points of simulation. We can explore the back-and-forth influences between our sources, sources which are more eruptions of a given "now" that are continually intersecting other moments of "now." Throughout this essay, we have stressed that there is a process by which the assumed "original" or underlying source not only effects influence on "copies" that follow it, but also are affected by those copies. The image of Cornelius in Acts 10 is given a fresh, different nuance following, for example, the missional deviation. To return to Acts 10 is to really read the Gentile mission and the apostolic division of the world through a new lens. Acts 10 has become something new. Indeed, through simulation it veers from itself through difference. All becomes simulacra. This insight reveals the falsity of assumptions about representation and identity in the Acts tradition.[66] We often work from the assumptions that one is representing the true Cornelius story and later apocryphal work is not. What if neither are representing, but rather each is creating something new for their audiences?

Fourth, how does this text continue an intensity of difference (along a spectrum) in the Acts tradition? Exploring these differences via Deleuze allows us to avoid a clear, categorical binary "demarcation" of difference, such as the canonical and the apocryphal. The study of ancient to medieval Christian texts has been burdened by canonical bias, where a Baudrillard approach to simulation has romanticized the canonical and denigrated the apocryphal. From Baudrillard's perspective, the apocryphal would constitute the perversion of the original through false representation. An outcome of such a view has resulted in non-canonical works being valued only when they are deemed early and useful for better understanding the canonical works. The study of New Testament apocrypha has long suffered from such a bias in scholarship. Even the study of manuscripts have long been conducted to reconstruct some "original" recension, rather than appreciating each manuscript as a moment of creativity.[67] A Deleuzian approach,

66. See fn. 41 above.
67. In an important study of the variants of the Apocryphon of John, Karen King long ago argued just this point. See King, "Approaching the Variants of the *Apocryphon of John*," in *The Nag Hammadi Library After Fifty Years: Proceedings of the 1995 Society of Biblical Literature Commemoration* (ed. John D. Turner and Anne McGuire; NHMS, 45; Leiden: Brill, 1997), 105–37. She insightfully observes: "Rather than see

however, allows us to better appreciate the production, transformation, and consumption of religious texts by diverse people in diverse communities engaged in diverse moments of interpretation. None are any more "real" or "authentic" than another, except perhaps from the perspective of those producing simulations. Indeed, the canonical—as category—still is useful when it is evoked and played with by social actors who are playing with their traditions. The Acts of Cornelius, for example, points to its own "original" or canonical source as part of its own generative act of producing an "authentic" work that transforms the canonical (indeed, subsumes the canonical to the apocryphal by overtly subsuming the apocryphal to the canonical). Again, we return to the playfulness of disparity.

To study the Acts simulacrum—as one example of Christian textual traditions to which we can apply critical theories—through a Deleuzian lens is to study the epistemological processes whereby social and intellectual histories create and recreate meanings. If we can only know things not only *through* but *as* expressions, then there can be no original or authentic (contra Baudrillard), in the sense of the originary-to-the-copy. Rather, they are both expressions and both original; they function as nodes in a reciprocal exchange of value. Thus, each one serves the function of being both the copy and the source for the other. The original and the copy collapse into each other by necessity. This is the rhizome, the simulacra of identity liquidation and identity generation *through* such liquidation. The authentic, therefore, is the simulacrum functioning as the original for the original which is not the simulacrum. The nodes in meaning go beyond the generative to the interdependent. They rely upon each other for their authenticity, their originality, and thus their value—yet value or reliance within given generative contexts (what Stanley Fish called the interpretative community). This is the semantic domain through which the rhizome grows and is nourished. The semantic, to use once again the planting metaphor, is not a single pot for a single plant. That singular (if it could exist at all) ceases to be a rhizome, as its solitary existence merely is the illusion of the *sui generis*. Rather, the semantic is the flower bed, the garden if you will, through which the generative is continually at work. If there are grand narratives, or grand interpretative structures,

---

the tendencies of a version as the distortion of the hypothetical 'original,' tendencies can be analyzed as evidence of the meaning and practices (the social and intellectual history) of the audiences who knew the *Apocryphon of John*. In this approach, the 'tendencies' of the texts are no longer perceived as 'corruptions' or 'distortions' that must be removed in order to reveal the original practices of the 'circles' around the *Apocryphon of John*; they are instead important keys to understanding the history of such 'circles.' Privileging the 'original' with regard to 'reliability' effectively erases or at least devalues the text's history and performances, which are keys to social and intellectual history" (132–3).

these are the product—indeed, the "grand" rhizome—of the garden, at a given moment, taken in reflexively and creating a new simulation. It is the pause. The pause is the grand rhizome, the broad and bold statement: this is history, this is reality, this is the great design, the movement from something to something. We may call this the paradigm, the frame, the narrative, the perspective. Perhaps even the statement of self-importance, of hubris. Whatever we call it, it remains another simulacrum, though one functioning to hold—indeed, to contain—all other simulacra within a class (to evoke theories on class and class inclusion/exclusion). Yet, even the simulacra are containers in that they hold other simulacra in their claims to not be simulacra or to be simulacra that point to the original (the original as generative rhizomes of the copy, thereby given the status of the original yet no more original than the scholia, the gloss, the marginalia). That which is called "authentic" is only authentic through the lens of the interpretative; thus, the interpretative is the authentic rather than that which is pointed to as the authentic. There is a necessary contradiction in that the interpretative relies upon the authentic to hold authenticity of voice while that authenticity of voice is what lends authenticity to the object called the authentic (the latter's own authenticity now dependent upon the voice granting authenticity). To call something a copy is to try to contain copies, and such efforts at classification are acts of functional imposition or interpretation. They are themselves processes of simulation, moments of disparity and thus creativity. Here is where we tackle the hermeneutical, and here is where the hermeneutical collapses into its own creativity, its own originality. The circular discourse of the "real" and the "authoritative" only exists within the garden of the simulacra. Other gardens will carry different claims of the authoritative. Thus, there are multiple originals as there are multiple copies or derivatives. If these dependencies and independencies can be theorized along such lines, then it makes sense to claim that there is no such thing as an apocryphal text vis-à-vis the canonical text. Both serve as canonical and apocryphal. Indeed, to be canonical—and to hold canonical meaning and thus, for diverse social actors in various contexts, meaningfulness—is to be dependent upon the apocryphal or the derivative. Such dependency results in the insight that the canonical is the derivative or, in Deleuze's terms, the simulacrum within a network or web of nodes/pauses of interdependent simulacra. Thus, there is no original, only the original derived from the rhizome.

Biographical Notes

Matthew G. Whitlock (PhD, The Catholic University of America, 2008) is Associate Professor of New Testament at Seattle University. His research focuses on Acts of the Apostles, the Apostle Paul, New Testament Poetry, Critical Theory, and Science Fiction. His publications have focused on topics ranging from New Testament poetry in the *Catholic Biblical Quarterly* to the Body without Organs and Christianity in *Deleuze and Guattari Studies*. He is currently working on two books on dialectical images, one on images from the Science Fiction of Philip K. Dick and images from the letters of Paul, and the other on the theme of fame in images from the life of Kurt Cobain and early Christian writings about Jesus of Nazareth.

Philip L. Tite (PhD, McGill University, 2005) is a specialist in early Christian studies with strong interests in method and theory in the academic study of religion, engaging research on ancient Gnosticism, ancient martyrdom, apocryphal traditions, religion and violence, and social scientific approaches to the study of religion. He is the founding editor of Studies in Ancient Religion and Culture, served as editor of the Bulletin for the Study of Religion for nine years, and is the author of numerous books and articles. Dr. Tite is an affiliate lecturer at the University of Washington in Seattle and an instructor at Youngstown State University.

Bibliography

Aichele, George. *Simulating Jesus: Reality Effects in the Gospels*. Abingdon: Routledge, 2014. https://doi.org/10.4324/9781315729237
Alliez, Eric, and Michel Feher. "Notes on the Sophisticated City," *Zone* 1.2 (1986): 40–55.
Baudrillard, Jean. *Simulacra and Simulation*. Translated by Sheila Faria Glaser. Ann Arbor: The University of Michigan Press, 1994. https://doi.org/10.3998/mpub.9904
Berressem, Hanjo. "Crystal History: 'You Pick Up the Pieces. You Connect the Dots,'" 216–8 in *Time and History in Deleuze and Serres*. Edited by Bernd Herzogenrath. London: Bloomsbury, 2012.
Borges, Jorge Luis. *Collected Fictions*. Translated by Andrew Hurley. New York: Viking, 1998.
Bovon, Francois. "Canonical and Apocryphal Acts of the Apostles," *Journal for the Study of the New Testament* 11 (2003): 165–94. https://doi.org/10.1353/earl.2003.0019
Braun, Willi. "The Past as Simulacrum in the Canonical Narratives of Christian Origins," *Religion & Theology* 8 (2001): 213–28. https://doi.org/10.1163/157430101X00107
Burke, Tony, and Witold Witakowski. "The Acts of Cornelius the Centurion," 337–61 in *New Testament Apocrypha: More Noncanonical Scriptures*. Edited by Tony Burke and Brent Landau. Grand Rapids, MI: Eerdmans, 2016.
Butts, Aaron Michael. "Ethiopian Christianity," 366–410 in *Eastern Christianity; A Reader*. Edited by James E. Walters. Grand Rapids, MI: Eerdmans, 2021.
Cobb, L. Stephanie. "Polycarp's Cup: *Imitatio* in the *Martyrdom of Polycarp*," *Journal of Religious History* 38.2 (2014): 224–40. https://doi.org/10.1111/1467-9809.12008
Colebrook, Claire. *Gilles Deleuze*. Routledge Critical Thinkers. Abingdon: Routledge, 2002. https://doi.org/10.4324/9780203241783

Deleuze, Gilles. "Plato and the Simulacrum." Translated by Rosalind Krauss. *October* 27 (Winter 1983): 45–66. https://doi.org/10.2307/778495
—*Dialogues*. Translated by H. Tomlinson and B. Habberjam. New York: Columbia University Press, 1987.
—*Difference and Repetition*. Translated by Paul Patton. Revised edition. New York: Columbia University Press, 1994.
Deleuze, Gilles, and Félix Guattari. *Anti-Oedipus*. Translated by Robert Hurley, Mark Seem, and Helen R. Lane. New York: Viking, 1977.
—*What Is Philosophy?* New York: Columbia University Press, 1996.
Esler, Philip F. *Ethiopian Christianity: History, Theology, Practice*. Waco, TX: Baylor University Press, 2019.
Foakes-Jackson, F. J., and Kirsopp Lake, eds. *The Beginnings of Christianity, Part I: The Acts of the Apostles*. 5 volumes. London: Macmillan, 1920–1933.
Haile, Getachew. "The Letter of Archbishops Mika'el and Gäbrə'el Concerning the Observance of Saturday," *Journal of Semitic Studies* 26.1 (1981): 73–8.
—"Religious Controversies and the Growth of Ethiopic Literature in the Fourteenth and Fifteenth Centuries," *Oriens Christianus* 65 (1981): 102–36.
—"The Cause of the Ǝstifanosites: A Fundamentalist Sect in the Church of Ethiopia," *Paideuma* 29 (1983): 93–119.
—"A Hymn to the Blessed Virgin from Fifteenth-Century Ethiopia," *Worship* 65 (1991): 445–50. https://doi.org/10.1093/jss/26.1.73
Holland, Eugene. "Non-Linear Historical Materialism; Or, What is Revolutionary in Deleuze and Guattari's Philosophy of History?" 17–30 in *Time and History in Deleuze and Serres*. Edited by Bernd Herzogenrath. London: Bloomsbury, 2012.
Keener, Craig S. *Acts: An Exegetical Commentary*. 4 volumes. Grand Rapids, MI: Baker, 2012–2015.
King, Karen. "Approaching the Variants of the *Apocryphon of John*," 105–37 in *The Nag Hammadi Library after Fifty Years: Proceedings of the 1995 Society of Biblical Literature Commemoration*. Edited by John D. Turner and Anne McGuire. Nag Hammadi and Manichaean Series, 45. Leiden: Brill, 1997. https://doi.org/10.1163/9789004439740_012
Lacan, Jacques. *The Four Fundamental Concepts of Psychoanalysis*. Translated by Alan Sheridan. New York: Norton, 1981.
Lampert, Jay. *Deleuze and Guattari's Philosophy of History*. London: Continuum, 2006. https://doi.org/10.5040/9781472546258
Martin, Jean-Clet. *Variations: The Philosophy of Gilles Deleuze*. Translated by Constantin V. Boundas and Susan Drykton. Edinburgh: Edinburgh University Press, 2010. https://doi.org/10.1017/UPO9780748642342
Massumi, Brian. "Realer than Real: The Simulacrum according to Deleuze and Guattari," *Copyright* 1 (1987): 90–7.
Merrin, William. "Did You Ever Eat Tasty Wheat: Baudrillard and the Matrix," *Scope: An Online Journal of Film Studies*, May 2003. https://www.nottingham.ac.uk/scope/documents/2003/may-2003/merrin.pdf
Moss, Candida R. *The Other Christs: Imitating Jesus in Ancient Christian Ideologies of Martyrdom*. Oxford: Oxford University Press, 2010. https://doi.org/10.1093/acprof:oso/9780199739875.001.0001
Öztürk, Seyda. "Simulation Reloaded." *Cinetext*, August 2003. http://cinetext.philo.at/magazine/ozturk/seyda_ozturk-simulation_reloaded.pdf
Piovanelli, Pierluigi. "Connaissance de dieu et sagesse humaine en Éthiopie: Le traité

Explication de la Divinité attribué aux hérétiques 'mikaélites,'" *Muséon* 117.1–2 (2004): 193–227. https://doi.org/10.2143/MUS.117.1.504583

Read-Heimerdinger, Jenny, and Josep Rius-Camps. *The Message of Acts in Codex Bezae: A Comparison with the Alexandrian Tradition.* 4 volumes. London: T&T Clark, 2004–2009.

Roffe, Jonathan. "Simulacrum," 253 in *The Deleuze Dictionary*. Edited by Adrian Parr. Revised edition. Edinburgh: Edinburgh University Press, 2010.

Sharpe, Eric J. *Comparative Religion: A History*. 2nd edition. London: Open Court, 1986).

Smith, Daniel W. "Platonism—The Concepts of the Simulacrum: Deleuze and the Overturning of Platonism," 3–26 in *Essays on Deleuze.* Edinburgh: Edinburgh University Press, 2012.

Thompson, Richard P. "Reading Beyond the Text, Part I: Poetics, Rhetoric, and Religious Texts from the Greco-Roman World," *ARC: The Journal of the Faculty of Religious Studies, McGill University* 28 (2000): 115–42.

—"Reading Beyond the Text, Part II: Literary Creativity and Characterization in Narrative Religious Texts of the Greco-Roman World," *ARC: The Journal of the Faculty of Religious Studies, McGill University* 29 (2001): 81–122.

Tite, Philip L. "A Polite Conversation, an Edict, and a Sword: A Look at the *Martyrdom of Julius the Veteran*," *Journal of Theological Studies* NS 70.1 (2019): 184–238. https://doi.org/10.1093/jts/fly179

Trouillot, Michel-Rolph. *Silencing the Past: Power and the Production of History*. Boston: Beacon, 1995.

Tyson, Joseph B. *Marcion and Luke-Acts: A Defining Struggle*. Columbia, SC: University of South Carolina Press, 2006.

Williams, James. "Deleuze," in *Encyclopedia of Aesthetics.* 4 volumes. Edited by Michael Kelly. New York: Oxford University Press, 1998.

Winter, Bruce W., ed. *The Book of Acts in First Century Setting*. 5 volumes. Grand Rapids, MI: Eerdmans, 1993–1996.

Chapter Eight

Face-ing the Nations: Becoming a Majority Empire of God Reterritorialization, Language, and Imperial Racism in Revelation 7.9-17

Sharon Jacob

No Hindu who has received an English education ever remains sincerely attached to his religion. It is my firm belief [so they always were] that if our plans of education are followed up, there will not be a single idolater among the respected classes in Bengal thirty years hence.[1]

—Donald Eugene Smith

And they cried out in *a loud voice*: "Salvation belongs to our God, who sits on the throne, and to the Lamb."[2]

—Revelation 7.10

The production of nation and nationhood is based in the unanimity of language. The language of people speaking in one voice signifies nations as stable, fixed, and homogenous entities. Timothy Brennan observes, "Nations, then, are imaginary constructs that depend for their existence on an apparatus of cultural fictions in which imaginative literature plays a decisive role."[3] Written texts promoting a sense of nationhood become fundamentally political to the transformation of nations into "distinctively uniform" entities.[4] In other words, the birth of a nation, relying on the imaginary, is brought into existence through written words. Although the book

---

1. Donald Eugene Smith, *India as a Secular State* (Princeton, NJ: Princeton University Press, 1963), 339. Also cf. Lord Thomas Babington Macaulay, "Minute on Education," 2 February 1835, published in Henry Sharp, selections from the *Educational Records, Bureau of Education, India* I (Calcutta, 1920).
2. The translation that I will be using in this essay is the New Revised Standard Version. Italics here are my own.
3. Timothy Brennan, "The National Longing for Form," in Bill Ashcroft, Gareth Griffiths, and Helen Tiffin, eds., *The Post-Colonial Studies Reader* (2nd edn.; New York: Routledge, 1995), 128–32, here 130.
4. Brennan, "The National Longing for Form," 130. Speaking about novels in the post-war period, Brennan points out: "The idea of nationhood is not only a political plea, but a formal binding together of disparate elements. And out of the multiplicities of culture, race, and political structures, grows also a repeated dialectic of uniformity and specificity: of world culture and national culture, of family and of people."

of Revelation never once uses the word nationalism, the text articulates in its pages a nationalized vision of a sovereign, yet limited empire of God.[5] The author of Revelation presents the divine empire of God as an alternative to the Roman Empire.[6] However, this divine empire in the book of Revelation, morphed into a nationalized vision, is imagined as a community comprised of various nations that are assimilated into one imperial vision of God.[7] The collective communal consciousness of nations envisioned by John of Patmos, which is embedded into a nationalized language, produces a "uniquely uniformed" free nation under God.

This essay focuses on Revelation 7.9-17, which gestures toward a national vision of the divine empire, where people from all the nations, tribes, and languages gather before the Lamb and cry out in one voice and in one language. Giles Deleuze and Félix Guattari in *A Thousand Plateaus* comment on the role of language in relation to obedience: "Language is not made to be believed but to be obeyed, and to compel obedience."[8] Language prefigures as a tool of obedience in Revelation 7.9-17, used to not only compel obedience among the various nations, but to allow for the recognition of these nations by replacing their native language with Greek, one of the official languages of the Empire.

Continuing further, Deleuze and Guattari write: "We can conceive of several ways for a language to homogenize, centralize ... The scientific enterprise of extracting constants and constant relations is always coupled

---

5. Benedict Anderson, "Imagined Communities," in Ashcroft, Griffiths, and Tiffin, eds., *Post-Colonial Studies Reader*, 123–6, here 124. I draw on the work of Anderson, who defines nation as "... an imagined political community—and imagined as both inherently limited and sovereign."

6. Susan R. Garrett, "Revelation," in *Women's Bible Commentary: Expanded Edition* (ed. Carol A. Newsom and Sharon H. Ringe; Louisville, KY: Westminster John Knox, 1998), 469–74, here 469. Garrett points out how the New Jerusalem is an alternative city to Rome: "Some of the book's most important symbols use feminine imagery. The new Jerusalem is envisioned as 'coming down out of heaven from God, prepared as a bride adorned for her husband' (21:2). At the opposite extreme, the city of Babylon (a symbolic name for Rome) is portrayed as a whore, 'holding in her hand a golden cup full of abominations and the impurities of her fornications' (17:4)."

7. Anderson, "Imagined Communities," 125. Anderson argues that the nation is imagined as a community "because, regardless of the actual inequality and exploitation that may prevail in each, the nation is always conceived as a deep, horizontal comradeship. Ultimately it is this fraternity that makes it possible, over the past two centuries, for so many millions of people, not so much to kill, as willingly to die for such limited imaginings."

8. Gilles Deleuze and Felix Guattari, *A Thousand Plateaus: Capitalism and Schizophrenia* (trans. Brian Massumi; Minneapolis, MN: University of Minnesota Press, 1987), 76.

with the political enterprise of imposing them on speakers and transmitting order-words."[9] The language of the empire imposed onto the bodies of the various nations compels assimilation, and so assemblages are inserted into a nationalized vision of the divine empire by the author of Revelation. Deleuze and Guattari further note: "Not only is language always accompanied by faciality traits, but the face crystallizes all redundancies, it emits and receives and recaptures signifying signs. It is a whole body unto itself: it is like the body of the center of significance to which all of the deterritorialized signs affix themselves, and it marks the limit of their deterritorialization."[10] The facialization of these nations occurs as their native languages are deterritorialized and replaced/reterritorialized by the language of the empire. Such a reterritorialization of the nations, I argue in the case of Revelation 7.9-17, allows nations to be "facialized" by constructing them as recognizable, controllable, and comprehensible entities as they are inserted into the nationalistic vision of the divine empire of God.[11]

Historical and Literary Contexts of Revelation 7.9-17

Focusing on the historical and the literary context of Revelation, this section of the essay is divided into two parts. The first part, entitled "Revelation: Mimicking Derision and the Empire of God," begins with a brief summary of the historical context of the book of Revelation before moving into the discussion of postcolonial theory and its application to the text of Revelation. This section looks at the way colonized people internalize the culture of the colonizer by using strategies of mocking and mimicking. It is important to note that postcolonial biblical scholars interpreting the book of Revelation have aptly demonstrated the ways in which the performance of mimicking the colonizer's culture exposes both the desire and the derision of the oppressed for the dominant and their culture. The second part focuses on the scholarly discussion revolving around the identity of the nations

---

9. Deleuze and Guattari, *A Thousand Plateaus*, 101. Deleuze and Guattari explain order words as follows: "We call *order-words*, not a particular category of explicit statements (for example, in the imperative), but the relation of every word or every statement to implicit presuppositions, in other words, to speech acts that are, and can only be, accomplished in the statement." A detailed discussion on order-words can be found on p. 79.

10. Deleuze and Guattari, *A Thousand Plateaus*, 115.

11. Deleuze and Guattari, *A Thousand Plateaus*, 178. Deleuze and Guattari argue that the faciality machine works to detect the deviances, wherein which, the White man is the signifier against which all other races are judged. They write: "If the face is in fact Christ, in other words, your average ordinary White Man, then the first deviances, the first divergences, are racial: yellow man, black man, men in the second or third category—They must be Christianized, in other words, facialized."

mentioned in Revelation 7.5-8, in what leads into 7.9-17. This part follows two scholars, Christopher Smith and Richard Bauckham, and their discussions revolving around the order in which the nations are presented in 7.5-8.

A. Revelation: Mimicking Derision and the Empire of God

It is clear when reading Revelation that Rome figures as a prominent character in the text. In her commentary on Revelation, Susan R. Garrett comments on the hostile relationship between John of Patmos and Rome.[12] Scholars note that the scathing critique on the Roman Empire demonstrates that the author may have been a Palestinian Jew who had come to the Asia Minor in the aftermath of the Jewish defeat in the first revolt against Rome, which took place between 66–73 CE.[13] Although, there is some debate as to when the book of Revelation was written, most scholars agree that this text would have been written at the end of the reign of emperor Domitian.[14] The violent nature of the text had led to the assumption that Revelation was a reflection of the persecution faced by John of Patmos and his followers at the hands of the Domitian.[15] However, recent scholarship has illustrated that the historical evidence of persecution has been dependent on the book of Revelation and therefore is rendered unreliable.[16] In fact, scholars have noted that this text is addressed to those Christian believers who had taken a lax attitude toward the Roman Empire and its imperial values. Garrett observes: "John feared for the salvation of the churches, whose members were becoming morally lax and conforming too readily to the standards of the larger culture (see 2:14-15, 20-23; 3:1-3, 15-17)."[17] For John of Patmos, then, the Christian community's collusion with the Roman

---

12. Garrett, "Revelation," 470.
13. Garrett, "Revelation," 470.
14. Tina Pippin and J. Michael Clark, "Revelation/Apocalypse," in *The Queer Bible Commentary* (ed. Deryn Guest, et al.; London: SCM Press, 2006), 753–68, here 753. They note: "The majority opinion is that an itinerate preacher-prophet named John wrote to seven churches in Western Anatolia at or near the end of the reign of the Emperor Domitian (81–95 CE)." Other scholars including John W. Marshall argue for dating Revelation earlier around 69 CE. For his detailed argument, see John W. Marshall, *Parables of War: Reading John's Jewish Apocalypse* (Waterloo, ON: Wilfred Laurier University Press, 2001), 88–97.
15. Garrett, "Revelation," 470. Garrett writes: "For centuries it was assumed that John and his readers were being persecuted by the emperor Domitian (who reigned from 81 to 96 CE) for failure to worship him in the imperial cult."
16. Garrett, "Revelation," 470. Garrett writes: "More recently it has been shown that the historical evidence for that persecution itself depends on the book of Revelation. Thus, the argument is circular and the conclusions unreliable."
17. Garrett, "Revelation," 470.

imperial ideology is both morally questionable and corrupts his vision of the divine empire that he presents as an alternative to Rome.

Revelation is explicitly addressed to seven urban churches in the Roman province of Asia that belonged to the colonizing campaigns dating back to the Greeks.[18] Wes Howard-Brook and Anthony Gwyther observe: "The people of the Roman province of Asia did not consider themselves to be subjugated or occupied by Rome. Unlike people in Judea, Gaul, or Britain, the people in Asia welcomed rather than resisted Roman rule."[19] The issue then for John of Patmos lies with the dominant culture of Rome and its influence on the Christian communities located in these seven cities in Asia Minor. In his essay, "Symptoms of Resistance in the Book of Revelation," Greg Carey points out that Revelation struggles to identify a movement by constructing its identity over against neither a church nor a foreign power, but against the dominant culture of its own time and place."[20] While I agree with Carey's analysis that this text seeks to construct its identity against the larger cultural context of its time and place, I argue that for John of Patmos the dominant Roman culture would still be seen as a foreign colonizing power that sought to influence, seduce, and coerce his Jewish-Christian community away from their native roots. In contexts that are colonized, the internalized culture of the colonizer is seen as foreign, threatening, and a corrupting influence on the general population. As a result, in the process of outwardly resisting the Roman Empire, John of Patmos internalizes the imperial values and reinscribes them in his vision.

The work of postcolonial theorists has played an important role in bringing to light the ways in which the relationship between the colonizer and the colonized is one of ambivalence, emanating desire and derision at the same time.[21] Drawing on the work of postcolonial theorist Homi Bhabha and his work on colonial mimicry, Stephen Moore finds mimicry present in the text

---

18. Stephen D. Moore, *Untold Tales from the Book of Revelation: Sex and Gender, Empire and Ecology* (Atlanta, GA: SBL Press, 2014), 16. Moore writes: "The history of colonization in Asia Minor extended back to the Hellenizing campaigns of Alexander the Great and his successors, who sowed Greek cities (poleis) throughout the region …"

19. Wes Howard-Brook and Anthony Gwyther, *Unveiling Empire: Reading Revelation Then and Now* (New York: Orbis Book, 1999), 91.

20. Greg Carey, "Symptoms of Resistance in the Book of Revelation," in *The Reality of Apocalypse: Rhetoric and Politics in the Book of Revelation* (ed. David L. Barr; Atlanta, GA: SBL, 2006), 169–80, here 175.

21. Moore, *Untold Tales from the Book of Revelation*, 25. Discussing the work of Homi K. Bhabha, *The Location of Culture,* Edward Said, *Orientalism,* and Gayatri Chakravorty Spivak, "Can the Subaltern Speak," Moore writes: "Bhabha's enabling assumption is that the relationship between colonizer and colonized is characterized by ambivalence instead, which is to say attraction and repulsion at one and the same time."

of Revelation. He observes: "Revelation presents us with a reverse scenario in which parody or mockery of the imperial order constantly threatens to topple over into mimicry, imitation, and replication."[22] Thus, the desire to envision an empire of God is recreated in the reflection of the derided empire of Rome.

B. Revelation 7.5-8: The Identity of the Nations

The role of the nations in Revelation 7.5-8 is an important one for understanding 7.9-17. Christopher R. Smith and Richard Bauckham have noted that this vision in Revelation is a transformation of the conventional Jewish messianic expectations into Jewish-Christian images.[23] Both Bauckham and Smith spend a considerable amount of time discussing the identity of the tribes listed in Revelation 7.5-8. However, while both are in agreement on their interpretative approach on the text for the most part, the divergence in their argument appears in the way each of them interpret the order of the tribes presented by John of Patmos in the book of Revelation. Richard Bauckham observes that the list of the tribes appearing in Revelation 7.5-8 does not follow the conventional order of the nations listed in contemporary Jewish texts. This deviation, he argues, is the result of a faulty memory on the part of the author of Revelation causing him to deviate from the normative order of the tribes. Meanwhile, Christopher Smith disagrees with this line of interpretation arguing that an author like John, who expects his audience to recognize the traditional image of the Jewish messianic expectation that he has painstakingly conjured up for his readers, would not suffer from a faulty memory and would not make a careless choice when it comes to the presentation of the nations in his text.[24] Smith instead notes that the change in the order of the list of the tribes in Revelation 7 must be seen as

---

For a detailed discussion cf. Homi K. Bhabha, *The Location of Culture* (New York: Routledge, 1994), 129–38.

22. Moore, *Untold Tales from the Book of Revelation*, 28.

23. Christopher R. Smith, "The Tribes of Revelation 7 and the Literary Competence of John the Seer," *Journal of the Evangelical Theological Society*, 38.2 (June 1995): 213–8, here 213. Smith, commenting on Richard Bauckham's interpretation of Revelation 7, notes: "We both understand the technique of the author of the book ... to be the ironic transformation of conventional Jewish messianic expectations into Jewish-Christian images."

24. Smith, "The Tribes of Revelation 7," 214. Smith points out, "How can we consider John an author who expected his audience to recognize a traditional image of Jewish messianic expectation, in order to appreciate its Christian transformation, if he was at the same time a 'writer who did not really care in what order he listed the tribes' and therefore presented them in a form that was not intelligible?"

"a purposeful innovation of a skilled writer" because John of Patmos reinterprets conventional Jewish images while also executing this plan successfully in his text. Furthermore, Smith insists that the change in the list of the tribes illustrates that "John may be beginning a Christian transformation even as he presents a Jewish expectation…"[25] Debating this notion, Bauckham argues: "It is in any case hard to see how a revision of the order of precedence among the tribes of Israel could represent the inclusion of Gentiles in the New Israel."[26] Instead, Bauckham notes that the Christian interpretation must be applied later in Revelation 7, in particular, John of Patmos envisions a Christian empire in Revelation 7.9-14.[27] Both Smith and Bauckham agree that the vision depicted in Revelation 7 gestures to a new divine order; however, their interpretations rely on different verses in the text. While Smith argues for the creation of the new Church as the new Israel based on the list of the tribes found in 7.5-8,[28] Bauckham argues for a literary linking of 7.5-8 with 7.9-17, suggesting that John of Patmos deliberately juxtaposes the images in 7.4-9, which contains the 144,000, to 7.9-17 where the great multitude from all nations, tribes, people, and languages are gathered.[29]

---

25. Smith, "The Tribes of Revelation 7," 216. Smith argues: "John elsewhere uses characters who are ostensibly 'Jews' to represent those who are 'Christians' (irrespective of their ethnicity). In Rev 12.17, for example, the 'offspring of the woman who wears a crown of twelve stars' (obviously an image of Israel) are explained to be 'those who keep the commandments of God and bear testimony to Jesus.' So it is not intrinsically improbable that some of the 'tribes of Israel' in Revelation 7 might stand for Gentiles if the changes John makes in the list of tribes are a purposeful Christian expression."
26. Richard Bauckham, "The List of the Tribes in Revelation 7 Again," *JSNT* 42 (1991): 99–115, here 102.
27. Bauckham, "The List of the Tribes in Revelation 7 Again," 106. Bauckham writes: "It follows that we should not look, as Smith does, for a Christian interpretation of the list of twelve tribes within 7:4-8. This image as such is a traditional Jewish image of the people of God called to military services in the messianic war. The Christian interpretation comes in 7:9-14, which shows the same people celebrating victory in heaven, but shows them to be an innumerable multitude of martyrs from all the nations."
28. Christopher R. Smith, "The Portrayal of the Church as the New Israel in the Names and Order of the Tribes in Revelation 7:5-8," *JSNT* 39 (1990): 111–8, here 115. Smith writes, "In summary, then, we find in Rev 7:5-8 a systematic reworking of a paradigmatic list of the sons of Israel grouped by maternal descent, whose otherwise perplexing features are clearly explained by the author's design of portraying the church as the New Israel."
29. Bauckham, "The List of the Tribes in Revelation 7 Again," 103. Bauckham writes: "The contrast is obvious in two respects: the 144,000 are counted, whereas the great multitude cannot be counted; the 144,000 are from all the nations, tribes, peoples, and languages."

Although both Bauckham and Smith make important observations in their essays, their interpretations, limited to a Christian vision, fail to take into account the traces of imperialism that appear as the undercurrent in this vision. It is important to note that although Bauckham acknowledges that for the author of Revelation the "antichrist" was the imperial power of Rome, he never applies imperialism as an interpretive lens in his reading of this pericope. As a result, I argue that the Christianized vision of John of Patmos recreated in Revelation 7.9-17 is not merely a transformation of the Jewish-Christian images, but is also an imperial vision that attempts to duplicate the Roman Empire, transforming nations and facializing them through the use of imperial language.

Concurrently, Håkan Ulfgard argues that a reading of Revelation 7 must consider the feast of the Tabernacle. Commenting on the view of other exegetes, Ulfgard notes, "In the literary composition, these people are described in contrast to the followers of the beast: they are virgins (14:4; cf. the great harlot of ch. 17) and they do not speak a lie (14:5; cf. the blasphemous speech in 13:6)."[30] Connecting this passage to Jewish rather than Hellenistic roots, Ulfgard argues that Revelation 7.9-17 alludes to the Exodus event, but John adds slight variation expanding this vision to a multitude in the hopes of expanding God's salvation all people.[31] He then references 7.3-4, where John says: "Do not harm the land or the sea or the trees until we put a seal on the foreheads of the servants of our God. Then I heard the number of those who were sealed: 144,000 from all the tribes of Israel." Ulfgard argues that those who receive the seal and those who belong to the multitude are the ones mentioned in the book of life.[32] He notes that readers are introduced to these "people of God" on Mount Zion in Revelation 14.1-5 and they sing the song of Moses and the Lamb by the sea of glass in 15.2-4. Continuing further

---

30. Håkan Ulfgard, *Feast and Future: Revelation 7:9-17 and the Feast of the Tabernacles* (Stockholm: Almqvist & Wiksell International, 1989), 76–7.

31. Ulfgard, *Feast and Future*, 78. Ulfgard writes: "The identification of the Christian people of God with Israel's twelve tribes is an Exodus-related feature referring to God's special protection over Israel during the whole Exodus event (from the Egyptian plagues and paschal deliverance until the entry into Canaan), which is combined with the remnant idea of the prophets, especially Ezek 9:4, as shown by the saving sign on the foreheads. Those who were to be protected are seen standing in God's presence, being protected, led, nourished and comforted by God and the Lamb. But John adds a new dimension: the multitude comes 'from every tribe etc.,' i.e. salvation is shared by people of all nations."

32. Ulfgard, *Feast and Future*, 79. Ulfgard writes, "From the broader perspective of the book, it is clear that those who are to receive the saving seal and those who belong to the multitude must be the ones whose names are written in the book of life (cf. 3:5, 13:8, 17:8, 20:15, 21:27)."

he notes: "The symbolic figure 144,000 is thus best understood as representing the people of God *in its totality* without racial or other distinction, and the juxtaposition of the 144,000 and the great multitude as in some way expressing the typical New Testament perspective of *already—not yet*."[33] Similar to Bauckham and Smith, Ulfgard also argues that John of Patmos draws on images from the Hebrew Bible and reinterprets them through a Christian lens.[34]

It is important to note that while these scholars acknowledge the presence of the Roman Empire and its role in the text neither of them attempt to interpret the vision in Revelation 7.9-17 through an imperial lens. However, it seems to me that the presence and influence of empire in this vision is undeniable. Furthermore, race is never considered as a hermeneutical lens to interpret this passage. Although Ulfgard describes the people in this text as "one people of God," he refuses to connect this vision to cultural assimilation and race.[35] He writes, "The difference between 7:1-8 and 9-17 lies therefore in perspective, not in an emphasis on racial distinction."[36] Thus, while the first eight verses of this chapter focus on listing the different tribes, their names and their numbers, the next verses complete the transformation describing the multitude through their clothes and their language. While I see Ulfgard's point, the issue of racial exclusivity brought about through language, dress, and ultimately assimilation cannot and must not be overlooked. In other words, this vision I would argue, while a Christianized vision of the Hebrew Bible, promotes a racial unity and superiority brought about through language and dress. In other words, Revelation 7.9-17 is a racialized vision that attempts to construct the unity of the nations through the use of both language and dress. Read through the work of Deleuze and Guattari, this passage presents the cultural assimilation of various nations through language and dress, creating a nationalized and racialized vision of the empire of God.

Language and Facialization:
Interpreting Revelation 7.9-17 through the Work of Deleuze and Guattari

> After this I looked, and there before me was a great multitude that no one could count, from every nation, tribe, people and language, standing before

---

33. Ulfgard, *Feast and Future*, 79. Also cf. George B. Caird, *A Commentary on the Revelation of St. John the Divine* (repr.; Peabody, MA: Hendrickson, 1995), 95.

34. Ulfgard, *Feast and Future*, 73.

35. Ulfgard, *Feast and Future*, 73. Ulfgard writes, "There is just one people of God in Rev, but it is described in a redundant language that overflows with Scriptural images."

36. Ulfgard, *Feast and Future*, 73.

the throne and before the Lamb. They were wearing white robes and were holding palm branches in their hands. And they cried out in a loud voice:

"Salvation belongs to our God,
who sits on the throne,
and to the Lamb."

—Revelation 7.9-10

This section will discuss two key points about language and nation. Here I explore the ways in which language plays an important role in the construction of the nation. Partha Chatterjee in his work describes this as "linguistic nationalism." In other words, official languages become the common thread that stitch together nations, binding the tongues of its citizens, weaving them into a unique tapestry that displays nationalism on the world stage. One of the ways that language evokes sentiments of nationalism among its citizens is to hark back to the past presenting it as glorious and nostalgic. When it comes to the language of Revelation, John of Patmos is writing in one of the official languages of the Roman Empire, which is Greek, more specifically Koine Greek. Interpretations of this text have already established that in the process of expressing his derision and disgust for Rome, John of Patmos is inadvertently seduced by the Empire and expresses his desire by mimicking imperial power in his text.[37] Thus, John of Patmos blurs the lines between the empire of God and the empire of Rome until they become indistinguishable. By drawing on the work of theorists and biblical scholars who use postcolonial hermeneutics as a lens to interpret texts, this section will also explore the ways in which minor languages spoken by the multitude in Revelation 7.9-17 are replaced by the major language of the Empire. I will attempt to connect the act of speaking the language of empire to the facialization of the various nations in this section.

The emergence of nation states speaking in the dominant language is performative of what Partha Chatterjee terms "linguistic nationalisms."[38] The unity of a nation is signified through language. Timothy Brennan observes:

---

37. Gilles Deleuze, "Nietzsche and Saint Paul, Lawrence and John of Patmos," in *Essays Critical and Clinical* (trans. Daniel W. Smith and Michael A. Greco; Minneapolis, MN: University of Minneapolis Press, 1997), 36–52 here 39. Deleuze, citing D. H. Lawrence, observes, "The collective soul does not simply want to seize power or to replace the despot. On the one hand, it wants to hate Caesar or the Roman Empire with all his heart. On the other hand, however, it also wants to penetrate into every pore of power, to swarm in its centers, to multiple them throughout the universe."

38. Partha Chatterjee, "Nationalism as a Problem," in Ashcroft, Griffiths, and Tiffin, eds., *Post-Colonial Studies Reader*, 122–8, here 126. Describing the three models of nationalism that emerged. Chatterjee writes: "The second 'model' was that of the linguistic nationalisms of Europe, a model of the independent national state which henceforth became 'available for pirating.'"

"The idea of nationhood is not only a political plea, but a formal binding together of disparate elements. And out of the multiplicities of culture, race, and political structure, grows also a repeated dialectic of uniformity and specificity."[39] At first glance, one can see that John of Patmos in his text is attempting to recreate a new empire of God that is in stark contrast to the Roman Empire. However, as we shall see, in the process of this recreation, the author also duplicates the Roman imperialism.

Revelation is a text filled with visions ranging from the fantastical, to mythical, and to the downright grotesque. It is no wonder that D. H. Lawrence called this book "perhaps the most detestable of all these books of the Bible."[40] The visions in the book of Revelation become tropes of the most scathing critique on the Roman Empire.[41] The Greek ἀποκάλυψις, commonly translated in English as apocalypse or revelation, refers to a dream or a vision that needs to be interpreted by a heavenly being.[42] Visions or dreams play an important role in the construction of nations. In other words, similar to the author of Revelation, who envisions a divine empire where the followers of Jesus are connected in a tight knit community, imaginings of nations attempt to create a community of fellow members connected through language and their national identity. Benedict Anderson proposes the following definition of the nation: "it is an imagined political community—and imagined as both inherently limited and sovereign. It is imagined because the members of even the smallest nation will never know most of their fellow-members, meet them, or even hear of them, yet in the minds of each lives the image of their communion."[43] John of Patmos, banished to the island of Patmos, is repeatedly shown visions about the new world that will replace the old world.[44] These visions, while highly symbolic and

---

39. Brennan, "The National Longing for Form," 130.

40. D. H. Lawrence, *Apocalypse and Writings on Revelation* (ed. Mara Kalnis; Cambridge: Cambridge University Press, 1980), 6. See also Deleuze, "Nietzsche and Saint Paul, Lawrence and John of Patmos," 36. Commenting on the description of Revelation by D. H. Lawrence Deleuze writes, "The Apocalypse is collective, popular, uncultivated, hateful, and savage—John of Patmos does not even assume the mask of the evangelist, nor that of Christ, he invents another mask, he fabricates another mask that unmasks Christ or, if you prefer, that is superimposed on Christ's mask."

41. See Moore, *Untold Tales from the Book of Revelation*, 15. Moore writes: "Critical scholars of Revelation have customarily read it as, perhaps, the most uncompromising attack on the Roman Empire."

42. See Howard-Brook and Gwyther, *Unveiling Empire*, 4: "Apocalypses can have a wide range of characteristics, but commonly include … a dream or vision that requires interpretation by a 'heavenly' agent."

43. Benedict Anderson, "Imagined Communities," 125.

44. Garrett, "Revelation," 469. Garrett notes: "The book of Revelation, or the

violent in nature, visualize the new world as peaceful, spiritually and culturally superior to the present age.[45] The new world invokes the past by glorifying its purity and cultural superiority and presenting it over and against the current world.[46] Imaginings of nations purposefully summon traditions of the past to undermine the cultural mores of the present. Frantz Fanon illustrates this urgency: "Because they [the native intellectuals] realize they are in danger of losing their lives, and thus becoming lost to their people, these men, hot headed and with anger in their hearts, relentlessly determine to renew contact once more with the oldest and most pre-colonial springs of life of their people."[47] Making a similar move in his text at many points, John of Patmos attempts to recreate the images of the pre-colonial past and reconnect his Christian community back to their native roots. In addition to this, the author, in Revelation 7.5-8, lists the names of the tribes from the Hebrew Scriptures, which is an attempt by the author to evoke in his readers their connection to their roots.

The violent and destructive language of the book of Revelation is directed towards the Roman empire. Wes Howard-Brook and Anthony Gwyther write: "Revelation casts a critical eye on Rome's economic exploitation, its politics of seduction, its violence, and its imperial hubris or arrogance."[48] Similar to the ways in which colonized people find the empire both seductive and repugnant at the same time, the author of Revelation characterizes Rome as both the seductive Whore and the personification of Satan.[49]

Apocalypse (Greek for 'revelation'), belongs to an ancient type of literature in which a seer describes symbolic visions of the heavens and secrets about the end of the age."

45. Howard-Brook and Gwyther, *Unveiling Empire,* 159. Brooks and Gwyther point out that "the contrast is manifest in the respective descriptions of the two cities. Babylon is depicted as corrupt and corrupting. The city is the dwelling place of evil, a smoking ruin. In contrast, New Jerusalem is depicted as the ideal city. It is filled with the glory of God."

46. Jorunn Økland, "Why Can't the Heavenly Miss Jerusalem Just Shut Up," in *A Feminist Companion to The Apocalypse of John* (ed. Amy Jill Levine and Maria Mayo Robbins; New York: T&T Clark, 2009), 88–105, here 100. Økland writes: "In Revelation, Babylon is the whore and the New Jerusalem is the pure bride (21.2, 9). Thus holiness is associated with virginity and holiness."

47. Frantz Fanon, "On National Culture," in Ashcroft, Griffiths, and Tiffin, eds., *Post-Colonial Studies Reader*, 117–9, here 119.

48. Howard-Brook and Gwyther, *Unveiling Empire*, 116.

49. Howard-Brook and Gwyther, *Unveiling Empire*, 116. "Rome was not an order with which one could cooperate. It was, instead, an incarnation of 'Satan.' It was both a ferocious Beast and a seductive Whore." I am also drawing on the work of Homi Bhabha, *Location of Culture*. Bhabha points out that "the black is both savage (cannibal) and yet the most obedient and dignified of servants (the bearer of food); he is the embodiment of rampant sexuality and yet innocent as a child; he is mystical, primitive, simple-minded

Moore writes: "Revelation's depiction of the 'other' empire, that of God and the Lamb, a mimicry that persistently blurs the boundaries between the two empires until it becomes all but impossible to say where one leaves off and the other begins."[50]

Imperial visions and language mimicked in the text of Revelation facialize the empire of God by constructing a unified vision of the nations under one God. While Revelation repeats imperial visions and language the construction of the divine empire is both similar and yet different from the Roman Empire. In *Difference and Repetition*, Deleuze writes, "The role of imagination, or the mind which contemplates in its multiple and fragmented states, is to draw something new from repetition to draw difference from it."[51] Chapter 7 extends the vision of John of Patmos from the first chapter. Howard-Brook and Gwyther write: "One of the greatest differences between Revelation and other New Testament texts is Revelation's portrayal of numerous scenes of liturgy and worship."[52] However, worship, especially in the book of Revelation, is a deeply political gesture.[53] The worship scene in the book of Revelation replicates the vision of the imperial courtroom that begins in chapter 5. Moore writes, "Roman imperial court is, in Revelation, merely a dim, distorted reflection of the heavenly courts …"[54] The heavenly kingdom, complete with the throne and the various nations standing before the Lamb (Rev. 7.9-10), resembles and repeats the imperial vision, hoping to overturn this vision by constructing something better. Deleuze writes, "… by simulacrum we should not understand a simple imitation but rather the act by which the very idea of a model or privileged position is challenged and overturned."[55] The assimilation of the var-

---

and yet the most worldly and accomplished liar, and manipulator of social forces," 118. In colonial contexts, Bhabha notes the ways the colonized are subjected to binarized descriptions of being manipulative and simpleminded. Similarly, Rome for John of Patmos is ferocious, savage, and uncivilized and yet, sophisticated, manipulative, desiring, and seducing. In other words, Rome is both disgusting and desiring at the same time for John of Patmos.

    50. Moore, *Untold Tales from the Book of Revelation*, 35.

    51. Gilles Deleuze, *Difference and Repetition* (trans. Paul Patton; New York: Columbia University Press, 1994), 76.

    52. Howard-Brook and Gwyther, *Unveiling Empire*, 197.

    53. Howard-Brook and Gwyther, *Unveiling Empire*, 206. Howard-Brook and Gwyther write: "All power is now acknowledged to belong to the One on the throne. Worship is shown to be primarily a political act: one worships whomever or whatever one affirms as possessing true power to affect peoples, the central currency of politics in all ages."

    54. Moore, *Untold Tales of Revelation*, 29.

    55. Deleuze, *Difference and Repetition*, 69.

ious nations repeated in the new vision in Revelation 7.9-17 is constructed as both different and yet strangely familiar.

Revelation is written in one of the two official languages of the Empire: Koine Greek. In "The Language of the Apocalypse," Allen Dwight Callahan observes "the author of the Apocalypse writes in the language of the eastern Roman Empire, modified in a provincial dialect. Drawing lexically and syntactically on Hebrew and Aramaic, its base is nevertheless the language of the dominant."[56] Writing in the language of the dominant gestures to the political stance that the author makes in his text. The desire to participate and perform the language of the Empire, even with an accent never ceases to end or be forgotten. In his essay, "The Alchemy of English," Braj B. Kachru writes, "The English language is a tool of power, domination and elitist identity, and of communication across continents."[57] The ability to speak in the language of the empire is about power, domination, and identity, "facializing" entire bodies of the other. So John of Patmos envisions in Revelation 7.9-10 all the nations speaking in one language.

> After this I looked and there was a great multitude that no one could count from every nation, from all tribes and peoples and languages, standing before the throne and before the Lamb, robed in white, with palm branches in their hands. They cried out in a loud voice saying, "Salvation belongs to our God who is seated on the throne and to the lamb.[58]"

The role of the nations in this passage is an important one. The text does not say much about who exactly these nations are. They are never named or identified in any way. One can assume, therefore, from the text that the

---

56. Allen Dwight Callahan, "The Language of the Apocalypse," *HTR* 88.4 (1995): 453–70, here 457. Also cf. Gilles Deleuze and Felix Guattari, *Kafka: Toward a Minor Literature* (trans. Dana Polan; Minneapolis, MN: University of Minnesota Press, 1986), 16–7. Commenting on Jewish Literature from Warsaw and Prague, Kafka argues that minor literature does not come from minor language rather it is the language constructed by a minority within the majority language. They write: "The impossibility of writing other than in German is for the Prague Jews the feeling of an irreducible distance from their primitive Czech territoriality. And the impossibility of writing in German is the deterritorialization of the German population itself, an oppressive minority that speaks a language cut off from the masses, like a 'paper language' or an artificial language that is all the more true for the Jews who are simultaneous, a part of this minority and excluded from it." In light of these words, the author of Revelation writing in the language of the dominant that almost but not quite sounds like the language of the empire ultimately creating a language of the dominant makes him at once included and excluded from the empire.

57. Braj B. Kachru, "The Alchemy of English," in Ashcroft, Griffiths, and Tiffin, eds., *Post-Colonial Studies Reader*, 272–6, here 272.

58. I am using the New Revised Standard Version in this essay.

multitude consisted of diversity not only in terms of people and ethnicity but also diversity in terms of languages. However, Acts stands in stark contrast to Revelation. In other words, contrasting Revelation 7.9-17 with Acts 2.1-4 presents an interesting perspective on the globalization of empire. Thus, on the one hand, the text of Revelation insists on a vision of a multitude that gathers together in front of the throne and before the lamb singing in one voice in the language of the empire. Acts 2.1-4, on the other hand, gathers all the disciples in one places where the Holy Spirit gives them the ability to speak in the languages of the various nations.[59] Simply put, while John of Patmos envisions the empire of God to be a homogeneous, monolingual entity where various nations are bound together by the major language of the empire, Acts imagines the empire of God to be a heterogenous, multilingual entity where the disciples are expected to speak in the minor languages of the various nations.

Revelation 7.9 suggests that the multitude contained people not only from every tribe or nation, but also different languages:

> After this I looked, and there before me was a great multitude that no one could count, from every nation, tribe, people and language, standing before the throne and before the Lamb.

Howard-Brook and Gwyther write: "The countless multitude from every nation, tribe, peoples, and language is *the new Israel*, the perfectly complete number represented by the twelve thousand from each of the twelve historic tribes. John's vision, as usual, reinterprets the biblical tradition."[60] Although interpretations such as there are helpful, the insertion of the critical theory, and in particular the use of Deleuze and Guattari, nuances the reading of this passage: the new Israel or the new Church is a multinational, multicultural, multilinguistic multitude, *but speaking in the language of the empire*.

In *The Location of Culture*, Homi K. Bhabha points out that "the nation fills the void left in uprooting of communities and kin, and turns that loss into the language of metaphor. Metaphor, as the etymology of the word

---

59. See Acts 2.1-4: "When the day of Pentecost had come, they were all together in one place. And suddenly from heaven there came a sound like the rush of a violent wind, and it filled the entire house where they were sitting. Divided tongues, as of fire, appeared among them, and a tongue rested on each of them. All of them were filled with the Holy Spirit and began to speak in other languages, as the Spirit gave them ability."

60. Howard-Brook and Gwyther, *Unveiling Empire*, 210. Also cf. Smith, "The Portrayal of the Church as the New Israel," 111. Smith writes: "The identity of the 144,000 'sealed out of all the tribes of Israel' in Revelation 7 has been the subject of considerable debate, in the pages of this journal among other places. Is this a symbol for the church, as some argue, or is the image to be understood in a more literal sense as of Jews or of Jewish Christians?"

suggests, transfers the meaning of home and belonging ..."[61] Unlike the modern-day immigrants that Bhabha mentions, who leave "home" on their own accord, John of Patmos is a refugee. It is interesting to note that the author of Revelation, envisioning the gathering of all the nations under one God, recreates his own metaphor of home and belonging. Bhabha continues:

> Gatherings of exiles and émigrés and refugees; gatherings in the ghettos or cafés of city centers; gathering in the half-life; half-light of foreign tongues, or in the uncanny fluency of another's language; gathering the signs of approval and acceptance, degrees, discourses, disciplines; gathering the memories of underdevelopment, of other worlds lived retroactively; gathering the past in a ritual of revival; gathering the present.[62]

The gathering in Revelation 7 presents a belonging embedded in the strictest form of cultural assimilation displayed through language and dress. Furthermore, John of Patmos attempts to revive the past memory of belonging and togetherness in the present by recalling the Hebrew Scriptures. In Revelation 7.9-17, John draws on the imagery found in Exodus to recreate his vision of a new nation of Israel. Ulfagard observes that "the passage about white-washed robes of God's redeemed people recalls Ex. 19:10, 14, where it is said that the children of Israel must 'wash their garments' in order to be ready for God's arrival on Mount Sinai."[63] Similarly, scholars like Smith and Bauckham argue that John of Patmos in 7.9-17 draws heavily on the Old Testament texts to recreate his vision of the salvation of Israel.[64] Up until now, scholarly interpretations of 7.9-17 have focused on the inclusion of Gentiles as part of the new Israel or the new church. While such interpretations are important, they nevertheless fail to take into account the ways in which the reinscription of the past presents the new empire of God as a homogenous, stable entity that promotes the cultural assimilation of its subjects through language and dress. Fanon writes: "The native intellectual who decides to give battle to colonial lies fights on the field of the whole continent. The past

---

61. Bhabha, *Location of Culture*, 200.
62. Bhabha, *Location of Culture*, 199.
63. Ulfagard, *Feast of the Tabernacle*, 83.
64. Smith, "The Tribes of Revelation 7," 216. Smith writes: "If we allow that John may be beginning a Christian transformation even as he presents a Jewish expectation, this possibility does not seem unreasonable. John elsewhere uses characters who are ostensibly 'Jews' to represent those who are 'Christians' (irrespective of their ethnicity)." Also cf. Richard Bauckham, "The list of the Tribes Again," 103. "Moreover, just as in 5:6, the image which conveys John's Jewish Christian interpretation of Jewish hopes is a scriptural one, so in 7:9 the image of the innumerable multitude from all nations is a scriptural allusion. It echoes God's promise to the patriarchs that their descendants would be innumerable (Gen. 13:16; 15:5; 32:12; Hos. 1:10; Jub. 13:20; 14:4-5; Heb. 11:12, cf. Gen. 22:17; 26:4; 28:14; Jub. 18:15, 25:16; 27:23; Lad. Jac 1:10)."

is given back its value. Culture, extracted from the past to be displayed in all its splendor, is not necessarily that of his own country."[65] Extracting the Hebrew scriptures from his past, John of Patmos recreates the memory of belonging within his community just as he begins putting the foundations of the new world in place. Simply put: in the text of Revelation, the foundations of the new world, built upon the memories and remains of the precolonial past, attempt to conceptualize a new empire of God.

Scholars have noted that the list of the tribes appearing in Revelation 7.5-8 is somehow expanded beginning at verse 9, therefore leading to a Christian transformation of this vision.[66] Other scholars have argued that the vision present in chapter 7 when contrasted with chapter 5 must be read as a Christian interpretation of a Jewish messianic expectation.[67] While both these interpretations focus on the transformation of the images in 7.9-17, none of them take into account the imperial context of John of Patmos and its effects on this passage. The reinscription of the Roman empire in 7.9-17 envisions an alternative empire of God, that while different is at the same time, founded on the same imperial values of Rome.[68] Benedict Anderson, citing the work of Ernest Gellner, notes: "With a certain ferocity Gellner makes a comparable point when he rules that 'Nationalism is not the awakening of nations to self consciousness: it invents nations where they do not exist.'"[69] The gathering before the throne and the before the Lamb reinserted into the imperial vision bring these nations into existence. Deleuze and Guattari note that "the form of subjectivity, whether consciousness or passion, would remain absolutely empty if faces did not form loci of

---

65. Frantz Fanon, "On National Culture," in *Colonial Discourse and Post-Colonial Theory: A Reader* (ed. Patrick Williams and Laura Chrisman; New York: Columbia University Press, 1994), 36–52, here 38.

66. See Smith, "The Portrayal of the Church as the New Israel," 117. Smith writes: "Suffice to say that in general terms, it is virtually impossible to account for the unusual order and composition of the list of tribes by interpreting it as descriptive of ethnic Israel. But seeing in this list a portrayal of the church as the New Israel, consistent with NT theology, resolves the difficulties quite simply."

67. Bauckham, "The List of the Tribes Again," 103. Bauckham writes: "The contrasting images are parallel to those of 5:5-6: the 144,000 are the Israelite army of the Lion of Judah, while the international multitude are the followers of the slaughtered Lamb. The purpose of the contrast is the same as in 5:5-6: to give a Christian interpretation of an element of Jewish messianic expectation."

68. Stephen D. Moore, *Empire and Apocalypse: Postcolonialism and the New Testament* (Sheffield: Sheffield Phoenix Press, 2006), 110. Moore writes: "Colonial mimicry results when the colonizer's culture is imposed on the colonized and the latter is lured or coerced into internalizing and replicating it."

69. Anderson, "Imagined Communities," 124. Also cf. Ernest Gellner, *Thought and Change* (London: Weidenfeld & Nicholson, 1964), 169.

resonance that select the sensed or mental reality and make it conform in advance to a dominant reality."[70] The subjectivity of the nations, tribes, and people in the text of 7.9-17 is brought into existence in verses 10-11:

And they cried out in a loud voice: "Salvation belongs to our God, who sits on the throne, and to the Lamb." All the angels were standing around the throne and around the elders and the four living creatures. They fell down on their faces before the throne and worshiped God,

The faceless nations, people, and tribes gathered before the throne and the lamb— facialized through imperial language—are immediately defaced as they fall on their faces.

In John's vision the multilinguistic nations sing praises to the new emperor, namely the Lamb, but as the text reminds us, "they cry out in a loud voice." Although the text never explicitly states what language all these nations cry out in, the song that they sing gestures to the notion that the languages of all these nations, people, and tribes is one.[71] John of Patmos re-envisions the multilingual vision of Israel into a monolingual empire. Deleuze and Guattari write: "The unity of language is fundamentally political. There is no mother tongue, only a power takeover by a dominant language that advances along a broad front, and at times swoops down on diverse centers simultaneously."[72] The various languages of the nations are replaced/deterritorialized by Koine Greek, the language of the empire. Deleuze and Guattari in their first theorem on deterritorialization write: "Reterritorialization must not be confused with a return to a primitive or older territoriality: it necessarily implies a set of artifices by which one element, itself deterritorialized serves as a new territoriality for another, which has lost its territoriality as well."[73] The loss of the native languages into one language of praise is then, I would argue, a kind of reterritorializing.

In current contexts where globalization and capitalism are running the world economy, countries rely on this form of reterritorialization through languages in order to validate their presence and participate in the competition on the global scale. As a result, we see this form of reterritorialization through languages in modern India. In her article "Englishing India: Reinstituting Class and Social Privilege," Modhumita Roy writes, "English was the language of the rulers; its acquisition meant social and economic

---

70. Deleuze and Guattari, *A Thousand Plateaus*, 168.
71. The Greek for loud voice is "μεγάλη φωνῇ." This phrase alone occurs 18 times in Revelation. See discussion in David E. Aune, "The Protective Sealing of the 144,000 (7:1-17)," in *Word Biblical Commentary: Revelation 17-22* (Grand Rapids, MI: Zondervan, 1988), 424–55.
72. Deleuze and Guattari, *A Thousand Plateaus*, 101.
73. Deleuze and Guattari, *A Thousand Plateaus*, 174.

gains. For those who came from inconspicuous economic backgrounds and were otherwise without the prospect of a job, English was a technical language with a wholly instrumental purpose."[74] The effects of learning English, the language of the empire, are felt even today in postcolonial India. Dale Hudson writes, "Indian customer service operators (CSO's) and others working in India's business processing outsourcing (BPO) and information technologies enabled services (ITES) sectors, 'neutralize' their accounts into 'global English' …"[75] English in India is not just the language of power and privilege, it becomes a language that unifies the world and its economics. Therefore, the language of power replacing the native language works to homogenize, centralize, and standardize heterogenous nations.

Turning our attention back to the text of Revelation, the song sung by the nation in 7.10 is described as a song of celebration and praise. Bhabha writes, "If the spirit of the Western nation has been symbolized in epic and anthem, voiced by a 'unanimous people assembled in the self presence of its speech,' then the sign of colonial government is cast in a lower key, caught in the irredeemable act of writing."[76] While John of Patmos never mentions the presence of nation, nationalism, or the national anthem in his text, the song of praise in verse 10 gestures to an ancient national anthem that signifies the allegiance of the various nations to the throne and the Lamb. The gesture of allegiance is then completed by the multitudes in verse 11: "They fell down on their faces before the throne and worshiped God, saying: 'Amen! Praise and glory and wisdom and thanks and honor and power and strength be to our God for ever and ever. Amen!'" Anderson writes: "Coming to maturity at a stage of human history when even the most devout adherents of any universal religion were inescapably confronted with the living pluralism of such religions, and the allomorphism between each faith's ontological claims and territorial stretch, nations dream of being free, and, if under God, directly so."[77] The nations in Revelation 7.9-17, freed by John of Patmos, become sovereign nation states placed directly under the only and ultimate authority, the God of Israel.

The languages spoken by the nations in Revelation 7.10 are minor

---

74. Modhumita Roy, "Englishing India: Reinstituting Class and Social Privilege," *Social Text* 39 (1994): 83–107, here 97.

75. Dale Hudson, "Undesirable Bodies and Desirable Labor: Documenting the Globalization and Digitization of Transnational American Dreams in Indian Call Centers," *Cinema Journal* 49.1 (Fall, 2009): 82–102, here 82.

76. Bhabha, *Location of Culture*, 132. Also cf. Jacques Derrida, "The Violence of the Letter," in *Of Grammatology* (trans. G. Chakravorty Spivak; Baltimore, MD: Johns Hopkins University Press, 1976), 109–52, here 134.

77. Anderson, "Imagined Communities," 125.

languages that exist only in relation to the dominant language. Deleuze and Guattari argue that minor languages must be evaluated and understood in relation to both their mother tongue as well as the dominant language of the colonial empire.[78] They note, "Minor languages do not exist in themselves: they exist only in relation to a major language and are also investments of that language for the purpose of making it minor."[79] As Deleuze and Guattari explain, minor and major is not about being quantitative but rather about a standard.[80] In 7.10, the imperial language becomes the constant, the standard against which the languages of the nations are not only pitted but slowly are decentered. They continue, "the majoritarian as a constant and homogenous system; minorities as subsystems and minoritarian as a potential, creative, and created, becoming."[81] The becoming of minority languages has already been established by R. H. Charles in his book, *The Revelation of St. John*. Charles writes, "How are we to explain the unbridled license of his [the author of Revelation] Greek constructions? The reason clearly is that, while he writes in Greek, he thinks in Hebrew."[82] Reading the words of Charles in conjunction with the work of Deleuze and Guattari, one can argue that the author of Revelation while thinking in the minor language writes in the major language.

The author produces a form of "ghetto Greek." Callahan notes that some New Testament scholars argued that, "A third assessment [is] that the author of the work wrote in a pidginized 'ghetto Greek' of a diasporan Jewish community that spoke an assimilated form of the language with a strong Semitic accent."[83] In Revelation 7.9-17, the language of the nations reterritorialized by Greek can be imagined as a "pidginized" Greek that is spoken from a facialized nation with a strong native accent. Deleuze and Guattari write: "It is futile to criticize the worldwide imperialism of a language by denouncing the corruptions it introduces into other languages—For if a language such as British English or American English is major on a world scale, it is necessarily worked upon by all the minorities of the world, using very diverse

---

78. Deleuze and Guattari note that "the Bantu dialects must be evaluated not only in relation to the mother tongue but also in relation to Afrikaans as a major language, and English as a counter-major language preferred by blacks" (*A Thousand Plateaus*, 102).

79. Deleuze and Guattari, *A Thousand Plateaus*, 105.

80. Deleuze and Guattari, *A Thousand Plateaus*, 105. Deleuze and Guattari write: "Majority implies a constant of expression or content, serving as a standard measure by which to evaluate it."

81. Deleuze and Guattari, *A Thousand Plateaus*, 106.

82. R. H. Charles. *The Revelation of St. John* (ICC; 2 vols.; New York: Scribner's, 1920), 1.

83. Callahan, "The Language of the Apocalypse," 464.

procedures of variation."[84] Imagining the nations present in the text speaking a native form of Greek, albeit with an accent, demonstrates a nationalized vision of the divine empire. Bhabha writes, "Once the liminality of the nation-space is established, and its signifying difference is turned from the boundary 'outside' to its finitude 'within', the threat of cultural difference is no longer a problem of 'other' people. It becomes a question of otherness of the people-as-one."[85] The gathering of the great multitude comprising of the nations, tribes, people, and languages, who once were standing outside the boundaries of the Jewish-Christian vision of John of Patmos, are now ushered into the vision as the threat of their cultural difference is covered under their white robes and the language of God. At the same time, this new empire while based in the image of the old empire is somehow different. The idea of simulacrum comes into play in this text.

One could argue, that the multitude in Revelation 7.10 construct their own language, a language that at once belongs to the empire and at the same time has stark differences from it. The modern context of call centers helps in understanding this phenomenon better. Hudson points to the ways nations speaking minority languages shift their language and reveal the slippage between fantasy and reality. He writes, "During her interview, call-center manager Mandavi is interrupted by an incoming call, revealing a shift in the tone of her voice …"[86] The shift in the tone is illustrative of the ways in which the subjects in call centers perform for their viewer. Revelation 7.9-17 illustrates a similar kind of shift, with the multitude switching their tone as they move from their native language into the language of the dominant. At the same time, this switch produces a hope to assimilate and become part of the majoritarian. Hudson writes, "… CSO faces based solely on auditory telepresense of 'neutralized' accents, figuratively 'taking the face off' the body of labor."[87] In the text, the facialized multitudes speaking the language of the dominant are de-faced, "They fell down on their faces before the throne and worshiped God," (7.11), their faces are separated from their bodies as they continue to sing praises to God.

The ability to speak in the language of the empire is no ordinary feat and in fact is both political and racial. To speak in the language of the empire is not just about assimilation, as has been established above, but also about the facialization of the multitude. Deleuze and Guattari write, "European racism as the white man's claim has never operated by exclusion, or by the

---

84. Deleuze and Guattari, *A Thousand Plateaus*, 102.
85. Bhabha, *Location of Culture*, 215.
86. Hudson, "Undesirable Labor and Desirable Bodies," 95.
87. Hudson, "Undesirable Labor and Desirable Bodies," 95.

designation of someone as Other: it is instead in primitive societies that the stranger is grasped as an 'other.'"[88] Grasping the other in colonial contexts often occurs through language. Sir Charles Trevelyan was a colonial administrator in India and worked in Calcutta in the 1850s and 1860s. He had numerous publications and worked to improve the condition of the native Indian population. In his work, *On the Education of People of India*, Trevelyan illustrates the ways in which learning the language of the empire creates a false sense of hope and desire in the minds of colonized Indians. The desire then of colonized Indians was to see themselves as equals. He writes: "we have gained everything by our superior knowledge; that it is this superiority which has enabled us to conquer India, and to keep it; and they want to put themselves as much as they can upon an equality with us."[89] The ability to speak in the language of the empire works in two ways: one, the empire is able to grasp, to understand the "other" making them strange and yet familiar, and second, it allows for the ways in which the other can aspire to become an equal in the empire.[90]

Drawing on the documentary *John and Jane*, Hudson depicts the ways in which employees in CSOs (Customer Service Outsourcing) come to understand and struggle with their own identity. He writes, "Nicholas [real name Nikesh Soares] laments that he will never be able to speak as 'they' do and imagines highways full of clean cars and air."[91] To speak in the language of the empire is to be facialized as a people and as a nation. Janell Watson argues that, "For Deleuze and Guattari, the face of Christ is neither representation nor image, but rather a powerful new form of coding, an overcoding of the body by the face. In order to fully grasp the politics of the face, it is useful to imagine people without faces, but with beautifully expressive bodies."[92] Shifting back to the biblical text, the multitude in this text are just that bodies without faces. Their faces are hidden from the gaze of the reader.

Language embedded in the face of the "other" makes them familiar. In Revelation 7.13-14, John says: "Then one of the elders asked me, 'These in white robes—who are they, and where did they come from?' I answered,

---

88. Deleuze and Guattari, *A Thousand Plateaus*, 178.
89. C. E. Trevelyan, *On the Education of the People of India* (London: Longman, Orme, Brown, Green, & Longman, 1838), 176.
90. Here I draw on the work of Bhabha, *Location of Culture*, 101. Bhabha writes: "Therefore despite the 'play' in the colonial system which is crucial to its exercise of power, colonial discourse which is crucial to its exercise of power, colonial discourse produces the colonized as a social reality which is at once an 'other' and yet entirely knowable and visible."
91. Hudson, *Undesirable Labor and Desirable Bodies*, 99.
92. Janell Watson, "The Face of Christ: Deleuze and Guattari on the Politics of Word and Image," *The Bible and Critical Theory* 1.2 (2005): 1–14, here 8.

'Sir, you know.' And he said, 'These are they who have come out of the great tribulation; they have washed their robes and made them white in the blood of the Lamb.'" This verse is often interpreted through a baptismal lens. Ulfgard notes that "the baptismal reference is especially emphasized by Kraft, Prigent, and Schüssler Fiorenza. Like many others, Kraft notes the possible allusion to Gen. 49:11."[93] On the other hand, scholars like Ulfgard depart from this view and instead argue that "the multitude in their white-washed robes are depicted as a true congregation of God analogous to Israel at Sinai."[94] However, when read through the work of Deleuze and Guattari, the white-washed robes worn by the multitude illustrate a form of cultural assimilation that attempts to first Christianize the nations by making them speak in the language of the dominant and then pledge their allegiance to the throne of God. Simply put: the nations in the text of Revelation minimize their deviance by masking their difference through language and dress. Deleuze and Guattari write: "The deterritorialization of the body implies a reterritorialization on the face; the decoding of the body implies an overcoding by the face."[95] The decoded bodies of the multitude hidden under the white robes are overcoded in their faces as they sing the anthem of praise before God. Deleuze and Guattari continue: "The difference between our uniforms and clothes and primitive paintings and garb is that the former effect a facialization of the body…"[96] The different garbs of the nations are stripped as their bodies are covered with white robes that seek to minimize their difference and create the illustration of people-as-one within the national boundaries imagined by the author of Revelation. Simply put, the bodies of the multitude are finally facialized before God.

---

93. Ulfagard, *Feast and the Future,* 82. Ulfgard summarizes the arguments of all the three scholars as follows. Heinrich Kraft in his book *Die Offenbarung des Johannes* (HNT, 16a; Tübingen: Mohr Siebeck, 1974. While Kraft draws connection of the white robes in Rev. 7.9-17 to Gen. 49.11, he goes further to argue that the robes symbolize the ritual of baptism. Similarly, Pierre Prigent in his work, *L'Apocalypse de saint Jean* (CNT, 14; Paris: Delachaux et Niestlé, 1981), 123, 126, also connects the white robes and the blood of the Lamb to the act of baptism. Elisabeth Schüssler Fiorenza makes a similar argument in her work entitled, *Invitation to the Book of Revelation: A Commentary on the Apocalypse with Complete Text from the Jerusalem Bible* (Garden City: 1981), 93. Thus, while she argues that this text alludes to baptism she interprets the great multitude to consist of both Christians and all those who suffered in the last great tribulation regardless of their relationship with the Lamb.
94. Ulfagard, *Feast and the Future*, 84.
95. Deleuze and Guattari, *A Thousand Plateaus*, 181.
96. Deleuze and Guattari, *A Thousand Plateaus*, 181.

Conclusion

Language plays an important role in Revelation 7.9-17. The vocalization of the nations manifested through their song and their dress facializes them in the text. At the same time, speaking the imperial language creates ways for nations to envision themselves as becoming a part of the empire. Language then, helps in constructing the identity of the other or to put it simply, facializes the bodies of these nations. Deleuze and Guattari write:

> Whatever the differences between significance and subjectification, whichever prevails over the other in this case or that, whatever the varying figures assumed by their de facto mixtures—they have it in common to crush all polyvocality, set up language as a form of exclusive expression, and operate by signifying biunivocalization and subjective binarization.[97]

Thus, imperial language reterritorialized on the lips of imperialized "other" displaces, deterritorializes, and finally crushes the polyvocal languages of the nations. The desire to speak and sound like the empire is a desire to assimilate into the empire and allows one to imagine being transported into a place that is at once strange and yet remarkably familiar at the same time.[98] In other words, reterritorialized imperial language placed on the lips of colonized subjects while seeking to facialize them also alienates them from their own subjectivity. The polyvalent languages spoken by the minority nations, people, and tribes inserted into monolithic and homogenous language of the empire compels assimilation. This assimilation not only makes nations recognizable, but their ability to speak the major imperial language makes them comprehensible on the global stage. The assemblages of the nations disunited and heterogenous are produced into a major monolithic empire that is facialized through language. Deleuze and Guattari write, "If the face is in fact Christ, in other words, your average ordinary White Man, then the first deviances, the first divergences types, are racial: yellow man, black man, men in the second or third category. They are also inscribed on the wall, distributed by the hole. They must be Christianized, in other words, facialized."[99] The facialization of these nations, illustrated through an overt and deliberate reterritorialization of their language and dress, racialized in

---

97. Deleuze and Guattari, *A Thousand Plateaus*, 180.
98. Celia M. Britton, *Edourd Glissant and Postcolonial Theory: Strategies of Language and Resistance* (Charlottesville, VA: University of Virginia Press, 1999), 83. Britton points to this idea using the work of Glissant who, "... emphasizes the importance of the mimetic drive's verbal dimension: to 'be' the white Frenchman is above all to speak like he does," and Glissant explains "the desiring violence of speech in Martinique as above all a desire to be other and to be elsewhere."
99. Deleuze and Guattari, *A Thousand Plateaus*, 178.

order to familiarize, constructs a nationalized vision where only one nation, speaking one language, wearing one dress, gathers to worship only the one and true God.

Biographical Note

Sharon Jacob is Associate Professor of New Testament at Pacific School of Religion. Dr. Jacob earned her Masters of Divinity from Lancaster Theological Seminary and Masters of Sacred Theology from Yale University. She earned her PhD from Drew University. Her research interests include gender and sexuality studies, feminist theory, race and whiteness theory, and postcolonial theory. Her publications include a monograph entitled, *Reading Mary alongside Indian Surrogate Mothers: Violent Love, Oppressive Liberation, and Infancy Narratives* (New York: Palgrave, 2015). She has also co-authored an essay entitled, "Flowing from breast to breast: An Examination of Dis/placed Motherhood in Black and Indian West Nurses," in *Womanist Biblical Interpretations: Expanding the Discourses* (Atlanta, GA: Society of Biblical Literature Press, 2016). Her essay entitled "Imagined Nations, Real Women: Politics of Culture and Women's Bodies. A Postcolonial, Feminist, and Indo-Western Interpretation of 1 Timothy 2:8-15," in *Asian American Biblical Hermeneutics* was published by T&T Clark in 2019. More recently her essay entitled, "Jezebel and Indo-Western Women: Nation, Nationalism, and the Ecologies of Sexual Violence in Revelation 2: 20-25" in *Ecological Solidarities: Mobilizing Faith and Justice for an Entangled World (World Christianity)* was published by Penn State University Press, 2019.

Bibliography

Anderson, Benedict. "Imagined Communities," 123–6 in Ashcroft, Griffiths, and Tiffin, eds., *The Post-Colonial Studies Reader*, 1995.

Ashcroft, Bill, Gareth Griffiths, and Helen Tiffin, eds. *The Post-Colonial Studies Reader.* 2nd edn. New York: Routledge, 1995.

Aune, David E. "The Protective Sealing of the 144,000 (7:1-17)," 424–55 in *Word Biblical Commentary: Revelation 17–22*. Grand Rapids, MI: Zondervan, 1988.

Bauckham, Richard. "The List of the Tribes in Revelation 7 Again," *Journal for the Study of the New Testament* 42 (1991): 99–115. https://doi.org/10.1177/0142064X9101304206

Bhabha, Homi K. *The Location of Culture*. New York: Routledge, 1994.

Brennan, Timothy. "The National Longing for Form," 128–32 in Ashcroft, Griffiths, and Tiffin, eds., *The Post-Colonial Studies Reader*, 1995.

Britton, Celia M. *Edourd Glissant and Postcolonial Theory: Strategies of Language and Resistance*. Charlottesville, VA: University of Virginia Press.

Caird, George B. *A Commentary on the Revelation of St. John the Divine*. Reprint. Peabody, MA: Hendrickson, 1995.

Callahan, Allen Dwight. "The Language of the Apocalypse," *Harvard Theological Review* 88.4 (1995): 453–70. https://doi.org/10.1017/S0017816000031710
Carey, Greg. "Symptoms of Resistance in the Book of Revelation," 169–80 in *The Reality of Apocalypse: Rhetoric and Politics in the Book of Revelation*. Edited by David L. Barr. Atlanta, GA: Society of Biblical Literature, 2006.
Charles, R. H. *The Revelation of St. John*. International Critical Commentary. 2 volumes. New York: Scribner's, 1920.
Chatterjee, Partha. "Nationalism as a Problem," 126–8 in Ashcroft, Griffiths, and Tiffin, eds., *The Post-Colonial Studies Reader*, 1995.
Deleuze, Gilles. *Difference and Repetition*. Translated by Paul Patton. New York: Columbia University Press, 1994.
—"Nietzsche and Saint Paul, Lawrence and John of Patmos," 36–52 in *Essays Critical and Clinical*. Translated by Daniel W. Smith and Michael A. Greco. Minneapolis, MN: University of Minneapolis Press, 1997.
Deleuze, Gilles, and Felix Guattari. *Kafka: Toward a Minor Literature*. Translated by Dana Polan. Minneapolis, MN: University of Minnesota Press, 1986.
—*A Thousand Plateaus: Capitalism and Schizophrenia*. Translated by Brian Massumi. Minneapolis, MN: University of Minnesota Press, 1987.
Derrida, Jacques. "The Violence of the Letter," 109–52 in *Of Grammatology*. Translated by G. Chakravorty Spivak. Baltimore, MD: Johns Hopkins University Press, 1976.
Fanon, Frantz. "On National Culture," 36–52 in *Colonial Discourse and Post-Colonial Theory: A Reader*. Edited by Patrick Williams and Laura Chrisman. New York: Columbia University Press, 1994.
—"On National Culture," 117–9 in Ashcroft, Griffiths, and Tiffin, eds., *The Post-Colonial Studies Reader*, 1995.
Garrett, Susan R. "Revelation," 469–74 in *Women's Bible Commentary: Expanded Edition*. Edited by Carol A. Newsom and Sharon H. Ringe. Louisville, KY: Westminster John Knox, 1998.
Gellner, Ernest. *Thought and Change*. London: Weidenfeld & Nicholson, 1964.
Howard-Brook, Wes, and Anthony Gwyther. *Unveiling Empire: Reading Revelation Then and Now*. New York: Orbis Book, 1999.
Hudson, Dale. "Undesirable Bodies and Desirable Labor: Documenting the Globalization and Digitization of Transnational American Dreams in Indian Call Centers," *Cinema Journal* 49.1 (Fall, 2009): 82–102. https://doi.org/10.1353/cj.0.0164
Kachru, Braj B. "The Alchemy of English," 272–6 in Ashcroft, Griffiths, and Tiffin, eds., *The Post-Colonial Studies Reader*, 1995.
Kraft, Heinrich. *Die Offenbarung des Johannes*. Handbuch zum Neuen Testament, 16a. Tübingen: Mohr Siebeck, 1974.
Lawrence, D. H. *Apocalypse and Writings on Revelation*. Edited by Mara Kalnis. Cambridge: Cambridge University Press, 1980.
Macaulay, Lord Thomas Babington. "Minute on Education," 2 February 1835. Published in Henry Sharp, selections from the *Educational Records, Bureau of Education, India* I. Calcutta, 1920.
Marshall, John W. *Parables of War: Reading John's Jewish Apocalypse*. Waterloo, ON: Wilfred Laurier University Press, 2001.
Moore, Stephen D. *Empire and Apocalypse: Postcolonialism and the New Testament*. Sheffield: Sheffield Phoenix Press, 2006.
—*Untold Tales from the Book of Revelation: Sex and Gender, Empire and Ecology*. Atlanta, GA: Society of Biblical Literature, 2014. https://doi.org/10.2307/j.ctt9qh21k

Økland, Jorunn. "Why Can't the Heavenly Miss Jerusalem Just Shut Up," 88–105 in *A Feminist Companion to The Apocalypse of John*. Edited by Amy Jill Levine and Maria Mayo Robbins. New York: T&T Clark, 2009.

Pippin, Tina, and J. Michael Clark. "Revelation/Apocalypse," 753–68 in *The Queer Bible Commentary*. Edited by Deryn Guest, et al. London: SCM Press, 2006.

Prigent, Pierre. *L'Apocalypse de saint Jean.* Commentaire du nouveau testament, 14. Paris: Delachaux et Niestlé, 1981.

Roy, Modhumita. "Englishing India: Reinstituting Class and Social Privilege," *Social Text* 39 (1994): 83–107. https://doi.org/10.2307/466365

Schüssler Fiorenza, Elisabeth. *Invitation to the Book of Revelation: A Commentary on the Apocalypse with Complete Text from the Jerusalem Bible*. New York: Garden City, 1981.

Smith, Christopher R. "The Portrayal of the Church as the New Israel in the Names and Order of the Tribes in Revelation 7:5-8," *Journal for the Study of the New Testament* 39 (1990): 111–8. https://doi.org/10.1177/0142064X9001203907

—"The Tribes of Revelation 7 and the Literary Competence of John the Seer," *Journal of the Evangelical Theological Society* 38.2 (June 1995): 213–8.

Smith, Donald Eugene. *India as a Secular.* Princeton, NJ: Princeton University Press, 1963.

Trevelyan, C. E. *On the Education of the People of India*. London: Longman, Orme, Brown, Green, & Longman, 1838.

Ulfgard, Håkan. *Feast and Future: Revelation 7:9-17 and the Feast of the* Tabernacles. Stockholm: Almqvist & Wiksell International, 1989.

Watson, Janell. "The Face of Christ: Deleuze and Guattari on the Politics of Word and Image," *The Bible and Critical Theory* 1.2 (2005): 1–14. https://doi.org/10.2104/bc050004

PART III
Alain Badiou

Chapter Nine

Alain Badiou and Early Christian Texts

Matthew G. Whitlock

Introduction

Nietzsche wrote that a philosophy is always the biography of the philosopher. Maybe a biography of the philosopher by the philosopher himself is a piece of philosophy.[1]

—Alain Badiou, "Philosophy as Biography"

To recast Badiou's words above: perhaps the best way of providing context for a philosopher's life is hearing a philosopher talk about his autobiography as philosophy. Alain Badiou did such an act on 13 November 2007, when recounting nine "stories" in his life.[2] This nine-story recollection will serve as a guide for understanding the context of Badiou's theories as they apply to early Christianity—especially as a way of understanding the model Badiou sets for a transdisciplinary approach to early Christian texts. So we will mark—in the words of Walter Benjamin—quite precisely the sites where Badiou gained possession of his truths. For the most part, we will follow the order of Badiou's own articulation of these sites, but at times we will change the order. Embedded in these nine stories are also connections to the three essays that follow and ideas for future Badiou and early Christian studies projects.

I. Parentage and Philosophy: The Matheme and the Poem

Badiou first sets his philosophical work within the context of his parents and their education. Both parents attended École Normale Superieure, his

---

1. Alain Badiou, "Philosophy as Biography," *The Symptom* 9 (2007), http://www.lacan.com/symptom9_articles/badiou19.html. Badiou begins his lecture with this Nietzsche quote.
2. Badiou, "Philosophy as Biography." Badiou ends this lecture with poetry by Saint-John Perse, where Badiou picks up the line "I shall inhabit my name." To Badiou, "this is precisely what philosophy tries to render possible for each and every one." And as for biography's relation to this philosophical task, Badiou says, "to constantly begin again the search for the conditions which the proper name of each one can be inhabited."

mother earning a degree in French literature, his father a degree in mathematics. Alain himself was an alumnus from École Normale Superieure, but with a degree in philosophy, which he describes as "the only possible way to assume the double filiation and circulate freely between the literary maternity and the mathematical paternity."[3] The result is a unique philosophical language, which Badiou highlights: "the language of philosophy always constructs its own space between the matheme and the poem, between the mother and the father, after all."[4] Both math and poetry serve as key components of Badiou's four truth procedures in his philosophy: science, art, love, and politics, with math a key component of science, and poetry of art.[5]

Mathematics is the ground of Badiou's philosophy.[6] Similar to Deleuze's suspicions about language, Badiou does not see any language—and especially language grounded theology (even in its secularized form)[7]—capable of being the basis for ontology and theory.[8] According to John Mullarkey, Badiou's distrust of language roots in his ideas about truth's universality. For Badiou, "truth is not relative to language (acclaim to which he ascribes to the 'sophists')"; math, unlike language, is universal and not "culturally conventional."[9] What is more, Badiou wants to avoid grounding his theory in a metaphysics of the one, which is connected to assumptions about God, the infinite, and the finite.[10] So he begins his magnum opus, *Being and Event*,

   3. Badiou, "Philosophy as Biography."
   4. Badiou, "Philosophy as Biography."
   5. For math and poetry as exemplars of truth procedures in science and art respectively, see Hollis Phelps, *Alain Badiou: Between Theology and Anti-Theology* (Durham: Acumen, 2013), 96.
   6. Phelps, *Between Theology and Anti-Theology*, 3. Phelps points out that Badiou, in fact, tries to re-ground philosophy (and ontology) in mathematics.
   7. Phelps, *Between Theology and Anti-Theology*, 4–6, 21.
   8. See John Mullarkey "Deleuze," in *Alain Badiou: Key Concepts* (ed. A. J. Bartlett and Justin Clemens; Durham: Acumen, 2010), 168–75, here 169–70. Mullarkey states: "Deleuze shares with Badiou his issues with linguistic philosophies (Rorty and Wittgenstein, say, would be enemies for both). Deleuze clearly rejects the power of language in theory, seeking a non-linguistic semiotics of direct sensation … He wants to replace the linguistically dominated semiological approach with a 'semiotics'—a system of images and signs independent of language."
   9. Mullarkey "Deleuze," 169–70.
   10. On Badiou's avoidance of a metaphysics of the one, see Ed Pluth, *Badiou: A Philosophy of the New* (Key Contemporary Thinkers; Cambridge: Polity Press, 2010), 30. On how this metaphysics brings about false assumptions about the finite and infinite, see Phelps, *Between Theology and Anti-Theology*, 38–50. On Badiou's use of mathematics being "an anti-religious or anti-theological gesture," see Hollis Phelps, "Alain Badiou (1937-)," in *Religion and European Philosophy: Key Thinkers from Kant to Žižek* (ed. Philip Goodchild and Hollis Phelps; New York: Routledge, 2017), 438–51, here 439–40. But this gesture should not be misunderstood as a call to abandon theology

with the following assertion: "the one is not."[11] Like Deleuze, Badiou asserts that multiplicity—as opposed to the one—is a given.[12] But for Badiou mathematics is the best place to consider multiplicity. In *Being and Event,* Badiou also asserts "mathematics is ontology."[13] The mathematics Badiou turns to is set theory, and according to Pluth, "... one of the reasons why Badiou wants to give ontology over to set theory is exactly because set theory does not limit us to considerations of natural objects and objects of experience; it allows for a far more expansive, indeed non-human, take on the multiple."[14] Set theory, in short, allows us to see multiplicity (and infinity) apart from language and apart from experience. Set theory also allows us to see, in Phelps's words, the operations in which we experience "the world as unified, as one."[15] Reality, indeed, is "pure and inconsistent multiplicity"; however, there is also something secondary to this multiplicity, an operation where we "count as one," in which we organize and structure.[16] Hence, "part of the goal of Badiou's ontology," according to Phelps, "is to understand this operation itself, that is, the movement from inconsistent multiplicity to consistent multiple."[17] It is this quest for understanding this operation from multiplicity to consistent multiple that informs the study of early Christian texts. While historical approaches have disclosed the diversity and multiplicity of early Christian texts (and that they are embedded in historical contexts), there is a need for philosophically informed approaches that help us understand

---

and religious studies. Phelps accordingly argues that Badiou's assertions are "most pertinent for theology" and religious studies (440, 449–50).

11. Alain Badiou, *Being and Event* (trans. Oliver Feltham; London: Continuum, 2005), 23; translation of *L'Etre et l'événement* (Paris: Seuil, 1988).

12. Badiou and Deleuze agree on this point; however, they do not agree on the starting point, which for Badiou is mathematics and set theory. See Mullarkey, "Deleuze," 174: "Badiou concedes that Deleuze was on the right track to think in terms of multiplicities, but adds that he was not successful in this endeavor because he missed the correct starting point for thinking the multiple. For Badiou, the science of the multiple *qua* multiple must be set theory, because it is the theory of the multiple in the purest sense, which, through its axioms and theorems, articulates all that can be said about the pure multiple."

13. Badiou, *Being and Event*, 4. Phelps, *Between Theology and Anti-Theology*, 19, notes that the statement "mathematics is ontology" is "not a statement about being; rather, it positions mathematics as the discursive vehicle through which being qua being can be though and expressed."

14. Pluth, *A Philosophy of the New*, 43. See also, Phelps, *Between Theology and Anti-Theology*, 18: "Mathematics avoids admitting the finite into its thought in both form and content."

15. Phelps, "Alain Badiou," 440–1.
16. Phelps, "Alain Badiou," 440–1.
17. Phelps, "Alain Badiou," 440–1.

how truths are derived from this multiplicity. Hence, in this volume, both Bruce Worthington ("Christianity Appears First, as Itself") and Hollis Phelps ("Recapitulating the Event: Reading Irenaeus with Badiou") use Badiou's theories to derive truths from the quest from early Christianity, from the historical Jesus to Paul to Irenaeus.[18] More will be said about both pieces in the final section of this chapter.

Badiou himself, in *Saint Paul: The Foundation of Universalism*, turns to early Christianity to trace the "count as one" operation as it is derived from multiplicity. Part of this process involves "naming," that is, using language to name "the event" as it is derived from the multitudinous situation. For Badiou, Paul is a model of this procedure. And given Paul's role in "naming," Badiou calls Paul "a poet-thinker of the event."[19] This is where Badiou's parentage comes into play, that is, the convergence of matheme and the poem. And herein lies a paradox in Badiou's thinking: math and poetry converge, even if the latter is secondary in the procedure of "the event." As I noted above, poetic language is not the ground of Badiou's ontology—for it is mythical and mystifying, according to Phelps, and not "cold" and "deductive" like the matheme.[20] What is more, it cannot fully describe what is outside its context, that is, the event. Poetry and language, in other words, are embedded in the multiplicity of situations and cannot be separated from them, unlike math. However, at the same time, one must use language to articulate "the event" and truth. Phelps states: "the subject must necessarily use the language of the situation to produce terms that connect multiples to name the event."[21] Yet this language does not have a referent—for what it is trying to name is the event, which is not part of the situation. Phelps continues: "The names that the subject uses are thus not primarily representative in function, since truth, as something that is always to

---

18. Both pieces also serve as starting points for understanding Badiou's theory of the event, especially in light of early Christian studies.

19. Alain Badiou, *Saint Paul: The Foundation of Universalism* (Stanford, CA: Stanford University Press, 2003), 2.

20. Phelps, *Between Theology and Anti-Theology*, 20, 22. This is also where Badiou's "anti-theology" comes into play as well. Badiou is avoiding the mystical and theological language of "the one," which is not. Yet, as Phelps points out, Badiou's philosophy does not avoid this language altogether, but remains "captive to theology, conditioned by certain theological concepts, even if Badiou fails to acknowledge as much" (p. 130).

21. Phelps, *Between Theology and Anti-Theology*, 77. Also, in the Badiou's philosophy, "the subject" is much more complex and involved than the individual subjectivity. For an introduction to "the subject" in Badiou, see Pluth, *A Philosophy of the New*, 104–27. See section below on Badiou: Marxism, Maoism, and the Subject for a brief description of Badiou's conception of the subject.

come, is strictly speaking incalculable."²² Yet this language, this poetic language, is necessary: "It is precisely poetic nomination that allows an event to be susceptible to an interventional decision, making the production of truth possible."²³ So poetic language "pushes the limits of language 'so as to effect a powerful anticipation.'"²⁴ On the limits of language to describe an event and truth, and at the same time, on the pursuit of the expression of the effects of an event and truth, see Paul's letters, for example: "all creation is groaning together" and "we also groan" (Rom. 8.21-23); "the Spirit itself intercedes with inexpressible groanings" (Rom. 8.26); "heard ineffable things, which no one may utter " (2 Cor. 12.4). Paul knows that what he is naming cannot be named, but he strives to name it in his letters anyway, often through metaphor and poetic and unusual language.²⁵ In sum, Phelps, quoting Badiou, sums up this poetic function in Badiou's writings well:

> There is a close relationship ... between nomination and how Badiou understands the creativity of poetry and poetic language. Indeed, in so far as poetry for Badiou is not primarily descriptive or expressive but creative, Badiou claims that "every name of an event or of the evental presence is in its essence poetic."²⁶

Because of his parents, Badiou's "double filiation" with poetry and math does not cease at philosophy; indeed, it extends to politics. Both his parents were politically active. What is also worth noting, which Badiou notes out in the fifth "act" of "Philosophy as Biography," is his father's political activity: he was mayor of Toulouse, France, as a member of the Socialist Party, and he was part of the resistance in World War II. On the latter point, Badiou comments elsewhere: "... it was very early on that my father introduced me to his own resistance as purely logical. From the moment that the country was invaded and subjugated by the Nazis, he said, there was nothing else for it than to resist. It was no more complicated than that. But then

---

22. Phelps, *Between Theology and Anti-Theology*, 78. Note also that Deleuze and Guattari see language as non-representational, but for different reasons. See Whitlock and Tite, Chapter 7 this volume.
23. Phelps, *Between Theology and Anti-Theology*, 97. On intervention and naming, see p. 151: "Because the event is undecidable from the perspective of the situation, an interventional decision is required to name the event, making it available for thought and the subsequent development of truth through fidelity."
24. Phelps, *Between Theology and Anti-Theology*, 98. Phelps's quote here is from Alain Badiou, *Handbook of Inaesthetics* (trans. Alberto Toscano; Stanford, CA: Stanford University Press, 2004), 23.
25. On Paul's use of unusual language and metaphor, see Beverly Roberts Gaventa, *Our Mother Saint Paul* (Louisville, KY: Westminster John Knox, 2007).
26. Phelps, *Between Theology and Anti-Theology*, 58; Badiou, *Handbook of Inaesthetics*, 26.

my father was a mathematician."²⁷ Here Badiou sees mathematics as a "war machine" (to use Deleuze's phrase) for political thought and action: "Mathematics provides philosophy as a weapon, a fearsome machine of thought, a catapult aimed at the bastions of ignorance, superstition, and mental servitude."²⁸ And not only did his parentage play a role in making his philosophy into a mathematical, poetical, and political war machine, but also the events of 1968 and the various responses to them, the topic of our next section.

II. Politics and Philosophy: 1968, the Paris Commune, and Pauline Communities

Just as 1968 brought about the convergence of Deleuze and Guattari into Deleuzoguattarian thought, May 1968 sparked a key moment in Badiou's own thinking. In "Philosophy as Biography," in his sixth story, Badiou refers to the events of 1968 and those who later renounced these events, that is, the new philosophers of the 1970s. This renouncement is a driving force in Badiou's philosophy. Badiou asks: "How is it possible that one can cease being the subject of the truth? How is it possible that one return to the routine of the world?"²⁹ According to Badiou, May 1968 was his "Road to Damascus" experience.³⁰ More specifically—as Pluth observes in the opening of his *A Philosophy of the New*—it was a retrospective look at the activism of 1968 that sparked Badiou's thinking. For he saw many of his peers form "a strong hostility toward their former militant engagement."³¹ What is important here is the question driving Badiou's philosophy, as articulated by Pluth: "What are the conditions under which a militant engagement can continue, instead of burning out or reversing?"³² Seeing the militant engagement and activism of 1968 fade, Badiou sought ways of viewing change and continuance through the lens of philosophy, more specifically, through a systematic philosophy focusing on events and fidelity to them. For Badiou, philosophy's duty is "to continue," that is, "to stay not only within the vividness of the event, but within its becoming."³³ This philosophy of fidelity draws heavily from early Christian literature: Paul's uncontested letters, which we

---

27. Alain Badiou, *Metapolitics* (trans. Jason Barker; London: Verso, 2005), 6.
28. Alain Badiou, *Theoretical Writings* (ed. and trans. Ray Brassier and Alberto Toscano; London: Continuum, 2004), 16; quoted in Phelps, *Between Theology and Anti-Theology*, 21–2.
29. Badiou, "Philosophy as Biography."
30. Pluth, *A Philosophy of the New*, 18.
31. Pluth, *A Philosophy of the New*, 1.
32. Pluth, *A Philosophy of the New*, 1.
33. Badiou, "Philosophy as Biography."

will return to at the end of this section.³⁴ Here it is important first to point out another event Badiou references in his writing: the Paris commune.

In *The Communist Hypothesis,* Badiou refers to the Paris Commune (founded on 18 March 1871) while recounting a commentary on the commune by Julien Gracq, who himself was commenting on a commune leader. When on the brink of the commune being massacred by state forces (in late April 1871), one of its leaders "wanders like a lost dog from one barricade to another" and can only think to distribute "in disorderly fashion vouchers for herrings."³⁵ He says, "Leave me alone … I need to think alone." Later, as Gracq speculates, the leader is haunted by the voices of the massacred asking him: "Where are the orders? Where is the plan?" Applying this situation to our own time (as well as the student uprisings in France in 1968), Badiou warns: "I write here so that neither I nor my interlocutors—intellectual or not—ever become the one who, all told, can only meet the great dates of history by distributing herring vouchers."³⁶ Even more, Badiou writes about his purpose in recounting this story: "to contribute, however slightly, to preventing us (as inheritors of the Cultural Revolution and May 1968) from becoming '*dealers in herring vouchers.*'"³⁷ To Badiou, now is the time to think and plan.

---

34. Unlike Deleuze and Guattari, who intentionally created and changed their language in order to avoid systematization, Badiou sought a more systematic approach. See Hollis Phelps, "Alain Badiou": "Badiou's project … can be understood as an attempt to develop a rational, systematic philosophy, centered on the development of a mathematical, deductive ontology and non-objective theory of truth and the subject" (p. 438).

35. See Alain Badiou, *The Communist Hypothesis* (trans. David Macey and Steve Corcoran; London: Verso, 2010), 160–1: "A kind of atrocious nausea arises while following the *Ubuesque* masquerade, the pathetic disorder, of the last pages wherein the unfortunate Commune delegate—no longer daring to show his sash which he clasped under his arms in a newspaper—a sort of incompetent district official, of petroleur Charlot leaping between shell blasts, incapable of doing anything at all, treated harshly by the rebels who bare their teeth, wanders like a lost dog from one barricade to another distributing in disorderly fashion vouchers for herrings, bullets, and fire, and imploring the spiteful crow—which was hard on his heels, because of the fix into which he had plunged it—pitifully, lamentably, 'Leave me alone, I ask you. I need to think alone.' In his exile as a courageous incompetent, he must have sometimes awoken at night, still hearing the voices of all the same people who were to be massacred in a few minutes, and who cried so furiously at him from the barricade, 'Where are the orders? Where is the plan?'"

36. Alain Badiou, *Theory of the Subject* (trans. Bruno Bosteels; London: Continuum, 2009), xlii; translation of *Théorie du sujet* (Paris: Éditions du Seuil, 1982).

37. Badiou, *The Communist Hypothesis*, 160–1. Note that Badiou recounts this story twice in his major works, almost thirty years apart: *Théorie du sujet* (1982) and *The Communist Hypothesis* (2010). On this and Badiou's "herring voucher" comment and its relation to his philosophy, see Ed Pluth, *Badiou: A Philosophy of the New,* 11.

In this volume, while Bruce Worthington and Hollis Phelps discuss Badiou's theories centering on the event and evental recurrence (theories derived from the matheme and the poem), James Crossley discusses Badiou's thinking on revolution and politics, using it as a starting point of his essay, noting Badiou's dissatisfaction with how revolutionary sparks fade, a fading exemplified both in the early Christian communities and in Marxism, from Jesus to Paul (and later deutero-Pauline writings and communities), and from Marx to Lenin (and later Stalin). Crossley also contemporizes this pattern in comparing liberal, grass-roots movements (e.g., Bernie Sanders in America and Jeremy Corbyn in England) to less radical, neo-liberal movements, movements which have in many ways left behind liberal ideology. Tracing how radical movements fade or endure or evolve is important for early Christian studies—for it is easy to overlook these later processes in favor of glorifying their origins. Badiou's focus in relation to this point, that is, in following the consequences of an event versus glorifying in the original event itself, is captured well in his *Being and Event*: "What the doctrine of the event teaches us is rather that the entire effort lies in following the event's consequences, not in glorifying its occurrence."[38]

III. Seized by Events: Responding to an Unheard Appeal

Continuing to frame his philosophy in the context of his parents, Badiou recalls a story about his mom at the age of 81, when she told him that, before meeting Badiou's father, she had a "devouring passion" for her philosophy teacher, who ultimately "had gone off with someone else."[39] Badiou sees the humor in this story: Badiou is a "consolation," having "done nothing else except accomplish the desire of [his mother]," that is, becoming a philosophy teacher himself.[40] What is most important to Badiou, however, is what this story says about philosophy: first, there is always a next step in philosophy; second, "in the most unconscious manner," a philosopher responds to an appeal that he or she "has not even heard."[41] This illustrates well Badiou's conception of the subject, which is certainly broader than the individual, individual choices, and individual actions. The subject does not seize the event, but the event seizes the subject. Ed Pluth ties together this point with what we discussed in the prior section (i.e., the continuance of the event):

---

38. Badiou, *Being and Event*, 210.
39. Badiou, "Philosophy as Biography."
40. Badiou, "Philosophy as Biography."
41. Badiou, "Philosophy as Biography." Badiou says, "As myself, in the most unconscious manner, I never did anything as a philosopher except respond to an appeal that I had not even heard."

Badiou's goal is not to trigger events, and it is not about trying to convince anyone to join a particular movement. Badiou's formalized in-humanism is supposed to show us instead how the new happens, how it emerges not at all without human practice, but not with the full knowledge and choice and freedom of any of its participants either. And as a practical humanism, his system is supposed to give individuals the wherewithal to continue with these procedures that seize them.[42]

IV. Early Christian Studies and Badiou: Finding "the Raw" in the Present

Another story Badiou recounts is his arrival in Paris in 1955, at the age of 18, at the time of the war in Algeria. As a student, he joined the protests in Paris to stop the war, where "the police are waiting for [them] with their cloaks, and [they] were joyfully knocked senseless." In response, Badiou and his fellow demonstrators continued to protest. "We had to do it again," says Badiou.[43] Badiou recalls these events not simply to highlight the importance of political engagement, or to call for more scholar-activists. He derives something from these events that can inform scholarship, especially informing scholarship that does not engage "the pure present." He says, "something of the contemporary is always raw." What's more, "philosophy must testify to this raw or take place within it."[44] Similar to Benjamin, a scholar does not simply catalogue the past, but understands that this cataloguing takes place in the present, in its raw moments, moments not to be ignored or escaped. Without engagement in these raw moments, scholarship faces the danger of repeating only what is in its current field, within its discipline, within the language of its own situation, within the status quo, within the "dominant state of affairs," as Badiou names it in the context of politics.[45]

V. A Philosophy Seductively Hostile to the Normal Regime of Seductive

Badiou, in his next story, reminiscences about his early encounters with seduction and love before his arrival in Paris in 1955. As noted above, the young Badiou was a French provincial, and Badiou notes that within this context he encountered a majority of girls who were "still raised in

---

42. Pluth, *A Philosophy of the New*, 184.
43. Badiou, "Philosophy as Biography."
44. Badiou, "Philosophy as Biography."
45. On Badiou and politics, see Phelps, *Between Theology and Anti-Theology*, 102–8. Here Phelps quotes Badiou, speaking about a collective politics that looks to new possibilities, "not the dominant state of affairs" (Badiou, *The Meaning of Sarkozy* [trans. David Fernbach; London: Verso, 2008], 11).

religions." This led to a unique kind of seduction: "the young man who knows how to refute the existence of God is more seductive than the one who could propose to the girl a game of tennis."[46] So he paraded his refutations of the existence of God. From this, Badiou concludes that philosophy is seduction. Though he acknowledges "philosophy argues against the seduction of images," philosophy is "being seductively hostile to the normal regime of seductive."[47] In his philosophy—as in Benjamin's, Deleuze's, and Butler's—there is suspicion of the seduction of the status quo, a suspicion which pushes scholarship toward creativity, to move beyond the situation in which it finds itself and be seduced by the new and unfamiliar, or even the unfamiliar in the familiar.

VI. Badiou: Marxism, Maoism, and the Subject

Badiou recounts another story on politics, one tied to Marxism and equality, and philosophy's relationship with both. "Truth is universal," says Badiou, and "in a radical sense, the anonymous equalitarian for-all, the pure for-all, constitutes it in its being."[48] Like Benjamin and Deleuze, Badiou interacts with Marxist thought.[49] Badiou also delves into Maoist thought, which was not unique to political thought in France in the late 1960s, especially in relation to its anti-hierarchical ideology.[50]

Although 1968 draws attention to a key point in the emergence of Badiou's philosophy, Badiou himself also points to his work as a journalist in Belgium in 1960, where he encountered striking mine workers, who "reorganized the entire social life of the country." Badiou comments: "I was from then on convinced ... that philosophy was on that side." From this

---

46. Badiou, "Philosophy as Biography."
47. Badiou, "Philosophy as Biography." Badiou argues: "philosophy argues against the seduction of images and I remain Platonist on this point. But it also argues in order to seduce. We can thus understand the Socratic function of corruption of the youth. Corrupting youth means being seductively hostile to the normal regime of seduction. I maintain and I repeat that is the destiny of philosophy to corrupt the youth, to teach it that immediate seductions have little value, but also that superior seductions exist."
48. Badiou, "Philosophy as Biography."
49. See, e.g., Badiou, *The Communist Hypothesis*; Phelps, *Between Theology and Anti-Theology*, 106. Phelps (2) discerns two phases in Badiou's thought: the first is based on a Marxist framework (as articulated above), culminating in 1985; the second in based on a mathematical framework, as delineated in *Being and Event*.
50. See Pluth, *A Philosophy of the New*, 19–24, 109. Pluth outlines (22–4, 109) how Badiou's interaction with Maoist thought gives birth to Badiou's *Theory of the Subject* (1982). This Maoist framework, according to Pluth, is coupled with Badiou's analysis of Christian thought (109).

experience, Badiou draws three points about truth as it relates to equality. First, truth "depends on an irruption, not a structure."[51] Second, "truth is universal ... the pure for-all" (as quoted above). Third, "truth constitutes the subject," and the subject does not constitute the truth.[52] This third conclusion expresses well Badiou's conception of the subject. The subject is not individual consciousness, but, as Pluth summarizes, the subject is "the real presence of change in a given situation."[53] It is disruptive, dynamic, and collective. It is fashioned by the event.[54] It is faithful to the event. It names it. But it is neither the foundation nor the cause of it.[55]

VII. Badiou's Literary Voice and the Category of Love

In an "erotic" story, Badiou brings to the fore the torments of sexuality in the 1950s and 1960s. Here he mentions his first novels: *Almagestes* (1964) and *Portulans* (1967), where he notes that "this [sexual] torment is certainly still very perceptible." From this he concludes: "Desire is not a central category for philosophy, and cannot be."[56] Instead, he argues, "love, not desire, must instantly return into the constitution of the concept." Two points are noteworthy for our purposes here. First, in true transdisciplinary style, Badiou does not limit himself to philosophical prose, but writes novels and plays, and, in fact, also composes *The Incident at Antioch: A Tragedy in Three Acts* (2013), a play in which he modernizes the conflict at Antioch between Paul and Peter, changing Paul to the modern revolutionary Paula.[57] Robert Seesengood sums up the play well:

---

51. Badiou, "Philosophy as Biography."
52. Badiou, "Philosophy as Biography."
53. Pluth, *A Philosophy of the New*, 23, 108, 114, 118, 120, and 145. See also Hollis Phelps and Bruce Worthington. "Alain Badiou and the Book of Acts," *Bible and Critical Theory* 12.2 (2016): 104–23, here 107, n. 7; Phelps, *Between Theology and Anti-Theology*, 74.
54. Pluth, *A Philosophy of the New*, 113.
55. Pluth, *A Philosophy of the New*, 112.
56. Badiou, "Philosophy as Biography."
57. Alain Badiou, *The Incident at Antioch: A Tragedy in Three Acts* (trans. Susan Spitzer; New York: Columbia University Press, 2013); translation of *L'Incident d'Antioche: Tragedie en trois actes*. For a review of Badiou's play as it relates to Pauline studies, see Robert Paul Seesengood, "Review of Alain Badiou, *The Incident at Antioch: A Tragedy in Three Acts*," *The Bible and Critical Theory* 10.1 (2014): 88–91. For Badiou's other literary works, see Alain Badiou, *L'Echarpe rouge* (Paris: Maspéro, 1979); *Ahmed le subtil* (Arles: Acts Sud, 1994); *Ahmed the Philosopher: 34 Short Plays for Children* (trans. Joseph Litbak; New York: Columbia University Press, 2014); *Le Second Procès de Socrate* (Arles: Actes Sud, 2015).

Paula, a young statist, converted into a Marxist revolutionary. Act I revolves around Paula's conversion. Act II follows the calcification of revolution into a new tyranny, with the conflict between Paula and Cephas as crescendo. Act III, at "Nicea," explores the final failure of revolution by descent into tyranny, with Paula continuing to struggle to hold on to her idealism. Antioch is set in a modern age (though it is unclear where this modern state-system exists). The play follows the rise of the radical anti-statists into power and the imposition of a new regime of terror and oppression.[58]

While, as Seesengood points out, Badiou certainly misses the nuances of Paul's experience and plays into stereotypical depictions of Paul's conflict with Peter (e.g., freedom versus law), Badiou uses the story to underscore the patterns he sees in revolutions, patterns James Crossley covers in his chapter below.

Second, like Paul (i.e., 1 Cor. 13.1-13; Gal. 5.6, 13), love is a "central category" of Badiou's philosophy and differs from desire.[59] For Badiou, love is one of the aforementioned four truth procedures: science, art, love, and politics.[60] Love is not pure unity, not two becoming one.[61] Love is multiple; love is disjunctive. This idea of two becoming one, according to Badiou, is a misconception. Badiou here stays true to two of his philosophical principles we have already discussed above: multiplicity and "the one is not." So he states that the idea of two becoming one—a "fusional conception of love"—is "a *suppression of the multiple.*"[62] While this volume covers Badiou's conceptions of the event and revolution—and outside of the typical Badiou-Paul paradigm—one gap to be filled in early Christian scholarship is a dialectic between Badiou's and Paul's conceptions of love and desire, of the one and the many.

VIII. A Return to Parentage: Plato (Forms) and Badiou's Father (Mathematics)

In his eighth "story," Badiou returns to his roots when he discusses his "mathematician father," linking this heritage with Plato's forms, quipping, "obviously, in the eyes of the psychoanalyst, means that my desire is only

---

58. Seesengood, "Review of Alain Badiou, *The Incident at Antioch*," 88.
59. On love, see Badiou, "What Is Love?" (trans. Justin Clemens), *Umbr(a)* (1996): 37–53.
60. On these four truth procedures, see Badiou, *Logics of Worlds*, 70–80; Pluth, *A Philosophy of the New*, 147–50; Phelps, *Between Theology and Anti-Theology*, 87–120. On p. 173, Phelps also links other Badiou writings with each of these four procedures.
61. Here I follow Phelps on Badiou and love, *Between Theology and Anti-Theology*, 98–102.
62. Badiou, "What Is Love?" 38.

there to sublimate the image of my mathematician father."[63] In combining both the mathematics and Platonic forms, Badiou remains faithful to the "pure form," which for him is found in mathematics. He also remains committed to the multiple over the one, unlike Plato. Hence, Badiou describes his philosophical project as articulating a "Platonism of the multiple."[64] This unique combination of Platonism and multiplicity results in useful truth procedures, ones, for example, that do not strand historians in contextual particulars, but at the same time acknowledges the uniqueness of these particulars.[65] This is true, for instance, for political truth procedures. Perhaps a connection back to Badiou's Marxism (see Badiou: Marxism, Maoism, and the Subject, above) illustrates this point. Ed Pluth states:

> Structurally speaking, [Badiou's] view is that mass political movements will always refer to communist invariants—equality, freedom from oppression, and so on. But each political situation will require its own *particular* (local) incarnation of these invariants. This point practically requires a break with classical Marxism on Badiou's part, and it is very nearly an ahistorical point, as it amounts to the claim that there is a truth in politics that traverses human history, concerning the assertion of a generic humanity.[66]

Pluth's point here crystallizes Badiou's value for (Marxist-) historical analysis of early Christians texts: one can, with the utmost rigor and care, understand particular, local, contextual, and historical situations of texts, while at the same time identify invariants in new situations.[67]

What's more, one can point to invariants without a reactionary appeal to origins, without absolutizing them, and without policing their extensions and trajectories (in the light of absolutizing them).[68] Badiou, as Phelps demonstrates in his essay below, sees faithfulness to an event as non-reactionary,

---

63. Badiou, "Philosophy as Biography."

64. Badiou, *The Century,* 165–6; *Manifesto for Philosophy,* 104. See Pluth, *A Philosophy of the New,* 32.

65. Again, see Worthington's essay below concerning the historical particulars of early Christianity and how Badiou's philosophy helps us derive truth from their cultural and contextual constraints.

66. Pluth, *A Philosophy of the New,* 156. Earlier, Pluth describes Badiou's theoretical work as the pursuit of "the formal resemblances among different historical periods," resulting in a "conceptual framework ... that can be used to outline the structure of ... disparate situations" (p. 3).

67. Of course, this point is one of contention between Deleuze and Badiou. Deleuze sees a return to transcendence here. See Phelps, *Between Theology and Anti-Theology,* 151.

68. On absolutizing the event and policing extensions of it, see Henry Krips, "The Politics of Badiou: From Absolute Singularity to Objet-a" (paper presented at the plenary session in the Bradshaw Lecture Series "Event and Process," December 2007), 19.

that is, with a future orientation in mind, with the idea of resurrecting and recapitulating and extending truths out of the event. In another place, Phelps and Worthington note: "truths have their origin in events and may, at times, recall that origin and its sense *for their ongoing construction and extension.*"[69] And in another place, Phelps notes: "Events are ruptures that have the potential to force absolutely *new trajectories* in situations, trajectories that correspond to the production of truth."[70] In short, although Badiou lays claim to invariants through Plato, his focus is on how they resurrect or reoccur or emerge over time. Hence, Pluth sums up Badiou's theory as one of emergence: "Badiou's fusion of a study of structures with a study of events ... is really an attempt to develop a theory of change, or *a theory of emergence* of genuine novelty in human situations."[71]

IX. Badiou's Philosophical Parentage: Sartre, Lacan, and Althusser

In his ninth "story," Badiou claims he has maintained his fidelity to three thinkers, three masters: Sartre, Lacan, and Althusser, "disparate" masters to whom Badiou claims to have kept his fidelity.[72] First, drawing on Lacan's "discourse of the master," and without shame, Badiou asserts the necessity of intellectual masters, who "must be combined and surmounted," but must not be denied.[73] In Lacan, Badiou also finds the connection between "a theory of subjects and a theory of forms." This connection serves as the basis for Badiou's theory of the subject (discussed above). The subject, therefore, is "not at all of a psychological character, but is an axiomatic and formal question."[74] Second, in Sartre's existentialism, Badiou finds that "philosophic concept is not worth an hour of toil ... if it does not clarify and ordain the agency of choice, of the vital decision."[75] For Badiou, decision plays an ongoing and central role in the process of fidelity, as well as its relation to the subject.[76] Third, Badiou names his teacher, Louis Althusser, who certainly impacted Badiou's explorations into Marxist thought, and also impacted his theory of the subject. Pluth, on Badiou's conception the subject, asserts the influence of both Sartre and Althusser here: "... the

---

69. Phelps and Worthington. "Alain Badiou and the Book of Acts," 107. Italics are my own.
70. Phelps, *Between Theology and Anti-Theology*, 11.
71. Pluth, *A Philosophy of the New*, 6. Italics are my own.
72. Badiou, "Philosophy as Biography."
73. Badiou, "Philosophy as Biography."
74. Badiou, "Philosophy as Biography."
75. Badiou, "Philosophy as Biography."
76. See Pluth, *A Philosophy of the New*, 97.

rights and privileges of the free, conscious human subject (Sartre) versus the assertion of the predominance of a-subjective, non-conscious, processes and systems, with a devaluing of the (humanist) subject as a thing of pure ideology (Althusser)."[77] Also from his teacher Badiou found the value and uniqueness of philosophy, a philosophy that "must be separated from what is not philosophy."[78] It this type of philosophy—one not vaguely generalist, but also radically disciplinary and interdisciplinary—that this volume aims to dialogue with.

Key Concepts and Theories in this Volume and Beyond

Pluth points out that Badiou's work did not a have large reception in English in the 1970s and 80s, even when French theory was garnering attention. Pluth attributes this lack of attention to Badiou's work not fitting "into any categories or schools."[79] Even today, after gaining attention across disciplines, Badiou's philosophical, trans-, and interdisciplinary efforts are not typical, ranging from mathematics, to political events, to the Apostle Paul. And it is only after he composed his work on Paul that Badiou's theories gained an audience in early Christian Studies and theology. This audience, however, largely focuses on "Badiou and Paul," and the interaction of Badiou's philosophy with early Christian studies, theology, and religious studies is too often limited to this category.[80] As a result, the following three chapters do not limit Badiou's theories to Paul, but extend them to other areas, from the historical Jesus to Paul, from Paul to John, and ultimately to Irenaeus.

A. Bruce Worthington: Christianity Appears First, as Itself

Bruce Worthington brings Badiou's theory of the event into dialogue with the study of early Christian origins, where historical analyses sometimes work from the assumption that *"nothing is sui generis, nothing is unique,"* assuming that "historical subjects and events can always be located within a context, and therefore do not exceed their own ideological, linguistic, or cultural constraints." These analyses, argues Worthington, leave data about early Christianity within their particular historical contexts without examining their relation to truth and Christianity's uniqueness and novelty. Badiou's work offers philosophical methods for drawing truths from historical

---

77. Badiou, "Philosophy as Biography."
78. Badiou, "Philosophy as Biography."
79. Pluth, *A Philosophy of the New*, 22.
80. See Phelps, "Alain Badiou," 449.

situations, as well as for understanding how historical movements, such as Christianity, can be understood as new and unique. On the latter point, Worthington begins by quoting Deleuze—"to find the conditions under which something new is produced"—and then applies Badiou's theory of the event to understand the conditions under which Christianity was produced, concluding that "Christianity constitutes a new truth" and exists "on the very first day of its appearance." Worthington's chief reference points, in order, are Badiou's *Logics of Worlds*, *Being and Event*, and *Saint Paul: The Foundation of Universalism.*

In the first section, Worthington delineates scholarship's move away from Protestant theology's tendency to describe a "unique" and "pristine" and original Christianity, one that contrasts the supposed "later institutional corruptions." While this move has certainly been beneficial in understanding the diversity of Christian origins, it also has not recognized "the evental character of many of its primary texts." As a result, reflection on "an originary event" in the study of Christian origins has been dismissed. So Worthington offers a philosophical inquiry via Badiou into the idea of an originary event without recourse to "theological speculation." In the second section, Worthington begins his analysis with Badiou's theory of the event, starting with Badiou's concept of the "evental site," which serves as the site within a historical situation where the new and unnamable occurs. It is here where the originary event of early Christianity ("Jesus has been resurrected") is not simply a modification "of its pre-existing cultural situation." Rather, the event exceeds it. In the third section, Worthington considers Badiou's concept of "intervention," wherein "an undecidable event" meets "an interventional decision of the subject," which names the event. The result is "historical novelty." Yet this novelty is not expressed by the "clever invention of novel terms," nor solely by language of the historical situation. Rather, it is expressed by evoking prior situations and events, and combining them with the new event. Next, in the fourth section, Worthington considers Badiou's concept of evental fidelity, which involves militant fidelity to what is a new given situation, which "cannot fall under the categories of existing knowledge of the situation." Here Worthington underscores the key point of his chapter: in early Christian studies, "the scholarly act of 'comparison' [is] extremely difficult, especially with texts, like Paul's letters, that are derived from the consequences of a [new] event." Finally, in the final section, Worthington demonstrates the value of Badiou's philosophy, which offers a methodology that "accounts for diverse responses to events," that is, the diversity of early Christian texts, yet, at the same time does not bracket off what is originary in early Christianity.

B. James Crossley:
Towards a Vulgar Marxist Reading of Christian Origins Today

James Crossley, in his own words, composes an "anachronistic and absurdist argument which simultaneously makes a serious point." Perhaps the chapter can also be depicted in Benjamin's terms, as one composed of dialectical images, or even more in Badiou's terms, as one looking for formal patterns between different historical periods.[81] Crossley begins with the following comparison, which he derives from Badiou: Paul is to Christ what Lenin is to Marx. In short, in making the comparison, he provides an analysis of the first century of the Jesus movement through the lens of historical materialism.

In the first section, "Jesus, Revolution, and Historical Materialism," Crossley examines the Jesus movement through the lens of "vulgar Marxism" or historical Marxism. Here he focuses on Jesus not simply as an individual revolutionary, but as one in the midst of socio-economic changes that spark revolution: "it might be more helpful to understand the categories of 'revolution' and 'revolutionary' in less individualistic terms and more in terms of socio-economic changes in the tradition of historical materialism, broadly understood." It is both the material changes and perceptions of these changes that spark revolutionary movements, leading Crossley to conclude "the Jesus movement did not just spontaneously emerge from nowhere." And this emergence was not simply reformist, but revolutionary, where the Gospel tradition makes "claims that are not those of the bleeding-heart liberal reformist, but those of an overthrowing of the order, a stark eschatological role reversal of rich and poor, the impossibility of rich people being saved, the incompatibility of God and Mammon, hostility to wealth, and concerns about debt and poverty."

In the second section, "Revolutionary Millenarianism," Crossley outlines "the shifts in, and explosions of, ideas and thinking" that result from social upheavals and revolutions, pointing to Christopher Hill's Marxist reading of the English revolution and civil wars, and ultimately to a "transition to capitalist democracies and empires." Reading the Jesus movement as a similar type of upheaval leads Crossley explain the emergence of Christianity. While Jesus can be depicted as bringing upheaval (e.g., as "a socially castrated itinerant leader of a queer family"), depictions also emerge of him in "conventional masculinized constructions." In the third section, this type of emergence leads to "Bureaucratizing the Revolution," depicted in the move from Lenin to Stalin, where revolution becomes appropriated from above.

---

81. Pluth depicts Badiou's philosophy as "pursuing the formal resemblances among different historical periods" (*A Philosophy of the New*, 3; see also 5, 11).

Paul is the first figure to do so. Crossley states: "Borrowing from Badiou, we might note that the revolutionary potential became encapsulated by the Event of Christ's death and resurrection which now opened up radical possibilities and demanded fidelity to the Event." Paul introduces this fidelity. And while "Paul was undeniably an anti-imperialist" he was also "a tactical Leninist" who "would know when to act and when not to act, hence statements about restraining revolutionary fervor and obeying the authorities." Here Crossley also parallels Paul's and 1 Peter's policing of fidelity with that of twentieth-century British communism. And for Crossley, Johannine literature represents "the ideological hardening" after revolution. In the final section, Crossley turns to our time, from Occupy to Corbyn, and points out how "the language of the radical Christian tradition has been employed" in these movements. And he ponders "whether Partyism or the Church keep radical ideas alive, even if sometimes they seem against their own radical interests."

C. Hollis Phelps: Recapitulating the Event: Reading Irenaeus with Badiou

In this chapter, Hollis Phelps considers Irenaeus' second-century idea of recapitulation in light of Badiou's concept of evental recurrence. Through Badiou's philosophy, Phelps offers a reassessment of an allegorical reading of scripture, often dismissed by biblical scholarship as "pre-critical" and as an escape from the historical. Phelps, however, through both Irenaeus and Badiou, reads "recapitulation in terms of a materialist understanding of history." Given that there are excesses in events—ones not captured in the present—Phelps argues that allegory captures these events. For events, in their excesses, strain to be realized both retroactively and anticipatorily. So Phelps aims "to provide a general outline for a recovery of allegory as a method for grasping this excess, as constitutive of history itself." This method "recognizes a pluralism at work in texts and our approach to them, without *necessarily* dismissing other, viable readings, including the literal, relatively plain sense on the surface."

In the first section, "Allegory, Typology, and History," Phelps outlines Irenaeus' critique of the Gnostics, who according to Irenaeus read allegorically in order to support already held positions and devalue "materiality both textually and historically." Phelps argues that Irenaeus also read allegorically, but materially, reading history in terms of excess. Here he points to the work of Stanislas Breton, where he shows, through his analysis of the Apostle Paul, that events are "haunted by '[a] kind of "excess" [that] makes the identity of these events tremble, conferring on them a futural excess.'" It is in this material, "futural excess" where both retroaction and anticipation occur in interpretation, that is, in recapitulation. In the second section, "Badiou's Philosophy of the Event," Phelps discuss three key concepts in Badiou's philosophy of the event: intervention, evental recurrence, and the idea of a resurrection of truths. These concepts intersect with Irenaeus' method of recapitulation, setting a modern philosophical foundation for an allegorical-yet-materialist interpretation of scripture and history. In the third section, "Recapitulation: Reading Irenaeus with Badiou," Phelps concludes by "draw[ing] out a materialist conception of time from Badiou's philosophy, one that, moreover, contributes to grasping the basic structure of recapitulation as it is found in Irenaeus' theology." As a result of this analysis, Phelps concludes with "a rethinking of allegory as a materialist form of interpretation, because … history itself is allegorical."

D. For Further Consideration:
Beyond Paul, Love and Desire, and Poetic Language

Here I underscore three launching points for further study of Badiou and early Christians, all three of which I discussed above. First, Badiou's philosophy offers early Christian studies more than just "Badiou and his book on Paul." Badiou's conversation needs to expand beyond what he discusses about Paul, expanded throughout canonical and non-canonical early Christian texts. What is more, his philosophy, like the philosophies of Benjamin, Deleuze, and Butler, needs to challenge the categories and lenses through which we view early Christian texts. Second, Badiou's philosophy of love offers intersections with early Christian texts and their receptions, especially in love's relationship to desire. Finally, Badiou's assertions about poetic language's striving to describe what is not yet describable offers a new, modern philosophical approach to early Christian apocalyptic literature.

Biographical Note

Matthew G. Whitlock (PhD, The Catholic University of America, 2008) is Associate Professor of New Testament at Seattle University. His research focuses on Acts of the Apostles, the Apostle Paul, New Testament Poetry, Critical Theory, and Science Fiction. His publications have focused on topics ranging from New Testament poetry in the *Catholic Biblical Quarterly* to the Body without Organs and Christianity in *Deleuze and Guattari Studies*. He is currently working on two books on dialectical images, one on images from the Science Fiction of Philip K. Dick and images from the letters of Paul, and the other on the theme of fame in images from the life of Kurt Cobin and early Christian writings about Jesus of Nazareth.

Bibliography: Primary Literature and Key Secondary Texts

Included below are the major works of Alain Badiou and other short works cited in this chapter and the chapters that follow. For a comprehensive list of his "Shorter Works," see Hallward, *Badiou: A Subject to Truth*, 429–35, and http://egs.edu/faculty/alain-badiou/bibliography. The original French publications are listed for the sake of presenting a chronology of Badiou's work.

A. Primary Literature: Major Works on Philosophy and Theory

The Concept of the Model: An Introduction to the Materialist Epistemology of Mathematics. Edited and translated by Zachary L. Fraser and Tzuchien Tho. Melbourne: re.press, 2007. Translation of *Le Concept de modèle: Introduction à une épistémologie matérialiste des mathématiques.* Paris: Maspéro, 1975.
Théorie de la contradiction. Paris: Maspéro, 1975.
De l'idéologie. Paris: Maspéro, 1975.
Theory of the Subject. Translated by Bruno Bosteels. London: Continuum, 2009. French. Worthington Stuff in Biography. Translation of *Théorie du sujet.* Paris: Éditions du Seuil, 1982.
Peut-on penser la politique? Paris: Seuil, 1982.
Being and Event. Translated by Oliver Feltham. London: Continuum, 2005. Translation of *L'Etre et l'événement.* Paris: Seuil, 1988.
Manifesto for Philosophy. Translated by Norman Madarasz. Albany, NY: State University of New York Press, 1999. Translation of *Manifeste pour la philosophie.* Paris: Seuil, 1989.
Number and Numbers. Cambridge: Polity Press, 2008. *Translation of Le Nombre et les nombres.* Paris: Seuil, 1990.
Rhapsody for the Theatre. Translated by Bruno Bosteels. London: Verso, 2013. Translation of *Rhapsodie pour le théâtre.* Paris: Le Spectateur français, 1990.
D'un désastre obscur (Droit, Etat, Politique). Paris: L'Aube, 1991.
Conditions. Translated by Steven Corcoran. London: Continuum, 2009. Translation of *Conditions.* Paris: Seuil, 1992.
Ethics: An Essay on the Understanding of Evil. Translated by Peter Hallward. London: Verso: 2001. Translation of *L'Ethique: Essai sur la conscience du mal.* Paris: Hatier, 1993.
On Beckett. Edited by Nina Power. Translated by Alberto Toscano. Clinamen Press, 2003. Translation of *Beckett: L'incrévable désir.* Paris: Hachette, 1995.
Deleuze: The Clamor of Being. Translated by Louise Burchill. Minneapolis, MN: University of Minnesota Press, 2000. Translation of *Gilles Deleuze: "La clameur de l'Etre."* Paris: Hachette, 1997.
Saint Paul: The Foundation of Universalism. Translated by Ray Brassier. Stanford, CA: Stanford University Press, 2003.Translation of *Saint Paul et la foundation de l'universalisme.* Paris: Presses Universitaires de France, 1997.
Metapolitics. Translated by Jason Barker. London: Verso, 2005. Translation of *Abrégé de métapolitique.* Paris: Seuil, 1998.
Briefings on Existence: A Transitory Ontology. Translated by Norman Madarasz. Albany, NY: State University of New York Press, 2003. Translation of *Court traité d'ontolgie transitoire.* Paris: Seuil, 1998.

Handbook of Inaesthetics. Translated by Alberto Toscano. Stanford, CA: Stanford University Press, 2004. Translation of *Petit manuel d'inésthétique*. Paris: Seuil, 1998.
Infinite Thought: Truth and the Return to Philosophy. Translated by Oliver Feltham. London: Continuum, 2003.
Badiou: Theoretical Writings. Translated and edited by Ray Brassier and Alberto Toscano. London: Continuum, 2004.
The Century. Translated by Alberto Toscano. Cambridge: Polity Press, 2007. Translation of *Le Siècle*. Paris: Seuil, 2005.
Logics of Worlds: Being and Event 2. Translated by Alberto Toscano. London: Continuum, 2009. Translation of *L'Etre et l'événement: Tome 2, Logiques des mondes*. Paris: Seuil, 2006.
The Meaning of Sarkozy. Translated by David Fernbach. London: Verso, 2008. Translation of *De quoi Sarkozy est-il le nom?* Nouvelles Editions Lignes, 2007.
Second Manifesto for Philosophy. Translated by Louise Burchill. Malden: Polity Press, 2011. Translation of *Second Manifeste pour la Philosophie*. Paris: Fayard, 2009.
The Communist Hypothesis. Translated by David Macey and Steve Corcoran. London: Verso, 2010. Translation of *L'hypothése communiste*.
What Is Philosophy? A Lecture by Alain Badiou. Edited by Srdjan Cvjeticanin. New York: Atropos Press, 2015.

Novels and Plays

Almagestes. Paris: Seuil, 1964.
Portulans. Paris: Seuil, 1967.
L'Echarpe rouge. Paris: Maspéro, 1979.
Ahmed le subtil. Arles: Acts Sud, 1994.
The Incident at Antioch: A Tragedy in Three Acts. Translated by Susan Spitzer. New York: Columbia University Press, 2013. Translation of *L'Incident d'Antioche: Tragedie en trois actes*.
Ahmed the Philosopher: 34 Short Plays for Children. Translated by Joseph Litbak. New York: Columbia University Press, 2014.
Le Second Procès de Socrate. Arles: Actes Sud, 2015.

B. Primary and Secondary Literature: Life, Context, Work, and Concepts

Badiou, Alain. "What Is Love?" Translated by Justin Clemens. *Umbr(a)* (1996): 37–53.
—"Philosophy as Biography." *The Symptom* 9 (2007). http://www.lacan.com/symptom9_articles/badiou19.html.
Baki, Burhanuddin. *Badiou's* Being and Event *and the Mathematics of Set Theory*. London: Bloomsbury, 2015.
Bartlett, A. J., and Justin Clemens, eds. *Alain Badiou: Key Concepts*. Durham: Acumen, 2010. https://doi.org/10.1017/UPO9781844654703
Bosteels, Bruno. *Badiou and Politics*. Durham, NC: Duke University Press, 2011. https://doi.org/10.1215/9780822394471
Feltham, Oliver. *Alain Badiou: Live Theory*. London: Continuum, 2008. https://doi.org/10.5040/9781472546098
Gillespie, Sam. *The Mathematics of Novelty: Badiou's Minimalist Metaphysics*. Melbourne: re.press, 2008.

Hallward, Peter. *Badiou: A Subject of Truth.* Minneapolis, MN: University of Minnesota Press, 2003.
Lecercle, Jean-Jacques. *Badiou and Deleuze Read Literature.* Edinburgh: Edinburgh University Press, 2010, 2012. https://doi.org/10.3366/edinburgh/9780748638000.001.0001
Norris, Christopher. *Badiou's* Being and Event: *A Reader's Guide.* London: Continuum, 2009.
Pluth, Ed. *Badiou: A Philosophy of the New.* Key Contemporary Thinkers. Cambridge: Polity Press, 2010.

C. Secondary Literature: Theology, Religious Studies, and Biblical Studies

Blanton, Ward, and Hent De Vries. *Paul and the Philosophers.* New York: Fordham University Press, 2013.
Caputo, John, and Linda Alcoff. *Saint Paul among the Philosophers.* Bloomington, IN: Indiana University Press, 2009.
Clemens, Justin, and Jon Roffe. "Philosophy as Anti-Religion in the Work of Alain Badiou," *Sophia* 47: 345–58. https://doi.org/10.1007/s11841-008-0078-z
Critchley, Simon. *Faith of the Faithless: Experiments in Political Theology.* London: Verso Books, 2012.
Gaventa, Beverly Roberts. *Our Mother Saint Paul.* Louisville, KY: Westminster John Knox, 2007.
Gignac, Alain. "Taubes, Badiou, Agamben: Contemporary Receptions of Paul by Non-Christian Philosophers," 155–99 in *Reading Romans with Contemporary Philosophers and Theologians.* Edited by David Odell-Scott. New York: T&T Clark, 2007.
Harink, Douglass. *Paul, Philosophy, and the Theopolitical Vision: Critical Engagement with Agamben, Badiou, Žižek, and Others.* Eugene, OR: Wipf & Stock.
Miller, Adam. *Badiou, Marion, and St. Paul: Immanent Grace.* London: Continuum, 2008.
Phelps, Hollis. *Alain Badiou: Between Theology and Anti-Theology.* Durham: Acumen, 2013. https://doi.org/10.4324/9781315729862
—"Alain Badiou (1937-)," 438–51 in *Religion and European Philosophy: Key Thinkers from Kant to Žižek.* Edited by Philip Goodchild and Hollis Phelps. New York: Routledge, 2017. https://doi.org/10.4324/9781315642253-37
Phelps, Hollis, and Bruce Worthington. "Alain Badiou and the Book of Acts." *Bible and Critical Theory* 12.2 (2016): 104–23.
Reynhout, Kenneth. "Alain Badiou: Hidden Theologian of the Void?" *The Heythrop Journal* 52.2: 219–33. https://doi.org/10.1111/j.1468-2265.2008.00415.x
Seesengood, Robert Paul. "Review of Alain Badiou, *The Incident at Antioch: A Tragedy in Three Acts,*" *The Bible and Critical Theory* 10.1 (2014): 88–91.

D. Other Secondary Literature
(Including Works on both Deleuze and Badiou)

Fields, A. Belden. *Trotskyism and Maoism: Theory and Practice in France and the United States.* Brooklyn, NY: Autonomedia, 1988.
Krips, Henry. "The Politics of Badiou: From Absolute Singularity to Objet-a." Paper

presented at the plenary session in the Bradshaw Lecture Series "Event and Process," December 2007.

Mullarkey, John. "Deleuze," 168–75 in *Alain Badiou: Key Concepts*. Edited by A. J. Bartlett and Justin Clemens. Durham: Acumen, 2010. https://doi.org/10.1017/UPO9781844654703.018

Smith, Daniel. "Badiou and Deleuze on the Ontology of Mathematics," 77-93 in *Think Again: Alain Badiou and the Future of Philosophy*. Edited by Peter Hallward. London: Continuum, 2004.

Chapter Ten

Christianity Appears First, as Itself

Bruce Worthington

Introduction

One of the more popular assumptions of contemporary biblical scholarship is that, in regards to the ancient world, "*nothing is sui generis, nothing is unique.*"¹ In many ways this has been the mantra, not only of those engaged in the study of comparative religions, but across the discourse of New Testament studies—in order to understand the meaning of early Christian text and practice, it should be located within the dialectical conditions of its cultural situation, which is, late second Temple Judaism and the Roman Empire (for all that means).

This truism is a product of methodological assumptions that guide the practice of biblical studies, in particular, the assumption that historical subjects and events can always be located within a context, and therefore do not exceed their own ideological, linguistic, or cultural constraints. While such assumptions are extremely helpful in identifying the common relationship between historical subject and context, the notion that "nothing is unique" is philosophically untrue—new truth conditions continue to occur, often in ways that exceed the boundaries of their own cultural situation(s). As Ward Blanton notes, such a truism is indicative of a general "forgetting" of philosophy in biblical studies, with what appears to be an over-reliance on the analytical category of comparison.² This fascination with comparison has

---

1. This type of scholarship was originally represented by the Chicago School of History of Religions, in particular the work of Mircea Eliade throughout the 1960s and 1970s. The goal of the Chicago School was—through the use of socio-scientific methods—to analyze religion as a unique human phenomenon, best understood through a comparative approach. The mantle has since been taken up by Jonathan Z. Smith, in particular his work *Map Is Not Territory: Studies in the Histories of Religions* (Chicago, IL: University of Chicago Press, 1993 [1978]); and *Drudgery Divine: On the Comparison of Early Christianities and the Religions of Late Antiquity* (New York: Routledge, 2013 [1990]), and Burton Mack, *A Myth of Innocence: Mark and Christian Origins* (Minneapolis, MN: Augsburg Fortress, 1988).

2. Blanton notes that "forgetting philosophy has taken a heavy toll on our ability to produce creative new historiographical modes of thinking about early Christian

neglected one of the chief ends of philosophy, which, as Deleuze notes, is "to find the conditions under which something new is produced."[3]

An honest objection may, perhaps, be made by history of religions scholars like Jonathan Z. Smith, who assume that in most cases, when an argument is being presented for a sui generis element within early Christianity, this is most likely driven by theological presuppositions, and thus, not a "category of critical scholarship at all."[4] To be fair, the comparative approach to the study of religion has proven to be a useful analytical strategy, particularly in its ability to value a greater plurality of textual data, allowing scholars to work without, necessarily, recourse to miraculous events, dramatic breakthroughs, or personal experience. This has provided an appropriate place for biblical scholarship within the context of the public university and the general discourse of the humanities.[5] While the mantra "nothing is sui generis" is helpful in many cases, does it have to be that every time scholars identify a unique element within a cultural situation, that they are performing an intellectual "exorcism" or "purgation?"[6] Do not the evental character of many early Christian texts themselves show a concern for miraculous events and dramatic breakthroughs? The unquestioned insistence on the comparative approach reveals an intriguing philosophical question—how might we account for the production of novel truth conditions within a cultural situation? How can these insights be applied to the formal study of Christian origins?

---

religion." See Ward Blanton, *Displacing Christian Origins: Philosophy, Secularity, and the New Testament* (Chicago, IL: University of Chicago Press, 2007), 2. I agree with this sentiment, and this piece reflects a general attempt to reincorporate philosophy back into the hermeneutical assumptions of origins scholarship.

3. Gilles Deleuze and Claire Parnet, *Dialogues* (trans. Barbara Habberjam, et al.; rev. edn.; New York: Columbia University Press, 2007), vii.

4. Mack, *A Myth of Innocence*, 8. Smith, in *Drudgery Divine*, notes "the most frequent use of the terminology of the 'unique' within religious studies is in relation to Christianity; the most frequent use of this term within Christianity is in relation to the so-called 'Christ-event,'" 38.

5. Fitz John Porter Poole provides a helpful definition of the comparative approach used by Smith, Mack, and others: "Comparison does not deal with phenomena in toto or in the round, but only with an aspectual characteristic of them. Analytical control over the framework of comparison involves theoretically focused selection of significant aspects of the phenomena and a bracketing of the endeavor by strategic ceteris paribus assumptions." See Poole, "Metaphors and Maps," *JAAR* 54.3 (1986): 411–98, here 414–5. In the case of applying Poole to the study of Christian origins, the practice of "bracketing" is normally used in relation to miraculous events like the resurrection, healing miracles, etc.

6. Smith, *Drudgery Divine*, 143.

The work of Alain Badiou articulates, in perhaps the clearest fashion, how a truth may proceed in a manner that is sui generis relative to its cultural situation, without immediate recourse to theological speculation. So, the goal of this chapter is to reintroduce novelty as a category of critical scholarship in Christian origins without formal reference to traditional theology, in order to give a fuller account of the eventual character of Christian origins, beyond the popular analytical category of comparison.[7]

Novelty and Protestant Theology

It is clear to me that the work of Jonathan Z. Smith, Burton Mack, and the "comparative approach to the study of religion" is an important corrective against earlier Protestant theological depictions of Christian origins, particularly depictions that function as apologetics for early Christianity against the background of Greek Platonism, or as anti-papal attacks on Roman Catholicism.[8] Here, Protestant Christian origins scholarship functions not only to establish early Christianity as unique—and therefore superior—with respect to other religions, but also with respect to itself: early Apostolic faith against the corruptions of the "institutionalized" church of the second century CE.[9] Here is an example of such a problematic, uniquely Protestant approach to Christian origins by theologian Arthur Darby Nock: "such (linguistic) usages are the product of an enclosed world living its own life, a ghetto culturally and linguistically if not geographically."[10] The development of a unique or "pristine" original Christianity has been influential for Protestant theology, its non-derivative nature supporting the Protestant historiographic myth we may be familiar with: pure eventual origins that suffered later institutional

---

7. In order to accomplish this task, I will use Badiou's most thorough and recent account of novelty, found in *Logics of Worlds*, but also, at times, rely on *Being and Event*, along with the popular *Saint Paul: The Foundation of Universalism*. See Alain Badiou, *Saint Paul: The Foundation of Universalism* (trans. Ray Brassier; Stanford, CA: Stanford University Press, 2003 [translation of *Saint Paul et la foundation de l'universalisme*. Paris: Presses Universitaires de France, 1997]); *Being and Event* (trans. Oliver Feltham; London: Continuum, 2005 [translation of *L'Etre et l'événement*. Paris: Seuil, 1988]) and *Logics of Worlds: Being and Event 2* (trans. Alberto Toscano; London: Continuum, 2009 [translation of *L'Etre et l'événement: Tome 2, Logiques des mondes*. Paris: Seuil, 2006]).

8. Smith notes "the pursuit of the origins of the question of Christian origins takes us back, persistently, to the same point: Protestant anti-Catholic interpreters." *Drudgery Divine*, 34.

9. Smith, *Drudgery Divine*, 43.

10. Arthur Darby Nock, "The Vocabulary of the New Testament," *JBL* 52.2 (1933): 131–9, here 138.

corruptions.[11] In order to confront the dominance of Protestant theology within the study of Christian origins, scholars have relied chiefly on a comparative approach that has purposefully bracketed out references to originary events, miracles, or dramatic breakthroughs in their account of early Christian material. Ron Cameron and Merrill Miller, both active in the Society of Biblical Literatures annual section on "Christian Origins," explain their decision to limit the event in this way:

> Our aim is to redescribe the data of Christian origins in such a way as to contribute to the construction of another theoretical model: which is not focused on personal experience, transforming events, and dramatic breakthroughs; which does not imagine religion as a sui generis category, and thus, an unfathomable mystery, nor regards 'origins' as a cipher for unique encounters with divinity.[12]

The benefit of such an approach is to establish analytical parameters for the discourse of origins beyond simply Protestant theological speculation. Rejecting a single, novel point of origin for early Christianity opens up the space to carefully reconstruct alternative Christianities like we might find in "Q" or the Gospel of Thomas—groups which seemed to function with little formal reference to a single event, or novel point of origin. Here the reconstruction of Q and the discovery of the Gospel of Thomas in recent history point towards the need for identifying a diverse spectrum or multiple of early Christianities, some without reference to key events like the resurrection of Jesus. The comparative model allows "alternative" Christianities to sit alongside other more familiar narratives in the same analytical matrix, and has, generally, colored our picture of Christian origins with greater diversity.

Lost in the comparative approach to the study of Christian origins is, however, an appreciation for the evental character of many of its primary texts. If "there is no single moment, single cause, single concept, or single unique feature" that accounts for the diversity of material in early Christianity, how might we make sense of documents that point to a single moment, single cause, or single unique feature for their existence?[13] If we are to deal responsibly with texts that have an "evental character," should not their "evental" character be included in the reconstruction of Christian origins? How can we include the "evental" nature of many early Christian texts with-

---

11. Smith, *Drudgery Divine*, 43.
12. Ron Cameron and Merrill P. Miller, "Conclusion: Redescribing Christian Origins," in *Redescribing Christian Origins* (ed. Cameron and Miller; Leiden: Brill, 2004), 497–516, here 498.
13. Contra William Arnal and Russell McCutcheon, "The Origins of Christianity Within, and Without, 'Religion': A Case Study," in *The Sacred Is the Profane: The Political Nature of "Religion"* (New York: Oxford University Press, 2013), 31–56, here 50.

out recourse to speculative Protestant theology? It appears to me—to echo the sentiments of Ward Blanton—that recent Christian origins scholarship has collapsed into a self-protective intellectual complacency, one that in the interest of secularity, has dismissed the "event" as a key feature of early Christian identity. So, what is needed is not another Protestant "revival" in origins scholarship, but, instead, a critical mode of philosophical inquiry that can formally include "novelty, miraculous events, and dramatic breakthroughs" as legitimate categories of study. Alain Badiou's theory of the event provides an opportunity for careful reflection on how the study of Christian origins may include novel truth conditions, an originary event, a miracle, an anomaly—without, necessarily, resorting to theological speculation, scholarly exorcism, or purgation.

The Evental Site

Space does not permit here a full explication of Badiou's theory of truth or the event, nor am I willing to rehearse all the criticisms levelled against Badiou, especially after *Being and Event*.[14] It suffices to say that one of the most significant criticisms Badiou has received is regarding the relationship between event and context, namely, how do events occur within a cultural situation? What is the event's relationship to its world? If a truth appears, at times, as novel to its cultural situation, how is this so?[15] Many of these questions have been answered in *Logics of Worlds*, and this is instructive for how we might think about truth and event as it pertains to Christian origins.[16]

---

14. For criticism of Badiou, see Stephen Fowl, "A Very Particular Universalism: Badiou and Paul," in *Paul, Philosophy, and the Theopolitical Vision* (ed. Douglas Harink; Eugene, OR: Cascade Books, 2010), 119–34; Benjamin Dunning, *Christ Without Adam: Subjectivity and Sexual Difference in the Philosophers Paul* (New York: Columbia University Press, 2014; Roland Boer, *Criticism of Heaven: On Marxism and Theology* (Leiden: Brill, 2006), 343–59; Simon Critchley, "On the Ethics of Alain Badiou," in *Alain Badiou: Philosophy and its Conditions* (ed. G. Riera; Albany, NY: SUNY Press, 2005), 215–35. For a full explanation of Badiou's general oeuvre as it pertains to the study of religion, the best work is certainly Hollis Phelps, *Alain Badiou: Between Theology and Anti-Theology* (Durham: Acumen, 2013).

15. By "cultural situation," I simply mean what are the cultural or linguistic particularities that comprise an historical situation.

16. I realize that Badiou rejects the formal connection between early Christianity and "truth," insofar as, for Badiou, the resurrection of Jesus is "pure fable." See *Saint Paul*, 4. I apply the philosophy of Badiou to early Christianity simply because Badiou *already has*. For more on the complicated application of Badiou to religion, see the references above in fn. 14.

For Badiou, the production of a truth does not occur outside of a traditional cultural situation, it is not, for instance, that early Christianity develops wholly outside of the dialectical conditions of second Temple Judaism and the Roman Empire as an "enclosed ghetto." This is, perhaps, due to Badiou's assumption that early Christianity—in particular Pauline Christianity—was not (unlike Qumran) a sectarian movement. Instead, for Badiou, the event occurs within what Badiou calls an "evental site," and simply establishes what is new or unnameable within a given cultural situation, mobilizing elements of the evental site, but adding its own presentation to the mix.[17] Badiou suggests, "Every radical transformational action originates in a point, which, inside a situation, is an evental site."[18] This mitigates against the modern Protestant notion of "origins" mentioned above, namely by Nock: that early Christianity developed in an "enclosed world living its own life."[19]

The development of the notion of "evental site" is to avoid what Badiou fears most: a "speculative leftism" that imagines events as wholly self-authorizing.[20] Instead, based on Badiou's concept of "evental recurrence," there is an essential historicity to early Christianity that structures the event of the resurrection backwards to the event of Adam, and forward to the event of the Parousia.[21] This notion of recurrence is an essential "link" to the cultural situation of early Christianity, in particular its relationship to Judaism, which so fills the texts of early Christian material. Badiou explains evental recurrence like this:

> The intervention is based upon the circulation, within the Jewish milieu, of another event, Adam's original sin, of which the death of Christ is the relay ... Christianity is structured from the beginning to end by evental recurrence, moreover, it prepares itself for the divine hazard of the third event, the last judgment.[22]

A truth, for Badiou, contains all of the elements that make up a particular cultural situation, yet mobilizes the elements of the situation in light of the event, which is, for our purposes, "Jesus has been resurrected." For Badiou, the event contains all the elements of the evental site, and, on the other hand, itself.[23] Badiou explains the relationship between context and evental site in this way, regarding the Paris communes of 1871: 18 March (the

---

17. Badiou, *Being and Event*, 182.
18. Badiou, *Being and Event*, 176.
19. Nock, "The Vocabulary of the New Testament," 138.
20. Badiou, *Being and Event*, 210.
21. Badiou, *Being and Event*, 213.
22. Badiou, *Being and Event*, 213.
23. Badiou, *Being and Event*, 179. This notion of evental recurrence is, in my

Paris communes) is a site because, besides everything that appears within it under the evasive transcendental of the world "Paris in Spring 1871," it too appears, as the fulminant and entirely unpredictable break with the very thing that regulates its appearance.[24]

So, for our purposes, we could say the event "Jesus has been resurrected" contains everything that makes up the evental site, that is, Judea as a Roman province in the first century. There you will find the Pharisees, the Temple, the Romans, Peasants, Synagogues, the Sanhedrin, Galilee, maybe some Stoics, Epicureans, the Judeans, perhaps even linguistic conditions like Greek, Latin, Aramaic, and so on. However, as much as the event organizes and mobilizes linguistic and cultural elements of the site, the evental site is only, ever, a condition of being for the event itself.[25] Here is an important point: the dialectical conditions of the evental site do not positively produce the event in question, nor is the event an internal combination of the situation "Jew and Greek"; rather, the evental site is only the "minimal effect of structure which can be conceived," and does not strictly coincide with the event itself.[26]

Most of contemporary scholarship on Christian origins—as it eliminates the event—can only conceive of early Christianity as a modification to the internal combination of the cultural situation "Jew and Greek," to various degrees. The typical assumption "nothing is sui generis" suggests that events fit, always, within the established transcendental conditions of a world, and are merely modifications of its pre-existing cultural situation. This assumption abolishes the intensities to which subjects, at times, attach themselves to the consequences of an event, and diminishes the transgressive nature of events as nothing more than a typical cultural dialectic.[27]

Now, there are many occasions when an evental site appears, but no event happens, at least in the formal sense of Badiou's terminology. This is due to the aleatory conditions of the event itself. Were the emergence of early Christianity simply a combination of elements common to its cultural situation "Jew and Greek," it would not formally constitute an evental site; instead, we might be tempted to designate early Christianity as many scholars now do—as a slight modification to the logic of second Temple Judaism and the

---

opinion, overlooked by Benjamin Dunning in his characterization of Badiou in *Christ Without Adam*.

24. Badiou, *Logics of Worlds*, 365.
25. Badiou, *Being and Event*, 179.
26. Badiou, *Being and Event*, 182.
27. By using the term "subject," Badiou suggests, "We could say that a subject is an operative disposition of the traces of the event and of what they deploy in the world." See *Logics of Worlds*, 33–4.

Roman Empire.[28] In our case, the event "Jesus has been resurrected" mobilizes common elements of the site, but adds its own presentation to the mix, such that the event is unrecognizable, or, "an entirely abnormal multiple," that is, foolishness to Greeks and a stumbling block to Jews (1 Cor. 1.23).[29] This is what it means for Badiou to suggest that the event establishes a truth that is "generic" to its cultural situation, meaning that the evental truth—although appearing within an evental site—is unnameable by the language of the resources of the situation alone.[30] For Badiou, the evental site is a reflexive multiplicity, which belongs to itself, and thereby transgresses the laws of being, which, for our purposes, is represented by the dialectical combination Jew and Greek. All of this is to say that perhaps biblical scholars may find some temporary relief in the notion that Early Christianity did not just appear on its own—the event can only, ever, occur within a situation, and an evental site guided by its own internal linguistic and cultural conditions.

It should be noted that none of the specific factors of the situation constitute the event itself; in fact, the status of the event "Jesus has been resurrected" is undecidable from the perspective of the cultural situation.[31] Although the event is a source of novelty for the cultural situation, it is, as Phelps notes, more important for us to follow its consequences, which is to say, identify the process of intervention in early Christian thought and practice.[32]

Intervention and Early Christianity

The average early believer had a tough decision to make: to locate the statement "Jesus has been resurrected" within the original site of faith, or to establish the event's supernumerary name in the world, despite the odd appearance it assumes. While previously I had suggested that the event does not flow logically from the dialectical conditions "Jew and Greek," here the process of intervention draws out its dialectic support from the event itself, and circulates this truth throughout the entirety of the cultural situation.[33] It is the relationship between an undecidable event and the interventional decision of the subject that historical novelty results.[34] Again, as stated previously, an intervention is not the clever invention of novel terms or phrases, rather an intervention consists in "evoking the previous situation"

---

28. Badiou, *Logics of Worlds*, 372.
29. Badiou, *Being and Event*, 175.
30. Badiou, *Being and Event*, 338.
31. Phelps, *Alain Badiou*, 56.
32. Phelps, *Alain Badiou*, 64.
33. Badiou, *Being and Event*, 217.
34. Badiou, *Being and Event*, 231.

and using the situation precisely to create its own rationality, in light of the new event.[35] For Badiou, intervention cannot legitimately operate according to the idea of a primal event, as events are always linked in terms of consequences with other events.[36] An excellent example of an intervention is, perhaps, the relationship between Adam and Christ, as articulated by Paul in Romans 5.12-21. In this example, the event of the resurrection is contrasted with the sin of Adam—both constitute events in the formal sense—yet are linked in terms of meaning: "For if the many died by the trespass of the one man, how much more did God's grace and the gift that came by the grace of the one man, Jesus Christ, overflow to the many" (Rom. 5.15).

Here Paul can only ever use the language of the situation, and the logic of the eventral site to makes an interventional decision regarding Adam and Christ. For Paul to talk about Adam alone would not necessarily constitute an intervention as such; however, it is the combination of Adam's sin and Christ's resurrection—two events linked—that place into circulation an historical novelty, a sui generis interpretation of the human condition in Romans 5. Paul's interpretation of the typology "Adam-Christ" is hardly a disavowal, or antagonistic rejection of Judaism, nor does it reflect the logic of Marcion and others who can find no truth in God of the Old Testament; rather, Paul's intervention is a strange one insofar as it places into circulation the logic of the resurrection, and requires a revision of the past in light of the new truth revealed in the event of resurrection.[37] At the same time, Paul's intervention is not a summary of the common conditions of Judaism at his time, it does not reflect "institutional logic" regarding Christ and Adam, nor can it be said that his intervention logically flows from the cultural dialectic commonly understood as Jew-Greek. Here, an intervention puts the event "Jesus has been resurrected" into circulation for the cultural situation, making the resurrection susceptible to the unfolding of its consequences within history.[38]

---

35. Badiou, *Being and Event*, 185.
36. Badiou, *Being and Event*, 210.
37. Regarding Paul's intervention in Rom. 5.12-21, Badiou has this to say "The intervention is based upon the circulation, within the Jewish milieu, of another event, Adam's original sin, of which the death of Christ is the relay. The connection between original sin and redemption definitively founds the time of Christianity as a time of exile and salvation. There is an essential historicity to Christianity which is tied to the intervention of the apostles as the placement-into-circulation of the event of the death of God; itself reinforced by the promise of a Messiah which organized the fidelity to the initial exile. Christianity is structured from beginning to end by eventral recurrence, moreover, it prepares itself for the divine hazard of the third event, the Last judgement, in which the ruin of the terrestrial situation will be accomplished, and a new regime of existence will be established" (Badiou, *Being and Event*, 213).
38. Phelps, *Alain Badiou*, 59.

Note, for purposes related to the study of Christian origins, that the interventional decision is the "unfolding of the consequences of the event," and not the result of philosophical contemplation, an exercise in comparative philology, or a large theological treatise. Because an intervention is not a comparative exercise, it possesses the property of belonging to itself—what is presented in the act of intervention is the event's consequences, not just in glorifying its occurrence.[39] As such, the intervenor (the early believer) can be both entirely accountable for the regulated consequences of the event, and entirely incapable of boasting that they ever played a decisive role in the event itself.[40] Here the event serves as a sort of grace to the subject—not in the theologically loaded sense of the term—but rather in the sense that the intervenor had nothing to do with the occurrence of the event in the world.[41] The early Apostles are not "heroes of the event"—they proclaim the consequences of an event they had absolutely nothing to do with.

In order for the act of intervention to occur, Badiou mentions that it requires a kind of preliminary separation from the immediate law of the situation, or from whatever governs the cultural situation.[42] The intervention, in many ways, constitutes a "militant act," insofar as it violates not only the immediate legal context of Roman law, but also the general law(s) of the cultural situation. As the event and its intervention do not flow from the axiomatic conditions that govern the situation, the proclamation of the event constitutes, in some sense, an illegal act.

Fidelity (Rule of Faithful Connection)

It is the process of fidelity that leads us, perhaps, closest to identifying the sui generis nature of an eventual truth. A fidelity, for Badiou, is a set of procedures which discern and introduce into circulation those multiples that are related to an event.[43] Fidelity is not a subjective quality, a virtue, or an illumination; nor is it a matter of knowledge. Fidelity is not the work of an expert:

---

39. Badiou, *Being and Event*, 211.
40. Badiou, *Being and Event*, 207.
41. For more on Badiou's notion of eventual grace, see Adam Miller, *Badiou, Marion, and Saint Paul: Immanent Grace* (London: Continuum, 2008). Here Miller states: "I understand Badiou's work as a direct response to this question (of immanent grace). It is explicitly grounded in an attempt to 'tear the lexicon of grace ... away from its religious confinement' in the obscurity of transcendence," 111. For more on materialist grace, consult the excellent work of Roland Boer in *Criticism of Heaven*, 343–59. The chapter carefully deals with the notion of materialist or immanent grace, from the perspective of both Alain Badiou and Slavoj Žižek.
42. Badiou, *Being and Event*, 209.
43. Badiou, *Being and Event*, 232.

it is, instead, the work of a militant.[44] Fidelity to the evental truth, established through the act of intervention, is (to quote Hollis Phelps) "a string of statements, or 'minimal reports' that group together multiples connected to the event, mobilizing them in the production of a truth."[45] An example of militant fidelity is, perhaps, the speech of Steven in Acts 7.1-60, which organizes multiples connected to the event (the history of Israel, etc.) in the production of a truth—Jesus has been resurrected. So, for instance, the speech of Steven organizes, within the situation, another legitimacy of conclusions regarding the history of Israel. The results of this fidelity, from the perspective of the state of the situation (here, the Sanhedrin), appears to be nonsensical, and (as seen from the reaction of the speech), is met with a certain degree of hostility from representatives of the situation. Note that Steven can only use the language of the situation, yet the evental truth establishes a new meaning to the history of Israel in Acts 7.[46] The operator of a fidelity, and their illegal conclusions regarding the consequences of the event, constitutes a sui generis act in early Christian subjectivity. So, when trying to understand the unique logic of an evental fidelity, no amount of comparative knowledge will suffice, because a fidelity is distinctly different, or unassignable to the state of the situation.[47] Fidelity is, to quote Badiou, "another mode of discernment: one which ... represents a mode of discernment different from that represented by the knowledge of the situation."[48] Because evental fidelity represents something new with respect to the situation, it cannot fall under the categories of existing knowledge of the situation—this makes the scholarly act of "comparison" extremely difficult, especially with texts, like Paul's letters, that are derived from the consequences of an event.

Minimal and Maximal Consequences of the Event

We can modestly say that there are some early Christian texts that evince very little reference to the event of the resurrection (see GThomas and Q), while others reveal a strong evental character (see Acts, Paul's letters, Hebrews, 1 Peter). What are we to make of this strange and diverse

---

44. Badiou, *Being and Event*, 329.
45. Phelps, *Alain Badiou*, 71.
46. I realize that many scholars dismiss the historicity of Acts and the speech of Steven in Acts 7. Here is not the place to engage in a debate regarding the historicity of Acts, but it is simply enough to say that Badiou himself relies on Acts in *Saint Paul* to develop his notion of early Christian subjectivity, in particular the character of Paul and his Damascus Road experience as "event."
47. Badiou, *Being and Event*, 237.
48. Badiou, *Being and Event*, 329.

multiple? One choice—made by J. Z. Smith, Burton Mack and others—has been to bracket references to the event in order to highlight the diverse and exceptional character of GThomas, Q, and some portions of Mark.[49] Here, larger notions of novelty and event in the canonical gospels are the result of social self-definition and mythmaking, meaning, basically, that early Christians fabricated the event of the resurrection in order to differentiate themselves from their main competitors in Judaism.[50] This elimination of the event as a popular assumption in Origins scholarship is reminiscent of the situation described by Badiou in *Being and Event*:

> Historians can enumerate "everything delivered by the epochs as traces and facts," they can "inventory all of the elements of the evental site," but this "may well lead to the one of the event being undone to the point of being no more than the forever infinite numbering of the gestures, things and words that co-existed with it."[51]

Perhaps instead of eliminating evental reflection in our reconstruction of Christian origins, I suggest it is time to develop a methodology that can include reference to originary or novel events, without, necessarily, formal reference to traditional theology. To do this would provide a new, philosophically rigorous analytical framework for how we think about radical change in the first century. The work of Badiou is particularly instructive for this new approach, insofar as his methodology accounts for diverse responses to events, which can account more fully for the sheer variety of data that appears in the period of Christian origins. Eliminating references to novel events "apriori" does nothing to represent the diversity of responses to the resurrection by the earliest Christians, instead, it fashions a particular perspective on Christian origins that fits within the vision of what is already credible within secular modernity.[52]

---

49. Mack is most explicit in his elimination of "evental" texts here: "the three collections of major significance for the teachings of Jesus are Q, the Gospel of Thomas, and sets of chreiai used by Mark in the composition of his gospel." See Burton Mack, *The Christian Myth: Origins, Logic, Legacy* (New York: Continuum, 2001), 41. None of these three text groups mention the resurrection of Jesus, and therefore reflect a more credible "historical" Jesus for Mack.

50. Mack, *A Myth of Innocence*, 13.

51. Badiou, *Being and Event*, 180.

52. This situation is reminiscent of what Ward Blanton has already suggested in *Displacing Christian Origins*: "Thus, Derrida notes, critical interpreters of religion ... sometimes presented their own thought as a kind of 'purified' or 'originary' version of the religious tradition they criticized, doing Christianity one better, as it were, in the polemical struggle to establish the parameters of the religion itself." See Blanton, *Displacing Christian Origins*, 8.

For Badiou, there are a variety of responses to the event, a spectrum that can be divided into weak and strong, or, responses with non-maximal consequences and those with maximal consequences.[53] What differentiates a weak singularity from a strong singularity is the "properly evental character" of the latter, meaning, the force of the consequences drawn from the event, and whether these can be said to break with the laws of the cultural situation.[54] For Badiou, there are those early believers that seek to locate the event "within the traditional site of faith," meaning, an attempt to locate the meaning of the resurrection as a slight modification to its current cultural situation.[55] In this case the meaning of the statement "Jesus has risen" has minimal consequences, and is incorporated into the traditional site of faith in a dialectical manner as a "fulfillment of tradition," or the like. For Badiou, these are "reactive subjects" that organize the denial of the events formal novelty, treating it as a simple deformation of admitted forms.[56] We might think of the highly rhetoricized "Judaizers," or the character of Peter in Galatians in this manner.

Conversely, on the other side of the spectrum of responses to the event, are those early Christian groups and letters that draw maximal consequences from the statement "Jesus has been resurrected," meaning that the resurrection, in some sense, does not fall under the categories of existing knowledge of the situation and is a break in the fundamental laws of appearing in the world of the first century. On this side of the spectrum, we might locate the writings of Paul, and perhaps the book of Revelation. Many of the other canonical books of the New Testament, and other early Christian writings of the first and second century CE fall within this spectrum somewhere, and if we had more time it would be valuable to position early Christian writings in terms of their fidelity to the consequences of the event. The philosophical apparatus of Badiou, when applied to the discourse of Christian origins, represents a fuller, more colorful spectrum of responses to the event of resurrection, beginning with those groups with nearly zero consequences and those groups that did draw maximal consequences from the event. Both can be included in a more authentic account of Christian origins, one that need not sever ties with the evental character of some of its most cherished texts.

---

53. Phelps, *Alain Badiou*, 63.
54. Phelps, *Alain Badiou*, 63.
55. Badiou, *Saint Paul*, 23.
56. Badiou, *Logics of Worlds*, 73.

Conclusion—Christianity Appears First as Itself

The discourse of Christian origins and the comparative approach to religion have offered much to the advancement of human knowledge within the humanities. This is an unmistakable development away from clumsy categories of traditional theology, towards a more rigorous analytical framework of sociological comparison. It is an achievement. However, in insisting on this comparative approach, we have lost sight of the importance of novelty, and failed to provide an analytical framework for how we might think about radical change, both in the first century, and even now. We have, essentially, forgotten about philosophy, and its role, which is simply "to find the conditions under which something new is produced."[57] I offer the philosophy of Badiou as one way (perhaps among many ways) to philosophically reinvigorate the discourse of Christian origins, allowing us to give a more honest account of the variety of responses to the event, in a manner that respects both maximal, and non-maximal responses to the resurrection of Jesus in the first and second century CE.

What do I mean, then, when I suggest, "Christianity appears first as Itself"? Badiou suggests that "every world is capable of producing its own truth, within itself," that is, a truth that is not dialectically related to its cultural situation.[58] A truth for Badiou is a radical exception to its historical context, which means, at times, there are events and subjectivities that appear in the world that reveal the limits of a strictly comparative analytical approach to the study of history. For a real source of change in the world, an exception is required, an exception to the laws of being, as well as to the regulation of its logical consequences—a new truth requires its own indexing.[59] The comparative approach to the study of religion is insufficient to this task.

So, if early Christianity constitutes a new truth, then it exists, absolutely, on the very first day of its appearance—in the politically inexistent world on the eve of the resurrection.[60]

Biographical Note

Bruce Worthington completed his PhD at Wycliffe College, University of Toronto, where he teaches part-time. Bruce is the editor of two volumes,

---

57. Deleuze and Parnet, *Dialogues*, vii.
58. Badiou, *Logics of Worlds*, 8.
59. Phelps, *Alain Badiou*, 63.
60. Phelps, *Alain Badiou*, 63.

Reading the Bible in an Age of Crisis (Fortress, 2015) and *The Visible Shape of Christ's Life in Us* (Wipf & Stock, 2019). In addition to his academic work, Bruce is an accomplished touring musician and has charted two successful radio singles on Canadian country radio.

Bibliography

Arnal, William, and Russell McCutcheon, "The Origins of Christianity Within, and Without, 'Religion': A Case Study," 134–70 in *The Sacred Is the Profane: The Political Nature of "Religion."* New York: Oxford University Press, 2013. https://doi.org/10.1093/acprof:oso/9780199757114.003.0008

Badiou, Alain. *Saint Paul: The Foundation of Universalism.* Translated by Ray Brassier. Stanford, CA: Stanford University Press, 2003. Translation of *Saint Paul et la foundation de l'universalisme.* Paris: Presses Universitaires de France, 1997.

—*Being and Event.* Translated by Oliver Feltham. London: Continuum, 2005. Translation of *L'Etre et l'événement.* Paris: Seuil, 1988.

—*Logics of Worlds: Being and Event 2.* Translated by Alberto Toscano. London: Continuum, 2009. Translation of *L'Etre et l'événement: Tome 2, Logiques des mondes.* Paris: Seuil, 2006.

Boer, Roland. *Criticism of Heaven: On Marxism and Theology.* Leiden: Brill, 2006. https://doi.org/10.1163/ej.9789004161115.i-472

Blanton, Ward. *Displacing Christian Origins: Philosophy, Secularity, and the New Testament.* Chicago, IL: University of Chicago Press, 2007. https://doi.org/10.7208/chicago/9780226056883.001.0001

Cameron, Ron, and Merrill P. Miller, eds. "Conclusion: Redescribing Christian Origins," 497–516 in *Redescribing Christian Origins.* Leiden: Brill, 2004.

Critchley, Simon. "On the Ethics of Alain Badiou," 215–35 in *Alain Badiou: Philosophy and its Conditions.* Edited by G. Riera. Albany, NY: SUNY Press, 2005.

Deleuze, Gilles, and Claire Parnet. *Dialogues.* Translated by Barbara Habberjam, et al. Revised edition. New York: Columbia University Press, 2007.

Dunning, Benjamin. *Christ Without Adam: Subjectivity and Sexual Difference in the Philosophers Paul.* New York: Columbia University Press, 2014. https://doi.org/10.7312/dunn16764

Fowl, Stephen. "A Very Particular Universalism: Badiou and Paul," 119–34 in *Paul, Philosophy, and the Theopolitical Vision.* Edited by Douglas Harink. Eugene, OR: Cascade Books, 2010.

Mack, Burton. *A Myth of Innocence: Mark and Christian Origins.* Minneapolis, MN: Augsburg Fortress, 1988.

—*The Christian Myth: Origins, Logic, Legacy.* New York: Continuum, 2001.

Miller, Adam. *Badiou, Marion, and St. Paul: Immanent Grace.* London: Continuum, 2008.

Nock, Arthur Darby. "The Vocabulary of the New Testament," *Journal of Biblical Literature* 52.2 (1933): 131–9. https://doi.org/10.2307/3259389

Phelps, Hollis. *Alain Badiou: Between Theology and Anti-Theology.* Durham: Acumen, 2013. https://doi.org/10.4324/9781315729862

Poole, Fitz John Porter. "Metaphors and Maps," *Journal of the American Academy of Religion* 54.3 (1986): 411–98. https://doi.org/10.1093/jaarel/LIV.3.411

Smith, Jonathan Z. *Map Is Not Territory: Studies in the Histories of Religions.* Chicago, IL: University of Chicago Press, 1993 [1978].
—*Drudgery Divine: On the Comparison of Early Christianities and the Religions of Late Antiquity.* New York: Routledge, 2013 [1990]. https://doi.org/10.4324/9781315040905

Chapter Eleven

Towards a Vulgar Marxist Reading of Christian Origins Today

James Crossley

Introduction

In this chapter I want to utilize a traditional subgenre of the academic essay: the anachronistic and absurdist argument which simultaneously makes a serious point. It is therefore fitting that I turn to Slavoj Žižek and his development of Alain Badiou's (non-original) comparison of Paul as "Lenin for whom Christ will have been the equivocal Marx."[1] Žižek formulates the argument as follows:

> Paul goes on to his true Leninist business, that of organizing the new party called the Christian community. Paul as a Leninist: was not Paul, like Lenin, the great "institutionalizer," and, as such, reviled by the partisans of "original" Marxism-Christianity? Does not the Pauline temporality "already, but not yet" also designate Lenin's situation in between two revolutions, between February and October 1917? Revolution is already behind us, the old regime is out, freedom is here—*but* the hard work still lies ahead.[2]

I want to develop this alarming analogy to some of its more absurdist conclusions, and it is in this sense that I am seeing it as a "vulgar Marxist" approach. It may be more conventional to define "vulgar Marxism" as hard economic determinism—the study of Christian origins could certainly do with more economic vulgarity, and I will not entirely ignore such questions—but the version I use here is not alien to the use of the insult.[3] Keeping up the kind of vulgarism I have in mind, or rather criticisms that buy into it, we might already note that the history of Marxism (and Christianity-as-Marxism) is often seen as "the revolution that failed," from radical

---

1. Alain Badiou, *Saint Paul: The Foundation of Universalism* (Stanford, CA: Stanford University Press, 2003), 2.
2. Slavoj Žižek, *The Puppet and the Dwarf: The Perverse Core of Christianity* (Cambridge, MA: MIT Press, 2003), 9.
3. For a convenient summary of the uses of "vulgar Marxism," see McKenzie Wark, "Four Cheers for Vulgar Marxism!!!!" *Public Seminar* (25 April 2014), http://www.publicseminar.org/2014/04/four-cheers-for-vulgarity/.

origins to totalitarian empire. Here we might think of Mikhail Bakunin's famous reading of one potential future of Marxism as a "red bureaucracy":

> The reasoning of Marx ends in absolute contradiction. Taking into account only the economic question, he insists that only the most advanced countries ... are most capable of making social revolution ... This revolution will expropriate either by peaceful, gradual or violent means, the present property owners and capitalists. To appropriate all the landed property and capital, and to carry out its extensive economic and political programs, the revolutionary State will have to be very powerful and highly centralized. The State will administer and direct the cultivation of the land, by means of salaried officials commanding armies of rural workers organized and disciplined for that purpose. At the same time, on the ruins of existing banks, it will establish a single state bank which will finance all labour and national commerce ... For the proletariat this will, in reality, be nothing but a barracks: a regime, where regimented workingmen and women will sleep, wake, work, and live to the beat of a drum; where the shrewd and educated will be granted government privileges ... There will be slavery within this state, and abroad there will be war without truce, at least until the "inferior" races, Latin and Slav, tired of bourgeois civilisation, no longer resign themselves to the subjection of the State, which will be even more despotic than the former State, although it calls itself a Peoples' State.[4]

This logic was, of course, most famously popularized by George Orwell in his journalistic treatment of the Spanish Civil War and in his most celebrated novels, *Animal Farm* and *Nineteen Eighty-Four*. Notwithstanding the problems of authoritarianism, Orwell's (somewhat simplistic) vision (which he also assumes applies in many ways to religion) became influential to the point where liberal journalists now readily invoke Orwell's radical credentials to attack and slur any leftist resurgence. In more classic Marxist terms, Orwell's vision (at least in its reception) does not account for the significance of power in organization and discipline in defending revolutionary fervour, facing up to fascist threats, dealing with competing internal interests, or surviving against the overwhelming power of capitalism and imperialism.[5] In terms of Christianity, we are likewise back to that age-old question of whether it would have survived if it simply continued a romantic attachment to the eschatological enthusiasm of the historical Jesus without the structured "church" that followed. What I want to do in the rest of this chapter is to cast Christian origins in a vulgarized reading of Marxist history before seeing that the absurdity of such vulgarism in fact brings us

---

4. Mikhail Bakunin, *Selected Works* (New York: Alfred A. Knopf, 1972), 283–4.
5. Paul Preston, "George Orwell's Spanish Civil War memoir is a classic, but is it bad history?" *Observer* (7 May 2017).

directly to pressing questions of today, both in terms of historical analysis and political change.[6]

Jesus, Revolution, and Historical Materialism

Perhaps it is better to see Jesus more in the figure of the revolutionary rather than Marx proper. But what does it even mean to call Jesus a "revolutionary"? That depends on how the question is framed.[7] It is possible, as a long, noble scholarly tradition has claimed, that he was something akin to an armed bandit leader (cf. Mark 15.7, 16, 27) who wanted to overthrow whatever authorities, possibly with an angelic assist, and that this was covered up by apologetic Gospel writers. It is possible that he preached a message of radical nonviolence or promoted a radical model of egalitarian, brokerless communities in Galilee. But the problem such models face is the problem many historical Jesus studies face: how can we establish such reconstructions with any degree of certainty, particularly if they work with the idea of a successful Gospel coverup? Instead, it might be more helpful to understand the categories of "revolution" and "revolutionary" in less individualistic terms and more in terms of socio-economic changes in the tradition of historical materialism, broadly understood. Here we should look at the changes taking place in Galilee and Judea which helped articulate the ideas associated with the Jesus movement.

By "historical materialism, broadly understood" I mean a Marxist dialectical reading of history which was famously and arguably most conveniently summarized in (of all places) the popular magazine, *Life*, in an article on Marx by Hubert Kay:

---

6. The anachronistic historical essay has far more honourable antecedents. As a young man facing the very real possibility of death in the face of fascism and the Second World War, Christopher Hill wrote a historical piece on the significance of English Revolution and its victories for liberty which part explained the need to fight Nazi Germany. See Christopher Hill, *The English Revolution 1640* (London: Lawrence & Wishart, 1940). In my case, I am implicitly critiquing my argument about libertarianism and the tension between radicalism and reaction in *Jesus and the Chaos of History: Redirecting the Quest for the Historical Jesus* (Oxford: Oxford University Press, 2015), or rather developing the missing component of what happens when radicalism comes good on its promise to take power. And, yes, it is notable that the previous reading and the present reading stand either side of the enthusiasm generated by the near-miraculous emergence of Corbynism. If the reader wants to keep up the Marxist analogy, see this as an extended exercise in self-criticism.

7. For a summary of the issues and history of the scholarship see Fernando Bermejo-Rubio, "Jesus and the Anti-Roman Resistance: A Reassessment of the Arguments," *JSHJ* 12 (2014): 1–105.

> In the Marxian view, human history is like a river. From any given vantage point, a river looks much the same day after day. But actually it is constantly flowing and changing, crumbling its banks, widening and deepening its channel. The water seen one day is never the same as that seen the next. Some of it is constantly being evaporated and drawn up, to return as rain. From year to year these changes may be scarcely perceptible. But one day, when the banks are thoroughly weakened and the rains long and heavy, the river floods, bursts its banks, and may take a new course.
>
> This represents the dialectical part of Marx's famous theory of dialectical (or historical) materialism.[8]

In Marxism, of course, class-conflict, exploitation, and ownership of the means of production are integral to such historical change. At this point, I would rein in any vulgarism associated with stages of history associated with classical Marxism and suggest that in this instance class conflict and modes of production should be thought of in terms of the town-countryside relationship. Here we might think about how urban elites extract resources and surplus from the agrarian workforce (cf. Sir. 38.24-34) and how the relatively rare phenomenon of social unrest, and accompanying millenarianism, maybe more likely occur when urbanization and demands are intensified (cf. *Ant.* 18.269-75).[9]

Some of the bursting of the banks in Galilee and Judea can be seen in the developments of major building projects and the reactions to them, and they help us understand what should be a basic point, namely that the Jesus movement did not just spontaneously emerge from nowhere. As Jesus would have been growing up in Galilee, there was the building and re-building of significant urban centres, Tiberias and Sepphoris, while the Jerusalem Temple had itself become an extensive building project in Judea. In such contexts, the dislocation of land can become a major factor in unrest and dissatisfaction. Josephus' description of the building of Tiberias gives us some indication of the dislocations involved:

> Tiberias … The new settlers were a promiscuous rabble, no small contingent being Galilean, with such as were drafted from territory subject to him [Herod Antipas] and brought forcibly to the new foundation. Some of these were magistrates. Herod accepted as participants even poor men who were brought in to join the others from any and all places of origin. It was in question whether some were even free beyond cavil. These latter he often and in large bodies liberated and benefited imposing the condition that they should

---

8. Hubert Kay, "Karl Marx," *Life* (18 October 1948): 63–75, here 66–7.
9. A classic treatment is John H. Kautsky, *The Politics of Aristocratic Empires* (Chapel Hill, NC: University of North Carolina, 1982), 278–303, which was influential on John D. Crossan, *The Birth of Christianity: Discovering What Happened in the Years Immediately after the Execution of Jesus* (Edinburgh: T&T Clark, 1998).

not quit the city, by equipping houses at his own expense and adding new gifts of land. For he knew that this settlement was contrary to the law and tradition of the Jews because Tiberias was built on the site of tombs that had been obliterated, of which there were many there. And our law declares that such settlers are unclean for seven days. (*Ant.* 18.36-8)

These developments in Galilee and Judea would contribute to the historical materialist river taking a new course in the full-scale revolt against Rome in 66–70 CE, where Josephus suggests that there were feelings of great hatred toward Sepphoris and Tiberias (*Life* 30, 39, 66-8, 99, 374-84). It would be a category error to see the non-mention of Tiberias and Sepphoris in the Gospel tradition as having any relevance here. In this materialist reading, what we are dealing with is how urbanization in Galilee and Judea were part of the generation of historical change, irrespective of what individual actors personally made of changes or whether they were even aware of them having relevance in their lives.

Nevertheless, perceptions still remain important in such materialist readings. The ongoing debates about Galilee and Galilean archaeology in relation to the historical Jesus often vacillate between hard conflict-based approaches to the Gospel tradition and a more prosperous Herodian economy.[10] Archaeology of 20s Galilee as it stands probably cannot tell us much about the standards of living at the time or whether there were simmering resentments. But a conflict-based approach does not have to be quite as vulgar as an unambiguous rise or fall in the standard of living. Indeed, from Josephus' description above, we should probably be thinking more about some very different material changes for, and responses from, a range of people with a more complex mix of reactions, from anger through opportunism to accepting change whether in their economic interests or not. Moreover, unequal distribution of resources—with all the potential for antagonisms between owners and producers—would not necessarily have satisfied all. In this sense, *perception* is as important as material measurements in terms of assessing conflict. If people did not perceive changes for the better, it matters little if contemporary historians of Christian origins

---

10. The major treatment of a more prosperous Herodian economy against conflict-based readings are Morten Horning Jensen, *Herod Antipas in Galilee* (Tübingen: Mohr Siebeck, 2006); Morten Horning Jensen, "Herod Antipas in Galilee: Friend or Foe of the Historical Jesus?" *JSHJ* 5 (2007): 7–32; Helen K. Bond, *The Historical Jesus: A Guide for the Perplexed* (London: Bloomsbury/T&T Clark, 2012), 75–7. There are numerous conflict-based readings of Herodian Galilee. Classic treatments include Richard Horsley, *Jesus and the Spiral of Violence: Popular Jewish Resistance in Roman Palestine* (San Francisco, CA: Harper & Row, 1987); K. C. Hanson and Douglas E. Oakman, *Palestine in the Time of Jesus: Social Structures and Social Conflicts* (Minneapolis, MN: Augsburg Fortress, 1998).

would have told them that they were materially better off. The Marxist historian Eric Hobsbawm (whose spectre often haunts this debate) was careful in his wording of peasant land occupations where he saw peasant reaction being due to alienation "in a manner which they do not regard as valid."[11]

The material changes and perception of changes inevitably involved in the building projects of Sepphoris, Tiberias, and the Jerusalem Temple were not always perceived for the better if the Gospel tradition is anything to go by. And what we see in the Gospel tradition are claims that are not those of the bleeding-heart liberal reformist, but those of an overthrowing of the order, a stark eschatological role reversal of rich and poor, the impossibility of rich people being saved, the incompatibility of God and Mammon, hostility to wealth, and concerns about debt and poverty (e.g., Mark 10.17-31, 11.15-17; Matt. 6.24//Luke 16.13; Matt. 6.25-34//Luke 12.22-31; Matt. 11.8//Luke 7.25; Luke 6.20-26//Matt 5.3-12; Luke 12.57-59//Matt. 5.25; Luke 14.12-24//Matt. 22.1-14; Matt. 5.40-42, 6.12, 18.23-35, 25.31-46; Luke 4.18, 6.20-25, 6.35, 12.13-21, 16.1-8, 16.19-31; cf. *1 Enoch* 98.2, 102.9-11; *Thom.* 64). This does not automatically mean that we have recovered the words and deeds of the historical Jesus. But it is likely that such a heavy concentration of themes attested independently in sources and forms points us in the direction of a theme in the earliest traditions and thus provides us with embedded perceptions concerning the material changes taking place in Galilee and Judea, even if traditional tropes were employed.

Revolutionary Millenarianism

Such thinking was also part of the millenarianism associated with the Jesus movement: the imminent kingdom of God. Indeed, this is the sort of millenarianism or utopianism (whether reactionary or revolutionary) that can occur in upheavals in agrarian societies and witnessed in first-century Palestine, as the references to bandits, prophets, and millenarian figures like John the Baptist or Theudas might suggest. Gerhard Lenski's classic cross-cultural analysis of the "priestly class" in agrarian societies remains helpful here. Lenski's "priestly class" was broadly understood as figures who mediate between humanity and the divine and could take different forms and titles. The priestly class could be part of the elite and use divine authority to officiate channels of salvation and thus support the status quo. However, access to the divine can be ambiguous and if it functions outside the official system it can support economic redistribution and the interests of the lower end of

---

11. Eric J. Hobsbawm, *Uncommon People: Resistance, Rebellion and Jazz* (London: Abacus, 1998), 224.

the social structure.[12] Obviously, Lenski's model is too vulgar for our tastes, but it remains useful in that direct access to the divine from outside the more official channels of salvation have historically posed conflict and tensions. To anchor this in the first century, the notion of charismatic authority and access to the divine are issues raised in the Gospels, notably in relation to healing and exorcism and John the Baptist (e.g., Mark 1.23-27, 2.1-12, 3.21-30, 11.27-33).

One of the most dramatic parallels (certainly in Marxist historiography) is the English Revolution. Perhaps the most famous Marxist reading of the seventeenth century is Christopher Hill's account of the civil wars as a bourgeois revolution paving the way for longer term capitalist development. As part of this "revolution," Hill famously gave much attention to radical developments "from below" (e.g., Gerrard Winstanley, Diggers, Levellers, etc.) which would have to be dealt with, tamed, domesticated, or supressed.[13] This "world turned upside down" provided a context for radical claims concerning democracy, sexuality, theology, God, education, millenarianism, and so on, a process which finds a parallel phenomenon in Christian origins.[14] Hill's Marxist approach may have gone out of fashion but the general materialist point is important as it still shows that the chaos of this "world turned upside down" fed into longer term changes, suppression and/or developments in science, theology, literature, politics, democracy, philosophy, and so on, all to be taken up in the Enlightenment.[15] Even if scholarship has watered down Hill's historical materialism, its role in helping us understand the transition to capitalist democracies and empires, at least in England, remains.

That such upheavals and revolutions contribute to shifts in, and explosions of, ideas and thinking (whether revolutionary, reactionary, creative,

---

12. Gerhard E. Lenski, *Power and Privilege: A Theory of Social Stratification* (New York: McGraw-Hill, 1966), 263–5. In the British Marxist tradition see also the classic treatment in Rodney H. Hilton, "Peasant Society, Peasant Movements and Feudalism in Medieval Europe," in Henry A. Landsberger (ed.), *Rural Protest: Peasant Movements and Social Change* (New York: Macmillan, 1973), 67–94, e.g., 89–90.

13. Christopher Hill, *The World Turned Upside Down: Radical Ideas during the English Revolution* (London: Temple Smith, 1972).

14. See, for example, Dale C. Allison, *Jesus of Nazareth: Millenarian Prophet* (Philadelphia, PA: Fortress Press, 1998), 78–94; Dale C. Allison, *Constructing Jesus: Memory, Imagination, and History* (London: SPCK, 2010), 85–8, who approaches the historical Jesus from the perspective of cross-cultural millenarian groups. Cf. Christopher Rowland, *Christian Origins: An Account of the Setting and Character of the Most Important Messianic Sect of Judaism* (London: SPCK, 1986), 87–91, 111–7.

15. Michael Braddick, *God's Fury, England's Fire: A New History of the English Civil Wars* (London: Allen Lane, 2008), xxv.

culturally bizarre, peaceful, violent, or accidental) which may have huge long-term impacts, be clamped down almost immediately, or have potential unrealized, ought to be a basic materialist point. Clearly, understanding the material changes in Galilee and Judea help us understand some major historical changes, such as the emergence of Christianity and the consolidation of Judaism among the rabbis, both of which looked quite different after what had happened in the first century. We can see how this would have affected a range of ideas which would likewise not remain quite the same. In terms of constructions of gender and sexuality, we might think of how Jesus might have been expected to take on the role as the head of the household and produce children for the perpetuation of the family. Halvor Moxnes has argued that he was instead remembered as a socially castrated itinerant leader of a queer family in a world where expected household patterns were being threatened, a theme which looks early given its attestation across sources and forms (e.g., Mark 3.20-22, 31-35; 10.29-30; Mark 6.5-6// Matt. 13.58; Matt. 8.22//Luke 9.60; Matt. 10.34-36//Luke 12.51-53// *Thom.* 16.1-4; Matt. 10.37//Luke 14.26; Matt. 19.10-12).[16] Like the violent revolutionary Simon bar Giora shortly after him (*War* 4.505-8, 538), Jesus was also remembered for his association with women who would no doubt have been assumed to be part of this new family in Mark's retelling of Jesus' final Passover rather than the familiar thirteen men (Mark 14.12-26).[17] Even crucifixion would suggested the idea of a feminized passive victim of masculinized Roman dominance. This gendered reaction would no doubt have been an option from the moment it was known that death as a criminal was going to happen.

But this was not the emergence of liberal democratic notions of gender, Christianity was hardly progressive as we would understand it (nor has the history of Communism always been), and the social constraints of the time meant that more conventional masculinized constructions were employed or even intensified. Acts of sexual restraint could still be seen as a special gift for those with the (manly) ability (cf. Matt. 19.10-11); the alternative households still had a particularly dominant father, namely the one who was in heaven (cf. Matt. 23.9); and while marriage may have been queered, people could be expected to turn into (warlike) angels (cf. Mark 12.18-27;

---

16. Halvor Moxnes, *Putting Jesus in His Place: A Radical Vision of Household and Kingdom* (Louisville, KY: WJK, 2003).

17. The classic treatment of women and revolutionary change is Elisabeth Schüssler Fiorenza, *In Memory of Her: A Feminist Theological Reconstruction of Christian Origins* (2nd edn.; London: SCM, 1994). On the cultural assumptions of Jesus' last Passover, at least as presented by Mark, see Maurice Casey, *Jesus of Nazareth: An Independent Historian's Account of His Life and Teaching* (London: T&T Clark, 2010), 429–37.

Luke 20.34-36). Jesus as victim of Roman power could be reimagined (and perhaps simultaneously) as a heroic or noble martyr or masculinized as someone capable of taking a serious beating. Nevertheless, things were not the same, which of course they would not be, dialectically speaking. As Coleen Conway reminds us, despite the masculinized constructions of gender, Mark still presents a "passive emasculated victim who suffers a humiliating death … it is as if the author cannot fully dismiss the ignominy of the crucifixion."[18] Nevertheless, Christianity would be forever haunted by uncomfortable sayings about eunuchs, family, women's authority, alongside uncomfortable sayings about the fate of the damned rich, which would reappear throughout the history of Christianity.

Bureaucratizing the Revolution: From Lenin to Stalin

With the death of Jesus, his followers inherited these chaotic ideas which would, by our anachronistic formula, function like Christopher Hill's notion of the revolution within the revolution, whereby the revolutionary energy would be ready to be appropriated from above. The revolutionary moment of Jesus' millenarianism might now be cast in materialist terms of the "political miracle." The unexpectedness of the revolutionary moment and the building of a post-revolutionary society against the odds might alternatively be seen as bringing us to our Lenin figure: Paul. The Leninist idea of revolution-as-miracle involved tension between the hard work of organization (e.g., party structure, propaganda) and the enthusiasm of the unexpected and spontaneous. As the Marxist-Leninist (with Chinese characteristics) Roland Boer has argued, the reception of this tradition in subsequent Marxist thought in notions of ruptures, eschatological moments, Messianic time, and Events (e.g., Benjamin, Jameson, Agamben, Badiou, Žižek) has typically stressed one-sided versions of this tension, that is, the spontaneous.[19] Our Lenin figure, however, clearly embraced the necessity of organization and consolidation of the movement. Borrowing from Badiou, we might note that the revolutionary potential became encapsulated by the Event of Christ's death and

---

18. Coleen M. Conway, *Behold the Man: Jesus and Greco-Roman Masculinity* (Oxford: Oxford University Press, 2008), 89, 100.

19. Roland Boer, *Lenin, Religion, and Theology* (New York: Palgrave Macmillan, 2013), 135–74. Some of these suggestions may be qualified, as Boer does. Žižek, for instance, can make arguments about Leninist organization and institutionalization. See, e.g., Žižek, *The Puppet and the Dwarf*, 9; Jodi Dean, *Žižek's Politics* (New York: Routledge, 2006), 179–203. Cf. Slavoj Žižek, *Violence: Six Sideways Reflections* (London: Profile Books, 2009), e.g. 6–8, 213–7.

resurrection which now opened up radical possibilities and demanded fidelity to the Event.[20]

To take yet another anachronistic parallel to help this reading of Christian origins, we might turn to the contemporary revolution in Rojava, northern Syria.[21] A group of volunteers from the British Isles and Ireland called the Bob Crow Brigade have thrived and assisted in this "beacon of egalitarian politics and progressive policies." But they additionally saw what was happening in Rojava as the first step towards a democratic or bourgeois revolution which, according to one conventional Marxist reading, would be the requirement for a socialist revolution to take off. A full communist revolution had not happened because, they argued, that while there had been some redistribution of land, some communes, some cooperatives, and so on, there had not been "mass expropriation of the local bourgeoisie" for that would involve countless small traders and, as an agricultural region, Rojava was reliant on cross-border trade. The stage after the democratic/bourgeois revolution was the beginning of the class struggle within the revolution and this involved the creation of industry and a developed proletariat. Here, we also get a Marxist-Leninist critique of the "ultra-left" who in this instance, the Bob Crow Brigade argued, were not concerned with developing a left-wing analysis. Instead, this group was worrying too much that ideas of "direct democracy, autonomy, ecology and feminism" did not become "infected with forbidden and unclean ideas, such as support for Parties, stages of revolution, national liberation, vanguards etc." By way of contrast, these volunteers "welcome[d] this infection" as part of "the reality of socialist struggle."[22]

Borrowing loosely from Ward Blanton's analysis of the political Paul then and now, we might see the the Bob Crow Brigade as a group of contemporary Pauline materialists.[23] Recast in the era of Paul, this is when set parties representing the interests of Jews and Gentiles were being established to widen the scope of the movement beyond the constrained revolutionary moment (e.g., Gal. 2.1-10; cf. Acts 15). Pragmatism was combined with authority to bring together diverse groups and identities under Christ, even if full equality was not being realized in the present (e.g., Gal. 3.28). There has been a lot of

---

20. Badiou, *Saint Paul*.
21. James Crossley, *Cults, Martyrs, and Good Samaritans: Religion in English Political Discourse* (London: Pluto, 2018), 162–99.
22. Kevin Hoffmann, "Interview with the Bob Crow Brigade in Rojava." *Kevin Hoffmann* (1 November 2016), http://kevinhoffmann.blogsport.eu/2016/11/01/interview-with-the-bob-crow-brigade-in-rojava/.
23. Ward Blanton, *A Materialism for the Masses: Saint Paul and the Philosophy of Undying Life* (New York: Columbia University Press, 2014).

discussion of Paul as either an openly anti-imperial figure, which can often be too vulgar even for this analysis, or as a cipher for scholars' edgy liberal credentials by saying Paul was nothing of the sort. But in one sense, Paul was undeniably an anti-imperialist: anyone expecting the kingdom predicted by Jesus would know it would bring a necessarily violent end to the violence of Roman imperialism. Yet in the present, a tactical Leninist like Paul would know when to act and when not to act, hence statements about restraining revolutionary fervour and obeying the authorities (Rom. 13.1-10).[24]

To help us understand this we might turn to the role of Communist parties. In Britain, as Stephen Woodhams has pointed out, being a pre-1956 Communist was "a serious calling," that the Party "would support a self-nurtured respectability," that the image of the Communist was as a "serious citizen," and there was a "necessity to maintain civility" whether in the home or in the street. The Party was not, Woodhams argued, about "being subversive and undermining values of decency," but was instead about "re-enforcing them all the stronger." Such an emphasis on seriousness and the maintenance of self-respect could be said to provide cohesion "in a world where all around were apparently lost to the lure of transient pleasures."[25] Raphael Samuel similarly recalled the "lost world of British Communism" as a serious-minded, intellectual lifestyle of "strictness" and "clean living," eschewing "foul language" of the "politically illiterate."[26] In this respect we might recall how shocked some of the Marxist establishment were with flamboyant radicalism of the 1960s, most infamously the case of Adorno when faced with rebellious students.[27]

The serious-minded public behaviour is something that the author of 1 Peter would have appreciated (e.g., 1 Pet. 1.13-16, 2.1-2, 2.11-25, 4.7-19) and which was anticipated in the Paulinist discipline in everyday conduct, from strict ethical behaviour in the world (e.g., Gal. 5.19-21; 1 Cor. 6.9-20) to policing the body in public, including a good Soviet haircut for the men

---

24. Compare the similar argument (made by plenty of others) in Jacob Taubes, *The Political Theology of Paul* (Stanford, CA: Stanford University Press, 2004), 40–1.

25. Stephen Woodhams, *History in the Making: Raymond Williams, Edward Thompson and Radical Intellectuals 1936–1956* (London: Merlin Press, 2001), 103–4, 106.

26. Raphael Samuel, *The Lost World of British Communism* (London: Verso, 2006), 185–200.

27. Theodor W. Adorno, "Resignation (1969)," in *Critical Models: Interventions and Catchwords* (New York: Columbia University Press, 2005), 289–93. For general discussion see, e.g., Lorenz Jäger, *Adorno: A Political Biography* (New Haven, CT: Yale University Press, 2004), 192–208; Stefan Müller-Doohm, *Adorno: An Intellectual Biography* (Cambridge: Polity, 2005); Detlev Claussen, *Theodor W. Adorno: One Last Genius* (Cambridge, MA; Belknap Press of Harvard University Press, 2008), 1–2, 10, 201, 332–9.

(1 Cor. 11.14). Similarly, influences from different sides, from opposition to change through to identity politics and radical liberalism, were beginning to be constructed as ideological deviations, whether demands for new male recruits were to adhere to ideas that circumcision was central to the group's identity or that undisciplined spirit-fuelled enthusiasm (1 Cor. 12) or potentially anarchic living apart from the Law could now be the way forward. To quote Paul, "'All things are lawful,' but not all things are beneficial. 'All things are lawful,' but not all things build up" (1 Cor. 10.23; cf. 1 Cor. 6.12-20). Put another way, Paul anticipates Žižek's favored quip from Stalin (and found in Lenin) in response to "Which deviation is worse, the Rightist or the Leftist one?": "They are both worse!" Placed in the Stalin-Žižek line, the leftist deviation is "objectively" nothing more than a rightist deviation in that it effectively acts against the success of the revolution.[28]

This is not the place to assess fully whether Stalin was or was not a legitimate or inevitable development of Lenin, or indeed whether both or either were a legitimate or inevitable development of Marx and Marxism. But Lenin was not completely removed from what happened with Stalin, just as Paul was not removed from what happened in Johannine thought. In our Stalinist era, the past of the historical Jesus got airbrushed to conform with the present more than any other canonical Gospel, or in the Stalin-Žižek line, here is how history could get read retroactively so that the truth likewise becomes clear retroactively (cf. John 2.22 "After he was raised from the dead, his disciples remembered that he had said this").[29] As the kingdom did not come and the second coming had not happened when expected, so the figure and his early followers who made such problematic predictions no longer said such things as previously understood (John 3.3, 5) or are now corrected accordingly (e.g., John 21). While the benefits of the realized eschatology of the Christ-socialist moment could be located in the present, the full global Christ-Communism would be inaugurated in distant Communist future, as indeed Boer suggests of Stalinist thought itself in relation to notions of the delay in the Parousia.[30] In the present, there is effectively

---

28. E.g., Slavoj Žižek, *Less Than Nothing: Hegel and the Shadow of Dialectical Materialism* (London: Verso, 2012), 72. Cf. Vladimir Ilyich Lenin, *What Is to Be Done? Burning Questions for Our Movement* (1902), available https://www.marxists.org/archive/lenin/works/1901/witbd ("We confess that we find it difficult to say which of these resolutions is the better one. In our opinion they are both worse.")

29. Žižek, *Less Than Nothing*, 72. On John's Gospel see Maurice Casey, *Is John's Gospel True?* (London: Routledge, 1996); Casey, *Jesus of Nazareth*, 511–25; Crossley, *Jesus and the Chaos of History*, 48–62.

30. Roland Boer, "Stalin and Proleptic Communism," *Politics, Religion & Ideology* 17 (2016): 162–71.

Actually Existing Christ-Socialism in one group threateningly surrounded by the world and so the boundaries around the in-group and its ideology are firm (e.g., John 1.10-13). The power of the charismatic authority of Jesus and Paul now gets harnessed into foregrounding a fully deified cult of personality (e.g., John 5, 10.11-18, 10.31-42, 14.6). Authority and the ideologically correct line get hardened in John's Gospel, including through valorizing love and loyalty among fellow believers to the point of death for the new society (e.g., John 15.13, 16.2). This sort of ideological hardening meant clearing out the problematic deviants who do not hold the Party line (e.g., John 6.60-66). The Johannine letters even give us a Trotsky figure constructed as against the revolution, namely the figure of Diotrephes who was deemed to take on a deviant authority and liable to make false allegations (3 John 9-10).

Christian Origins: A Tale for Our Time

No doubt we could continue the parlor game of comparing Christian origins and Marxist history (was Irenaeus Mao?). An absurd thought experiment this all may be and, furthermore, we should never fool ourselves that progressive values were generated before their time in Christian origins. But some of the questions raised do not go away so easily: would not ultra-leftism (Christian or left wing) have lacked the discipline, authority, and power to survive? Does not the Partyism or the Church keep radical ideas alive, even if sometimes they seem against their own radical interests? What were the internal impulses and external pressures that led to Christianity as another empire or led to Russia ending up as another twenty-first century capitalist country? These are comparative historical questions that a future essay might explore with greater contextualization, detail, and cultural sensitivity than necessarily presented in an essay such as this. Such a history would avoid the narrative of the Great Man practically changing everything and pay far greater attention to a historical materialist of the emergence and survival of the Jesus movement and Christianity. This should not be confused with a hard-deterministic reading of history with no role for the individual. On the contrary, a historical materialist view should see nothing inevitable about change and development but rather as a complex dialectical process. Nevertheless, such a history should not lose sight of the ways in which movements develop, succeed, and change (possibly directly against the wishes, interests, and intentions of the early adherents). This chapter has posed some anachronist ways this process might be understood.

This may all be an anachronistic thought-experiment, but the seemingly long-forgotten ideas raised here have returned to prominence in the West. While still within their respective liberal-democratic systems, Jeremy Corbyn and (to lesser extent) Bernie Sanders represent unexpected developments in two countries which have epitomized neoliberalism and the apparent death of the Left, and yet have now attracted a serious rethinking of Partyism, Party discipline, organization, electoral alliances and popular support, the development of leftist cultures, and so on. In America, Jodi Dean has especially stressed the combination of the unpredictable spontaneity of the crowd and the hard work of involvement in or building a party to bring about revolutionary change with reference to both Sanders and Communist theory and practice. She has rethought these issues in light of the recurring problems of housing, indebtedness, and ubiquitous use of technology at home and work as an updating of contemporary form of class struggle, of those proletarianized under communicative capitalism.[31] In the UK, and facing similar issues under the contradictions of neoliberalism, the enthusiasm, hard work and occasional discipline, of the Corbynite group Momentum was for a time crucial in keeping Corbynism alive in the face of threats from the traditional media and centrist politicians in his own party but also bringing the socialist wing of the Labour Party close to power. And none of this is alien to or distanced from Christian discourses. From Occupy through Rojava to Corbyn, the language of the radical Christian tradition has been employed in the development of a new leftist hegemony in the latest instalment of the historical-material process. In one sense these are not purely "leftist" or "Christian," as if such categories can be so easily distinguished, but rather both, or at least both have a shared and ongoing history. Such a materialist understanding of history acknowledges that there have been historic failures and successes in such egalitarian and redistributive outbursts. Today, in the post-2008 era of the crises of neoliberalism, the questions are now pressing ones for the Left in the renewed quest to not only keep alive but sustain the radical impulses associated with both the radical Christian tradition and Marxism in the face of contemporary capitalist and imperialist power.

Biographical Note

James Crossley is Professor of Bible, Culture, and Politics at St. Mary's University, London, and Academic Director of the Centre for the Critical Study of Apocalyptic and Millenarian Movements for the Panacea Charitable Trust. His is author of numerous publications on Christian origins and religion in English politics, including *Cults, Martyrs and Good Samaritans: Religion in Contemporary English Political Discourse* (Pluto, 2018). His

---

31. Jodi Dean, *The Communist Horizon* (London: Verso, 2012); Jodi Dean, *Crowds and Party* (New York: Verso, 2016).

new book is *Spectres of John Ball: The Peasants' Revolt in English Political History, 1381–2020* (Equinox, 2022).

Bibliography

Adorno, Theodor W. "Resignation (1969)," 289–93 in *Critical Models: Interventions and Catchwords*. New York: Columbia University Press, 2005.
Allison, Dale C. *Jesus of Nazareth: Millenarian Prophet*. Philadelphia, PA: Fortress Press, 1998.
—*Constructing Jesus: Memory, Imagination, and History*. London: SPCK, 2010.
Badiou, Alain. *Saint Paul: The Foundation of Universalism*. Stanford, CA: Stanford University Press, 2003.
Bakunin, Mikhail. *Selected Works*. New York: Alfred A. Knopf, 1972.
Bermejo-Rubio, Fernando. "Jesus and the Anti-Roman Resistance: A Reassessment of the Arguments," *Journal for the Study of the Historical Jesus* 12 (2014): 1–105. https://doi.org/10.1163/17455197-01202001
Blanton, Ward. *A Materialism for the Masses: Saint Paul and the Philosophy of Undying Life*. New York: Columbia University Press, 2014. https://doi.org/10.7312/columbia/9780231166911.001.0001
Boer, Roland. *Lenin, Religion, and Theology*. New York: Palgrave Macmillan, 2013. https://doi.org/10.1057/9781137314123
—"Stalin and Proleptic Communism," *Politics, Religion & Ideology* 17 (2016): 162–71. https://doi.org/10.1080/21567689.2016.1222940
Bond, Helen K. *The Historical Jesus: A Guide for the Perplexed*. London: Bloomsbury/T&T Clark, 2012. https://doi.org/10.5040/9780567691194
Braddick, Michael. *God's Fury, England's Fire: A New History of the English Civil Wars*. London: Allen Lane, 2008.
Casey, Maurice. *Is John's Gospel True?* London: Routledge, 1996.
—*Jesus of Nazareth: An Independent Historian's Account of His Life and Teaching*. London: T&T Clark, 2010. https://doi.org/10.5040/9780567691224
Claussen, Detlev. *Theodor W. Adorno: One Last Genius*. Cambridge, MA: Belknap Press of Harvard University Press, 2008. https://doi.org/10.4159/9780674029590
Conway, Coleen M. *Behold the Man: Jesus and Greco-Roman Masculinity*. Oxford: Oxford University Press, 2008.
Crossan, John D. *The Birth of Christianity. Discovering What Happened in the Years Immediately after the Execution of Jesus*. Edinburgh: T&T Clark, 1998.
Crossley, James. *Jesus and the Chaos of History: Redirecting the Quest for the Historical Jesus*. Oxford: Oxford University Press, 2015. https://doi.org/10.1093/acprof:oso/9780199570577.001.0001
—*Cults, Martyrs, and Good Samaritans: Religion in English Political Discourse*. London: Pluto, 2018. https://doi.org/10.2307/j.ctv3mt8w5
Dean, Jodi. *Žižek's Politics*. Routledge: London, 2006.
—*The Communist Horizon*. London: Verso, 2012.
—*Crowds and Party*. London: Verso, 2016.
Hanson, Kenneth C., and Douglas E. Oakman, *Palestine in the Time of Jesus: Social Structures and Social Conflicts*. Minneapolis, MN: Augsburg Fortress, 1998.
Hill, Christopher. *The English Revolution 1640*. London: Lawrence & Wishart, 1940.

—*The World Turned Upside Down: Radical Ideas during the English Revolution.* London: Temple Smith, 1972.
Hilton, Rodney H. "Peasant Society, Peasant Movements and Feudalism in Medieval Europe," 67–94 in *Rural Protest: Peasant Movements and Social Change* Edited by Henry A. Landsberger. New York: Macmillan, 1973. https://doi.org/10.1007/978-1-349-01612-9_2
Hobsbawm, Eric J. *Uncommon People: Resistance, Rebellion and Jazz.* London: Abacus, 1998.
Hoffmann, Kevin. "Interview with the Bob Crow Brigade in Rojava," *Kevin Hoffmann* (1 November 2016). http://kevinhoffmann.blogsport.eu/2016/11/01/interview-with-the-bob-crow-brigade-in-rojava/
Horsley, Richard. *Jesus and the Spiral of Violence: Popular Jewish Resistance in Roman Palestine.* San Francisco, CA: Harper & Row, 1987.
Jäger, Lorenz. *Adorno: A Political Biography.* New Haven, CT: Yale University Press, 2004.
Jensen, Morten Horning. *Herod Antipas in Galilee.* Tübingen: Mohr Siebeck, 2006.
—'Herod Antipas in Galilee: Friend or Foe the Historical Jesus?' *Journal for the Study of the Historical Jesus* 5 (2007): 7–32. https://doi.org/10.1177/1476869006074934
Kautsky, John H. *The Politics of Aristocratic Empires.* Chapel Hill, NC: University of North Carolina, 1982.
Kay, Hubert. "Karl Marx," *Life* (18 October 1948): 63–75.
Lenin, Vladimir Ilyich. *What Is to Be Done? Burning Questions for Our Movement* (1902). Available https://www.marxists.org/archive/lenin/works/1901/witbd
Lenski, Gerhard E. *Power and Privilege: A Theory of Social Stratification.* New York: McGraw-Hill, 1966.
Moxnes, Halvor. *Putting Jesus in His Place: A Radical Vision of Household and Kingdom.* Louisville, KY: Westminster John Knox, 2003.
Müller-Doohm, Stefan. *Adorno: An Intellectual Biography.* Cambridge: Polity, 2005.
Preston, Paul. "George Orwell's Spanish Civil War memoir is a classic, but is it bad history?" *Observer,* 7 May 2017.
Rowland, Christopher. *Christian Origins: An Account of the Setting and Character of the Most Important Messianic Sect of Judaism.* London: SPCK, 1986.
Samuel, Raphael. *The Lost World of British Communism.* London: Verso, 2006.
Schüssler Fiorenza, Elisabeth. *In Memory of Her: A Feminist Theological Reconstruction of Christian Origins.* Second edition. London: SCM, 1994.
Taubes, Jacob. *The Political Theology of Paul.* Stanford, CA: Stanford University Press, 2004.
Wark, McKenzie. "Four Cheers for Vulgar Marxism!!!!" *Public Seminar* (25 April 2014). http://www.publicseminar.org/2014/04/four-cheers-for-vulgarity/
Woodhams, Stephen. *History in the Making: Raymond Williams, Edward Thompson and Radical Intellectuals 1936–1956.* London: Merlin Press, 2001.
Žižek, Slavoj. *The Puppet and the Dwarf: The Perverse Core of Christianity.* Cambridge, MA: MIT Press, 2003. https://doi.org/10.7551/mitpress/5706.001.0001
—*Violence: Six Sideways Reflections.* London: Profile Books, 2009.
—*Less Than Nothing: Hegel and the Shadow of Dialectical Materialism.* London: Verso, 2012.

Chapter Twelve

Recapitulating the Event: Reading Irenaeus with Badiou

Hollis Phelps

In what follows, I attempt to read Irenaeus' notion of recapitulation, that is, the notion that Christ summarizes, repeats, and redeems the "transgression" of Adam and Eve, in light of Alain Badiou's philosophy of the event. Specifically, I relate recapitulation to Badiou's notion of evental recurrence as a means of showing the similar, material structure at work in both thinkers. To be clear, the point of what follows is not an attempt at a theological recovery of the notion of recapitulation. Irenaeus' theology of redemption, in my view, remains a largely mythological construct, grounded in the specificity of Eve and Adam, Mary and Christ. It is, rather, an attempt to read the notion of recapitulation in terms of a materialist understanding of history, relying on Badiou's notion of the event.

Such an approach may, at first glance, strike the reader as counterintuitive at best. Irenaeus, of course, does emphasize the historicity of redemption over against his so-called Gnostic opponents, but he does so by relying on an allegorical, and specifically, typological method, which reads texts and past occurrences as containing an extra-historical sense. Critical readers have long dismissed this sort of interpretative undertaking as fundamentally naïve, in the sense that it plays fast and loose with its materials for the purpose of a pre-determined, theological gain. Nevertheless, I suggest that Irenaeus' use of typology should not be classified along these lines, at least wholly. Irenaeus does, to be sure, rely on an allegorical method that seems out of touch with contemporary, critical methods, but he does so, I suggest, because history is for him allegorical, constituted through a certain excess that drives history, an excess that for him, nevertheless, takes on a mythological form. My attempt to draw this out from the notion of recapitulation, then, may also serve as an attempt to provide a general outline for a recovery of allegory as a method for grasping this excess, as constitutive of history itself.

A word about my reading of Irenaeus: like much early theology, Irenaeus draws heavily on images and tropes from scripture as a means to support his claims. Indeed, especially in Irenaeus' case, his use of scripture is an essential tool for combating what he takes as the heresy of his opponents.

Scripture, however, is by no means systematic, and neither is Irenaeus' theology. Many conceptual difficulties emerge throughout *Against Heresies*, difficulties present in the materials he uses themselves, and I do not attempt to iron these out.[1] Rather, I filter my reading of Irenaeus through his notion of recapitulation, drawing out the logic it entails. From a philosophical and theological perspective, recapitulation is arguably the most interesting aspect of the text, but it is also the point at which a dialogue between Irenaeus and Badiou is most apparent and fruitful.

To make the argument, the first part of this essay focuses on Irenaeus' critique of an allegorizing reading of scripture, as it is found among his opponents in his work *Against Heresies*. Drawing on Paul and the work of Stanislas Breton, I draw out another understanding of allegory which reads history in terms of excess, which I discuss in more detail in regard to Irenaeus in the third part of the essay. The second part of the essay focuses on Badiou's philosophy of the event, focusing specifically on the notions of intervention, eventual recurrence, and the idea of a resurrection of truths. Doing so allows me to draw out a materialist conception of time from Badiou's philosophy, one that, moreover, contributes to grasping the basic structure of recapitulation as it is found in Irenaeus' theology, as I discuss in the third part of the essay. I conclude with some brief remarks of how the ground covered throughout may contribute to a rethinking of allegory as a materialist form of interpretation, because, as I suggest, history itself is allegorical.

Allegory, Typology, and History

One of Irenaeus' main complaints against his Gnostic opponents is that they derive their doctrines at least in part from a faulty reading of scripture.[2] Rather than reading scripture in terms of its "order" and "continuity" with respect to the material locus of salvation in history, the heretics, as Irenaeus calls them, "dissolve the members of the truth. They transfer and transform,

---

1. Irenaeus, *Against Heresies* (trans. Alexander Roberts and William Rambaut; *Ante-Nicene Fathers*, 1; ed. Alexander Roberts, James Donaldson, and A. Cleveland Coxe; Buffalo, NY: Christian Literature Publishing, 1885). All subsequent references are given parenthetically, and refer to book and chapter number.
2. "Gnosticism" is, of course, a problematic category as a way of generalizing the diversity of views lumped under it. I use the term throughout primarily for convenience, and my discussion of it vis-à-vis Irenaeus draws only on his characterizations in *Against Heresies*. Such an emphasis is only meant to shore up the specificity of Irenaeus' own thought as he presents it. For a critical discussion of the term as a category, see for instance Michael Allen Williams, *Rethinking "Gnosticism": An Argument for Dismantling a Dubious Category* (Princeton, NJ: Princeton University Press, 1996).

making one thing out of another and thus lead many astray by the badly constructed phantom that they make out of the Lord's words they adjust" (I, 8.1). In order to prop up their doctrines, Irenaeus contends, they ignore the teaching of the prophets and the transmission of the apostles, and instead seek out a supposed mysterious content hidden in and underneath the text, the sense of which is accessible to the select few in the know. Simply put, Irenaeus' "heretics" read scripture allegorically, as a means to drawing out and thus supporting the positions that they already hold in advance. They are, he says,

> eager to adapt things well said to things they have badly invented. They try to draw their proof not only from the Gospels and the writings of the Apostle, changing the interpretations and twisting the exegesis, but also from the law and the prophets. Since they encounter many parables and allegories which can be taken in various ways, they adjust what is ambiguous to their fiction through exegesis and lead captive, far from the truth, those who do not preserve a firm faith in one God the Father Almighty and in one Jesus Christ the Son of God. (I, 3.6)

His opponents' method, in this sense, corresponds to their doctrines themselves, insofar as the latter point to the assumed reality of salvific knowledge and wisdom above and beyond the contingencies of history. They devalue the materiality, both textually and historically, in favor of a disembodied, individual illumination. In sum, the heretics teach a doctrine "the prophets did not proclaim, the Lord did not teach, and the apostles did not transmit" (I, 8.1).

Against the "gnosis" of his opponents, then, Irenaeus stresses the embodied nature of salvation, as continuous with the history out of which it emerges. Indeed, as I will discuss below, this is in many ways the whole point of the notion of recapitulation. Nevertheless, in terms of Irenaeus' approach to scripture, over-against the individualized approach of his opponents he stresses the importance of "apostolic succession" as a means of grounding and transmitting the gospel. He writes that the economy of salvation is known "only through those whom the Gospel came to us; and what they then first preached they later, by God's will, transmitted to us in the scriptures so that it would be the foundation and pillar of our faith (I Tim. 3.15)" (III, 1.1). Such succession, moreover, forms the basis of the church, "in which the tradition from the apostles has always been preserved by those who are from everywhere, because of its more excellent origin" (III, 3.2). The emphasis on apostolic succession and the church provides Irenaeus with a given context for reading scripture and understanding God's plan for salvation. And both of these, Irenaeus contends, are resolutely historical. Hence his general dismissal of allegory, or at least a certain type of it, as inadequate, that is, unfaithful to the sense of scripture and history transmitted through the prophetic and apostolic archive. So, for instance, when Irenaeus discusses the events leading up to and comprising the eschaton, he notes that we should not "try to understand such prophecies as allegories" (V, 35.1). The events related to the end, that is, "cannot be understood as occurring in the supercelestial realms," but rather "will take place in the times of the kingdom, when the earth has been renewed by Christ and Jerusalem has been rebuilt after the model of the Jerusalem above" (V, 35.2).

Before proceeding, it is worth stopping for a moment to dwell on the nature of allegory, as a means of understanding Irenaeus' specific complaint. Despite Irenaeus' attempt to distance himself and the substance of Christianity from allegorical interpretations of scripture, such approaches were a mainstay of early, medieval, and early-modern Christianity, and its surrounding cultures more generally. Without going here into a full-fledged theory, allegorical readings of texts for the most part focused on drawing out "hidden" meanings behind the literal content, as a way of conveying moral, political, and spiritual truths above and beyond a text's relatively clear sense. Contemporary biblical scholars and other interpreters generally regard such interpretative approaches as pre-critical. So understood, an allegorical approach remains largely useless for grasping the socio-historical sense of a given text, even if it remained a popular device.

It is not surprising, then, that despite Irenaeus' reservations, his own reading of prior traditions can also be said to rely on allegory, and specifically typology, especially with regard to his notion of recapitulation. The more immediate inspiration for the latter is, however, Paul, and so in this sense Irenaeus can claim apostolic warrant. In Romans 5, Paul juxtaposes Adam and Christ, associating the former with sin, law, death, and the like and the latter with obedience, grace, and eternal life. One can, of course, read Paul here in disjunctive terms, in the sense that Christ institutes a radical novelty that breaks with the prior arc that had, in his view, governed history up to Christ's death and resurrection. Generally speaking, such a reading has been crucial to the popular and, to a certain extent, theological reception of Paul in Protestant Christianity, with its emphasis on a sharp distinction between law (Judaism) and grace (Christianity).[3] Contemporary biblical scholars have, of course, criticized that view by situating Paul squarely in his context, and it is clear from Paul himself that he does not understand

---

3. The disjunctive reading has also, unfortunately, been one of the drivers of Christian anti-Semitism. The literature on this subject is, at this point, well-established, and there is no need to rehearse it here. But for a discussion of some of the key issues, see for instance Daniel Boyarin, *A Radical Jew: Paul and the Politics of Identity* (Berkeley, CA: University of California Press, 1997).

his emphasis on grace in the supercessionist terms that would later form the mainstream of the Christian theological, ecclesial, and interpretative traditions. Paul notes later on in Romans, for instance, that salvation in Christ does not obviate God's covenant with Israel but, rather, serves as a means of grafting the Gentiles into that covenant (Rom. 11.17).

Nevertheless, even in Romans 5, Paul's juxtaposition of Adam and Christ functions not so much to dichotomize the relationship between sin and, by extension, law with grace but rather to knot them together. Although on the surface Adam and Christ function as opposites, the deeper logic of Paul's argument sees them in continuity with each other, with Christ unraveling and ultimately reversing what was done in Adam. Paul writes:

> Therefore just as one man's trespass led to condemnation for all, so one man's act of righteousness leads to justification and life for all. For just as by one man's disobedience the many were made sinners, so by one man's obedience the many will be made righteous. But law came in, with the result that the trespass multiplied; but where sin increased, grace abounded all the more, so that, just as sin exercised dominion in death, so grace might also exercise dominion through justification leading to eternal life through Jesus Christ our Lord. (Rom. 5.18-21)

This is why, in 1 Corinthians 15, Paul refers to Jesus as the "second" or "last" Adam. Paul notes that the "first man [Adam] was from the earth, a man of dust; the second man is from heaven. As was the man of dust, so are those who are of the dust; and as is the man of heaven, so are those who are of heaven. Just have we have borne the image of the man of dust, we will also bear the image of the man from heaven" (vv. 46-49).

Now, particularly in reference to Paul's claim in I Corinthians 15, it is tempting to read Paul's use of allegory, and specifically typology, immaterially and a-historically. Paul's contrast between the "spiritual" and the "physical," "heaven" and "earth," would seem to support such a reading. Indeed, such is a common complaint against allegorical interpretations of scripture more generally, as we see even for Irenaeus. In his introduction to the history and use of allegory, Jeremy Tambling, for instance, traces Christian reliance on allegory as an interpretative strategy directly back to Paul. Allegory, on this account, becomes a means of re-reading texts, and specifically the Hebrew Bible/Old Testament, "outside the rigid constraints of the literal, outside the letter of the law."[4] Tambling goes on to note that "[t]hinking allegorically means escaping the material; so St Paul's successors in biblical interpretation disregarded the literal meaning of the Bible in their reading."[5]

---

4. Jeremy Tambling, *Allegory* (London: Routledge, 2010), 22.
5. Tambling, *Allegory*, 22.

To be sure, allegorical interpretations of scripture can at times border on the excessive, as Irenaeus exhibits with respect to his opponents. Nevertheless, a more generous view of an allegorical approach to reading would stress that it is not so much about denying any so-called literal reading but, rather, drawing out multiple meanings that cannot be reduced to the literal. Otherwise put, it recognizes a pluralism at work in texts and our approach to them, without *necessarily* dismissing other, viable readings, including the literal, relatively plain sense on the surface.[6] Moreover, although Paul relies on a series of disjunctions that would seem to function as a way of "escaping the material," his pairing of Adam and Christ via typology actually serves to historicize the economy of salvation, at least it seems so on his view.

Stanislas Breton's reading of Paul is important for grasping this point. Breton pushes the notion of a pluralism at work in texts, which I mentioned above, toward the ontological register. For Breton, allegory is not merely a method applied to texts but, in addition, corresponds to history itself. That is to say, allegory is possible as a means of interpretation because history is, in a certain sense, allegorical. Historical events, according to Breton, are not merely self-identical, reducible to what we might consider their surface-level significance. Events, rather, are haunted by "[a] kind of 'excess' [that] makes the identity of these events tremble, conferring on them a futural excess."[7] Being, in this sense, is a being-toward, meaning that events strain toward a future through which they will become what they are within the contingent play of history. For this reason, Breton notes that, for Paul, the economy of salvation cannot be reduced to pure succession, as if Christ merely comes after Adam. The economy of salvation, rather, evinces that history "obeys a law of progressive determination." Breton writes further:

> Each epoch has a singular style of interpretation. Abraham is not Moses. The time of kings, dominated by the figure of David, is not that of the Babylonian exile. The era of prophecy allows us to privilege the sorrowful figure of Jeremiah. And the "servant of Yahweh" in Isaiah (53.1ff) forms a kind of hallmark of the figurative tradition thanks to the precision of its features, in which the Christians (cf. Acts 8.26-35) like to read the passion and death of Christ. Each epoch thus entrusts to the following one the task of adding, as in the margins of a sketch, the specific mark of its originality. It all happens as if time, imagined as a scriptural space, integrates the differences inscribed

---

6. I draw the term "pluralism" to describe allegory from Henri de Lubac, *Medieval Exegesis* (vol. 1; trans. Mark Sebanc; Grand Rapids, MI: Eerdmans, 1998), 31. See also R. P. C. Hanson, *Allegory and Event: A Study of the Sources and Significance of Origen's Interpretation of Scripture* (Louisville, KY: Westminster John Knox Press, 2002).

7. Stanislas Breton, *A Radical Philosophy of Saint Paul* (trans. Joseph N. Ballan; New York: Columbia University Press, 2011), 64.

within it as it moves along, so that it might eventually outline, under the invisible hand that guides those differences, the self-portrait of Christ.[8]

Now, it is important to emphasize that Breton's notion of excess, which allegory marks and untangles, cannot be reduced to a vulgar Hegelian reading that would understand events as containing *in nuce* their later, historical significance.[9] Events, in other words, are not auto-affective or self-fulfilling but aleatory, wracked with the contingency of their appearing. It is rather the case that the possibility ostensibly contained in an event is imposed on it from the discontinuity of a later event, which will retroactively create a sequence between the two. Breton, for example, notes, "The sequence in which they take place has nothing like a sufficient reason that would unite the efficiency of causality with the infirmity of the 'sign.'"[10]

The possibilities contained in events are thus animated, or made actual, by the force of the future. Events, and the history or economy to which they belong, takes the form of retroaction and anticipation. Breton thus writes,

> Retrospection is a regressive march, but one that returns, each time it stops, in the prospective design of the future. Where we might distinguish two movements, the allegorical method invites us to discern the correlative aspects of a single process, for the *going back* toward the past is also, and indissolubly, the *moving forward* of the past toward "the One who comes."[11]

This is the structure, Breton argues, that we see in Paul and his use of the biblical traditions available to him to construct the significance of Christ within the economy of salvation. But we also see it at work more deliberately in Irenaeus and, moreover, in the philosophy of Alain Badiou. Focusing on the interplay of retroaction and anticipation in more detail in Badiou's philosophy provides of way of further grasping the sense of recapitulation in Irenaeus.

Badiou's Philosophy of the Event

A detailed overview of Badiou's complex system is well beyond the scope of this chapter. Suffice it to say that central to Badiou's philosophy is the notion of the event. At an intuitive level, an event is simply an unanticipated

---

8. Breton, *A Radical Philosophy of Saint Paul*, 65.
9. Badiou himself relies on such a reading of Hegel in *Saint Paul: The Foundation of Universalism* (trans. Ray Brassier; Stanford, CA: Stanford University Press, 2003), 65–74, to emphasize the importance of the resurrection over-against Christ. Badiou himself, however, presents a more complex reading of Hegel in *Theory of the Subject* (trans. Bruno Bosteels; London: Continuum, 2009), 3–50.
10. Breton, *A Radical Philosophy of Saint Paul*, 66.
11. Breton, *A Radical Philosophy of Saint Paul*, 67.

rupture in a situation (*Being and Event*) or world (*Logics of Worlds*).[12] An event breaks with the rules that normally govern a situation or world, proposing to it a novel opportunity, one that has the potential to radically reshape the context in which it occurs. Badiou gives numerous examples of events throughout his work, drawn from the spheres of science, art, poetry, and love, the four domains in which recognized truth procedures can occur.[13] Although each of these spheres has particular formal features that mark them as distinct, what each share is a potential to disrupt, even to the point of how we understand these domains themselves. The occurrence of an event, and the sequence of truth it initiates, implies that things will never be the same again.

In more formal terms, events "are singular multiplicities, which are presented but not represented. These are multiples which belong to the situation without being included in the latter: they are elements but not subsets."[14] Although we cannot here develop the intricacies of Badiou's ontology, suffice it to say that the rudimentary relationship that governs all situations is that of belonging and, by extension, inclusion. Badiou draws the language, here, from set theory, but at a basic level what it implies is that the way in which situations are organized has nothing to do with any substantial qualities but just the fact of organization itself. Situations become situations, that is, when something is counted as *belonging* to that situation. Since what belongs is essentially multiple, the various parts of the "something" in question can also be counted, or *included* in the situation. All situations, in this sense, are counted at least twice: first, at the level of belonging, or the structure of the situation; second, at the level of inclusion, the meta-structure or state of a situation. Badiou also marks the difference between these two operations as that between presentation (belonging) and representation (inclusion).[15]

An event emerges in the difference between belonging and inclusion, which Badiou also refers to as the point of excess in a situation. Now, for Badiou, all historical situations are more or less constituted on the basis of this excess. The maintenance of any situation, its relative stability, depends

---

12. Alain Badiou, *Being and Event* (trans. Oliver Feltham; London: Continuum, 2005); Alain Badiou, *Logics of Worlds* (trans. Alberto Toscano; London: Continuum, 2009).

13. These domains are recognized and discussed throughout Badiou's work, but for an introduction to how these function within the context of his philosophy, see the essays gathered in Alain Badiou, *Infinite Thought* (trans. and ed. Oliver Feltham and Justin Clemens; London: Continuum, 2004).

14. Badiou, *Being and Event*, 174.

15. I am, of course, offering an extremely condensed picture here, but all this is outlined in in detail in Parts I and II of *Being and Event*.

upon minimizing the gap between belonging and inclusion as much as possible. Otherwise put, the goal is to count the count, so to speak, representing what has been presented in the structure of the situation at the level of its state or metastructure. Representation is thus an attempt to control a situation, to ward off any potential that its logic may be disrupted by an abnormality. Nevertheless, because Badiou's ontology mandates that being is an essentially inconsistent multiplicity, or void, based on the in-existence of the one, it is impossible to fully secure inclusion in terms of belonging, especially when we are speaking of contingent historical sequences and formations. Badiou thus notes that the "form-multiple of historicity is what lies entirely within the instability of the singular; it is that upon which the state's metastructure has no hold. It is a point of subtraction from the state's re-securing of the count."[16]

Badiou refers to this point of subtraction as an evental site, which is an "entirely abnormal multiple; that is, a multiple such that none of its elements are presented in the situation."[17] An evental site belongs to its situation, but what composes it, its various elements or parts, are not represented by and for the situation. Badiou will insist that such a site is thus "on the edge of the void."[18] The distinction here is crucial. Because the site belongs to its situation but its elements do not, the latter circulate in the situation without themselves being presented. The elements of the evental site, in this sense, thus constitute an uncounted, and thus unaccounted for, excess for the situation.

It is from this excess that an event may emerge, but "may" is the operative word, here: there is no necessary connection between an evental site and an event. That is to say, although an evental site is prerequisite for the existence of an event, the former is always "only ever a *condition of being* for the event."[19] An evental site, that is, "merely opens up the possibility of an event," but it is "always possible that no event actually occur."[20] To use a different philosophical terminology, an evental site is a necessary, but not sufficient, condition for an event. Indeed, technically speaking, a site is only qualified as evental retroactively, through the actual occurrence of an event. It is the event itself, in this sense, that shows the possibilities inherent in its situation, and not the other way around: to adopt the latter stance would amount to essentializing the relationship between the two.

As I will point out in a moment, drawing an event from its site and putting it into circulation in a situation is a radically contingent affair, and

16. Badiou, *Being and Event*, 174.
17. Badiou, *Being and Event*, 175.
18. Badiou, *Being and Event*, 175.
19. Badiou, *Being and Event*, 179; original emphasis.
20. Badiou, *Being and Event*, 179.

depends on what Badiou refers to as intervention. Nevertheless, for now we can note that Badiou formally defines an event in the following way: "*I term event of the site X a multiple such that it is composed of, on the one hand, elements of the site, and on the other hand, itself.*"[21] On the one hand, and as mentioned above, an event is composed of a situation's excess, defined locally as those elements in a site that are not represented in the situation. On the other hand, an event belongs to itself, which means that it presents itself as the condensation of the situation's excess over-against its exclusion by the state of the situation. As Badiou puts it, an event "presents itself as an immanent résumé and one-mark of its own multiple"; an event is "supernumerary to the sole numbering of the terms of its site, despite it presenting such a numbering. The event is thus clearly the multiple which both presents its entire site, and, by means of the pure signifier of itself immanent to its own multiple, manages to present the presentation itself, that is, the one of the infinite multiple that it is."[22] Ontologically speaking, Badiou will maintain that an event refers to "what-is-not-being-qua-being," since being as such prohibits self-belonging.[23] But what this means in more concrete terms is that an event is always irreducible to the conditions that govern a particular situation, including the various historical determinants and acceptable forms of knowledge therein. To call the event "irreducible" is not to suggest by any means that it is a-historical, a sort of miraculous exception to what is.[24] It is, rather, to say that situations are always essentially incomplete: there is always something that evades the count, which is where events come in.

Nevertheless, because an event occurs as an exception to what is, its occurrence is, strictly speaking, undecidable from the perspective of the situation to which it belongs. Another way to put the matter is to say that it is impossible to delineate an event with respect to the governing knowledge of its situation. With a clear nod to Pascal, Badiou notes that an event's existence thus relies on a wager, on an actual decision for its belonging to the situation. Although the occurrence of an event cannot be reduced to a decision, only a wager marks an event as an event. The wager, then, is essential for putting an event into circulation in the situation, even though qua event it can never be reduced to its situation. If it could be so reduced,

---

21. Badiou, *Being and Event*, 179; original emphasis.
22. Badiou, *Being and Event*, 180.
23. Badiou, *Being and Event*, 184–90.
24. This is, of course, a common complaint made against Badiou's notion of the event. See, for instance, Daniel Bensaïd, "Alain Badiou and the Miracle of the Event," in *Think Again: Alain Badiou and the Future of Philosophy* (ed. Peter Hallward; London: Continuum, 2004), 94–105.

or legitimatized according to established conditions and conventions, one would get rid of the need for a wager, which is akin to denying the event itself. Badiou thus notes that "one can only hope that this wager never becomes legitimate, inasmuch as any legitimacy refers back to the structure of the situation."[25]

Badiou gives the term "intervention" to this wager on an event, which refers to "any procedure by which a multiple is recognized as an event."[26] Intervention assumes the inherent undecidability of whether an event belongs to the situation in which it occurs, but it decides on this undecidability. There is, however, a certain amount of paradox at work here, for once an event is decided upon, an event is, in effect, canceled or annulled qua event, since it then becomes a term of the situation. As a way of remedying this paradox, Badiou insists on a gap between an event itself as undecidable and its name or, put more exactly, the various acts of nomination that render it susceptible to decision and help chart its trajectory. Intervention, the wager on an event, lies closer to nomination than the event itself, which must always exist in a sort of indeterminable liminal space. Badiou writes:

> The act of nomination of the event is what constitutes it, not as real—we will always posit that this multiple has occurred—but as susceptible to a decision concerning its belonging to a situation. The essence of the intervention consists—within the field opened up by an interpretive hypothesis, whose *presented* object is the site (a multiple on the edge of the void), and which concerns the "there is" of an event—in naming this "there is" and in unfolding the consequences of this nomination in the space of the situation to which the site belongs.[27]

Hinging intervention on nomination, however, results in a similar circle. That is, pushing the possibility of intervention, and the sequence that it institutes, onto the event's name does little more than substitute the name for the event itself. The novelty that the event may portend, in this sense, appears on the surface as the result of a theoretical sleight of hand.

It is at the point of this impasse that Badiou introduces the notion of eventual recurrence. Badiou writes of this notion:

> It is certain that the event alone, aleatory figure of non-being, founds the possibility of intervention. It is just as certain that if no intervention puts it into circulation within the situation on the basis of an extraction of elements from the site, then, lacking any being, radically subtracted from the count-as-one, the event does not exist. In order to avoid this curious mirroring of the

---

25. Badiou, *Being and Event*, 201.
26. Badiou, *Being and Event*, 202.
27. Badiou, *Being and Event*, 203.

event and the intervention—of the fact and the interpretation—*the possibility of the intervention must be assigned to the consequences of another event.* It is eventual recurrence which founds intervention. In other words, there is no interventional capacity, constitutive for the belonging of an eventual multiple to a situation, save within the network of consequences of a previously decided belonging. An intervention is what presents an event for the occurrence of another. It is an eventual between-two.[28]

What Badiou suggests, here, is that intervention is never direct, never a mirror of the event on which it ostensibly wagers. Events certainly occur, but their interpretative entrance into circulation in their situation via intervention is always disjunct or, as he puts it, diagonal. That is, intervention occurs less in relation to the event to which it ostensibly refers than to a prior, previously-decided eventual sequence. Or, rather, intervention is the between-space of events: intervention, that is, anticipates eventual novelty through retroaction. Badiou writes, for instance, that "intervention is a line drawn from one paradoxical multiple, which is already circulating, to the circulation of another, a line which scratches out. It is a *diagonal* of the situation."[29]

On the one hand, the notion of eventual recurrence combats what Badiou refers to as "speculative leftism." Although Badiou often uses lofty terms for the event, terms that imply that an event constitutes an almost miraculous break in history, he is otherwise skeptical of any attempt to assign to an event a "radical beginning."[30] This is just what speculative leftism attempts to do, in that it "imagines that intervention authorizes itself on the basis of itself alone; that it breaks with the situation without any other support than its own negative will."[31] Speculative leftism, then, constitutes an "imaginary wager," in that it "fails to recognize that the real of the conditions of possibility of intervention is always the circulation of an already decided event."[32] Speculative leftism is a species of anti-philosophy, which rejects the cold, hard work of deduction, so as "to break in two the history of the world," as Badiou quotes that pre-eminent of anti-philosophers, Nietzsche.[33]

On the other hand, because eventual recurrence rejects any sort of absolute novelty that would be utterly disjoined from its past and future, eventual

---

28. Badiou, *Being and Event*, 209.
29. Badiou, *Being and Event*, 210; original emphasis.
30. Badiou, *Being and Event*, 210.
31. Badiou, *Being and Event*, 210.
32. Badiou, *Being and Event*, 210.
33. Badiou, *Being and Event*, 210. See also Alain Badiou, "Who is Nietzsche?," *Pli* 11 (2001): 1–11. I have discussed the category of anti-philosophy at length as an essential feature of Badiou's philosophy in Hollis Phelps, *Alain Badiou: Between Theology and Anti-Theology* (Durham: Acumen, 2013), 87–120.

recurrence, as part and parcel of intervention, provides the conditions for a theory of time. Badiou writes:

> Time—if not coextensive with structure, if not the *sensible form of Law*—is intervention itself, thought as the gap between two events. The essential historicity of intervention does not refer to time as a measurable milieu. It is established upon interventional capacity inasmuch as the latter only separates itself from the situation by grounding itself on the circulation—which has already been decided—of an evental multiple. This ground alone, combined with the frequentation of the site, can introduce a sufficient amount of non-being between the intervention and the situation in order for being itself, qua being, to be wagered in the shape of the unpresentable and the illegal, that is in the final resort, as inconsistent multiplicity. Time is here, again, the requirement of the Two: for there to be an event, one must be able to situate oneself within the consequences of another.[34]

Intervention contains the very substance of time, which is shaped through the relationship between events, spread out of course among the various domains in which events can occur: science, art, politics, and love.

As Badiou notes in *Logics of Worlds*, there is an eternity at work in this conception of time, an eternity shaped through the material force of events. I will return to this notion momentarily, but for now, it is worth mentioning that when Badiou attempts to illustrate the notion of evental recurrence in *Being and Event*, he turns to the Christian narrative. Indeed, riffing on one of Lacan's claims that, among religious options, Christianity comes closest to the question of truth, Badiou notes that "[a]ll the parameters of the doctrine of the event are thus disposed in Christianity."[35] To be sure, from within the strictures of Badiou's ontology, Christianity remains beholden to "an ontology of presence" condensed in a pre-Cantorian articulation of infinity. Nevertheless, "at the heart of Christianity there is that event—situated, exemplary—that is the death of the son of God on the cross."[36]

The death of Christ is not, as Badiou points out, an isolated occurrence. It occurs in the midst of human life, which functions as the site of the event, as a means of registering its ultimate sense. The cross, Badiou notes, names life "summoned to its limit, to the pressure of its void, which is to say in the symbol of death, and of cruel, tortured, painful death."[37] Nevertheless, the

---

34. Badiou, *Being and Event*, 210; original emphasis.
35. Badiou, *Being and Event*, 212.
36. Badiou, *Being and Event*, 212. Badiou's reading of Christianity, in this sense, is different from the Pauline version he gives in *Saint Paul*. On Badiou's reading of Paul, Christ's death is not so much an event but its site; death, in other words, organizes the possibility of resurrection, which is the event proper for Badiou's Paul. See *Saint Paul*, 65–74.
37. Badiou, *Being and Event*, 212.

intervention on this event, its interpretation, cannot and does not rest on the cross alone, in an absolutist sense. Rather, the apostles unravel its sense progressively via nomination by situating it in relation to other events, namely Adam's original sin and the Last Judgment. Badiou writes:

> The intervention is based upon the circulation, within the Jewish milieu, of another event, Adam's original sin, of which the death of Christ is the relay. The connection between original sin and redemption definitively found the time of Christianity as a time of exile and salvation. There is an essential historicity to Christianity which is tied to the intervention of the apostles as the placement-into-circulation of the event of the death of God; itself reinforced by the promise of a Messiah which organized fidelity to the initial exile. Christianity is structured from beginning to end by eventurecurrence; moreover, it prepares itself for the divine hazard of the third event, the Last Judgement, in which the ruin of the terrestrial situation will be accomplished, and a new regime of existence will be established.[38]

Christ's death certainly constitutes an event, but the sense of it as an event, its eventness, so to speak, is only legible in light of original sin. The latter functions as the locus for intervention, but that locus, in turn, forms the body of the new eventual sequence found nascently in Christ's death on the cross. This is why, Badiou says, Christ's death is the "relay" of the original event. Moreover, Christ's death will become the opportunity to name a third event, the Last Judgment, the anticipation of which gives sense to the entire sequence via the medium of the cross. Eventual recurrence thus structures the Christian narrative through retroaction and anticipation, that is, under the mode of the future anterior. Indeed, this structure is doubled, in the sense that the meaning of original sin, which constitutes the basis of intervention, only makes sense retroactively, in light of its relay in the death of Christ; that death, in turn, only makes sense in light of the anticipation of judgment. The between-two of Christ's death on the cross, then, constitutes the Christian sense of time itself, as a diagonal of linked events. As Badiou puts it, "As soon as this interventional decision is taken, everything is clear, and the truth circulates throughout the entirety of the situation, under the emblem which names it: the Cross."[39]

Now, it is important to emphasize that, on Badiou's account, the situating of events in relationship to each other via eventual occurrence has no necessity about it, similar to what we saw with Breton in the previous section. For instance, original sin may, indeed, contain the seeds of Christ's death, but it only does so via the retroaction of that death. Otherwise put, it is intervention that connects events, and not events that shape intervention, at least in any substantial, auto-affective sense. This is because events are

---

38. Badiou, *Being and Event*, 213.
39. Badiou, *Being and Event*, 217.

fundamentally discontinuous, and only rendered legible after the fact via intervention. Any continuity among events is solely the result of an interpretative, retroactive decision, which forms the basis of evental recurrence. Badiou thus notes that the "intervention wagers upon a discontinuity with the previous fidelity solely in order to install an unequivocal continuity."[40]

Nevertheless, Badiou's insistence on the aleatory nature of events and the contingency of their recurrence does not prevent him from risking assigning a certain eternality to sequences, as mentioned above. Although interpreters have often focused on Badiou's doctrine of the event, in many ways the latter is only a means to an end. Badiou's notion of the event, that is, forms the basis of a theory of truths, which is arguably his main concern. This is evident, I think, in *Being and Event*, but it is explicit in *Logics of Worlds*, in which he argues against a certain "democratic materialism" that would reduce thought to bodies and languages. Badiou's counter-claim, "There are only bodies and languages, except that there are truths," thus serves as a sort of guiding axiom for *Logics of Worlds* but also, we could add, his philosophy as a whole. Insisting on the "except that" of truths, however, also necessitates thinking their persistence across time, despite the various discontinuities that the events on which they are based pose. Badiou will thus insist that once truths "have appeared, they compose an a-temporal meta-history."[41]

Nevertheless, despite the obvious Platonic hue that this notion of an "a-temporal meta-history" of truths has, truths remain contingent processes in the material world. The meta-history involved, that is, is not otherworldly, but situated in truths themselves or, more precisely, in the relay among truths via evental recurrence. In *Logics of Worlds*, the latter still remains operative, but in a different key, specifically in the notion of the resurrection of truths. Badiou outlines a formal theory of the subject in *Logics of Worlds*, which complicates the notion of the faithful subject as it is outlined in *Being and Event*.[42] The faithful subject remains central to *Logics of Worlds*, but in addition Badiou outlines two deviations from it, the reactive subject and the obscure subject. Whereas the faithful subject, as the name suggests, acts in fidelity to an event, the reactive subject resists the novelty of an event by attenuating it; the obscure subject, in contrast, actively opposes an event, occulting it by appealing to supposed substantial, transcendent principles. The obscure subject, Badiou writes, "calls on an atemporal fetish: the incorruptible and invisible over-body, be it City, God, or Race."[43]

---

40. Badiou, *Being and Event*, 219.
41. Badiou, *Logics of Worlds*, 9.
42. See Badiou, *Being and Event*, 391–409.
43. Badiou, *Being and Event*, 60.

What is important for my purposes, however, is that there are actually two figures of the faithful subject, or two destinations. Badiou notes that his division of the faithful subject in two is meant in part to address "the complexity of the subjective field in its historical scansion."[44] As mentioned above, one never really acts on an event directly, at least in most circumstances; a subject's relationship to an event is determined by the relationship that that event maintains with other events. In *Being and Event*, such a relationship, which finds its structure in retroaction and anticipation, goes under the name eventual recurrence, but Badiou describes a similar structure in *Logics of Worlds* under the notion of the resurrection of truths. Events, and the truths constructed from them, are on Badiou's account fragile, shot through with indeterminacy and uncertainty. That is just what it means to be undecidable from the perspective of a situation. The appearance of a truth via fidelity to an event, in other words, is not a guarantee of its continuance, especially given its susceptibility to denial and occultation. Truths, for lack of a better word, can be lost, but never absolutely.

This is where the notion of resurrection comes in. Resurrection names the procedure by which truths can be reappropriated or reactivated in a different context; to run with the metaphor, resurrection names the conversion of a once occulted truth from death to life. As Badiou puts it, "We will call this destination, which reactivates a subject in another logic of appearing-in-truth, *resurrection*. Of course, a resurrection presupposes a new world, which generates the context for a new event, a new trace, a new body—in short, a truth-procedure under whose rule the occulted fragment places itself after having been extracted from its occultation."[45] In *Logics of Worlds*, the possibility of resurrection depends on the eternality of truths, as mentioned above. As Badiou says again, "every truth is eternal; of not truth can it be said, under the pretext that its historical world has disintegrated, that it can be lost forever."[46] Badiou will thus say that resurrection names a "supplementary destination of subjective forms."[47]

Nevertheless, if we fold the notion of resurrection into the notion of eventual recurrence, resurrection is, for the most part, the primary form that fidelity takes in the production of truths. What resurrection implies, in other words, is a relay between truths: one reappropriates another truth in a different logic of appearing or world as a means of forcing the creation of a new truth, which will be sequentially connected with its past eventual impetus.

---

44. Badiou, *Being and Event*, 62.
45. Badiou, *Being and Event*, 65.
46. Badiou, *Being and Event*, 66.
47. Badiou, *Being and Event*, 66. Badiou labels his own reading of Paul in exactly these terms. His reading is, he says, a "reactivation" of Paul." See Badiou, *Saint Paul*, 2.

An occulted truth, for instance, serves as material for the creation of a new truth—and so on and so forth. Once again, we find ourselves within the structure of retroaction and anticipation, the future anterior of events and the truth procedures that issue from them.

Recapitulation: Reading Irenaeus with Badiou

In what follows, I read Irenaeus' notion of recapitulation in light of the basic framework of retroaction and anticipation that I have drawn out from Badiou's notion of the event, along with its attendant notions of intervention, eventual recurrence, and the resurrection of truths. Doing so, I contend, provides a way to read Irenaeus through a materialist lens, even if the content of his claims remains, for the most part, mythological. But it is not just a matter, here, of fitting Irenaeus and his notion of recapitulation into a foreign framework. The sense of Badiou's theory of the production of truths, as outlined above, is, I claim, already found with Irenaeus himself, and Badiou implicitly acknowledges as much in his use of the Christian narrative as an exemplar of the structure of eventual recurrence.

Against so-called Gnostic speculation, which generally devalues history as evil and reduces Christ to an ultimately disembodied spiritual phantom, Irenaeus emphasizes the irreducibly historical character of the incarnation. Now, to be sure, the notion of incarnation implies, to a certain extent, an a-historical core, much as does Badiou's notion of the eternality of truths. The Word of God, that is, still *becomes* human, which logically and theologically entails the priority, or pre-existence, of the Word over and above the history into which the Word enters. As with Badiou, what matters, however, is the manner in which this moment in which the eternal and the temporal collide is grasped. For Irenaeus, and unlike his opponents, the incarnation is not an instance of an "impossible Christ" who "come[s] down into Jesus," as if Jesus' body, his flesh and blood, were inconsequential. Rather, the human element, the incarnation's historicity, is all-important, even down to the suffering that Jesus endures. Contra the "impossible Christ," Irenaeus emphasizes that "Jesus, since he was Christ, suffered for us, slept and rose again, descended and ascended (Eph. 4.10), the Son of God became Son of Man" (III, 18.3).

But nor is Jesus "a mere man begotten by Joseph" (III, 19.1). Although writing well before the doctrine of Christ's two natures would receive its classical articulation at Chalcedon, Irenaeus hinges the notion of recapitulation, and the redemption it entails, on the interplay of the human and the divine or, more properly put, the gap between the two. On the one hand, it is essential that Jesus qua Christ be fully human, that he enter the human condition in its entirety, even up to death. Only a human being, that is, can recapitulate the human condition, and show what human beings can and should be. Irenaeus writes, for instance, that the Son of God

> was made in the likeness of sinful flesh to condemn sin and expel it, thus condemned, from the flesh (Rom. 8.3) and also to call man to become like him, assigning him to God as imitator (Eph. 5.1), raising him into the kingdom of the Father and giving him the ability to see God and comprehend the Father. This Word of God which dwelt in man was made Son of man to accustom man to perceive God and to accustom God to dwell in man, according to the good pleasure of the Father. (III, 19.3)

Likewise, he notes, "For if flesh and blood were not to be saved the Word of God would not have become flesh (John 1.14) and if the blood of the just were not to be requited the Lord would not have had blood" (V, 14.1). Otherwise put, the Son of God, qua Christ, has to take on "perishability" and "mortality" in order to convert these aspects of the human condition into "imperishability" and "immortality" (III, 19.1). To quote Irenaeus again, "And how could we have been united with imperishability and immortality unless imperishability and immortality had first been made what we are, so that what was perishable might be absorbed by imperishability, and what was mortal by immortality (I Cor. 15.53-54), 'that we might receive adoption as sons' (Gal. 4.5)?" (III, 19.1).

Nevertheless, Christ's humanity must also be exceptional, irreducible to the human condition up to his incarnation. Although the exceptional character of Christ is, in one way or another, part and parcel of virtually all theological formulations of his person, Irenaeus' articulation of it differs importantly from later formulations. To give just one example, take Athanasius' formulation in *On the Incarnation*. For Athanasius, prior to their disobedience human beings were originally united with the Word of God, a union which protected them, so to speak, from the natural state of corruption and mortality. Death does not enter the picture as a punishment per se but, rather, as the result of the dissolution via sin of the bond between God and humans. Athanasius writes:

> For because of the Word dwelling with them, even their natural corruption did not come near them, as Wisdom also says: God made man for incorruption, and as an image of His own eternity; but by envy of the devil death came into the world. But when this had come to pass, men began to die, while corruption thence-forward prevailed against them, gaining even more than its natural power over the whole race, inasmuch as it had, owing to the transgression of the commandment, the threat of the Deity as a further advantage against them.[48]

---

48. Athanasius, *On the Incarnation* (Crestwood, NY: St. Vladimir's Seminary Press, 2003), 5.2.

Christ, in essence, restores this bond, re-establishing what was broken through transgression. Christ "turn[s] them again toward incorruption, and quicken[s] them from death by the appropriation of His body and by the grace of the Resurrection, banishing death from them like straw from the fire."[49]

The outcome, for Irenaeus, is largely the same, but the starting point differs, at least to a certain extent. Irenaeus does, of course, rely on the language of sin as a transgression throughout his discussion of the impact of the incarnation, and considers human beings as enslaved to "the primal disobedience" (III, 19.1). But it is less clear that for Irenaeus Christ's recapitulation of human being and history is a restoration of a prior state or bond. Irenaeus, for instance, notes that those who remain enslaved to transgression are "not yet mingled with the Word of God the Father nor sharing in freedom through the Son" (III, 19.1). He goes on to say that human beings only "mingle" with the word as the result of recapitulation: "For this the Word of God became man, and the Son of God Son of man, that man, mingled with the Word and thus receiving adoption, might become a son of God" (III, 19.1). Christ's death and resurrection, his recapitulation of human historicity, is less a restoration and more a novelty, a novelty that by definition is certainly potential in human beings but that does not come to fruition until the incarnation.

This is why, coupled with imagery of a "fall," Irenaeus also insists on a more progressive view of salvation, which takes the exposure to corruptibility as essential to what human beings will become via Christ's entrance into history. The whole affair, for Irenaeus, seems more of a learning process for immature humanity than anything else. Irenaeus, for example, writes:

> This, then, was God's generosity. He allowed man to pass through every situation and to know death and then come to the resurrection from the dead, and learning by experience that from which he had been liberated, might always be grateful to the Lord, having obtained the gift of imperishability from him, and might love him more, for "he to whom more is forgiven loves more" (Luke 7.42-47). (III, 19.3)

Indeed, Irenaeus relies on the metaphors of "growth" and "increase" to indicate how the economy of salvation works. Noting the importance of imitating Christ's "works and doing his words" as a means of "communion with him," Irenaeus writes that "we who are newly created receive growth from him who was perfect before the whole creation, who alone is excellent and good" (V, 1.1). Likewise, referring to the Eucharist, he notes, "And because we are his members (I Cor. 6.15) and are nourished by means of the creation

---

49. Athanasius, *On the Incarnation*, 8.

... he declared that the cup from the creation is his blood, out of which he makes our blood increase, and the bread from the creation is his body, out of which he makes our body grow" (V, 2.2). All in all, for Irenaeus, salvation is about "progress in being," rather than a reversion to a primordial state (V, 36.1).

Such progress, however, hinges on the uniqueness of Christ in his humanity. Communion with God has to pass through humanity, since it is the human being that is at issue. Otherwise put, only a real human being can effect salvation for human beings. This should be obvious, based on what has been stated above and considering the locus of salvation, for Irenaeus. Theoretically, God could have fashioned an entirely new creature, but this would void the notion of recapitulation, which just *is* how God's economy of salvation works. Irenaeus writes that God did not "take dust anew" to fashion Christ, so "that there would not be another fashioning nor another work fashioned to be saved but that the same being might be recapitulated, with the likeness preserved" (III, 21.9). In order for Christ to recapitulate Adam, they must both possess a "like origin" (III, 21.10).

The problem, of course, is that no normal human being fits the required bill, due to humanity's exposure to corruption and mortality. Drawing on various biblical texts, Irenaeus writes that "not one among the sons of Adam is properly called God and Lord" (III, 19.2). Christ, then, has to be human, but not "a mere man begotten by Joseph" (III, 19.1). Hence the need for a human, but more "brilliant origin," that is, "the brilliant birth from the Virgin" (III, 19.2).[50] On the one hand, being born of Mary gives Jesus a human lineage, one that, moreover, stretches back to Adam, at least according to the genealogy that Luke gives in his gospel. Irenaeus writes that Christ, as Word of God, recapitulates "Adam in himself, [and] from Mary still a virgin rightly received the generation that is the recapitulation of Adam" (III, 21.10). It is thus from Mary that Christ receives his humanity, and not just formally but actually, down to the latter's most mundane features. "Why would Christ have come down into her if he was to receive nothing from her?" Irenaeus asks rhetorically. "And if he had received nothing from Mary he would never have taken foods derived from the earth; after fasting forty days like Moses and Elijah he would not have felt hunger because his body needed food ... All these are signs of the flesh taken from the earth, which he recapitulated in himself, saving what he had formed" (III, 22.2).

Mary's real analogue, however, is Eve. Recapitulation cuts two ways here. First, Irenaeus plays with the notion of virginity to connect Mary and

---

50. Irenaeus is here referring to Isa. 53.8 and 7.14, respectively.

Eve on the basis of the dialectic between disobedience and obedience. At the time of Eve's seduction and disobedience, she is, like Mary, a "betrothed virgin" (V, 19.1).[51] But whereas Eve's virginity functions as a precursor to disobedience, Mary's virginity becomes the mark of obedience, meaning that she recapitulates Eve's prelapsarian state as a means of salvation. Irenaeus writes:

> For just as Eve had Adam for a husband but was still a virgin ... and by disobeying became the cause of death for herself and the whole human race, so also with Mary, with a husband predestined for her but yet a virgin, was obedient and became the cause of salvation for herself and the whole human race. (III, 22.4)

In effect, what Mary's virginal obedience does is unravel Eve's disobedience, reversing the course, so to speak, of history. Mary's virginity effects a "recycling" for Eve:

> For what had been tied cannot be loosed unless one reverses the ties of the knot so that the first ties are undone by the second, and the second free the first: thus it happens that the first tie is unknotted by the second and the second has the place of a tie for the first ... So too the knot of Eve's disobedience was loosed by Mary's obedience, for what the virgin Eve had bound by her unfaith, the virgin Mary loosed by her faith. (III, 22.4)

Second, Irenaeus doubles back Mary's recapitulation of Eve into Adam, as a means of understanding Christ's recapitulation of Adam and, thus, humanity as a whole. I have already indicated above the way that virginity functions to connect Eve and Mary, but Irenaeus also rules out Joseph as Jesus' father in similar fashion. It is necessary for Christ not to be the product of an earthly father, not only due to "primal disobedience" but also because Adam himself was uniquely fashioned. Adam, to put it straightforwardly, was not the product of an earthly father either, but was rather directly fashioned by God out of the materials of the earth. Irenaeus writes, "If then the first Adam (I Cor. 15.45) had had a man for father and had been born of the seed of a man, the heretics could rightly say that the second Adam (15.47) was generated by Joseph. But if the first Adam was taken from the earth and fashioned by the Word of God, it was necessary, working in himself the recapitulation of

---

51. Like much of the Christian theological tradition, Irenaeus places the blame on Eve, even though the myth in Genesis clearly indicates that Adam was with her. That reading has, unfortunately, done much at both a theological and material level to reinforce various forms of patriarchy, in the church but in culture more generally. Such patriarchy is, moreover, further reinforced in the focus on virginity. Although it is important to emphasize the theological function that the connection between Eve and Mary has for Irenaeus within his doctrine of recapitulation, it remains the case that his articulation relies on sexist assumptions and paradigms.

Adam, possessed a like origin" (III, 21.10). That "like origin" assures, for Irenaeus, that Christ recapitulates the same humanity that he is, while also functioning as a sort of inclusive exclusion that actually makes recapitulation possible.[52]

Now, this notion of recapitulation obviously relies on a mythology that is, to be blunt, impossible to accept as literal, for numerous reasons. But, if we follow Badiou, we can extract the material core on which the doctrine appears to be built. Granted, from a strictly theological perspective, it may be impossible to dissociate the core from the myth, especially since the latter has salvation as its locus. There are, of course, other models of redemption available in the theological tradition, which run the gamut from the more to less mythological. Any theological use of recapitulation, however, must contend with the way in which Eve and Mary, Adam and Christ, function as relays of redemption based on the assumed specificity of their persons, and Irenaeus, as mentioned, rules out treating them as mere allegories.

But the structure present in the notion, the core around which the drama of redemption revolves, assumes the importance of retroaction and anticipation, as we find it in Badiou's theory of eventual truths. Adam and Eve's transgression functions as an "event" that exposes humankind to corruption and perishability, but the ultimate sense of this "event" is only legible retroactively, via Christ's introduction of incorruption and imperishability through his incarnation, life, and death. The former anticipates the latter, but such anticipation only properly appears retroactively, in the Christ-event's recapitulation of the Adam-and-Eve-event. Christ's recapitulation of the original event, moreover, anticipates a third event, the "resurrection of the just" (V, 33.4) and the renewal of the earth (V, 35.2). Again, though, it is this third event that will ultimately indicate the real sense of the second: Christ's resurrection anticipates it, but only inchoately; the upshot of the resurrection for history entire will only have become apparent once human beings "take back their bodies and rise perfect, that is, bodily, as also the Lord rose, and thus will come to the vision of God" (V, 31.2). The relationship between events here is also, moreover, redoubled individually, in the couplings Eve/Mary and Adam/Christ. The former individual in each pair anticipates the latter, but the meaning of the former for history can only be grasped retroactively, in the relay that the latter institute. In sum, Irenaeus' notion of recapitulation has the structure of eventual recurrence, which for Badiou is the substance of time and history itself, and—conversely—Badiou's notion of

---

52. The language of "inclusive exclusion" comes from Giorgio Agamben. See Giorgio Agamben, *Homo Sacer: Sovereign Power and Bare Life* (trans. Daniel Heller-Roazen; Stanford. CA: Stanford University Press, 1998), 1–29.

evental recurrence finds an impetus in Irenaeus, in a theological articulation of the trajectory of history. We might say, in this sense, that Badiou "recapitulates" Irenaeus, endowing the latter's notion with a formality that allows for its non-theological, material use.

Conclusion

I mentioned above Breton's notion of allegory, as indicating a certain excess that haunts historical events. Allegory is not for Breton only a method of interpretation, a means of drawing out a "spiritual" sense that works behind the scenes, so to speak, of literal sense. Allegory is, rather, the nature of history itself, in that events always contain more than what they initially indicate. The "more" that events contain, however, can only properly be grasped retroactively, in light of their contingent futures.

We see a similar notion of excess at work, I think, in both Irenaeus and Badiou. Irenaeus rejects so-called Gnostic allegory for its tendency to devalue the historical, but this does not amount to a wholesale rejection of allegory itself: he relies, rather, on a typological interpretation of scripture generally, via Paul, condensing the salvific sense of history into the material figures of Adam, Eve, Mary, and Christ. The structure of recapitulation gives to these figures more than their respective self-identities contain, meaning that they each harbor an excess that becomes legible through the interplay of anticipation and retroaction. Likewise, with Badiou, events are always in excess over the situation in which they occur, but this excess is doubled in the interrelation among events marked in the notion of eventual recurrence. The latter notion understands events, again, through anticipation and retroaction, but that particular structure only works if events themselves strain toward more than they initially contain, so to speak. Indeed, for Badiou, it is this excess that makes time itself possible, which also means that time can never be reduced to simple occurrence. My reading of the relationship between Irenaeus and Badiou, then, may contribute to the construction of a materialist theory of allegory, one that allows us to read history allegorically, in the sense outlined above, because it is always already allegorical. Recapitulation, on my account, is not just a theological model but, perhaps, helps us grasp the movement of history, at least once shorn of its mythological components.

Biographical Note

Hollis Phelps is an Associate Professor of Interdisciplinary Studies in the Department of Liberal Studies at Mercer University, Macon GA (USA). He is the author of *Alain Badiou: Between Theology and Anti-Theology* and co-editor of *Religion and European Philosophy: Key Thinkers from Kant to Zizek*, both published by Routledge. His most recent book is *Jesus and the Politics of Mammon*, published by Cascade Books.

Bibliography

Agamben, Giorgio. *Homo Sacer: Sovereign Power and Bare Life*. Translated by Daniel Heller-Roazen. Stanford, CA: Stanford University Press, 1998.

Athanasius. *On the Incarnation*. Crestwood, NY: St. Vladimir's Seminary Press, 2003.

Badiou, Alain. "Who is Nietzsche?" *Pli* 11 (2001): 1–11.

—*Saint Paul: The Foundation of Universalism*. Translated by Ray Brassier. Stanford, CA: Stanford University Press, 2003.

—*Infinite Thought*. Translated and edited by Oliver Feltham and Justin Clemens. London: Continuum, 2004.

—*Being and Event*. Translated by Oliver Feltham. London: Continuum, 2005.

—*Logics of Worlds*. Translated by Alberto Toscano. London: Continuum, 2009.

—*Theory of the Subject*. Translated by Bruno Bosteels. London: Continuum, 2009. https://doi.org/10.5040/9781350252042

Bensaïd, Daniel. "Alain Badiou and the Miracle of the Event," 94–105 in *Think Again: Alain Badiou and the Future of Philosophy*. Edited by Peter Hallward. London: Continuum, 2004.

Boyarin, Daniel. *A Radical Jew: Paul and the Politics of Identity.* Berkeley, CA: University of California Press, 1997.

Breton, Stanislas. *A Radical Philosophy of Saint Paul*. Translated by Joseph N. Ballan. New York: Columbia University Press, 2011.

Hanson, R. P. C. *Allegory and Event: A Study of the Sources and Significance of Origen's Interpretation of Scripture*. Louisville, KY: Westminster John Knox Press, 2002.

Irenaeus, *Against Heresies*. Translated by Alexander Roberts and William Rambaut. *Ante-Nicene Fathers*. Volume 1. Edited by Alexander Roberts, James Donaldson, and A. Cleveland Coxe. Buffalo, NY: Christian Literature Publishing, 1885.

de Lubac, Henri. *Medieval Exegesis*. Volume 1. Translated by Mark Sebanc. Grand Rapids, MI: Eerdmans, 1998.

Phelps, Hollis. *Alain Badiou: Between Theology and Anti-Theology*. Durham: Acumen, 2013. https://doi.org/10.4324/9781315729862

Tambling, Jeremy. *Allegory*. London: Routledge, 2010. https://doi.org/10.4324/9780203462126

Williams, Michael Allen. *Rethinking "Gnosticism": An Argument for Dismantling a Dubious Category*. Princeton, NJ: Princeton University Press, 1996. https://doi.org/10.1515/9781400822218

PART IV
Judith Butler

Chapter Thirteen

Judith Butler and Early Christian Texts

Matthew G. Whitlock

Introduction

Part of what a body does (to use the phrase of Deleuze, derived from his reading of Spinoza) is to open onto the body of another, or a set of others, and for this reason bodies are not self-enclosed entities. They are always in some sense outside themselves, exploring or navigating their environment, extended and even sometimes dispossessed through the senses. If we can become lost in another, or if our tactile, motile, haptic, visual, olfactory, or auditory capacities comport us beyond ourselves, that is because the body does not stay in its own place, and because dispossession of this kind characterizes bodily sense more generally.[1]

—Judith Butler, "Body Vulnerability, Coalition Politics"

... precisely because bodies are formed and sustained in relation to infrastructural supports (or their absence) and social and technological networks or webs of relation, we cannot extract the body from its constituting relations—and those relations are always economically and historically specific.[2]

—Judith Butler, "Body Vulnerability, Coalition Politics"

In contextualizing the work of Judith Butler, I want to return to Benjamin's thought image of the archaeological dig, of marking "the exact location" where one enters into a vertical dig into the past. It is in the quest for "the exact location" where we question not only where the dig begins, but who or what is doing the digging in the present location. The answer for Butler would be concrete: bodies. However, the exactness of "bodies" certainly comes into question in Butler's work, especially since bodies are cited, reiterated, and defined by the norms of the location where the dig begins. In her

---

1. Judith Butler, *Notes Toward a Performative Theory of Assembly* (Cambridge, MA: Harvard University Press, 2015), 149. Butler is referring to a chapter in Gilles Deleuze's work on Spinoza: Gilles Deleuze, *Notes towards a Performative Theory: Spinoza* (trans. Martin Joughin; New York: Zone Books, 1992), 217–34. Here Deleuze asserts that Spinoza considers two fundamental questions as equivalent: "*What is the structure (fabrica) of a body?* And: *What can a body do?*" (p. 218). In other words, "relations are inseparable from the capacity to be affected," and "what a body can do corresponds to the natures and limits of its capacity to be affected" (p. 218).

2. Butler, *Performative Theory of Assembly*, 148.

early work, Butler rightly questions how we have defined the body, and as a result, introduces us to gender fluidity, both socially and materially, both in terms of gender and sex. In her later work, Butler extends her conceptions of the body to bodies, and how bodies are connected: namely, how they form coalitions, how they are vulnerable to other bodies, how they are vulnerable to precarity, and how they are vulnerable to institutions and infrastructures (or lack thereof). Butler's approach to bodies adds complexity to the question we began with: who or what is doing the vertical dig into the past? But the layers of the dig are not only vertical, as Benjamin describes, but also horizontal. And the layers cannot be stringently defined and demarcated by lines. The layers are overlapping, interconnected, and fluid.

In Butler's words, "the body never exists in an ontological mode that is distinct from its historical situation."[3] That is, "precisely because bodies are formed and sustained in relation to infrastructural supports (or their absence) and social and technological networks or webs of relation, we cannot extract the body from its constituting relations."[4] So it is not a sole, individual, unconnected body that digs into the past, into early Christian history. Rather, they are bodies, bodies *formed and sustained* by relations, connections, coalitions, corporations, communities, laws, and desires.

In her earliest work, *Subjects of Desire,* an analysis of twentieth-century French theorists and Hegelian philosophy, Butler turns to Julia Kristeva for a critique of Hegel, a critique from an "embodied" and "gendered" point of view.[5] "Kristeva's purpose," according to Butler, "is to explode this monadic structure of the subject through a return to the body as a heterogeneous assemblage of drives and needs."[6] Two important points about Butler's theories can be drawn from this. First, for Kristeva and for Butler, the body must be at the forefront in discussions about the subject.[7] Second, the heterogeneity of the body—whether a body of an individual or a body of people—must also be at the forefront of understanding the subject, a heterogeneity in contrast to the misleading "monadic structure of the subject."

---

3. Butler, *Performative Theory of Assembly,* 148.
4. Butler, *Performative Theory of Assembly,* 148.
5. Judith Butler, *Subjects of Desire: Hegelian Reflections in Twentieth-Century France* (New York: Columbia University Press, 1987), 232–8.
6. Butler, *Subjects of Desire,* 232. Note here that, similar to Deleuze and Badiou, Kristeva argues for the value of poetic language. For Kristeva, poetic language ruptures monadic structures. In Butler's analysis, Kristeva sees a return to heterogeneity "through the medium of poetic language," focusing on the "plurivocity of meanings" of poetic language, its "rhythms and sounds."
7. Butler, *Subjects of Desire,* 232. This focus on the body is made in contrast to Hegel's view of the subject, one that, according to Butler and Kristeva, "denies the materiality of the body and the psychosomatic origins of affective life."

This understanding also extends to history: recognizing "complex bodies in complex historical situations."[8] And this understanding, in the words of Sara Salih, calls for a "history of bodies" that is not reductive, a call that extends into the study of the history of early Christian texts and their receptions (that is, both their authors and readers), texts and receptions that cannot be separated from bodies, bodies connecting vertically and horizontally, flowing into one another, vulnerable to one another, resisting demarcations.[9]

The two following chapters apply Butler's theories on the body and bodies, especially focusing on *Bodies That Matter*: Valérie Nicolet's "Paul Exposed: Reading Galatians with Judith Butler" and Peter Anthony Mena's "Mattering Bodies." Before introducing these two chapters and other key ideas that can be derived from Butler's work, we consider the context of Butler's work.

The Context of Judith Butler's Work (1956–)

Butler was born 24 February 1956 in Cleveland, Ohio. Butler's Jewish heritage and upbringing has had a strong impact on her philosophy. As a youth, Butler was active in her Jewish community, attending Jewish schools until attending Bennington College and Yale University, where she earned her PhD. It was her experience in her community that first sparked her interest in philosophy. In a 2013 interview with Michael Roth, Butler addressed what first sparked her interest in philosophy:

> I was introduced to philosophy in my synagogue. And I had a rabbi who was reading Spinoza and Martin Buber, who also had strong interests in literary criticism, and so one would find Erich Auerbach in the middle of his sermon … He was a stunning individual and also a professor of religion. I guess there was one point where I became a disciplinary problem in the Hebrew school class, and they sent me to the rabbi. And he said, "Well, we're not going to send you back to that class. Your punishment is that you will have to do a tutorial with me."
>
> And I was very thrilled. And I was about fourteen, and he asked me what I wanted to work on. And I said, "Well, I want to know whether there are seeds of fascism in the tradition of German idealism. I want to know why Spinoza was excommunicated from the synagogue (I was feeling some identification)."
>
> And I wanted to know about existential theology.[10]

---

8. Butler, *Subjects of Desire*, 237.
9. Sara Salih, *Judith Butler* (London: Routledge, 2002), 40. Here Salih is referring to Butler's critique of Foucault. Specifically, her critique calls for "a history of bodies that does not reduce culture to the imposition of the law upon the body."
10. Judith Butler and Michael Roth, "A Conversation at Wesleyan University's

Butler, therefore, roots her thought in the continental philosophical tradition quite early. She recalls discovering and reading Kierkegaard and Spinoza in her parent's basement, and then taking "Introduction to Philosophy" and "Introduction to Ethics" college classes while in high school.[11] In graduate school, Butler's interest in Hegelian philosophy grew into her dissertation at Yale, which in turn developed into her first book *Subjects of Desire: Hegelian Reflections in Twentieth-Century France*. The French philosophers that Butler covers here include Kojève, Sartre, Derrida, Foucault, Lacan, Deleuze, and Kristeva. While other topics and names other than Hegel come to the fore in discussions about Butler's work, Hegel remains important to her work, especially the concept of dialectic. Sara Salih accordingly notes: "very few critics and academics would associate Butler with Hegelian philosophy in the first instance, yet it is impossible to overestimate the influence of [Hegel] on Butler's work."[12] Butler herself claims that the interplay between desire and recognition in Hegel's philosophy played a vital role in her own thinking on both concepts, especially in connection with feminism and gender.[13]

Butler's comment in the Roth interview about "the seeds of fascism" is also revealing. Members from her mother's side of her family perished in the Holocaust. Her intellectual formation grows out of a collective reflection about fascism and anti-Semitism in the twentieth century, as Vikki Bell asserts in "Mimesis as Cultural Survival: Judith Butler and Anti-Semitism." Here Bell aims "to give Butler's work [on gender] a genealogy that traces the notion of mimesis back into work which employed the concept within socio-theoretical responses to anti-Semitism."[14] Specifically, Bell points to the work of Adorno and Horkheimer in the *Dialectic of Enlightenment* and Jean Paul Sartre's *Anti-Semite and Jew*. "This is not a straightforward trajectory," according to Bell, "since although Sartre's work was clearly important for Butler's intellectual development, these would not be connections that she herself would emphasize, nor maybe even accept as important."[15] What Bell emphasizes, however, is how this trajectory brings light to Butler's "socio-political vision," which involves both the recognition

---

Center for Humanities," 2013, https://www.youtube.com/watch?v=Rf4px4KyqbY. This brief interview gives a holistic view of Butler's philosophy, connecting together her interest in continental philosophy, feminism, and gender.

11. Butler and Roth, "A Conversation."
12. Salih, *Judith Butler*, 1.
13. Butler and Roth, "A Conversation."
14. Vikki Bell, "Mimesis as Cultural Survival: Judith Butler and Anti-Semitism," *Theory, Culture, and Society* 16.2 (1999): 133–61, here 134.
15. Bell, "Mimesis as Cultural Survival," 158.

that identities are not constituted by essences, and that normative identities, which often masquerade as essences, can be exposed by subversive acts that reveal the masquerade (e.g., by drag).[16] On normative identities and how theorizing about them connects twentieth-century philosophy with Butler's work, Bell writes:

> I focus on Judith Butler's highly influential work on gender ... in order to suggest that it reveals a certain feminist inheritance of an emphasis on mimesis and imitation that resonates with the ways in which theoreticians responded to the calamitous events of essentialists politics and versions of belonging that were central to the political vision of Hitler's National Socialism and to the events of the Second World War.[17]

What is important for the purposes of this introduction is how Butler's work cannot be viewed apart from important twentieth-century philosophies, philosophies critiquing essentialism and essentialist politics and responding with non-essentialist theories and practices, ones that preserve both difference and cultural identity. Indeed, for Butler these philosophies join with her views on gender and sexuality in order to break apart and open up categories themselves. In light of her studies of philosophy and her activism in the areas of gender and feminism, Butler recalls:

> Some people said, "You're such a feminist. Why don't you do feminist scholarship?"
>
> I thought, "Oh no, I don't want to do feminist scholarship. I just want to read my continental philosophy over here, and then have my feminist activism over there."
>
> But then I was invited to write on De Beauvoir and Wittig, and that involved me in a kind of critique of dominant forms of feminism at the time that seemed to assume that ... to be recognized as a "woman" you had to be within a certain kind of heterosexual frame or you had to have a particular relationship to the maternal. And I fought against that, and I wanted to open up the category, and I wanted to say that the category misrecognizes certain people, or fails to recognize them altogether.[18]

---

16. Though noting commonalities in the trajectory (i.e., anti-essentialism, mimesis, and cultural survival), Bell acknowledges key differences within the trajectory of responses to anti-Semitism, from Adorno, Sartre, and later twentieth-century scholarship, chiefly the work of Daniel Boyarin and Jonathan Boyarin, "Diaspora: Generation and the Ground of Jewish Identity," *Critical Inquiry* 19 (1993): 693–725. See Bell, "Mimesis as Cultural Survival," 150–60, for an insightful and nuanced analysis of the commonalities and differences within the trajectory she proposes.

17. Bell, "Mimesis as Cultural Survival," 134.

18. Butler and Roth, "A Conversation." On the influence of De Beauvoir and Wittig, see Butler's first two major essays: "Sex and Gender in Simone de Beauvoir's *Second Sex*," *Yale French Studies* 72 (1986): 35–41; "Variations on Sex and Gender: Beauvoir,

So it was the combination of Butler's activism and her work on continental philosophy, as well as her work on De Beauvoir and Wittig, that was a key transitional moment in her work. Bell, in quoting Butler's second book, *Gender Trouble*, demonstrates why. Here Bell notes Butler's analysis of De Beauvoir's idea of "becoming," linking it to Butler's anti-essentialist critiques:

> ... if gender is something that one becomes—but never be—then gender is itself a kind of becoming or activity, and that gender ought not be conceived of as a noun or a substantial thing or a static cultural marker, but rather an incessant and repeated action of some sort.[19]

The logic behind Butler's claim is clear: if gender is "becoming," then it cannot be some static, pre-existing identity or form; it is, in other words, not an identity pre-determined by the body or sex. Instead, it is determined by *performativity*—repeated and iterative acts. It is enacted upon by cultural norms. Bell sums up Butler's concept of gender performativity:

> Although gender is generally understood to be interior, stable and causative, it is better interrogated, Butler is suggesting, as a cultural fiction, as a way of producing the effect of "identity," and therefore, as the exterior, contingent resultant of repeated "acts, gestures, enactments" ...[20]

A key qualification here—and one that Butler underscores in her third book, *Bodies That Matter*—is that gender performativity is iterative, and just because gender is not static does not mean that it is instantly plastic and malleable by one act. Gender identity is formed through iterative acts, and it is iteratively enacted upon by societal norms. It is "at once socially constructed and at the same time self-constituting," according to Butler.[21] Butler asserts: "The theory of the performativity of gender was one in which we all are constantly constituting ourselves according to certain norms ... It focuses on agency and acts. And yet, at the same time, we're being formed by institutions. We're being called names. We're having norms imposed on us."[22]

The location of this formation is the body, something which Butler also underscores in *Bodies That Matter*.[23] The body is the location of iterative acts, and the body is also acted upon, especially through speech acts,

---

Wittig, and Foucault," in *Essays on Politics of Gender in Late-Capitalist Societies* (ed. Seyla Benhabib and Drucilla Cornell; Cambridge: Polity Press, 1987), 129–42.

19. Judith Butler, *Gender Trouble: Feminism and the Subversion of Identity* (New York: Routledge, 1999 [1990]), 112. Quoted in Bell, "Mimesis as Cultural Survival," 136.

20. Bell, "Mimesis as Cultural Survival," 136.

21. Butler and Roth, "A Conversation."

22. Butler and Roth, "A Conversation."

23. Judith Butler, *Bodies That Matter: On the Discursive Limits of "Sex"* (New York: Routledge, 1993).

through citation.[24] Bodies, according to Salih, "are never merely described," but "they are always constituted in the act of description."[25] For example, Butler famously points to the birth of a child, when the family proclaims, "It's a girl." Here Butler asserts, "Femininity is thus not the product of a choice, but the forcible citation of a norm."[26] Speech acts, indeed, are intricately connected with the body.[27] In her fourth book, *Excitable Speech,* Butler expands on the role speech acts have in the construction of identity, where she takes on hate speech, where "we're being called names" and "we're having norms imposed on us."[28] Yet, there is agency here. But effective opposition to hate speech is not found in censorship, argues Butler. Instead, Butler reaffirms what she argued in her earlier works: namely, effective opposition is found in performativity, in repetition, in mimicry (e.g., subversively re-appropriating the word "queer").[29]

A transitional point in Butler's work involves expanding her ideas about the body and performativity into a broader understanding of bodies, that is, she transitions into examining in what ways bodies are interdependent and connect, in what ways they "speak" and are silenced, in what ways are they are included and excluded, in what ways they are precarious, and in what ways precarity brings about connections between marginalized groups. Hence, Butler herself addresses this transition, which interlocutors label as a move from performativity to precarity, though Butler maintains a strong connection between the two concepts.[30] Although those looking for a connection between the two often are, according to Butler, "looking for a biographical answer, it is still a theoretical concern." Butler does, however, point to the response of the United States to 9/11.[31] In a moment when the United States could have realized its interconnectivity to and reliance on the broader world, it instead closed itself off in an effort to secure itself. Butler saw this as a moment to think about interconnectivity, to think about the body in its broader sense, leading her to consider bodies of the vulnerable.

---

24. Butler derives these ideas from J. L. Austin (speech acts) and Derrida (citationality). She is also working with Louis Althusser's idea of interpolation.

25. Salih, *Judith Butler*, 88–9.

26. Butler, *Bodies That Matter,* 232. See also Salih, *Judith Butler*, 88–90.

27. For a concise summation of Butler's theory on the interrelation between speech acts and the body, see Amy Hollywood, "Performativity, Citationality, Ritualization," *History of Religions* 42.2 (2002): 93–115, here 99–100. Hollywood, most importantly, links Butler's ideas on performativity to ritual in this essay.

28. Judith Butler, *Excitable Speech: A Politics of Performative* (New York: Routledge, 1997).

29. Recall Vicki Bell's article above, "Mimesis as Cultural Survival."

30. See Butler, *Performative Theory of Assembly*, 26–7.

31. Butler and Roth, "A Conversation."

"It seems I was concerned with queer theory and the rights of sexual and gender minorities," claims Butler, "and now I am writing more generally about the ways in which war or other social conditions designate certain populations as ungrievable."[32] This writing includes Butler's work on Israel's treatment of Palestinians: *Parting Ways: Jewishness and the Critique of Zionism*.[33]

The coupling of performativity with precarity also involves how marginalized groups respond as bodies. In her work on performativity, Butler argues that "certain acts that individuals could perform would or could have a subversive effect on gender norms."[34] In her more recent work, Butler concentrates on "how precarity ... might operate, or is operating, as a site of alliance among groups of people who do not otherwise find much in common and between whom there is sometimes even suspicion and antagonism."[35] These alliances are examined in *Notes Toward a Performative Theory of Assembly*. In her discussion on performativity and precarity, Butler affirms one constant in her work: "identity politics fails to furnish a broader conception of what it means, politically, to live together, across differences, sometimes in modes of unchosen proximity ..."[36]

Key Concepts and Theories Covered in this Volume

Butler's concepts and theories offer challenging lenses through which to view early Christian texts. Her theories themselves perform, breaking categories and teleological assumptions. And because of this, like the three other critical theorists in this volume, a systemic Butlerian philosophy is difficult to capture, other than a philosophy of process and becoming. To return to the start of this chapter: the place at which our dig into the past begins is a fluid one. It is difficult to demarcate with standard categories, and even new ones. Valérie Nicolet reminds us of this fluidity at the end of her chapter: "Perhaps that is what a dialogue with Butler can teach us ... the necessity to propose possible interpretations and the correlated need to recognize that our interpretations will never be the definite ones, but only another critical repetition, curious and eager to be challenged by other readers."

What is more, along with Butler's critique of fixed categories, through which gender and identity categories of early Christian studies are

32. Butler, *Performative Theory of Assembly*, 26.
33. Judith Butler, *Parting Ways: Jewishness and the Critique of Zionism* (New York: Columbia University Press, 2013).
34. Butler, *Performative Theory of Assembly*, 26.
35. Butler, *Performative Theory of Assembly*, 26.
36. Butler, *Performative Theory of Assembly*, 26.

challenged and opened, Butler's critique of quests for origins, essences, and ends also challenges the study of early Christianity. Indeed, Butler's theories on gender intricately connect with this critique. Sara Salih sums up this connection well: "It is because, like the 'subjects' she discusses, Butler's works themselves are part of a process of a becoming which has neither origin nor end; indeed, in which origin and end are rejected as oppressively, perhaps even violently, linear or 'teleological.'"[37] Butler's works themselves, as Salih points out, are performative. They perform against what they call out: linear, origin-based, teleological assumptions. Butler's own work not only offers a check on assumptions about essence-based categories in early Christian studies (e.g., gender and sex) but also offers a check on its linear, origin-based, teleological assumptions.[38] Because of this subversive, Butlerian "performance"—a dialectical performance perhaps akin to Benjamin, Deleuze and Badiou—we cannot place her ideas into firm categories and "use" them to study early Christianity. But we can perform along with Butler's ideas. We can examine points within Butler's "performance" and explore how they would perform with early Christian texts. In the next two chapters, Valérie Nicolet and Peter Anthony Mena read the Apostle Paul and Origen alongside Butler. Nicolet focuses on gender performativity in relation to Paul's letters, specifically Galatians. Mena focuses on *Bodies That Matter*, and expands Butler's work to an even broader understanding of bodies, to non-human ones.

A. Valérie Nicolet: Paul Exposed—Reading Galatians with Judith Butler

Nicolet's reading of Paul with Butler offers "a way out of a binary reading of Paul." Her reading reframes scholarly discussions on topics such as Paul and the Law and Paul and Gender, highlighting "the ambiguity of [Paul's] liberating practices." Read in light of Butler's theories, especially those in *Bodies That Matter*, Paul's letters are both "disciplinary" and "liberating," and fit neither "progressive" nor "conservative" categories. In Nicolet's words, "Paul's rhetoric offers grips for resistance practices, but, at other moments of [Galatians], his discourse aims to discourage exactly the kind of queer embodying of gender that his rhetoric could allow." In short, Paul's letters both transgress norms and constrain with norms, something one would expect in light of Butler's work on power.

---

37. Salih, *Judith Butler*, 3.
38. The reason certain scholarly categories and practices are firmly in place is because of performance and iteration, not simply because they hold essence or truth. And the way they are countered is not simply through one act or speech act of truth, but through repeated, subversive, scholarly performance.

In the first part of her chapter, Nicolet introduces Butler's key issues and concepts in *Bodies That Matter*, including Butler's rejection of an autonomous subject and, at the same time, her affirmation of agency. The subject is formed through the repetition of norms, but these norms can also be challenged in abject spaces, where the repetition of norms is potentially disrupted. This disruption involves repetition itself: "disrupted repetition" and "imperfect imitation." Even more, it involves constant twisting and queering, largely because even disruptions themselves, according to Nicolet, can be restrictive when repeated. With this tension in mind, Nicolet shows how "Butler's work asks how Paul reinscribes and repeats the norms of gender, of social class, of ethnicity, of age," but at the same time, liberates from the law and norms. Nicolet shows how Butler's work helps highlight both reinscription and liberation in Paul's work.

In the second part of her chapter, "Reading Paul with Butler," Nicolet turns to Paul, focusing on how his iterations of norms produce both subjects (insiders) and abjects (outsiders) in Galatians, especially in relation to the law and familial norms, focusing on how discourse and practices reinforce gender norms and also challenge them. These norms are reinforced by repetition, by using the law as a tool to control imitation, and by imitating Christ. In doing so, abject spaces are created. In these spaces, norms are destabilized. While Paul's diminutive language in Galatians (i.e., slave of Christ, weakness of the flesh, Paul as birthing mother, slaves of one another, and stigmata) serve to establish his own ethos as leader, this language also serves as a "destabilizing power, perhaps most of all for those who would not necessarily have been intended as the recipients of this language." What's more, if imitating and repeating Christ produces free Jewish males, stabilizing boundaries of masculinity, it also produces abject spaces where norms can be queered and penetrated by women, slaves, and children.

Nicolet concludes her chapter by asserting the ambiguity of Paul's message and calling for queer critiques in Pauline studies. Nicolet notes that "any liberating discourse is also always at the same time a disciplining discourse" and "any 'in-group' discourse unfailingly creates an 'out group.'" Boundaries are always drawn. But there is also always a need for queer critique to "constantly shift boundaries that are/seem settled or fixed" in scholarship.

B. Peter Anthony Mena—Mattering Bodies: Animacy and Justice in Origen's On First Principles

Peter Anthony Mena reads Origen's *On First Principles* alongside Judith Butler's *Bodies That Matter*, expanding Butler's theories about bodies to non-human bodies, to all matter. In doing so, Mena views the body beyond the human body, or even animate bodies, offering "something ... oriented toward justice for all matter ... a justice that extends beyond care for only matter viewed as animate." As a result of this new materialist dialogue across ages, Mena argues for seeing the material world not simply as our "common home but, rather, as our kin." Mena's argument has three sections: Language Matters, Ancient Matters, and Butler's *Bodies That Matter*.

In the first section—"Language Matters"—Mena points to Mel Chen's theory of *animacy* and proposes language that undermines "problematic binaries in the service of opening up the capacity to speak of nonhuman matter in terms that better capture its relationship with, or effect on all human and nonhuman matter." To develop this, Mena uses the work of Sonia Hazard, Bruno Latour, and Deleuze and Guattari to show how binaries such as living/non-living or subject/object fail to articulate how "each part is equally important" in an assemblage and how each part is connected to form an assemblage greater than its individual parts. To Mena, this calls for a "decentering [of] the human as either the subject for analysis or *the* component upon which other lesser components act upon." Mena ends this section by posing the following question: "How might a different cosmology enliven our understanding of the environment and all matter—human and non-human alike?" Mena next turns to earlier Christian cosmologies to see if there is "attentiveness toward non-human matter that does not include its dominance and oppression."

In the second section—"Ancient Matters"—Mena examines the work of Plato and Origen. Here Mena discusses the "*thingness* of *things*, and their relationship to and with human animals." In linking this section to the prior one, Mena argues how "language is a key component to how these relationships function and what our understanding of all non-human matter is reliant on." So he examines the language of Origen and then Plato. Here Mena finds egalitarian and kinship language as opposed to simply hierarchal language. Specifically in Origen's work, Mena finds that "all matter is created in order to house fallen souls. All matter is imbued with something of the divine and all matter is connected by way of familial-like connections, or kin networks."

In his third section—Butler's *Bodies That Matter*—Mena underscores an important point in Butler's work on human bodies and gender: how language imposes hierarchies on bodies. Mena then expands Butler's work to non-human bodies, connecting it to Origen and Plato, asking what qualifies as a viable body. Just as Butler calls for a "radical rearticulation as what qualifies as bodies that matter," so Mena, through his analysis of Origen, calls for rearticulation of all matter, of "all matter as connected in kinship."

C. For Further Consideration:
Assemblies in Early Christianity and American Politics

Butler's most recent work on alliances and assemblies informs not only the current political milieu in the United States, but also how we view political bodies in Acts of the Apostles and early Christianity. Butler's theories on political bodies in *Notes Toward a Performative Theory of Assembly* challenge how we think about assemblies, both today (e.g., assemblies in America before, during, and after the election Donald Trump) and in ancient texts (i.e., the assemblies in Acts of the Apostles). Concerning the latter, her work highlights *how* the narrative of Acts of the Apostles, for example, tells its story of assemblies through a rhetoric of assembly. Concerning the former, her work highlights how political assemblies—both assemblies of Trump supporters and assemblies of those protesting his administration's speech-acts and policies—"speak" in our modern context, whether by the political bodies alone or by rhetoric about them. Both situations spark a series of questions similar to the ones Butler herself raises in *Notes Toward a Performative Theory of Assembly*, especially concerning precarity and performativity, suggesting an avenue for further analysis of assemblies in early Christianity and modern politics, with Butler's theories and questions mediating between the ancient and modern image.

As I have pointed out in a previous piece, Acts of the Apostles sets up a dynamic where the narrator describes events and then various speakers (i.e., from Peter to Paul) interpret these events, usually in the form of speeches.[39] What is more, the interpretations explain God's hand in the events. Two conclusions can be drawn from this dynamic: first, speech-acts about God's agency are used to underscore the significance of events, usually justifying them; second, a *modus operandi* of the early Church involves speaking about God-events to and for its assemblies, a *modus operandi* found not only in Acts of the Apostles, but also in Paul's letters. One type of event common in Acts of the Apostles is the persistent growth of its assemblies, summed in its summary sections (Acts 2.41; 4.4; 5.14; 6.1, 7; 9.31; 11.21, 24; 12.24; 14.1; 19.20), which are generalizations and serve a rhetorical purpose in the narrative.[40] At an early point in the narrative, this growth is interpreted not by an

---

39. See Matthew G. Whitlock, "From the Acts of the Apostles to Paul: Shaking off the Muffled Majesty of Impersonal Authorship," in *Unity and Diversity in the Gospels and Paul: Essays in Honor of Frank J. Matera* (ed. Christopher Skinner and Kelly Iverson; Early Christianity and Its Literature, 7; Atlanta, GA: Society of Biblical Literature, 2012), 149–72.

40. See Joseph A. Fitzmyer, *The Acts of the Apostles* (AB, 31; New York: Doubleday, 1998), 97–8.

Apostle, but ironically by a member of the Sanhedrin, Gamaliel (5.35-39). He compares the assemblies of Jesus' followers to those of Theudas, who claimed "to be someone important," who had "about four hundred men" join him, and who was killed. And as a result, "all those who were loyal to him were disbanded and came to nothing" (v. 36). He also compares the assemblies to those of Judas the Galilean, who "drew people after him," and who perished. As a result, "all those who were loyal to him were scattered" (v. 37). He concludes that if these assemblies of Jesus' followers are of "human origin, it will destroy itself." But he says, "if it comes from God," they will not be able to be destroyed (vv. 38-39). The implication is that what makes large assemblies persist, what makes these bodies viable, is God-sponsorship. And what makes large assemblies dissipate, not viable, is lack of God-sponsorship, or simply being of human origin. And those that oppose large assemblies sponsored by God are potentially God-haters (θεομάχοι).

Now let us shift to our era. There is a threefold concern in the Trump administration and among its supporters about assemblies and legitimization: (1) the size of his crowds, (2) the size of the crowds of political rivals, and (3) God's sponsorship of his presidency and God's lack of sponsorship of his opponents.[41] On the former two, Trump persistently generalizes and exaggerates the size of his crowds and the crowds of rivals in order to legitimize his cause and delegitimize the cause of others.[42] On the latter, Trump's Christian supporters refer to God's hand in him being president.[43] Acts' similar rhetorical use of crowd size and God sponsorship (and non-sponsorship)

---

41. After his impeachment, for example, Trump asserted that Debbie Dingell's husband did not look down on them from heaven, but up from hell. Eileen Sullivan, "Debbie Dingell Calls for Civility after Trump Insults Her Late Husband," *USA Today* (19 December 2019), https://www.usatoday.com/story/news/politics/2019/12/19/debbie-dingell-responds-trump-attacks/2696844001/.

42. See Salvador Rizzo, "President Trump's Crowd-Size Estimates: Increasingly Unbelievable," *The Washington Post* (19 November 2019), https://www.washingtonpost.com/politics/2018/11/19/president-trumps-crowd-size-estimates-increasingly-unbelievable/; Ashley Parker and Annie Linskey, "'The Lines Keep Getting Longer': Crowd Size Takes Center Stage in 2020 Race as Warren Event Rivals Trump," *The Washington Post* (17 September 2019), https://www.washingtonpost.com/politics/the-lines-keep-getting-longer-crowd-size-takes-center-stage-in-2020-race-as-warren-event-rivals-trump/2019/09/17/14112608-d960-11e9-ac63-3016711543fe_story.html. On self-legitimization of the state, see Butler, *Performative Theory of Assembly*, 19: "… the signifying effect of the assembly, its legitimation effect, can function precisely through orchestrated enactments and orchestrated media coverage, reducing and framing the 'popular' as a strategy of the state's self-legitimation."

43. Eugene Scott, "Comparing Trump to Jesus, and Why Some Evangelicals Believe Trump is God's Chosen One," *The Washington Post* (18 December 2019),

poses important questions. Does crowd size alone legitimize a political movement? What is it about the physical presence of bodies that "speaks," both in the age of modern media and in the Greco-Roman world? Do crowds need a speaker to speak for their cause(s)? Who has the authority to speak for crowds? And if one speaks for the crowd, is it possible to find a message that encompasses both its unity and diversity? Does persistent and stable crowd size suggest "divine-sponsorship"? What makes one want to make this claim?

In the context of the Trump administration, the answers to these questions of divine sponsorship, at least for those who do not support the administration, are no. But at the same time, do appeals to crowd size and persistence in Acts of the Apostles bring the same response, especially among non-Trump supporters who identify as Christians? Why or why not? Do crowd size and the persistence of the crowd size make a movement viable in Acts? And do other factors aside from crowd size and an authoritative claim of God-sponsorship legitimize the movement in Acts? Are there other factors of legitimization in Acts of the Apostles?

Butler's work helps address these questions, or more appropriate for Butler's own *modus operandi*, helps pose further questions. Butler's concern in *Notes Toward a Performative Theory of Assembly* involves those who assemble because of precarity. They assemble precisely because they have been placed in precarious situations by those in power. They assemble together to gain power against precarity.[44] This distinction is key to understanding modern images of assemblies, such as Black Lives Matter, the Women's March, or Occupy Wallstreet. This distinction is also key in the context of reception of early Christian texts, such as Acts of the Apostles. By whom is the rhetoric of crowd size being used? By whom is the rhetoric of God-sponsorship being used? In the history of Christian reception, at what points does the rhetoric change hands between those threatened by precarity and those in power? Acts of the Apostles provides an interesting context to examine these questions. It is at a threshold between precarity and power, as the poor community, which originates in Jerusalem, moves towards the powers in Rome. Here I suggest that Acts offers an ancient context in which to explore today's assemblies, creating a dialectical image, an image with Butler's questions and theories mediating. What is more, aside

---

https://www.washingtonpost.com/politics/2019/11/25/why-evangelicals-like-rick-perry-believe-that-trump-is-gods-chosen-one/.

44. See Butler, *Performative Theory of Assembly*, 58: "sometimes it is not a question of first having power and then being able to act; sometimes it is a question of acting, and in the acting, laying claim to the power one requires. This is performativity as I understand it, and it is also a way of acting from and against precarity."

from the questions of legitimization, there are also questions about how crowds "speak," and whether the one speaking for crowds truly represents the crowds. And to what extent is unity in message and practice projected onto these crowds (see Acts 2.42-47)?

Butler asks four types of questions about political bodies, especially applying them to bodies facing precarity. I list each of these and couple them with a question about the study of early Christianity. First, Butler asks questions about the physical presence of assemblies and how they speak without speaking, and how they "speak" as an empowered body made up of bodies facing precarity.[45] These bodies, indeed, are performative, performative without speaking. How, then, do bodies speak in early Christianity without speaking? How are they performative? Second, Butler asks questions about the transience of assemblies: "How, then, do we think about these transient and critical gatherings?":

> Popular assemblies form unexpectedly and dissolve under voluntary or involuntary conditions, and this transience is, I would suggest, bound up with their "critical" function. As much as collective expressions of the popular will can call into question the legitimacy of a government that claims to represent the people, they can also lose themselves in the forms of government that they support and institute.[46]

In applying Butler's questions and observations about transient and critical gatherings, we perhaps should not simply ask whether gatherings are transient, but *when and whether the critical function of gatherings persists* in early Christianity? Third, Butler asks questions about a gathering's unifying "voice."[47] She asks how a gathering speaks in comparison to how a speaker speaks for it. She states:

> Although we often think that the declarative speech act by which "we the people" consolidates its popular sovereignty is one that issues from such an assembly, it is perhaps more appropriate to say that the *assembly is already speaking before it utters any words*, that by coming together it is *already* an enactment of a popular will: that enactment signifies quite differently

---

45. See Butler, *Performative Theory of Assembly*, 18: "Indeed, we have to rethink the speech act in order to understand what is made and what is done by certain kinds of bodily enactments: the bodies assembled 'say' we are not disposable, even if they stand silently." See also pp. 19, 25, 55, 75, 84, 88, 94. Butler asserts just as political bodies can legitimize the state, so can bodies threaten the state through delegitimation (83). She also considers the effects of technology it frames assemblies without words (92–4; 100–2).

46. Butler, *Performative Theory of Assembly*, 7: See also pp. 20–2: "Gatherings are necessarily transient, and that transience is linked to their critical function."

47. See Butler, *Performative Theory of Assembly*, 27, 77, 82–3, 112–3, 119, 160.

from the way a single unified subject declares its will through a vocalized proposition.[48]

Butler's words here certainly raise questions when coupled with Acts of the Apostles and early Christian literature. How did early Christian gatherings already speak before they uttered words? How did these enactments signify "quite differently from the way a single unified subject [e.g., a gospel writer, an epistle writer, a speaker in a narrative] declares its will through a vocalized proposition"?

Finally, Butler asks what makes an assembly good? For Butler, we ought not simply assume the positive value of "bodies on the street"; the phrase "can refer equally well to right-wing demonstrations, to military soldiers assembled to quell demonstrations and seize powers, to lynch mobs or anti-immigrant populist movements taking over public space." Butler then asks: "Under what conditions do we find bodies assembled on the street to be a cause for celebration, or, what forms of assembly actually work in the service of realizing greater ideals of justice and equality, even the realization of democracy itself?"[49]

Whereas dueling voices in the first centuries of Christianity have garnered most of our attention, Butler's focus on non-speaking or prior-to-speaking bodies is worthy of consideration when looking at early Christian texts. We are not granted the lens of viewing these bodies in such a way. We view them only after they are spoken about, only after they are framed. But we can ask questions about how bodies and assemblies are described, and how the "good" and "bad" ones are framed in narratives or epistles. Finally, given that precarity and critique are the unifying bonds in Butler's theories on assembly, can we also hypothesize that precarity and critique are the unifying bonds of diverse, early Christian gatherings, rather than an ideology one writer later projects onto them (e.g., Acts 2.42)?

While the questions above are certainly not new to the study of early Christian texts, Butler's questions serve as unique entry points for analyzing early Christian bodies and assemblies, and not with an ecclesial or missional lens, but with the lens of critical theory, with the lenses of precarity and performativity.

---

48. Butler, *Performative Theory of Assembly*, 156. See also p. 26, where Butler's comments about how assemblies can also "quickly renamed" by the voice of the opponent (e.g., as "unrest" or "riots").

49. Butler, *Performative Theory of Assembly*, 124.

Biographical Note

Matthew G. Whitlock (PhD, The Catholic University of America, 2008) is Associate Professor of New Testament at Seattle University. His research focuses on Acts of the Apostles, the Apostle Paul, New Testament Poetry, Critical Theory, and Science Fiction. His publications have focused on topics ranging from New Testament poetry in the *Catholic Biblical Quarterly* to the Body without Organs and Christianity in *Deleuze and Guattari Studies*. He is currently working on two books on dialectical images, one on images from the Science Fiction of Philip K. Dick and images from the letters of Paul, and the other on the theme of fame in images from the life of Kurt Cobain and early Christian writings about Jesus of Nazareth.

Bibliography: Key Primary and Secondary Texts

For a complete bibliography of Judith Butler, see https://egs.edu/faculty/judith-butler/bibliography.

A. Primary Literature (Major Works)

"Sex and Gender in Simone de Beauvoir's *Second Sex*," *Yale French Studies* 72 (1986): 35–41. https://doi.org/10.2307/2930225

Subjects of Desire: Hegelian Reflections in Twentieth-Century France. New York: Columbia University Press, 1999 [1987].

"Variations on Sex and Gender: Beauvoir, Wittig, and Foucault," 129–42 in *Essays on Politics of Gender in Late-Capitalist Societies*. Edited by Seyla Benhabib and Drucilla Cornell. Cambridge: Polity Press, 1987.

"Foucault and the Paradox of Bodily Inscriptions," *Journal of Philosophy* 86 (1989): 601–7. https://doi.org/10.5840/jphil198986117

Gender Trouble: *Feminism and the Subversion of Identity*. New York: Routledge, 1999 [1990].

Bodies That Matter: *On the Discursive Limits of "Sex"*. New York: Routledge, 1993.

Excitable Speech: *A Politics of Performative*. New York: Routledge, 1997.

The Psychic Life of Power: Theories in Subjection. Stanford, CA: Stanford University Press, 1997.

Antigone's Claim: Kinship between Life and Death. New York: Columbia University Press, 2000.

Giving an Account of Oneself. New York: Fordham University Press, 2005.

Precarious Life: The Powers of Mourning and Violence. London: Verso, 2005.

Parting Ways: Jewishness and the Critique of Zionism. New York: Columbia University Press, 2013.

Notes Toward a Performative Theory of Assembly. Cambridge, MA: Harvard University Press, 2015.

Senses of the Subject. New York: Fordham University Press, 2015.

The Force of Nonviolence: The Ethical in the Political. London: Verso, 2020.

B. Co-Authored Books

Butler, Judith, Seyla Benhabib, Drucilla Cornell, and Nancy Fraser. *Feminist Contentions: A Philosophical Exchange*. London: Routledge, 1995.
Butler, Judith, John Guillory, and Kendall Thomas. *What's Left of Theory? New Work on the Politics of Literary Theory*. London: Routledge, 2000.
Butler, Judith, Ernesto Laclau, and Slavoj Žižek. *Contingency, Hegemony, Universality: Contemporary Dialogues on the Left*. London: Verso, 2000.
Butler, Judith, and Athena Athanasiou. *Dispossession: The Performative in the Political: Conversations with Athena Athanasiou*. Cambridge: Polity Press, 2013.

C. Secondary Literature: Theology, Religious Studies, and Biblical Studies

Armour, Ellen T., and Susan M. St. Ville. *Bodily Citations: Religion and Judith Butler*. New York: Columbia University Press, 2006.
Boyarin, Daniel. *Galatians and Gender Trouble: Primal Androgyny and the 1st Century Origins of a Feminist Dilemma. Protocol of the Colloquy of the Center for Hermeneutical Studies. 5 April 1992*. Edited by Christopher Ocker. Berkeley, CA: Center for Hermeneutical Studies, 1995.
Boyarin, Daniel, and Jonathan Boyarin. "Diaspora: Generation and the Ground of Jewish Identity," *Critical Inquiry* 19 (1993): 693–725. https://doi.org/10.1086/448694
Fitzmyer, Joseph A. *The Acts of the Apostles*. Anchor Bible, 31; New York: Doubleday, 1998.
Hollywood, Amy. "Performativity, Citationality, Ritualization," *History of Religions* 42.2 (2002): 93–115. https://doi.org/10.1086/463699
Hornsby, Teresa J. "The Annoying Woman: Biblical Scholarship after Judith Butler," 71–89 in Armour and St. Ville, *Bodily Citations*, 2006.
—"The Dance of Gender: David, Jesus, and Paul," *Neotestamentica* 48.1 (2014): 75–91.
Jacobs, Brianne. "An Alternative to Gender Complementarity: The Body as Existential Category in the Catholic Tradition," *Theological Studies* 80.2 (2019): 328–45. https://doi.org/10.1177/0040563919836243
Jodamus, Jonathan. "Gendered Ideology and Power in 1 Corinthians," *Journal of Early Christian History* 6.1 (2016): 29–58. https://doi.org/10.1080/2222582X.2016.1184884
Nicolet, Valérie. "Hagar: The Monster in the Closet," in *Contentious Bodies: Queering Pauline Epistles and Interpretations*. Edited by Joseph Marchal. Atlanta, GA: SBL Press, forthcoming.
Whitlock, Matthew G. "From the Acts of the Apostles to Paul: Shaking off the Muffled Majesty of Impersonal Authorship," 149–72 in *Unity and Diversity in the Gospels and Paul: Essays in Honor of Frank J. Matera*. Edited by Christopher Skinner and Kelly Iverson. Early Christianity and Its Literature, 7. Atlanta, GA: Society of Biblical Literature, 2012.

D. Other Secondary Literature

Bell, Vicki. "Mimesis as Cultural Survival: Judith Butler and Anti-Semitism," *Theory, Culture, and Society* 16.2 (1999): 133–61. https://doi.org/10.1177/02632769922050584
Deleuze, Gilles. *Notes towards a Performative Theory: Spinoza*. Translated by Martin Joughin. New York: Zone Books, 1992.

Parker, Ashley, and Annie Linskey. "'The Lines Keep Getting Longer': Crowd Size Takes Center Stage in 2020 Race as Warren Event Rivals Trump." *The Washington Post* (17 September 2019). https://www.washingtonpost.com/politics/the-lines-keep-getting-longer-crowd-size-takes-center-stage-in-2020-race-as-warren-event-rivals-trump/2019/09/17/14112608-d960-11e9-ac63-3016711543fe_story.html (accessed 18/11/2021).

Puar, Jasbir. *Terrorist Assemblages: Homonationalism in Queer Times*. Durham, NC: Duke University Press, 2007. https://doi.org/10.1215/9780822390442

Rizzo, Salvador. "President Trump's Crowd-Size Estimates: Increasingly Unbelievable." *The Washington Post* (19 November 2019). https://www.washingtonpost.com/politics/2018/11/19/president-trumps-crowd-size-estimates-increasingly-unbelievable (accessed 18/11/2021).

Salih, Sara. *Judith Butler*. London: Routledge, 2002. https://doi.org/10.4324/9780203118641

Scott, Eugene. "Comparing Trump to Jesus, and Why Some Evangelicals Believe Trump is God's Chosen One." *The Washington Post* (18 December 2019). https://www.washingtonpost.com/politics/2019/11/25/why-evangelicals-like-rick-perry-believe-that-trump-is-gods-chosen-one/ (accessed 18/11/2021).

Sullivan, Eileen. "Debbie Dingell Calls for Civility after Trump Insults Her Late Husband." *USA Today* (19 December 2019). https://www.usatoday.com/story/news/politics/2019/12/19/debbie-dingell-responds-trump-attacks/2696844001/

Chapter Fourteen

Paul Exposed: Reading Galatians with Judith Butler

Valérie Nicolet

Bodies That Matter, Judith Butler's follow up work to *Gender Trouble*, impresses by the breadth of its erudition.[1] It spans Aristotle, Foucault, Irigaray, Plato, Lacan, Freud, and Žižek, while also making use of various artistic examples (perhaps most famously *Paris is Burning* by Jennie Livingstone, but also novels by Willa Cather, and Nella Larsen's *Passing*) to expand Butler's analysis of body and sex. My use of Butler in this chapter will, by force, be restricted and will concentrate only on certain elements of the sweeping thought she develops in *Bodies That Matter*. Butler herself seems to encourage this use of her work in her introduction to *Bodies That Matter*:

> Taking the heterosexual matrix or heterosexual hegemony as a point of departure will run the risk of narrowness, but it will run it in order, finally, to cede its apparent priority and autonomy as a form of power. This will happen within the text, but perhaps most successfully in its various appropriations. Indeed, it seems to me that one writes into a field of writing that is invariably and promisingly larger and less masterable than the one over which one maintains a provisional authority, and that the unanticipated reappropriations of a given work in areas for which it was never consciously intended are some of the most useful.[2]

Without claiming that my re-appropriation of Butler might be most useful in general, I do think that Butler's work in *Bodies That Matter* questions Pauline scholarship in two directions, which constitute the main pay-offs for reading Butler and Paul together: (1) it proposes a way out of a binary reading of Paul, and (2) it affirms the necessity of a queer critique of readings of Paul. This queer critique demands that the various repetitions of Paul by scholars be constantly redirected and reframed. Before I get to this, however, I take the following steps. First, I present elements drawn out of Butler's work that are helpful for the analysis of Paul, particularly the process of creating and repeating norms, as well as the ambiguity of liberating

---

1. Judith Butler, *Gender Trouble: Feminism and the Subversion of Identity* (London: Routledge, 1990); *Bodies That Matter: On the Discursive Limits of 'Sex'* (London: Routledge, 1993).
2. Butler, *Bodies That Matter*, xxvii.

practices. I also provide a brief summary of other works in biblical scholarship engaging Butler. In my second part, I proceed to read Paul with Butler and I explore two themes more in depth: (1) the strategies that Paul uses to produce subject and abject spaces, with a focus on the role of the law in Paul's rhetoric and (2) the gender boundaries that are drawn by Paul's rhetoric. In giving attention to gender boundaries, I not only explore how masculinity is framed by Paul, but also how some bodies question Paul's gender boundaries. Finally, I return to the pay-offs of reading Paul with Butler, proposing that Butler's theoretical work helps us to understand both the disciplinary and liberating dimensions of Paul's letters, offering a model to map why Paul's letters include traction both for transgressive practices and disciplining discourse. I hope that the interaction with Butler might highlight the fact that approaches which try to figure out whether Paul is progressive or rather conservative do not sufficiently consider the rhetorical and strategic dimensions of his letters.

Concepts in Butler and Brief Survey of Some Uses of Butler in Biblical Scholarship

Concepts in Butler: Repeating Norms and the Ambiguity of Liberating Practices

In the preface to *Bodies That Matter*, Butler describes the struggle provoked by her analysis of gender in *Gender Trouble*, a struggle between a choosing subject and constraints that produce gender and that seem to discard the notion, or even the possibility, of an autonomous subject. She rejects the idea of a choosing subject, but she is also concerned in preserving practices—here practices that embody gender—as spaces where critical agency, resistance, can be put into action.[3] She writes: "But if there is no subject who decides on its gender, and if, on the contrary, gender is part of what decides the subject, how might one formulate a project that preserves gender practices as sites of critical agency?"[4] The tension between construction and agency motivates Butler's project in *Bodies That Matter*. She proposes to see how "sex" is materialized, how it does not precede gender, how it is not simply what one has, but that "sex" also functions as a norm, which, repeated and reiterated, defines which bodies can be understood and accepted.[5] She explores the implications of this conception of sex in various

---

3. Butler, *Bodies That Matter*, viii–x.
4. Butler, *Bodies That Matter*, ix.
5. Butler, *Bodies That Matter*, xii: "'Sex' is, thus, not simply what one has, or a static description of what one is: it will be one of the norms by which the 'one'

examples that question and push her to reflect further. In these examples, she seeks to highlight the repetition of norms.

This repetition of norms contributes to the creation of spaces where subjects are formed, subjects that correspond to the dominant heterosexual norm, allowing certain identifications and making some impossible.[6] Next to the subjects produced by the dominant norms—subjects who are recognized as bodies that matter, that comply and function properly—Butler highlights the "simultaneous production of a domain of abject beings, those who are not yet 'subjects', but who form the constitutive outside to the domain of the subject."[7] Butler insists that one cannot have a subject space without its correlative abject space. The forces of exclusion at work in the creation of subjects produce "a constitutive outside to the subject, an abjected outside."[8] For Butler, the subject cannot emerge without this "domain of abjection."[9] Inside this domain of abjection, one might be able to identify practices of resistance. Because subjects are produced through the constant reiteration of norms, disruption in the repetition of these norms might function to challenge the production of bodies that matter.

Repetition is a key concept in Butler's understanding of law. When Butler thinks about the law in *Bodies That Matter*, she insists on the notion of "citationality."[10] She challenges the idea that a law, here the law of sex, has a "separable ontology," which precedes its expression as law.[11] On the contrary, she argues that law is produced by citation of the law: "the citation of the law is the very mechanism of its production and articulation."[12] To put it a bit crudely, the more one repeats a law, as if it has power, the more one contributes to reinforcing this power. Eventually, it appears as if this power in fact precedes the law and contributes to its efficiency. Yet, in fact, as Butler identifies, the force of the law is directly correlated to its repeated citation. Thus, one might find precisely in the citation the space to perhaps

---

becomes viable at all, that which qualifies a body for life within the domain of cultural intelligibility."

6. Butler, *Bodies That Matter*, xiii: "At stake in such a reformulation of the materiality of bodies will be the following: … a linking of the process of 'assuming' a sex with the question of *identification*, and with the discursive means by which the heterosexual imperative enables certain sexed identifications and forecloses and/or disavows other identifications."

   7. Butler, *Bodies That Matter*, xiii.
   8. Butler, *Bodies That Matter*, xiii.
   9. Butler, *Bodies That Matter*, xiii.
  10. Butler, *Bodies That Matter*, xxi.
  11. Butler, *Bodies That Matter*, xxiii.
  12. Butler, *Bodies That Matter*, xxiii.

produce a different kind of law, to "cite" the law differently, to "reiterate and coopt its power."[13]

Because repetition is key in providing power to the law, disrupted repetition, imperfect imitation can function as practices of resistance. Butler indicates that "threat and disruption" might be a "critical resource in the struggle to rearticulate the very terms of symbolic legitimacy and intelligibility."[14] When one reproduces norms in a disrupted fashion, it might be possible to transform the boundaries that delineate the insider group. At the same time, Butler understands that, if the production of subjects is the result of reiteration of norms, even repeated disruptions and contestations of the norms, queering of the norms, can end up becoming oppressive and restrictive. She thus insists on the necessary transient and instable quality of queerness. The queer subject can never and should never be fixed. Queer contestation needs to "remain that which is, in the present, never fully owned, but always and only redeployed, twisted, queered from a prior usage and in the direction of urgent and expanding political purposes."[15]

In the spirit of this volume, which seeks to represent "our age in the age during which early Christian texts arose" and thus to use critical theory to "expose hidden assumptions in both ages," Butler creates space to showcase questions which are not the explicit questions of the early texts of Christianity, but which function powerfully in the rhetoric and practices of these texts and in their reception. Butler's work asks how Paul reinscribes and repeats the norms of gender, of social class, of ethnicity, of age that surround him. It allows identifying the constraints that mark Paul's world, and how Paul might play with them, how he uses their productive force and how he can also be overwhelmed by the productive force of constraints. It helps to name the norms that Paul idealizes and naturalizes in his discourse. Furthermore, it shows that Paul's rhetoric, because it seeks to set boundaries and works with insider/outsider mechanisms, can have diverse effects, both disciplinary and liberating. Butler's work explicitly shows why Paul's rhetoric of freedom is also disciplinary rhetoric. It exposes Paul's rhetoric as a discourse that repeats various norms to shape identity. In a critique informed by Butler, Paul's enterprise of creating Christ-believer subjects—an insider group of saved people—also means the production of an outsider group (no matter how large or small) of rejected people.

Thus, keeping Butler in mind, we should not be surprised that Paul can be at the same time perceived as a resource when it comes to elaborating a

---

13. Butler, *Bodies That Matter*, xxiii.
14. Butler, *Bodies That Matter*, xiii.
15. Butler, *Bodies That Matter*, 173.

theology which frees human beings from the grasp of the law (as Paul was for Luther, for example), and at the same time be perceived as homophobic and misogynistic, successfully imposing structures of power on his addressees, which preclude the manifestation of autonomous subjects. Butler, far from providing the keys to decide how one should read Paul, helps to understand why both readings of Paul are possible. Her analysis of norms, and the repetition of norms, accounts for the workings and dynamics of power networks inside Paul's letters, and sheds light on the diverse effects Paul's letters have had over the centuries. At the same time, a perspective informed by Butler also makes it clear that it is impossible to say which reading of Paul is more correct, closer to Paul's mind, than another. Because of the nature of Paul's letters as disciplinary, aimed at education, one cannot reach the essential sense of Paul's letters. It is possible to expose some strategies, ignore others, highlight certain aspects and downplay others, but it is impossible to get to the meaning, let alone the mind, of Paul, since what is accessible in the letters are strategies of power.

Butler and Paul:
Brief Survey of Some Uses of Butler in Biblical Scholarship

From these rather general observations, I now argue how Butler's work can provide tools for reading Paul's letters, specifically Galatians. The work of Butler and the questions she asks in *Gender Trouble* and *Bodies That Matter* have had some impact in biblical studies. Often Butler's theoretical work has allowed scholars to question the androcentric presupposition of biblical texts, or to highlight dynamics of power in passages.[16] Jonathan Jodamus's work in "Gendered Ideology and Power in 1 Corinthians" is representative of this interaction with Butler's work.[17] Jodamus explicitly indicates that one of the aims of his reading is to "unearth gender ideology" in 1 Corinthians.[18] Identifying "discursive and reiterated practices" allows him to see the power at work in Paul's rhetoric to shape and "regulate" bodies.[19] Through Butler, Jodamus identifies to what degree Paul's discourse,

---

16. Without being explicitly named, it seems that at least a Butlerian-inspired theory informs Lone Fatum's reading of 1 Thessalonians in her article "Brotherhood in Christ: A Gender-Hermeneutical Reading of 1 Thessalonians," in *Constructing Early Christian Families: Family as Social Reality and Metaphor* (ed. Halvor Moxnes; London: Routledge, 1997), 183–97.

17. Jonathan Jodamus, "Gendered Ideology and Power in 1 Corinthians," *Journal of Early Christian History* 6.1 (2016): 29–58.

18. Jodamus, "Gendered Ideology and Power in 1 Corinthians," 34.

19. Jodamus, "Gendered Ideology and Power in 1 Corinthians," 40: "[Butler] argues for an understanding of power that operates through 'discursive practices' and points to

and its acceptance by the Corinthian community, becomes normative and normalized.[20] Butler is used here as an ally to identify ideological points of pressure in Paul's discourse and to indicate how Paul's power over the communities is in fact constructed only through the communities' acceptance of his authority.[21]

In his reading of Galatians, Daniel Boyarin has a more genealogical use of Butler.[22] Starting with Butler's re-elaboration of Simone de Beauvoir's critique of the body/mind division, Boyarin, taking up Butler's questions and making them his own, seeks to find out how the masculine came to symbolize "disembodied universality," while the feminine functioned as "disavowed corporeality."[23] For him, the response to these questions lies in the myth of the primal androgyne, as it can be found in the writings of Philo of Alexandria, for example.[24] In this case, Boyarin uses Butler's work as the impulse to do the genealogy of a problem and, perhaps, propose a first solution. It also allows Boyarin to offer a response to a problem inside Pauline scholarship, namely the tension between an affirmation such as the one found in Galatians 3.28, which seems to erase gender differences, and statements such as those found in 1 Corinthians 11.3-16 and 14.34-36, which seem to reinscribe them.[25] Finally, in a more meta-theoretical move, Butler can also be used to question the position of biblical scholars, feminist or queer, inside the industry of the discipline. As Teresa Hornsby points out, Butler has successfully highlighted that works of resistance and of liberation also contribute to disciplining and oppressing.[26] In her own use of

---

the construction of the subject as a product of power. By this estimation, discursive and reiterated practices function as power to produce regulated bodies."

20. Jodamus, "Gendered Ideology and Power in 1 Corinthians," 41.

21. Jodamus, "Gendered Ideology and Power in 1 Corinthians," 42.

22. Daniel Boyarin, *Galatians and Gender Trouble: Primal Androgyny and the 1st Century Origins of a Feminist Dilemma. Protocol of the Colloquy of the Center for Hermeneutical Studies. 5 April 1992* (ed. Christopher Ocker; Berkeley, CA: Center for Hermeneutical Studies, 1995), 1–38.

23. Butler, *Gender Trouble*, 16: "Through what act of negation and disavowal does the masculine pose as a disembodied universality and the feminine get constructed as a disavowed corporeality?"

24. Boyarin makes reference to at least two texts by Philo: *Allegorical Interpretation of Genesis* and *On the Creation*. Both are quoted in the Loeb Classical Library: Philo, *On the Creation: Allegorical Interpretation of Genesis 2 and 3* (trans. F. H. Colson and G. H. Whitaker; LCL, 226; Cambridge, MA: Harvard University Press, 1929).

25. Boyarin, *Galatians and Gender Trouble*, 3: "This myth, I suggest, encodes the dualist ideology whereby a spiritual androgyny is contrasted with the corporeal (and social) division into sexes up until at least some feminist theory of the present moment."

26. Teresa J. Hornsby, "The Annoying Woman: Biblical Scholarship after Judith

Butler, Hornsby seeks to challenge "some assumptions of heteronormative structure and disrupts some constructions of the term *woman*."[27]

In the following section, I focus my analysis on Galatians and look at two aspects of Paul's rhetoric that connect with Butler's critique particularly well. First, I explore the way that Paul seeks to shape the identity of his addressees and of his community, and how he creates insider and outsider groups. In the construction of these groups, several strategies, reminiscent of Butler's concepts, are used: Paul relies on imitation and repetition to produce the subjects he desires in his communities. Paul's language relies on the role of the law, but also on imitation both of Christ and of himself to shape an insider group, who receives benefits from its belonging to the Christ community. On the outside of this group lie the abject bodies, who hold the potential to destabilize the norms carefully articulated by Paul. One can see traces of this destabilization in the belittling language Paul uses, but also, and perhaps more efficiently—as we will see—in the embodying of Christ by bodies which do not correspond to the norms delineated by Paul's rhetoric.

The second aspect analyzed in this section has to do with categories of masculinity and femininity, and the way they are re-used and re-configured in Paul's discourse. Here too, albeit more briefly, I will delineate aspects of Paul's discourse that reinforce ancient categories of male and female, as well as spaces in Paul's language, and, more importantly, in the practices of the communities, that challenge these categories.

Reading Paul with Butler

Producing Subjects and Abjects in Galatians

In Galatians, Paul constructs *nomos* as a problematic notion that threatens the freedom of his addressees. *Nomos* is associated to various, mostly negative, metaphors which I propose to explore here. I am approaching the topic of the law in Galatians with the idea that, as David Kaden has emphasized, "law does not exist as a ready-made object," but rather is constructed through various discursive practices.[28] In this approach, I focus on the Butlerian notions of citationality and performance, and I treat *nomos* in

---

Butler," in *Bodily Citations: Religion and Judith Butler* (ed. Ellen T. Armour and Susan M. St. Ville; New York: Columbia University Press, 2006), 71–89.

27. Hornsby, "The Annoying Woman," 86.

28. David A. Kaden, *Matthew, Paul and the Anthropology of Law* (Tübingen: Mohr Siebeck, 2016), 4: "I am not treating law (or unwritten customs or rules in the case of the ethnographies) as a ready-made object—comprised of an essential group of traits—that exists apart from the discursive processes and social relations that make its emergence possible."

Paul as not pre-existing its use in Galatians but as being created by the discourse on and around the law in Galatians. Of course, because Galatians is a letter, and thus inscribes itself in the context of previous communication, *nomos* in Galatians is already pre-constructed when the addressees (historical or not) encounter it in the text of the letter. For the historical addressees, *nomos* carries everything that would have been evoked by *nomos* in a Hellenistic Jewish and Roman context.[29] For the present addressees, *nomos* is pre-determined by volumes of previous scholarship. Yet, Butler's insistence on law being produced by the citation of the law itself invites us to explore *nomos* as it is constructed through the various discursive practices of the letter, as it emerges from the network of relations of power that enable its discursive formation.[30] In relationship to power, law is thus "an effect of power": "it is a site that gets constituted as an object in the sphere of the exercise of power, and, once constituted, can become a relay of power."[31]

Consolidating Norms: Law and its Relationship to Family Language
In Galatians, two passages inscribe the law inside relationships characteristic of the family: 3.23-27 and 4.1-5. In Galatians 3.23-27, *nomos* is presented as something that keeps "us" corralled (ἐφρουρούμεθα συγκλειόμενοι) until "the faith about to come has been revealed."[32] *Nomos* is here famously compared to a παιδαγωγὸς, the slave responsible for bringing children to their various activities. Obvious also from Galatians 3.23-27 is that this state of being under the control of *nomos* is intended as temporary, a preparation time until "faith comes" (ἐλθούσης δὲ τῆς πίστεως) and "we" is freed from the παιδαγωγὸς, in order for "all" to become "sons of God" (υἱοὶ θεοῦ).[33]

---

29. Kaden, *Matthew, Paul and the Anthropology of Law*, 22. Kaden makes a similar point: "… I am initially accepting that certain domains of knowledge—e.g. scholarship on law in early Judaism and Christian origins, and the field of anthropology of law—have constituted a series of social practices as the discursive object 'law.'"

30. To use more foucaultian language, see for example Michel Foucault, *History of Sexuality, Volume 1: An Introduction* (New York: Vintage Books, 1990), but also *The Archaeology of Knowledge and the Discourse of Language* (New York: Pantheon Books, 1972). A similar argument that helped delineate my own thought is found in Kaden, *Matthew, Paul and the Anthropology of Law*, 22: "… sexuality or law are not fully formed entities that preexist in any meaningful sense their own emergence … Sexuality or law *become* objects of discourse because relations of power make possible their emergence."

31. Kaden, *Matthew, Paul and the Anthropology of Law*, 26.

32. I do not think that it is necessary here to identify who exactly this "us" covers. I am rather convinced that it is aimed at non-Jewish Christ believers (and not at Jewish Christ believers) but I do not think that this identification is fundamental for my argument here.

33. I am here of the opinion that the *pistis* under discussion, that is awaited and

Nomos is associated to a temporary immature stage, aimed to be discarded, to attain divine, mature sonship. What is most interesting, regardless of whether παιδαγωγὸς intends a positive or a negative judgment on *nomos*, is that it inscribes *nomos* in familial relationships, and even more precisely, in the universe of children's education.

In the second passage, Galatians 4.1-5, one finds a similar attention to childhood. In verse 1, the future heir (ὁ κληρονόμος) is presented in his infant stage (νήπιός), a stage that makes him like a slave. In this situation, the little child is under the control of guardians and managers (ὑπὸ ἐπιτρόπους ἐστὶν καὶ οἰκονόμους), slave positions in the household, just like the παιδαγωγὸς. Again, this stage is but temporary since the young heir is poised to fully inherit his sonship (υἱοθεσίαν) at the time set by the father. *Nomos* is explicitly used only in verses 4 and 5, to qualify the birth of Jesus and to indicate who needs to be freed from the law, just like in Galatians 3.23. Being under the law is furthermore paralleled with being enslaved to the elements of the world (ὑπὸ τὰ στοιχεῖα τοῦ κόσμου), a state characteristic of those who are only infants.[34] Here too, *nomos* is firmly inscribed in the pattern of relationships inside the household. At the same time, if *nomos* is enmeshed inside familial power relationships, so are Paul's addressees (and Paul himself, since he includes himself in the first-person plural, and probably also in the everyone of 3.26). These games of power inside the household construct a discursive object associated with *nomos*. One can interrogate what is the "particular discursive context" of family in which Paul's language is inscribed.[35]

a. Imitation and Repetition. In the passages I have quoted above, Paul's addressees and Paul himself are reminded of their experiences as children. The experiences to which he appeals (being under the supervision of a παιδαγωγὸς, and of ἐπιτρόποι and οἰκονόμοι, having the perspective to inherit and have full access to the father's estate) suggest the context of a household organized around a *paterfamilias* and including several slaves.[36]

---

needs to come, is the one of Christ. Again, I do not think that my position on this debated exegetical issue here affects the discussion of family relationships very much.

34. Once more, the precise meaning of τὰ στοιχεῖα τοῦ κόσμου (in my opinion, elements associated with ancient astrology and magical practices) is not fundamentally important here. It is more fundamental for my project to see that this stage, serving the elements of the world, is also associated with childhood.

35. Kaden, *Matthew, Paul and the Anthropology of the Law*, 169.

36. Family as a topic of historical interest has emerged in the 1980s and has become a rather widely-studied phenomenon also in New Testament and Early Christianity Studies. A state of research is found in Beryl Rawson, "'The Roman Family' in Recent Research: State of the Question," *BibInt* 11.2 (2003): 119–38. It is part of a special

In these relationships, Paul treats his addressees as little children, dependent on other persons for their well-being, until they reach proper maturity. Central to this traditional religious learning is imitation. As Jacob L. Mackey indicates, imitation allows children to become active acquirers of ritual norms.[37] As children repeat what they see, it becomes authoritative. To say it with Butler, as religious behavior is reiterated, cited, it becomes authoritative and the imitation itself contributes to giving it its essential character. "What" is imitated is thus the site of power struggles and requires disciplining. Mackey writes: "Teaching, character-building and proper socialization required Roman adults to limit the space within which children could exercise their imitative agency, that is, to mediate children's access to models of thought, speech and action."[38]

b. Nomos as a Tool to Control Imitation. When Paul evokes the universe of the little child in this section of Galatians 4, it might be possible to think of this construction of childhood as participating in the development of a person's agency and subjectivity, through among other things imitation.[39] It would thus be important to control what is accessible to repeat and imitate. Several things are mentioned that limit the options given to the Galatian little children: they are like slaves, under ἐπιτρόπους καὶ οἰκονόμους, they are enslaved to στοιχεῖα τοῦ κόσμου, and if one admits that 3.23 and 24 might be connected to the same experience, they are guarded by the law, the παιδαγωγὸς. Against interpretations that have criticized using Roman guardianship laws to understand these figures,[40] John Goodrich inscribes

---

edition of *Biblical Interpretation* on "family." More recently, *Acta Patristica et Byzantina* also had a special edition on "family" as a strategy: *Acta Patristica et Byzantina* 21.2 (2010). For Early Christian studies, see also: Carolyn Osiek and David L. Balch, *Families in the New Testament World: Households and House Churches* (Louisville, KY: Westminster/John Knox, 1997); Halvor Moxnes, ed., *Constructing Early Christian Families: Family as Social Reality and Metaphor* (New York: Routledge, 1997).

37. See for example, Jacob L. Mackey, "Roman Children as Religious Agents. The Cognitive Foundations of Cult," in *Children and Everyday Life in the Roman and Late Antique World* (ed. Christian Laes and Ville Vuolanto; London: Routledge, 2017), 179–97, here 179 and 181.

38. Mackey, "Roman Children as Religious Agents," 181–2.

39. For the idea of childhood as a phase of the construction of agency and subjectivity, see Ville Vuolanto, "Experience, Agency, and the Children in the Past: The Case of Roman Childhood," in Laes and Vuolanto, eds., *Children and Everyday Life in the Roman and Late Antique World*, 11–24, here 19. He quotes Mary Jo Maines, "Age as a Category of Historical Analysis: History, Agency, and Narratives of Childhood," *Journal of the History of Childhood and Youth* 1.1 (2008): 114–24, here 119.

40. John K. Goodrich, "Guardians, not Taskmasters: The Cultural Resonances of Paul's Metaphor in Galatians 4.1-2," *JSNT* 32.3 (2010): 251–84, here 254, refers in

the ἐπίτροποι and οἰκονόμοι firmly in that context. For him, both terms were used during the Greek and Roman periods "to identify the slave or freedmen agents and administrators who managed the estates of their principals."[41] These two terms were probably interchangeable.[42] The function of these tutors in Roman guardianship especially for minors (*tutela impuberis*) would have been primarily the protection of the minor, but also the protection of patrimony.[43] Goodrich's final conclusion highlights that, in the metaphors used by Paul, his addressees are "cast as children, and the law as a temporarily authorized custodian."[44]

The purpose of the system of Roman guardianship was protection and fructification. It was presented as being in the best interest not only of the various guardians but also of the heirs under *tutela*.[45] If Roman guardianship laws were in the mind of both Paul and his addressees when he coined, and they heard, the metaphors of children and various guardians, it would reinforce a discourse that constructs human beings as in danger, in need of protection and incapable of making their own decisions. These human beings could not be trusted to make the right decisions or to manage their lives and their selves in a correct manner. In this rhetorical construction, *nomos* is thus presented as a power, which keeps human beings out of trouble, and helps bring them to maturity. It is established for the protection and the education of the heir.

Nomos is a device that free, independent, male adults can employ to contribute to the proper disciplining of small, immature, children, as well as women and foreigners. It has only limited power, the power to contain and discipline, until the proper time, just as the παιδαγωγὸς, ἐπίτροποι and

---

particular to the work of James M. Scott, *Adoption as Sons of God: An Exegetical Investigation into the Background of ΥΙΟΘΕΣΙΑ in the Pauline Corpus* (Tübingen: Mohr Siebek, 1992), who reads the passage in the light of the Hebrew Bible and proposes to see in the ἐπίτροποι and οἰκονόμοι Egyptian taskmasters. The reference would then be to Israel's enslavement in Egypt, before the exodus.

41. Goodrich, "Guardians, not Taskmasters," 265. He refers to evidence in Aristotle (*Pol.*1255b 35-47), Xenophon (*Oec.* 1344a), but also Matt. 20.8 and Luke 12.42. He also mentions non-literary evidence from Egypt, and inscriptions in Asia Minor (Roman Bithynia, Pisidia, Galatia).

42. Goodrich, "Guardians, not Taskmasters," 268.

43. Goodrich, "Guardians, not Taskmasters," 270.

44. Goodrich, "Guardians, not Taskmasters," 272.

45. See for example, Goodrich, "Guardians, not Taskmasters," 270 which quotes the *Digest* as a late source based on earlier practices. It defines *tutela* as "force and power granted and allowed by the civil law over a free person, for the protection of one who, on account of his age, is unable to protect himself of his own accord" (*Dig.* 26.1.1; translation from Alan Watson, *The Digest of Justinian*, [Philadelphia, PA: University of Pennsylvania Press, 1998]).

οἰκονόμοι only have a limited authority, controlled by the *paterfamilias*, who is ultimately the one in charge for bringing the child to full maturity and autonomy. In the context of Galatians, Paul claims that this power is offered to God's own son, who gifts sonship at the fulfilling of time (Gal. 4.4-5) and thus liberates the Galatians from tutelage. By extension, Paul also attributes this power to himself and to those who remain faithful to him. *Nomos* is a powerful concept in the hands of those who know how to wield it. Combined with kinship language, it constructs the *ethos* of the community. Both *nomos* and family language about inheritance and sonship contribute to discipline a community that needs to see itself as constituted of sons and heirs to God's promise (Gal. 4.7). The members of the community go from childhood to adulthood, but also from slavery and imprisonment to freedom, and from tutelage to full enjoyment of the inheritance, and this is partly made possible by the guardianship of the law.

c. Imitation of Christ/Paul as Discipline and Education. As free adult males, the Christ believers constitute an "in group" that has Christ as model. Even though Galatians does not explicitly use the language of imitation, the *topos* of imitation appears strongly in passages like 1 Corinthians 11.1 ("Be imitators of me, as I am of Christ"), 1 Corinthians 4.16 ("I appeal to you, then, be imitators of me") and Philippians 3.17 ("Be co-imitators[46] of me").[47] Imitation contributes to educating the communities. In Galatians, a similar element of education is present in the language of "putting on Christ" (Gal. 3.27).[48] Christ, and by implication Paul, should be imitated and used as models for the behavior of the communities. In putting on Christ, the Christ believers become one in Christ, and become heirs according to the promise (Gal. 3.29). Their status as heirs, as sons inside the *oikos* of God is ensured. As Bert Jan Lietaert Peerbolte and Leendert Groenendijk show, the heavy use of family language in Paul is "indicative of his attempts to establish a social identity and to reinforce cohesion of the Christ groups he had raised in analogy with the tightest model of social belonging in the period in which

---

46. The formula is a bit different here: Συμμιμηταί μου γίνεσθε: "be co-imitators of me." In 1 Cor. 11.1 and 1 Cor. 4.16, one finds: μιμηταί μου γίνεσθε: "be imitators of me."

47. Eph. 5.1 ("Therefore be imitators of God, as beloved children"), whose Pauline authorship is debated, could also be added to this list. It modifies the imitation motif a little bit, when it demands imitation of God, but the next verse introduces a concrete dimension of imitation of Christ in the aspect of love: "and live in love, as Christ loved us and gave himself up for us, a fragrant offering and sacrifice to God."

48. This language is also present in Rom. 13.14. It is found also in several other points in the Pauline letters, but not with Christ as an object. See for example Rom. 13.12, 1 Cor. 15.53-54, 2 Cor. 5.3, 1 Thess. 5.8. It also makes its way in the so-called deutero-pauline literature: Eph. 6.11-15 and Col. 3.10-12.

Christianity surfaced, viz. the family."[49] In this new family, it is important to ensure education and socialization through imitation.[50]

Paul does not invent these pedagogical practices. It echoes language found in sapiential literature, for example. One can take the example of Sirach,[51] who presents the sage as the summit of the sapiential edifice. For Benjamin G. Wright, the sage "mediates Wisdom in whatever form she might take."[52] As Wright indicates, the sage is not just "an instructor," but "more importantly," "an exemplar."[53] Wright explains that "Ben Sira constructs the ideal sage"[54] for his students, shows this ideal picture to this students, and then, so to speak, steps into that delineated picture to indicate that, while he is that ideal figure, his students can become it as well. Something similar is at work in Paul's educational project. He has an ideal image in his messianic figure, and just as he can become like Christ, and truly embody Christ, so his Christ believers can do the same, provided they follow his instructions.[55] The example of Ben Sira shows how Paul, in framing his modeling of the communities in the terms of becoming like him to embody Christ, also becomes a gatekeeper (to use Wright's term) for access to Christ. Just as "Ben Sira transforms the indirect knowledge of hearing into the direct knowledge of seeing, and in the process … steps into the picture frame of the ideal sage, where he has drawn that ideal for his students,"[56] in the

---

49. Bert Jan Lietaert Peerbolte and Leendert Groenendijk, "Family Discourse, Identity Formation, and the Education of Children in Earliest Christianity," *Annali di storia dell'esegesi* 33.1 (2016): 129–49, here 132.

50. Peter Gemeinhardt, "In Search of Christian Paideia: Education and Conversion in Early Christian Biography," *Zeitschrift für antikes Christentum* 16 (2012): 88–98, discusses the example of the *Pseudo-Clementine Homilies*, a text that, in its oldest layer, can be dated to 220 CE, and in its final form to c. 300–320 CE. Gemeinhardt indicates that for the *Pseudo-Clementines*, Greek rhetorical education is not sufficient, and that "true knowledge" is acquired "only by following the model of Peter who in turn is the primordial imitator of Christ" (94). Perhaps it is possible to see here an alternative model of education to polytheist learning, influenced by the language found in Paul's letters.

51. Claudia V. Camp, *Ben Sira and the Men Who Handle Books: Gender and the Rise of Canon-Consciousness* (Sheffield: Sheffield Phoenix Press, 2013), xi, dates Sirach to the early second century BCE.

52. Benjamin G. Wright, "Where is the Torah in Ben Sira?" unpublished paper given at the 9th Enoch Seminar in Camaldoli, 18–23 June 2017.

53. Wright, "Where is the Torah in Ben Sira?"

54. Wright, "Where is the Torah in Ben Sira?" The idea of stepping into the figure is also Wright's.

55. Wright, "Where is the Torah in Ben Sira?" Wright says that for Ben Sira's students it is "insufficient to imitate the sage; they must work to become what the sage is" (and what Ben Sira already is, I would presume). The same could be said of Paul's community. The language of imitation intends to lead to embodying of Christ.

56. Wright, "Where is the Torah in Ben Sira?" See also, Benjamin G. Wright,

same manner, Paul draws the ideal image of the one who embodies Christ perfectly and steps into that picture frame, inviting his audience to follow him. This type of instruction, focusing on behavior to become a true Christ believer, is also found in later texts, such as the *Didache*. The *Didache* insists on establishing "the right type of behaviour" to allow for baptism.[57] Later authors, such as Clement of Alexandria, elaborate a specifically Christian *paideia*, with "Christ as the ultimate instructor."[58] While in Paul we do not have clear evidence of the teaching that accompanied the ritual of baptism,[59] his insistence on imitation and embodying of Christ before and after baptism[60] produces norms. The norms to become a Christ believer are not only constructed by Paul to correspond to the ideal of the free adult male, they are now projected onto his person, ensuring that his communities, if they want to incarnate Christ, become just like Paul, free adult males. These are the subjects produced by Paul's idealization and repetition of certain norms into law. The ideal of the free male heir constructed by Paul's language in Galatians 4 becomes the norm and is naturalized.

d. Creating the Outsider. This construction of the identity of the community is inevitably purchased at the expense of an Other, the "not free," "not male," "not adult" who are part of Paul's community, the abject space corollary of the subject space produced by Paul's community-modelling discourse. If, as Butler shows, these spaces are produced by repetition and reiteration of certain norms, one might be able to identify practices of resistance inside the domain of abjection, not quite appropriate repetitions that

---

Praise Israel for Wisdom and Instruction: Essays on Ben Sira and Wisdom, the Letter of Aristeas and the Septuagint (Leiden: Brill, 2008).

57. Lietaert Peerbolte and Groenendijk, "Family Discourse," 138.

58. Lietaert Peerbolte and Groenendijk, "Family Discourse," 139. For *paideia* in Early Christianity, the classic work is Henri-Irénée Marrou, *Histoire de l'éducation dans l'antiquité* (6th edn.; Paris: Éditions du Seuil, 1965); more recently see Peter Gemeinhardt, *Das lateinische Christentum und die antike pagane Bildung* (Tubingen: Mohr Siebeck, 2007); Karl Olav Sandnes, *The Challenge of Homer: School, Pagan Poets and Early Christianity* (London: T&T Clark, 2009).

59. Lietaert Peerbolte and Groenendijk, "Family Discourse," 137 who indicate that "during the early decades of the movement the genre of baptismal instruction had apparently not yet developed." They argue that there is "no evidence of a kind of instruction to converts who were preparing for baptism." I would agree that there is no evidence for "the genre of baptismal instruction" but narrative reconstructions such as those found in Acts 8.35 and Acts 16.14-32 point to some instruction given to individuals before their baptism.

60. Here too Paul fits into the larger movement of the Christ believers who, as Lietaert Peerbolte and Groenendijk, "Family Discourse," 139, point out, used ethical instructions not just before baptism, but also for members of the communities.

allow for the boundaries of the in and out groups to shift a little. The disruption of the repetition of the norms might challenge the production of bodies that matter. One way of reaching these disruptions is to reconstruct and reclaim the voices of the silenced bodies in Paul's letters.[61] Here, I do not aim at historical reconstruction; rather I am looking at Paul's own language in Galatians and trying to identify destabilizing elements in Paul's rhetoric itself, not developing whether these elements were used by Paul's audience. For my purpose here, it suffices to show that there are elements in Paul's language that have the potential to question the naturalization of norms embodied by Paul himself. The presence of these elements would contribute to explain why Paul is perceived sometimes as rather hierarchical and sometimes as egalitarian.[62]

Destabilizing Norms

Inside Paul's discourse in Galatians, one can identify at least two elements that have the potential to question the fossilization of boundaries created by Paul's disciplining discourse: the use of belittling language and the way this language could have functioned for slaves, women, and children. This second element implies more hypothetical work, the first one involves a closer reading of the text.

a. Diminutive Language. The first element has often been noticed in Paul's discourse, and might be less apparent in Galatians than in other letters: Paul

---

61. See, for example, several works which build on the methodology delineated by Elisabeth Schüssler Fiorenza, *Wisdom Ways: Introducing Feminist Biblical Interpretation* (Maryknoll, NY: Orbis, 2001); Antoinette Clark Wire, *The Corinthian Women Prophets:. A Reconstruction through Paul's Rhetoric* (Eugene, OR: Wipf & Stock, 2003 [Minneapolis, MN: Fortress Press, 1990]); Joseph A. Marchal, *Hierarchy, Unity and Imitation: A Feminist Rhetorical Analysis of Power Dynamics in Paul's Letter to the Philippians* (Atlanta, GA: SBL Press, 2006); Davina Lopez, *Apostle to the Conquered: Reimagining Paul's Mission* (Minneapolis, MN: Fortress Press, 2010); Brigitte Kahl, *Galatians Re-imagined: Reading with the Eyes of the Vanquished* (Minneapolis, MN: Fortress Press, 2010).

62. In her study of Paul's language of motherhood and infancy, Jennifer Houston McNeel, *Paul as Infant and Nursing Mother: Metaphor, Rhetoric, and Identity in 1 Thessalonians 2:5-8* (Atlanta, GA: SBL Press, 2014) summarizes the work done on the maternal images found in Paul. On the "egalitarian" side, she indicates the work of Kathy Ehrensperger, *That We May Be Mutually Encouraged: Feminism and the New Perspective in Pauline Studies* (New York: T&T Clark, 2004) and, on the hierarchical side, Elizabeth A. Castelli, *Imitating Paul: A Discourse of Power* (Louisville, KY: Westminster John Knox, 1991). She sees the work of Beverly Roberts Gaventa, *Our Mother Saint Paul* (Louisville, KY: Westminster John Knox, 2007), as escaping this binary approach of Paul.

will sometimes use a language that praises weakness. For example, Brigitte Kahl argues that "when the Christ-following Galatians declared that their identity was defined not by the imperial *koinon* established by Rome but by the new messianic *koinōnia*, they practically became nonpersons, nobodies themselves—anti-selves, like the barbarians they had once been ..."[63] For Kahl, the community of Christ believers founded by Paul embodies an ethics radically different from the imperial hierarchy and offers an organization entirely different from the one of the Empire. It does not propose another empire;[64] it proposes a new community which is a "noncompetitive and nonhierarchical body of 'new life.'"[65] Without going as far as Kahl in seeing Paul establish a new fundamentally egalitarian order (I think Butler prevents us from doing that), I would agree that Paul's language of inversion and diminution can contribute to questioning hierarchical boundaries.

In Galatians, Paul's language of diminution is not as obvious or present than in a letter like 1 Corinthians for example (1 Cor. 4.7-12; 11.7-30) or in Paul's auto-presentation as a slave in Romans 1.1 or Philippians 1.1. The context of Galatians, where Paul's apostleship and authority are challenged (see Gal. 1.1, 11-12, 15-16; 2.1-11) explains why Paul presents himself in a more forceful and explicitly authoritative manner. Yet, even in this letter, there are a couple of instances where Paul uses language potentially challenging to the norms of a patriarchal and hierarchical organization. Most of this language comes at the end of the letter, in chapters 5 and 6, when Paul gives his final instructions to the community, but before I turn to that section of the letter, there are two other places that warrant discussion.[66]

i. Slave of Christ. In Galatians 1.10, Paul presents himself as "a slave of Christ" (Χριστοῦ δοῦλος). This self-presentation as slave occurs in a section where Paul forcefully insists that he is not trying to please human beings, but is only concerned with persuading God. Dale B. Martin has carefully analyzed Paul's use of slavery metaphor in his monograph *Slavery*

---

63. Kahl, *Galatians Re-Imagined*, 245.
64. Kahl, *Galatians Re-Imagined*, 266: "[The messianic transformation] is a metamorphosis that does not simply replace one empire with another empire, the kingdom of Caesar with a counter-kingdom of God; rather, it establishes an *other* order that is different."
65. Kahl, *Galatians Re-Imagined*, 289.
66. Hans Dieter Betz, *Galatians: A Commentary on Paul's Letter to the Churches in Galatia* (Philadelphia, PA: Fortress Press, 1979), 22, identifies 5.1–6.10 as the *Exhortatio*, the parenetic section of the letter, and 6.11-18 as the *Conclusio*, the postscript written in the hand of Paul which "serves to authenticate the letter, to sum up its main points, or to add concerns which have come to the mind of the sender after the completion of the letter."

as Salvation[67] and has emphasized the ambiguous ways in which it could be used, precisely because of its connections with the complex social organization of the Roman Empire.[68] Depending on one's position on the social ladder, one had a different evaluation about being called a slave. The positive meaning related to slavery depends upon the level of the slave and the status of the slave's master,[69] but Martin remarks that, for a good portion of the population, calling oneself or others a slave would not necessarily be humiliating.[70] In fact, in the context of the patron-client system, if the master one served was powerful and occupied a high-status position, the slave of that person, especially if he (or, more rarely, she) was in a managerial position, carried some of the authority of the master and could occupy an enviable position inside that system.[71] Richard Horsley, building on others, has since challenged the notion that managerial slaves would have benefited from a higher position. He writes: "Such slaves' position was thus also always insecure at best. Their masters retained the power to torture and kill even the most powerful managerial slave."[72] In the immediate context of Galatians, I tend to think that the expression "slave of Christ" does not have a strong derogatory meaning. It comes in a passage where Paul emphasizes his higher faithfulness to the God of Israel and his Messiah, a

---

67. Dale B. Martin, *Slavery as Salvation: The Metaphor of Slavery in Pauline Christianity* (New Haven, CT: Yale University Press, 1990).

68. Martin, *Slavery as Salvation*, 60: "The evaluative ambiguity of the terminology (is it shameful or honorable? Powerful or powerless?) corresponded to the social ambiguity of Greco-Roman slavery."

69. Martin, *Slavery as Salvation*, 49.

70. Martin, *Slavery as Salvation*, 76: "… calling someone a slave—among the lower strata of the population—would not necessarily be so humiliating. Such people would hear Paul's claim that he is a slave without the negative evaluation that accompanies such terminology in philosophical discourse. These untrained hearers, therefore, could conceivably grant to Paul's self-description a positive valuation, if he is a slave not of some lowly, unimportant person but of a person of power and high status."

71. Martin, *Slavery as Salvation*, 49. Also Allen Dwight Callahan, "Paul, *Ekklêsia*, and Emancipation in Corinth: A Coda on Liberation Theology," in *Paul and Politics: Ekklesia, Israel, Imperium, Interpretation* (ed. Richard Horsley; London: Trinity Press International, 2000), 216–23, here 220: "Manumission is, however, an emancipatory practice, in that it finds a space and place for freedom in the limits of Roman slavery."

72. Richard A. Horsley, "The Slave Systems of Classical Antiquity and Their Reluctant Recognition by Modern Scholars," *Semeia* 83–84 (1998): 19–66, here 56. See also: Orlando Patterson, *Slavery and Social Death: A Comparative Study* (Cambridge, MA: Harvard University Press, 1982). Sheila Briggs, "Paul on Bondage and Freedom in Imperial Roman Society," in Horsley, ed., *Paul and Politics*, 110–23, here 118 shares this evaluation: "… when salvation itself is seen as a process of domination, then the critique of social arrangements, resulting from processes of domination, is made, to say the least, more difficult."

faithfulness that guarantees not only the truth of Paul's message but also the value of Paul's person, emphasizing Paul's direct link with his lord, Christ, and his independence from any other human authority (see for example Gal. 1.1: "Paul an apostle—sent neither by human commission nor from human authorities, but through Jesus Christ and God the Father"; Gal. 1.11-12: "For I want you to know, brothers, that the gospel that was proclaimed by me is not of human origin; for I did not received it from a human source, not was I taught it, but I received it through a revelation of Jesus Christ"; Gal. 1.15-16: "But when God, who had set me apart before I was born and called me through his grace, was pleased to reveal his Son to me, so that I might proclaim him among the Gentiles, I did not confer with any human being …"). His service to Christ emphasizes his autonomy from other apostles in Jerusalem and works to enhance his status in the Galatian community.

ii. Weakness in the Flesh. In Galatians 4.13-14, as well as 4.19, Paul refers to his own person with belittling language. Yet, in both cases, this language also functions to construct Paul as the privileged channel for the transmission of the person of Christ. In Galatians 4.13-14, Paul refers to the fact that he came to evangelize in Galatia because of a weakness in the flesh (δι' ἀσθένειαν τῆς σαρκὸς). He also indicates that this condition of his flesh put the community to the test, but that they did not despise or reject him. In fact, quite the contrary happened, since Paul was welcomed ὡς ἄγγελον θεοῦ, like a messenger of God, and even more so ὡς Χριστὸν Ἰησοῦν, like Christ Jesus. His weakness is the opportunity for a christophanic event. There is a link here with the idea more fully developed in 2 Corinthians that the apostles have the good news of Christ in "clay jars," so that it is made clear that their power comes from God and not human beings (2 Cor. 4.7). It is possible to see this language as continuing the traditions of the prophets before Paul and of the seers gifted with apocalyptic revelations. Far from being a deterrent, Paul's weakness (whatever it might be)[73] reveals the power of God, and makes room for a christophany. In the end, Paul "as the apostle and 'imitator' of Christ, represents Christ."[74] Even his weakness contributes to Paul's authority, as a vessel for Christ.

---

73. This weakness is also mentioned in 2 Cor. 12.7. Interpretations abound on what it might be. Betz, *Galatians*, 225 is correct in my opinion when he points out that Paul uses metaphorical and demonological language to talk about his illness, not medical vocabulary.

74. Betz, *Galatians*, 226.

iii. Paul as Birthing Mother. A bit further on, in a plea asking the Galatians to listen to him, he addresses them as "his children"[75] (τέκνα μου). One would then expect a father metaphor, in a parallel to 1 Corinthians 4.15 ("For though you might have ten thousand guardians in Christ, you do not have many fathers. Indeed, in Christ Jesus I engendered[76] you through the gospel"); 1 Thessalonians 2.11 ("As you know, we dealt with each one of you like a father with his children,") and Philemon verse 10 ("I am appealing to you for my child, Onesimus, whom I have engendered during my imprisonment"). The notion of the spiritual father would be familiar in the Greco-Roman world from the mystery cults for example,[77] and would contribute to the hierarchical organization of the world around the figure of the *paterfamilias*. In Galatians 4.19, Paul however takes the family relationship in another direction and presents himself as in the throes of labor pains (ὠδίνω). The verb he uses describes Paul "as a mother giving birth to a congregation" that needs to be formed in the shape of Christ.[78] For Hans-Dieter Betz, the metaphor achieves more than just comparing Paul to a mother; it shows that Paul "understands his own mission as giving birth to Christian [sic] churches."[79] Betz indicates that there are some parallels in Gnostic literature, notably in Hermes Trismegistos,[80] and that, in its figurative sense, ὠδίνω is found in Philo and the magical papyri.[81] Betz sees this image as working to shape identity: it produces Christ inside the believers, as a "foetus," and it makes the Christian community into "a living organism."[82] Others have argued the

---

75. There is a textual variant here, where several manuscripts read τεκνια and not τεκνα. I follow NA 28, which chooses τεκνα. Τεκνα is also found in 1 Cor. 4.14.
76. The verb γεννάω is used by Paul both for women giving birth (Rom. 9.11; Gal. 4.23, 24, 29 [although Gal. 4.23 and 29 are ambiguous because they could also refer to the fact of engendering a child, in the sexual act involving a man and a woman]) than for the male act of engendering (1 Cor. 4.15; Phlm. 10).
77. See Betz, *Galatians*, 234.
78. Betz, *Galatians*, 233.
79. Betz, *Galatians*, 233.
80. Betz, *Galatians*, 233. Betz quotes Codex VI, tractate 6. On Hermes Trismegistos, see the recently published: Anna Van den Kerchove, *Hermès Trismégiste: Le messager divin* (Paris: Entrelacs, 2017).
81. See Betz, *Galatians*, 234 and notes 160 and 161. For the references in Philo: *De Sacrificiis Abel et Caini* 3.102; *Quod deterius potiori insidari soleat* 127; *De cherubim* 42, 57; *De posteritate Caini* 135; *Quod Deus sit immutabilis* 14, 137; *De confusione linguarum* 21; *De agricultura* 101; *De migratione Abrahami* 33; *Legum allegoriarum libri* 1.74. For the magical papyri: *Papyri graecae magicae* (ed. Albert Henrichs; 2 vols.; Stuttgart: Teubner, 1973–1974), 2.92.
82. Betz, *Galatians*, 235.

importance of the apocalyptic context for the image, as inscribing Paul's own missionary efforts in God's apocalyptic plan for the world.[83]

In this case, again, it is unsure whether the image would really have functioned to diminish the status of Paul, and in particular whether it questioned his masculinity, when he presents himself as a "female—identified male."[84] I will return to the issue of Paul's masculinity below, as another dimension of the production of subjects and abjects, but for now, I want to highlight the function of the motherhood metaphor in the rhetoric of Galatians. In the context of an apocalyptic worldview, the image might have more to do with the labor needed "to bring about the new age"[85] rather than with gender perception, even if gender norms can also be challenged by the image.[86] There is transgressive potential in the image for sure, and it might have been appropriated by some readers (then and today) to shift some boundaries around gender roles and the incarnation of motherhood, but this transgressiveness is not made explicit by Paul.

iv. Slaves of Each Other. I now turn to a section where the language of role reversal and service is made more obvious by Paul. Starting in Galatians 5.13, Paul opens a parenetic section where he demands that his addressees "become enslaved to one another, through love" (διὰ τῆς ἀγάπης δουλεύετε ἀλλήλοις). In the context of the overall argument of Galatians, where Paul has critiqued the members of the community for wanting to be enslaved to lower elements again, among them the law (Gal. 4.9, 4.21) and has exhorted them to freedom (5.1: "Τῇ ἐλευθερίᾳ ἡμᾶς Χριστὸς ἠλευθέρωσεν· στήκετε οὖν καὶ μὴ πάλιν ζυγῷ δουλείας ἐνέχεσθε."), the demand to become slaves of one another a couple of verses later poses a strong ethical exigency for the new community: enslavement is acceptable only if it is for the sake of the members of the Christ believing community, embodying the ethics of love

---

83. See J. Louis Martyn, *Galatians: A New Translation with Introduction and Commentary* (New York: Doubleday, 1997), 427–30. Martyn sees the apocalyptic language as a contribution to the creation of God's people. Also Gaventa, *Our Mother Saint Paul*, and Susan G. Eastman, *Recovering Paul's Mother Tongue: Language and Theology in Galatians* (Grand Rapids, MI: Eerdmans, 2007). For a discussion of the scholarship on motherhood language, see McNeel, *Paul as Infant and Nursing Mother*, 2–8.

84. Gaventa, *Our Mother Saint Paul*, 14, as quoted by McNeel, *Paul as Infant and Nursing Mother*, 7.

85. McNeel, *Paul as Infant and Nursing Mother*, 5.

86. Sandra Hack Polaski, *A Feminist Introduction to Paul* (Saint Louis, MO: Chalice, 2005), 24–5 notes the transgressive potential of a man representing himself in "drag." See on the cross-dressing potential of Paul's metaphor, my article "Monstrous Bodies in Paul's Letter to the Galatians," in *Bodies on the Verge: Queering Pauline Epistles* (ed. Joseph A. Marchal; Atlanta, GA: SBL Press, 2019), 115–41.

characteristic of the Christ believers. This ethics, reinforced later in Galatians 6.2 ("bear one another's load and thus you fulfill the law of Christ"), has, as a corollary, the fact of crucifying the flesh and its passions ("The ones belonging to Christ have crucified the flesh, along with its passions and its desires," Gal. 5.24). This new behavior, characteristic of the eschatological community, means imitation of Christ to help each other. The language of bearing one another's burden is more developed in Romans 14 and 1 Corinthians 8, where the rights of those who are more advanced in faith are limited for the sake of the weaker brother. In all these passages, Paul insists that, in the Christ-believing community, it is a mistake to think oneself superior to another. Rather, as he states in Galatians 6.3, "if they think they are something when they are nothing, they deceive themselves." The Christ believers are reminded of the necessity to remain humble, presumably since individual values and characteristics do not matter in comparison to belonging to Christ (see Gal. 3.28). This community ethics makes room for an organization alternative to the patriarchal household.

v. The Stigmata of Jesus. Finally, in a passage written in his own hand (Gal. 6.11), Paul goes back to his self-presentation, and insists upon two things: that boasting can only occur in the cross of Christ (6.14) and that he carries upon his body the marks of Jesus (ἐγὼ γὰρ τὰ στίγματα τοῦ Ἰησοῦ ἐν τῷ σώματί μου βαστάζω; 6.17). From these last passages in Galatians, one can draw out two observations about Paul's understanding of the world and of himself. First, the apocalyptic context of his thought relativizes the values of the world. Galatians 6.15 highlights this dimension as well: at the end of a letter almost entirely concerned with the appropriateness (or lack thereof) of circumcision, Paul can affirm that neither circumcision nor uncircumcision are of any importance in comparison to the new creation. The overall eschatological context of Paul's mission does mean that human differences eventually lose their importance in the face of the imminent new creation. Again, Paul's interpreters encounter language that has the potential to destabilize established boundaries. Second, Paul ends his letter by re-affirming "his self-description as a representative of the crucified Christ" (see also 1.10).[87] The word used for "marks" is στίγμα, related to the verb στίζω, meaning "to prick." The word can refer to marks that animals, but also slaves and soldiers, bore on their bodies to indicate to whom they belonged. It could also be used to refer to religious tattooing.[88] Betz

---

87. Betz, *Galatians*, 323.
88. See Gerhard Friedrich Kittel, ed., *Theologisches Wörterbuch zum Neuen Testament Band Sieben Σ* (Stuttgart: W. Kohlhammer Verlag, 1964), 657–64. As examples of

indicates that the term "originally refers to the marks of religious tattooing," a phenomenon "widely used in the Hellenistic world."[89] For Betz, however, the term has been spiritualized by Paul and refers to the troubles he faced during his missions.[90] In that sense, the description would not be understood as self-humiliating; rather, it would be part and parcel of the final section of the letter, which Betz describes as *conquestio*, where the defendant insists upon his value by describing his "worth, his manly pursuits, the scars from wounds received in battle ..."[91] As Betz indicates, the mention of the στίγματα contributes to building Paul as "the apostle of Christ ...; as the 'slave of Christ' (1:10), he represents Christ as in a christophany (4:13-14)."[92] Paul's self-presentation as the authorized representative of Christ among the Galatians is consistent throughout the letter and contributes to the affirmation of his authority. Even if Paul's language about himself does not necessarily mean a self-lowering of himself, one can ask how this language could have functioned for those who had no power in Paul's society: the slaves, the women, the children.

b. Repeating Christ for Abject Bodies. The previous analysis has shown that Paul's usage of belittling language does not necessarily mean a diminution of his own authority. This language aims at positioning Paul as the representative of Christ in the Galatian community, and consolidates Paul's position as the legitimate leader of the community. Yet, this language does carry destabilizing power, perhaps most of all for those who would not necessarily have been intended as the recipient of this language. What would it have meant for people who were not free adult males (the ideal addressees of Paul) to repeat Christ, to embody Christ, to become like him? How did Paul's strategies of community-building work on slaves (both male and female), on women, on children? When Paul writes in Galatians 3.28 that "there is no longer Jew, nor Greek, no longer slave, nor free, no longer male and female" to emphasize the unity of the believers in Christ (οὐκ ἔνι Ἰουδαῖος οὐδὲ Ἕλλην, οὐκ ἔνι δοῦλος οὐδὲ ἐλεύθερος, οὐκ ἔνι ἄρσεν

---

religious tattooing, Kittel mentions the cult of Dyonisus (3 Macc. 2.29), and Is. 44.5 as an example of sacred stigmatizing. In that sense, στίγμα has a positive content.

89. Betz, *Galatians*, 324.

90. Betz, *Galatians*, 324. The same reading is proposed by Kittel, *Theologisches Wörterbuch*, 663: "Die Deutung der στίγματα τοῦ Ἰησοῦ auf Wunden und Narben des Apostels bleibt somit die wahrscheinlichste."

91. See Betz, *Galatians*, 323, quoting Quintilian, *Instituio oratoria* 6.1.21 (trans. H. E. Butler; LCL). There is now a new edition of Quintilian, *The Orator's Education, Volume III: Books 6-8* (ed. and trans. Donald A. Russell; LCL, 126, Cambridge, MA: Harvard University Press, 2002).

92. Betz, *Galatians*, 325.

καὶ θῆλυ· πάντες γὰρ ὑμεῖς εἷς ἐστε ἐν Χριστῷ Ἰησοῦ), he does not erase the social differences of his time. As Boyarin argues, he speaks ideally of an eschatological community, and yet, in the practical world, differences are very much maintained, as evidenced by Paul's discussions of concrete problems in the community (1 Cor. 11.2-16 to cite only one).[93] In everyday life, differences between male and female, slaves and free, are very much maintained as the later Pauline tradition will show, notably in the household codes (Eph. 5.22–6.9; Col. 3.18–4.1; Tit. 2.1-10; 1 Timothy 2 reflects similar patriarchal organization, as well as 1 Tim. 5.1-6, 6.1-2). The simple presence of these many instructions in literature that claims Pauline authorship reflects the possible tensions that Paul's ideal language of erasure of differences might have provoked in the historical communities. Butler's work on boundaries and repetitions of norms should also make us attentive to the potential for queerness contained in any citation of the law.

i. Women and Paul's Message. For example, we can point out that for a young female non-Jewish enslaved body, marginalized through multiple criteria in the ancient world (age, sex, social status, race), the exhortation to put on Christ or to be morphed into Christ (Gal. 3.27 and 4.19) would function very differently than for a free Jewish adult male. At first, this exhortation might simply seem meaningless: a female slave does not have the necessary freedom to choose to embody the *ethos* of Christ. She seems to be a by-product of strategies aimed at producing free adult male, a mere abject body. Yet, Butler highlights that even the abject space produces a being who can queer norms and appropriate them for themselves. We might not be able to historically reconstruct women's exact practices, but they might have been able to perform being in Christ in their own way. One can seek traces of these appropriations of Christ in the abject spaces in the mention of women prophets in Corinth, in the martyr figures of earliest Christianity,[94] and in the monasteries where women might have found ways

---

93. See Boyarin, *Galatians and Gender Trouble*, 18, for example: "In Corinthians, therefore, Paul produces a theology of the body which balances and completes, but does not contradict, the theology of the spirit of Galatians … In the life of the spirit, in Paul as in Philo, there may be no male and female, but in the life of the body there certainly is."

94. On female martyrs from a specifically gender perspective: see Todd Penner and Caroline Vander Stichele, *Contextualizing Gender in Early Christian Discourse: Thinking beyond Thecla* (London: T&T Clark, 2009); Peter-Ben Smit, "Thecla's Masculinity in the *Acts(of Paul) and Thecla*," in *Biblical Masculinities Foregrounded* (ed. Ovidiu Creangă and Peter-Ben Smit; Sheffield: Sheffield Phoenix Press, 2014), 245–67; Gail P. C. Streete, *Redeemed Bodies: Women Martyrs in Early Christianity* (Louisville, KY: Westminster John Knox, 2009); Brooke Nelson, "A Mother's Martyrdom: Elite Christian Martyrdom and the *Martyrdom of Domina*," *Journal of Feminist Studies in Religion*

of life that allowed them to fit themselves inside the structures of patriarchy in a different manner.⁹⁵ Putting on Christ might have meant greater autonomy and agency, by giving them access to a powerful male figure. For these women, the Jesus movement might have provided a way of modifying gender boundaries. This is a second element that our reading with Butler might highlight.

ii. Gender Boundaries in Galatians: Masculinity and Femininity. The difficulty with identifying how gender boundaries might or might not be queered is that we have very little access to the way women themselves perceived their role and status in the early decades of the Jesus movement. It is not my aim here to proceed to this type of reconstruction. I merely want to point out that Butler's work in *Bodies That Matter* allows us to say that, theoretically, there were spaces for abject people in the ancient world to push against the boundaries of race, gender, social status, and age. Yet, Butler also shows that these types of practices of resistance do not mean that the edifice of patriarchal ideology is simply dismantled. Practices of resistance are inscribed inside a rhetoric of power that reproduces and repeats dominant norms. Inside Galatians, I have pointed out spaces where Paul's rhetoric offers grips for resistance practices, but, at other moments of the letter, his discourse aims to discourage exactly the kind of queer embodying of gender that his rhetoric could allow. In this section, I am looking at language used by Paul that reinforces his position as male, and constructs the position of those who oppose him as female.⁹⁶ I have mentioned how the

---

32.2 (2016): 11–26; Gillian Cloke, "*Mater* or Martyr: Christianity and the Alienation of Women within the Family in the Later Roman Empire," *Theology and Sexuality* 5 (1996): 37–57; Stephanie Cobb, *Dying to Be Men: Gender and Language in Early Christian Martyr Texts* (New York: Columbian University Press 2008).

95. On women in the monasteries and how it affected questions of gender, see: Rebecca Krawiec, *Shenoute and the Women of the White Monastery: Egyptian Monasticism in Late Antiquity* (New York: Oxford University Press, 2002). For a resource book: Ross S. Kraemer, ed., *Maenads, Martyrs, Matrons, Monastics: A Sourcebook on Women's Religions in the Greco-Roman World* (Philadelphia, PA: Fortress Press, 1988). Stephen J. Davis, "Crossed Texts, Crossed Sex: Intertextuality and Gender in Early Christian Legends of Holy Women Disguised as Men," *JECS* 10 (2002), 1–36. Elizabeth A. Clark, "Ascetic Renunciation and Feminine Advancement: A Paradox of Late Ancient Christianity," *Anglican Theological Review* 63.3 (1981): 240–57. Elizabeth Castelli, "Virginity and its Meaning for Women's Sexuality in Early Christianity," *Journal of Feminist Studies in Religion* 2.1 (1986): 61–88.

96. For an understanding of gender in the ancient world, and particularly masculinity: Maud W. Gleason, *Making Men: Sophists and Self-Presentation in Ancient Rome* (Princeton, NJ: Princeton University Press, 1995); Janice Capel Anderson and Stephen D. Moore, "Taking It Like a Man: Masculinity in 4 Maccabees," *JBL* 117 (1998): 249–73;

reference to "marks on the body" could be perceived as language that presented Paul in a manly fashion, and I turn now to a famous insult in the letter to the Galatians. In 5.12, Paul wishes his adversaries would castrate themselves (Ὄφελον καὶ ἀποκόψονται οἱ ἀναστατοῦντες ὑμᾶς), effectively making eunuchs out of them, at least rhetorically.[97]

Masculinity and Paul's Message
Discussion of this invective brings us into the construction of masculinity in the ancient world. As Karin B. Neutel and Matthew R. Anderson note, building on Maud Gleason's work, "male genitals did not an ancient man make."[98] It was rather one's social and political power that constitutes (and proves) maleness.[99] As Neutel and Anderson indicate, maleness was thus performed, and implied various qualities (courage, action dignity and most of all control),[100] but anatomy did play a role: "Masculinity 'was a language that anatomical males were taught to speak with their bodies.'"[101] Even if circumcision was criticized by Romans as being the mark of licentiousness, Jewish males, and in particular Philo, reproduce the understanding of gender common in the ancient world.[102] For Neutel and Anderson, Paul is particular because he manages to offend the construction of masculinity

---

Ralph M. Rosen and Ineke Sluiter, *Andreia: Studies in Manliness and Courage in Classical Antiquity* (Leiden: Brill, 2003); Jennifer Larson, "Paul's Masculinity," *JBL* 123 (2004): 85–97; Colleen M. Conway, *Behold the Man: Jesus and Greco-Roman Masculinity* (Oxford: Oxford University Press, 2008); Craig A. Williams, *Roman Homosexuality* (Oxford: Oxford University Press, 2010); Deryn Guest, *Beyond Feminist Biblical Studies* (Sheffield: Sheffield Phoenix Press, 2012); Claudia V. Camp, *Ben Sira and the Men Who Handle Books*; Ovidiu Creangă, ed., *Men and Masculinity in the Hebrew Bible and Beyond* (Sheffield: Sheffield Phoenix Press, 2010); Ovidiu Creangă and Peter-Ben Smit, eds., *Biblical Masculinites Foregrounded*. And also, Michel Foucault, *History of Sexuality* (3 vols.; London: Allen Lane, 1979; London: Penguin Books: 1990 and 1992). French original: *Histoire de la sexualité* (3 vols.; Paris: Gallimard, 1976 and 1984).

97. I also discuss this passage, thinking more about it with monster theory, in "Monstrous Bodies in Paul's letter to the Galatians."

98. Karin B. Neutel and Matthew R. Anderson, "The First Cut is the Deepest: Masculinity and Circumcision in the First Century," in Creangă and Smit, eds., *Biblical Masculinities Foregrounded*, 228–44, here 229. See also Gleason, *Making Men*.

99. Neutel and Anderson, "The First Cut is the Deepest," 229.

100. Neutel and Anderson, "The First Cut is the Deepest," 229.

101. Neutel and Anderson, "The First Cut is the Deepest," 229, quoting Gleason, *Making Men*, 70. They indicate that representations of the penis were available in nude statues, and people knew the ideal looking penis: "relatively small and covered with a foreskin tapering to a petite point. Even in rare depictions of erect penises, the glans was often still covered, signaling a man's respectability and self-control" (229).

102. See Neutel and Anderson, "The First Cut is the Deepest," 230–3, 237. ("In other words, the core values expected of males were the same [between Jews and Greco-

of both Jews and nations: he offends "pious Jewish ideals of masculinity by spiritualizing and perhaps even implicitly abolishing circumcision."[103] And yet, according to Neutel and Anderson, he also does not correspond to Greco-Roman ideals of masculinity when he preaches "a circumcised" and "deeply humiliated divine saviour."[104] For Neutel and Anderson, Paul's presentation of Jesus goes so far as to propose "a kind of deconstruction of conventional masculinity implicit in Paul's description of himself, his message, and his messiah."[105] However, as Neutel and Anderson also note, Paul in his own rhetoric "seeks to dominate his opponents," and, in that trait, he reproduces conventional notions of ancient masculinity.[106] His comment about the castration of his opponents falls into that rhetorical strategy. Not only does it play on the Greco-Roman despising of circumcision (in a letter heavily marked by opposition to the practice!),[107] but it also denies his opponents the right to be perceived as male and feminizes them, thus devaluing their discourse.[108] At the same time, Paul is able to reinforce his own position as the male in charge, a position he has already asserted in previous passages, notably Galatians 3.23–4.5 where he presents himself as the person who can help the Galatians mature into free adult sons, confirming the authority he has assumed at the beginning of the letter already.

Romans], despite the diametrically opposed physical ways in which the communities sought to engender and reinforce these values.")

103. Neutel and Anderson, "The First Cut is the Deepest," 239.

104. Neutel and Anderson, "The First Cut is the Deepest," 229. On the masculinity of Jesus, see Brittany E. Wilson, "Gender Disrupted: Jesus as a 'Man' in the Fourfold Gospel," *Word and World* 36.1 (2016): 24–35, and Teresa J. Hornsby, "The Dance of Gender: David, Jesus, and Paul," *Neotestamentica* 48.1 (2014): 75–91.

105. Neutel and Anderson, "The First Cut is the Deepest," 240.

106. Neutel and Anderson, "The First Cut is the Deepest," 240.

107. Neutel and Anderson, "The First Cut is the Deepest," 240.

108. Eunuchs are critiqued in Deut. 23.2; Lev. 22.25 prohibits the sacrifice of castrated animals. Josephus depicts a very negative picture of eunuchs: *Ant.* 4.290-291. The same is true for Philo: *Spec. Leg.* 3.40-42 and *Deus Imm.* 111. In Is. 56.4-5, there is a prophecy that eunuchs will be saved along with everyone else in the end times, and, of course, Acts 8.26-40 presents a eunuch who is baptized. On eunuchs, see Vern L. Bullough, "Eunuchs in History and Society," in *Eunuchs in Antiquity and Beyond* (ed. Shaun Tougher; London: The Classical Press of Wales and Duckworth, 2002), 1–17. Matthew Kuefler, *The Manly Eunuch. Masculinity, Gender Ambiguity, and Christian Ideology in Late Antiquity* (Chicago, IL: University of Chicago Press, 2001). On the eunuch of the book of Acts: Marianne B. Kartzow and Halvor Moxnes, "Complex Identities: Ethnicity, Gender and Religion in the Story of the Ethiopian Eunuch (Acts 8: 26-40)," *Religion and Theology* 17 (2010): 184–204.

Gender Boundaries and Bodies

If Paul, thus, at least in Galatians, is the male in control, able to birth other free, adult heirs, all other bodies, women, slaves, and children, are constructed as the feminine. For Paul, these boundaries are not fluid, in particular because he wants to dissociate his communities from the vices that characterize polytheists (see Gal. 5.19-21 but the vice list here matches other vice lists in the Pauline correspondence: Rom. 1.29-31, 13.13; 1 Cor. 5.10-11, 6.9-10; 2 Cor. 12.20-21).[109] Combined with the vice lists, Paul's binary understanding of gender means that those who commit the vices are also those whose masculinity is called into question. They lack the control associated with masculinity. Masculinity for Paul has nothing to do with uncontrolled bodily functions.[110] In light of Butler's analysis in *Bodies That Matter*, it is interesting to notice that understanding masculinity as disconnected from the body requires "that women and slaves, children and animals be the body, perform the bodily functions that it will not perform."[111] She adds that "the prohibition of sexual impropriety secures the impenetrability of masculinity."[112] Male bodies are defined and constructed through their removal from bodily functions, which consolidates the boundaries around the male bodies. In Galatians, Paul excludes children, castrates, slaves, and their descendants (see 4.30: "throw out the slave child and her son, for the son of the child slave will not inherit with the son of the free woman") from the sphere of the promise, thus securing a stable boundary, an impenetrable boundary, around the male, mature heirs of the promise of God. Butler asks the following question, equally relevant for Paul: "would the terms 'masculine' and 'feminine' still signify in stable ways, or would the relaxing of the taboos against stray penetration destabilize these gendered positions in serious ways?"[113] It might be possible to say that as women or slaves penetrated the Jesus movement, they could have assumed qualities that were traditionally associated with the

---

109. See Hornsby, "The Dance of Gender," 78 and 85: "Paul wants to dissolve certain boundaries (those separating Jew from Gentile), so he dispenses with certain laws (namely those having to do with food and circumcision). However, Paul seeks to strengthen the delineations between Christians [sic] and pagans and he does this by a heightened focus on sex and gender. Gender, for Paul, must be fixed, or there is no foundation."

110. See Boyarin, *Gender Trouble*, 20–1, where he argues that the erasure of gender differences was only spiritual, and furthermore meant the return to an androgynous original. For a woman to achieve some autonomy, she had to renounce her body and her sexuality, and become like a man.

111. Butler, *Bodies That Matter*, 21.
112. Butler, *Bodies That Matter*, 23.
113. Butler, *Bodies That Matter*, 23.

ancient male and challenged some gender boundaries as well as developed different uses and interpretations of the body.

Where Do We Go from There?

In my opinion, there are two connected benefits of reading Paul in dialogue with Butler.

Ambiguity of Paul's Enterprise

First, it invites the escape of binary readings of Paul, readings which have often been part of the history of scholarship and end up opposing Paul with an Other: Christianity versus Judaism, Faith versus Law, Grace versus Works, Universalism versus Particularism. Butler exposes the fundamental ambiguity of Paul's enterprise, and the Christian enterprise. Any liberating discourse is also always at the same time a disciplining discourse. Any "in-group" discourse unfailingly creates an "out group." Butler is aware that one cannot and should not simply erase boundaries, and that they are in fact necessary for building community. When it comes to Paul, this insight renders us attentive to the fact that it is useless to try to define Paul as progressive or conservative. As boundaries are crossed, they are also recreated. Both moments are necessary. Reading with Butler reminds one of the necessity of a queer critique to constantly shift boundaries that are/seem settled or fixed.

The Need for Queer Critique: Reading with the Abject Body and Camp

This queer critique, and this is the second element, can take place, in Pauline scholarship, through a process of repetition and imitation, but with constant redirecting. As scholars repeat the process and notions of scholarship before them, they can repeat with some differences, and redirect the scholarly effort in (at least) two directions. First, one can read with abject bodies. This is, for me, not necessarily a plea to reach and reconstruct the historical reactions of these abject bodies (although we can and need to be reminded of the voices that are silenced in Paul's letters, and in the letters born of the Pauline tradition). Rather, it is an effort to reconstruct other narratives based on the same characters. One powerful example (which I discuss elsewhere)[114] is the re-appropriation of the figure of Hagar by womanist theo-

---

114. "Biblical Hermeneutics of Imagination: Reading the Bible with Theory/ies in Western Europe (Feminist, Gender-Critical, Queer, Postcolonial Approaches)," in *Christentum und Europa. XVI. Europäischer Kongress für Theologie (10.-13. September*

logians, who, when they read with Hagar, construct a new identity for a marginalized figure inside the Pauline corpus and for themselves.[115]

Another strategy, less connected to traditional biblical scholarship, is related to the notion of "camping," as discussed by Susan Sontag in her "Notes on 'Camp.'"[116] In "Notes on 'Camp," Sontag proposes some "jottings" about "camp," which she defines as a sensibility marked by its love of the unnatural, the artifice and the exaggerated.[117] She sees "camp" embodied particularly in Art Nouveau, which perceives a potential for beauty in every object, and converts objects in what they are not. (Sontag gives the example of the late 1890 métro entrance in Paris, designed by Hector Guimard. These entrances are framed by doors which look like orchid stems.) The elements that interest me in Sontag's musings on "camp" have to do with the potential contained in "camp" for subverting things, for pushing, as Sontag says, the metaphor of "life as theater."[118] "Camp" can "be serious about the frivolous, and frivolous about the serious."[119] In addition, as Melissa Wilcox notes, camp can also take "a traditional cultural object or practice that has become slightly antiquated, an object of nostalgic and even saccharine affection in some areas of mainstream culture and re-invigorat[e] it with an ironic, queer twist that can be respectfully subtle, cunningly subversive, or blatantly shocking."[120]

Without being "camp" in all the ways that Sontag enumerates, it appears that the order of the Sisters of Perpetual Indulgence present an interesting

2017 in Wien) (ed. Michael Meyer-Blanck; Leipzig: Evangelische Verlagsanstalt, 2019), 424–34.

115. See for example, Delores S. Williams, *Sisters in the Wilderness: The Challenges of Womanist God-Talk* (New York: Orbis Books, 1993), also by Delores S. Williams, "Hagar in African American Biblical Appropriation," in *Hagar, Sarah and Their Children: Jewish, Christian and Muslim Perspectives* (ed. Phyllis Trible and Letty M. Russell; Louisville, KY: Westminster John Knox Press, 2006), 171–84. Also, Vanessa Lovelace, "'This Woman's Son Shall Not Inherit with My Son': Towards a Womanist Politics of Belonging in the Sarah-Hagar Narratives," *The Journal of the Interdenominational Theological Center* 41 (2015): 63–82; Renee K. Harrison, "Hagar Ain't Workin', Gimme Me Celie: 'A Hermeneutic of Rejection and a Risk of Re-appropriation,'" *Union Seminary Quarterly Review* 58.3 (2004): 38–55.

116. "Camping" is discussed by Susan Sontag, "Notes on 'Camp,'" in *Against Interpretation and Other Essays* (ed. Susan Sontag; New York: Picador, 1990), 275–92. The essay itself dates to 1964.

117. "Camping" and "Camp" come from the French verb "camper" in the meaning to embody someone, to act, as used in the expression "camper un personnage."

118. Sontag, "Notes on 'Camp,'" 290.

119. Sontag, "Notes on 'Camp,'" 288.

120. Melissa Wilcox, *Queer Nuns: Religion, Activism, and Serious Parody* (New York: New York University Press, 2018), 96.

potential for embodying religion, and here catholic religion, as "camp," as Wilcox also develops.[121] The order of the Sisters of Perpetual Indulgence reproduces some of the key elements of Catholicism in their organization in various houses, in their hierarchy, and in the process to become a sister.[122] Yet, they use the codes of traditional nunneries in order to exaggerate and queer them, repeating Catholic traditions and values to not only reach people outside traditional Catholicism, but also to propose a different position on questions that are difficult for traditional Catholicism. They reach people marginalized and persecuted by traditional Christianity and combat bigotry and often their own rejection by traditional Christianity through an irreverent use of the language and practices of traditional religion. They embody Christian values in drag, for a purpose often at odds with the traditional values of Christianity. By camping religion, they manage to queer it, and yet they also go back to the heart of the Christian message, in liberating human beings from guilt. Their artificiality and exaggeration in dress and makeup allows them to be light and playful about serious questions, such as the HIV/AIDS epidemic, homophobia, the attitude of Christian churches towards LGBTQI+ people, while at the same time addressing these questions on the ground with people directly affected by them.

In the Sisters' camping, or serious parody, as Wilcox terms it, one can find the kind of critical repetition analyzed by Butler in *Bodies That Matter*.

---

121. The Sisters of Perpetual Indulgence is an order of "queer nuns," which first appeared in 1979. On their website, here is how they present themselves: "The Sisters of Perpetual Indulgence® is a leading-edge Order of queer nuns. Since our first appearance in San Francisco on Easter Sunday, 1979, the Sisters have devoted ourselves to community service, ministry and outreach to those on the edges, and to promoting human rights, respect for diversity and spiritual enlightenment. We believe all people have a right to express their unique joy and beauty and we use humor and irreverent wit to expose the forces of bigotry, complacency and guilt that chain the human spirit" (www.thesisters.org, accessed on 14 July 2017). Of course, one could argue that Catholicism as a religion might have "camp" potential. For an in-depth analysis of the Sisters, see Wilcox, *Queer Nuns*. I thank Andreas Ihlang Berg for bringing Melissa Wilcox's work to my attention.

122. See the information about becoming a sister, https://www.thesisters.org/become-a-nun, which echoes the traditional language of religious calling: "Being a Sister requires a lot of different skills and an investment in time, energy and money. In evaluating a potential new member, we look at a number of things. We look for drive, passion and commitment; a desire to perform *community service*; the ability to handle many tasks with *grace*; *honesty* and a *genuine* character; good people skills and the ability to interact with others in a *meaningful* way" (italics mine). Wilcox also notes the rather elaborate (although differing from house to house) ranking system of the Order: one begins one's trajectory in the order as a postulant (in some orders, you have a stage of aspirancy), then as novice, finally becoming a Fully Professed Sister, with full rights and responsibilities in the house. See Wilcox, *Queer Nuns*, 4 and 10–3.

Wilcox, using Linda Hutcheon's language, describes the parody that takes place in the Sisters' practice as "repetition with critical distance."[123] In this form of repetition or imitation that opens spaces for resistance, Wilcox sees the Sisters as not only "camping but also reclaiming in all seriousness cultural figures [nuns] that have proven oppressive to queer individuals and communities."[124] For Wilcox, this serious parody allows the Sisters to also argue that they might in fact transmit "the most authentic, best forms of the religion by which they and their communities have often been repressed."[125] In their transgressive imitation, they contribute to modifying the form of the original they claim to reproduce (here, specifically Roman Catholicism).

In their parodic, yet serious, repetition, they actualize the Christian message of grace, the drive towards universalism and care for the weakest member, the potential for subverting hierarchical and patriarchal organization, present in the Pauline letters. And yet, in a context where Christianity has often proved harmful and hurtful to queer communities, it is precisely the boundaries erected around sexuality and gender through the endless repetition of the same Pauline letters that the Order of the Sisters of Perpetual Indulgence must joyfully transgress to embody a new kind of Christianity.[126]

Where does it leave us then, in terms of radical, Butlerian imitation and its impact on Paul's letters? Can one move from an endless critique and transgression to communities that construct a theology and a hermeneutic? To spaces that settle and establish themselves? As Wilcox has shown, the Sisters have struggled with precisely these questions, especially at the end of the eighties, when the Sisters of Perpetual Indulgence became a legal corporation.[127] While for some it was a "betrayal of [the] anarchist roots"[128] of the movement, it also proposes one possible answer to the question often asked of queer, transgressive movements about the constructive side of their criticism. I believe that repetition offers at least a first way to reflect upon that question.

As I have tried to show, Paul's letters (and in particular the most famous and important ones to Christianity, like Romans and Galatians) have been

---

123. Wilcox, *Queer Nuns*, 70 quoting Linda Hutcheon, *A Theory of Parody: The Teaching of Twentieth-Century Art Forms* (2nd edn.; Champaign: University of Illinois Press), 6.

124. Wilcox, *Queer Nuns*, 70.

125. Wilcox, *Queer Nuns*, 90.

126. Not all Sisters would see the order as embodying Christianity, of course. Some Sisters are quite critical of religion in general and Christianity in particular. But others also see the order as a better incarnation of Roman Catholicism. See Wilcox, *Queer Nuns*, particularly 87–95.

127. Wilcox, *Queer Nuns*, 58.

128. Wilcox, *Queer Nuns*, 58.

repeated almost *ad nauseam* by commentators and interpreters. Queer repetitions not only disrupt "proper" interpretations of Paul, just as camping nuns trouble our understanding of traditional nuns, but they also encourage us to seize the liberating aspects of Paul's letters and to use them, as is needed in diverse contexts, to create communities bold enough to advocate for the rights of oppressed people and humble enough to identify their own mechanisms of power and oppression.[129] Resistance also needs to open itself to subversive criticism. I think this can only happen if one takes the risk to propose possible interpretations, possible embodiments of communities, knowing that, as soon as one does so, one will be open to criticism and to re-evaluation. But, as Wilcox concludes one of her chapters, "if fabulously sexy queer nuns can exist, then perhaps anything is possible …"[130] even interpretations not doomed to endlessly repeat themselves, even communities that explicitly recognize the need for criticism and dialogue. Perhaps that is what a dialogue with Butler can teach us when we read Paul's letters: the necessity to propose possible interpretations and the correlated need to recognize that our interpretations will never be the definite ones, but only another critical repetition, curious and eager to be challenged by other readers.

Biographical Note

Since 2013, Valérie Nicolet is Associate Professor at the Institut protestant de théologie (faculté de Paris), where she teaches New Testament and Ancient Greek. In her research, she focuses on the Pauline letters. At the moment, she is working on the rhetorical construction of the law in Galatians. Her scholarship highlights interdisciplinary approaches, more prominently with philosophy, and recently, with queer theory. She has published a book on the construction of the self in Romans, *Constructing the Self: Thinking with Paul and Michel Foucault* (Tübingen: Mohr Siebeck, 2012).

Bibliography

Anderson, Janice Capel, and Stephen D. Moore. "Taking It Like a Man: Masculinity in 4 Maccabees," *Journal of Biblical Literature* 117 (1998): 249–73. https://doi.org/10.2307/3266982

Betz, Hans Dieter. *Galatians: A Commentary on Paul's Letter to the Churches in Galatia.* Philadelphia, PA: Fortress Press, 1979.

Boyarin, Daniel. *Galatians and Gender Trouble: Primal Androgyny and the 1st Century*

---

129. See also Wilcox, *Queer Nuns*, 139 for example. Wilcox extensively discusses the politics of gender and race at stake in the Sisters' organization.

130. Wilcox, *Queer Nuns*, 103.

Origins of a Feminist Dilemma. Edited by Christopher Ocker. Protocol of the Colloquy of the Center for Hermeneutical Studies. 5 April 1992. Berkeley, CA: Center for Hermeneutical Studies, 1995.

Briggs, Sheila. "Paul on Bondage and Freedom in Imperial Roman Society," 110–23 in Horsley, ed., *Paul and Politics*, 2000.

Bullough, Vern L. "Eunuchs in History and Society," 1–17 in *Eunuchs in Antiquity and Beyond*. Edited by Shaun Tougher. London: The Classical Press of Wales and Duckworth, 2002. https://doi.org/10.2307/j.ctv1n35846.5

Butler, Judith. *Gender Trouble: Feminism and the Subversion of Identity.* London: Routledge, 1990.

—*Bodies That Matter: On the Discursive Limits of "Sex".* New York: Routledge, 1993.

Callahan, Allen Dwight. "Paul, *Ekklêsia*, and Emancipation in Corinth: A Coda on Liberation Theology," 216–23 in Horsley, ed., *Paul and Politics*, 2000.

Camp, Claudia V. *Ben Sira and the Men Who Handle Books: Gender and the Rise of Canon-Consciousness.* Sheffield: Sheffield Phoenix Press, 2013.

Castelli, Elizabeth. "Ascetic Renunciation and Feminine Advancement: A Paradox of Late Ancient Christianity," *Anglican Theological Review* 63.3 (1981): 240–57.

—"Virginity and its Meaning for Women's Sexuality in Early Christianity," *Journal of Feminist Studies in Religion* 2.1 (1986): 61–88.

—*Imitating Paul: A Discourse of Power.* Louisville, KY: Westminster John Knox, 1991.

Cloke, Gillian. "*Mater* or Martyr: Christianity and the Alienation of Women within the Family in the Later Roman Empire," *Theology and Sexuality* 5 (1996): 37–57.

Cobb, Stephanie. *Dying to Be Men: Gender and Language in Early Christian Martyr Texts.* New York: Columbian University Press 2008. https://doi.org/10.7312/cobb14498

Conway, Colleen M. *Behold the Man: Jesus and Greco-Roman Masculinity.* Oxford: Oxford University Press, 2008. https://doi.org/10.1177/135583589600300504

Creangă, Ovidiu, ed. *Men and Masculinity in the Hebrew Bible and Beyond.* Sheffield: Sheffield Phoenix Press, 2010.

Creangă, Ovidiu, and Peter-Ben Smit, eds. *Biblical Masculinities Foregrounded.* Sheffield: Sheffield Phoenix Press, 2014.

Davis, Stephen J. "Crossed Texts, Crossed Sex: Intertextuality and Gender in Early Christian Legends of Holy Women Disguised as Men," *Journal of Early Christian Studies* 10.1 (2002): 1–36. https://doi.org/10.1353/earl.2002.0003

Eastman, Susan G. *Recovering Paul's Mother Tongue: Language and Theology in Galatians.* Grand Rapids, MI: Eerdmans, 2007.

Ehrensperger, Kathy. *That We May Be Mutually Encouraged: Feminism and the New Perspective in Pauline Studies.* New York: T&T Clark, 2004.

Fatum, Lone. "Brotherhood in Christ: A Gender-Hermeneutical Reading of 1 Thessalonians," 183–97 in *Constructing Early Christian Families: Family as Social Reality and Metaphor*. Edited by Halvor Moxnes. London: Routledge, 1997.

Foucault, Michel. *The Archaeology of Knowledge and the Discourse of Language.* New York: Pantheon Books, 1972.

—*History of Sexuality.* 3 volumes. Volume 1; London: Allen Lane, 1979. Volumes 2 and 3; London: Penguin Books: 1990 and 1992. French original: *Histoire de la sexualité.* 3 volumes. Paris: Gallimard, 1976 and 1984.

—*History of Sexuality. Volume 1: An Introduction.* New York: Vintage Books, 1990.

Gaventa, Beverly Roberts. *Our Mother Saint Paul.* Louisville, KY: Westminster John Knox, 2007.

Gemeinhardt, Peter. *Das lateinische Christentum und die antike pagane Bildung.* Tubingen: Mohr Siebeck, 2007. https://doi.org/10.1628/978-3-16-151340-4

—"In Search of Christian Paideia: Education and Conversion in Early Christian Biography," *Zeitschrift für antikes Christentum* 16 (2012): 88–98. https://doi.org/10.1515/zac-2012-0008

Gleason, Maud W. *Making Men: Sophists and Self-Presentation in Ancient Rome.* Princeton, NJ: Princeton University Press, 1995. https://doi.org/10.1515/9780691187570

Goodrich, John K. "Guardians, Not Taskmasters: The Cultural Resonances of Paul's Metaphor in Galatians 4.1-2," *JSNT* 32.3 (2010): 251–84. https://doi.org/10.1177/0142064X09357677

Guest, Deryn. *Beyond Feminist Biblical Studies.* Sheffield: Sheffield Phoenix Press, 2012.

Harrison, Renee K. "Hagar Ain't Workin', Gimme Me Celie: 'A Hermeneutic of Rejection and a Risk of Re-appropriation,'" *Union Seminary Quarterly Review* 58.3 (2004): 38–55.

Hornsby, Teresa J. "The Annoying Woman: Biblical Scholarship after Judith Butler," 71–89 in *Bodily Citations: Religion and Judith Butler.* Edited by Ellen T. Armour and Susan M. St. Ville. New York: Columbia University Press, 2006.

—"The Dance of Gender: David, Jesus, and Paul," *Neotestamentica* 48.1 (2014): 75–91.

Horsley, Richard A. "The Slave Systems of Classical Antiquity and Their Reluctant Recognition by Modern Scholars," *Semeia* 83–84 (1998): 19–66.

—ed. *Paul and Politics: Ekklesia, Israel, Imperium, Interpretation.* London: Trinity Press International, 2000.

Hutcheon, Linda. *A Theory of Parody: The Teaching of Twentieth-Century Art Forms.* 2nd edn. Champaign: University of Illinois Press.

Jodamus, Jonathan. "Gendered Ideology and Power in 1 Corinthians," *Journal of Early Christian History* 6.1 (2016): 29–58. https://doi.org/10.1080/2222582X.2016.1184884

Kaden, David A. *Matthew, Paul and the Anthropology of Law.* Tübingen: Mohr Siebeck, 2016. https://doi.org/10.1628/978-3-16-154077-6

Kahl, Brigitte. *Galatians Re-imagined: Reading with the Eyes of the Vanquished.* Minneapolis, MN: Fortress Press, 2010. https://doi.org/10.2307/j.ctv19cwb7n

Kartzow, Marianne B., and Halvor Moxnes. "Complex Identities: Ethnicity, Gender and Religion in the Story of the Ethiopian Eunuch (Acts 8: 26-40)," *Religion and Theology* 17 (2010): 184–204. https://doi.org/10.1163/157430110X597827

Kraemer, Ross S., ed. *Maenads, Martyrs, Matrons, Monastics: A Sourcebook on Women's Religions in the Greco-Roman World.* Philadelphia, PA: Fortress Press, 1988.

Krawiec, Rebecca. *Shenoute and the Women of the White Monastery: Egyptian Monasticism in Late Antiquity.* New York: Oxford University Press, 2002. https://doi.org/10.1093/0195129431.001.0001

Kuefler, Matthew. *The Manly Eunuch: Masculinity, Gender Ambiguity, and Christian Ideology in Late Antiquity.* Chicago, IL: University of Chicago Press, 2001.

Laes, Christian, and Ville Vuolanto, eds. *Children and Everyday Life in the Roman and Late Antique World.* London: Routledge, 2017. https://doi.org/10.4324/9781315568942

Larson, Jennifer. "Paul's Masculinity," *JBL* 123 (2004): 85–97. https://doi.org/10.2307/3268551

Lietaert Peerbolte, Bert Jan, and Leendert Groenendijk, "Family Discourse, Identity Formation, and the Education of Children in Earliest Christianity," *Annali di storia dell'esegesi* 33.1 (2016): 129–49.

Lopez, Davina. *Apostle to the Conquered: Reimagining Paul's Mission.* Minneapolis, MN: Fortress Press, 2010.

Lovelace, Vanessa. "'This Woman's Son Shall Not Inherit with my Son': Towards a Womanist Politics of Belonging in the Sarah–Hagar Narratives," *The Journal of the Interdenominational Theological Center* 41 (2015): 63–82.

Mackey, Jacob L. "Roman Children as Religious Agents: The Cognitive Foundations of Cult," 179–97, in Laes and Vuolanto, eds., *Children and Everyday Life*, 2017.

Maines, Mary Jo. "Age as a Category of Historical Analysis: History, Agency, and Narratives of Childhood," *Journal of the History of Childhood and Youth* 1.1 (2008): 114–24. https://doi.org/10.1353/hcy.2008.0001

Marchal, Joseph A. *Hierarchy, Unity and Imitation: A Feminist Rhetorical Analysis of Power Dynamics in Paul's Letter to the Philippians.* Atlanta, GA: Society of Biblical Literature Press, 2006.

Marrou, Henri-Irénée. *Histoire de l'éducation dans l'antiquité.* 6th edn. Paris: Éditions du Seuil, 1965.

Martin, Dale B. *Slavery as Salvation: The Metaphor of Slavery in Pauline Christianity.* New Haven, CT: Yale University Press, 1990. https://doi.org/10.2307/j.ctt1xp3tkh

Martyn, J. Louis. *Galatians: A New Translation with Introduction and Commentary,* New York: Doubleday, 1997. https://doi.org/10.5040/9780300261691

McNeel, Jennifer Houston. *Paul as Infant and Nursing Mother: Metaphor, Rhetoric, and Identity in 1 Thessalonians 2:5–8.* Atlanta, GA: Society of Biblical Literature Press, 2014. https://doi.org/10.2307/j.ctt9qh222

Moxnes, Halvor, ed. *Constructing Early Christian Families: Family as Social Reality and Metaphor.* New York: Routledge, 1997.

Nelson, Brooke. "A Mother's Martyrdom: Elite Christian Martyrdom and the *Martyrdom of Domina*," *Journal of Feminist Studies in Religion* 32.2 (2016): 11–26. https://doi.org/10.2979/jfemistudreli.32.2.03

Neutel, Karin B., and Matthew R. Anderson, "The First Cut is the Deepest: Masculinity and Circumcision in the First Century," 228–44 in Creangă and Smit, eds., *Biblical Masculinities Foregrounded*, 2014.

Nicolet, Valérie. "Biblical Hermeneutics of Imagination: Reading the Bible with Theory/ies in Western Europe (Feminist, Gender-Critical, Queer, Postcolonial Approaches)", 424–34 in *Christentum und Europa. XVI. Europäischer Kongress für Theologie (10.-13. September 2017 in Wien)*. Edited by Michael Meyer-Blanck. Leipzig: Evangelische Verlagsanstalt, 2019.

—"Monstrous Bodies in Paul's Letter to the Galatians," 115–41 in *Bodies on the Verge: Queering Pauline Epistles.* Edited by Joseph A. Marchal. Atlanta, GA: Society of Biblical Literature Press, 2019. https://doi.org/10.2307/j.ctvh4zh7m.8

Osiek, Carolyn, and David L. Balch. *Families in the New Testament World: Households and House Churches.* Louisville, KY: Westminster/John Knox, 1997.

Patterson, Orlando. *Slavery and Social Death: A Comparative Study.* Cambridge, MA: Harvard University Press, 1982.

Penner, Todd, and Caroline Vander Stichele. *Contextualizing Gender in Early Christian Discourse: Thinking beyond Thecla.* London: T&T Clark, 2009.

Philo. *On the Creation: Allegorical Interpretation of Genesis 2 and 3.* Translated by F. H. Colson and G. H. Whitaker. Loeb Classical Library, 226. Cambridge, MA: Harvard University Press, 1929. https://doi.org/10.4159/DLCL.philo_judaeus-allegorical_interpretation_genesis_i_ii.1929

—*Papyri graecae magicae*. Edited by Albert Henrichs. 2 volumes. Stuttgart: Teubner, 1973–1974.
Polaski, Sandra Hack. *A Feminist Introduction to Paul.* Saint Louis, MO: Chalice, 2005.
Quintilian, *The Orator's Education, Volume III: Books 6–8.* Edited and translated by Donald A. Russell. Loeb Classical Library, 126. Cambridge, MA: Harvard University Press, 2002.
Rawson, Beryl. "'The Roman Family' in Recent Research: State of the Question," *Biblical Interpretation* 11.2 (2003): 119–38. https://doi.org/10.1163/156851503765661249
Rosen, Ralph M., and Ineke Sluiter. *Andreia: Studies in Manliness and Courage in Classical Antiquity.* Leiden: Brill, 2003. https://doi.org/10.1163/9789047400738
Sandnes, Karl Olav. *The Challenge of Homer: School, Pagan Poets and Early Christianity.* London: T&T Clark, 2009.
Schüssler Fiorenza, Elisabeth. *Wisdom Ways: Introducing Feminist Biblical Interpretation.* Maryknoll, NY: Orbis, 2001.
Scott, James M. *Adoption as Sons of God: An Exegetical Investigation into the Background of ΥΙΟΘΕΣΙΑ in the Pauline Corpus.* Tübingen: Mohr Siebek, 1992.
Smit, Peter-Ben. "Thecla's Masculinity in the *Acts (of Paul) and Thecla*," 245–67 in Creangă and Smit, eds., *Biblical Masculinities Foregrounded,* 2014.
Sontag, Susan. "Notes on 'Camp,'" 275–92 in Sontag, *Against Interpretation and Other Essays.* New York: Picador, 1990.
Streete, Gail P. C. *Redeemed Bodies: Women Martyrs in Early Christianity.* Louisville, KY: Westminster John Knox, 2009.
The Sisters of Perpetual Indulgence. www.thesisters.org (accessed 14 July 2017).
Van den Kerchove, Anna. *Hermès Trismégiste: Le messager divin.* Paris: Entrelacs, 2017.
Vuolanto, Ville. "Experience, Agency, and the Children in the Past: The Case of Roman Childhood," 11–24 in Laes and Vuolanto, eds., *Children and Everyday Life*.
Watson, Alan. *The Digest of Justinian.* Philadelphia, PA: University of Pennsylvania Press, 1998.
Wilcox, Melissa. *Queer Nuns: Religion, Activism, and Serious Parody*. New York: New York University Press, 2018.
Williams, Craig A. *Roman Homosexuality.* Oxford: Oxford University Press, 2010.
Williams, Delores S. *Sisters in the Wilderness: The Challenges of Womanist God-Talk.* New York: Orbis Books, 1993.
—"Hagar in African American Biblical Appropriation," 171–84 in *Hagar, Sarah and Their Children: Jewish, Christian and Muslim Perspectives.* Edited by Phyllis Trible and Letty M. Russell. Louisville, KY: Westminster John Knox Press, 2006.
Wilson, Brittany E. "Gender Disrupted: Jesus as a 'Man' in the Fourfold Gospel," *Word and World* 36.1 (2016): 24–35.
Wire, Antoinette Clark. *The Corinthian Women Prophets: A Reconstruction through Paul's Rhetoric.* Eugene, OR: Wipf & Stock, 2003. [Minneapolis, MN: Fortress Press, 1990].
Wright, Benjamin G. *Praise Israel for Wisdom and Instruction: Essays on Ben Sira and Wisdom, the Letter of Aristeas and the Septuagint.* Leiden: Brill, 2008. https://doi.org/10.1163/ej.9789004169081.i-364
—"Where is the Torah in Ben Sira?" Unpublished paper given at the 9th Enoch Seminar in Camaldoli, 18–23 June 2017.

Chapter Fifteen

Mattering Bodies:
Animacy and Justice in Origen's *On First Principles*

Peter Anthony Mena

The radical attempt to think incommensurate queer inhumanity is a denaturalizing and unsettling of the settled, sedimented, and often ferocious world of recalcitrant anti-inhumanity. Queer thought is, in large part, about casting a picture of arduous modes of relationality that persist in the world despite stratifying demarcations and taxonomies of being, classifications that are bent on the siloing of particularity and on the denigrating of any expansive idea of the common and commonism.[1]

—José Esteban Muñoz, "Theorizing Queer Inhumanisms"

Which bodies come to matter—and why?[2]

—Judith Butler, *Bodies That Matter*

It is a curious thing, I think, to use a "new materialist" approach to reading ancient Christian literature. The curiosity does not arise simply because of the seeming contradictory word play with *new* and *ancient*. Nor, do I believe, is it a curious thing to use such literary and methodological tools to read ancient literature anew. Many far more adept and knowledgeable scholars of ancient Christianity have already carved a path for such transgressive and fruitful readings to be respected and taken seriously. This volume of essays is a testament to those scholars and the work they have done to make the use of critical theory as a hermeneutic for understanding the rich literature of earliest Christianities. Still, it is a curious thing to bring together seemingly disparate ideas and thinkers—separated by more than a millennium—into a coherent argument for understanding ancient cosmologies and ecologies in new, and I hope, insightful ways. For this reason, what follows is much less an argument than ruminations on these ideas. It is the case that I believe there is much to be gained by placing these ideas and thinkers in "conversation" with one another. What emerges for me, at least (and I hope for others too), are more questions and ideas inclined towards

---

1. José Esteban Muñoz, "Theorizing Queer Inhumanisms: The Sense of Brownness," in *GLQ* 21.2–3 (2015): 209–10.
2. Judith Butler, *Bodies That Matter* (New York, NY: Routledge, 1993), xii.

justice-oriented understandings of bodies—including all non-human bodies and for that matter, all matter.

I want to take into consideration the ideas of the early Christian philosopher-theologian, Origen of Alexandria. It is my contention that his cosmogony, laid bare in his *On First Principles*, coupled with the work of philosopher Judith Butler—especially from her *Bodies That Matter* (and most especially critiques of her ideas)—might offer us a glimpse of possibilities. How did some early Christians understand the material world that engulfed them? How did they understand humanity's place in the grand cosmos? What, if anything, do their cosmogonies have to offer our contemporary ruminations on the cosmos, ecological devastations, the treatment of non-human animals, and the treatment of all matter—human and non-human alike? While serious and deep consideration of these and other related questions is far too grand for the scope of this essay, I offer here some seeds of thought on what Origen (and through Origen, Platonic thought), has to offer our modern ideas and approaches to justice-oriented and sustainable living.

In part, what I would like to consider is how new materialist thought further nuances Butler's important (even if lacking in some respects) contributions to a more justice-oriented understanding of the human body and how that might be extended to other non-human bodies—to all matter. It is indeed my belief that Origen has much to offer to our understandings of the cosmos and its genesis, and therefore how we might conceive of all matter—not only theologically, but also ethically and culturally (which is not to say, of course, that ethics and culture are not theological matters!).

In *On First Principles*, Origen details the creation and telos of the cosmos and all the visible and invisible bodies that materialize within it. And while he demonstrates an ambivalence toward matter, it is an ambivalence that establishes a complex hierarchical and simultaneously egalitarian understanding of matter. Thus, the wordplay often invoked within new materialist thinking—that is, "matter that matters"—takes on a particular understanding when reading *On First Principles* with an eye toward questions of theology, social justice concerns, and even movements such as Black Lives Matter.

I will bring together several seemingly dissimilar thinkers and fields of inquiry in order to reflect on Origen's theology, rooted in Hellenistic philosophy—the zeitgeist of second- and third-century Christian politics—and I will suggest that Origen has something important to offer our current moment. That *something* is oriented toward justice for all matter—and it is a justice that extends beyond care for only matter viewed as animate. So, in part, one of the questions I wish to pose is: what happens when we consider all created matter as taking part in the *imago dei*? This would, perhaps, entail a reimagining of the creation narratives found in *Genesis*, but, as I will demonstrate, one of the most skilled and revered biblical exegetes from antiquity, lays the foreground for such a transgressive reading and reimagining.

Furthermore, what might such a reading offer, or, why would it matter? I believe that we might take from ancient theologians, like Origen, an understanding of the created universe as connected through a kind of kinship that would allow for an extension of love and justice to *all* matter—something akin to Ada María Isasi-Díaz's *Kindom of God*.[3] And while the focus of this essay rests primarily on a reading of *On First Principles* (and peripherally, Plato's *Timaeus*) that is centered on the cosmological bodies of the sun, the moon, and the stars, I argue that this kind of thinking would force us to not only reimagine what all matter is constituted of or imbued with, but it will also necessitate a reconsideration of the very language we use to describe such things. For example, how might our thinking and actions be shifted when we speak of the planet and the environment not as our "common home" but, rather, as our kin—as part of our familial and communal networks—more than simply the place in which humanity dwells? Would then, an encyclical titled "Care for our Common Kin"—with the same subject matter as Pope Francis's *Laudato Si*, have different impacts and implications for human treatment of the environment? I answer that question in the affirmative and so, undergirding my thought in this essay is the idea that understanding and speaking of all matter differently—as matter that *matters*—has the potential to lead us toward more just ecological practices. What I am reaching for, desiring even, is what José Esteban Muñoz calls a "sense of brownness"—where *brownness* is "an expansive category that stretches outside the confines of any group formation and, furthermore, outside the limits of the human and the organic."[4] Muñoz uses brownness—a term he recognizes as indebted to the "histories of theorizing blackness and queerness"—as a conceptual category that hones in on the relationality of all matter in the service of decentering the human. This move is a radical one, as Muñoz suggests in the epigraph to this essay. But it is one that invites a relational mode of being centered on justice for all matter.

---

3. Ada María Isasi-Díaz, *La Lucha* Continues: *Mujerista* Theology (Maryknoll, NY: Orbis Books, 2004). See especially "*Identifícate con Nosotras*: A *Mujerista* Christological Understanding," 240–65. While Isasi-Díaz uses the "kin-dom" of God to name a theological paradigm rooted in Latina/o/x conceptions of "*la familia*," this is not explicitly extended to non-human animals and non-human matter. I believe, however, that a reconception of "*la familia*" can be extended to include theses facets of ecological interconnectedness.

4. José Esteban Muñoz, "The Sense of Brownness," 209–10.

Language Matters

A shift in language is at the heart of scholar and theorist Mel Chen's work with animacies and its corollary in new materialist thought. Chen defines the term *animacy* as that which "has been described variously as a quality of agency, awareness, mobility, and liveness."[5] They describe the term's contents and contestations:

> Using animacy as a central construct, rather than say, "life" or "liveliness"— though these remain a critical part of the conversation ... helps us theorize current anxieties around the production of humanness in contemporary times, particularly with regard to humanity's partners in definitional crime: animality (as its analogue or limit), nationality, race, security, environment, and sexuality. Animacy activates new theoretical formations that trouble and undo stubborn binary systems of difference, including dynamism/stasis, life/death, subject/object, speech/nonspeech, human/animal, natural body/cyborg. In its more sensitive figurations, animacy has the capacity to rewrite conditions of intimacy, engendering different communalisms and revising biopolitical spheres, or, at least, how we might theorize them.[6]

According to Chen, a consideration of animacy gets at undermining problematic binaries in the service of opening up the capacity to speak of nonhuman matter in terms that better capture its relationship with, or effect on all human and nonhuman matter. Chen's theories on animacy contribute to the ever-growing work in theories of affect. I offer a brief example to better understand the contributions of new materialist thought on constructing language.

Theorist and anthropologist Bruno Latour famously ruminates on the now well-known dictum of the National Rifle Association: "Guns don't kill people, people kill people." But as Sonia Hazard has described, Latour's work reveals the falseness of this maxim by suggesting that once a person picks up a gun, they have been affectively changed and are no longer exactly the same person as they once were.[7] Hazard writes:

> Guns, among other things, when connected with humans, make up new networks or assemblages that embolden or enable certain kinds of actions, specifically killing. (One would not use the barrel of a gun to arrange a bouquet of roses, after all.) A shared human recognition of the gun's violent potential— drawn from, say, the news and films—induces an affective reaction on the part of the holder, who might feel powerful and dangerous. The physical heft of the

---

5. Mel Chen, *Animacies: Biopolitics, Racial Mattering, and Queer Affect* (Durham, NC: Duke University Press, 2012), 3.
6. Chen, *Animacies*, 3.
7. Sonia Hazard, "The Material Turn in the Study of Religion," in *Religion and Society: Advances in Research* 4 (2013): 58–78.

gun and the contours and textures of its surfaces may reinforce such feelings and accentuate an inclination to violence. Its trigger, which is shaped to accommodate a finger, directs human activation of a bullet. And of course, the speed of the bullet enables a murder far more easily than if one set out to kill with his or her bare hands. According to Latour, when a person kills with a gun, it is not only the person who kills. It is the larger assemblage that kills. Its murderous agency is distributed across its many parts including a finger, a trigger, a bullet, a human brain, violent films, and so on. Agency is always complex agency, unlocalizable and distributed across assemblages of both humans and things.[8]

Hazard and others use the term assemblages, from Deleuze and Guattari, in order to describe the entangled network of relations between things—subjects and objects, that work in tandem affecting each other working in unison as part of an assemblage or apart as plugged into other assemblages. The point being, that as a component of an assemblage, each part is equally important and therefore decentering the human as either the subject for analysis or *the* component which other lesser components act upon.

Similarly, Chen highlights the way that hierarchies of animacy further undermine the project of new materialist thinking. Chen uses linguistic theories to get at this problem and thereby suggests the important implication of new materialist thought. They write:

> … consider the phrase "the hikers that rocks crush": what does this mean? The difficulty frequently experienced by English speakers in processing this phrase has much to do with the inanimacy of the rock (which plays an agent role in relation to the verb crush) as compared to the animacy of the hikers, who in this scenario play an object role. "The hikers that rocks crush" thus violates a cross-linguistic preference among speakers. Yet more contentious examples belie the apparent obviousness of this hierarchy, and even in this case, *it is within a specific cosmology* that stones so obviously lack agency or could be the source of causality. What if nonhuman animals, or humans stereotyped as passive, such as people with cognitive or physical disabilities, enter the calculus of animacy: what happens then?[9]

Chen's provocative question alludes to what the stakes are for new materialist paradigms. And their provocations inspire some of my own questions and thoughts here: How might a different cosmology enliven our understanding of the environment and all matter—human and non-human alike? More importantly, might earlier Christian cosmologies give precedence for an attentiveness toward non-human matter that does not include its dominance and oppression?[10]

---

8. Hazard, "The Material Turn in the Study of Religion," 66.
9. Chen, *Animacies*, 2–3 (emphasis mine).
10. More recently, Virginia Burrus has posed the same question in her *Ancient*

Ancient Matters

The turn to the material is both a methodological possibility as well as a subject matter worthy of its own analysis by scholars. Patricia Cox Miller considers the range of options for ancient writers to communicate their own turn to the material in late antiquity.[11] For Miller, Christians of the late Roman and early Byzantine worlds attempted to make meaning of their worlds by relying on what she has termed "the corporeal imagination." According to Miller, Christians imagined matter (for her purposes, most explicitly, bodily matter) as sites for the elaboration of "spiritual presence, power, and activity."[12] Miller highlights a variety of ways in which Christian authors in late antiquity turned their focus to bodily matter and attempted to articulate the human body in art, literature, architecture, and other cultural artifacts. Miller relies on "thing theory" exemplified by the work of Bill Brown.[13] Brown, borrowing from Heidegger's distinctions between objects and things, posited that an object becomes a thing once it ceases to function as its intended purpose. At the precise moment an object fails to function as it is intended to, the relationship between the object and the human changes. As an example, Brown turns to A. S. Byatt's *The Biographer's Tale*: "Fed up with Lacan as with deconstructions of the Wolf-Man, a doctoral student looks up at a filthy window and epiphanically thinks, 'I must have things.' He relinquishes theory to relish the world at hand: 'A real, very dirty window, shutting out the sun. A thing.'"[14] The *thingness* of *things*, and their relationship to and with human animals, is precisely what I am interested in considering further. As Chen notes above and Brown's reading of Byatt exemplifies, language is a key component to how these relationships function and on what our understanding of all non-human matter is reliant. In this way, Judith Butler's consideration of matter as always in a state of becoming through language, is evoked here.[15] I will say more on this below, but for now, I simply want to note that critiques of Butler too often quickly dismiss the important function of language in shaping embodiment and relationality.

Miller argues that Christians from the fourth to sixth centuries developed strategies for articulating the saintly body—post-mortem—as more

---

Christian Poetics: Cosmologies, Saints, Things (Divinations: Rereading Late Ancient Religion; Philadelphia, PA: University of Pennsylvania Press, 2019), especially 1–4.

11. Patricia Cox Miller, *The Corporeal Imagination: Signifying the Holy in Late Ancient Christianity* (Philadelphia, PA: University of Pennsylvania Press, 2009).
12. Miller, *Corporeal Imagination*, 2.
13. Bill Brown, "Thing Theory," *Critical Inquiry* 28 (2001): 1–21.
14. Brown, "Thing Theory," 1–2.
15. Judith Butler, *Bodies That Matter*.

than just matter, but also a conduit for the divine. So primarily her work focuses on relics, hagiographies, and icons. In doing so, Miller argues that Christians retained the body, wrote the body, and depicted the body as more than matter. These strategies, according to Miller, "required the development of interpretive finesse so that the excess, the surplus value of things could be engaged and celebrated in non-idolatrous fashion."[16] While Miller's work doubly signals a turn to the material—first in her scholarship as a methodology for considering Christianity in late antiquity, then again in her analysis of the Christian authors of late antiquity who attempted to make meaning out of bodily matter, *The Corporeal Imagination* still hinges on human bodily matter. And therefore, in many ways Miller continues to center the human as the point of reference for analysis. Still, her work which is focused on the later fourth century and beyond, helps reorient our understandings of ancient Christian ideas about matter.

More recently, Virginia Burrus has turned to the material in her reading of ancient Christian texts. In her *Ancient Christian Ecopoetics*, Burrus demonstrates how "[a]ncient Christians seem to experience no sharp disjunction between the human and more-than-human world." She writes:

> They understand all things to be active, relational and elusive—that is to say, alive in some sense or potentially so. Such an animist sensibility is not sustained only, or even primarily, through the teaching of theologians; indeed, Christian doctrine is often at odds with it. It is sustained rather through the cultivation of a range of embodied habits and feelings in which *things* feature as importantly as people do. In fact, ancient Christianity is in many respects less a set of beliefs than an array of practices that nurture a style of living reverently, mindful of the power inhering in all beings.[17]

Burrus situates Origen's *On First Principles* (as well as his *Against Celsus*) as indicative of this theologically rooted, animist sensibility. Coincidentally, Burrus's rendering of ancient Christian theological and animist thinking as a "range of embodied habits and feelings," is relevant to José Esteban Muñoz's sense of brownness that I opened with in the epigraph. More precisely, it is reminiscent of what he calls "feeling brown" in which he attempts to "move beyond notions of ethnicity as fixed (something people are) and instead understand it as performative (what people do)."[18] While Muñoz is concerned with thinking about racialized differences in this way in order to provide a "reinvigorated and nuanced understanding of ethnicity,"[19] I am

---

16. Miller, *Corporeal Imagination*, 2.
17. Burrus, 212. Emphasis in original.
18. José Esteban Muñoz, "Feeling Brown: Ethnicity and Affect in Richard Bracho's *The Sweetest Hangover (and Other STDs)*," *Theatre Journal* 52.1 (2000): 67–79.
19. Muñoz, "Feeling Brown," 70.

connecting his ideas with Burrus's assertion that ancient Christians were implicated in similar frameworks of differentiating humanness from everything else through embodied habits and feelings or "affective differences," as Muñoz calls them, in order to suggest similar strategies for understanding difference.

In order to critically engage Origen's theological claims about matter, one must also comprehend an understanding of the soul and its function for early Christian thinkers as well as its reflection of the Hellenistic worldview. As Mark Edwards has noted:

> [A] large number of theologians have abandoned the belief in a discrete and immortal soul. Although it seemed to be the indispensable leaven of Christian thought and practice from antiquity to the present, this belief is now pronounced to be contrary to the spirit of the Bible ... On this view the Church Fathers, handicapped by a knowledge of Greek that our education spares us, hardly knew what they were doing when they superimposed the metaphysics of Plato on the parables of Jesus; consequently they can be at once forgiven and ignored.[20]

But if we choose not to ignore Origen and instead attempt to understand his theology, his worldview, and his Christo-Platonic cosmology, we might better glimpse early Christian ideas of the material world—the ecosystems—of which they saw themselves as a part.

Origen's contemplation of souls leads him to a distinctly complex view of bodies. And here I use the term bodies to refer to all matter as receptacles (in Platonic terms) for something akin to a soul or nous. Bodies contain *something*—and for Origen that something was something of the divine. Regarding corporeality as such with an ambivalence bordering on contempt, he nonetheless finds some bodies more beautiful than others. Indeed, in *On First Principles* he discovers a beauty and perfection in the sun, moon, and stars reminiscent of the glory of celestial bodies on display in Plato's *Timaeus*—a dialogue in which the lead interlocutor, Timaeus, presents an argument and articulation of the origin of the physical world and its inhabitants and their relationship to the larger cosmos. As we shall see, the *Timaeus* looms large in Origen's understanding of the material world. In *On First Principles*, Origen uses the idea of beauty to indicate levels of transgression by describing the opulent beauty of the sun, moon, and stars and contrasting it dramatically with the grosser, heavier, corporeality of humans and other earthborn creatures. Although Origen's notion of beauty thereby binds the visible body to a hierarchical paradigm, he regards the invisible souls as equal in making and differing only in the degree of their fall (or turning away) from God. Thus,

---

20. Mark Edwards, *Origen Against Plato* (Burlington, VT: Ashgate, 2002), 81.

in Origen we find an egalitarian model of creation juxtaposed with a hierarchical paradigm that links differentiations of embodiment and beauty with a pre-existent fall. This egalitarian model links all souls, regardless of their corporeality in the universe, that is, their embodied existence, as part of one larger familial network. The kinship metaphors invoked in Francis of Assisi's much later and well-known "Canticle of the Sun," are heirs of Origen's thought. The sun, moon, and stars are the siblings of humanity and of all created life. And, according to Origen, in their celestial bodies they are the most perfect and beautiful of all of God's children. But are these siblings without rivalry? What, furthermore, are the implications of such astral beauty for understanding human bodies in their relation to both beauty and desire?

Regarding Origen's exposition on celestial bodies and that which imbues them, one can put aside for now the heart of the "Origenist controversy" and rely on Rufinus's translated text available in extant.[21] Both Jerome and Justinian's fragments alluding to his ideas about the sun, moon, and stars are similar and nuanced in their variances.[22] It is also worth noting that Rufinus, a strict apologist for Origen's writings, makes little effort to revise (or re-write) this particular section of *On First Principles* in order to make it fit into a less controversial, theologically acceptable framework (something he acknowledges that he intentionally does in other parts of Origen's text)—indicating that Origen's theological framework for these astral bodies had not fallen completely out of favor by the later fourth and early fifth centuries when Jerome and Rufinus were debating over these ideas.[23]

Unlike Plato, Origen does not maintain that the celestial bodies are divinities themselves. In the *Timaeus*, Plato refers to celestial bodies as "the heavenly kind of gods (οὐράνιον θεων)" (40a).[24] Plato reveres these divinities as

---

21. Part of the controversy surrounding Origen's writings centers around the accuracy of their translation into Latin. Although Jerome takes issue with Rufinus's translation, there is little variance between his and Rufinus's translation with regard to the celestial bodies.

22. See *On First Principles* (trans. G. W. Butterworth; New York: Harper & Row, 1966), 62–3, where Butterworth writes, "Jerome claims to give Origen's own words. In another passage he gives Origen's doctrine as follows: 'the sun itself and the moon and the whole host of the stars are souls of creatures once rational and incorporeal, but now subject to vanity, that is to fiery bodies, which we in our ignorance and simplicity call the lights of the world.' Justinian also (Ep. Ad Mennam-Mansi IX. 513) charges Origen with saying that 'the sky and the sun and moon and stars and the waters above the heavens are living and rational powers.' Rufinus has apparently toned down the original and changed its order, but he does not seem to have omitted much at this point."

23. See Rufinus's Preface to *On First Principles*.

24. I am working with *Timaeus* (trans. R. G. Bury; Cambridge, MA: Harvard University Press, 1929).

having the most perfect shape. Their bodies then, become ones which were created in the highest attainable image. In a text where image and image-making lead to hierarchical natures in created life, the celestial "forms" are the most beautiful because of their bodily shapes. They are created in spherical bodies, not only as a prototype of that which already existed in the Platonic "Model"—the heavenly ideal of which the created universe is a copy—but also in emulation of the spherical bodily shape of the cosmos. So, there is in these beautiful bodies, an excess—a doubling over—of image. They are at once an image *from* the Model and also an image *of* the Model.

The beauty of these bodies comes into play, not only in their perfect spherical shapes, but in their adornment of garments. Plato's Demiurge decidedly "fashions the stars out of fire (ἰδέαν ἐκ πυρός)," but the sun he clothes in a light bright enough to be seen throughout the entirety of heaven. This is done so that the lesser celestial bodies can view the sun and imitate its perfect actions and movements. The stars, however, are made up of fire in order that "they be as bright as possible to behold and as fair (λαμπρότατον ἰδεῖν τε κάλλιστον εἴη)" (40a). Origen will later detail at length the beauty of these bodies and their consequential vanity. For Plato however, it is enough to say that these bodies are not only beautiful simply by the nature of their creation and shape, but also because they are composed of an elemental make-up which not only allows their beauty to be beheld by all other matter, but also contributes to that very same ideal beauty.

But with what exactly are these bodies imbued? It is not enough to accept that Plato assumes them to be of the "divine class," which he of course claims, but what exactly does it mean to be of the divine class? Before they were generated into their perfect spherical bodies, Plato refers to these proto-celestial bodies simply as "forms." As the Demiurge creates the world, it relies on "the Model," or Plato's "παραδείγματος"—the perfect ideal which necessitated that these forms, already existent in the Model, be molded into their perfect celestial bodies for the created world. The bodies contain rationality and intelligence. Being forms that are perceived by reason, they are set in motion by the demiurge thereby exemplifying their intelligence. Earlier in his text, Plato explains how motion is set just so in intelligible beings: "And he compassed them about with the motion that revolves in the same spot continually, and he made the one circle outer and the other inner. And the outer motion he ordained to be the motion of the same, and the inner motion the motion of the other" (36c).

It is through this perfect, spherical motion that the celestial bodies express their beauty and intelligence. Origen also perceives the motion of celestial bodies to exemplify this intelligence. He writes, "And since the stars move with such majestic order and plan that never have we seen their course deflected in the slightest degree, is it not the height of stupidity to say that such order, such exact observance of rule and plan, is accomplished by things without reason" (7.3)? Here Origen alludes to what will be detailed in full in *On First Principles*—his belief that non-human matter, such as the celestial bodies in the heavens, share much with human matter. As Alan Scott has convincingly argued, Origen's ideas, rooted in Hellenistic ideals, asserted that these astral bodies were just as alive as humanity. And furthermore, these bodies had the ability to cognate, to sin, and to turn away from, and inevitably back towards, God.[25] According to Origen and other contemporary thinkers, we are linked to one another—like kin—with similar attributes such as reason and intelligibility, and in possession of something like a soul.

Another characteristic sets these bodies apart from other created bodies. Plato regards celestial bodies as deities. And although he makes slight mention of it, it should not be without special notice that these are the only visible deities. He writes, "... let this account suffice us, and let our discourse concerning the nature of the visible and generated gods have an end" (40d). This demand is made just before Timaeus goes on to discuss the other divinities, which by their *invisibility*, may have caused reason for doubted existences:

> ... and we must trust to those who have declared it aforetime, they being, as they affirmed, descendants of gods and knowing well, no doubt, their own forefathers. It is, as I say, impossible to disbelieve the children of gods, even though their statements lack either probable or necessary demonstration ... we must follow custom and believe them. (40 d-e)

Plato's *Timaeus* elucidates the importance of the body and beauty within cosmogonic terms. The intelligible rationalities are formed by the creating Demiurge into perfect spherical bodies and set into perfect intelligent motion. They are either formed from or adorned with fire in order to make them more beautiful as well as to allow the rest of creation to observe their beauty. The visibility of their beautiful bodies is also a mark of their existence. There is no room for doubt here; and, with the elevated status as deities in the *Timaeus*, they are marked as the only visible gods.

While Origen does not elevate the position of celestial bodies to the status of deities, he is sympathetic to Plato's interpretation of the body and beauty. Origen views all created beings to be like Plato's "forms." They are equal in status and creation as *noetic* beings imbued with the *Logos*. In the familial terms employed by ancient Christians, a creator God is positioned

---

25. Alan Scott, *Origen and the Life of the Stars: A History of an Idea* (Oxford Early Christian Studies; Oxford: Oxford University Press, 1991).

as parent and all created matter is conceived of as God's children. According to Origen's soteriology, these *noetic* beings, siblings in relation to each other, are at first bodiless. Along with the *Logos* contained within each of these beings, they were also granted the gift of free will. Because of this gift, each of these beings decidedly turned away from God and "fell" to varying degrees. Origen's God was one of fire and light and so he uses the terms of "cooling" and "darkness" to describe the degrees to which the *noetic* beings fell. It is through the fall that they ceased being simply a *nous*—a noetic being—and became souls. It was because of the fall that the creator God was forced to create the material world with heaven and the seas and various kinds of bodies, in order to contain the fallen souls. And it is during the fall that some souls were placed within the celestial bodies to reside in the heavens of the cosmos.[26] This point in *On First Principles* is vital: all matter is created to house fallen souls. All matter is imbued with something of the divine and all matter is connected by way of familial-like connections, or kin networks.

The celestial bodies are important to Origen because they exemplify the fluidity and mobility of souls. Thus, souls are able to descend further from or ascend closer to God. He insists on refuting the claims made by other Christians who state that the sun, moon, and stars are not changing beings. He writes, "First, then, let us see what reason itself can discover about the sun, moon and stars, namely, whether it is correct to suppose, as some do, that they are exempt from the possibility of change" (2.2). Origen finds it necessary to prove his idea of "*noetic* siblings" because, for him, it explains the current status of nature and the world around him, as well as furthering understanding of the age to come, when his current world ceases to exist. In other words, through this interpretation of scripture he is able to discern that although in different bodies (human, non-human, celestial, angelic, or aerial) after the fall, all souls continue to contain a part of the God that created them and, in the end, will be called back to that God along with the rest of creation. He writes, "When Christ shall have delivered up the kingdom to God, the Father, then those living beings, because they have before this made part of Christ's kingdom, shall also be delivered up along with the whole of that kingdom to the rule of the Father; so that, when 'God shall be in all', they also, since they are part of all, may have God even in themselves, as God is in all things" (7.5). Furthermore, the celestial bodies, as well as all created matter, are for Origen living beings inasmuch as humans

---

26. See John Anthony McGuckin, ed., *The Westminster Handbook to Origen* (London: Westminster John Knox Press, 2004).

are living beings. They possess free will and reason which allows them to make choices that can improve or worsen their embodiment.

Origen, it has been argued, is ashamed of the body. Historian of Christianity Virginia Burrus notes, "Even the staunchest contemporary scholarly defenders of the Alexandrian must face the embarrassing disdain for carnality conveyed by Origen's soteriology, which strains towards an end in which all differences will dissolve like flesh, as souls merge with God in a union of perfect love."[27] Bodies are created to house fallen beings and are therefore constant reminders of creation turning away from its creator. However, contained within these concepts of bodies and shame, Origen has established a hierarchy of shame that correlates with the substance of the body. Angelic and celestial bodies are of higher regard, aerial (demonic) bodies of lesser, and human and non-human bodies fall somewhere in the middle. In part, these differences allow Origen to create meaning within an unjust world where some are rulers while others are ruled. But even more so, it explains passages of scripture which allude to God being a part of and contained within everything.[28]

So what do we make of these celestial bodies and by extension of all non-human matter? Are they similar to Plato's celestial bodies endowed with beauty and visible to all? Origen does talk of these particular bodies as being ones in which beauty is a defining characteristic. The sun, moon, and stars are some of the more perfect bodies in the cosmos. Not simply because of the lesser degree to which they have fallen, but because God has created beautiful bodies in which they reside. Their bodies, Origen finds scriptural evidence for this, are subjected to vanity. They become the subjects of vanity not by their own will but because of the will of God. In order to be obedient to God, they must endure their own beauty. Even here when Origen seems to have become comfortable with *a kind of body*, he reveals he is not.

Though celestial bodies are the most beautiful and the most perfect, they are still houses of corruption, reminders of a fall from which the inner souls desire to be released in re-unification with God. These beautiful bodies then are nothing more than prison cells. The souls contained within these cells are self-sacrificing. Residing in these beautiful bodies for the good of all created life, at the will of God and being subject to vanity, they long for release from these chains. Their self-sacrificing nature only serves to augment their already beautiful and perfected bodies. Or, perhaps, they are not self-sacrificing at all. Origen suggests that they may simply be holding up their part of a bargain

---

27. See Virginia Burrus, *Saving Shame: Martyrs, Saints and Other Abject Subjects* (Philadelphia, PA: University of Pennsylvania Press, 2008), 64–5.
28. 1 Cor. 15.28.

made with God when their souls originally fell. Origen writes, "… because he who subjected it promised those who were being given over unwillingly to vanity that on the fulfillment of their splendid work of service they should be delivered from this bondage of corruption and vanity …" (7.5). Thus, for Origen, the souls imbued within celestial bodies are at the same time self-sacrificing and self-serving.

Butler's Bodies That Matter

Returning to Butler, in her *Bodies that Matter*, she attempts to consider the hierarchies imposed on particular bodies. Now, again, Butler is concerned only with human bodies. She does not extend the definition of body, its ontology, or its production through discourse to non-human matter. She does however, through her rehearsal of Plato and feminist philosopher Luce Irigaray's reading of the *Timaeus*, consider hierarches of matter in which human matter is stratified into hierarchies across gender lines, and non-human animal matter is understood as lower than human matter. Considering Plato, she writes: "But this prior cosmogony calls to be rewritten, for if a man is at the top of an ontological hierarchy, and woman is a poor or debased copy of man, and beast is a poor or debased copy of both woman and of man, then there is still a *resemblance* between these three beings, even as that resemblance is hierarchically distributed."[29] It is precisely this resemblance where I am attempting to connect the dots. In Plato first, then later in Origen, the resemblance is akin to the kin networks I am attempting to name. And although hierarchies persist in both Origen and Plato, I think Origen's complex understanding of matter still has something important to offer our own perspectives on non-human matter.

In this way, Butler poses provocative and telling questions. She queries:

> How, then, can one think through the matter of bodies as a kind of materialization governed by regulatory norms in order to ascertain the workings of heterosexual hegemony in the formation of what qualifies as a viable body? How does the materialization of the norm in bodily formation produce a domain of abjected bodies, a field of deformation, which, in failing to qualify as the fully human, fortifies those regulatory norms? What challenge does that excluded and abjected realm produce to a symbolic hegemony that might force a radical rearticulation as what qualifies as bodies that matter, ways of living that count as "life," lives worth protecting, lives worth saving, lives worth grieving?[30]

---

29. Butler, *Bodies That Matter*, 17 (emphasis in the original).
30. Butler, *Bodies That Matter*, xxiv.

Butler's focus on human matter continues to trap us in an understanding of matter as produced through discourse and arranged in hierarchies in which some matter matters more than others. Her questions are vital ones, to be sure. In an era in which Black communities in the United States are increasingly targeted for state-sanctioned violence and some immigrants are being refused entrance into the United States while undocumented families are being torn apart and children are being placed in cages, an era in which queer people of color are increasingly met with challenges to their existence and women continue to be assaulted, victimized, and scapegoated, an era in which economic disparity increases along with the devastation enacted onto the earth, in this era, as in the many before it, Butler's questions must be at the forefront of any and all social, legal, cultural, economic, and theological considerations. For this reason, it is important, I believe, to extend her understanding of bodies to all matter—human and non-human alike. In this way, I am struck by the words of Virginia Burrus, in the preface to her work on ancient Christian ideas of shame, flesh, and embodiment:

> In what seems by now a predictable gesture, [my students] have recoiled from the manifestations in ancient Christian texts of self-hatred expressed above all in the loathing of the flesh. The students who voice such concerns respect and even powerfully identify with the yearning for transcendence, transformation, and freedom also evident in those same texts. But they resist—they struggle to resist—transcendence bought at the expense of the shaming of the body (above all the sexual body), transcendence that produces flesh in and through shame, inscribing it as a matter of shame—the shame of matter itself. Many of them do not fail to note that women, sexual and racial minorities, and the poor or uneducated seem to carry more than their fair share of the burden of such shame, or that the planet itself groans with the painfully destructive effects of the shame that nature is forced to bear. Armed with the doctrines of divine creation and incarnation, desiring to affirm the goodness of materiality, the poignancy of transience and finitude, the gift of sentience, my students still often seem to fight a losing battle against a theological tradition that remains to this day marked by its shameful shame of the flesh.[31]

Here Burrus connects human and non-human matter in her analysis of how ancient Christians thought and wrote about bodily matters. It is an important connection to make and one that has inspired me to consider further how someone like Origen of Alexandria may have understood the world and ecosystems he inhabited. Furthermore, what might that understanding offer our contemporary moment in which not all matter matters to all people?

Origen views his brother sun and sister moon as souls much like his own. At the end of time these beings will be released from their celestial bodies

---

31. Burrus, *Saving Shame*, xi–xii.

in the like manner that Origen will be released from his human body. The egalitarianism of Origen's cosmology is established with the creation of the *nous,* but it disappears with his hierarchical paradigm of bodies. He will return to his egalitarian sentiments with the re-unification of the souls with God, but in the meantime, some bodies are not only better than others, but they exceed in beauty as well.

There are definite similarities between Origen's view of celestial bodies and Plato's. Beauty is a characteristic of the bodies in both the *Timaeus* and *On First Principles*. Celestial beings are formed into bodies that are beautiful because of their purpose and perception. The light of which they are made up is the cause of their beauty and is the purpose of their existence. Unlike Plato's deities however, Origen's celestial bodies are bound to the best of what is bad—a body. While these bodies are closer to God than human bodies and all non-human matter residing on the earth, they are still temples of corruption and subject to vanity. For Origen then, even the beautiful, perfect bodies of the sun, moon, and stars, are equally disdained for being exactly what they are, bodies. And although Origen has this view of matter—a view that seemingly disparages matter—he still understands all matter as connected in kinship. I wonder then, what might we gain if we too understood our siblings in this way?

Biographical Note

Peter Anthony Mena is Assistant Professor of Theology and Religious Studies in the Department of Theology and Religious Studies at the University of San Diego. He is a historian of Christianity with expertise in Christian late antiquity and interests in the literature and cultures of the late-ancient Mediterranean as well as in contemporary literary and critical theories. Mena uses postcolonial, gender and queer theories, and cultural studies as an approach to study the past with the goals of considering current political, social, cultural moments. His award-winning monograph, *Place and Identity in the Lives of Antony, Paul, and Mary of Egypt: Desert as Borderland* (Palgrave Macmillan, 2019), uses the work of Chicana writer, Gloria Anzaldúa, to consider the descriptions of space and identity in ancient Christian hagiographies.

Bibliography

Brown, Bill. "Thing Theory," *Critical Inquiry* 28 (2001): 1–21. https://doi.org/10.1086/449030

Burrus, Virginia. *Saving Shame: Martyrs, Saints and Other Abject Subjects.* Philadelphia, PA: University of Pennsylvania Press, 2008. https://doi.org/10.9783/9780812201512

—*Ancient Christian Poetics: Cosmologies, Saints, Things*. Divinations: Rereading Late Ancient Religion. Philadelphia, PA: University of Pennsylvania Press, 2019. https://doi.org/10.9783/9780812295726

Butler, Judith. *Bodies That Matter.* London: Routledge, 1993.

Chen, Mel. *Animacies: Biopolitics, Racial Mattering, and Queer Affect*. Durham, NC: Duke University Press, 2012. https://doi.org/10.1215/9780822395447

Edwards, Mark. *Origen Against Plato.* Burlington, VT: Ashgate, 2002.

Hazard, Sonia. "The Material Turn in the Study of Religion," *Religion and Society: Advances in Research* 4 (2013): 58–78. https://doi.org/10.3167/arrs.2013.040104

Isasi-Díaz, Ada María. La Lucha *Continues*: Mujerista *Theology*. Maryknoll, NY: Orbis Books, 2004.

McGuckin, John Anthony, ed. *The Westminster Handbook to Origen.* London: Westminster John Knox Press, 2004.

Miller, Patricia Cox. *The Corporeal Imagination: Signifying the Holy in Late Ancient Christianity.* Philadelphia, PA: University of Pennsylvania Press, 2009. https://doi.org/10.9783/9780812204681

Muñoz, José Esteban. "Feeling Brown: Ethnicity and Affect in Richard Bracho's *The Sweetest Hangover (and Other STDs)*," *Theatre Journal* 52.1 (2000): 67–79. https://doi.org/10.1353/tj.2000.0020

—"The Sense of Brownness," in *GLQ* 21.2–3 (2015): 209–10.

Origen. *On First Principles*. Translation by G. W. Butterworth. New York: Harper & Row, 1966.

Plato. *Timaeus*. Translation by R. G. Bury. Cambridge, MA: Harvard University Press, 1929. https://doi.org/10.4159/DLCL.plato-philosopher_timaeus.1929

Scott, Alan. *Origen and the Life of the Stars: A History of an Idea*. Oxford Early Christian Studies. Oxford: Oxford University Press, 1991.

Index of Biblical References

Page numbers with the suffix 'n' refer to footnotes (e.g. 199n).

Old Testament/Hebrew Bible

Genesis		Exodus		Isaiah	
1	91	19.10	199	7.14	287n
1–11	36	19.14	199	44.5	335n
2	57			53.1	273
2.4–11.8	81	Leviticus		53.2	70
2.24	131	12–13	138	53.8	287n
3	36	12.2-8	138	56.4-5	339n
13.16	199n	15	138		
15.5	199n	15.19-24	138	Ezekiel	
22.17	199n	22.25	339n	1.1-27	68
26.4	199n			9.4	191n
28.14	199n	Deuteronomy			
32.12	199n	23.2	339n	Hosea	
49.11	206	23.10	138	1.10	199n
		23.12-14	138		
		30.12-14	136n		

New Testament

Matthew		23.9	259	10.29-30	259
5.3-12	257	25.31-46	257	11.15-17	257
5.25	257	26.28	89	11.27-33	258
5.40-42	257	27.45	165	12.18-27	259
6.12	257	27.54	165, 168	14.12-26	259
6.24-34	257	28.16-20	168	15.7	254
8.22	259			15.16	254
10.34-37	259	Mark		15.27	254
11.8	257	1.23-27	258	15.33	165
15.38	259	2.1-12	258	15.39	165, 168
18.23-35	257	3.20-22	259	16.14-16	168
19.5	131	3.21-30	258		
19.10-12	259	3.31-35	259	Luke	
20.8	324n	6.5-6	259	4.18	257
22.1-14	257	10.17-31	257	6.20-26	257

Luke (cont.)		8.26-35	273	1 Corinthians	
6.35	257	8.26-40	339n	1.11-12	133n
7.25	257	8.35	327n	1.23	243
7.42	286	9.31	306	3.4	133n
9.60	259	10	164–5, 167,	3.22	133n
12.13-31	257		170–1, 176,	4.7-12	329
12.42	324n		178	4.14	332n
12.51-53	259	10.3-6	164	4.15	332
12.57-59	257	10.6	166n	4.16	325
14.12-24	257	10.9-17	166	4.17	133n
14.26	259	10.22	166	5.9	133
16.1-8	257	11.19-20	167	5.10-11	340
16.13	257	11.21	306	6.1-20	137
16.19-31	257	11.24	306	6.9-10	340
20.34-36	260	12.24	306	6.9-20	262
22.19	89	14.1	306	6.12-20	263
23.44	165	15	261	6.15	286
23.47	165, 168	16.14-35	327n	6.15-16	129, 131, 134
24.44-49	168	18.3	137	7.1	133
		19.20	306	8	134, 334
John				8.1–11.1	137
1.10-18	264	Romans		10.23	263
1.14	285	1.1	329	11.1	325
2.22	263	1.26-27	134	11.1-30	329
3.3	263	1.29-31	340	11.2-16	336
3.5	263	5	271–2	11.3	140
5	264	5.12-21	244n	11.3-16	319
6.60-66	264	5.15	244	11.14	263
10.31-42	264	5.18-21	272	11.23-24	133
14.6	264	6.15-23	114n	12	263
15.13	264	8.21-23	217	12.12-27	129
16.2	264	8.26	217	12.14-20	133
21	263	9.11	332n	12.27	127, 129, 133
		10.6-7	136n	12.28-30	141
Acts		10.9	136n	13.1-13	224
1–9	165	11.17	272	14.34-36	319
2.1-4	198	12.4-5	127, 129	15	272
2.41	306	13	5n	15.28	362
2.42	310	13.1-10	262	15.45	288
2.42-47	309	13.12	325n	15.46-49	272
4.4	306	13.13	340	15.47	288
5.14	306	13.14	325n	15.53-54	285, 325n
5.35-39	307	14	334	16.1-4	133
6.1	306	15.25-28	133	16.10	133n
7	246, 306			16.15-18	133n

Index of Biblical References

2 Corinthians	
4.7	331
5.3	325n
8–9	133
12.4	217
12.7	331n
12.20-21	340

Galatians	
1.1	329, 331
1.10	334–5
1.10-12	329
1.11-12	331
1.13-16	159
1.15-16	329, 331
2.1-10	261
2.1-11	329
2.7-8	166
2.12	167
3.23	322
3.23–4.5	339
3.23-24	323
3.23-27	321
3.26	322
3.27	325, 336
3.28	261, 319, 334–5
3.29	325
4	323, 327
4.1-5	321–2
4.4-5	325
4.5	285
4.7	325
4.9	333
4.13-14	331, 335
4.19	331–2, 336
4.21	333
4.23-24	332n
4.29	332n
4.30	340
5.1	333
5.1–6.18	329n
5.6	224
5.12	338
5.13	224, 333
5.19-21	262, 340
5.24	334
6.2-3	334
6.11	334
6.14-15	334
6.17	334

Ephesians	
4.10	284
5.21–6.9	141
5.22–6.9	336
6.11-15	325n

Philippians	
1.1	329
1.13	133
2.19	133n
2.23-24	133n
2.26	133n
2.28-29	133n
3.17	325
4.18	133n

Colossians	
3.10-12	325n
3.18–4.1	141, 336

1 Thessalonians	
2.11	332
5.8	325n

1 Timothy	
2	336
3.15	270
5.1-6	336
6.1-2	336

Titus	
2.1-10	336

Philemon	
10	332

Hebrews	
11.12	199n

James	
8	138

1 Peter	
1.13-16	262
2.1-2	262
2.11–3.12	141
2.11-25	262
4.7-19	262

3 John	
9-10	264

Revelation	
2.14-15	187
2.20-23	187
3.1-3	187
3.5	191n
3.15-17	187
4–5	50
5	196, 200
5.1	59
5.5-6	200n
5.6	199n
7.1-8	192
7.3-4	191
7.4-9	190
7.5-8	187, 189–90, 195, 200
7.9	198
7.9-10	193, 196–7
7.9-17	119–20, 184–7, 189–93, 197–204, 206–7
7.10	184, 203
7.10-11	201–2, 204
7.13-14	205
12.17	190n
13.6	191
13.8	191n
14.1-5	191
15.2.4	191
17	191

Revelation (*cont.*)
17–18	50	21	50, 60	22.1	57
17.4	185n	21.1-22	57	22.3	57
17.8	191n	21.2	185n, 195n	22.5	57
20–22	57	21.9	195n	22.14	57
20.12-15	50	21.18-20	63	22.15	58
20.15	191n	21.24	57	22.19-21	57
		21.27	57, 191n		

Index of Classical References and Authors

Page numbers with the suffix 'n' refer to footnotes (e.g. 324n).

Aristotle			Plato			Plotinus	
Politicus				147n, 224-6,		*Enneades*	
1255b 35-47		324n		305		9.7	81

Rhetorica   *Phaedo*   Quintilian
I.7.1-2   169   64a   77   *Instituio oratoria*
96–107   77   6.1.21   335n

Hermes Trismegistos
Codex VI, 6   332   *Politicus*   Socrates
269c–273e   86   77

Hesiod
Theogony   *Theaetetus*   Xenophon
507   86   155c-d   72   324n

Papyri graecae   *Timaeus*   *Oeconomicus*
magicae (PGM)   352, 357, 365   1344a   324n
332   36c   359
40a   358-9
40d-e   360

Index of Early Christian Writings

Page numbers with the suffix 'n' refer to footnotes (e.g. 170n).

Acts of Cornelius		4.2 (EMML 1824)		Augustine	
	159, 162, 177		172, 174–5	*City of God, The (Civ.)*	
1.1-2	165	5.4	170n		72
1.1-3	170n	5.8 (EMML 1824)		1.18	73
1.1-9	163		172	4.14	83
1.2	164, 168	5.8-9 (EMML 1824)		12.14	83
1.2-3	166		175	14.8	73
1.4	167	5.9b (EMML 1824)		14.28	90
1.7	166		172	20.23	71, 73
1.7-8	167	6.1-5	163		
2.1	167	6.3	170n	*Confessions*	
2.1–3.9	163			2.1	74, 78
2.3	170n	Acts of Maximilian		3.1	81
2.3 (EMML 1824)		3.4	166	3.4	88
	171, 174			4.4	85
2.3-4	168	Acts of Philip		4.4-12	77
2.6-7	169	6.8-11	168	4.6	90
2.7	170n			5.6	69
2.9 (EMML 1824)		Acts of Thomas		5.19	71
	171		168	7.10	73
2.11 (EMML 1824)				7.10-11	78
	171, 174–5	Acts of Thomas and His		8.9-12	88
2.13 (EMML 1824)		Wonderworking Skin		8.12	79
	171, 174		168	8.17	88
3.4	170			9.10	78, 85
3.7	170	Acts of Thomas and		10.8	82
3.7 (EMML 1824)		Matthias		10.27	88
	171, 174–5		168	11.20	78
3.8 (EMML 1824)				11.27	78
	172, 174	Apocryphon of John		12.5	91
3.9 (EMML 1824)			178n, 179n	12.6	77, 85
	172, 175				
4 (EMML 1824)	172	Athanasius		*Ennarations on the*	
4.1-2	170n	*On the Incarnation*		*Psalms*	
4.1–5.11	163	5.2	285		66
		8	286		

Index of Early Christian Writings 373

On the Predestination of the Saints (Praed.)
ch. 37   69

On Rebuke and Grace (Corrept.)
ch. 14   69

Codex Bezae
          151–2, 154

Didache
          327

Gospel of Peter
15-22   165
39-42   163

Gospel of Thomas
          239, 246–7
16.1-4   259
64   257

Gregory of Tours
Glory of the Martyrs
          170

History of Philip
          168

History of Simon Cephas, Chief of the Apostles
6.1-7   168
7.1-6   166n

Irenaeus
Against Heresies
          269

I, 3.6   270
I, 8.1   270
III, 1.1   270
III, 3.2   270
III, 18.3 284
III, 19.1 284–6
III, 19.1-2 287
III, 19.3 285–6
III, 21.9-10   287
III, 21.10 289
III, 22.2 287
III, 22.4 288
V, 1.1   286
V, 2.2   287
V, 14.1   285
V, 19.1   288
V, 31.2   289
V, 33.4   289
V, 35.1-2 271
V, 35.2   289
V, 36.1   287

Justinian
Digest of Justinian

26.1.1   324n

Ep. Ad Mennam-Mansi
IX. 513   358n

Letter of Peter to Philip
          168

Martyrdom of Conon
2.5   169

Martyrdom of Fructuosus and Companions
3   166
4.3   166

Martyrdom of Julius the Veteran
2.3   169

Martyrdom of Montanus and Lucius
17.4   166
22.3   166

Martyrdom of Perpetua
9   169

Martyrdom of Polycarp
           166
7   169
9   169

Martyrdom of Potamiaena and Basilides
8-9   166

Origen
On First Principles
           351–2, 356–8, 365
2.2   361
7.3   360
7.5   361, 363

Index of Jewish Writings

Page numbers with the suffix 'n' refer to footnotes (e.g. 339n).

1 Enoch		**Ladder of Jacob**		*De sacrificiis Abel et Caini*	
98.2	257	1.10	199n		
102.9-11	257			3.102	332n
		3 Maccabees			
Josephus		2.29	335n	*De specialibus legibus*	
Jewish Antiquities				3.40-42	339n
4.290-291	339n	**Philo**			
18.36-38	256	*On the Creation: Allegorical Interpretation of Genesis 2 and 3*		*Legum allegoriarum libri*	
18.269-275	255			1.74	332n
			319n		
Jewish War, The				*Quod deterius potiori insidari soleat*	
4.505-508	259				
4.538	259	*De agricultura*		127	332n
		101	332n		
Life				*Quod Deus sit immutabilis*	
30	256	*De cherubim*			
39	256	42	332n	14	332n
66-68	256	57	332n	111	339n
99	256			137	332n
374-384	256	*De confusione linguarum*			
				Sirach	
Jubilees		21	332n		326
13.20	199n			38.24-34	255
14.4-5	199n	*De migratione Abrahami*			
18.15	199n			**Zohar**	
25.16	199n	33	332n	*Bereshit*	
27.23	199n			1.15a	91
		De posteritate Caini			
		135	332n		

Index of Modern Authors

Page numbers with the suffix 'n' refer to footnotes (e.g. 24n).

Adorno, Theodor W. 1, 2, 6–7, 9–11, 13–18, 20, 24n, 101n, 262
Agamben, Giorgio 79n, 289n
Aichele, George 44n, 116n, 149n, 152n
Alliez, Eric 159n
Allison, Dale C. 258n
Anderson, Benedict 185, 194, 200, 202
Anderson, Matthew R. 338–9
Arendt, Hannah 74–6, 84
Arnal, William 239n
Artaud, Antonin 130n, 142
Athanasiou, Athena 26n
Aune, David E. 57–8, 60, 201n

Baden, Joel S. 4n
Badiou, Alain viii, 6n, 10n, 11n, 213–31, 238, 240–9, 252, 260–1, 274–83
Bakunin, Mikhail 253
Baldwin, James 5
Ballard, Susan 101–3, 114n
Balzac, Honoré de 52
Bauckham, Richard 187, 189–91, 199–200
Baudelaire, Charles 16–7, 84
Baudrillard, Jean 147–51, 153–5
Bell, Vikki 298–300, 301n
Benjamin, Andrew 52n, 56n
Benjamin, Walter vii, 6–7, 10, 12–4, 16–9, 21, 23, 25, 35–46, 50–6, 62–3, 66–93
Bensaïd, Daniel 277n
Bermejo-Rubio, Fernando 254n

Berressem, Hanjo 151n, 157n, 160
Betz, Hans Dieter 329, 331n, 332, 334–5
Bhabha, Homi K. 188–9, 195n, 196n, 198–9, 202, 204, 205n
Bielik-Robson, Agata 14n
Blanton, Ward 27, 28n, 213, 247n, 261
Bloch, Ernst 23
Boer, Roland 36–7, 41, 240n, 245n, 260, 263
Bond, Helen K. 256n
Borges, Jorge Luis 148
Bould, Mark 25n
Bovon, Francois 161n
Boyarin, Daniel 271n, 319, 336, 340n
Braddick, Michael 258n
Brand, Karen 132n, 144
Braun, Willi 149n, 150–1, 155n
Brecht, Berthold 23
Brennan, Timothy 184, 193–4
Breton, Stanislas 230, 269, 273–4
Briggs, Sheila 330n
Britt, Brian 40
Britton, Celia M. 207
Bronner, Stephen Eric 2, 11n, 20n
Brook, Wes Howard 57n, 188
Brown, Bill 355
Buck-Morss, Susan 25, 26n, 41n, 52n
Burke, Tony 162, 163n, 171n
Burrus, Virginia 354, 356, 362, 364
Butler, Judith 2n, 4n, 6n, 9n, 11n, 12, 19, 26, 77–8, 295–306, 307n,

308–10, 314–18, 337, 340, 343, 350–1, 355, 363–4
Butts, Aaron Michael 173n, 175n

Caird, George B. 192n
Callahan, Allen Dwight 197, 203, 330n
Cameron, Ron 239
Camp, Claudia V. 326
Canavan, Gerry 23, 24n
Carey, Greg 188
Casey, Maurice 263n
Castelli, Elizabeth A. 328n
Charles, R. H. 203
Chatterjee, Partha 119, 193
Chen, Mel 305, 353–5
Clark, J. Michael 187n
Cobb, L. Stephanie 166n
Cohen, Jared 112n
Colebrook, Claire 3, 22, 103, 109–10, 153, 156
Collins, John, J. 59n
Conway, Coleen M. 260
Crockett, Clayton 115
Crossan, John Dominic 7–8
Crossley, James 229–30, 261
Culp, Andrew 3n, 112, 115

Danker, F. 129n
Darrow, Geof 113
Davies, Philip R. 4n, 12
De Beauvoir, Simone 319
De Landa, Manuel 142–3
De Lubac, Henri 273n
Dean, Jodi 260n, 265
Deleuze, Gilles 3, 6, 8n, 25n, 99–102, 105–12, 114–6, 119–21, 127–8, 130–43, 147–8, 151n, 154–61, 185–6, 193, 194n, 196, 197n, 198, 200–1, 203–7, 217n, 237, 249, 295
Derrida, Jacques 202n, 247n
Dickinson, Colby 15, 19, 44n
Dieterlen, Germaine 136n

Dosse, François 105–7, 109, 111, 115
Dunning, Benjamin 240n, 242n

Eagleton, Terry 53n
Edwards, Mark 357
Ehrensperger, Kathy 328n
Eiland, Howard 7n, 17–8, 35, 38–40, 45, 51n, 91
Eliade, Mircea 83–4
Engels, Friedrich 2n
Esler, Philip F. 172n, 173n

Fanon, Franz 195, 200
Fatum, Lone 318n
Feher, Michel 159n
Ferris, David 53–4
Fish, Stanley 177
Foakes-Jackson, F. J. 152n
Fredriksen, Paula 67n
Freud, Sigmund 86, 92

Garrett, Susan R. 185, 187, 194
Gaventa, Beverly Roberts 217n, 328n, 333n
Gellner, Ernest 200
Gemeinhardt, Peter 326
Gilloch, Graeme 51n
Gleason, Maud W. 337n, 338
Goodrich, John K. 323–4
Gordon, Lewis R. 11–2
Green, Steve 4
Griaule, Marcel 136n
Groenendijk, Leendert 325–7
Guattari, Félix 3, 6, 99–102, 105–6, 109, 114–6, 119–20, 128, 130–8, 140–3, 156n, 160–1, 185–6, 197n, 198, 200–1, 203–7, 217n
Gwyther, Anthony 57n, 188, 194–6, 198

Haile, Getatchew 172n, 173–4
Hanssen, Beatrice 52n
Harris, Jan Ll. 45n
Harrison, Renee K. 342n

Harvey, David 139n
Hazard, Sonia 353–4
Helmling, Steven 9–11, 13, 14n, 15–6, 19n, 20–1, 100
Hill, Christopher 229, 254n, 258, 260
Hilton, Rodney, H. 258n
Hobsbawn, Eric J. 257
Hoffmann, Kevin 261
Hoggart, Richard 54
Holland, Eugene 157n
Hollywood, Amy 301n
Horkheimer, Max 1–2, 11n
Hornsby, Teresa J. 319–20, 339n, 340n
Horsley, Richard A. 330
Howard-Brook, Wes 188, 194–6, 198
Hudson, Dale 202, 204–5
Hutcheon, Linda 344

Isasi-Díaz, Ada María 352

Jacob, Sharon 20, 119–21
Jacobs, Julia 5n
Jauss, Hans Robert 5n, 22
Jay, Martin 51n
Jennings, Michael W. 7n, 17–8, 35, 38–40, 45, 51n, 91
Jensen, Morten Horning 256n
Jodamus, Jonathan 318
Justaert, Kristien 13n, 135–6

Kachru, Braj B. 197
Kaden, David A. 320–2
Kafka, Franz 197n
Kahl, Brigitte 329
Kähler, Martin 127n
Kaplan, Aryeh 68–9, 91
Kautsky, John H. 255n
Kay, Hubert 254–5
Keener, Craig S. 152
Kelhoffer, James A. 27n, 28n
Khatib, Sami 56
Kim, Yung Suk 20

King, Karen 178n
Kittel, Gerhard Friedrich 334n, 335n
Klein, Melanie 138
Kloppenborg, John S. 127n
Koester, Craig R. 57
Kraft, Heinrich 206
Krips, Henry 225n

Lake, Kirsopp 152n
Lamm, Spencer 113n
Lampert, Jay 157n
Lane, Richard J. 51n, 56
Lawrence, D. H. 193n, 194
Lenski, Gerhard E. 257–8
Leslie, Esther 51n
Lessing, Gotthold 127n
Levenson, B. Carl 43–4, 69, 71n, 74n
Lietaert Peerbolte, Bert jan 325–7
Linskey, Annie 307n
Lovelace, Vanessa 342n
Lyons, William John 12n, 26

McCutcheon, Russell 239n
McDannell, Colleen 25
McGuckin, John Anthony 361n
Mack, Burton 236n, 237n, 247
Mackey, Jacob L. 323
McLean, Bradley H. 103–4, 116–8, 127n, 128n
McNeel, Jennifer Houston 328n, 333n
Magister, Simon 162
Maines, Mary Jo 323n
Marantz, Andrew 113n
Marrou, Henri-Irénée 327n
Marshall, John W. 187n
Martin, Dale B. 329–30
Martyn, J. Louis 333n
Marx, Karl 2n, 86, 138–9
Massumi, Brian 132, 149n, 154, 156, 158n
Mena, Peter Anthony 304–5
Merrin, William 149n

Miller, Adam 245n
Miller, Frank 113
Miller, Merrill P. 239
Miller, Patricia Cox 355–6
Miller, Tyrus 27n
Missac, Pierre 55n
Moore, Stephen D. 57–9, 188–9, 194n, 196, 200
Moss, Candida R. 4n, 166n
Moxnes, Halvor 259
Mullarkey, John 121n, 214, 215n
Muñoz, José Esteban 350, 352, 356
Myles, Robert 7–8, 108

Neocleous, Mark 139n
Neutel, Karin B. 338–9
Nicolet, Valérie 303–4
Niemoczynsk, Leon 135
Nietzsche, Friedrich 83, 103, 158
Nigianni, Chrysanthi 140n
Nock, Arthur Darby 238, 241
Novis, Kenneth 110n

Økland, Jorunn 195
Orwell, George 253
Öztürk, Seyda 149n

Parker, Ashley 307n
Parnet, Claire 143, 237, 249
Parr, Adrian 116n
Patton, Paul 115
Pérez, R. 120n
Phelps, Hollis 27, 214n, 215–7, 221n, 222n, 224n, 230–1, 240n, 243–4, 246, 248–9, 279n
Piketty, Thomas 54
Piovanelli, Pierluigi 172n, 175n
Pippin, Tina 59n, 187n
Pluth, Ed 10n, 214n, 215, 218, 219n, 220–3, 224n, 225–7, 229
Poe, Edgar Allen 68, 70
Pol-Droit, Roger 111
Polaski, Sandra Hack 333
Poole, Fitz John Porter 237n
Preston, Paul 253

Prigent, Pierre 206
Prigogine, Ilya 142–3
Proust, Marcel 88–90

Rawson, Beryl 322n
Read-Heimerdinger, Jenny 152n
Richter, Gerhard 15, 20–2, 55n
Ricoeur, Paul 86
Rius-Camps, Josep 152n
Rizzo, Salvador 307n
Robinson, Andrew 116
Roffe, Jonathan 147n, 155n
Rose, Jonathan 54
Roth, Michael 297–301
Rowland, Christopher 258n
Roy, Modhumita 201–2

Said, Edward 188n
Salih, Sara 2n, 6n, 9n, 12, 297–8, 301, 303
Samuel, Raphael 262
Sartre, Jean Paul 71
Sauvagnargues, Anne 105
Schmidt, Eric 112n
Scholem, Gershom 41n, 56n, 71, 80, 92
Schreber, Daniel Paul 139–40, 142
Schüssler Fiorenza, Elisabeth 206, 259n, 328n
Scott, Alan 360
Scott, Eugene 307n
Scott, James M. 323n
Seesengood, Robert Paul 42–3, 59n, 223–4
Sharpe, Eric J. 160n
Sherman, Jacob Holsinger 135
Shildrick, Margrit 138
Shklovsky, Viktor 23n
Smith, Christopher R. 187, 189–91, 198n, 199–200
Smith, Daniel W. 147n, 155n, 158, 159n, 161
Smith, Donald Eugene 184
Smith, Jonathan Z. 236n, 237–9
Smith, Mitzi J. 20

Sneer, Itay 6n
Sontag, Susan 130n, 342
Spinoza, Baruch 130
Spivak, Gayatri Chakravorty 188n
Steinberg, Michael, P. 36n
Stengers, Isabelle 142–3
Sullivan, Eileen 307n
Sutin, Lawrence 25
Suvin, Darko 23–4, 25n, 26, 114n

Talbert, Charles H. 58n
Tambling, Jeremy 272
Taubes, Jacob 262n
Taylor, Paul A. 45n
Terdiman, Richard 17
Thompson, Richard P. 165n
Thurman, Howard 20
Tihanov, Galin vii, 24n
Tite, Philip L. 118, 169n
Trevelyan, C. E. 205
Trouillot, Michel-Rolph 150
Tyson, Joseph B. 152n

Ulfgard, Håkan 191–2, 199, 206

Van de Wiel, Raymond 108
Vander Stichele, Caroline 104n, 116n
Vuolanto, Ville 323n

Wachowski, Lana and Lilly 113
Wark, McKenzie 252n
Watson, Francis 136n
Watson, Janell 205
Whitlock, Matthew G. 118
Wilcox, Melissa 342–5
Williams, Delores S. 342n
Williams, James 111, 157n, 159–61
Williams, Michael Allen 269n
Wilson, Brittany E. 339n
Winter, Bruce, W. 152n
Witakowski, Witold 162, 163n, 171n
Wohlfarth, Irving 38, 41n
Woodhams, Stephen 262
Worthington, Bruce 4n, 227–8
Wright, Benjamin G. 326
Wright, N. T. 8, 108

Žižek, Slavoj 252, 260n, 263

Index of Subjects

Page numbers with the suffix 'n' refer to footnotes (e.g. 168n).

abject bodies (outsiders) 304, 316, 320, 327–8, 335–7, 341
abject spaces 304, 315–6, 327–8, 336
absurdist and anachronistic analysis 252–65
Acts of Cornelius 162–76
   Ethiopic translation 162, 164, 168n, 171–6
   Gentile mission motif 163, 166–8, 171, 178
   martyr motifs 165–6, 168–70
   sources 164, 177–9
Acts of the Apostles 111, 118, 149–54, 158n, 159, 161n, 162–4, 177
   assemblies 306–10
   baptism 327n, 339n
   Cornelius' story 118, 162–7, 170–1, 176, 178
   fidelity 246
   and Revelation 198
   as simulacrum 111, 149–54, 158n, 159, 161n
Adam–Christ connection 244, 271–3, 281, 287–90
Adorno, Theodor W.
   and Benjamin vii, 6, 10, 13, 15–8, 40
   with Horkheimer 1, 2, 7, 298
   immanent critique 9, 10–14, 101
   strangeness/shock 20–1, 24n
Allbright College library 42–3, 61
allegorical interpretation 230–1, 268–74, 290
Althusser, Louis 226–7

anachronistic and absurdist analysis 252–65
angel of history 43–4, 80–2, 86–7, 93
Angelus Novus (Klee) 40, 80–2, 87
animacy 304–5, 353–4
Anti-Oedipus (Deleuze and Guattari) 6, 99–102, 106–7, 128, 132
anticipation *see* retroaction and anticipation
arcades
   New Jerusalem 58, 62
   Paris 17, 36, 42, 50–3, 56
   Arcades Project, The (Benjamin)
   dialectical images vii, 14, 17–8, 25
   Marxism 39–40
   Paris 17, 36, 42, 50
   structure of 50, 52, 55, 63
assemblages
   Butler 296
   Deleuze and Guattari 103, 144, 155n, 186, 207, 305, 354
assemblies 306–10
Augustine 66–7, 69–79, 81–93
   Benjamin, imagined dialogue with 66–7, 70–1, 76–9, 89–92
   biography 66, 69, 74, 81
   City of God, The 71–3, 83, 90
   Confessions 69, 71, 73–4, 76–9, 81–2, 85, 88–91
   redemption 66, 69, 83, 85
aura 38, 42, 44–6, 84–5, 87, 90
authenticity

Index of Subjects   381

Acts tradition 153, 161, 177, 179–80
Deleuze 110, 118, 147, 158–9, 177
see also origins of texts/ideas
authority
  charismatic 258, 264
  of Christ 140, 264, 325
  of Paul 264, 319, 331, 335
  of texts 44–6, 118, 150–1, 165, 177, 180

Badiou, Alain
  Being and Event 214–5, 220, 238n, 240–8, 275–83
  biography 213–4, 217, 220–2, 224–6
  evental recurrence 230–1, 241, 244n, 268–9, 278–84, 289–90
  intervention 217, 228, 241, 243–6, 278–82, 284
  Logics of Worlds 240, 242–3, 248–9, 275, 280, 282–3
  multiplicity 215–6, 224–5, 243, 275–80
  "Philosophy as Biography" 213–4, 217–8, 220–3, 225–7
  resurrection of truths 27, 231, 269, 282–4
  Saint Paul: The Foundation of Universalism 216, 238n, 240n, 246n, 252, 260, 280n
baptism 167, 206n, 327
Baudelaire, Charles 16–8, 40, 46, 84–5, 89, 93, 107
Baudrillard, Jean 118, 147–50, 153–6, 178
beauty
  classical ideas of 88n, 357–60, 362, 365
  modern ideas of 22, 46, 53, 70, 84, 342, 343n
becoming

Acts simulacrum 118, 156, 160, 176–7
Badiou 218
Butler 300, 302–3
Deleuze 111, 118, 127, 156, 160, 203
phase space theory 143
Being and Event (Badiou) 214–5, 220, 238n, 240–8, 275–83
belonging 198–9, 275–6, 279, 299
Benjamin, Walter 35–46, 50–63, 66–93
  and Adorno vii, 6, 10, 13, 15–8, 40
  angel of history 43–4, 80–2, 86–7, 93
  Augustine, imagined dialogues with 66–7, 70–1, 76–9, 89–92
  aura 38, 42, 44–6, 84–5, 87, 90
  on Baudelaire 17–8, 40, 46, 84–5, 89, 93
  biography ix, 38–41, 66, 75–6
  on Capra film 6–8
  chess-playing automaton 43–4, 67–71
  constellations vii, 13–5, 18, 20–1, 25
  language and translation 14–5, 36–7
  on libraries 50, 54–5, 62–3
  messianic themes 43–4, 50, 55–6, 62, 66
  progress 42–4, 50–1, 55–6, 61, 70, 72, 74–5, 80–2
  redemption 66, 70, 73–4, 76, 86, 90–1
  regression 86–8
  urban life 36, 39, 42–3, 50–3, 56, 62–3
Bible, popular status of 4–5
binary categories, escape from 178, 303, 305, 314, 340–1, 353–4
Bloch, Ernst 23
Bob Crow Brigade 261
bodies

abject bodies 304, 316, 320, 327–8, 335–7, 341
  Butler 295–7, 300–2, 304–10, 318–9
  early Christian view of humanness 356–7
  non-human bodies 305, 351, 353, 360–1, 364
  performativity 300–1, 309, 340
  precarity 296, 301–2, 308–10
  and the soul 357, 360–3, 365
  webs of relation 296–7, 301
Bodies That Matter (Butler)
  introduction to 300–1, 315–7
  and *On First Principles*, Mena's reading of 305, 350–1, 355, 363–4
  and Paul, Nicolet's reading of 303–4, 314–5, 317–8, 337, 340, 343
"body without organs" 127–44
  "body of Christ without organs" 116–8, 127–30, 132–44
  paranoid/schizoid 129, 139–41, 143–4
  passive syntheses 117–8, 129, 136–42
Boy with Machine (Lindner) 101–2, 114
bracketing 237, 239–40, 242, 247
Braun, Willi 150–1, 155n
Brecht, Berthold 23, 40–1, 70
Breton, Stanislas 273–4, 290
bricolage 55, 63
British communism 230, 262
brownness 352, 356
Butler, Judith 295–310
  assemblies 306, 308–10
  biography ix, 297–8
  bodies 295–7, 300–2, 304–10, 318–9
  congealed ideologies 9n, 12, 14
  essences 299–300, 303

  gender 2n, 296, 298–304, 315, 317–20, 337, 340
  imitation 299, 304, 317, 323, 344
  knowledge, limits of 19, 26
  norms 2n, 300–4, 315–20
  performativity 300–3, 309, 320, 336, 340
  precarity 296, 301–2, 308–10
  see also Bodies That Matter (Butler)

"camp" 342–5
canonical/non-canonical texts
  Acts simulacrum 147–54, 157–9, 161–2, 176, 178–80
  bracketing 247
  minor/major status 3, 20–2, 120–1
  rhizomes 104
  strangeness 21–2, 26
Capital (Marx) 138–9
capitalism
  Christianity and 108
  commodification 1, 50, 53, 139
  contemporary 112, 201, 265
  English Revolution, consequence of 229, 258
  insatiability of 60
  "Power Plant" 113–4
  surplus value 136, 138–9, 255
Capra, Frank 6–8
Catholicism 69, 107, 154, 238, 343–4
celestial bodies 352, 357–61, 364–5
"Chambermaids' Romances of the Past Century" (Benjamin) 42, 50, 54
charismatic authority 258, 264
chess-playing automaton 43–4, 67–71
children, in Galatians 304, 322–5, 327, 335
Christ *see* Jesus Christ
Christian community
  "body of Christ without

organs" 116–8, 127–30, 132–44
  in Galatians (Paul) 320, 325, 327, 329, 331–6
  organization and discipline 252–3, 260–4, 341
Christian texts *see* early Christian texts, introduction to
citationality 301n, 316–7, 320–1, 336; *see also* speech acts
cities *see* urban life
classification 106, 117–8, 138, 180, 317, 350; *see also* insider/outsider mechanisms; norms
cognitive estrangement vii, 23–4
commodification 1, 50, 53, 56, 101, 139
"common sense" ideas 6, 10, 14, 18–9, 111, 115, 120
communism 72–4, 106, 219, 230, 262
community *see* Christian community
comparison, analytical category 228–9, 236–9, 245–6, 249
congealment 9–15, 19–20
conjunctive synthesis 117–8, 129, 136, 141–2, 144
connective synthesis 117–8, 129, 136–7, 144
constellations vii, 13–5, 18, 20–1, 25
consumerism 2, 42, 53–4, 57–9
Corbyn, Jeremy 264–5
Corinthians, 1 318
Cornelius *see* Acts of Cornelius
cultural assimilation 192, 199, 206–7
culture industry 1–9, 14, 16, 22, 27
"Culture Industry, The" (Horkheimer and Adorno) 1–2

Davy, Marie-Madeleine 107
De Beauvoir, Simone 300

De Quincy, Thomas 17
death 76–7, 83, 85–6
  of Benjamin ix, 40, 66, 75
  of Deleuze 111–2
Deleuze, Gilles
  biography ix, 105–7, 109, 111–2
  Butler's use of 295
  "From Christ to Bourgeoisies" 107–8
  and "common sense" 6, 111, 115, 120–1
  Difference and Repetition 6, 25n, 110–2, 155n, 196
  minor/major literature 3, 22, 120–1
  science fiction 25n, 113
  simulacra 118, 148, 150, 154–8, 164, 177
  surplus value 138–9
  see also "body without organs"
Deleuze, Gilles, and Félix Guattari
  Anti-Oedipus 6, 99–102, 106–7, 128, 132
  language, role of 119–21, 185–6, 192, 201, 203–7
  minor/major literature 3, 20–2, 120–1
  rhizomatic networks 99–101, 103–5, 112
  What is Philosophy? 106, 116
Deleuzian hermeneutics 176–80
desiring machines 102, 114, 117–8, 134
desiring-production 118, 132–4, 139–41, 143–4
deterritorialization 106, 119–20, 142, 186, 197n, 201, 206–7
dialectical images 14–22
  Arcades Project, The vii, 14, 17–8, 25
  assemblies 308
  Benjamin and Augustine, as example of 43–4, 67
  Benjamin and John of Patmos, as example of 42–3

constellations vii, 13–4, 25
Lenin and Paul, as example
    of 229
Suvin 23–6
dialectical materialism *see* historical
    (dialectical) materialism
Difference and Repetition
    (Deleuze) 6, 25n, 110–2, 155n,
    196
disjunctive synthesis 117–8, 129,
    136–41, 144
dress 192, 199, 206–7

early Christian texts, introduction to
    concealment 9–14
    culture industry 1–9
    dialectical image 14–22
    estrangement 23–8
empire of God
    language, role of 119–20, 185–6,
        192–4, 196, 198, 201, 204
    Rome, comparison 119, 189,
        192–4, 196, 199–200
English language 197, 201–3
English Revolution 229, 254n, 258
environmental themes 351–2, 354
essence of texts/ideas
    angel of history 80, 82, 93
    "body without organs" 139
    Christian texts/Christianity 4,
        104, 111, 118, 147, 153–4,
        160, 318
essential historicity 241, 244n,
    280–1, 286
essentialism 45, 299–300, 303
estrangement and strangeness vii,
    13, 21–8, 110
eternity
    Athanasius 285
    Augustine 73, 83–4, 93
    Augustine and Benjamin,
        imagined dialogue 77–8, 90
    eternal life through Christ 271–2
    eternality of truth 280–4
    Plotinus 81
    relating to texts 22, 157
Eucharist 89n, 133
Eve–Mary connection 287–90
evental recurrence 230–1, 241,
    244n, 268–9, 278–84, 289–90
evental site 228, 236, 240–3, 247,
    249, 276
events
    bracketing of 237, 239–40, 242,
        247
    event-patterns 70–1
    and excess 230, 273–7, 290
    fidelity 217n, 218, 228, 230,
        245–6, 248, 261, 282–3
    intervention 217, 228, 241,
        243–6, 278–82, 284
    Jesus' resurrection 228, 230, 239,
        240n, 241–4, 246–9, 261
    naming of 216–17, 223, 228,
        241, 243, 278, 280–1
    speech acts to interpret 306
evil 57, 71, 73–4, 80–1, 83
excess
    early Christian theories of the
        body 356, 359
    and events 230, 268–9, 273–7,
        290
    see also surplus value

facialization 120, 186, 191–3,
    196–7, 201, 204–7
fall, the 37, 78, 81, 93, 357–8,
    361–3
familial relationships
    kinship of all matter 305, 352,
        358, 360–1, 363, 365
    Paul's rhetorical uses of 321–6,
        331–4
Fascism and Nazism
    Badiou's response to 217
    Benjamin's death ix, 40, 66, 75
    Benjamin's response to 41, 44,
        46, 62, 72–3, 82, 85
    Butler's response to 297–9
    Deleuze's response to 105–6

Hill's response to 254n
fatherhood/*paterfamilias*
   metaphor 322, 325, 331–2, 334
females, in Galatians 304, 328,
   332–3, 335–7, 340–1
femininity 319–20, 339
feminism 261, 298–9, 319, 363
fidelity
   applied to early Christianity 248,
      261
   and events 217n, 218, 228, 230,
      245–6, 282–3
   to thinkers 226
flanerie 40–1, 55, 78, 84–5
flows, "body without
   organs" 117–8, 129–39, 141, 144
Frankfurt School *see* Institute for
   Social Research (ISR)
Freudian psychoanalysis 102, 114
"From Christ to Bourgeoisies"
   (Deleuze) 107–8

Galatians 248, 218, 320–41
   Christian community in 320, 325,
      327, 329, 331–6
   family, language of 321–6, 331–4
   gender in 303–4, 319–20, 324–5,
      327–8, 333, 335–41
gender
   Butler 2n, 296, 298–304, 315,
      317–20, 337, 340
   fatherhood/*paterfamilias*
      metaphor 322, 325, 331–2,
      334
   femininity 301, 319–20, 339
   in Galatians 303–4, 319–20,
      324–5, 327–8, 333, 335–41
   identities 299–302
   masculinity 259–60, 304, 319–
      20, 333, 338–41
   and performativity 300–3, 336–8,
      340
Gentiles 163, 166–8, 171, 178, 199
gentrification 42, 50, 52–4, 58–60
Gnosticism 268–9, 284, 290, 332

Gracq, Julien 219
Greek language 193, 197, 201, 203
Green, Steve 4–5
Guattari, Félix 106–7; *see also*
   Deleuze, Gilles, and Félix
   Guattari

Hagar 341–2
Halbwachs, Pierre 107
Hebrews 60, 246
Hegel, Georg Wilhelm
   Friedrich 296, 298
historical analyses 7–8, 11–2, 114n,
   225, 227, 254
historical-critical method 11–2, 23,
   110, 159n
historical (dialectical)
   materialism 67, 70–1, 93n, 229,
   254–8, 264–5
historical positivism 103–4
history
   allegorical 230–1, 268–74, 290
   angel of history 43–4, 80–2,
      86–7, 93
   bodies 295–7
   historical Jesus 7–8, 27, 149,
      227, 247n, 253–7, 263
   reading historically,
      Benjamin 21–2, 23n, 36n
   see also eternity; events; "On
      the Concept of History"
      (Benjamin); progress
Hobby Lobby 4
Holocaust ix, 66, 73, 75, 105, 298
Horkheimer, Max 1–2, 7, 298
humans
   decentering of 305, 352, 354,
      356–7
   siblings with all matter 358, 361,
      365

identities 299–302, 304, 325, 327;
   see also gender; race and racial
   identity

illusions 42, 45–6, 50, 67, 138–9, 179; *see also* phantasmagoria
imitation
    Butler 299, 304, 317, 323, 344
    of Christ 286, 304, 320, 325–7, 331, 334
    see also mimicry
immanence 135–6, 144
immanent critique 9–14, 22, 101
imperialism 184–208
    contemporary pressures 265
    language, role of 119–20, 185–6, 190–9, 201–8
    mimicking the colonizer 119–20, 186–9, 193, 196, 200n
    Paul 230, 262, 329
    in Revelation 119–20, 185–9, 190–208
    Rome/empire of God, comparison 119, 189, 192–4, 196, 199–200
incarnation of Christ 136, 284–7, 289
India 201–2, 204–5
insider/outsider mechanisms 304, 315–17, 320, 325, 327–8, 336–7, 341
Institute for Social Research (ISR) 2, 6, 10, 17, 22–3, 39
intervention 217, 228, 241, 243–6, 278–82, 284
Irenaeus 230–1, 268–71, 273, 284–90
Israel 189–90, 195–201

Jerusalem Temple 255–6
Jesus Christ
    Adam–Christ connection 244, 271–3, 281, 287–90
    Augustine 83, 88
    authority of 140, 264, 325
    "body of Christ without organs" 116–8, 127–30, 132–44
    death on the cross, as event 280–1
    historical Jesus 7–8, 27, 149, 227, 247n, 253–7, 263
    imitation of 286, 304, 320, 325–7, 331, 334
    incarnation of 136, 284–7, 289
    as mass-reproduced "object" 45
    resurrection of 228, 230, 239, 240n, 241–4, 246–9, 261
    as revolutionary 254, 259
Jesus movement 229, 254–5, 257, 264
John of Patmos 50, 56–8, 63, 119, 185, 187–9, 191–7
Judaism
    and Acts of Cornelius 166, 168–9
    Benjamin 39, 40, 55, 82
    Butler 297, 302
    Jewish mysticism 40–1, 66
    and masculinity 338–9
    messianic themes 55, 71, 189, 200, 203–4
    relationship to Christianity 173–4, 236, 241–2, 244, 247, 341
    and Revelation 187–91, 197n, 198n, 199n
    other mentions 27, 60, 92–3, 259, 271

Kabbalah 68, 91–2
Kafka, Franz 73, 86, 197n
Klee, Paul 40, 80–2, 87
Kommerell, Max 35
Korsch, Karl 39
Kristeva, Julia 296

Lacan, Jacques 106, 226
language
    animacy and relationality 352–5
    belittling/diminutive 320, 328–9, 331, 335
    Benjamin 14–5, 36–7

Deleuze and Guattari 119–21,
    185–6, 192, 201, 203–7
  of familial relationships 321–6,
    331–4
  and imperialism 119–20, 185–6,
    190–9, 201–8
  minor/major status 119–21,
    202–4, 207
  naming of events 216–7, 223,
    228, 241, 243, 278, 280–1
  and nationhood 119–20, 184–6,
    192–204, 206–8
  poetic 46, 214, 216–17, 231, 296
  speech acts 300–1, 306, 308–10
law
  citationality 301n, 316–7, 320–1,
    336
  Paul's rhetorical uses of 315,
    318, 320, 322–3, 333
Lenin, compared to Paul 252, 260,
  262–3
libraries 42–3, 50, 54–5, 59, 61–3
Lindner, Richard 101–2, 114
linguistic nationalism 193–4
literal interpretation 129, 271–3,
  289–90
"Literary History and Literary
  Scholarship" (Benjamin) 21, 23n,
  36n
literature, minor/major status 3, 22,
  120–1
Living Book 50, 60, 63
Logics of Worlds (Badiou) 240,
  242–3, 248–9, 275, 280, 282–3
Luke, Gospel of 118, 152n, 164

machines
  "body without organs" 117–8,
    130–8, 144
  Boy with Machine
    (Lindner) 101–2, 114
  Deleuze and Guattari 99, 101–3,
    114–5
  "Power Plant, The" 113–4
  war machines 115, 218

Maelzel 68
males/men 325, 327, 335–6,
  339–40; *see also* masculinity;
  patriarchal households
Mann, Thomas 91
Mannlein 70–2, 74–6, 80
Maoism 222
maps, texts as 148–53, 158, 160,
  164
marginalization 19–21, 120,
  301–2; *see also* canonical/non-
  canonical texts; insider/outsider
  mechanisms
Mark, Gospel of 152, 247
Marseille 42, 50–3, 56
martyr motifs 165–6, 168–70
Marx, Karl 2n, 39, 138–9
Marxism
  Badiou 222, 224–6, 229, 252
  Benjamin 39–40, 44, 67, 70–1,
    73, 80, 93n
  Deleuze 138–9
  historical (dialectical)
    materialism 67, 70–1, 93n,
    229, 254–8, 264–5
  vulgar Marxism 229, 252–3,
    255–6, 258, 262
Mary–Eve connection 287–90
masculinity 259–60, 304, 319–20,
  333, 338–41
materialism
  historical (dialectical) 67, 70–1,
    93n, 229, 254–8, 264–5
  new materialism 350–1, 353–4
  see also "body without organs"
mathematics 214–8, 224–5, 227
Matrix, The 113–4, 149n
matter
  early Christian theories of 355
  hierarchies of 351–2, 354, 363
  kinship of 305, 352, 358, 360–1,
    363, 365
  non-human/non-living 305, 351,
    353, 360–1, 364

mediation, by theory vii, 17–9, 25, 43, 59, 103
memory 17, 19, 36, 63, 82–4, 89–93
messianic themes
   Augustine 66, 73
   Augustine and Benjamin, imagined dialogue 76, 79, 91
   Benjamin 43–4, 50, 55–6, 62, 66
   in Galatians 326, 329
   Judaism 55, 71, 189, 200, 203–4
   in Revelation 43, 56, 59, 63, 189, 200
millenarianism 257–60
mimesis 298–9
mimicry
   of imperial colonizers 119–20, 186–9, 193, 196, 200n
   simulacra 156
   subversive use of 301
minor/major languages 119–21, 202–4, 207
modernity/modernism 25, 39, 43, 53, 56, 85, 160
montage 13, 17, 41, 43–4, 52, 60; *see also* bricolage
motherhood metaphor 332–3
Mr. Robot 1
multiplicity
   Badiou 215–6, 224–5, 243, 275–80
   Deleuze and Guattari 102
   rhizomatic networks 104

naming of events 216–7, 223, 228, 241, 243, 278, 280–1
nations, in Revelation 119–20, 184–6, 189–90, 192–204, 206–8
Nazism *see* Fascism and Nazism
New Jerusalem 11, 42–3, 50–3, 56–9, 62–3
new materialism 350–1, 353–4
Nietzsche, Friedrich 83, 103, 279
nomos 320–5
non-canonical texts *see* canonical/non-canonical texts

normative identities 299–302, 304
norms
   Butler 2n, 300–4, 315–20, 337
   disruption of 303–4, 315–7, 319, 328, 336–7, 342–5
   in Galatians, Nicolet's reading of 323, 327–9, 333, 336–7
Notes Toward a Performative Theory of Assembly (Butler) 295, 302, 306, 308
novelty/the new
   Acts simulacrum 157–62, 164–5, 178, 180
   Benjamin 80, 87, 90
   "body without organs" 131, 135, 142–3, 148
   Deleuze and Guattari 103, 106, 110–1, 115–6
   novel truth 227–8, 236–8, 240–1, 245–6, 249
novum vii, 23–4, 26–7

On First Principles (Origen) 351–2, 356–8, 360–1, 363, 365
"On the Concept of History" (Benjamin) 12, 40, 72, 74–5, 83, 85–7, 93
   Augustine and Benjamin, imagined dialogue 67, 70–1, 78–9, 89–92
ontology 202, 214–7, 273, 275–6, 280, 363
organs *see* "body without organs"
Origen
   On First Principles 351–2, 356–8, 360–1, 363, 365
   introduction to 19, 304–5
origins of texts/ideas 3–4
   Badiou 220, 225–6, 228, 247–9
   Benjamin 17, 23, 44–6, 84
   bracketing 237n, 239–40, 242, 247
   essentialism 45, 299–300, 303
   Protestant theology of 154, 228, 238–41

see also "body without organs";
essence of texts/ideas;
simulacra
"other" 70, 205, 207
outsiders *see* abject bodies (outsiders); insider/outsider mechanisms
overcoding 118, 128, 141, 143, 205–6

palimpsest 16–17, 26, 101
paranoid "body without organs" 129, 139–41, 143–4
Paris
  arcades 17, 36, 42, 50–3, 56
  Badiou 218–9, 221
  Deleuze's birthplace 105
  flâneur, Benjamin relates as 40, 55, 84
  Paris commune 219, 242
passive synthesis 117–8, 129, 136–42, 144
patriarchal households 322, 325, 331–2, 334
patterns, Augustine and Benjamin 43–4, 66, 69–72, 76–8
Paul
  Adam–Christ connection 271–3, 290
  and Augustine 79, 88
  Badiou 216–7, 223–4, 227
  binary categories 303, 314, 341
  "body of Christ without organs" 117–8, 127–9, 131, 133–4, 140–1
  Christ, imitation of 320, 325–7, 331, 334
  Christ, marks of 334–5, 338
  imperialism 230, 262, 329
  Lenin, comparison to 252, 260, 262–3
  see also Galatians
performativity 300–3, 309, 320–1, 336–8, 340, 356
Peter, 1 230, 246

phantasmagoria 25–6, 53, 56, 58–60, 62, 90; *see also* illusions
phase space theory 118, 142–3
philosophy
  Badiou 213–4, 217–8, 230–1, 236–7, 249
  Butler's study of 297–8
  Deleuze's study of 109–11
"Philosophy as Biography" (Badiou) 213–4, 217–8, 220–3, 225–7
Plato and Platonism
  and Augustine 83, 86, 88
  and Badiou 224–6, 238
  and Deleuze 111, 154, 155n, 158–60
  Timaeus 352, 357–60, 365
poetic language 46, 214, 216–17, 231, 296
popular culture 1–6, 9–10, 25
"Portrait of Walter Benjamin, A" (Adorno) 6n, 10
postcolonial theory 186, 188–9, 193, 202
"Power Plant, The" (Darrow) 113–4
precarity 296, 301–2, 308–10
progress
  angel of history 43–4, 80–2, 86–7, 93
  Augustine 73–4, 83–4
  Augustine and Benjamin, imagined dialogue 78, 89
  Benjamin 42–4, 50–1, 55–6, 61, 70, 72, 74–5, 80–2
  John of Patmos 50
proletariat 51–4, 59, 139, 253, 261, 265
Protestant theology 154, 228, 238–41
Proust, Marcel 88–90, 93
psychoanalysis 102, 106, 114, 224–5

Q source 152, 239, 246–7
queer theory

Butler 301–2, 304, 314, 317, 319
"camp" 341–5
Jesus, depictions of 229, 259
Muñoz 350, 352
Paul's letters, disruption of norms in 303–4, 319, 328, 336–7, 345

race and racial identity 20, 192, 204–5, 207–8, 356
radical impulses 2–3, 7, 9, 19, 265
raw, the 221
Reading, PA 42–3, 60
recapitulation 230–1, 268–71, 284–90
redemption
    Augustine 66, 69, 83, 85
    Augustine and Benjamin, imagined dialogue 79, 91
    Benjamin 66, 70, 73–4, 76, 86, 90–1
regression 86–8
repetition
    congealment 10–1
    historical 82–3, 86
    of norms 304, 315–18, 320, 322–3, 327–8, 336, 341, 343–5
    and performativity 12n, 300
    simulacra 111, 148, 155, 176
    see also evental recurrence
repression 117–18, 136, 138–44
repulsion 139–40, 144, 188n
resemblance 154–6, 161n
resistance
    Badiou's political activities 219–22
    of "body without organs" 142
    disruption of norms 303–4, 315–7, 319, 328, 336–7, 342–5
    to Nazism 105, 107, 217
    to the Roman Empire 119, 188–9
resurrection of Jesus 228, 230, 239, 240n, 241–4, 246–9, 261
resurrection of truths 27, 226, 231, 269, 282–4

reterritorialization 119–20, 186, 201, 203, 206–7
retroaction and anticipation
    Badiou 230, 276, 279, 281–4, 289–90
    Benjamin 21–2
    Breton 274, 290
    Paul and John 263
Revelation 8, 11, 21, 42–3, 56, 184–208, 248
    imperialism 119–20, 185–9, 190–208
    Jesus' resurrection, event consequences 248
    messianic themes 43, 56, 59, 63, 189, 200
    nations 119–20, 184–6, 189–90, 192–204, 206–8
    New Jerusalem 11, 42–3, 50, 56–9
revolution
    art/literature 1–2
    Badiou 219–22, 224
    Benjamin 82, 86
    Christianity as revolutionary movement 229, 252–7, 259, 264
    millenarianism 257–60
    organization and discipline for 252–3, 260–5
rhizomatic networks
    Acts simulacrum 159–60, 164, 170–2, 176–7, 179–80
    Deleuze and Guattari 99–101, 103–5, 112
    passive synthesis 137
Rojava 261
Roman Empire
    Augustine 72, 83
    "body without organs" 117
    empire of God, comparison 119, 189, 192–4, 196, 199–200
    John of Patmos' relationship with 50, 56–8, 119, 185, 187–9, 191–7

Koine Greek language 193–4, 197, 201

sabbath 173–5
sacred texts, reproducibility 44–5
Saint Paul: The Foundation of Universalism (Badiou) 216, 238n, 240n, 246n, 252, 260, 280n
salvation, economy of 270, 273–4, 286–8
San Antonio 42, 62
Sanders, Bernie 265
Sartre, Jean Paul 226, 298
schizoid "body without organs" 129, 139–41, 143–4
Scholem, Gersholm 40–1
science fiction 23–5, 86, 112–4
Second World War ix, 40, 105–6, 217, 299
semblances 156, 161–4, 176–7
Sepphoris 255–6
set theory 215, 275
Shakespeare, thought experiment 3, 22, 110
simulacra
    Acts simulacrum 111, 118, 147–54, 157–79
    Baudrillard 118, 147–50, 153–6, 178
    Deleuze 118, 148, 150, 154–8, 164, 177
    Deleuzian hermeneutics 176–80
    in Revelation 196, 204
simulation 148–51, 153, 156, 162, 176–80
Sisters of Perpetual Indulgence 342–4
slaves, in Galatians 304, 321–3, 327, 329–30, 333–5
souls 357, 360–3, 365
speech acts 300–1, 306, 308–10
Spinoza, Baruch 130, 295, 297
Stalin 263
state apparatus
    Greco-Roman 134, 141, 144

overcoding the body 118, 128, 141, 143, 205–6
war machines 115, 218
strangeness and estrangement vii, 13, 21–8, 110
student riots 1968 106–7, 218–9
subject, the
    Badiou 220, 223, 226
    Butler 296–7, 304, 315–7
    decentering the human 305, 352, 354
    as insider 304, 317, 320, 327–8
Subjects of Desire (Butler) 296–8
subversion
    and British Communism 262
    Butler 14, 299, 301–3, 344
    "camp" 342
    mainstreaming of 7–8
    minor/major literature 120–1
    see also norms, disruption of
surplus value 129, 136, 138–40, 144, 255, 356; *see also* excess
Suvin, Darko vii, 23–6
synthesis 13, 18; *see also* passive synthesis
system, the
    incorporation into 2–4, 9–11
    protection of 3, 5–7, 9, 14, 18, 20, 46
    see also capitalism; norms
systematic philosophy 218–9

"The Turk" 68, 70–2, 80
theology 70–1, 80, 154, 228, 238–41
"Theses on the Philosophy of History" (Benjamin) 41, 43, 55
Thousand Plateaus, A (Deleuze and Guattari)
    language, role of 185–6, 201, 203–7
    rhizomes 99–101, 105
Tiberias 255–6
Timaeus (Plato) 352, 357–60, 365
time

Augustine and Benjamin,
  imagined dialogue 90–2
evental recurrence 244n, 269,
  279–81, 289–90
historical repetition 82–3, 86
messianic time 43–4, 73, 91
see also eternity
Timothy, 2 60
transcendence 74, 117, 127, 129,
  135–6, 144
transdisciplinary theories 25–7,
  40–1, 213, 223, 227
tree-like structures 4n, 99, 103–5
tribes, list in Revelation 189–90,
  195, 200
Trinitarianism 164, 171–5
Trump, Donald 306
truth
  eternality of 280, 282–4
  and intervention 217, 241, 244–6
  and multiplicity 216, 224–5, 243
  novel truth 227–8, 236–8, 240–1,
    245–6, 249
  resurrection of 27, 226, 231, 269,
    282–4
  retroactively clear 263
  truth procedures 214, 224–5,
    275, 284
  and universality 214, 222–3
typology 244, 268, 271–3, 290

universality 6, 12, 157, 214, 222–3,
  319

"Unpacking My Library"
  (Benjamin) 50, 54–5, 62–3
urban life
  Benjamin 36, 39, 42–3, 50–3, 56,
    62–3
  city streets, wandering 52, 78–9,
    84
  New Jerusalem 42–3, 50–3,
    56–9, 62–3
  US cities, contemporary 60–2

visions 194–6, 200
vulgar Marxism 229, 252–3, 255–6,
  258, 262

webs of relation 296–7, 301, 354
West Reading public library 42–3, 61
What is Philosophy? (Deleuze and
  Guattari) 106, 116
women *see* females, in Galatians
"Work of Art in the Age of
  Technological Reproducibility,
  The" (Benjamin) 38–9, 44–6
worship
  in Acts of Cornelius 163–4,
    171–2, 174–5
  in Revelation 119–20, 196,
    200–2, 206, 208

You Can't Take It With You
  (Capra) 6–8

Studies in Ancient Religion and Culture

Series Editors:
Philip L. Tite, University of Washington
Michael Ng, Seattle University
https://www.equinoxpub.com/home/studies-in-ancient-religion-and-culture/

Published:
Critical Theory and Early Christianity
Edited by Matthew G. Whitlock

Death's Dominion: Power, Identity, and Memory at the Fourth-Century Martyr Shrine
Nathaniel J. Morehouse

Social and Cognitive Perspectives on the Sermon on the Mount
Edited by Rikard Roitto, Colleen Shantz, and Petri Luomanen

The Complexity of Conversion: Intersectional Perspectives on Religious Change in Antiquity and Beyond
Edited by Valérie Nicolet and Marianne Bjelland Kartzow

Theorizing "Religion" in Antiquity
Edited by Nickolas P. Roubekas

Forthcoming:
An Embodied Reading of The Shepherd of Hermas: The Book of Visions and its Role in Moral Formation
Angela Kim Harkins

John Cassian and the Creation of Monastic Subjectivity
Joshua Schachterle

Worth More than Many Sparrows: Essays in Honour of Willi Braun
Edited by Sarah E. Rollens and Patrick Hart

www.ingramcontent.com/pod-product-compliance
Lightning Source LLC
Chambersburg PA
CBHW070008010526
44117CB00011B/1467